Ensemble

Charlotte Algie

In the sense that it can equally describe a compositional process or a component that could be an outcome of such a process, or both, ensemble is always an animated composition, flickering between conceptual and physical conditions. Ensemble is a specific assembly of multiple dissimilar parts articulated collectively by relational means. Its wholes, though unstable, are characterized by a tendency for totalization and conclusion, in time, in three dimensions, in mixed-media and through space, across multiple autonomous characters, in sculptural or pictorial realms, via configuration and reconfiguration.

This volume is a projective art history of ensemble as form and politics, and a critical introduction to a possibility for new architectural wholes. It uses theories of ensemble to speculate on both alternative extensive staging of design objects in architecture, and other resistant assemblies of the corps of architects. Ensemble is a lens to theorize object-parts and states at once, together.

Today, the ensemble is a central principle of nascent developments in probabilistic mathematics. Here, the critical logic of ensemble is a function fundamental to the development of artificial intelligence algorithms, thus both increasingly pervasive and especially urgent to rapid redefinitions of space, city and social production. Statistical ensembles, adaptation of Markov processes, produce and are produced by a highly circumscribed definition of creativity: a predictive state inherently based on a chain of linked, given events. The logic of ensemble within computational intelligence is predicated on the established patterns of the database. It uses it to effectively simulate imaginative problem solving, via a computational method particularly incapable of differentiating from consolidated modes of injustice or implicit power structures. Thus, as much as it is a neoclassical compositional principle, the ensemble is urgent to revisit today as it changes and shifts into new critical focus. How are the new ensembles different? Are they different at all?

This architecture and that architecture. While one architecture demonstrates a limited critical response to ensemble's mathematics—a fact this issue also seeks to address—art and architectural theory can be characterized today as a general field of play predominantly engaged in seeking a larger database. Coincident cycles of human-computer relations and their newer reproductions explore the possibility that the contemporary architectural tendency is tightly bound to implicit computational mathematics as they pervasively supervene on subjectivities of the designer and designed. This volume intends a newly interdisciplinary history of composition. In this history, the question remains open of a structural compatibility between the Markov chain and the neoclassical ensemble of state architecture. From this speculation, the generative thesis projects to a new design method to exploratively connect the actual constructive and projective modes of computational composition to material design process.

A progressive architecture after biographically authored interchanges with proprietary software products: Ensemble is extensive process. It is a design beyond a critical or complicit integration of the line-language of private property. Ensemble as theory is intended as a challenge to supersede a century of critical focus on the singular, authored calibration of a design, by one author or at one place, with a finite set of stakeholders, whatever its projective or retroactive associations, histories narratives, or technical domains. Ensemble draws from mixed-media art practices and electrical circuitry. It connects building matter with a charge and direction, and to states in time. Without resorting to the exhausted juridical regime of the twentieth-century city, without imposing any one of the multiple dimensions of meaning on a design act in advance, an ensemble is an architecture of territory. Ensemble, this volume intends, generates its territory and its social resonance actively and simultaneously and constantly anew alongside design creation. That is, ensemble is posed as a new critical design approach capable of co-configuring architecture's intellectual and material territorial conditions, together. After the work of self-evident justification through embodied process, and beyond any design defense via biographical basis when articulated case-by-case, ensemble is a territory of multiples related in space and time, an architecture of the city. It provides a way to rethink object form such that it persistently implies and generates alternative territorial conditions.

The volume that follows is both about and is an ensemble of a kind. The thematic assembly of the volume is grounded in the organizational anti-matter of architectural form—empire, or, lately, many other generalized extractive centralization conditions like artificial intelligence. Matter and organization of an ideological constellation connect, in the case of the Vichy regime, to a set of cultural, historical and material relations that are in some ways persistent and in other ways resistant. Coffins reappear as iconographic symbols of anti-colonial protest in 1878 in Dublin and today in Kolkata. Other multiple objects interpolate processes in art practice: Bremner's grey architecture, Tursack's multiple readings toward a possible new art production, Jarzombek's ghostly matter and form. The utopian projection is a castigation of immediate politics in Burioni's de la Valle just as it is in Mitchell's King Camp Gillette, the Royal Jubilee is a site of resistance and formation in Crinson's Dublin and Loring's Joseph Urban. The architecture of the elite home is a kernel of political appropriation in both Durga Puja and Palm Beach. Theological assemblies of American architects correspond to the ritual basis of Kolkata's new urban systems. Empire is the heterogeneous collection, according to Bowes, and also still a symbology of expropriation and reconstitution, as per Le Roux, rejoindered by many others here. The living pictures of Guha-Thakurta's Durga Puja combine with active theses of the design practices profiled in this volume. The possibility of a nomadic economy and its forms is explored in Mongolia and in Bengal and interwoven in a broader reading. New architectural event spaces emerge across language as kernels of a resistant politics. Ensemble the issue of Perspecta number fifty-two is a demonstration and a design brief.

Ensemble in architecture and its new possibilities are set out to be positively discerned, learned from even, through the center point of this issue —the contemporary Bengali city, theorized through the twin contributions of Swati Chattopadhahy and Tapati Guha-Thakurta and the photography of Arko Datto and Heyward Hart. Abundant open avenues remain for this research. This case demonstrates a designed material form as a switch in the city. It shows a paradigmatic possibility for a city of multiple incommensurate, even contradictory, states, and therein a possible critical stance to the overwhelming constraint of site in architectural production via the resistance of temporariness. Organizationally, and politically, the Bengal Durga Puja Festival is procured through nebulous self-organized political units. It has an origin and evolution deeply entwined with the city of Kolkata, founded as the fortified headquarters of the East India Company. As the festival expands today alongside the Hinduization of the Indian state, its documentation in this issue is especially important. To this condition, the volume entire is in many ways intended in ensemble, in new extensive and multiple formations and cycles of collective exchange.

Rural Functionalism in Vichy France

Jean-Louis Cohen

The architecture conceived during the four years of Nazi occupation in France—between the summers of 1940 and 1944—is generally considered to be branded with a seal of conservatism, or even to be plain reactionary.[1] It is tempting to test the validity of this judgment by looking at the intersection between architecture and another significant axis of policy of the regime presided over by Marshall Philippe Pétain—rural agenda. The Vichy program of reconstruction, accompanied by a focus on regions and the local, was sponsored by a state which, in other domains, had never been more centralized, but which celebrated rurality through figures of the village or the peasant.

An administrative division of territorial *départements* existed in France, resulting from the French Revolution. The Vichy regime intended to substitute these with provinces modeled on the Ancien Régime. In a letter written in December 1940 as message for the 110th birthday of Frédéric Mistral—the Provençal poet and tutelary figure of regionalism—Marshal Philippe Pétain underlines the conservatism of the provincial spirit: "oppose with fierce resistance everything that is downgraded, leveled, uprooted."[2] In the Appeal of June 25, 1940, a text written for Pétain by the philosopher Emmanuel Berl,rurality was established as a value of salvation. It affirms: "The earth does not lie, it remains your recourse, it is the homeland itself."[3] On August 22, 1940, a statement to the American press further specifies these thoughts: Pétain indicates that France "will become what it should never have ceased to be, an essentially agricultural nation. Like the giant of the fable, she will recover all her strength by reconnecting with the earth."[4]

Gerard Miller has shown the importance in this connection of the figure of the rural person. According to Pétain, it is necessary "that the rural person is highly honored, because he constitutes with the soldier the essential guarantees of the existence and the safeguarding of the country."[5] The rural person provides a moral example, as Pétain declared in 1936: "stubbornness in the daily effort, physical resistance, cautiousness toward any long-term forecasts and long-term decisions, a reasoned confidence, the taste for a rough and simple life; such are the virtues of our countrymen."[6]

Here, the two fields of Vichy politics were superimposed: regionalism was largely based on the celebration of the countryside, and rural space was considered within a regional perspective. These notions correspond to distinct speeches and programs, marked, in each case, by the seal of ambiguity characteristic of the years of the occupation. Each includes literary, artistic, and urbanistic and architectural registers. Under the occupation, regionalism and rurality tended to contaminate discourse and practice, forcing the most determined moderns to institute inflections in their approach. This led to cunning, sometimes subversive, strategies. The regionalist discourse percolated in the spheres of public policy and communication. The Charter of the reconstruction architect [*Charte de l'architecte reconstructeur*] reads as symptomatic of the prescriptions placed over signs of the "spiritual role" of the designer:

> Consider that for more than half a century, the small towns and the countryside have become ugly, the regional characters have disappeared. Yet, formerly,

> the work of men was at one with the landscape and with themselves; today it tends to become uniform from one region to another, disparate even in the same region and inhuman. It is therefore necessary, since the causes of evil are evident, to seek the means of combating them in future constructions. To that end, do not hesitate to look at the traditional houses of small towns and villages: masterpieces of the craftsmen of the past, they are the perfect expression of the ways of life of our ancestors.... Your first task will be to penetrate the spirit of the region in which you are to create. You must learn to know it well and, especially, to love it. This will not be delivered to you immediately, because if some of its characteristics are apparent, many others are hidden and require sensitivity, intuition and reflection to be revealed......[7]

One method is suggested:

> Study in a more detailed way, preferably with houses of exceptional aspect and strongly marked by the historical style, those which present the maximum of permanent characteristics, that is to say, characteristics which are retained over time. Do not disdain the simple houses: they are the strongest expression of the country. Finally, take as a base the type of house that you have found to offer the maximum number of typical characteristics and note the most important variants.... After having analyzed all these elements, it will be easy for you to make a synthesis which, having become familiar, will be for you of a precious help in the study of your projects. You will then be able to bring this spiritual element which makes, accordingly to whether it exists or is absent, either a human and living architecture or, on the contrary, a disappointing and dismal realization.[8]

In terms of architectural regionalism, France lagged behind Germany where the *Deutscher Bund Heimatschutz*, created in 1904 by Ernst Rudorff, had found its most active theoretician and propagandist in the person of Paul Schultze-Naumburg. The small green volumes of its *Kulturarbeiten*, published between 1902 and 1917 had declined principles at the scale of the town, landscape and house, and juxtaposed photographs of counter-examples identified throughout the countryside, proposing them as the recommended patterns. The message from Schultze-Naumburg on the rationality of traditional architectures announced word for word those of the *Charter*.[9]

In 1941, the weekly publication *L'Illustration*—read in all the bourgeois salons—devoted a special issue to reconstruction, which coincided with the promulgation of the *Charter*. In the lead essay, *La renaissance des villages de France*, critic Léandre Vaillat attempts to draw lessons from the failure of the "reconstitution" of devastated regions after 1918, and the episodes that followed. Vaillat introduced an inflated notion of "health," which he borrowed from Frederick Kiesler—who he probably did not realize was a Jew and a modern radical—making it the pivot of his argument for an architecture that could escape the tyranny of fashions launched since 1889 through the Expositions:

> We will not be able to build the village of tomorrow or adapt the village of the past to the life of today if, beforehand, we do not seek to ignore the visual habits installed in our memory by the brilliant but ephemeral spectacle of exhibitions. It is necessary that, by a sort of Jansenism, we absolutely forbid ourselves what is only fashion. The so-called schools of architecture throw themselves, as the case may be, in with the words beauty, solidity, practical qualities and economy: these are excuses for evading the essential. An American, Mr. Frédéric [sic] J. Kiesler, proposes to replace them by a single word: that of health. Moral health, which excludes the sophisms of architectural fashion. Physical health, which requires a construction of size to challenge a century at least, mainly when it is not a country house, a seasonal fantasy, but a rural house, the headquarters of culture. Only tolerated innovations that result from new needs. As for secular needs, it will always be necessary to return to the living elements, those which simply express the permanent needs of the human activity. In each of them we will quickly unravel the role of fashion and health.[10]

Vaillat was an indisputable champion for the regionalism he had advocated for over twenty-five years. With criticism hostile to the moderns, he evoked with regret the fact that the exhibition of regional architecture in the invaded provinces, which he had organized in 1917 in response to the destruction of the First World War, did not have any effect on the ground. Among the sources able to be used for a respectful reconstruction of regional character, Vaillat could not fail to cite the work of the architect Charles Letrosne, *Walls and roofs for the countryside of our home* [*Murs et les toits pour les pays de chez-nous*], published in 1923. Vaillat had, himself, written the preface to this set of three portfolios, presenting a collection of architectural solutions adjusted to the features of the typical historical architecture of the French regions: the post office or the town hall was shown adapted in the Alsatian, Corsican or Basque way, in watercolors that allowed a savoring of their character. Vaillat never ceased to advocate for regional architecture throughout the inter-war period, just as regionalist discourse was reinforced and diffused, as Jean-Claude Vigato has demonstrated, with accents that were both antimodern and politically reactionary.[11] As Camille Mauclair, the vibrant opponent of Le Corbusier, wrote in 1933 in his pamphlet *L'Architecture va-t-elle mourir?*, "Regionalism is the bane of communism."[12]

The reflection on region and rurality is not, however, the preserve of the political right, as shown by several displays at the Paris International Exposition in 1937. Here, the *Centre of the Regions* [*Le Centre Régional*] pavilions are assembled at the *l'Île des Cygnes*, many of them a modernized interpretation of historical constants; for example, there is the "village made of all the villages of France" ["*village fait de tous les villages de France*"], the Savoy Pavilion by Henri-Jacques Le Même.[13] The chief architect of the 1937 Exposition, Jacques Gréber, articulates "the most vivid illustration" of Letrosne's book (Letrosne had been the initial planner of the show): "the proof is, without any pastiche, made by the adaptation of modern needs to the immortal traditions imposed by climate, race, customs, and language, to bring out a form of living architecture that is indisputably more human and more sensitive than the mathematical and monotonous abstractions led by the sterile dogmas of the Esperantists of architecture."[14]

As for the *Centre of Rural Areas* [*Le Centre Rural*], which the Government of the *Front populaire* adds to the Exposition, this section brought together all the buildings of a theoretical village interpreted in a language of compromise between modern elements and stylized historical reminiscences. The overall project was prepared by André Leconte and Xavier Metz. The partnership of Guimpel, Hennequin, Japy and Martineau was responsible for the farm building in which a modernization of agriculture was staged. Charlotte Perriand and Fernand Léger installed a spectacular outdoor diorama. On the sidelines of the exhibition, the first International Congress of Folklore [*Congrès international du Folklore*] brought together historians, geographers, and ethnologists, under the direction of Paul Rivet, director of the Musée de l'Homme, and his collaborator Georges-Henri Rivière. A note found in the archives of André Hermant indicates that the modernist monthly *L'Architecture d'aujourd'hui* was preparing its own issue on regional architecture in 1939, revealing the intention of the moderns to dispute the exclusivity of the use of a popular notion of rural with their opponents, and also to note their concrete responses to the 1937 Exposition for wide circulation. Having assumed the position as editor of *Techniques et architecture*, Hermant entertained, during 1942 and 1943, a correspondence with Schultze-Naumburg, who was proposing to publish materials on French rural architecture and landscape design in Germany.[15]

From the very first months of the Vichy regime, regionalism was a strong component of Petain's discourse, as shown by his recruitment of Jean Charles-Brun—the founder of the regionalism movement—into the *Conseil national*, created on January 22, 1941. The Secretary General of Fine Arts [*secrétaire général des Beaux-Arts*] Louis Hautecœur did not hesitate to speak on the regional issue, although reconstruction was not a part of his responsibilities. He denounced with as much verve the notion of "imitating" internationalism as he did that of "modern" internationalism:

> Regional architecture must preserve all that is logical; it can remain faithful to the forms that have a purpose [*raison d'être*], but it cannot live pastiche, be pleased by the style of the "medieval inn" or the universal exhibition pavilion. It can not ignore modern needs and materials. It must adapt the lessons of the province to the necessities of changing life. Regional architecture, like any architecture, presupposes common sense, logic, measurement.[16]

The pages devoted to regionalism by the authors in other disciplines were innumerable. Landscape architect André Vera proposed an extension to the realm of gardens in 1941 in his *Manifesto for the Renewal of French Art* [*Manifeste pour le renouveau de l'art français*], published as an article in *Urbanisme* prior to becoming an autonomous volume.[17] In his 1942 article "*Régionalisme,*" Vera criticized the first reconstruction projects undertaken in the *department du Loiret*—notably in Gien: "on the banks of the Loire, in such a bombed city, the façades will be built in red bricks, the others black, arranged so as to draw diagonals. It is, it seems, in the tradition. This work, done with regularly calibrated bricks, regularly tinted, red or black, regularly laid down in the same vertical plane, regularly jointed, will not it produce a painful variegation? ... And can we only ask the masons to mitigate the hardness caused by the regularity of hue and calibration, to mount the facades in mill wings and to do everything a bit askew?"[18] The anaphora of Vera is a good example of the artisanal approach taken by the regionalists.

Remarkably, it was in 1942 that Georges Doyon and Robert Hubrecht published *The Rural and Bourgeois Architecture in France, A Study of the Techniques of the Past and their Applications to our Time* [*L'Architecture rurale et bourgeoise en France, étude sur les techniques d'autrefois et leurs applications à notre temps*]—the 434-page manuscript had been almost completely finalized in 1939.[19] In this text, Doyon and Hubrecht provided *reconstructeurs* a fairly systematic body of doctrine, based on the comparison of a large number of examples, and a practical manual containing easily transposable details. Doyon, a pupil of Victor Laloux and Charles Lemaresquier, was an architect in charge of major state buildings, and Hubrecht, a disciple of the conservative École des Beaux-Arts educators Charles Lemaresquier and Georges Gromort, was an architect. Hubrecht returned after the death of his colleague to write the many subsequent editions of the book, eliminating, prudently, its subtitle from the 1945 edition and thereafter.[20] The book had an encyclopedic dimension. It was not divided according to regions or provinces, although it addressed "northern" and "southern" houses in separate chapters. Rather, in an "analytical observation of the vast majority of old houses," Hubrecht focused on the "general characteristics of the House of France" which he relates to the "classical concept of architecture."[21] If a study of "craftmanship of details" [*"facture des details"*] and "constructive elements" occupies practically half of the work, it escapes the frequent fetishism of this type of literature in order to consider the houses in terms of their constitutive principles—masses and ordinances in particular but also the plan. The volume navigates between the analysis of the house as a totality and that of all the families of works that constitute it.

Much attention was paid to the grouping of houses in villages and towns, but also to squares and "urban groupings," although, by the authors' own admission, they pose these to be "problems that go beyond [their] work."[22] A certain historical fixation emerges: "we tried to convince our readers that the time with which we could most easily reconnect the chain is that of the flourishing of classical architecture in France, from the seventeenth to the nineteenth century, and that, because instructions of order are preponderant, and it is from the absence of analogous instructions that we suffer; and again, because that time is still sensitive to the traditions of guilds, without requiring the constant use of the whole of artisanal force, which, if it is not the natural fruit of a technique, not only scholarly but dynamic, leads only to fancies devoid of value, and are dangerous examples offered to all bad tastes."[23] This problematic developed by Doyon and Hubrecht is not radically antimodern and, to show it best, the authors reproduced the sketch of a "fishing hamlet in Brittany" by Le Corbusier, and a Breton house drawing by modernist André Lurçat. Prior to anything descriptive, the book was prescriptive, and intended to have a veritable use value: it concluded on "instructions" written for the use of the practitioners, and which show regard to "old advised practices" [*pratiques anciennes à conseiller*] as well as "modern habits to avoid" whether masonry, roofing, carpentry, carpentry or lock-smithing.

Also in 1942, a nationwide enactment took place through the provincial studies competitions organized by the Commissariat for Building Reconstruction [*Commissariat à la reconstruction immobilière*]. Published in the July-August issue of the conservative journal *L'Architecture française*, the program encouraged competitors to "use their memories only to create new works,"[24] thus dismissing any excessive mimicry. It is true that many prisoners invited to participate often had only memory at their disposal to elaborate the projects they sent to Paris, shown in the Palais de Chaillot from April 1 to October 15, 1942.[25] Both in the curvilinear galleries and alcoves of the building and on the pages of *L'Architecture française*, projects were presented according to the regions, the lion's share being reserved for the region of Île-de-France surrounding Paris. Other projects were designed by architects who had avoided captivity, such as Louis Arretche, who drew several rural buildings and town houses for Artois with a large team.

The vigorous public campaign to promote regionalism, spearheaded by the efforts of the administration, led various press to solicit work from the most prominent architects. In the rag newspaper *Les Nouveaux temps*, linked to the collaborationist Jean Luchaire, several of these efforts were interrogated. The director of the École des Beaux-Arts Paul Tournon considered this operation, "a vast analytical investigation tending to identify the reasons for certain constructive or plastic arrangements and to discover constants worthwhile for any time, [it] can be of the greatest aid for the architects called to build in regions of which they do not know the deep characteristics."[26] Auguste Perret was clear in his reaction: "regionalism? What a joke! Does a horse stop a locomotive? But today the regionalists seem less convinced of the future of the animal they launched, a little faster, onto rail ... This, moreover, will not stand before the realities. And they are the ones who control them. France will be, by force, rebuilt in a new style and with new techniques."[27]

In a brochure dedicated in 1943 to Olivier de Serres, who introduced modern agriculture in France at the end of the sixteenth-century, Jean Charles-Brun observed: "We had, for more than a century, lost ground as we detached from the earth.... I am thinking of the virtues proper of the soil and race, to the characteristics of this peasantry, the true strength of the nation, a school of patience and toil, a guardian of morality and family life."[28] Alongside Joan of Arc and Marshall Lyautey, de Serres was part of the Vichy regime's pantheon, and pilgrimages were organized to his former estate at Le Pradel in Villeneuve-de-Berg. The Musée national des Arts et Traditions Populaires created an interpretation center, inaugurated in July 1939 by Georges-Henri Rivière, the museum's founder, together with Marcel Maget and Guy Pison. With the support of the Minister of National Education [*ministre de l'Éducation nationale*] and the radical-socialist leader Jean Zay, Rivière began by creating a department, the Arts et Traditions Populaires (ATP), within the Musée de l'Homme in 1937. It would eventually become independent. The same year, the Exposition in Paris gave Rivière the opportunity to envision a prefiguration of the small regional museum [*Musée du Terroir*] in the *Centre rural*, using the example of the village of Romenay-en-Bresse. More importantly, Rivière organized the exhibition *The Rural House in France* [*La maison rurale en France*] at the Palais de Tokyo with the geographer Albert Demangeon: it centered on five types of buildings recreated through an installation in open space, a display that earned him many critics.[29] A useful comparison to develop more precisely would be the exhibition organized the previous year as part of the Milan Triennale, by Giuseppe Pagano under the title *Architettura rurale italiana*, which celebrated the "functionality" of rural dwellings and agricultural buildings.[30]

Rivière's display, developed with assistance of the ethno-historian André Varagnac, was installed in the west wing of the Palais de Chaillot. It both utilized existing collections and developed them in pronounced ways, particularly around the theme of rural culture. Rivière was an accomplished musician and had attended the courses of the *École du Louvre* while hanging out in the galleries of the *Musée d'Ethnographie* at the *Palais de Chaillot*, where he began his career. He had organized the legendary Dakar-Djibouti mission of 1931–33. At the International Congress of Folklore [*congrès international du folklore*] of 1937, Rivière was in contact with historians Lucien Febvre and Marc Bloch. Although it was a creation of the *Front populaire*, the Musée national des Arts et Traditions Populaires experienced an intense activity under the occupation. It became a national museum in 1941, allowing Rivière to remark: "other projects are engendered by new causes: the will of the French head of state is to give the country a regionalist structure, to animate foci of civilizations to give an important place to the rural people and artisans, and to inspire young people with love and respect for tradition. If we adopt our terminology... we would say that folklore as well as folk ethnography are called upon to benefit from the circumstances."[31]

In June 1941, Rivière took part in the exhibition *La France européenne* by setting up a "Normandy farm" in the Grand Palais and, in December of 1942, the *Exposition artisanale nationale* in the Pavillon de Marsan of the Louvre. Particularly important was the museum undertaking of four "Intellectual Worksites" [*Chantiers intellectuels*] organized by the General Delegation for National Equipment [*Délégation générale à l'équipement national*] to ostensibly fight against the unemployment of graduates, but which were incidentally used to help them to avoid compulsory labor service in Germany. More than a hundred people were put to work. The Worksites were supervised at the Ministry by the poet and resistance fighter Edmond Humeau. Worksite No. 909 dealt with "traditional furniture," No. 1810 with arts and craftsmanship, No. 1187 with the organization of the documentation of the museum. Worksite No. 1425 was devoted to a "*Survey of Regional Architecture*" and engaged about fifty architects.[32]

The operation was led by the architect and engineer Urbain Cassan—who served as president—and Pierre-Louis Duchartre—the museum specialist. Rivière was replaced by Pison upon the latter's return from captivity. He was joined by the architects Pierre Drobecq and Jean-Charles Moreux, as well as the ethnologist Marcel Maget. The text *Instructions for Investigators* [*Instructions pour les enquêteurs*], written by Cassan, Duchartre, Pison and Rivière, inscribes the operation in its political context: "a new France wants to find its way in the light of the traditions, to restore the rural population and to save the physical and moral health of its children, by a house policy." The authors invited young architects who, for the most part, were attached to the ideas of the modern movement to detect the "constants" that made it possible to define the "characteristic house" in each county.[33]

The *Survey of Regional Architecture* was based on the study of samples selected by the architects, sometimes on the basis of their aesthetic quality. Marie-Noëlle Denis has nonetheless compared the rigor of the dossiers created to those of the "descriptive systems of the natural sciences."[34] Based on the instructions of Pison, the survey team gathered texts and sketches according to a layout fixed to a standardized format, twenty-one by twenty-seven centimeters, with drawings standardized in terms of architectural scale and graphic conventions. The analysis was conducted using a notion of terrain in which buildings were not the only centers of interest: various uses and agricultural activities were also documented through oral surveys, and work in the archives of the land registry and among the notaries completed this, as well as collection of all possible visual and cartographic materials. In some cases, the study also focused on beliefs, rites, and magic or religious signs, moving from architecture to ethnography. Two centers coexisted in the organization of the project: the apartment of Rivière in the occupied zone, and an apartment in Montpellier, in the "free" zone.[35] A total of fifteen-thousand drawings were produced, corresponding to about twenty sites per each department, across seventy-seven of them. A total of about 1600 case studies of buildings were compiled.

In 1943, under the aegis of Maget, who had been trained as a psychologist and ethnologist and was the head of the service of the "rural civilization" [*civilisation paysanne*] of the National Rural Corporation [*Corporation nationale paysanne*], the investigation became more rigorous. It combined a historic study of the house in its natural environment, a precise and methodical description of the building, and an analysis of the adaptation of the built environment to the uses and the way of life of the occupants.

George-Henri Rivière was a member of the editorial board of *L'Architecture française*, but it was the journal *Techniques et architecture*, an offspring of the modernist *L'Architecture d'aujourd'hui*—the latter having been scuttled by its Jewish owner André Bloc in 1940—which gave the best coverage of the program. An issue entitled "*Techniques locales*" produced at the end of 1943 gave an initial assessment of the enterprise. Its strategy was presented by extracts from the report made by Pison at a conference held a year earlier at the École du Louvre, in the presence of officials such as André Prothin, head of city planning at the national level, academics, and also Le Corbusier who was acquainted with Rivière. Pison affirmed: "Our survey is a synthetic search, implementing the various disciplines that are interested in the rural house. From this point of view our research participates in science, insofar as it is related to human geography, economic and social history, and finally ethnography; It also participates in art, I mean architecture and agriculture."[36] Pison considers Albert Demangeon's geography and Marc Bloch's rural history as his main inspiration, stating: "there is an ethnographic way of studying human facts," and that, "participating in scientific research, our inquiry also participates art, in this case architecture and agriculture."[37] Above all, Pison presents his method as being both intensive and extensive: "[we have] endeavored to combine the two methods by determining, within the department assigned to each architect, the characteristic regions and in these regions, the centers of interest on which, at least initially, the investigation had to be carried out."[38]

In addition to benefits of a historical, geographical, ethnographic and museographic nature, Pison highlighted the architectural challenges: "While we will always have more agricultural machinery, a scientific agriculture will intensify and specialize production. Multiplied transport will bring materials created by the industry, with lands that will be regrouped, and new social structures that will emerge. Yet, we go imitating forms that, when they were alive, evolved, and which appear today only dissected or mummified? Let us therefore know that we must free ourselves, as architects enlightened by this experience of ethnography, from an obsolete regionalism. And direct our studies towards a bold functionalism. But this will be another lesson of our research—towards a humanist functionalism, not a restrictive one but one that exalts individual and social man."[39]

In a general overview, Urbain Cassan questioned the transformation of the characters of the rural house through time.[40] It was left to André Hermant to give a thorough examination: Hermant derived an initial assessment of the Worksites as they appeared to him: "1. The unsuspected diversity and interpenetration of local techniques whose distribution is far from correspondent to the simplistic delimitation of geographical or economic regions. 2. The multiplicity of factors to which these local techniques owe their origin and their justification, often very different from the truly local conditions that are the material resources and the climate. 3. The variability over time of some of these factors and, consequently, of these techniques themselves. Giving a clearer view of the past, this [...] documentation will provide a healthy lesson for the future."[41] Utilizing a remarkable graphic system, developed by Jean Bossu, who had been one of the most diligent draftsmen at the studio of Le Corbusier and Pierre Jeanneret in the mid-1930s, Hermant reinforced those theses that went against the regionalist postulates in his dossiers, grouping several case studies by *département*. Highlighting the geographical and economic data, he compares similarities and differences, especially as related to the organization of rural buildings and the structure of farms. These analyses define an approach that is not nostalgic, and in which the variety of architectural components can simply help identify a "local composition unit." Bossu presented his own investigations from Vendée, a *département* in western France, undermining the regionalist illusion with a provocative oxymoron: "the folklore of tomorrow will teach us that the regionalism of reinforced concrete lies in the difference of its interpretation from one country to another ... And we will speak the same language as yesterday, but with a renewed syntax."[42] In May 1944, Rivière sent Bossu a "note on the aesthetic characteristics of the French rural house," "in memory of our Vendées." Suspected of collaborationism after the liberation of France, Rivière was suspended from the direction of the ATP, leaving it provisionally in the hands of Marcel Maget, although the program undertaken during the war would be re-established in 1946. Urbain Cassan had become director general at the Ministry of Reconstruction, an institute led by his old friend Raoul Dautry. In 1946, he relied heavily on his experiences as part of Worksite No. 1425, for the publication of his book *People, houses, landscapes: Essay on the environment* [*Hommes, maisons, paysages; essai sur l'environnement*].[43]

The next year, in 1947, the journal *Techniques et architecture* returns to the experience of Worksite No. 1425. Rivière finally publishes the note sent to Bossu.[44] The principles of the *Chantiers intellectuels* appear in the volume in all their clarity, freed of the rigorous but constraining grid of Bossu that defined the previous publication. A "general study" on the Vercors was published as the introduction to the volume, by the historian Albert Soboul who would become an acknowledged specialist of the French Revolution. The case study of a Vercors farm is given in full form, making it possible to perceive all the layers of the analysis conducted by the investigators between 1941 and 1943. This reprised investigation would set in motion the publication of the *Corpus d'architecture rurale française*, led by Jean Cuisenier, successor of Rivière, while Rivière would go on to oversee the new building for the *Musée des Arts et Traditions Populaires* in the Bois de Boulogne, designed by architect Jean Dubuisson. Pison would, in 1958, design the agriculture display in the French pavilion of the Brussels Exposition assisted by young designer Paul Chemetov.

The allusion to the modernity of rural architecture was not totally incantatory. The *Techniques locales* issue of *Techniques et architecture* concludes with views of a farm at Grand Pouvreau, built in 1941 in the Vendée marshes, by the sculptor Joël Martel and the architect Gérald Hanning, whom the issue defines as "regional, without being regionalist." Martel and Hanning were friends of Bossu. Martel, a sculptor who had contributed to the Congress of Folklore of 1937 with a paper on "Construction moderne et folklore,"[45] was established in Vendée. Hanning was then a draftsman at the office Le Corbusier, for whom he began the study of the Modulor. In the Somme, a team formed by Bossu and the town planner Paul Dufournet focused on a project at the scale of the territory of the municipality of Le Bosquel that had completely burned down in 1940.[46] They conducted a study of the rural buildings there, and designed a detailed reconstruction of several large farms, including one named Quesnel. The reconstruction included consideration of housing and farm buildings. The light wood frames of Quesnel were also referenced in the work of Robert Le Ricolais, future professor of structures at the University of Pennsylvania. This remains undoubtedly the most concrete case of the implementation of the conclusions of the *Chantiers Intellectuelles*, Worksite No. 1425, a moment which cast an extremely long shadow on postwar architecture. FIG 1-17

1 Anatole Kopp, Frédérique Boucher, and Danièle Pauly. *L'architecture de la reconstruction en France, 1945–1953*. Paris: Éditions du Moniteur, 1982.

2 «Oppose une résistance farouche à tout ce qui vient nous déclasser, nous niveler, nous déraciner ;» Marshall Pétain, in Gérard Miller, *Les Pousse-au-jouir du maréchal Pétain* (Paris: Seuil, 2004), 124.

3 «La terre, elle, ne ment pas. Elle demeure votre recours. Elle est la patrie elle-même» Marshall Pétain, Appeal of 25 June 1940, in Miller, *Les Pousse-au-jouir*, 136.

4 «Redeviendra ce qu'elle n'aurait jamais dû cesser d'être, une nation essentiellement agricole. Comme le géant de la fable, elle retrouvera toutes ses forces en reprenant contact avec la terre.» Pétain in the American press, 22 August 1940, in Miller, *Les Pousse-au-jouir*, 134.

5 «Que le paysan soit hautement honoré, car il constitue avec le soldat les garanties essentielles de l'existence et de la sauvegarde du pays.» Marshall Pétain, Message of April 20, 1941, in Miller, *Les Pousse-au-jouir*, 133.

6 «L'obstination dans l'effort quotidien, la résistance physique, une prudence faite de prévisions à longues échéances et de décisions longuement mûries, la confiance raisonnée, le goût d'une vie rude et simple, telles sont les vertus de nos campagnards.» Marshall Pétain, tdiscourse in front of the memorial to the dead peasants of Capoulet-Junac, 17 janvier 1936, in Miller, *Les Pousse-au-jouir*, p. 135–136.

7 «Songez que, depuis plus d'un demi-siècle, les petites villes, les campagnes s'enlaidissent, les caractères régionaux s'effacent. Pourtant, jadis, l'œuvre des hommes faiait corps avec le paysage et avec eux-mêmes ; aujourd'hui elle tend à devenir uniforme d'une région à l'autre, disparate même dans une même région et inhumaine. Il faut donc, les causes du mal étant évidentes, chercher les moyens de les combattre dans les constructions futures. Pour cela, n'hésitez pas à regarder les maisons traditionnelles de petites villes et des villages: chefs-d'œuvre des artisans d'autrefois, elles sont l'expression parfaite des genres de vie de nos ancêtres. [...] Votre premier travail sera donc de vous pénétrer de l'esprit de la région dans laquelle vous allez créer. Il vous faut apprendre à la bien connaître et surtout à l'aimer. Elle ne se livrera pas tout de suite, car si certains de ses caractères sont apparents, beaucoup d'autres sont cachés et exigent pour se révéler de la sensibilité, de l'intuition et de la réflexion.» «Charte de l'architecte reconstructeur,» *L'Architecture française* 2, No. 4 (1941), 43.

8 «Étudiez d'une façon plus approfondie, de préférence aux maisons d'aspect exceptionnel et fortement marquées par le style historique, celles qui présentent le maximum de caractères permanents, c'est-à-dire des caractères qui se conservent dans le temps. Ne dédaignez pas les maisons simples : elles sont la plus forte expression du pays.

Prenez enfin comme base le type de maison que vous aurez jugé offrir le maximum de caractères typiques et notez-en les plus importantes variantes. [...] Après avoir analysé tous ces éléments, il vous sera facile d'en faire une synthèse qui, devenue familière, sera pour vous d'une aide précieuse dans l'étude de vos projets. Vous saurez alors apporter cet élément spirituel qui fait, suivant qu'il y existe ou qu'il en est absent, une architecture humaine et vivante ou au contraire une réalisation décevante et morne.» «Charte de l'architecte reconstructeur,» *L'Architecture française* 2, No. 4 (1941), 43.

9 Paul Schultze-Naumburg, *Kulturarbeiten*. Munich: Callwey, 1902–17.

10 «Nous ne saurons pas construire le village de demain ni adapter le village d'autrefois à la vie d'aujourd'hui si, au préalable, nous ne cherchons à faire abstraction des habitudes visuelles installées dans notre mémoire par le spectacle brillant mais éphémère des expositions. Il faut que, par une sorte de jansénisme, nous nous interdisions absolument ce qui n'est que mode. Les soi-disant écoles d'architecture se jettent, selon les cas, les mots de beauté, de solidité, de qualités pratiques et d'économie : ce sont là des excuses pour éluder l'essentiel. Un Américain, M. Frédéric J. Kiesler, propose de les remplacer par un seul mot : celui de *santé*. Santé morale, qui exclut les sophismes des modes architecturales. Santé physique, qui exige une construction de taille à défier un siècle au moins, principalement quand il s'agit non d'une maison de campagne, fantaisie saisonnière, mais d'une maison paysanne, quartier général de la culture. Seules selon tolérées les innovations qui résultent des besoins nouveaux. Pour ce qui est des besoins séculaires, il faudra toujours en revenir aux éléments vivants, ceux qui expriment simplement les besoins permanents de l'activité humaine. En chacun d'entre eux on aura vite fait de démêler la part de la mode et celle de la santé.» Léandre Vaillat, "La renaissance des villages de France", *L'Illustration*, No. 5124, May 24, 1941, n. p. See also "Nous avons à restaurer la France," *L'Illustration*, No. 5090 September 28, 1940, 95–71.

11 Jean-Claude Vigato, *L'architecture régionaliste: France, 1890–1950* (Paris: Norma, 1994).

12 «Le régionalisme est la bête noire du communisme.» Camille Mauclair, *La Crise du "panbétonnisme intégral". L'Architecture va-t-elle mourir ?* (Paris: Nouvelle Revue Critique, 1933), 88.

13 «Village fait de tous les villages de France». René Baschet, quoted in Vigato, *L'Architecture régionaliste*, 266.

14 «La preuve est faite que, sans aucun pastiche, l'adaptation des besoins modernes aux traditions immortelles qu'imposent le climat, la race, les coutumes et la langue permet de dégager une forme d'architecture vivante indiscutablement plus humaine et plus sensible que l'abstrait mathématique et monotone auquel aboutissent les dogmes stériles des espérantistes de l'architecture.» Jacques Gréber quoted in Vigato, *L'architecture régionaliste*, 267.

15 See among others: André Hermant, letter to Paul Schultze-Naumburg. July 13, 1943. Hermant archive. Cité de l'architecture et du patrimoine, Paris.

16 «L'architecture régionale doit conserver tout ce qui est logique ; elle peut demeurer fidèle aux formes qui ont une raison d'être, mais elle ne saurait vivre de pastiche, se plaire au style "hostellerie" ou pavillon d'exposition universelle. Elle ne peut méconnaître les besoins et les matériaux modernes. Elle doit adapter les leçons de la province aux nécessités de la vie changeante. L'architecture régionale, comme toute architecture, suppose le bon sens, la logique, la mesure». Louis Hautecœur, «Régionalisme et architecture», *L'Architecture française* 3, No. 15, 1942.

17 André Vera, *Manifeste pour le renouveau de l'art français*, Orléans, Imprimerie orléanaise, 1941.

18 «Au bord de la Loire, en telle ville bombardée, les façades seront construites en briques les unes rouges, les autres noires, disposées de façon à dessiner des diagonales. C'est, paraît-il, dans la tradition. Ce travail exécuté avec des briques régulièrement calibrées, régulièrement teintées, rouge ou noir, régulièrement posées à fleur d'un même plan vertical, régulièrement jointoyées, ne produira-t-il pas un pénible bariolage ? [...] Et peut-on seulement demander aux maçons pour atténuer la dureté causée par la régularité de teinte et de calibrage, de monter les façades en ailes de moulin et de tout faire un peu de guingois ?», ibid.

19 Georges Doyon and Robert Hubrecht, *L'Architecture rurale et bourgeoise en France, étude sur les techniques d'autrefois et leurs applications à notre temps* (Paris: Vincent, Fréal et Cie, 1942).

20 François Gebelin, "Georges Doyon, Robert Hubrecht. L'architecture rurale et bourgeoise en France," *Bulletin Monumental* 129, No. 3 (1971), 215–217.

21 Doyon and Hubrecht, *L'Architecture rurale*, 10.

22 Doyon and Hubrecht, *L'Architecture rurale*, 300.

23 «Nous avons essayé de convaincre nos lecteurs que l'époque avec laquelle nous pouvions le plus facilement renouer la chaîne est celle de l'épanouissement de l'architecture classique en France, du XVIIe au XIXe siècle, et cela parce que les consignes d'ordre y sont prépondérantes, et de c'est de l'absence des consignes analogues que nous souffrons ; et encore, parce qu'à cette époque les traditions des corporations sont encore sensibles, sans qu'elles nécessitent l'emploi constant du tout de force artisanal, lequel, s'il n'est pas le fruit naturel d'une technique, non pas seulement savante mais dynamique, n'aboutit qu'à des fantaisies dénuées de valeur, et sont des exemples dangereux offerts à tous les mauvais goûts.» Doyon and Hubrecht, *L'Architecture rurale*, 401.

24 «Ne faire appel à leurs souvenirs que pour créer une œuvre nouvelle » *L'Architecture française* 3, No. 21–22 (July–August 1942).

25 *L'Architecture française* 3, No. 23–24 (September–Octobre 1942).

26 «Une vaste investigation analytique tendant à dégager les raisons de certaines dispositions constructives ou plastiques et à découvrir des constantes valant pour toute époque, [il] pourra

être du plus grand secours pour les architectes appelés à construire dans des régions dont il ils ne connaissent pas les caractéristiques profondes.» Tournon, interview by Jean-Marc Campagne, *Les Nouveaux temps* 11 (August 1943). Republished in *L'Architecture française* 3, No. 35 (1943).

27 «Le régionalisme ? Quelle plaisanterie ! Est-ce qu'un cheval arrête une locomotive ? Mais, de jour en jour les régionalistes paraissent moins convaincus de l'avenir de l'animal qu'ils ont lancé, un peu vite, sur le rail... Ceci, d'ailleurs, ne tiendra pas devant les réalités. Et ce sont elles qui commandent. La France sera, *par force*, reconstruite dans un style neuf et avec des techniques nouvelles.» Perret, interview by Jean-Marc Campagne, *Les Nouveaux temps* 4, August, (1943). Republished in *L'Architecture française* 3, No. 35 (1943).

28 «Nous avions, depuis plus d'un siècle, perdu pied en nous détachant de la terre. [...] je songe aux vertus propres du sol et de la race, aux caractères de cette paysannerie, force véritable de la nation, école de patience et de labeur, conservatrice de la moralité et de la vie familiale.» Jean Charles-Brun, *Olivier de Serres, gentilhomme de la Terre* (Paris: Jean Renard, 1943), quoted in Jean-Michel Guieu, «Régionalisme et idée européenne».

29 Nina Gorgus, *Le magicien des vitrines ; le muséologue Georges-Henri Rivière* [1999], (Paris: Éditions de la Maison des sciences de l'homme, 2003), 104–108. On Rivière, see Germain Viatte, Marie-Charlotte Calafat, eds., *Georges Henri Rivière: voir c'est comprendre,* (Paris: Réunion des musées nationaux, 2018).

30 Giuseppe Pagano, Werner Daniel, *Architettura rurale italiana* (Milan: Hoepli, 1936).

31 «D'autres projets sont engendrés par des causes nouvelles : la volonté du chef de l'État français de donner au pays une structure régionaliste, d'animer des foyers de civilisations régionales, de rendre une place importante à la paysannerie et aux artisans, et d'inspirer aux jeunes l'amour et le respect des traditions. Si nous adoptons notre terminologie [...] nous dirions que le folklore autant que l'ethnographie folklorique sont appelés à bénéficier des circonstances.» Gorgus, *Le magicien des vitrines*, 124. See Christian Faure, *Le projet culturel de Vichy : folklore et révolution nationale, 1940–1944* (Paris: Presses du CNRS, 1989).

32 Marie-Noëlle Denis, « L'enquête d'architecture rurale (1940–1968), une étape dans la construction de l'ethnologie française », in Jacqueline Christophe, Denis-Michel Boëll, Régis Meyran, Michel Colardelle, Isac Chiva and Christian Bromberger, dir., *Du folklore à l'ethnologie* (Paris : Éd. de la Maison des sciences de l'homme, 2009), 49–61.

33 «Une France nouvelle veut retrouver sa route à la lumière des traditions, restaurer la paysannerie et sauver la santé physique et morale de ses enfants, par une politique de la maison.» Délégation générale à l'équipement national. Service des chantiers intellectuels et artistiques. *Enquête sur l'architecture régionale, instructions pour les enquêteurs du chantier 1425*, Paris, Bernard frères, 1941.

34 Denis, "L'enquête d'architecture rurale," 52.

35 Georges-Henri Rivière. "Le chantier 1425: un tour d'horizon, une gerbe de souvenirs." *Ethnologie française* 3, No. 1–2 (1973), 9–14.

36 Guy Pison, "L'enquête d'architecture rurale du chantier 1425." *Techniques et architecture* 3, No. 11–12 (November–December 1943), 312 & 324.

37 Pison, "L'enquête d'architecture rurale du chantier 1425," 312 and 324.

38 Pison, "L'enquête d'architecture rurale du chantier 1425," 312.

39 Guy Pison, "L'enquête d'architecture rurale du chantier 1425." *Techniques et architecture* 3, No. 11–12 (November–December 1943), 324.

40 Urbain Cassan, "Persistance et évolution des caractères de la maison rurale," *Techniques et Architecture* 3, No. 11–12 (November–December 1943), 276–278.

41 André Hermant, *Techniques et Architecture* 3, No. 11–12 (November–December 1943).

42 «Le folklore de demain nous apprendra que le régionalisme du béton armé [oxymore provocateur] réside dans la différence de son interprétation d'un pays à l'autre... Et nous parlerons le même langage qu'hier, mais avec une syntaxe renouvelée.» Jean Bossu, *Techniques et Architecture* 3, 11–12 (November–December 1943) 387.

43 Urbain Cassan, *Hommes, maisons, paysages ; essai sur l'environnement humain* (Paris : Plon, 1946).

44 Georges-Henri Rivière, "Formes ; note sur les caractères esthétiques de la maison rurale française," *Techniques et architecture* 7, 1–2 (January–February 1947), 25.

45 Joël Martel, "Construction moderne et folklore," in *Travaux du premier congrès international de folklore, Paris, 23–28 août 1937* (Tours: Arrault et Cie, 1938), 373–376.

46 *Urbanisme* 13, No. 101–102, Avril-Mai (1944), 72.

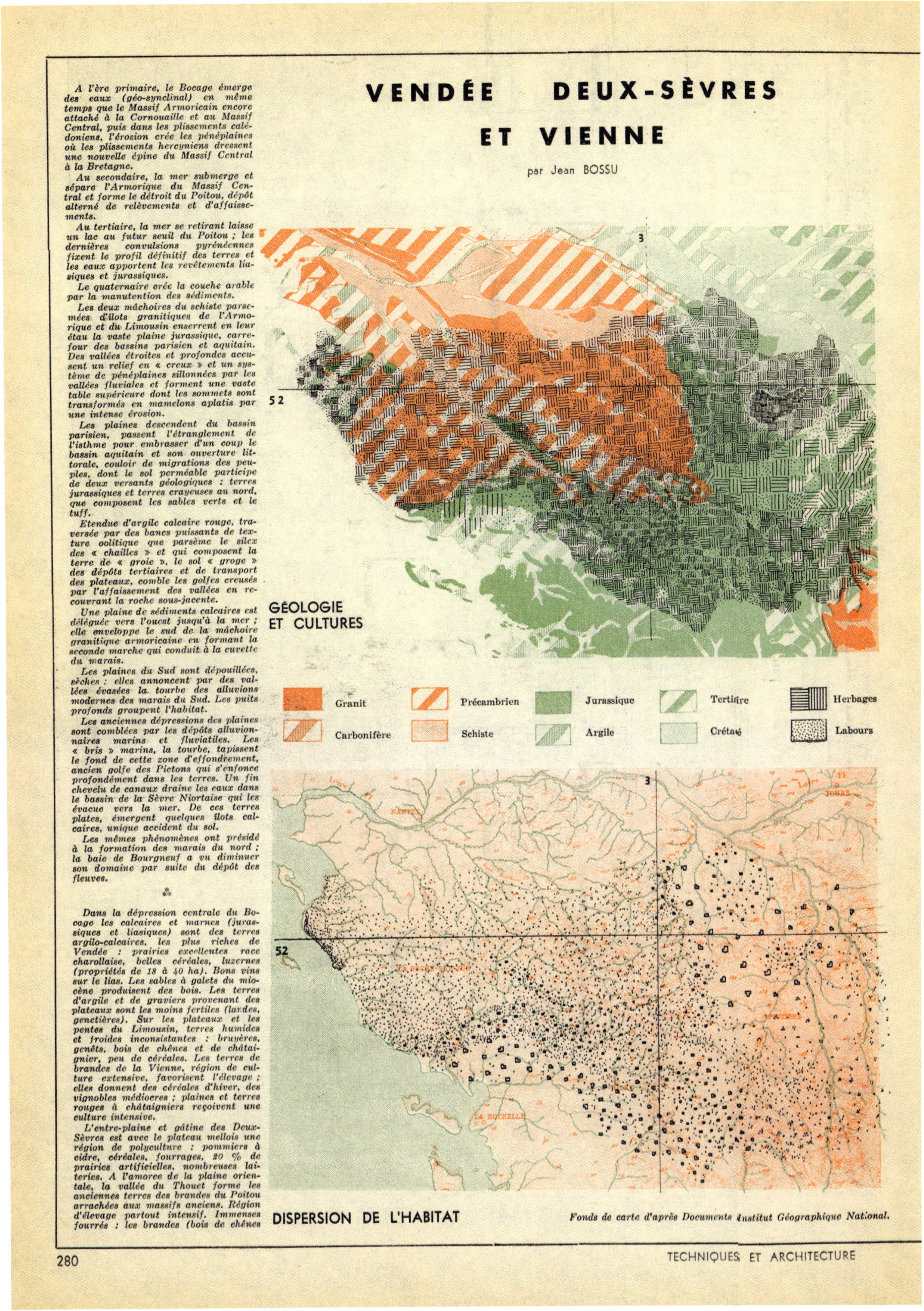

VENDÉE DEUX-SÈVRES ET VIENNE

par Jean BOSSU

A l'ère primaire, le Bocage émerge des eaux (géo-synclinal) en même temps que le Massif Armoricain encore attaché à la Cornouaille et au Massif Central, puis dans les plissements calédoniens, l'érosion crée les pénéplaines où les plissements hercyniens dressent une nouvelle épine du Massif Central à la Bretagne.

Au secondaire, la mer submerge et sépare l'Armorique du Massif Central et forme le détroit du Poitou, dépôt alterné de relèvements et d'affaissements.

Au tertiaire, la mer se retirant laisse un lac au futur seuil du Poitou ; les dernières convulsions pyrénéennes fixent le profil définitif des terres et les eaux apportent les revêtements liasiques et jurassiques.

Le quaternaire crée la couche arable par la manutention des sédiments.

Les deux mâchoires du schiste parsemées d'îlots granitiques de l'Armorique et du Limousin enserrent en leur étau la vaste plaine jurassique, carrefour des bassins parisien et aquitain. Des vallées étroites et profondes accusent un relief en « creux » et un système de pénéplaines sillonnées par les vallées fluviales et forment une vaste table supérieure dont les sommets sont transformés en mamelons aplatis par une intense érosion.

Les plaines descendent du bassin parisien, passent l'étranglement de l'isthme pour embrasser d'un coup le bassin aquitain et son ouverture littorale, couloir de migrations des peuples, dont le sol perméable participe de deux versants géologiques : terres jurassiques et terres crayeuses au nord, que composent les sables verts et le tuff.

Etendue d'argile calcaire rouge, traversée par des bancs puissants de texture oolitique que parsème le silex des « chailles » et qui composent la terre de « groie », le sol « groge » des dépôts tertiaires et de transport des plateaux, comble les golfes creusés par l'affaissement des vallées en recouvrant la roche sous-jacente.

Une plaine de sédiments calcaires est déléguée vers l'ouest jusqu'à la mer ; elle enveloppe le sud de la mâchoire granitique armoricaine en formant la seconde marche qui conduit à la cuvette du marais.

Les plaines du Sud sont dépouillées, sèches : elles annoncent par des vallées évasées la tourbe des alluvions modernes des marais du Sud. Les puits profonds groupent l'habitat.

Les anciennes dépressions des plaines sont comblées par les dépôts alluvionnaires marins et fluviatiles. Les « bris » marins, la tourbe, tapissent le fond de cette zone d'effondrement, ancien golfe des Pictons qui s'enfonce profondément dans les terres. Un fin chevelu de canaux draine les eaux dans le bassin de la Sèvre Niortaise qui les évacue vers la mer. De ces terres plates, émergent quelques îlots calcaires, unique accident du sol.

Les mêmes phénomènes ont présidé à la formation des marais du nord ; la baie de Bourgneuf a vu diminuer son domaine par suite du dépôt des fleuves.

⁂

Dans la dépression centrale du Bocage les calcaires et marnes (jurassiques et liasiques) sont des terres argilo-calcaires, les plus riches de Vendée : prairies excellentes race charollaise, belles céréales, luzernes (propriétés de 18 à 40 ha). Bons vins sur le lias. Les sables à galets du miocène produisent des bois. Les terres d'argile et de graviers provenant des plateaux sont les moins fertiles (landes, genetières). Sur les plateaux et les pentes du Limousin, terres humides et froides inconsistantes : bruyères, genêts, bois de chênes et de châtaignier, peu de céréales. Les terres de brandes de la Vienne, région de culture extensive, favorisent l'élevage ; elles donnent des céréales d'hiver, des vignobles médiocres ; plaines et terres rouges à châtaigniers reçoivent une culture intensive.

L'entre-plaine et gâtine des Deux-Sèvres est avec le plateau mellois une région de polyculture : pommiers à cidre, céréales, fourrages, 20 % de prairies artificielles, nombreuses laiteries. A l'amorce de la plaine orientale, la vallée du Thouet forme les anciennes terres des brandes du Poitou arrachées aux massifs anciens. Région d'élevage partout intensif. Immenses fourrés : les brandes (bois de chênes

GÉOLOGIE ET CULTURES

DISPERSION DE L'HABITAT

Fonds de carte d'après Documents Institut Géographique National.

280 TECHNIQUES ET ARCHITECTURE

FIG 1–17
Spreads from the "Techniques locales" issue of the journal *Techniques et architecture*, published in 1943.

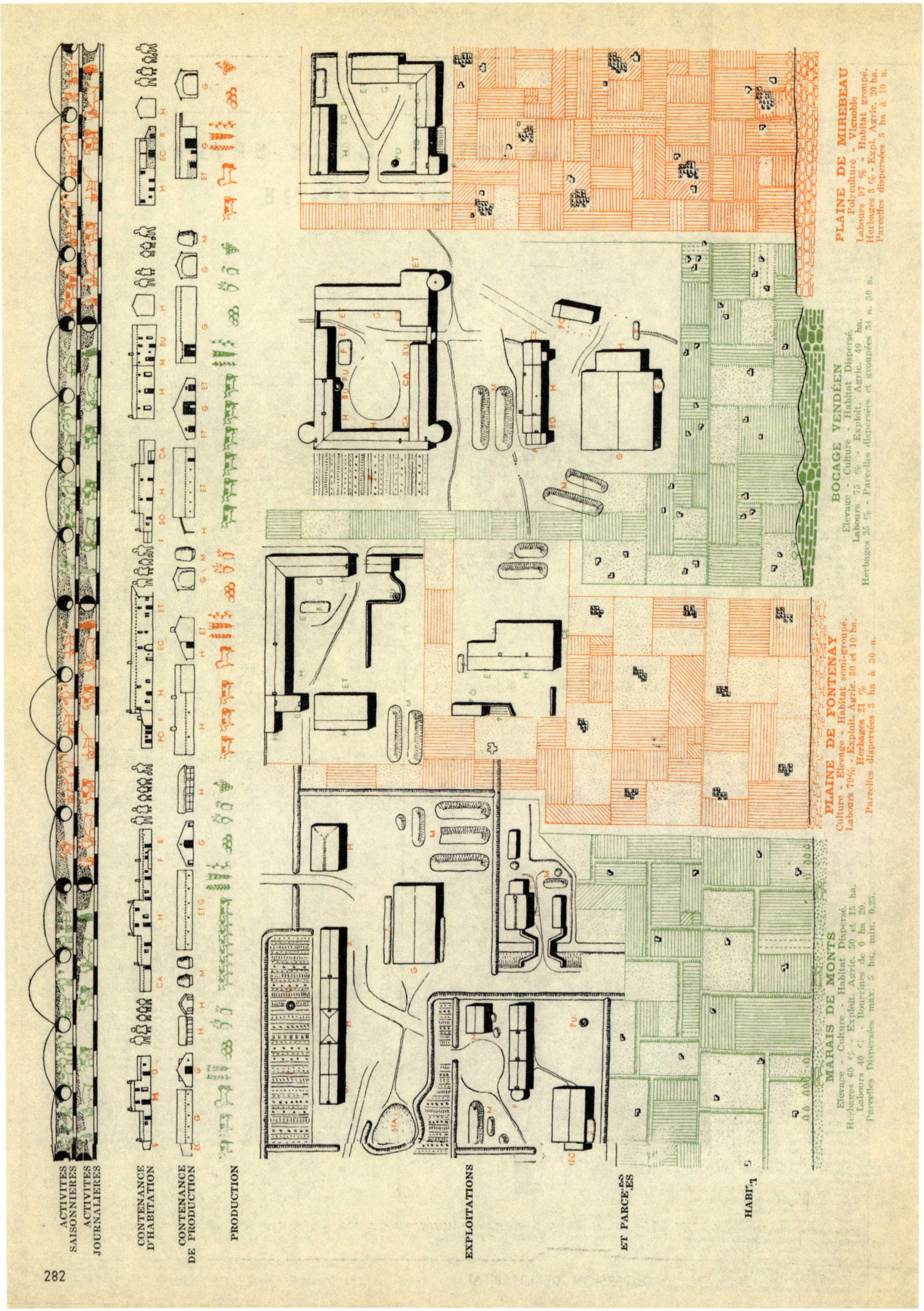
ACTIVITES SAISONNIERES
ACTIVITES JOURNALIERES
CONTENANCE D'HABITATION
CONTENANCE DE PRODUCTION
PRODUCTION
EXPLOITATIONS
MARAIS DE MONTS
Elevage - Culture - Habitat Dispersé.
Herbages 60 % - Exploit. Agric. 50 et 15 ha.
Labours 40 % - Bourrines de 0 ha 20.
Parcelles Dispersées max. 5 ha, min. 0,25.
PLAINE DE FONTENAY
Culture - Elevage - Habitat semi-groupé.
Labours 79% - Exploit. Agric. 30 et 10 ha.
Herbages 21 %
Parcelles dispersées 3 ha à 30 a.
BOCAGE VENDÉEN
Elevage - Culture - Habitat Dispersé.
Labours 75 % - Exploit. Agric. 40 ha.
Herbages 25 % - Parcelles dispersées et groupées 34 a. 30 a.
PLAINE DE MIREBEAU
Polyculture - Vignoble
Labours 97 % - Habitat groupé.
Herbages 3 % - Expl. Agric. 20 ha.
Parcelles dispersées 5 ha à 10 a.
282

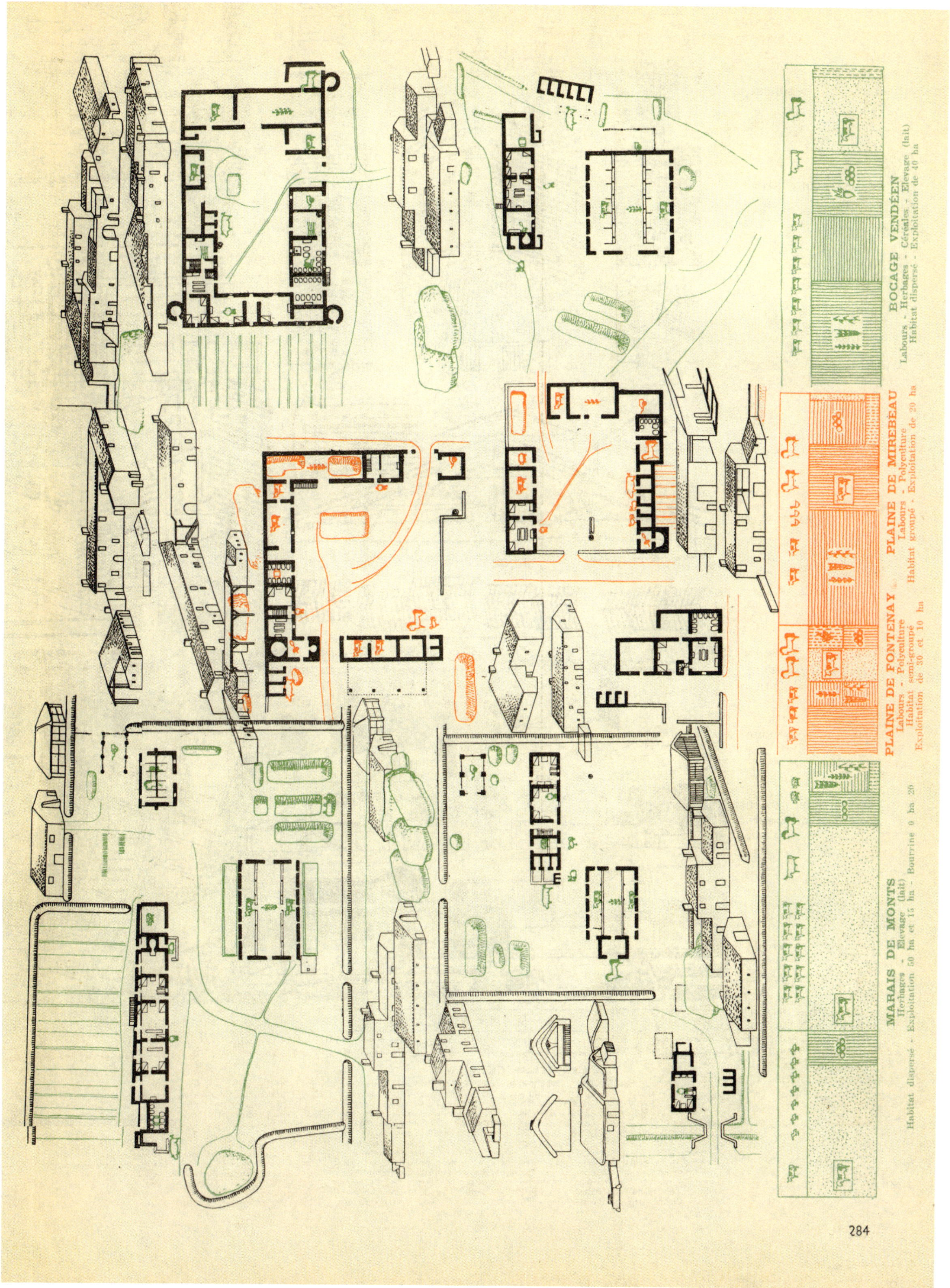
BOCAGE VENDÉEN
Labours - Herbages - Céréales - Elevage (lait)
Habitat dispersé - Exploitation de 40 ha
PLAINE DE MIREBEAU
Labours - Polyculture
Habitat groupé - Exploitation de 20 ha
PLAINE DE FONTENAY
Labours - Polyculture
Habitat semi-groupé
Exploitation de 30 et 10 ha
MARAIS DE MONTS
Herbages - Elevage (lait)
Habitat dispersé - Exploitation 50 ha et 15 ha - Bourrine 9 ha 20
284

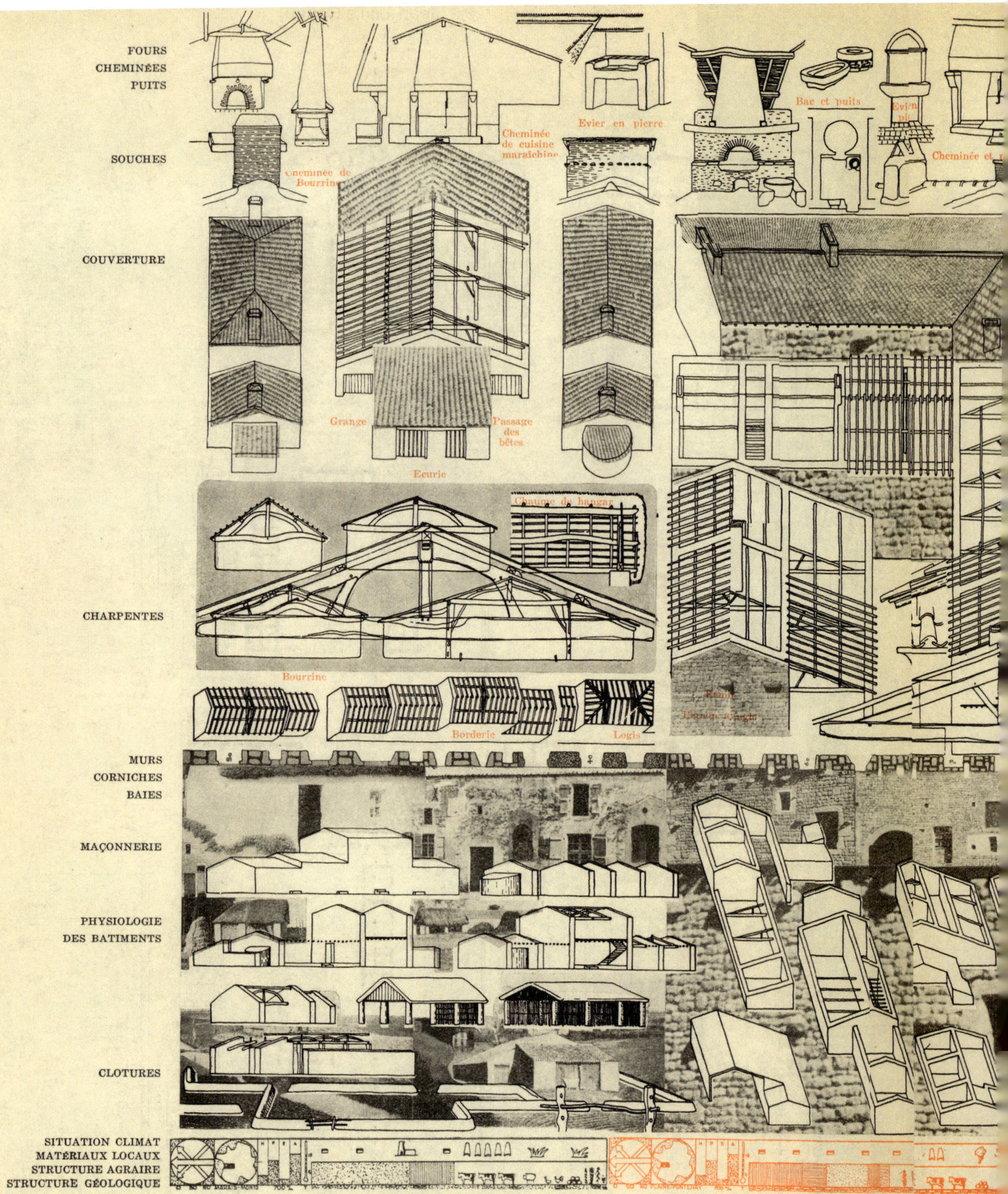

PAYS MARAICHIN

Habitat dispersé - Exploitations à bâtiments dissociés - L'habitation et ses servitudes affectent le « plan-wagon » - Locaux juxtaposés - Clôtures en levées de terre « Terriens » - Parfois plantées de haies - Murs des « Bourrines » en pisé terre, eau et sable (0 m. 40) - Sol en terre battue - Absence de cave - Exploitations : murs en moellons de calcaire (callorien) (0 m. 50- 0 m. 55) - Extérieurs et intérieurs crépis et chaulés - Sols carreaux terre cuite ou terre battue - Baies appareillées - linteaux bois ou appareillage pierre non apparent - Absence de plafond - Le plancher de volige est apparent - Charpente à ferme simple - Pièces travaillées (anciens logis seigneuriaux) (ormeau ou chêne) - Couverture en chaume (0 m. 30) (Bourrine) - Pente 40° - Roseau du Marais ou rouche - Tuiles creuses scellées au plâtre - Pente 18° - Corniche génoise - Souches en briques - Cheminées à hotte en plâtre - Foyer surélevé (D° pour four) - Evier en pierre, écoulement extérieur - Puits en pierre sans portique

285

PLAINE FONTENAISIENN

Habitat groupé ou semi-dispersé - Bâiments oupés en « blo
selon un plan en profondeur dans les ptites et yennes exploitat
et rassemblés autour d'une cour semi-fermée da les grandes ex
tations - Absence de clôture - Murs chainage ngle et moellons
calcaire tendre (0 m. 60) - Parement pparent Vieux passant
Encadrement des baies chaulé - Sols dalles pierres ou reaux terre cui
Absence de cave - Planchers portant sur murs de refer t poutres trans
sales - Charpente à ferme simple infendue (chêne) - lige en peupli
Couvertures en tuiles creuses (pente 19°) - Tuiles de fa scellées au plât
Corniche en pierre ou toiture en saillie sur façades (0 . 25) - Souches
briques enduites - Cheminée à manteau droit en pier et foyer surelev
Potager foucade - Ponnes à lessive - Evier en pierre av coulement extér
- Puits en moellons sans portique

BOCAGE VENDÉEN

Habitat dispersé - Deux types d'exploitation - 1º Bâtiments dispersés (récent) - Habitations selon un plan en longueur - 2º Bâtiments rassemblés autour d'une cour (ancien logis) - Clôtures : haies - Basses - Ronces - Murs en moellons de schiste et granit apparents ou partiellement noyés dans mortier de chaux (épaisseur 0 m.. 70) - Encadrement des baies chaulé - Sol affleurement schiste ou carreaux -ence de cave - Planchers portant sur murs de façade et poutres longitu-s (anciens planchers en boutilli) - Charpente à ferme simple - Pièces -ues et sculptées (chêne - orme - frêne) - Entraits reposant sur sablière -ige - Lattes de châtaignier ou bois blanc - Couverture en tuiles creuses - 19º) - Tuiles de faîte scellées au plâtre - Corniche génoise - Souche -ques - Cheminées à manteau droit en pierre - Foyer surélevé - Boulangerie -nes à lessive - Evier en pierre avec écoulement extérieur - Puits en pierre -ique en berceau

PLAINE DE POITIERS

Habitat groupé - Quelques fermes isolées - Bâtimens groupés autour d'une cour fermée - Clôture : murs de pierre sèch à proximité des bourgs - Murs constitués par chainage en pierre detaille - Remplissage en moellons de calcaire et craie tuffau tendre salpètreuse gélive - Parement apparent - Sols en dalles pierre ou terre battue - Caves fréquentes - Planchers reposant sur les refends et poutres transversales - Charpente à ferme simple refendue portant sur les chaînages - Volige : lattes de châtaignier - Couverture en tuiles creuses - Tuiles faîte non scellées (pente 21º) - Absence de corniche - Toiture en saillie sur les façades (0 m. 35) - Souches en pierre - Cheminées à manteau droit en pierre et foyer surelevé - Fournil - Hotte en pierre - Evier pierre avec écoulent extérieur - Puits en pierre sans portique

CHARENTES

par Robert GOUBERT

« Là comme un large fleuve aux eaux permanentes, depuis des milliers d'années ont passé des multitudes humaines et les produits qu'elles transportent. Le Nord et le Midi s'y sont rencontrés. »

BOISSONNADE.

A la hauteur du 45e et 46e degrés de latitude nord, axé sur les 2e et 3e degrés de longitude ouest de Paris, incorporée à la structure géologique secondaire qui s'étend des contreforts méridionaux du Massif Central à la côte Atlantique suivant une direction sud-est, nord-ouest, entre l'exhaussement du plissement hercynien poitevin et le bassin de la Garonne, la pénéplaine charentaise inclinée d'est en ouest, est engendrée par le large plissement tertiaire en éventail concomitant à la surrection du Limousin. Entre les deux synclinaux du seuil du Poitou et de Saintes, les sédiments de calcaire jurassique se déposent, étalant leur réseau de failles. Au sud du fleuve, l'érosion assouplit l'horizontalité des couches du calcaire crétacé ; les alluvions quaternaires se répandent sur les ondulations. Les dernières transgressions déposent sur la bordure côtière des couches marneuses et laissent émerger au-dessus des flots d'importants îlots calcaires : bastions naturels protégeant une côte abordée dès l'antiquité par les flottes conquérantes.

Pays de transition entre le Nord et le Midi, à la topographie atténuée, graduée d'ouest en est, au climat marin et continental tempéré, aux vents chauds, froids et humides, à la température douce, à la flore océanique et subméditerranéenne.

Région carrefour et frontière maritime, toujours convoitée pour la facilité de ses communications, elle est sectionnée par une croisée de pistes d'invasion qui se muent en collecteurs commerciaux et spirituels. La Chaussée des légions romaines : Médolianum Lugdunum (Saintes-Lyon) devient la voie du sel et du cognac, puis le Genève-Océan. Le chemin des Sarrasins, la route des pèlerins de Saint-Jacques-de-Compostelle et l'axe Paris-Madrid. Les langues d'oc et d'oïl s'y affrontent et y stabilisent leur frontière.

Les Charentes : ensemble des anciennes provinces d'Angoumois, d'Aunis et de Saintonge, issues des diocèses médiévaux de Saintes et d'Angoulême, des pagus gallo-romains d'Engolinensis, de Santonensis et de la cité gauloise des Santones, s'agglomèrent aujourd'hui, dans le cadre de la nouvelle division territoriale, aux départements révolutionnaires de la Vendée, de la Vienne et des Deux-Sèvres.

Le paysage géographique, ethnique, psychologique est sans cesse modifié sous la double action influente des colonisateurs et de l'indigène, à la poursuite de la meilleure utilisation des ressources locales et de la création de courants d'échange. Le Charentais est vigneron, cultivateur de blé et

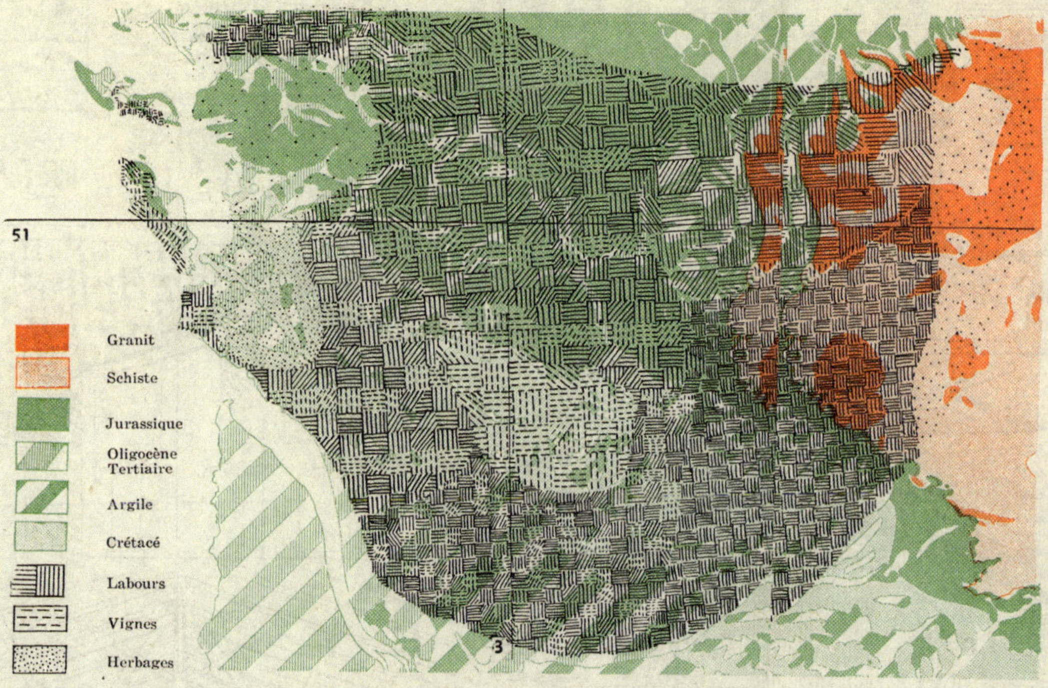

GÉOLOGIE ET CULTURES

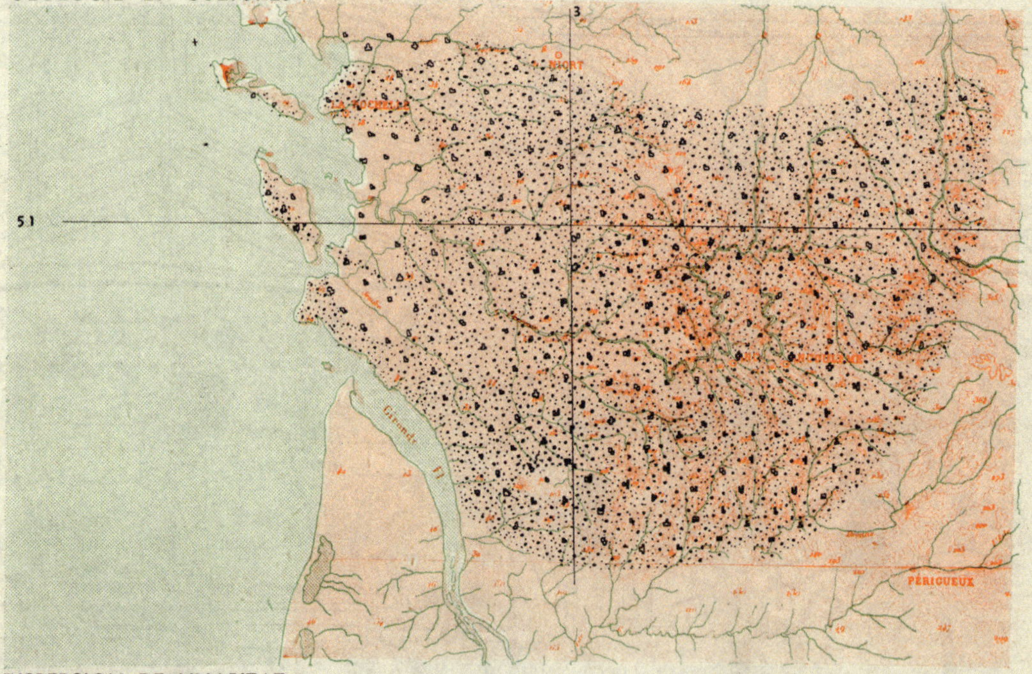

DISPERSION DE L'HABITAT

Fonds de carte d'après Documents Insbts Institut Géographique National.

GENRE DE VIE ET CARACTÈRE DE LA DEMEURE

Le paysan de la mer, autrefois saunier, aujourd'hui ostréiculteur, toujours occupé sur les « laisses » du rivage et les « prises » du marais, s'abrite encore dans la même petite demeure, blottie sous le même toit que ses « servitudes » ; limitée à deux pièces basses, soigneusement protégée du vent d'océan par un mur aveugle et ouverte au soleil levant, elle est coquettement parée de son diaphane badigeon blanc.

A partir du XVIIe siècle, le viticulteur de Grande-Champagne se doubla d'un distillateur et s'est replié si discrètement dans une cour bien close qu'il prit, sans doute, l'habitude de traiter sa récolte à l'abri de toutes indiscrétions. Il a dressé sa demeure sur la grande cour de service, d'où il peut assurer facilement la distillation, pendant les mois d'hiver et veiller au vieillissement de son « capital Cognac ». Paysan évolué, il semble tenir à avoir une façade architecturée et vouloir marquer son degré de fortune par l'enrichissement de son portail.

Le cultivateur du Ruffécois, proche de l'agriculteur du Poitou, vit simplement dans la cour de sa ferme, ouverte sur ses terres de culture. Son habitation, généralement sous le même toit que partie de l'exploitation, est d'expression modeste, dépouillée de tout souci de paraître.

L'éleveur du Confolentais a longtemps vécu en hobereau, au milieu de son domaine, dans un logis dressé à proximité de ses pacages, au milieu d'un parc boisé, d'où il pouvait diriger son exploitation. Son habitation, d'aspect rude, aime à s'orner d'une tourelle d'escalier, d'une lucarne ou d'une large cheminée...

SIMILITUDE, DIVERSITÉ

Sur le scur le sous-sol calcaire, parsemé de dépôts alluvionnaires, naires, l'habitant a trouvé partout, à courte portée de tée de sa fixation, les matériaux essentiels nécessaires à aires à la satisfaction de ses besoins de construction. Ation. Aussi, a-t-il généralisé la maçonnerie en moellon et llon et pierre de taille, la charpente en chêne et en ormen orme, la couverture en tuile. L'unité de ressources de ces de la structure géologique est cependant nuancée encée et offre une diversité d'expression : alors que le m le moellon de crétacé supérieur, de taille moyenne yenne a des angles émoussés, celui de jurassique, se e, se débite en éléments plats aux arêtes vives. Les s. Les parements de murs en l'un et l'autre ont des aspect aspects bien distincts. Les argiles du Confolentais donais donnent des tuiles d'un rouge plus sombre que celles celles du Pays Bas ou du Saintais ; la gamme

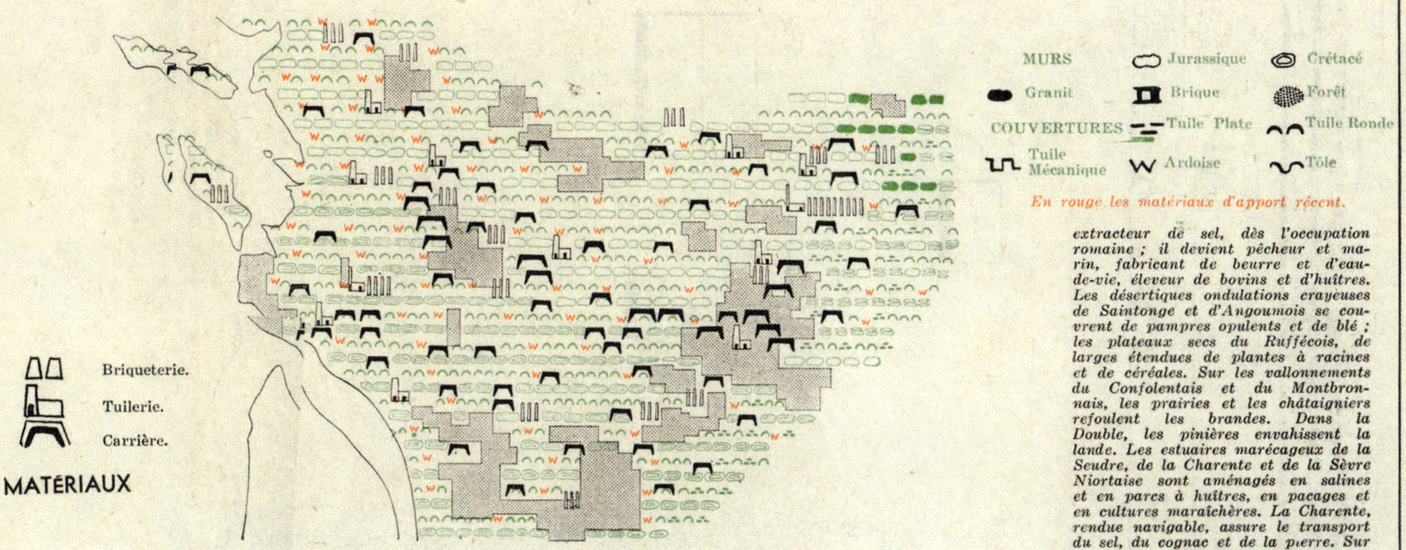

MATÉRIAUX

extracteur de sel, dès l'occupation romaine ; il devient pêcheur et marin, fabricant de beurre et d'eau-de-vie, éleveur de bovins et d'huîtres. Les désertiques ondulations crayeuses de Saintonge et d'Angoumois se couvrent de pampres opulents et de blé ; les plateaux secs du Ruffécois, de larges étendues de plantes à racines et de céréales. Sur les vallonnements du Confolentais et du Montbronnais, les prairies et les châtaigniers refoulent les brandes. Dans la Double, les pinières envahissent la lande. Les estuaires marécageux de la Seudre, de la Charente et de la Sèvre Niortaise sont aménagés en salines et en parcs à huîtres, en pacages et en cultures maraîchères. La Charente, rendue navigable, assure le transport du sel, du cognac et de la pierre. Sur son cours, des cités commerciales s'échelonnent entre Angoulême et la côte, sur laquelle se développent les deux grandes installations portuaires qui prolongent outre-océan les relations économiques.

Des races voisines et éloignées cohabitent. Les pêcheurs bretons et les marins flamands se fixent sur la côte et y pratiquent l'élevage de produits de la mer. Les Limousins viennent tenir commerce ou artisanat, les Vendéens introduisent l'élevage et la production beurrière après la grande crise phylloxérique du XIXe siècle.

Un élément permanent avec ses fluctuations de prospérité, d'appauvrissement domine l'économie charentaise : la fabrication du cognac. Les facteurs conjugués de la structure géologique, du climat et de l'activité persévérante de l'homme ont fait d'une région originairement pauvre, un des pays les plus riches de France. L'arrondissement de Cognac n'est il pas celui qui pourvoie le plus le Trésor ? Sur un sous-sol et un humus variés, au point de fusion des régimes océanique et continental, grâce à une laborieuse fixation séculaire, le grand crû des eaux-de-vie de Coganc ; celui de la Grande Champagne forme un noyau central environné de zones concentriques hiérarchisées par les variations de climat et de terrain auxquelles l'expérience du viticulteur charentais a su adapter des cépages idoines, perfectionner la distillation du vin et du vieillissement de l'eau-de-vie. Les vins d'Aunis, de Saintonge et d'Angoumois, fort appréciés dès le XIIIe siècle, des provinces centrale de la France et des pays nord-européens sont, à partir du XVIe siècle, transformés en eau-de-vie en Angleterre. Les Anglais imaginent plus intéressant d'effectuer cette transformation sur les lieux de production et introduisent au XVIIe siècle la technique de la distillation en Aunis et en Saintonge. Commence alors l'ère de grande prospérité du pays de Cognac qui diffuse son produit unique, d'universelle réputation, dont M. Robert Delamain a pu dire qu'il est une sorte de prodige naturel, un accident, un miracle.

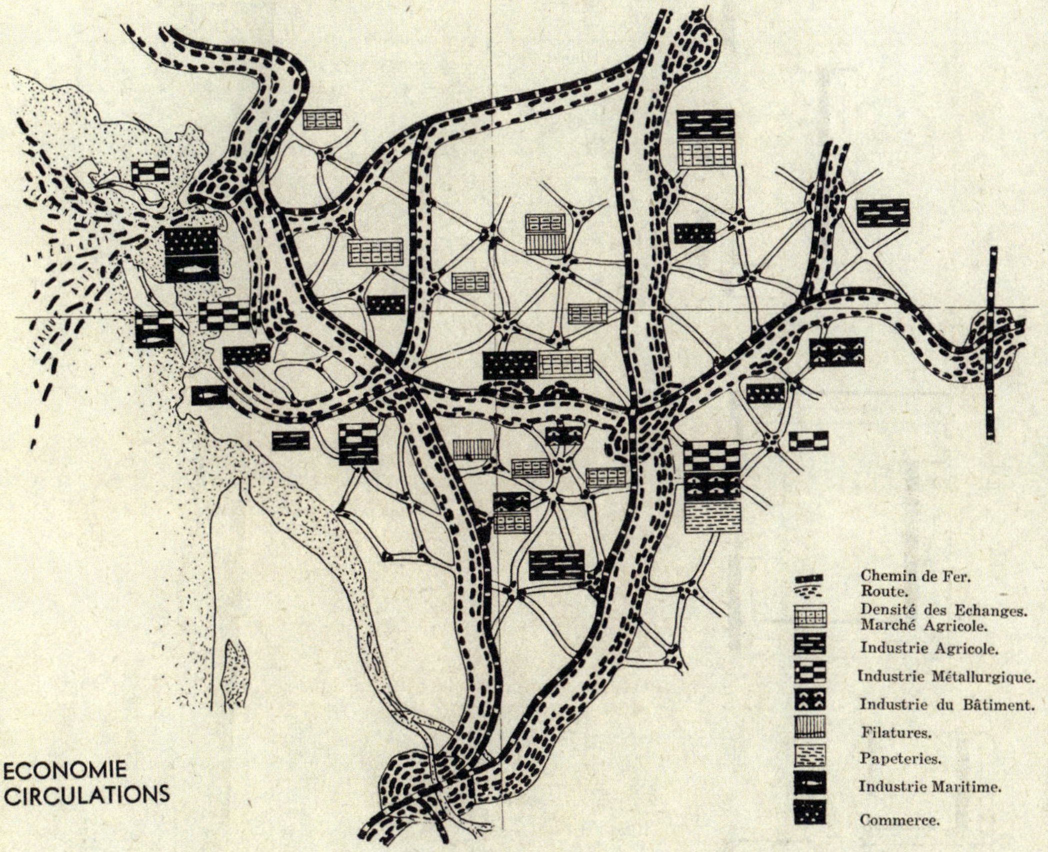

ECONOMIE
CIRCULATIONS

des unes et des autres s'étend d'un grenat violacé au jaune pâle, en passant par le vermillon.

La mise en œuvre d'un même matériau varie avec le degré de résistance du sol. Le mur en pierre calcaire est constitué différemment dans deux pays contigus. En Grande Champagne, où le sol pierreux affleure partout, les murs n'ont pas besoin d'être fondés ; le poids des lourdes toitures et des planchers est réparti par l'intermédiaire des chaînes en pierre de taille, dressées régulièrement au droit de la portée des fermes. La maçonnerie de moellons à deux parements n'a qu'une fonction de remplissage. Dans le Pays Bas de Cognac, zone d'affaissement, au fond de laquelle s'est déposé un épais limon argilo-marneux, la fondation des murs ne peut pas toujours atteindre le sol ferme ; on s'efforce donc de répartir le poids mort et la charge utile du bâtiment sur l'ensemble de leur base. Le mur en moellon, dépourvu de harpes, devient un élément portant. Les chaînages verticaux en pierre de taille sont remplacés par des chaînages horizontaux assurant un liaisonnement des deux parements dans toute sa hauteur. Ces adaptations à la nature du terrain d'assise engendrent deux traits morphologiques : tandis que les murailles de Grande Champagne sont rythmées verticalement par des harpes à redent, celles du Pays Bas le sont horizontalement par la ponctuation des lignes de boutisses saillantes. Les moyens humidifuges enrichissent aussi la gamme des éléments formels du mur ; la pratique de l'enduit du parement, destiné à le protéger contre l'humidité. Systématique sur la bordure côtière, avec l'agrément du chatoyant engobe blanc du badigeonnage au lait de chaux, elle alterne, à l'intérieur des terres, avec le parement apparent de calcaire ; offre une surface mouchetée sur le mur en schiste granitique dont elle obture les intervalles irréguliers laissés par la taille grossière du moellon rocailleux.

La diversité se manifeste encore dans le caractère des baies ; les portes d'accès sont plus basses dans le pays marin et celui des terres froides qu'au centre des Charentes : réduction due au souci de protection contre le vent d'une part, contre le froid de l'autre. Sur la côte elles sont vitrées ; dans le Confolentais, pleines et à double épaisseur. En Grande Champagne, elles sont pleines, à deux vantaux inégaux et surmontées d'une imposte vitrée.

(Suite p. 295.)

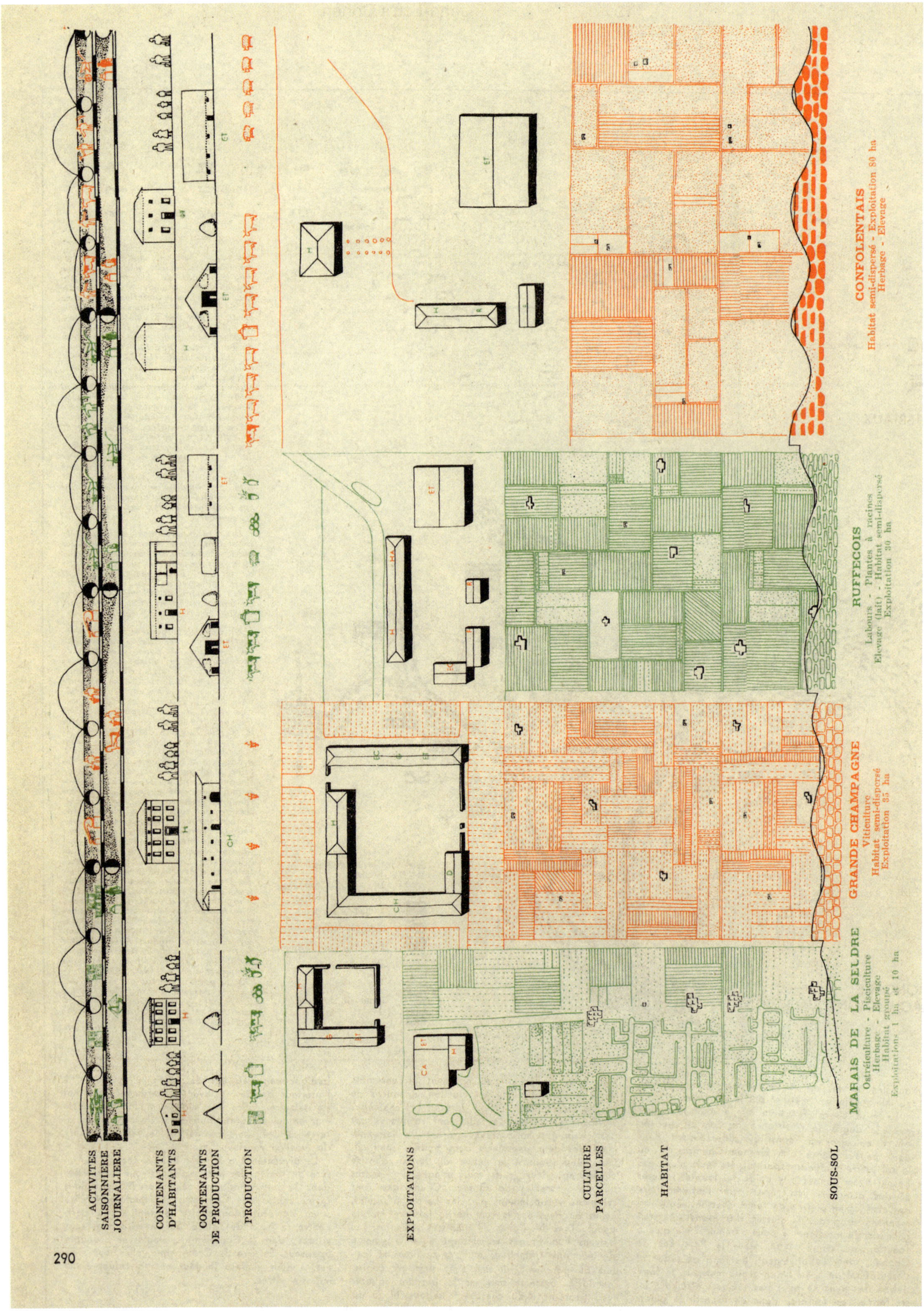
290
ACTIVITES SAISONNIERE JOURNALIERE
CONTENANTS D'HABITANTS
CONTENANTS DE PRODUCTION
PRODUCTION
EXPLOITATIONS
CULTURE PARCELLES
HABITAT
SOUS-SOL
MARAIS DE LA SEUDRE
Ostréiculture - Pisciculture
Herbage - Elevage
Habitat groupé
Exploitations 1 ha et 10 ha
GRANDE CHAMPAGNE
Viticulture
Habitat semi-dispersé
Exploitation 35 ha
RUFFECOIS
Labours - Plantes à racines
Elevage (lait) - Habitat semi-dispersé
Exploitation 30 ha
CONFOLENTAIS
Habitat semi-dispersé - Exploitation 80 ha
Herbage - Elevage

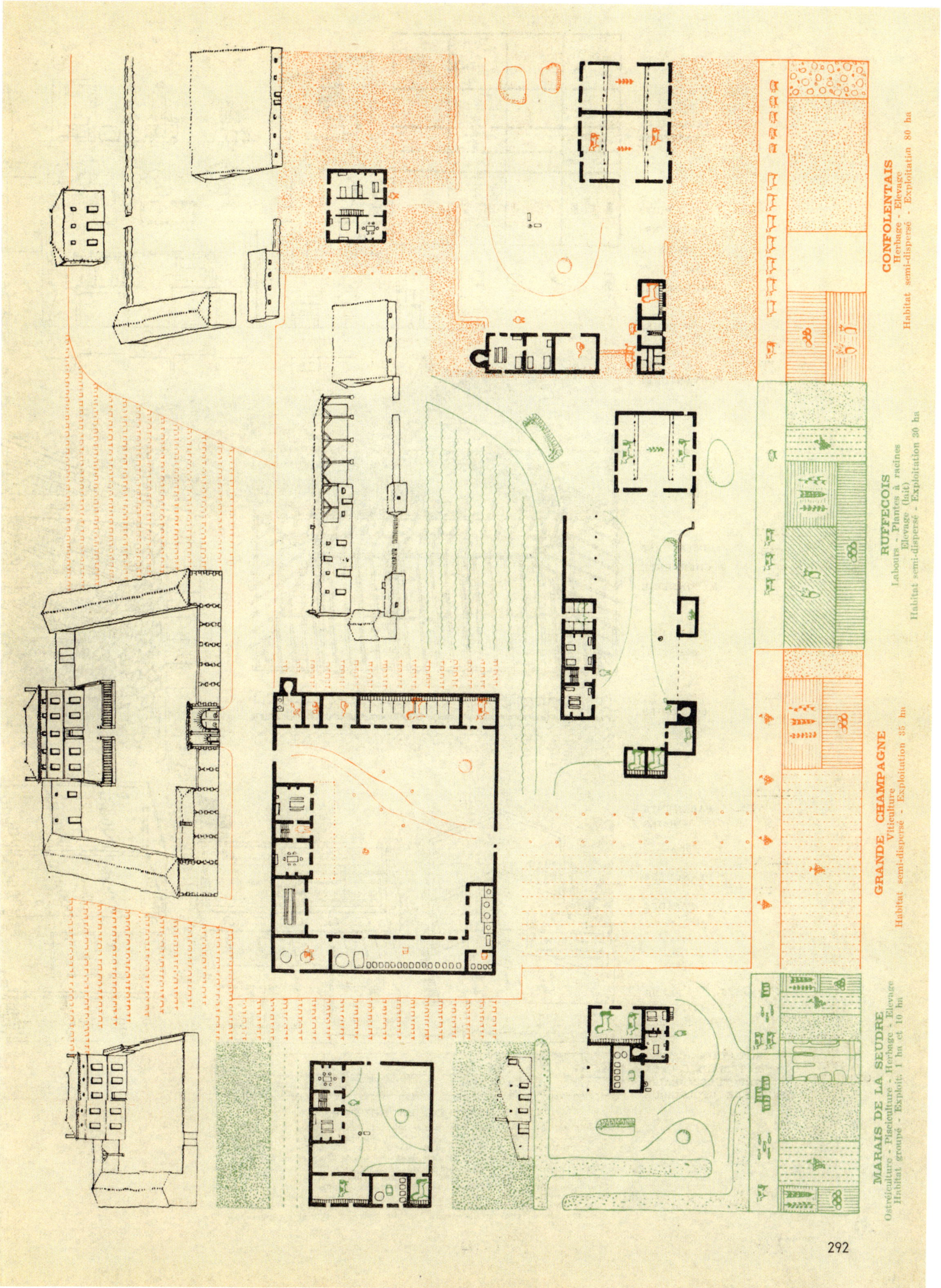
CONFOLENTAIS
Herbage - Elevage
Habitat semi-dispersé - Exploitation 80 ha
RUFFECOIS
Labours - Plantes à racines
Elevage (lait)
Habitat semi-dispersé - Exploitation 30 ha
GRANDE CHAMPAGNE
Viticulture
Habitat semi-dispersé - Exploitation 35 ha
MARAIS DE LA SEUDRE
Ostréiculture - Pisciculture - Herbage - Elevage
Habitat groupé - Exploit. 1 ha et 10 ha
292

MARAIS DE LA SEUDRE

Habitation et exploitation sous même toit ou indépendantes - Logement 2 pièces - Grenier bas à accès extérieur ou intérieur - Murs en moellons de calcaire enduits et chaulés (0 m. 55) - Planchers portants sur murs latéraux et de refend ou sur poutres transversales - Charpentes à fermes simples - Entraits posés sur sablière - Couverture en tuiles creuses (17°) - Corniches en « genoise » - Rives et faîtages scellés au mortier de chaux - Souches en pierre ou briques chaulées - Cheminées à manteau en pierre de taille ornée - Fournil, four avec cheminée à hotte - Bac à lessive en terre cuite - Eviers à écoulement libre - Puits en pierre de taille et moellons accompagnés de timbres abreuvoirs ; poulie portée par mât ou portique pierre ou fer

GRANDE CHAMPAG

Habitation et exploitation groupées autour d'une
4 pièces et un vestibule réparties par moitié en re
- Grenier haut à accès intérieur - Murs constitués
de taille calcaire et remplissage en moellons deux
apparents ou enduits (0 m. 65) - Planchers porta
refend et sur poutres transversales - Charpente
sur chainages en pierre - Entraits posés sur sabliè
creuses (19°) - Faitages scellés au mortier de cha
tenus par pierres posées - Corniches en pierre de
en pierre de taille - Cheminées à manteau en pi
Fournil : four avec cheminée à hotte - Deux bac
- Eviers à écoulement libre en niche dans l'épais
pierre de taille en portique

293

RUFFECOIS

Habitation et exploitation sous même toit ou indépendantes sur cour ouverte - Logement 2 pièces - Grenier à accès intérieur - Grands hangars à poteaux de bois ou piles de pierre - Grange étable à triple nef - Murs en moellons de jurassique à deux parements et blocage - Angles en pierre de taille (0 m. 65) - Planchers portant sur murs latéraux, murs de refend et poutres transversales - Charpentes à fermes simples - Entraits posés sur sablières - Charpente d'étable composée d'une ferme centrale simple portant sur poteaux flanquée de deux appentis - Couverture en tuiles creuses (19°) - Faîtages et rives scellés au mortier - Pas de corniches - Souches en pierre de taille ou en briques - Cheminées à hotte en moellons - Four à pain indépendant commun à plusieurs logis, avec ou sans auvent - Eviers à écoulement libre en niche dans l'épaisseur des murs - Citerne en pierre de taille avec levier de puisage à bras à contrepoids

CONFOLENTAIS

Habitation et exploitation indépendantes ou sous même toit sur cour ouverte - Logement de maîtres 4 pièces, 1 vestibule - De métayers 1 ou 2 grandes pièces - Grenier à accès intérieur - Grande grange-étable à triple nef - Murs en moellons de schiste granitique à deux parements et blocage partiellement enduits - Angle en blocs de granit taillés (0 m. 75) - Planchers portant sur murs latéraux, de refend et sur poutres transversales - Cloisons intérieures en pan de bois et pisé - Charpentes à fermes simples - Entraits posés sur sablières - Charpente d'étable composée d'une ferme centrale portant sur poteaux flanquée de deux appentis - Couverture en tuiles creuses (22°) non scellées - Pas de corniche - Souches en briques - Cheminées à hotte en moellons - Four à pain sous cheminée - Salle commune - Eviers à écoulement libre dans l'épaisseur des murs - Puits en pierre de taille accompagnés de timbres abreuvoirs

294

NIÈVRE · COTE D'OR

par Pierre POCORULL

La région étudiée est une zone située au centre le la France, entre le bassin de la Seine, le bassin de la Saône et la vallée de la Loire. Elle comprend à l'ouest, le Nvernais, à la limite du bassin parisien, et le Morvan, témoin avancé du Massif Central ; à l'est, une partie de la dépresson qui entre Vosges et Morvan constitue le seuil bourguignon. Pays ayant leurs caractéristiques propres, mais dont le rôe essentiel est de liaison.

GEOLOGIE ET CULTURES

Le Morvan constitué de terrains primitifs à dominante granit émerge au milieu des pays de substratum secondaire qui bordent le bassin parisien. Région jadis pauvre : élevage ; cultures.

Autour du Morvan, zone des terres pleines (argiles et marnes liasiques) travaillée par les eaux qui font reculer le plateau calcaire et dégagent par endroits le granit.

A l'ouest, au delà du Bazois, le Nivernais, pays secondaire faillé et disloqué N.-S., avec émergement granitique (Saint-Saulge) et affleurement primaire (La Machine), s'étend jusqu'à la vallée alluvionnaire de la Loire. Pays d'élevage (prés et embouches) et de cultures (céréales et racines pour les animaux). Vigne en régression.

A l'est du Morvan, le plateau calcaire pénètre intimement l'Auxois et se prolonge jusqu'aux marnes des pays de Langres et du Bassigny voisins des Vosges. Il est interrompu au centre par la vallée châtillonnaise, dépression argileuse orientée S.O.-N.E. Pays de culture extensive : élevage bovins (lait), ovins.

Au sud, La Côte borde le plateau le long de la plaine de Saône (viticulture). La plaine comprend : au nord, un pays au sol semblable au plateau, puis, plus au sud, les alluvions de la plaine dijonnaise et le bas pays (argiles ferrugineuses, éléments sableux). Pays de cultures spécialisées (limite nord du maïs) ; houblon ; culture maraîchère ; grande culture industrielle.

OROGRAPHIE — HYDROGRAPHIE CLIMAT ET HABITAT

Le Morvan, massif nivelé repris par l'érosion, est formé de cuvettes, de bosses aux sommets mal dégagés (800-900 mètres maxima). Climat rude et humide. Les eaux ruissellent sur le granit (Settons : 108 jours de gelées par an 1 m. 57 de pluie réparti sur près de 180 jours). Vents variant suivant les vallées (Château-Chinon : 174 jours à dominante W ; 155 jours dominante E.). Hameaux dispersés tous les 4 à 5 kilomètres. Economie extensive.

Zones des terres pleines : légères ondulations ; rivières aux méandres encaissés. Le bocage s'est substitué à la forêt. Buttes témoins environnées de sources autour desquelles se sont concentrés les villages ; fermes isolées peu nombreuses. Climat plus doux, mais subissant l'influence du Morvan. Pluies : Vitteaux 0 m. 81 ; Montbard : 0 m. 73.

A l'ouest, au delà du Bazois et de la cuvette des Amognes, les chaînes nord-sud des collines du Nivernais (altitude 300 à 350 mètres) se perdent au nord par le système oblique du Donziais et au sud sous les alluvions des pays entre Loire et Allier. Vallées peu inclinées où coule une rivière faisant des méandres dans les pâturages. Climat légèrement plus froid que celui du bassin parisien. Varzy : 9°11 moyenne. Pluie : 0 m. 75 répartis en 150 jours. 90 jours de gelée. Habitat groupé : bourgs; hameaux de quelques fermes.

A l'est de l'Auxois, s'amorce le plateau calcaire nivellé en partie (tasselots), et repris par l'érosion (vallées étroites et parallèles, petits vallons secs). Eaux souterraines avec ressurgescences. Au centre, la vallée châtillonnaise : légères ondulations, buttes témoins. Climat rude, continental. Pluies : Châtillon, 0 m. 76 ; Saint-Seine, 0 m. 91. Villages de plateaux installés dans les clairières avec quelques fermes aux limites ; villages groupés le long des vallées.

Au sud, la Côte et l'Arrière-Côte. Le plateau s'étage en gradins coupés par l'érosion (Combes). Population dense [illegible] à l'entrée des Combes.

La plaine : au nord de Dijon. pays semblable au plateau : plaines marécageuses de Tilles et de l'Ouche, drainées dès le XVIIIe siècle et Bas-Pays. Villages aux maisons éparpillées, construites sur le talus qui borde la Saône. Climat continental subissant l'influence du couloir rhodanien. Dijon : moyenne, 10°1. Vents : N. hiver et printemps ; S. et W, humidité. Pluies : 0 m. 60. 60 jours de gelées.

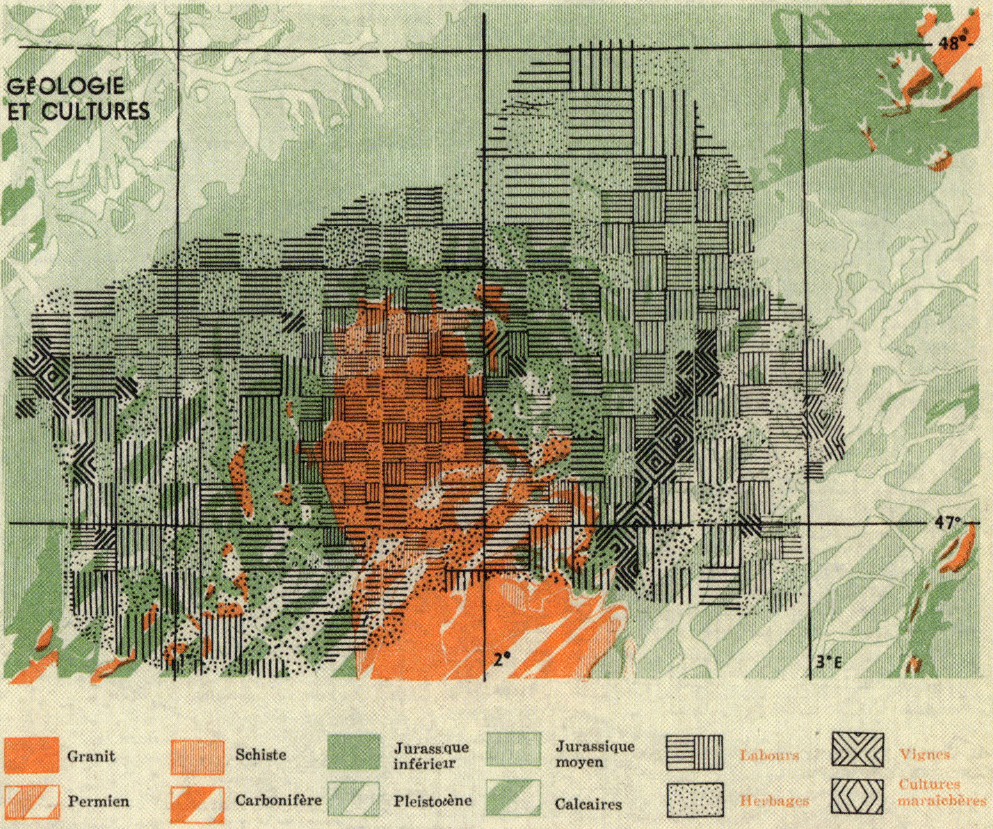

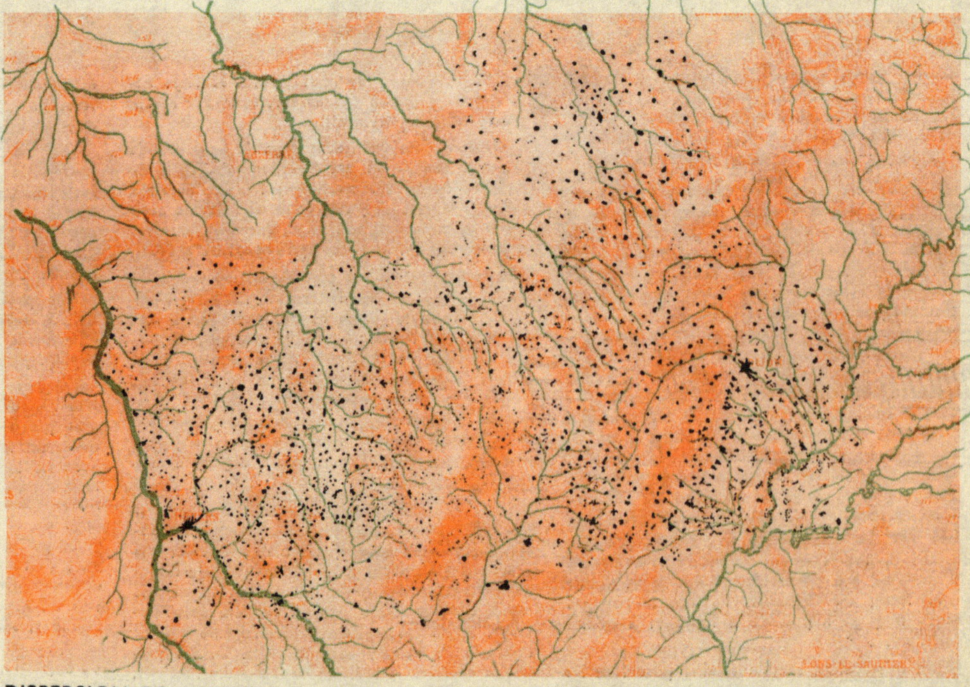

DISPERSION DE L'HABITAT

Fonds de carte d'après Documents Institut Géographique National.

REPARTITION IN DES MATERIAUX LIEUX DE ÐE PRODUCTION

*Les lieux de pro*ı *production sont passés, depuis un siècle, cle, de l'échelle locale à l'échelle régionale* ıale *et inter-régionale. qués, soit à cause* ıse *de difficultés économiques diverses (énergie, transports, cause de la qualité* ıité *des matériaux fabri-*

Les tuileries locales ont disparu, soit à miques diverses (énergie, transports, marché). Seules, sont en exploitation régulière les carrières dont la qualité de la pierre et les facilités de transports rendent l'exploitation rentable (exploitation locale sporadique).

Tuileries, carrières, fours à chaux ou à plâtre se répartissent suivant la nature du sol et les possibilités économiques.

Les murs. — *Le bois est éliminé du mur et remplacé par la pierre ou la brique, matériaux ininflammables donnant l'impression de la stabilité et de la richesse.*

Le matériau pierre est utilisé à l'échelle locale, même si sa qualité laisse à désirer on constate le fait et on le subit. Pierre calcaire jurassique dans le Nivernais et le plateau bourguignon. Pierre granitique dans le Morvan. La brique fait son apparition dans les constructions récentes ; dans certaines zones, son usage est très ancien : remplissage pans de bois, puis murs portants dès le XVIIIe *(région de Seurre).*

Couvertures. — *Le couvrant est la partie du bâtiment qui a le plus évolué, certains matériaux locaux étant peu compatibles avec l'économie actuelle.*

Le chaume disparaît, remplacé par la tuile plate dans le Nivernais dès le XVIIIe *et par l'ardoise d'Angers ou de Savoie dans le Morvan, au cours du* XIXe *et du* XXe. *En Bourgogne, la lave, matériau très lourd, peu pratique, est lentement éliminée par la tuile plate* (XVIIIe-XIXe) *et la tuile mécanique* (XXe). *La tuile canal est dans la côte et dans la partie sud de la montagne, à l'extrême limite de son influence (auvents, locaux secondaires, etc...). Elle disparaît.*

Les courants de circulation ont permis l'utilisation de matériaux usinés ou importés (dès le XIXe *: ardoise le long du val de Loire et dans le Nivernais ;* XXe *: tuile mécanique, matériau pratique et économique qui étend rapidement son domaine. La tôle ondulée ou les feuilles d'amiante-ciment plus récentes sont d'un emploi moins généralisé).*

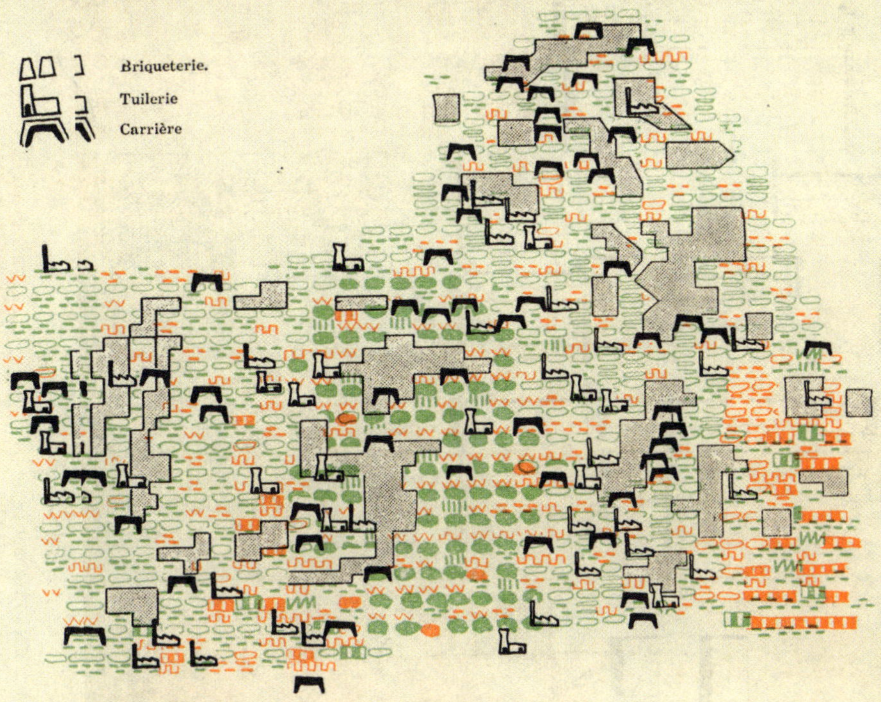

MATÉERIAUX *En rouge les matériaux d'apport récent.*

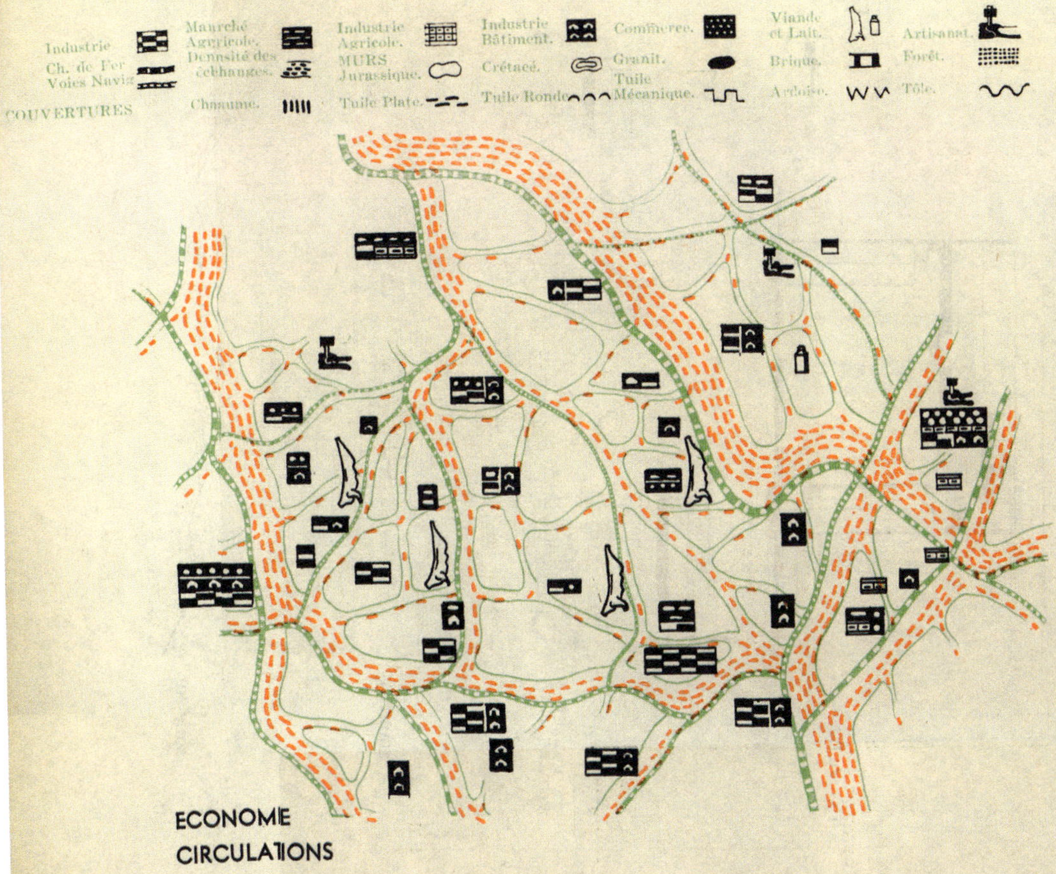

ECONOMIE - CIRCULATION

La Bourgogne est un pays de liaison. Le seuil entre Vosges et Morvan est utilisé pour les communications entre les pays méditerranéens et l'Europe du nord et du nord-est. La trouée entre Vosges et Jura, la percée de la vallée du Rhône et les facilités de passage entre la Loire et la Saône permettent la liaison E.-O. Les vallées de la Loire et de l'Allier sont aussi utilisées pour le trafic N.-S. et les relations entre Paris et le Massif Central. Des voies secondaires contournent le Morvan le long des terres pleines : dans les vaux d'Yonne et le Bazois, liaison entre Seine et Loire et dans l'Auxois route Paris-Méditerranée plus rapide que celle passant par Dijon.

Le Nivernais et le plateau bourguignon formaient à la fin du XVIIIe *une des régions les plus industrielles de la France : le minerai de fer trouvé sur place était traité dans les hauts fourneaux au bois ; une partie du fer était travaillée sur place : clouteries, tôleries de villages. Cette industrie locale a été ruinée dans la première moitié du* XIXe *par l'utilisation de la fonte au coke ; elle a de nos jours presque totalement disparu. Seules subsistent quelques usines situées sur des courants de circulation, appartenant à divers groupements métallurgiques. Les ressources minières sont exploitées à La Machine, à Epinac et dans le Synclinal, Blanzy, Montceau-les-Mines, Le Creusot, où sont installées les forges de la Société Schneider.*

Près des centres urbains, d'autres industries se sont développées. Industries du bâtiment : tuileries, ciments, agglomérés, céramiques, etc... Industries chimiques dont certaines transforment les produits agricoles (féculeries et distilleries de la Plaine, etc.).

Des usines de distillation du bois, des scieries, etc., vivent de l'exploitation des plaques forestières du Nivernais, du Morvan et du plateau bourguignon — le flottage du bois sur l'Yonne et la Cure a disparu depuis les débuts du XXe *(prix de revient trop élevé).*

Les poteries étaient jadis fabriquées dans bien des régions : Puisaye, Bazois, vallée de la Saône, etc... Dans les villages, cette industrie a disparu. Rarement subsiste une très petite entreprise évoluée, mais parfois des petites usines ont pu se développer : la qualité de la matière, la présence de la main-d'œuvre et les facilités de vente rendant l'exploitation intéressante.

Les viandes du Nivernais, de l'Auxois et du Morvan sont réparties *l'Auxois et du Morvan sont réparties* *sur les marchés de la région, de Paris et de Lyon. Le lait est distribué à l'échelle régionale.*

La production agricole ou les produits de l'élevage donnent lieu à des spéculations nationales, voire même internationales.

TECHNIQUES LOCALES 297

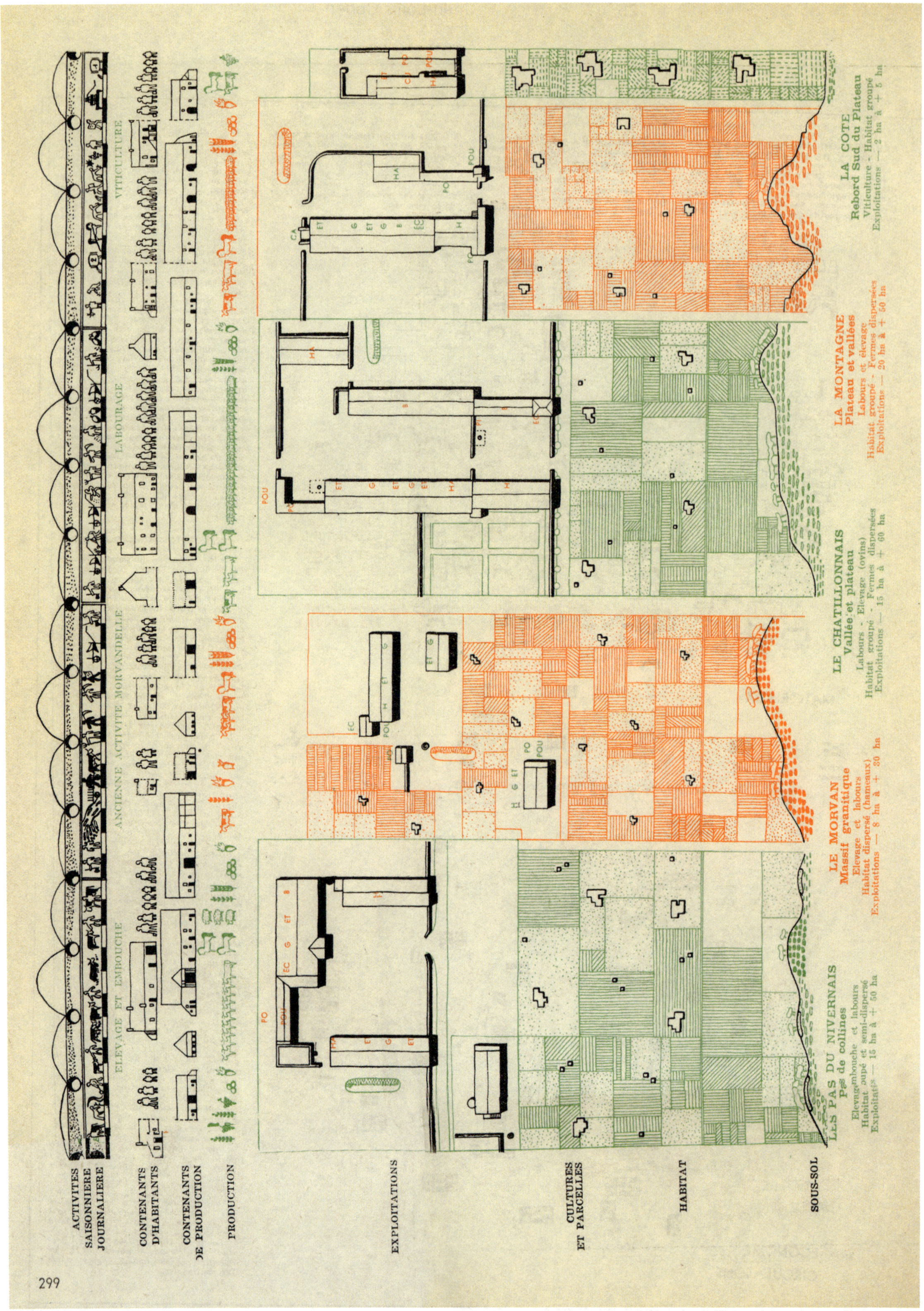

ACTIVITES SAISONNIERE JOURNALIERE
CONTENANTS D'HABITANTS
CONTENANTS DE PRODUCTION
PRODUCTION
EXPLOITATIONS
CULTURES ET PARCELLES
HABITAT
SOUS-SOL
ELEVAGE ET EMBOUCHE
ANCIENNE ACTIVITE MORVANDELLE
LABOURAGE
VITICULTURE
LES PAS DU NIVERNAIS
Pays de collines
LE MORVAN
Massif granitique
Elevage et labours
Habitat dispersé (hameaux)
Exploitations — 8 ha à + 30 ha
LE CHATILLONNAIS
Vallée et plateau
Labours - Elevage (ovins)
Habitat groupé - Fermes dispersées
Exploitations — 15 ha à + 60 ha
LA MONTAGNE
Plateau et vallées
Labours et élevage
Habitat groupé - Fermes dispersées
Exploitations — 20 ha à + 50 ha
LA COTE
Rebord Sud du Plateau
Viticulture - Habitat groupé
Exploitations — 2 ha à + 5 ha
299

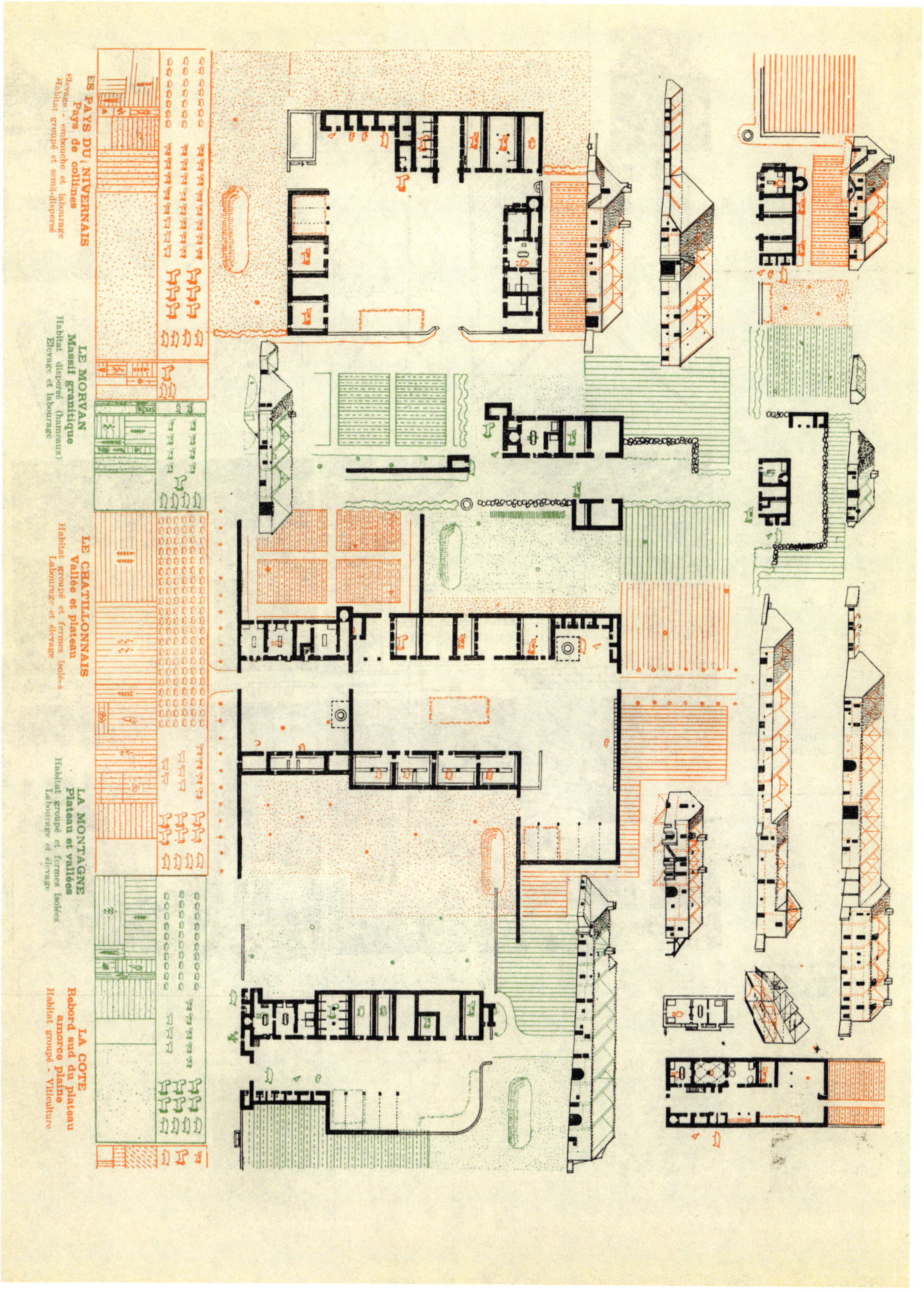
ES PAYS DU NIVERNAIS
Pays de collines
Elevage - embouche et labourage
Habitat groupé et semi-dispersé
LE MORVAN
Massif granitique
Habitat dispersé (hameaux)
Elevage et labourage
LE CHATILLONNAIS
Vallée et plateau
Habitat groupé et fermes isolées
Labourage et élevage
LA MONTAGNE
Plateau et vallées
Habitat groupé et fermes isolées
Labourage et élevage
LA COTE
Rebord sud du plateau
amorce plaine
Habitat groupé - Viticulture

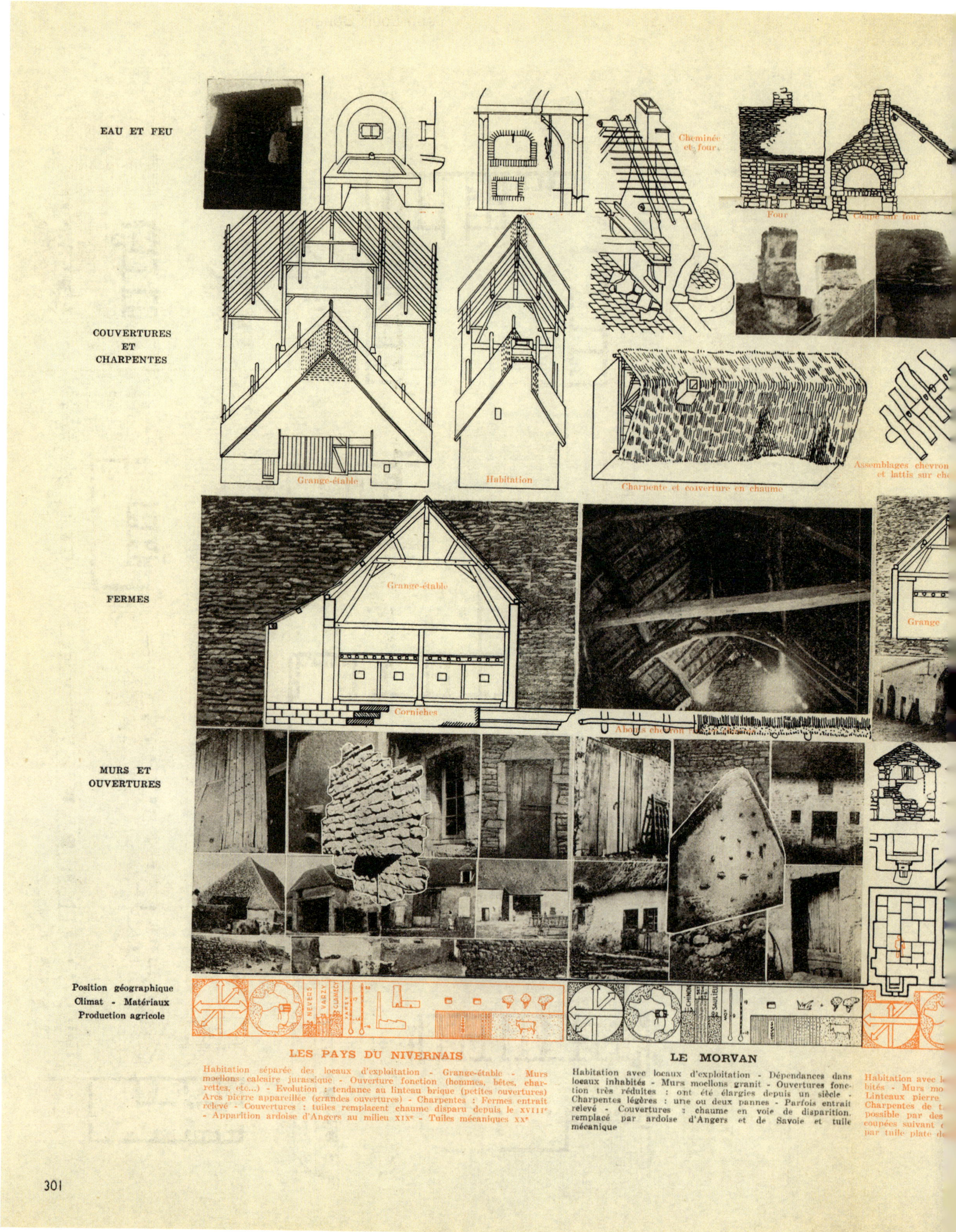

LES PAYS DU NIVERNAIS

Habitation séparée des locaux d'exploitation - Grange-étable - Murs moellons calcaire jurassique - Ouverture fonction (hommes, bêtes, charrettes, etc...) - Evolution : tendance au linteau brique (petites ouvertures) Arcs pierre appareillée (grandes ouvertures) - Charpentes : Fermes entrait relevé - Couvertures : tuiles remplacent chaume disparu depuis le XVIIIe - Apparition ardoise d'Angers au milieu XIXe - Tuiles mécaniques XXe

LE MORVAN

Habitation avec locaux d'exploitation - Dépendances dans locaux inhabités - Murs moellons granit - Ouvertures fonction très réduites : ont été élargies depuis un siècle - Charpentes légères : une ou deux pannes - Parfois entrait relevé - Couvertures : chaume en voie de disparition, remplacé par ardoise d'Angers et de Savoie et tuile mécanique

Habitation avec l
bités - Murs mo
Linteaux pierre
Charpentes de t
possible par des
coupées suivant
par tuile plate d

301

ONTAGNE

tions, Dépendances : Bâtiments inha- jurassique - Ouvertures fonction - urs sans évolution (dépopulation) - ections - Fermes remplacées le plus vertures « lave » (feuilles calcaire en voie de disparition - Remplacée et tuile mécanique XXe

LA COTE

Habitations avec locaux exploitation système dit en hauteur - Murs moellons calcaire jurassique - Ouvertures fonctions - Utilisation hardie de la pierre (dalles, trumeaux, poteaux, etc...) - Charpentes (grosses sections fermes chevillées) - Couvertures lave en voie de complète disparition remplacée par tuile plate dans le XVIIIe et par la tuile mécanique XXe

LA PLAINE VAL SAONE

Habitation avec locaux exploitation - Murs pans de bois et pierre ou brique suivant zones - Remplissages : terre ou brique - Evolution : disparition pan de bois, remplacé par la pierre ou la brique suivant la région - Le mur brique apparaît dès le début du XVIIIe (zone Seurre) - Couvertures : chaume presque complètement disparu - Remplacé depuis le XVIIIe par la tuile plate et la tuile mécanique XXe

BASSE NORMANDIE

par Raymond SENNEVAT

La présente étude, contrairement à celles précédemment exposées, ne porte pas sur une région complète, mais sur une parcelle territoriale de la province. La Basse-Normandie, qui comprend administrativement les départements du Calvados, de l'Orne et de la Manche, est composée de deux grandes régions naturelles : la région des Plaines et la région des Bocages, subdivisées en d'autres régions géographiques, historiques ou agricoles : le Lieuvin, le Pays d'Auge, les Plaines et Campagnes de Caen, d'Argentan, d'Alençon, le Pays d'Ouche, le Perche, le Merlerault, le Bessin, les Bocages de Vire, Passais, Mortainais, Avranchin, Coutançais, la Plaine de Saint-Lô, les Marais de Carentan, les Campagnes de Valognes, de Cherbourg, le Val de Saire, la Pointe de la Hague.

Il n'était pas possible, dans une étude restreinte, de passer en revue ces quelque vingt régions ; d'autre part, il semblait intéressant, en opposition avec les autres études, d'examiner d'une façon intensive, une parcelle du territoire français. Nous avons donc adopté le principe du prélèvement, prélèvement situé au centre de la région totale, d'environ 50 km. sur 62 km, et délimitée sensiblement ainsi : au nord, Caumont-l'Eventé (Haut-Bessin) ; au nord-est, Evrecy ; à l'est, Thury-Harcourt (Campagne de Caen), Flers; au sud, Domfront (le Passais) ; à l'ouest, Mortain (Mortainais) et Vire (Bocage Virois), représentant deux régions naturelles, plaine et bocage, subdivisées en cinq régions, soit géographique (Plaine de Caen), soit historique (Passais, Mortainais), soit agricole (Bocage de Vire, Haut-Bessin).

GEOLOGIE

Deux systèmes géologiques bien distincts:

Au nord-est, la Plaine de Caen, à la lisière occidentale du Bassin Parisien, et la partie bocagère à l'extrémité orientale du Massif Armoricain.

Le sous-sol de la plaine de Caen fait partie des terrains secondaires, jurassique, bradfordien supérieur, calcaire blanc à grain grossier, recouvert par des limons légèrement calcaires qui donnent à la plaine toute sa fertilité. Vers le bocage des terrains de liaison avec le primaire, tel le bajocien.

Le sous-sol du bocage, terrains primaires, précambrien, est formé en majeure partie par des Phyllades de Saint-Lô, assises disposées en bancs très redressés, schiste tendre bleu ou verdâtre. Vers le centre, une barre orientée est-ouest de schiste cambrien vert, bleuâtre ou rouge. Vers le sud apparaissent les affleurements granitiques, en particulier le granit de Vire, très typique c'est une roche à grain moyen, d'un gris bleuâtre, à mica noir utilisée à Montjoie, Gathemo, Coulouvray, pour la sculpture et les monuments funéraires. Le sol est argilo-siliceux, peu perméable à l'eau, propice aux herbages. Quelques fonds de vallées formés par des alluvions modernes.

OROGRAPHIE — HYDROGRAPHIE

Correspondant sensiblement à la distinction géologique, l'orographie présente :

Une partie de plaine mollement ondulée, la Plaine de Caen, dont les niveaux varient entre 35 et 100 m., avec des déclivités inférieures à 5 %, quelques grandes vallées ;

Une partie de bocage très différente, vers le nord, un grand plateau recoupé de vallées en tous sens, avec des cotes maxima de 200 à 360 m. ; en descendant vers le centre, nous quittons le plateau pour aborder un vallonnement plus serré ; puis, au sud, apparaissent les contreforts des collines de Normandie, ligne de partage des eaux entre les Bassins de la Manche et de l'Atlantique, orientée est-ouest, créant de grandes vallées recoupées par des vallées de ruissellement perpendiculaires, les cotes maxima variant entre 300 et 370 m., les pentes atteignant souvent 10 à 12 % ; c'est dans cette région qu'apparaissent les affleurements granitiques.

Cette ligne de partage des eaux détermine les deux Bassins hydrographiques de la Manche et de l'Atlantique.

Au nord, les cours d'eau faisant partie du Bassin de la Manche, coulant sud-nord et venant prendre source sur les pentes du plateau : l'Elle, la Drouve, l'Aure, la Seulle, l'Odon. Puis, prenant source sur le versant nord des collines ou le versant sud du plateau, la Vire et les affluents de l'Orne : la Drouance, le Noireau. Entre les deux chaînes de collines et suivant les grandes vallées est-ouest, la Sée et la Sélune qui se rejoignent dans la Baie du Mont-Saint-Michel.

Au sud, les cours d'eau faisant partie du Bassin de l'Atlantique, coulant nord-sud, affluents de la Mayenne : l'Egrenne et la Varenne, qui prennent leur source sur le versant sud des collines de Normandie.

Dans toute la partie bocagère, un réseau très serré de rivières, ruisseaux et rus, coulant par toutes les fissures et retenus par un sol imperméable. Dans la partie de plaine, au contraire, quelques cours d'eau d'un quadrillage très large.

Dans la Plaine de Caen, une première nappe d'eau importante à environ 6 m., une seconde nappe à 30 m. de profondeur. En Bocage, les eaux sont superficielles, abondantes et disséminées.

DEMOGRAPHIE

La densité de la population est variable entre les différentes régions : en plaine, 45 habitants au km^2 ; en bocage, 71 habitants, rapport normal. Alors qu'en plaine l'exploitation moyenne de 100 hectares occupe ou plutôt supporte 11 à 15 habitants, soit au maximum 6 ha 5 par habitant, en bocage la ferme moyenne de 20 hectares supporte 5 habitants, soit 4 ha par habitant et, si nous prenons des régions tel le Mortainais, dont la

Granit. — Primaire Silurien. — Primaire Précambrien. — Jurassique moyen. — Jurassique inférieur.

Labours. — Herbages.

OLOGIE - CULTURES

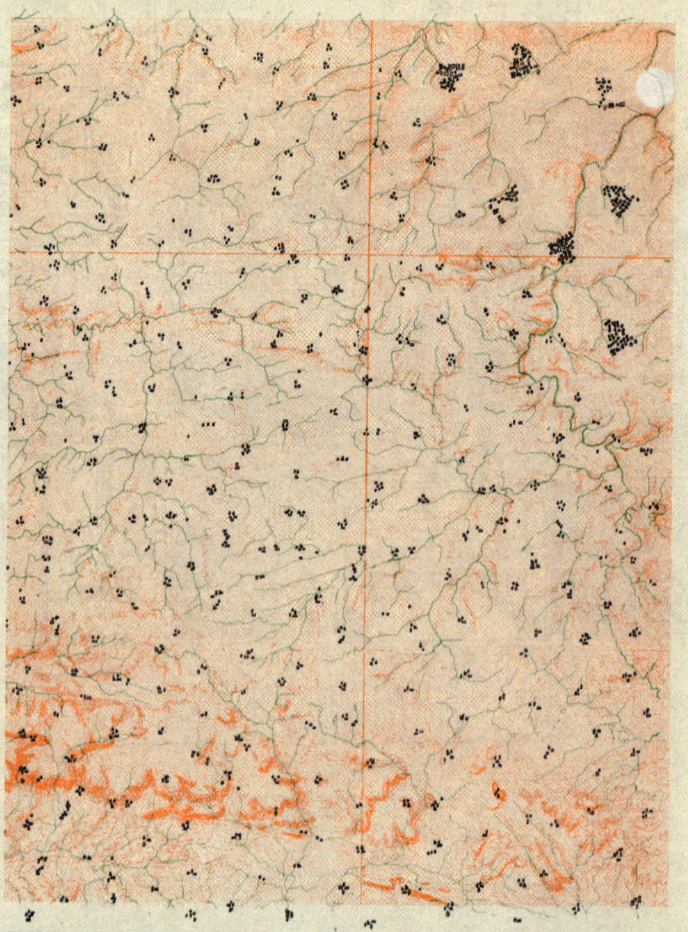

SPERSION DE L'HABITAT

Fonds de carte de l'Institut Géographique National.

304 TECHNIQUES ET ARCHITECTURE

Tides That Bind: Waterborne Trade and the Infrastructure Networks of Jardine, Matheson & Co.

G. A. Bremner

The Jardine Matheson Group, or Jardines as it is commonly known, is a corporate conglomerate with global business interests in industries as wide-ranging as shipping, property, financial services, retail, and hotel management. An umbrella for well-known holding companies such as Dairy Farm (comprising the Wellcome, Giant, Hero, and Yonghui supermarket chains in China and Southeast Asia), Jardine Cycle & Carriage (prestige motor sales), Astra International (vehicle manufacturing and palm oil), and the Mandarin Oriental hotel chain, it also manages Asian branches of Pizza Hut, KFC, and IKEA.[1] With more than 469,000 employees worldwide, Group revenues for 2018 amounted to approximately \$92.3 billion, with a pretax profit of \$4.931 billion.[2]

Jardines is the direct present-day manifestation of Jardine, Matheson & Co., an agency house firm established in Canton in 1832 by two enterprising Scotsmen, William Jardine (1784–1843) and James Matheson (1796–1878).[3] Thomas Keswick, an ancestor of the current owners, married Jardine's niece and was involved in the business from its inception. Familial connection was typical in the 1830s, and Scottish agency houses proliferated in the region following the abolition of the East India Company's trading monopoly in 1833.[4] Heavily invested in the China Trade, Jardine, Matheson & Co. rapidly positioned itself at the center of Britain's imperial economy in Asia via substantial trading interests in tea and opium, among other commodities.[5]

Corporate conglomerates today are sustained by the transfer of goods and services in specially demarcated Export Processing Zones, serviced through (and materialized by) a dense, largely obscure web of logistics and communications infrastructure. With complicated offshore financial and taxation arrangements operating across multiple domestic and international jurisdictions, these conglomerates exist as much in their infrastructural matrix as they do in actual personnel, buildings, and exchange commodities.[6] Their networked geography traces through nodal points in a way that is characteristically diffuse.[7] Multinational companies such as Jardines work to create *new* zones of corporate exchange in what Ash Amin has labeled "trans-territorial production" space, with boundaries, standards, and hierarchies that do not necessarily overlap with those of nation states or established trading blocs.[8] In this respect the commercial and regulatory "space" in which Jardines operates today can be seen as an evolved form of the international "free trade" environment inhabited by its distant forebears in 1840s Hong Kong.[9] And these conglomerates may be understood as the postcolonial counterparts of their colonial progenitors in the joint-stock trading monopolies and agency-house firms—only much larger, more sophisticated, and less accountable.[10]

Jardine Matheson's initial phases of development in the early nineteenth century are particularly relevant to the expansion of its built infrastructure. The company's earliest physical facilities for storage and distribution catalyzed and in turn generated new critical pressures for growth. In focusing on the formal and spatial structure of this organization, it is possible to reveal both its geographical shape and interconnectedness as a corporate mechanism. What, it may be asked, were the particular spatial and material features comprising its corporate structure, including dock, warehouse, office, and shipping facilities? How and why did such structures form a system as a whole, and operate to produce a 'zone' or territory that both defined and acted to protect British political interests in the region?[11] Put simply, how can material evidence such as buildings and other man-made structures be marshalled in making explicit the physical contours of a corporate organization such as Jardine Matheson?[12]

The driver for this expansion was tea-drinking culture in Britain, America, and Australasia. But to make sense of Jardine Matheson's entanglement within the commercial imperatives of the British imperial system it is necessary to move beyond traditional land-based conceptions of empire (what some have termed 'terracentrism'), particularly in the context of Asia, to an approach that is concerned more with a water- or ocean-based framework of analysis.[13] As Alison Games, David Hancock, Philip Stern, and H. V. Bowen among others have insisted, to fathom the quasi-imperial activity of corporate entities such as Jardine Matheson one must examine their networked constitution as much *between* as *across* traditional oceanic zones of analysis, whether Atlantic, Indian, or Pacific.[14] This is especially the case with Jardine Matheson, for it never understood itself as operating within or being restricted to any historiographically convenient geography.

Without a land-based trading domain, Jardine Matheson sought strategic relationships via oceans, ports, and rivers rather than railways, roads, and territorial districts. The services supplied to "upstream" and "downstream" chain partners of the business occupied a maritime world encompassing the Pearl River delta, South China Sea, and Bay of Bengal, as well as numerous other ports across the Pacific, Indian, and Atlantic Oceans.[15] The waterborne character of Jardine Matheson's commerce can thus be taken as the quintessential "image" of the company's trading environment, so much so that Matheson occasionally conducted business aboard the company's ships, especially during the First Opium War (1839–42).[16]

The insights of what have been termed transnational and oceanic histories are prescient.[17] In delineating a "connected history," as Simon Potter and Jonathan Saha have pleaded for in the spirit of Sanjay Subrahmanyan, I will attempt to achieve a new understanding of the "gray" architecture comprising Jardine Matheson's trade infrastructure and its associated spaces.[18] As Brian Larkin has noted, this requires an appreciation of the semiotic qualities of infrastructure, along with a consideration of how it addresses and constitutes subjectivity, including its technical operations.[19] The idea of the "network" and "networking" is of critical importance, as is the notion of littoral environments, with the infrastructures operating at the interface between land, sea, and/or river.[20]

A material and spatial history of this kind draws attention to the various and less visible ligatures (financial, informational, and transactional) that constitute the practice of building in all of its forms. Jardine Matheson was an ultra-mobile corporate entity, and the matrix it inhabited was in many ways the crystallization of its requirements for speed and efficiency of transaction. Its spatial and material features were the palpable "traces," as Latour would have it, of the specifically "nonsocial" dimensions of its network.[21] Yet in the process of their creation and use, these features assembled and tied the social together. The trading facilities described here may have been largely static, disparate, and subject to all the problems and vulnerabilities associated with man-made structures, but combined and viewed as part of a networked whole they unleashed vast potentials of commercial energy in the flow of goods and services. As part of a network driven by the economic rationality of capitalist logistics, no one building or space stood alone or was paramount: all were ultimately subservient to a larger extended structure.

In attempting to recover the complex spatial qualities of Jardine, Matheson & Co., my approach is by necessity more speculative than systematic, concerning only a small representative sample of instances relating to the China Trade and its infrastructure. Although the company's material assets and subsidiary holdings are vast, making a comprehensive account impractical, it is nevertheless possible to discern a certain logic and consistency to its formation from the few examples considered here. A cross section more than an overview, this analysis will present ways of exploring the significance of infrastructural buildings as a means of gauging, and thereby interpreting, the diffuse, circulatory, and transactional "shape" of a modern corporation, and especially what has been termed the "imperialism of free trade."[22]

Global Trade and the First Information Revolution

Some basic facts about Jardine, Matheson & Co. and its scope of operations are necessary to begin with. Initially the company was involved in what was known as the "country trade" throughout the Asia-Pacific region, involving the supply, transportation, and sale of goods and services between India, China, and the settlements of the Southeast Asian archipelago.[23] Carried out by the East India Company under the terms of its Royal Charter initially, the trade fell increasingly to "private" merchants from the late eighteenth century onward. The "free trade" environment that evolved after the reforms of the East India Company's trading monopoly in 1813 and 1833 allowed the agency houses conducting private commerce to grow and expand their businesses substantially. When it formally moved its base of operations to Hong Kong in 1843, Jardine Matheson was the region's leading agency-house firm.[24]

The rise of Jardine Matheson to market dominance was strongly implicated with the China Trade and the Canton "system" (1757–1842).[25] Under this arrangement foreign merchants were allowed access to the Chinese market with commercial activities restricted to the trading season (September to March) at a location beyond the walls of the southern Chinese city of Canton (Guangzhou), on the banks of the Pearl River (Zhujiang). FIG 1 It was an area comprising the so-called factories, or "hongs," of the local Chinese merchant elite. Over time this restricted area of the city steadily became Westernized as European and American merchants, including the East India Company, began expanding their trading activities with Qing China.[26]

FIG 2 Within the confines of this enclave, Jardine Matheson entrenched itself in the triangular trade network between India, China, and Britain involving opium, silver, and tea.[27] Through the proceeds of this trade the company was able to establish and consolidate a substantial business position, allowing it to forward integrate into related commercial activities such as shipping, insurance, and banking.[28]

The steady improvement of information supply and management was a key feature of the China Trade. As H. V. Bowen has observed, information management had been crucial to the business practices and success of the East India Company.[29] The professionalization of bureaucracy that characterized these corporate improvements can in many ways be viewed as inseparable from the wider advancement in techniques for the gathering, classification, and communication of data that occurred throughout the course of the eighteenth and early nineteenth centuries. Globally coincident transformations were historical part-and-parcel of what has since become known as the "first information revolution" or new "information society."[30] The epistolic territories that resulted were fundamental to the increasingly modern and efficient administration of British imperial and mercantile interests.[31]

Jardine Matheson's extended web of relationships, and the commercial intelligence that flowed across it, was in effect the organizational "architecture" that underpinned the company's business model.[32] As speed of traffic, efficiency of routing, access to finance, and ease of communications were critical to competitive advantage in what was essentially a series of interfirm transactions dealing in perishable goods, the "strength" of this information architecture was key. The ambition was to use information to form an economy of trust, and the primary factor was the ability to relay faithful intelligence concerning supply, demand, and risk.[33] Flows of intelligence are evident in the company's voluminous correspondence, as well as in trade papers such as the *Canton Register* (Jardine Matheson's biweekly publication).[34] Through its perfection of the techniques of information supply and management, Jardine, Matheson & Co. was able to guarantee a degree of market predictability that helped to offset risk.[35] As the company's lines of communication widened and grew during the 1830s and '40s, so did its market penetration, wealth, and influence.

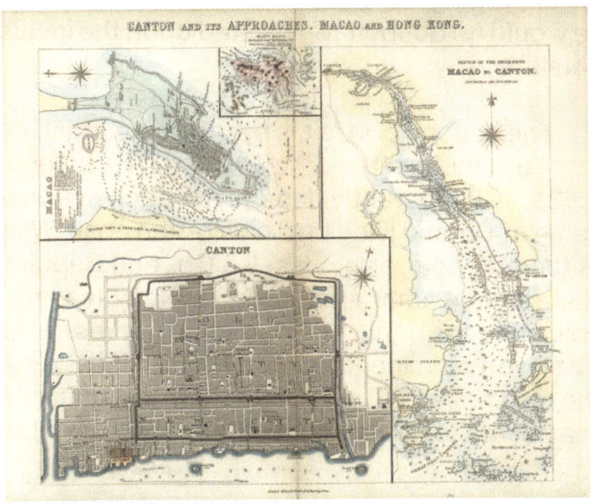

FIG 1
John Walker and Edward Belcher (1855), *Canton and its Approaches, Macao and Hong Kong*. Note the foreign 'Factories' district at bottom left of 'Canton' inset map.

FIG 2
Chinese artist (c. 1830s), *The Hongs of Canton*.

Insofar as the China Trade constituted a commercial and political space within which the actual differences between technical practices, procedures, and forms were actively reduced (with a view to creating common standards), it may be understood as a type of infrastructure.[36] The business practices of Jardine Matheson were very much concerned with integrating systems of production, bureaucracy, and logistics in order to create high degrees of connectivity while excluding (even punishing) commercial and political actors who failed to conform. Although not constituting monopolies as such, China Trade firms were collectively involved in the creation of a broad new commercial structure ("zone") in which the rules of engagement were increasingly complex and specialized, such that knowledge and/or contacts were requisite for participation.

William Jardine and James Matheson had become so wealthy and powerful by the 1840s, and the British exchequer so reliant on import duties from Chinese tea, that they and their proxies were able to intervene directly in British foreign policy, circumventing conventional routes of access to executive decision making via personal contacts and persistent lobbying.[37] Yet just as the apparent logic and benefits of free trade in the Asia-Pacific region were being touted as a universal good, resistance came from the Chinese imperial authorities. The British government reacted with direct violent intervention ("gunboat diplomacy") to generate the desired "market" conditions. Jardine and Matheson became members of parliament on their return from Asia (in 1841 and 1843, respectively), strengthening their influence over government policy on trade with China.

Connectivity and Facilities Infrastructure

The communications architecture described here calls to mind its corollary in the form of actual buildings. In the case of Jardine, Matheson & Co. these architectures were superimposed on one another. Both were respective outgrowths, and thus essential elements, of the business model and its inherent strategy, encompassing communication lines and physical plant, both terrestrial and maritime. Reliable channels of correspondence established the intellectual framework through which the company's political and financial ambitions could be met. As Carol Matheson Connell points out, this correspondence "was the principal means of setting rules, sharing market information, building relationships with suppliers and agents, communicating strategy to partners, training and disciplining agents, organizing industry support, and communicating with and influencing the British government."[38]

But Mark Crinson, Ben Marsden, and Crosbie Smith, among others, have argued that an approach emphasizing correspondence alone without acknowledging the physical facilities requisite to its maintenance and transmission risks perpetuating a basic historical inadequacy.[39] For instance, Crinson has observed how architecture and other forms of built infrastructure were integral to many of the practices and relationships that empire required for its advancement.[40] On this point David Hancock reminds us that Britain's "expanding imperial environment did more than influence the conduct of merchants; in creating the need for an infrastructure—shipping and trading services, physical plant, and voluntary and involuntary settlement opportunities—it increasingly provided the precondition for much wealth creation."[41] Although referring to the British Atlantic world of the mid-eighteenth century, these words also apply to the current context.

Working from the definition provided by Larkin, we may take "infrastructure" here to mean a built network that facilitates the flow of goods or ideas that allows for exchange over space. As a physical form it can be understood as shaping the nature of that network, the speed and direction of its movement, its temporalities, as well as its vulnerability to breakdown.[42] Thus the business correspondence of Jardine Matheson, and in turn the goods and services it described, was fundamentally reliant for its effective communication on the logistical potential of physical infrastructure, including the technologies that connected it across time and through space, such as shipping (and later telegraph cables). Security was paramount too. As Eve Tavor Bannet notes, the seas across which this correspondence moved were understood as spatial intervals via which the threads of mercantile and epistolary commerce were required to be knit securely. These seas were thus spaces that both government and merchants had a common interest in safeguarding, against both piracy and malevolent foreign interference.[43]

William Jardine and James Matheson were fully aware of the importance of facilities infrastructure in leveraging commercial advantage in this way. As Horatio Hardy—Jardine Matheson's London informant, and proprietor of the popular Jerusalem Coffee House—wrote to them following the parliamentary vote on the East India Company charter in 1833: "The whole of the [company's] commercial property is to be immediately given up when the Charter expires in April 1834, viz—warehouses, wharf, Docks, East India House, and the buildings with all commercial property in India."[44] The enforced relinquishing of this infrastructure obviously spelled the end of the East India Company as a commercial trading entity. The facilities described in Hardy's letter pinpoint precisely the critical dependence a pervasive commercial enterprise had on structures of this kind in fulfilling its core mission. Without them its ability to trade effectively ceased. Indeed by 1814 the Company was spending some £53,000 on expenses related to estate management, including an average of £31,807 per annum on warehouse maintenance alone.[45]

With this in mind, the infrastructural circuits that tightly bound the Jardine Matheson organization, along with those of the China Trade as a whole, had become indispensable to the maintenance and continued expansion of British interests in the region, not least revenue generation for the Crown. In this scenario the coalescence and exercise of these networks and their attendant infrastructures had become engines of power in their own right.[46] Thus although not setting out to exercise dominion as such, in the immediate post-East India Company trading environment, the China Trade had become an institution of its own, with ever-growing political ramifications. It had simply become too big to fail. From this perspective the buildings typical of Jardine Matheson's early growth emerge as central in another kind of architectural history.[47]

Factory, Port, Ship, and Godown

A useful way to analyze this type of building in the context of the China Trade is to consider two contemporary portraits. The first of these is the 1830s portrait of William Jardine by George Chinnery FIG 3 Apart from the sitter himself, the books and papers strewn across the table are immediately prominent, among them a bundle of correspondence and a ledger. On the floor, partly unfurled, resides what is most likely a map or shipping chart. The sitter clasps a quill, the tip of which is thoroughly blackened with ink owing to heavy use. With fist clenched, and wearing a concerted if rather enigmatic look, Jardine is presented to us as a man who means business in every sense of the term: calm and 'trustworthy,' if calculating. On closer inspection, however, the setting reveals peculiar detail. Unlike so many early nineteenth-century portraits of this type, where one might expect to see a picture of a classical ruin, a grand country house, or perhaps a family portrait, the background wall is set with a painting that depicts instead mere trading facilities—the *hongs*, or factories, of Canton. Moreover, we see numerous ships in the form of trading vessels. It was from amidst this jumble of structures that Jardine Matheson conducted business for a number of years before relocating to Hong Kong. Given the importance of Canton to Jardine, he would no doubt have insisted upon the inclusion of this detail.

The second portrait is by the same artist, only this time there are three sitters. FIG 4 Entitled *Dent's Verandah, Macao* (c.1842), it apparently depicts a French merchant by the name of Durand lying back in a rattan chair, William Hunter of the American firm Russell & Co., and Captain William H. Hall, later an admiral in the Royal Navy, leaning on the column to the right.[48] Of particular interest here is a map displayed prominently on the wall behind the sitters. One of the men has a cup of tea, and there is a mature poppy plant in a pot at the bottom right of the picture, symbolizing opium.

There are other instruments of the business depicted too, such as a barometer and a nautical telescope.

The symbols and instruments depicted in these images evoke a narrative reflecting the fundamental nature of the China Trade as one in a perpetual state of potential or actual movement and transaction. The maps in these images conjure an idea of seaborne mobility and trade rendered reliable by the exacting science of modern European cartography. These two images open windows onto a wider world of commercial promise—the painting of Canton in the one, the view beyond the veranda in the other—that offers the prospect of a connected world and its near unlimited potential for commodities-based exploitation, one that was only then beginning to take its modern form.

The architectural settings in both images are central to this understanding. The verandah upon which the sitters are positioned in the second image is that of Dent & Co.'s headquarters in Macao. This structure constituted the center of the company's system of transportation networks, connecting ship to port to warehouse throughout the region and beyond. In the portrait of Jardine, the painting on the wall draws our attention to Jardine Matheson's origins in Canton, where it initially occupied premises at Imperial Hong (No. 7), before taking up residence in No. 4, the Creek. In both cases, these buildings were used as offices and private accommodation, while nearly all were part of complexes incorporating godowns and other spaces associated with trade.[49]

FIG 4
George Chinnery (1842), *Dent's Verandah, Macao.*

FIG 3
William Jardine (c.1830s), *Thomas Goff Lupton.* Published by Leggatt & Co, after George Chinnery.

FIG 6
Chinese artist (1855), *Jardine, Matheson & Co.'s executive house and godowns, East Point, Hong Kong.*

FIG 5
William John Higgins (1824), *The Opium Ships at Lintin, China.*

Mobile infrastructure in the form of ships was also important. Owning ships (rather than hiring those owned by others) helped Jardine Matheson maintain greater control over the transportation of goods and security of information, as well as to grow the proprietary trading aspect of the business.[50] By 1843 the company owned at least twelve ships, and it is clear from its extant archive that much time and resources were devoted to acquiring and operating them.[51] Nautical holdings ranged from opium and tea clippers to receiving ships and hulks, as well as steamers from the late 1830s onward.[52] FIG 5 As moving spaces of containment and transfer, ships were in effect an extension of the factory and godown spaces into which they off-loaded and up-lifted their cargoes. It is therefore no coincidence that ships of various kinds appear prominently in nearly every image of Jardine Matheson facilities. FIG 6 Without this peripatetic infrastructure, the static facilities that comprised the transactional networks of Jardine Matheson's commercial "system" would have been inert. The significance of shipping in this regard, especially after the advent of the steamer, has parallels with the effects of the modern railway network on the global consolidation of European commerce and political power during the nineteenth century.[53]

Just as the commodities traded by Jardine Matheson may be considered proxy agents of the company, the methods and processes by which they were transferred can be understood as indicative of the founders' commercial ideology. To quote the vociferous British free-trade advocate Richard Cobden: "Not a bale of merchandise leaves our shores but it bears the seeds of intelligence and fruitful thought to the members of some less enlightened community."[54] Such objects—invested as they were with disparately sourced capital and emblazoned with the company's trademark—were agents of a different order in the forging of new relationships (spatial, commercial, and social). This concerns not only the nature and history of things, but also the networks of interaction between merchants and their cargoes.[55] In other words, the shifting space of the ship as it plied the trade routes back and forth created a new kind of culturally contingent spatiality by establishing an entwined dynamic between land and sea, factory and vessel.[56]

Fabricating British Dominion in Asia

Little is known about the premises of Dent & Co. in Macao beyond its similarity to the many other buildings erected in the "compradoric" classical style that characterized colonial architecture in the region.[57] FIG 7 Generally speaking, structures of this nature represented a category of facility that might otherwise be described as infrastructure. Its function was to account for, secure, and manage the commodities that corporate entities such as Jardine Matheson and Dent & Co. dealt in, principally opium.[58] Opium was the product that knitted the triangular system of the China Trade together, sustaining the solvency of British commerce in the region for nearly a century.

Britain's average balance-of-payments deficit with China during the period 1817–33 ran between £800,000 and £3 million per annum.[59] As China required very few commodities from either Britain or India, large amounts of gold and silver bullion were used to buy products such as tea and silk for shipment back to markets in Britain, Europe, and North America. This drain on cash reserves caused consternation among both the government and merchants, leading to the development of opium as a substitute form of remittance. By the late eighteenth century the East India Company had established a substantial manufacturing operation in Bengal, producing the coveted 'Patna' and 'Benares' varieties of opium that were shipped to China for consumption. This industry required an extensive and sophisticated large-scale infrastructure at both ends of the network, from production to distribution. FIG 8A, 8B, 9

FIG 7
George Chinnery (1838), *View of Macao.*

FIG 8B
Sita Ram, 'The opium godown or store within its compound at Patna,' from *Views by Seeta Ram from Patna to Benares 2*, 1814.

FIG 8A
Sita Ram, 'Watercolour of opium factory and godowns at Patna, India,' from *Views by Seeta Ram from Patna to Benares 2*, 1814.

Such facilities were strewn throughout the region, from Bombay and Calcutta to Singapore and Canton. Given the related nature of these structures, they naturally formed networks of storage and transshipping facilities for opium along the Pearl River and its estuary in strategic locations such as Whampoa, Lintin Island, Macao, and pre-cessation Hong Kong.[60] Since the importation and sale of opium to China had been officially banned by Imperial decree since 1729, smuggling depots at these and other locations were used increasingly as staging posts for the clandestine offloading of opium along the south China coast. The cash generated from this illicit trade was used to purchase goods such as tea in Canton, where they were stored and then shipped to key markets in the Atlantic. Reliable storage facilities were required for this racket: godowns, receiving ships, and hulks (essentially floating godowns) of various kinds funneled this contraband, creating a waterborne web of shipping conduits and littoral entrepôts that remained fundamental to the survival of the China Trade. FIG 10 The actors involved were equally diverse, ranging from Parsi brokers (such as the famous Jamsetjee Jejeebhoy), Western agents (including Jardine Matheson), and Chinese *cohong* merchants such as Houqua. Jardine Matheson's special relationship with Jejeebhoy enabled the company to deal in Malwa opium (via Bombay, outside of Indian government control), alongside the standard Patna and Benares varieties.[61] This highlights the collaborative transoceanic dimension of this commercial "regime" as it bound, in the words of Gregory Blue, "Indian peasants, British and Indian governments, a vast mass of Chinese consumers, and an array of Western, Parsee, Sephardic, and most of all Chinese merchants in an immense revenue-generating system."[62]

In terms of function, the buildings involved were often (but not always) hybrids comprising part house, part business premises, and part storage and transshipping depot (godown). On the whole the requirements were basic. Although other activities took place in these structures, including the entertainment of clients, ultimately they were business premises. The leases and subleases between Jardine Matheson and others that exist in the Jardine Matheson archive highlight both the routine nature of these structures and the matter-of-fact esteem in which they were held and used.[63] Their purpose was to serve as but one station among many in the networked spaces that constituted the Canton system and its global connections. As Stephen Lockwood, Cole Roskam, and others have observed, buildings of this kind were essentially economic mediators the function of which was to span both geographic and cultural distance. The real and symbolic value they had was almost exclusively bound up in the levels of comfort and organized storage capacity they could afford, and therefore the confidence they inspired in the minds of corporate executives and insurance brokers.[64]

This reveals something of these buildings' semiotic quality. The embodied 'functionalism' apparent in their form and purpose rendered them metapragmatic objects, "signs of themselves," to quote Larkin, that had meaning and effect within the confines of particular circulatory regimes.[65] This extended to their internal arrangements. FIG 11 As Hancock has argued, choosing a location for, erecting, and organizing the interior of business premises for operational efficiency including training, filing, and cleaning embodied a rational and disciplined revolution in business-management practice. To reiterate a point made earlier, this indicated wider information-processing developments that had transformed the modern world and spawned a "true bred" and worldly merchant class.[66] Moreover, in commodities-based industries such as the China Trade, associated storage and warehousing facilities signaled the scale of a business, the knowledge and skill of those involved (engendering trust), and potential profit margins.[67]

Concerning the factories in Canton, accounts of these mundane attributes typically describe structures of three stories:

> The lower floors were occupied by counting-rooms, godowns, and store-rooms, by the rooms of the Compradore [Chinese foreman], his assistants, servants and coolies, as well as by a massively built treasury of granite, with iron doors, an essential feature, there being no banks in existence. In front of each treasury was a well-paved open space, with table for scales and weights, the indispensable adjuncts of all money transactions. ... The second floor was devoted to dining and sitting rooms, the third to bedrooms. As almost all were provided with broad verandahs and the buildings put up with care, they were quite devoid of ornamental work.[68]

We glean further information about these structures from extant building documents and leases, such as the contract between B. C. Wilcocks (lessor) and Tsoey Hing and Acha (Chinese builders) for Nos. 1 and 2, Creek Hong, Canton, dated 1827. This document, although primarily a legal agreement between two parties, is significant for what it reveals about the building process and the seriousness with which it was undertaken. It refers to the reconstruction of the hong—possibly following the fire of 1822, for it explicitly indicates a process of "rebuilding" as opposed to repair

FIG 10
Detail of Whampoa: the anchorage, by Chinese artist, late 18th century. A number of godowns are shown in this image along the river bank.

FIG 9
W. S. Sherwill (c.1850) The Examining Hall, Opium Factory, Patna.

FIG 11
Chinese artist (early 19th century) Interior of a room in one of the factories, probably the British factory.

or refurbishment. What the contract also suggests is that although the land upon which the buildings sat was owned by local Chinese *cohongs*, the buildings themselves were paid for and thus presumably owned by individual agency houses under a system of leasehold.[69] As numerous other lease agreements for Canton factories in the Jardine Matheson archive reveal, the lessors were then free (it seems) to sublet or alienate the leases and their buildings to other foreign merchants, effectively converting factory buildings into commercial assets in their own right.[70]

The contract between Wilcocks and Tsoey Hing states that no "mud" was to be used anywhere in erecting the hong (i.e., no mat-shed) and that substantial materials were to be employed throughout: teak for doors, *chunam* for godown floors, solid brick for walls, granite for windowsills and the basement floor—all raised considerably above ground level to protect against dampness. The houses were to be supported on stone pillars and have marble floors. Venetian blinds were to be fitted to all windows. The basement and godown floors were to have twelve-foot-high ceilings, and the house floor was to be fifteen feet high. "Light ornamental work" was permitted to finish.[71] In addition to these basic provisions, three "treasuries," or strong rooms, were specified, to be made of "red stone" of "sufficient size and thickness." A plan for the whole is mentioned, but this appears to have been nothing more than a suggestive sketch, perhaps outlining the principal dimensions.[72] Externally, directions were given to look to other hongs for inspiration. For instance, it was specified that "Door at the Entrance of the Hong to be of Teak, constructed and finished like that at the H. E. I. C. Factory," and "front to be finished after the manner of Mr Sturgis's Factory." The contract was for $17,554 Spanish dollars (equivalent to approximately £650).

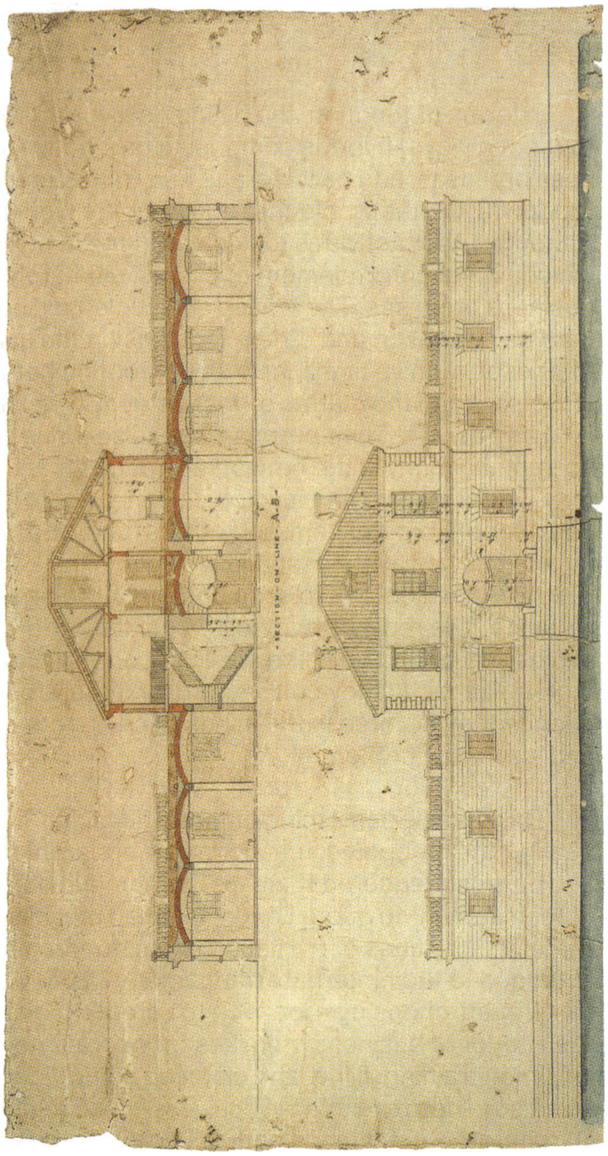

FIG 13
Elevation and section of opium godown (warehouse), Jardine, Matheson & Co., East Point, Hong Kong, c.1850s.

After Jardine Matheson relocated its base of operations to East Point, Hong Kong, in 1843, it quickly began erecting substantial purpose-built structures to facilitate its business interests. Among these were godowns for the storage and transshipment of opium. What is immediately apparent from an extant, professionally-drawn plan of one of these structures, is the care and precision with which it was assembled. FIG 12, 13 Security was clearly paramount: heavily rusticated walls of solid granite, three feet thick, characterize the structure, with a keeper's residence forming an upper story and rooms for Manila guards below. Nestled at the heart of the building was a treasury and shroffing room. These two spaces denote the presence of considerable amounts of cash in the form of silver coinage, the "shroffer" being the trained professional (usually Chinese) responsible for counting and assessing the quality of metal coins. The treasury was of course required for the secure storage of cash derived directly from the illicit trade in opium along the south China coast. Apart from its functional utility, the godowns projected an image of security and commercial confidence, creating the impression of a business built upon an infrastructure as solid and commanding as its position in the market.

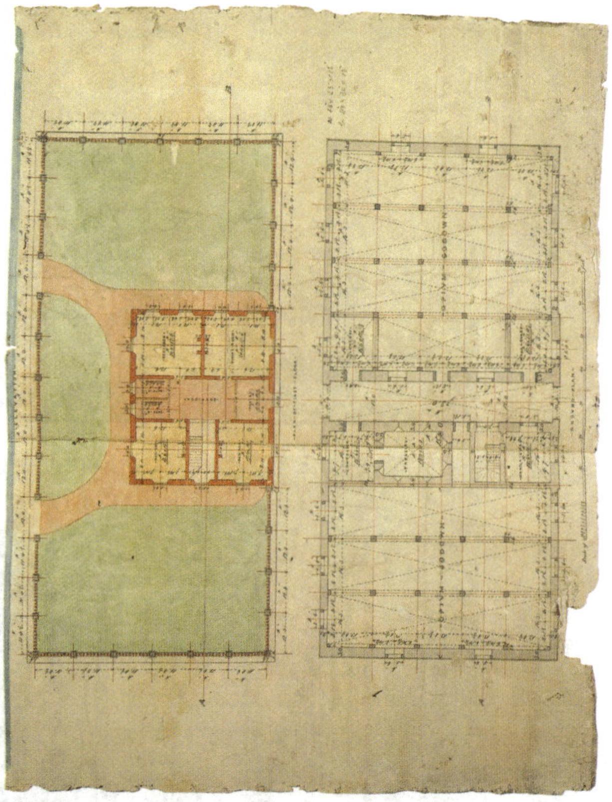

FIG 12
Ground-floor and upper-floor plan of opium godown (warehouse), Jardine, Matheson & Co., East Point, Hong Kong, c.1850s.

A rare plan in the Jardine Matheson archive shows how structures of this kind had evolved by the time of the Shamian concession in Canton in 1859. FIG 14 Owing to the availability of larger plots on the island, we begin to see a separating of the business premises (office and accommodation) from the warehousing facilities.[73] Although there is very little detail concerning materials or architectural décor, we can nevertheless see clearly how the spaces were organized.[74] The presence of certain rooms reveals this "dwelling house" to have been a tea-processing center. The front of house, on the ground floor immediately to the left of the public entrance, provided ample office accommodation, essential to the professional running of the business. Across the corridor was to be the largest space in the building, the tea muster and inspection room.[75] Immediately adjacent to this space, as in the company's opium godown at East Point, were a treasury and shroffing room, with the comprador's office tucked in behind. This arrangement indicates the proposed building as the infrastructural counterpart to the opium godown, located as it was at the Canton end of the supply chain, where tea was purchased using proceeds from opium sales.

Throughout the mid-nineteenth century Jardine, Matheson & Co. established business branches across East and Southeast Asia. In the treaty ports alone it had amassed five partners and twenty assistants by 1844, within two years of the conclusion of the First Opium War.[76] By 1880 the company had opened thirteen branches, and a further twelve by 1900.[77] Much trade was also handled via Singapore, Manila, and numerous ports in Japan. Facilities infrastructure of various kinds was required in each of these locations, whether owned or rented, including branch offices and godowns.

Modern Spatial Economies and the China Trade

Of particular importance with regard to these types of structure, including ships, is how the accounting practices employed in relation to them were as regular, systematic, and perfunctory as the structures themselves. This reflected a certain mentality of abstraction (collation, partition, and recording) common to the China Trade as a whole.[78] The huge number of ledgers kept in the Jardine Matheson archive illustrate the precision with which goods and property circulating within its commercial system were received, accounted for, processed, and transshipped. The patterns of recording are largely consistent, with entries for trademarks, volumes, agents, couriers, locations, and prices accompanied by related observations. FIG 15 Page after page and volume after volume these coordinates appear uniform and isotropic, with a seemingly dreary capacity for the infinite. The expanse of things recorded was enmeshed firmly within and thus subservient to the Cartesian regime that ordered the gridded pages comprising the ledgers, creating an analytical field that was at once optical, intellectual, and spatial.[79]

We may infer from the insights of Samuel Edgerton that the businessmen behind this regime were disposed to a visual and spatial world that accorded precisely with the tidy principles of mathematical order applied in their ledgers.[80] The elective affinities are especially strong between the functional spaces of storage and transshipment. As these "things" in transit appeared on one side of the register, assigned their rightful addresses within the matrix of cells making up the ledger, they simultaneously emerged on the other as they moved into and through the real spaces of ship, hulk, and godown. With this in mind, it is perhaps not entirely accidental that William Jardine, every bit a practical-minded businessman, was portrayed with the company ledgers positioned directly beneath an image of ships and factories.

Ship and godown may thus be understood as a kind of spatial analogue to the ledger, and vice versa.[81] FIG 16, 17 This testifies to the all-encompassing logic of the financial worldview characterizing the early development of the capitalist global economy, which had begun to bend all to its will, including the built environment. To be sure, architecture always corresponds to the economies prevalent in any given domain, whether financial, political, or intellectual. Much has been written in recent decades on the rational abstraction of modern science and its effects on the European architectural imagination.[82] But taken merely as an expression of the exchange economics associated with the China Trade, these infrastructures—connected as they were for reasons of commercial optimization—reflected new levels of pecuniary compliance, in terms of connectivity and bureaucratic rationalization. Despite their "metapragmatic" dimension as objects maintaining a certain aesthetic value, they were largely disembodied as works of architecture, and therefore empty of content.[83]

As Nathan Dunn had requested of Charles Magniac in 1823: a factory with godowns must "be built strong for the stowage of Cargo" and be "good ..., plain, [and] substantial."[84] Thus, just as the Cartesian techniques of representation conventional to the efficient conveyance of commercial data became increasingly important, so did organized infrastructure in the movement and manipulation of commodity objects.[85] Apart from tea and silk—the key goods shipped to European and North American markets—numerous other commodities comprising the China and "country" trades flowed along and through these spaces, including cotton, pepper, lumber, tin, and rice. The Jardine Matheson ledgers show the coming and going of these commodities with inexorable regularity, their quantities scrupulously recorded as they passed from one containment facility to another. What this bland, repetitive, and precise process also highlights is recording for the purposes of insuring goods and property to an appropriate standard. The China Trade was at times a risky business, and insurance played a key role in managing the commercial economy.

The buildings in which these goods were stored reveal the seriousness with which precautions against fire, flood, and theft were taken. Turning again to historic building contacts, we get a glimpse of the specifications demanded of such structures. For example, the 1859 contract between Thomas Hunt & Co. and Attuck (Chinese builder) for erecting a godown on Pedder's Wharf, Hong Kong Central, is instructive.[86] The terms of the general agreement include phrases such as "all proper and necessary materials" and "workmanlike manner"; works were to be performed and completed "according to the true intent and meaning" of the "Plans, Sections, Elevations, and Specifications" provided.[87] Such language was intended to obligate the builder legally to producing a solid, secure, and weatherproof receptacle of given dimensions and volume, which in turn demonstrated reasonable levels of capacity and security for purposes of business planning and insurance.[88] In the specification schedule it is noted that the building's foundations should be "built with large Granite Stones, in level courses, of headers and stretchers, laid alternately, ... the whole well consolidated with Chinam [sic] mortar." A granite plinth was to be raised two feet above ground level on these foundations, followed by solid walls eight inches thick of the "best Japan Brick." Floor joists were to be twelve-by-three-inch Oregon pine, and the flooring was to comprise seven-inch wooden planks, one and a half inches thick, fixed to "each joist with 2 nails 3" long." All windows were to be fitted with iron bars seven-eighths of an inch thick, with cross bars two and a half inches thick, "let well into the stone and run with lead." FIG 18 The document concludes with the following clause:

> The whole of the materials used to be of the best quality, and the whole of the work performed in a workmanlike manner to the entire satisfaction of Messrs Thos Hunt & Co: and under the supervision and direction of Mr S. B. Rawling [the engineer supplying the plans].[89]

Although the specification schedule for this godown is reasonably detailed, it could have been far more so, leaving little or no room for misinterpretation. A specification schedule for a hong to be erected for Jardine Matheson c. 1850 contains more than 180 separate entries covering all manner of items, including timber structural members and fittings, brick and stonework, brass door and window furniture, and ironwork.[90] In these contracts we also find specifications for materials coming from all over the Asia-Pacific region and beyond: bricks from Japan, red cedar from Australia, various types of Asian oak, Philippines hardwood, teak from India, Oregon joists from the United States, and iron from Europe. Indeed, the materials for Jardine Matheson's first substantial godown at Hong Kong were transferred entirely from Macao.[91] This demonstrates how such structures were co-productive of the system and its web of commercial relations. Standing as the literal embodiment (materially speaking) of the transactional dynamic that both drove and characterized the China Trade, they may be understood as the outcome of the circulation of materials that moved between one littoral environment and another within the wider confines of European enterprise and its associated commercial networks.

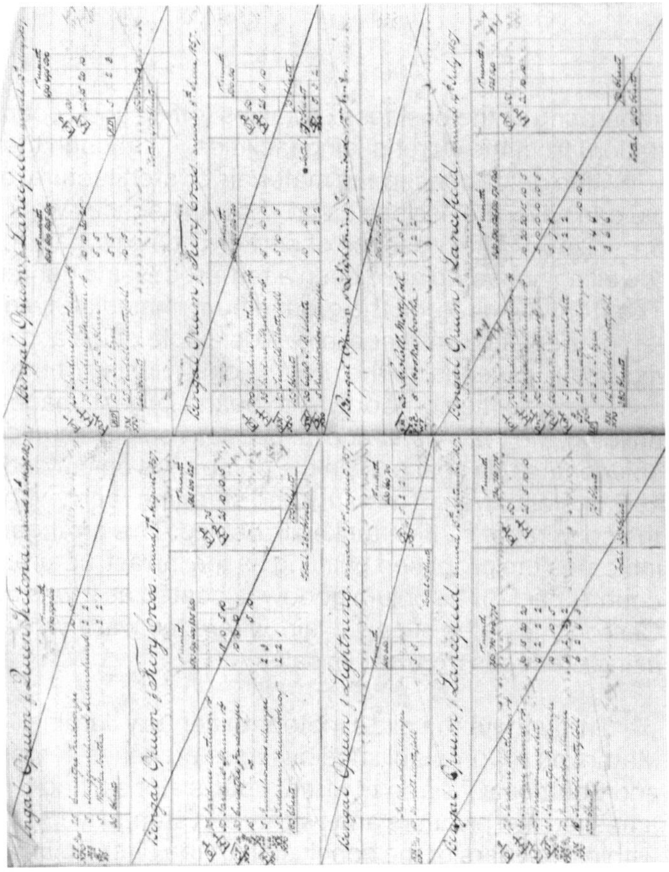

FIG 15
Page from Jardine, Matheson & Co. opium ledger (accounts), 1857.

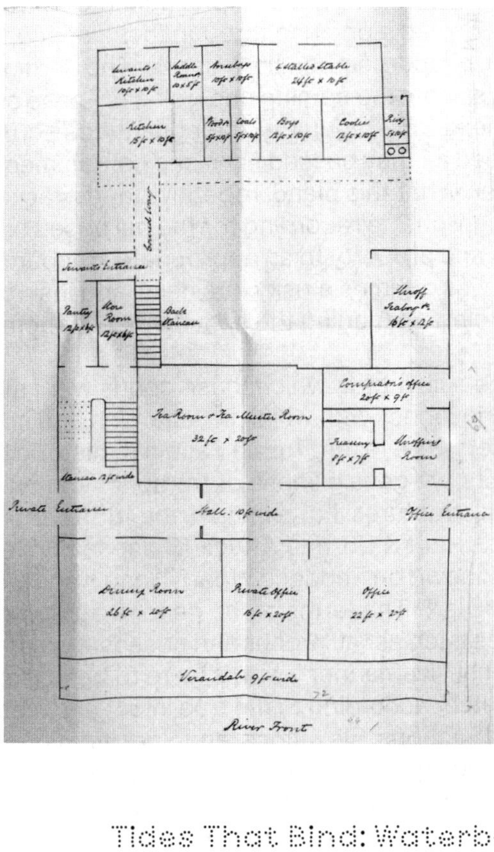

FIG 14
Sketch plan of proposed 'dwelling house' (i.e., tea processing factory) for Jardine, Matheson & Co., Shamian concession, Canton, 1859.

What is demonstrated by these attempts to orchestrate a system of common standards for the recording, storage, and insurance of commodities, along with the framing of legal agreements and construction techniques in relation to physical infrastructure, is the emergence of a technological zone. The China Trade clearly comprised a system that innovated financial instruments and management structures in the context of rapid capitalist and corporate expansion. In this respect a holding company or an accounting practice was as much a technical invention as a godown or a tea clipper: all were essential to producing an infrastructural system.[92]

Reach and Reproducibility Across the Network

In terms of appearance, godowns were typically modest. Although they often began life as "cutcha" structures in matshed or *attap* (palm leaf), they were usually quadrangular in form, built in brick or stone, and surmounted by a simple hipped or gable roof.[93] They differed from hong-style structures in that they were not normally conjoined with accommodation or office spaces. Built almost exclusively for the storage, preservation, and security of merchandise, windows were usually small and few in number. They could be freestanding or built in clusters, as illustrated in an early photograph of Jardine Matheson's base of operations in Hong Kong. FIG 19 Their minimal requirements tended towards standardization, with regional variations according to levels of professional design input, local building practice, and materials FIG 20. Although nothing more than warehouses, this typology perhaps characterizes the architectural experience of Jardine Matheson's global trading network more than any other. Whether in London, Bombay, Hong Kong, Singapore, or Sydney, the four square godown/warehouse was a familiar and commercially reassuring sight.

The resemblance among structures of this kind spread over wide geographical areas may be related to (and partly explained by) their relationship to regionally-inflected economies of administrative or commercial interaction and exchange.[94] Such patterns can be understood as resulting from the interconnectivity of littoral trading settlements, both coastal and oceanic.[95] Extrapolated to the context of the China Trade and its networks, such a geographical area constitutes a technological zone. Within such a zone architectural resemblance and standardization were logical, especially with respect to the relation between function and form that knitted the zone (and its networks) together into a larger, loosely coherent megastructure of sorts. As those involved in the trade moved along the circuitous routes comprising the zone, taking ideas and information with them, there was a propensity for emulation, if not replication, in building design as methods and practices were tested and standardized in search of efficient models. This led to the development of an inherently stable network of spaces that could be relied upon to facilitate trade.

To be sure, the development of this network's spatial manifestations (both "factories" and godowns) dates back to the very origins of European trade in Asia, in the sixteenth century.[96] By the eighteenth and nineteenth centuries it had begun to intersect with other networks of expertise, such as the Royal Engineers, who were encouraged to devise standardized forms of building design and construction and often provided professional architectural expertise to China Trade firms.[97] Therefore the sharing or pooling of professional building knowledge in this way was an important a factor.[98] The engineer S. B. Rawling, mentioned in the godown contract above, was one such expert whose engagement affirms the "diffusion" model of technology transfer outlined by Daniel Headrick.[99]

Structures of this kind within the circulatory networks of the China Trade proliferated over time and extended beyond warehousing facilities. Commercial expansion necessitated the erection and extension of port facilities such as wharfs, piers, and, with the coming of steam locomotion, coal stores. In the Jardine Matheson archive there exists an 1859 contract between the company and Chinese builder Yan-Lee for "a Sea Wall and Pier, Filling-in a certain quantity of the bay in front of their offices at East Point and erecting thereupon two Fireproof Godowns, a Treasury, [and] a Godown Keeper's house and offices." The plans were supplied by Scottish architect T. L. Walker, who had immigrated to Hong Kong in the 1850s.[100] A little earlier Jardine Matheson had set up John Lamont, a shipwright of Scottish origin, with his own slipway and godowns at its East Point base, where he repaired company ships. It was here that Lamont built Hong Kong's first steamer.

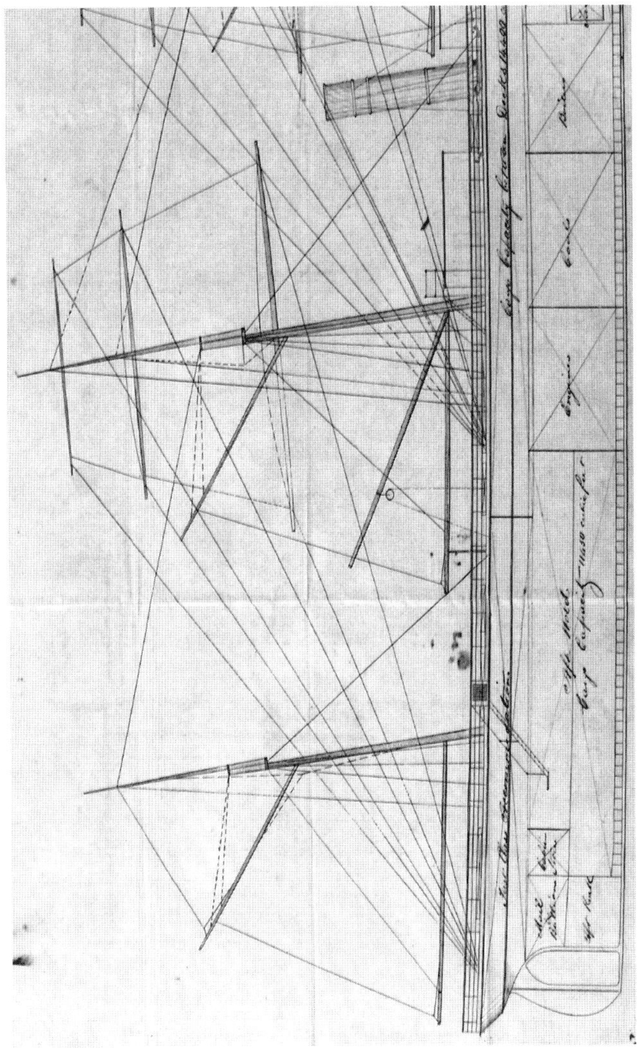

FIG 17
Rigging plan and longitudinal section of screw steamer 'Corea'. Drawn for Jardine, Matheson & Co. by William Denny & Brothers, Dumbarton.

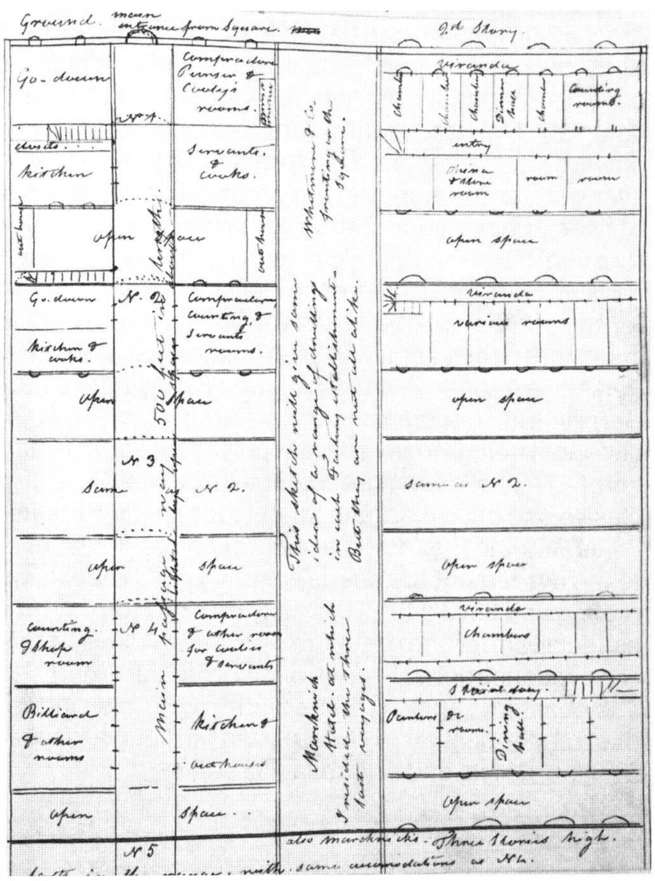

FIG 16
Plan of Imperial Factory, Canton, by Bryant Parrot Tilden c.1831–37.

FIG 19
East Point depot and trading facilities of Jardine, Matheson & Co. (c.1860s). Photograph by John Thomson. The company's godowns (warehouses) can be seen along the shore in the middle foreground.

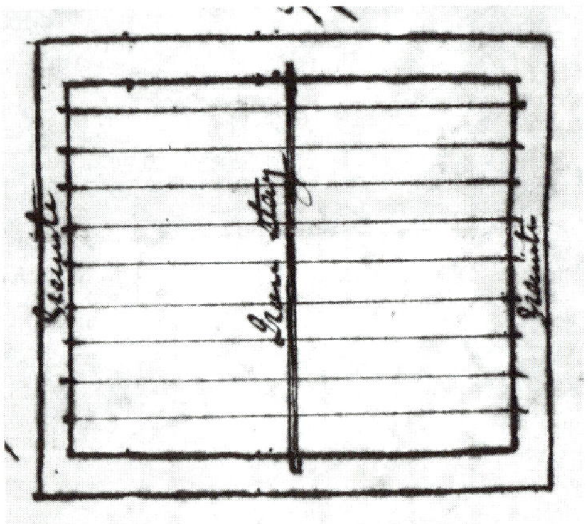

FIG 18
Detail sketch of godown (warehouse) window showing iron bar arrangement for security.

FIG 21
Borneo wharf, Singapore, 1885. Numerous coal stores required to service steamships can be seen in the foreground.

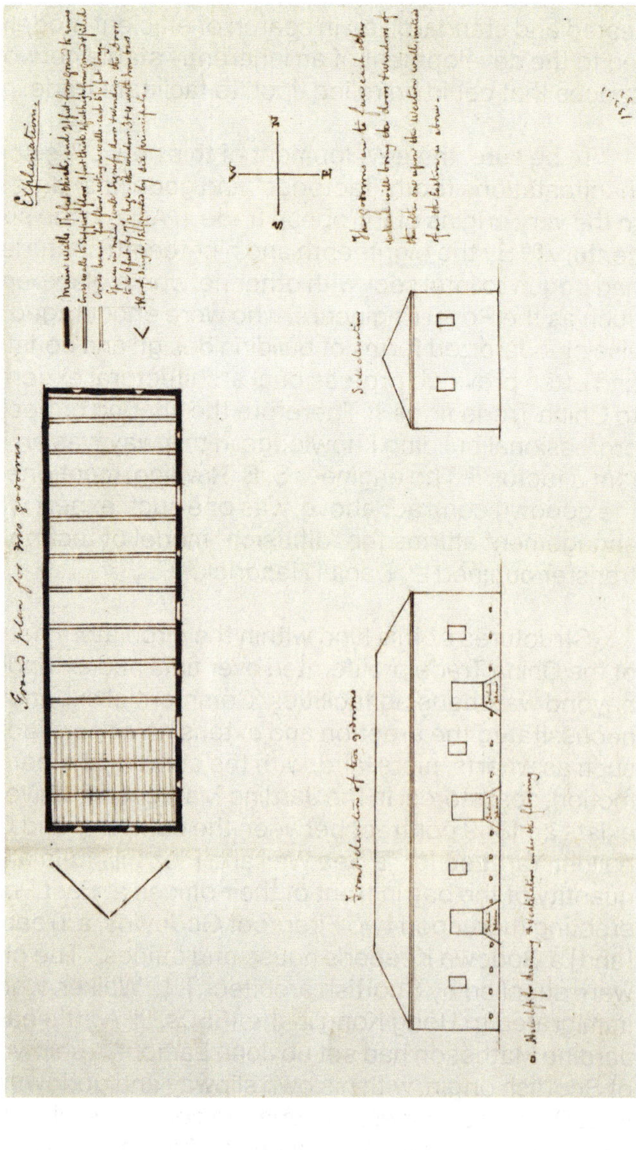

FIG 20
Ground plan and elevation for two godowns, (c.1846).

By the 1850s the power, speed, and increasing reliability of steam navigation had begun to transform the China Trade. Such vessels required frequent and abundant supplies of coal, distributed across the network of shipping routes that comprised the trade's infrastructural zone. From this time onward contracts for coal-storage facilities appear with ever greater frequency in the archive, such as that in 1857 between Lamont and Chung Asin for four sixty-by-forty-foot coal stores at East Point, and the 1853–5 agreement by Jardine, Skinner & Co. to lease land at Howrah, near Calcutta, for the erection of coal godowns.[101] Singapore was also an important coaling station for steamers rounding the Malay Peninsula into the South China Sea during this period.[102] Here, in 1853, recognizing the growing importance of long-distance steam-powered transportation, Jardine Matheson entered into a lease agreement with Jacob Clunis for exclusive use of a wharf and sheds for recoaling steamers at Pulau Brani, in the "new harbour" of Singapore.[103] According to the agreement the sheds were to be of timber with *attap* roofing and have a total capacity of 1,200 tons. Over time, especially after the great fire of 1877, buildings of this type were reconstructed in brick and corrugated iron. FIG 21 The coal that supplied these stations was also indicative of the "zone"—coming from places as far-flung as India (West Bengal), China, and Australia (Newcastle).

If the traditions of architectural history teach us that certain buildings demand attention for their historical significance, then the commercial structures highlighted here definitely stake a claim in that regard. Yet because they were neither grand nor designed by prominent architects, they have escaped consideration in the annals of architecture. This perceptual "displacement," as Larkin calls it, relates to infrastructure's ontology. As a physical entity, infrastructure is present to the senses but, owing to its radical instrumentality, tends to disappear from view as we focus on the objects it carries, transmits, or contains.[104]

Yet the buildings examined here are perhaps among the most important of all, comprising the foundation of a commercial system that transformed the modern world. As the "tools" that facilitated the fluvial and oceanic trade and "technological zones" that came to dominate the early development of the capitalist world system, they may be considered the architecture of globalization par excellence. Today Jardines is a global leader, and even a "poster boy" for multinational corporations, and it is clear that the company did not rise to dominance by luck or accident. Although there may be a certain romance around the group's beginnings as the brainchild of two business-savvy Scotsmen, it has always been an ambitious company that developed economic instruments and infrastructural techniques through rigorous processes of market scrutiny, evaluation, and participation. Moreover, it was an operation that had equally serious social and political consequences.

We have seen how the spaces of these "gray" architectures coalesced to form networks of infrastructure that, once engaged, and through their extension, wielded considerable commercial and political power as instruments of facilitation. They were the basis of a system that invoked and forced the mantra of "free trade" economics when and where it suited, and, because of its centrality to British imperial revenue streams, could call upon state aid in the form of military assistance to protect and enforce its claims. To be sure, the commercial structure of the China Trade followed its own internal logic, but once it achieved a certain scale it became politically entwined owing to the informal imperial commitments on the part of the state that it inevitably drew within its orbit. Despite the moral carping of W. E. Gladstone and the fictional parody of China Trade taipans by Benjamin Disraeli, the strategic interests at stake were simply too significant, and British foreign policy makers knew it.[105]

This analysis encourages us to view and value these "architectures" precisely for their grayness. They challenge our traditional notion of buildings as aesthetic architect-centered objects, highlighting instead their dissipated condition as points of intersection and exchange within much wider spheres of coexistence.[106] Therefore, rather than attempt to categorize them definitively in one way or another (in the classic Pevsnerian sense), we ought to recognize and consent to their inherently unstable and indeterminate status, taking this as the basis for their theoretical articulation. Indeed, this is one lesson we might take from the sociology and anthropology of infrastructure. Perceived in this way, buildings of this kind have the potential to emerge as useful points of reference and forms of evidence for the histories of both architecture and British imperialism.

1 "Return to China: A Grand Old Trading House Seeks a New Propellant," *The Economist*, July 4, 2015, 57.

2 See Jardine Matheson Group press release of February 28, 2019, accessed June 26, 2019, https://www.jardines.com/assets/files/NewsAndEvents/corporate-press-releases/jardine-matheson/results18.pdf

3 The Jardine Matheson Group traces its history directly to these origins. See http://www.jardines.com/the-group/history.html, accessed December 17, 2017. The company was effectively trading by 1828, when Jardine and Matheson took over the running of Magniac & Co. It was only the name that was not changed until 1832. See Alain Le Pichon, ed., *China Trade and Empire: Jardine Matheson & Co. and the Origins of British Rule in Hong Kong 1827–1843* (London: British Academy, 2006), 22–3.

4 Networks of Scottish patronage at home sustained trade abroad. This is part of a phenomenon that some historians have come to view as "Scotland's empire." For instance, see Tom Devine, *Scotland's Empire: The Origins of the Global Diaspora* (London: Penguin Books, 2012). The Scottish connection here is far from anomalous in the context of Asia, for the presence of Scots in the region was already considerable owing to their employment in the East India Company. See Andrew Mackillop, "Locality, Nation, Empire," in *Scotland and the British Empire*, ed. J. M. MacKenzie and T. M. Devine (Oxford, UK: Oxford University Press, 2011), 54–83. See also Le Pichon, *China Trade and Empire*, 6; George McGilvary, "Scottish Agency Houses in South-East Asia, c.1760–c.1813," in *The Scottish Experience in Asia, c.1700 to the Present: Settlers and Sojourners*, ed. T. M. Devine and Angela McCarthy (London: Palgrave Macmillan, 2016), 75–96; Susan Leiper, *Precious Cargo: Scots and the China Trade* (Edinburgh: National Museums of Scotland, 1997).

5 The nepotistic and Scots-centric structure of Jardine, Matheson & Co. is discussed in J. K. Fairbank, *Trade and Diplomacy on the China Coast: The Opening of the Treaty Ports 1842–1854* (Cambridge, MA: Harvard University Press, 1953), vol. 1, 62; vol. 2, 56–7.

6 For a history and analysis of Free Trade Zones (FTZs) and Export Processing Zones (EPZs), see Xiang-ming Chen, "The Evolution of Free Economic Zones and the Recent Development of Cross-National Growth Zones," *International Journal of Urban and Regional Research* 19 (1995): 593–621.

7 See Deborah Cowen's blog "Infrastructures of Empire and Resistance," accessed December 15, 2017, https://www.versobooks.com/blogs/3067-infrastructures-of-empire-and-resistance. See also Deborah Cowen, *The Deadly Life of Logistics: Mapping the Violence of Global Trade* (Minneapolis: University of Minnesota Press, 2014).

8 Ash Amin, "The European Union as More than a Triad Market for National Economic Spaces," in *The Oxford Handbook of Economic Geography*,

ed. Gordon L. Clark, Maryann P. Feldman, and Meric S. Gertler (Oxford, UK: Oxford University Press, 2000), 671–85.

9 Robert J. McCalla, "The Geographical Spread of Free Zones Associated with Ports," *Geoforum* 21 (1990): 126. For Jardine Matheson's part in this, see Alain Le Pichon, "From Monopoly to Free Trade: How the Introduction of Competition in the Tea Export Trade of China Heralded the End of the Hong System, 1833–1838," *Journal of the Royal Asiatic Society Hong Kong Branch* 54 (2014): 131–55.

10 The power such conglomerates wield through their multiple, overlapping, and nested forms of influence via transnational infrastructure space has been described by Keller Easterling as "extrastatecraft." See Keller Easterling, *Extrastatecraft: The Power of Infrastructural Space* (London: Verso, 2014).

11 For the idea of territorial production via infrastructure, see Kathy Velikov and Geoffrey Thün, "The Production of Territory," in *Infrastructure Space*, ed. Ilka and Andreas Ruby (Berlin: Ruby Press, 2017), 34–6.

12 See introduction to Louis P. Nelson, Architecture and Empire in Jamaica (New Haven and London: Yale University Press, 2016), 1–9. Daniel Maudlin and Bernard Herman have made the same point in relation to the Atlantic world. See introduction to *Building the British Atlantic World: Spaces, Places, and Material Culture, 1600–1850*, ed. Daniel Maudlin and Bernard L. Herman (Chapel Hill, NC: University of North Carolina Press, 2016), 1–28. As Andrew Barry and Timothy Mitchell have also argued, in tracing the connections between industrial infrastructures on the one hand, and transportation routes, financial instruments, and consumptive cultures on the other, we are in a better position to understand the peculiar political and economic forces (and relationships) that coproduced and sustained those connections. See Andrew Barry, "Technological Zones," *European Journal of Social Theory* 9 (2006), 239–53; Timothy Mitchell, "Carbon Democracy," *Economy and Society* 38 (2009): 422.

13 Rila Mukherjee, "Escape from Terracentrism: Writing a Water History," *Indian Historical Review* 41 (2014): 87–90.

14 Alison Games, *The Web of Empire: English Cosmopolitans in an Age of Expansion 1560–1660* (Oxford, UK: Oxford University Press, 2008); David Hancock, *Oceans of Wine: Madeira and the Emergence of American Trade and Taste* (New Haven and London: Yale University Press, 2009); Philip J. Stern, *The Company-State: Corporate Sovereignty and the Early Modern Foundations of the British Empire in India* (Oxford, UK: Oxford University Press, 2011); and H. V. Bowen, "Britain in the Indian Ocean Region and Beyond: Contours, Connections, and the Creation of a Global Maritime Empire," in *Britain's Oceanic Empire: Atlantic and Indian Ocean Worlds, c.1550–1850*, ed. H. V. Bowen, Elizabeth Mancke, and John G. Reid (Cambridge, UK: Cambridge University Press, 2012), 45–65. See also Kären Wigen, "Oceans of History," *American Historical Review* 111 (2006): 717–21; and Glen O'Hara, "'The Sea Is Swinging into View': Modern British Maritime History in a Globalised World," *English Historical Review* 124 (2009): 1109–34. For a historiographic overview of this method, see Sujit Sivasundaram, Alison Bashford, and David Armitage, eds., *Oceanic Histories* (Cambridge, UK: Cambridge University Press, 2017).

15 Carol Matheson Connell, "Jardine Matheson & Company: The Role of External Organization in a Nineteenth-Century Trading Firm," *Enterprise & Society* 4 (2003): 109–10.

16 Richard J. Grace, *Opium and Empire: The Lives and Careers of William Jardine and James Matheson* (Montreal and Kingston: McGill-Queen's University Press, 2014), 144–5.

17 For instance, see Pierre-Yves Saunier, *Transnational History* (London: Palgrave Macmillan, 2013), esp. 117–34; Sivasundaram, Bashford, and Armitage, *Oceanic Histories*. Concerning historical geography and empire, I refer in particular to the proposals of Alan Lester. For example, see Alan Lester, "Imperial Circuits and Networks: Geographies of the British Empire," *History Compass* 4 (2006), 124–41.

18 Simon J. Potter and Jonathan Saha, "Global History, Imperial History, and Connected Histories of Empire," *Journal of Colonialism and Colonial History* 16 (2015), accessed March 15, 2017, https://muse.jhu.edu/article/577738. For "gray" architecture, see G. A. Bremner, Johan Lagae, and Mercedes Volait, "Intersecting Interests: Developments in Networks and Flows of Information and Expertise in Architectural History," *Fabrications* 26 (2016): 236.

19 Brian Larkin, "The Politics and Poetics of Infrastructure," *Annual Review of Anthropology* 42 (2013): 329.

20 Much of what has been written on networking in relation to empire in recent years may be traced back to Frederick Cooper, whose basic definition I am working from here. See Frederick Cooper, "Networks, Moral Discourse, and History," in *Intervention and Transnationalism in Africa*, ed. Thomas M. Callaghy, Ronald Kassimir, and Robert Latham (Cambridge, UK: Cambridge University Press, 2001), 23–46.

21 Bruno Latour, *Reassembling the Social: An Introduction to Actor-Network-Theory* (Oxford, UK: Oxford University Press, 2005), 8–9.

22 John Gallagher and Ronald Robinson, "The Imperialism of Free Trade," *The Economic History Review* 6 (1953): 1–15.

23 For the history of the company's relationship to this trade, see introduction to Le Pichon, *China Trade and Empire*, 1–35. For a description of the types of trading activity the company was involved in along the China coast, see Robert Blake, *Jardine Matheson: Traders to the Far East* (London: Weidenfeld & Nicolson, 1999), 42–58.

24 Blake, *Jardine Matheson*, 20–36; Matheson Connell, "Jardine Matheson," 99–138. For the phenomenon of the agency house in general, see Maria Misra, "The Managing Agency Houses in the Era of High Imperialism, 1860–1919," in *Business, Race, and Politics in British India, c.1850–1960* (Oxford, UK: Oxford University Press, 1999), 17–64.

25 Paul A. Van Dyke, *The Canton System: Life and Enterprise on the China Coast, 1700–1845* (Hong Kong: Hong Kong University Press, 2005). See also Blake, "The Canton System," in *Jardine Matheson*, 16–29.

26 For a good overview of the Canton System's effects on the city of Guangzhou, see Patrick Conner, *The Hongs of Canton: Western Merchants in South China 1700–1900, as Seen in Chinese Export Paintings* (London: English Art Books, 2009); and Jonathan Farris, *Enclave to Urbanity: Canton, Foreigners, and Architecture from the Late Eighteenth to the Early Twentieth Centuries* (Hong Kong: Hong Kong University Press, 2017).

27 Matheson Connell, "Jardine Matheson," 114; Le Pichon, *China Trade and Empire*, 10.

28 This was characteristic of the growth of China agency-house firms. See Fairbank, *Trade and Diplomacy*, 61.

29 H. V. Bowen, *The Business of Empire: The East India Company and Imperial Britain, 1756–1833* (Cambridge, UK: Cambridge University Press, 2006), 151–81.

30 Daniel R. Headrick, *When Information Came of Age: Technologies of Knowledge in the Age of Reason and Revolution, 1700–1850* (Oxford, UK: Oxford University Press, 2000); Robert Darnton, "An Early Information Society: News and the Media in Eighteenth-Century Paris," *American Historical Review* 105 (2000): 1–35.

31 Eve Tavor Bannet, *Empire of Letters: Letter Manuals and Transatlantic Correspondence, 1688–1820* (Cambridge, UK: Cambridge University Press, 2005).

32 The idea of business "architecture" employed here is taken from Matheson Connell, "Jardine Matheson."

33 Matheson Connell, "Jardine Matheson," 116.

34 For Jardine's commercial intelligence and market strategy, see Grace, *Opium and Empire*, 137–43. For its importance to British commercial advantage and power overall, see John Darwin, *The Empire Project: The Rise and Fall of the British World System 1830–1970* (Cambridge, UK: Cambridge University Press, 2009), 36–9.

35 "Jardine Matheson's development of a pattern of external relationships ... foster[s] the flow of information, the knowledge with which to interpret it, the ability to influence others, and the reputation to attract and retain partners." In 1836–7 Jardine, Matheson & Co. captured a 41 percent share of the Chinese tea export market to Britain. See Le Pichon, "From Monopoly to Free Trade," 140; and Matheson Connell, "Jardine Matheson," 132.

36 Barry, "Technological Zones," 239–40; Cowen, *Deadly Life of Logistics*.

37 Duties for tea imports into the United Kingdom averaged 20.95 percent of total British customs duties between 1835 and 1858. For the significance of tea to the British exchequer in this regard, see J. Y. Wong, *Deadly Dreams: Opium, Imperialism, and the Arrow War (1856–1860) in China* (Cambridge, UK: Cambridge University Press, 1998), 343–54. For William Jardine's political access and activities, see Le Pichon, *China Trade and Empire*, 42–7; Nathan A. Pelcovits, *Old China Hands and the Foreign Office* (New York: King's Crown Press, 1948); Fairbank, *Trade and Diplomacy*, 81–2.

38 Matheson Connell, "Jardine Matheson," 122.

39 Mark Crinson, *Modern Architecture and the End of Empire* (Aldershot, UK: Ashgate, 2003); Ben Marsden and Crosbie Smith, *Engineering Empires: A Cultural History of Technology in Nineteenth-Century Britain* (London: Palgrave Macmillan, 2005). See also, Cowen, "Infrastructures."

40 Crinson, *Modern Architecture*, 4.

41 David Hancock, *Citizens of the World: London Merchants and the Integration of the British Atlantic Community, 1735–1785* (Cambridge, UK: Cambridge University Press, 1995), 37.

42 Larkin, "Politics and Poetics," 328.

43 Tavor Bannet, *Empire of Letters*, 230–31.

44 Hardy quoted in Le Pichon, *China Trade and Empire*, 30.

45 Bowen, *Business of Empire*, 287–8. See also "The East India Company Warehouses," in Margaret Makepeace, *The East India Company's London Workers: Management of the Warehouse Labourers, 1800–1858* (Martlesham, UK: Boydell & Brewer, 2010), 17–39.

46 It is worth noting the connection between East Indies commerce and elected MPs in the House of Commons. As late as 1820, for instance, up to 100 out of 658 Members of Parliament were holders of East India stock, causing no small conflict of interest. See Bowen, *Business of Empire*, 95–6.

47 For instance, see Sibel Zandi-Sayek, "The Unsung of the Canon: Does a Global Architectural History Need New Landmarks?" *ABE Journal* 6 (2014), accessed January 24, 2018, http://journals.openedition.org/abe/1271.

48 Jeremy Maas, *Victorian Painters* (London: Barrie and Rockliff, 1969), 117.

49 For a description of such structures, including their general appearance and internal arrangements, see Farris, *Enclave to Urbanity*, 19–30.

50 Matheson Connell, "Jardine Matheson."

51 Le Pichon, *China Trade and Empire*, 35; David R. MacGregor, *The Tea Clippers* (London: Percival Marshall & Co., 1952); Basil Lubbock, *The Opium Clippers* (Glasgow: Brown, Son & Fergusson, 1933); Alan Reid, "The Shipping Interest," in *The Thistle and the Jade: A Celebration of 175 Years of Jardine, Matheson & Co.*, ed. Maggie Keswick, revised and updated C. Weatherall (London: Frances Lincoln, 2008), 144–69. See also Jardine Matheson Archive, Cambridge University Library, series L and K.

52 Sensing the potential advantages, Jardine Matheson was keen to test steam technology as early as possible. See A. D. Blue, "Early Steamships in China," *Journal of the Hong Kong Branch of the Royal Asiatic Society* 13 (1973): 45–57. By the mid-1860s Jardine Matheson had purchased five Clyde-built steamers from Robert Napier & Sons. See *Illustrated London News*, May 11, 1867, 465.

53 For the impact of steam shipping on the British economy, see Charles K. Harley, "The Shift from Sailing to Steamships, 1850–1890: A Study in Technological Change and Its Diffusion," in *Essays on a Mature Economy: Britain after 1840*, ed. Donald N. McCloskey (London: Methuen & Co., 1971), 215–31.

54 Cobden quoted in Darwin, *Empire Project*, 36.
55 O'Hara, "The Sea Is Swinging," 1112.
56 This also recalls Michel de Certeau's space as "practiced place." See Michel de Certeau, *The Practice of Everyday Life*, trans. Steven Rendall (Berkeley: University of California Press, 1984), 117.
57 For "compradoric" classicism, see Conner, *Hongs of Canton*, 199 (and note 52). See also C. L. Yip, "Four Major Buildings in the Architectural History of the Hongkong and Shanghai Banking Corporation," in *Eastern Banking: Essays in the History of the Hongkong and Shanghai Banking Corporation*, ed. Frank H. H. King (London: Athlone, 1983), 113; Frank H. H. King et al., *The Hongkong Bank in Late Imperial China, 1864–1902* (Cambridge, UK: Cambridge University Press, 1987), 355–60. See also Cole Roskam, *Improvised City: Architecture and Governance in Shanghai, 1843–1937* (Seattle: University of Washington Press, 2019).
58 For Jardine Matheson's involvement in this trade, see Grace, *Opium and Empire*.
59 Le Pichon, *China Trade and Empire*, 17. A good account of how the opium trade worked between British India and China can be found in Michael Greenberg, *British Trade and the Opening of China 1800–42* (Cambridge, UK: Cambridge University Press, 1970), 104–43. See also Timothy Brook and Bob Tadashi Wakabayashi, "Introduction: Opium's History in China," in *Opium Regimes: China, Britain, and Japan*, ed. Timothy Brook and Bob Tadashi Wakabayashi (Berkeley: University of California Press, 2000), 5–7; C. A. Trocki, *Opium, Empire, and the Global Political Economy: A Study of the Asian Opium Trade 1750–1950* (London: Routledge, 1999), 88–108. For a comprehensive overview of the economics of trade between Britain, India, and China focusing on opium, see Wong, *Deadly Dreams*, 331–454.
60 For instance, see Paul A. Van Dyke, "Smuggling Networks of the Pearl River Delta before 1842: Implications for Macao and the American China Trade," in *Americans and Macao: Trade, Smuggling, and Diplomacy on the South China Coast*, ed. Paul A. Van Dyke (Hong Kong: Hong Kong University Press, 2012), 49–72. An example of this can be seen in Jardine Matheson's opium accounts for 1835, which reflect its arrival in Hong Kong. See Jardine Matheson Archive, A7/81. See also Gregory Blue, "Opium for China: The British Connection," in Brook and Tadashi Wakabayashi, *Opium Regimes*, 33–4.
61 Le Pichon, *China Trade and Empire*, 28. See also Jesse S. Palsetia, *Jamsetjee Jejeebhoy of Bombay: Partnership and Public Culture in Empire* (New Delhi: Oxford University Press, 2015), 21–35.
62 Blue, "Opium for China," 45.
63 See Jardine Matheson Archive, F14/1–18.
64 Stephen C. Lockwood, *Augustine Heard and Company, 1858–1862: American Merchants in China* (Cambridge, MA: East Asian Research Center, Harvard University, 1971), 115; Roskam, *Improvised City*.
65 Larkin, "Politics and Poetics," 336.
66 Hancock, *Citizens of the World*, 114.
67 Hancock, *Oceans of Wine*, 232. For the semiotic nature of the East India Company infrastructure, see Makepeace, "The East India Company Warehouses."
68 William C. Hunter, *The "Fan Kwae" at Canton Before Treaty Days 1825–44* (London: Kegan Paul, Trench & Co., 1882), 24. Although most of the factories dating from the post-1822 fire were of this kind, they were not all so mundane. The EIC "English" factory—among the first on the scene—may be considered a rather lavish affair by comparison, with no small amount of architectural pretension. Owing to its mighty influence and reputation prior to 1833, the company clearly had an image to uphold. In its Canton factory one could encounter "unbounded hospitality" amid the life-size portraits, silver plate, and "row of huge chandeliers" in the vast dining room overlooking the river. Admittedly the sight was "unique in that distant quarter of the world." 31.
69 See especially the 1847 agreement between the British Consul and Woo Eho for the lease of ground near Hog Lane in Canton, Jardine Matheson Archive, F14/10.
70 In a letter to Hollingwoth Magniac dated March 2, 1832, William Jardine describes disposing of the company's Creek Hong assets for $65,000 dollars, "we renting them from the Cohong." This suggests that he was selling the master lease along with its material assets. See Le Pichon, *China Trade and Empire*, 151. A lease agreement between Yrisarri & Co. and Charles Magniac dated March 24, 1823, states explicitly that they were leasing part of Imperial Hong (No. 7) from Magniac (who was leasing the property, plus land, from Houqua) and that they were entitled to sublet ("subset") it. Jardine Matheson Archive, F14/2. See also memorandum of agreement between Charles Magniac and Nathan Dunn for rebuilding of the factory at the front of Imperial Hong, Canton, in 1823, Jardine Matheson Archive, F14/4. For Magniac's original lease from Houqua, see "No. 1, Houqua's Agreement, 1823," Jardine Matheson Archive, F14/4. Jardine Matheson appears to have taken over this lease in 1844. See "Young Hoqua, the old E-wo Hong, Renewing agreement ... with Alex Matheson, 1844," Jardine Matheson Archive, F14/4 and 8.
71 "Contract for Building Three Factories in the Creek Hong," Jardine Matheson Archive, A8/121/42.
72 Occasionally a drawing is mentioned, but none remain. See note of agreement between Jardine, Matheson & Co. and Gibb, Livingston & Co. for the rebuilding of "House No. 6," Imperial Hong, Canton, in 1854, Jardine Matheson Archive, F14/4.
73 See also Roskam, *Improvised City*.
74 It is noted in an accompanying memo that the drawing had "no pretentions to accuracy, but would serve as the basis of a correct plan." See "Sketch of proposed arrangement for new House at Shamien, Canton," Jardine Matheson Archive, A8/106/1 (1 of 3).
75 In the memo accompanying the plan it stipulates that the north veranda "be narrowed to a mere passage, so as not to intercept light from the tearoom," Jardine Matheson Archive, A8/106/1 (1 of 3).
76 Fairbank, *Trade and Diplomacy*, 159n.

77 See Susumu Mizuta, "A Study on Jardine, Matheson & Co's Branch Buildings in the Far East: 1842–1929," presentation at the EAAC 2012 International Conference on East Asian Architectural Culture, Chinese University of Hong Kong, December 2012. I wish to thank the author for supplying me with a copy of this paper.

78 For instance, see A7 series in the Jardine Matheson Archive, Cambridge University Library.

79 This recalls Michel Foucault's idea of the "disciplinary" character of modern mechanisms of ordering and control. See Michel Foucault, *Discipline and Punish: The Birth of the Prison*, trans. A. Sheridon (London: Penguin Books, 1991).

80 Samuel Y. Edgerton, *The Renaissance Rediscovery of Linear Perspective* (New York: Harper & Row, 1975), 39.

81 For the general synergy of such technologies, see Bernhard Siegert, *Cultural Techniques: Grids, Filters, Doors, and Other Articulations of the Real* (New York: Fordham University Press, 2015), 97–120.

82 See scholars such as Rudolf Wittkower, who wrote *Architectural Principles in the Age of Humanism* (1949).

83 I am basing this idea on an observation made by Tony Ballantyne and Antoinette Burton on late-nineteenth-century bureaucratic technologies. See Tony Ballantyne and Antoinette Burton, *Empires and the Reach of the Global, 1870–1945* (Cambridge, MA: Harvard University Press, 2012), 82.

84 Memorandum of agreement between Charles Magniac and Nathan Dunn for rebuilding of Imperial Hong, Canton (1823), Jardine Matheson Archive, F14/4.

85 For the graphic representation of information in this way see Headrick, *When Information Came of Age*, 123–30.

86 Jardine Matheson Archive, F1/35.

87 See also Hunt & Co.'s contract with Young Yan for offices at Pedder's Wharf (1858), Jardine Matheson Archive, F1/33.

88 Such contracts were often enforced legally via the drawing up of a bond. See "Bond for securing Due performance of Contract by Yan-Lee, July 1859," Jardine Matheson Archive, A8/104/12.

89 Samuel Bartlett Rawling, Royal Engineers, provided the plans. Other engineers used by Jardine Matheson included Thomas Pearce and Thomas Larkins Walker.

90 Jardine Matheson Archive, A8/106/1 (1 of 3).

91 D. E. Evans, "Jardine, Matheson & Co.'s First Site in Hong Kong," *Journal of the Royal Asiatic Society Hong Kong Branch 8* (1968): 150.

92 On this relationship see Thomas P. Hughes, *Networks of Power: Electrification in Western Society, 1888–1930* (Baltimore: Johns Hopkins University Press, 1983), 1–17.

93 The term *cutcha* comes from a lease in the Jardine Matheson Archive, F14/18. For the meaning of the term, see Christopher Cowell, "The Kacchā-Pakkā Divide: Material, Space, and Architecture in the Military Cantonments of British India (1765–1889)," *ABE Journal* 9–10 (2016), accessed February 12, 2018, http://journals.openedition.org/abe/3224.

94 For instance, Thomas R. Metcalf, *Imperial Connections: India in the Indian Ocean Arena, 1860–1920* (Berkeley: University of California Press, 2007), 46–67. For Metcalf, the Raj in British India operated as a powerful administrative hub within the wider empire, affecting the political, economic, and cultural life of the entire Indian Ocean sphere of influence, including architecture. A similar argument has been made in relation to Catholic missionaries. See George Kubler, "Two Modes of Franciscan Architecture: New Mexico and California," in *Studies in Ancient American and European Art: The Collected Essays of George Kubler*, ed. Thomas F. Reece (New Haven and London: Yale University Press, 1985), 34–8.

95 Prita Meier, *Swahili Port Cities: The Architecture of Elsewhere* (Bloomington and Indianapolis: Indiana University Press, 2016). For Meier this is exemplified by Swahili port cities along the coast of East Africa and their commercial links with communities around the Indian Ocean and, in particular, the Arabian Sea.

96 Anthony D. King, *The Bungalow: The Production of a Global Culture* (Routledge & Kegan Paul: London, 1984), 14–17.

97 Cowell, "The Kacchā-Pakkā Divide," 33–48.

98 Susumu Mizuta, "The East Asian Branch Buildings of Jardine, Matheson & Co.," presentation at the 71st Annual International Conference of the Society of Architectural Historians, St. Paul, Minnesota, April 19, 2018.

99 This would be seen to represent the "third" category in Daniel Headrick's model of technology transfer: "cultural diffusion by Western experts." See Daniel R. Headrick, *The Tentacles of Progress: Technology Transfer in the Age of Imperialism, 1850–1940* (Oxford, UK: Oxford University Press, 1988), 10.

100 Jardine Matheson Archive, A8/104/12. See also contract for Jardine Matheson godowns at Tamsui (in Taiwan) dated 1863, Jardine Matheson Archive, A8/123/6.

101 Jardine Matheson Archive, F1/30 and F14/18.

102 Goh Chor Boon, *Technology and Entrepôt Colonialism in Singapore, 1819–1940* (Singapore: Institute of Southeast Asian Studies, 2013), 71–5.

103 Jardine Matheson Archive, F14/19.

104 Larkin, "Politics and Poetics," 329.

105 Wong, *Deadly Dreams*, 425–9.

106 This notion is taken from Doreen Massey, *For Space* (London: Sage, 2005), 63.

Dublin, 1897: The Art of (Architectural) Street Fighting

Mark Crinson

Magic-lantern slides projected across a Georgian square, a "glass-breaking epidemic" in the streets, a mock parade past monuments of colonial power, even a visit to the coffins of long-dead martyrs in a dusty crypt—all of these acts of appropriation and ritualized contestation upturned the symbolic order of the city, however briefly, and made a stage for the street theater of Irish nationalism. And these actions occurred over a day or so in 1897, in a moment of counterdemonstration against the official parades and ceremonies marking the Diamond Jubilee of Queen Victoria, the sixtieth anniversary of her reign, and the reassertion of continuing British rule. If there was an urban script, then the anti-Jubilee events of 1897 attempted to overwrite it. The "relics of civilized life" were taken out of the everyday world that naturalized them;[1] the streets were mobilized in militant rehearsal. The frame, the focus, and the target of this disorderly relation to the city was architecture. The temporality of protest was brought against another temporality: "the monuments which are [the people's] true masters."[2] As the Paris Communards had pronounced in 1871, a city thus perceived was "a permanent insult to the vanquished by the victors."[3]

In Ireland, actual attacks on buildings would become a notable feature of the "great unrest" of 1916–21, as well as the civil war that followed.[4] Some of Dublin's greatest architectural creations were seriously damaged during these years—three of its major public buildings in particular—by all three sides in the conflicts. The buildings attacked were not just Dublin's nodal points for law, trade, and communications but also its finest Georgian buildings and emblems of the Protestant Ascendancy. A 1922 print by Harry Clarke shows these once imposing buildings now damaged and stacked up, put into balance against rotting slums, with a female succubus looming between.[5] FIG 1 As anticolonial resistance, the events in the wake of the Easter Rebellion were to have significance for later independence movements around the world.[6] The history of this architectural violence was indigenous, starting some twenty years previously around resistance to the commemoration of Victoria's Jubilee through the practice of the "counterdemonstration."[7] This was a curious interim period in Dublin history. Sidelined from London's attention by the death of Charles Stewart Parnell, in 1891, this was a time W. B. Yeats referred to as the "long gestation," when cultural forces emerged as an alternative to a stalled parliamentary politics.[8] Considered

FIG 1
Harry Clarke, *The Last Hour of the Night*. Frontispiece to Patrick Abercrombie's *Dublin of the Future*.

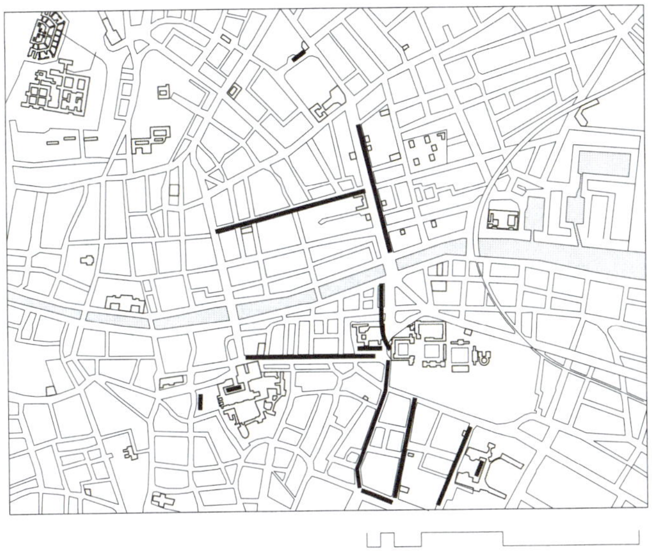

FIG 2
Streets marked to represent those with loyalist decorations.

in this light, the events of 1897 proposed a new tactic for staging protest within and against urban space. The targeting of monuments set a precedent for the rebellion of 1916. But the playful manipulation of lantern slide projections demonstrated a unique concept of resistance that would not be possible in later times of open violent conflict.

Queen Victoria was the first avowedly imperial monarch, and Ireland was Britain's first colony. There was bound to be dissension in 1897. Such an event could not go unopposed. This may be why, apart from a military spectacle in Phoenix Park, celebrations in June that year were largely unofficial, with the Irish nationalist Dublin Corporation most notable in absenting itself.[9] The conspicuously loyalist areas of the city could be mapped by Jubilee decorations, organized largely by private individuals and businesses, the "Court traders and the Protestant religious bodies."[10] FIG 2 Mainly they took the form of gas and electric illuminations on some of the main roads, particularly along Grafton, Dame, and Westmoreland Streets, and at the Trinity College end of College Green. As described in the *Freeman's Journal*, these streets had "the establishments of the purveyors to the Castle ... yet out of 124 houses in Grafton Street only 64 exhibited decorations; out of 82 houses in Dame Street only 19 were decorated; only 16 houses out of 37 in College Green; and 14 houses out of 41 in Westmoreland Street."[11] Loyal businesses and insurance offices in Dame and Dawson Streets displayed flags; some of the institutional buildings on Kildare Street and St. Stephen's Green were adorned with bunting. North of the River Liffey few streets marked their loyalty, although many businesses along Sackville, Henry, and Mary Streets were festooned.

Of individual buildings decorated across the city, the most notable were Trinity College, the Port & Docks Board House, the offices of the *Irish Times* and *Daily Express*, the National Insurance Office, the Kildare Street Clubhouse, the Guinness brewery buildings (an extravagant display), St. Werburgh's Church, Leinster House, the Constitutional Clubhouse, the Army and Navy Club, the City of Dublin Steam Packet Company, the Orange Hall (in Rutland Square), the Royal Irish Academy, and the Royal Dublin Society. No images survive of the decorations, so we are left to imagine their effects from photographs of similarly decorated buildings in London.[12] FIG 3 We are told that the most politically sensitive of all buildings, the Bank of Ireland (once the Irish parliament), had displays of an "elaborate character," including "devices showing the figures 37–97 [Victoria's reign had started in 1837] on all sides of the Bank and the letters VR [Victoria Regina]," and there were "four hundred and seventy electric lights, for the purpose of which a 25-horse power steam engine and dynamo [was] brought into requisition."[13]

FIG 3
Jubilee decorations in London.

Inevitably, differing opinions were expressed about how extensive these displays really were. The loyalist *Irish Times* reported "a great display of bunting," whereas the nationalist *Freeman's Journal* saw them as "on a very partial scale." The *Freeman's Journal* also described "the citizens generally making no sign" and "miles of street, in fact, being perfect blanks ... The demonstrations of what was called loyalty were of a kind to rejoice the hearts of the disloyal."[14] The nationalist *Irish Daily Independent* was distinctly unimpressed by the city's "very melancholy appearance. ... [It was] tawdry ... nondescript," and the decorations of the Bank of Ireland in particular did everything "to ruin the classic frontage of the beautiful building."[15] A different kind of criticism was that many of the loyal decorations were really for commercial purposes, "mere trade display. ... Almost everywhere from the midst of the decorations peeped plaster casts of the Royal Arms, which seemed to be adopted as an ornament to show off the line 'by royal appointment.'"[16]

Loyalist celebrations of Victoria's reign in Dublin were challenged by a series of anti-Jubilee counterdemonstrations encompassing a range of imaginative forms of resistance by militant nationalists. The most interesting parts of the anti-Jubilee were jointly organized by James Connolly and Maud Gonne for June 21 and 22, as an alternative to the loyalist events and decorations.[17] Connolly worked as an organizer for the Irish Socialist Republican Party and would go on to establish the Irish Citizen Army and be one of the leaders of the Easter Rising, in 1916. Gonne, English-born but an adopted Irish patriot, had supported the rent protests and became a flamboyant and controversial figure with both feminist and fascist sympathies. Gonne and Connolly were part of the 1798 Centenary Commemorative Committee, formed to find ways to mark the United Irishmen's Rising nearly a century before, and one of their methods for disrupting Victoria's Jubilee was to publicize the centenary of the uprising of 1798 during Jubilee days.[18]

FIG 4
The Sheares brothers' coffins in St Michan's crypt.

FIG 5
W. Curtis Green, Parliament House (now the Bank of Ireland).

If one aspect was an attempt to marginalize the Jubilee by foregrounding 1798, another was the attempts to mimic and satirize the imperial event as a prelude to the organizers' own program of events. Here the mockery of empire was folded into an extended version of nationalist rituals of commemoration, so that the past and its ghosts were reactivated in the face of a continuing history of oppression. An example of this was Gonne's attempt on June 20—designated that year as Decoration Day—to decorate the tombs of Irish rebels from 1798 in the churches of St. Michan's and St. Werburgh's as well as in Glasnevin Cemetery. These tombs were obscure and rather pathetic, but they formed counter-monuments in nationalist political symbolism. FIG 4 Then, as now, the tombs of the Sheares brothers, in the dark crypt of St. Michan's, were unkempt and cobwebby, in contrast to Dublin's public statues to William III, say, and the more recent monument to Daniel O'Connell, official unionist and Catholic nationalist icons, respectively. The marginal, subterranean location of the tombs spoke to a mythology, re-evoked by Gonne's visit, of a suppressed episode of revolutionary possibility. The neglected crypt incarnated the Gothick romance of unmourned heroes—and an improperly entombed folk memory.[19]

In this imaginary, the tombs of St. Michan's Church were associated with another monument to independence, of grander but equally bitter associations. After Gonne was barred from accessing the graves she wrote to the newspapers: "Is it not enough that they degrade with their hideous, vulgar Jubilee decorations our old Parliament House in College Green?"[20] She was referring to the repurposed Bank of Ireland. When Parliament House, the building at the center of Anglo-Irish rule before the Act of Union, was sold in 1803 and taken over by the Bank of Ireland, a political void was created within Ireland in terms of its powerlessness to represent itself and self-govern. It was also a void in the shape of the Parliament building, where a substitution had occurred, of neutral finance for a politics deemed too disorderly. According to this logic there had arisen a loyalist way of representing the building as almost incidental, as a touristic scenography historically distant and to be picturesquely viewed. FIG 5 The nationalist way of rendering the building was literally juxtaposed with Gonne's letter in the masthead of the *Freeman's Journal*, which had long used an image of Parliament House. FIG 6 Here the building was a daily reminder of what Ireland had lost and thus what it might regain, with the sun rising emblematically from behind the frontage of the old building, the logo "Ireland—A Nation" below it. It was both a flash of the past and a promise for the future, an ideal more than a building.

Gonne's visit to those sacred nationalist sites was hardly the trivial event it might appear, and it points to several important aspects of the counterdemonstrations and their organizers: First, a direct line to the nationalist press, which was essential to amplifying publicity, although little of this extended outside of Ireland.[21] Second, use of the historical resonances of architecture and urban space in the belief that a martyrology of rebellion was manifested in the neglected state of countermonuments celebrated annually on Decoration Day.[22] Third, rhetoric around the belief that a nationalist iconography was being sullied by the Jubilee and the assertion of alternative causes for commemoration. Gonne thus evoked the "Old Parliament House" as an icon of nationalist longing stolen by the Act of Union and besmirched by loyalist disrespect—an occluded monument linked with the occluded graves of hero-martyrs. Nationalist urban memory, then, was a matter both of countermonuments *and* of reclaiming established monuments.

The urban imaginary of the anti-Jubilee was informed by the extraordinary coverage of Jubilee celebrations in the British media. Before and after the event this reporting emphasized processions through London, Royal Navy reviews, mayoral deputations to the Queen, demonstrations of loyalty across the empire, attendance of exotic imperial troops, and the exemplary appearance of loyal representatives of the colonies in London.[23] FIG 7 "Rome is equalled," as *Le Figaro* put it.[24] For many Ireland's ambivalent and humiliating status was evidenced precisely in terms of a modern-day Rome parading itself indifferently in front of its colonial subjects. In the words of Irish MP Michael Davitt, it was a "carnival of conquest and snobbery."[25] Because it was ruled directly by London, Ireland had no official representatives at the London events. It was the "jarring note" or "the skeleton at the feast," as another Irish MP, John Dillon, told the House of Commons: "Why should we rejoice? ... We have no share in your festival."[26] In short, Ireland's disloyalty in 1897 and the absence of its representatives from the London celebrations marked it as the imperial exception. This is not, however, to downplay other anti-Jubilee protests in the empire.[27]

The main anti-Jubilee events were arranged for June 22, the day of the most elaborate formal celebration, in St. Paul's, London.[28] That evening the 1798 Centenary Committee met in Dublin's City Hall.[29] At 9:30 p.m. a parade (with ten thousand participants, according to Gonne) set out from Townsend Street with a mock coffin at its head. FIG 8 Accounts differ on the parade route: either it went through College Street, College Green, and Dame Street to Christ Church Place and returned the same way or it veered off Dame Street to Capel Street Bridge, was blocked by police, and then returned.[30] At College Green, on the return route, the police, along with reinforcements from nearby Dublin Castle, attempted to disperse demonstrators with baton charges.[31] Meanwhile Connolly, who was leading the parade, realized at O'Connell Bridge (or Capel Street Bridge, depending upon the report) that it could not continue and ordered that the coffin be dropped into the River Liffey. Many of the marchers—including Gonne and Yeats, but not Connolly, who had been arrested—headed northward up Sackville Street. Stones were thrown, particularly in Henry and Mary Streets.[32] Later, about 11 p.m., as Gonne was being escorted to Rutland Square to view a magic-lantern show, stones were thrown at the Bank of Ireland and the offices of Mutual Life Insurance Company. Yeats and Gonne ended up outside the National Club, on which the magic-lantern images were being projected. There they heard of another baton charge by the police and the death of an elderly woman caught up by the violence while watching the display. Afterward, walking down Sackville Street, Yeats and Gonne saw that many in the crowd were taking revenge for the earlier baton charges, stoning houses and shops that were decorated in support of the Jubilee.[33]

FIG 6
Masthead of *The Freeman's Journal*, 16 June, 1904.

FIG 7
The route of the royal procession, Diamond Jubilee, London. *Illustrated London News*, 12 June, 1897.

FIG 9
The coffin of the British Empire passing Dublin Castle. *Journal des Voyages*, 52, 28 November, 1897.

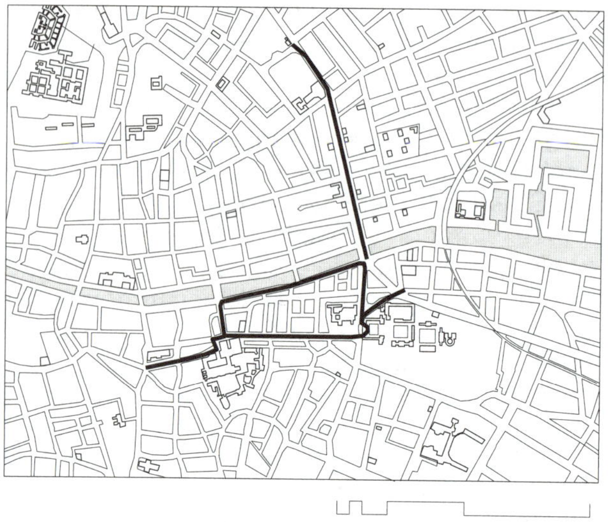

FIG 8
Streets marked to represent the route of the nationalist parade, Dublin.

FIG 10
The north-east corner of Parnell Square as it is today. The old National Club building is on the left with a sculptural ornament, added c.1900, over the door.

This program of resistance might be separated into three parts: First, the march and its associated theater of events; second, the magic-lantern display; and, third, the riots. All three are closely bound and reactive to the monuments, urban fabric, and associated meanings of the city around them. They must also be understood as interlinked parts of a sequence that is always focused on architecture.

The first of these counterdemonstrations, the march, clearly drew on the theatrical tradition of ritual and public performance in Irish nationalism, and it was a choreographed satire of certain elements of the loyal processions in British cities.[34] At the head of the parade was a large black coffin "symbolic of the fate of the British Empire."[35] FIG 9 It was carried on a wagonette or handcart made up as a mourning coach, its sides inscribed with the slogans *The Record Reign, Starved to Death, Evicted, Emigrated, Executed*, and *Done to Death*,[36] accompanied by the playing of a funeral march and the waving of black flags onto which Gonne had embroidered facts about the famines and evictions that occurred under Queen Victoria.[37] Leading the parade was an ad hoc hearse, in place of a royal carriage, and which bore declamations of failure, misgovernment, and exploitation, instead of pronouncements of triumph and fidelity. The official ceremonial liturgy was travestied by the music of mourning played not by a glittering military band but by workers "whose instruments were so old and battered that if they were broken by the police it would be no great loss."[38] When the march was balked, participants completed the anti-ceremony by tipping the coffin into the river, with the crowd chanting, "Here goes the coffin of the British Empire. To Hell with the British Empire!"[39]

The march responded closely to the streets it passed through, chosen precisely because they were shaped and layered by the urban forms of previous colonial regimes and their building campaigns. The counterdemonstrations were thus performed within and against an urban political history whose major components were well known to the participants: the statue of William III at College Green, often the target of previous attacks, whose horse was draped with green nationalist flags while the king was given a black flag and a tall hat; Dublin Castle, the seat of colonial power, where the parade stopped to chant; City Hall, a site of nationalist authority, where the march was joined by committee members preparing for the 1798 centenary.[40] In a more dispersed form, the march then passed Nelson's Pillar, halfway up Sackville Street, and the nationalist bronze heroes erected more recently by the Dublin Corporation to William Smith O'Brien (1870) and Daniel O'Connell (1882), also on Sackville Street (whose very name was then contested).[41] From one point of view, the repetition of the parade route south of the river was a mocking echo of the invocation of Rome in the grand official processional routes of London, the planning of which was well known in Dublin. From another point of view, the route marked out and made a claim to a circuit of institutional power in Dublin as yet untouched by the new symbolic geography of nationalist monuments then emerging north of the River Liffey.

The second part of the program of resistance was the magic-lantern display in Rutland Square. The lantern slides were projected from the northeast edge of the square onto a screen set up in front of a window of the National Club.[42] FIG 10 Sympathetic city electricians agreed to cause electrical faults at the right time so the images would be more visible. Turning the power off and on at will was a demonstration of potential trade union strength that was also evidenced in the blacking out of loyalist displays of electric decorations in shops. Gonne owned the lantern slides, and we know that they bore slogans and statistics, images of events in Irish history, nationalist heroes, and political prisoners.[43] The most remarkable of the slides came from a set of sixty taken the previous decade by photographers from the studio of William Mervyn Lawrence.[44] These recorded moments of eviction when the rural rent protest known as the Plan of Campaign, organized by the Land League between 1886 and 1890, came into conflict with the authorities.

Although it is not known precisely which images were shown, we can be confident about the kinds of images on display because the eviction photographs used a narrow range of tropes. FIG 11–16 Most of these scenes show the immediately pre- or post-climactic moment, a battering ram, mounted on its pole and pulley, either ready to make a cottage uninhabitable or having already battered holes in its walls. The camera looks from the viewpoint of police and bailiffs onto the action. It is on the side of authority, but it is also a witness, and so its products have a curious double, or ambivalent, function. The sequence of events is usually apparent: windows and doors are fortified, breaches are made in walls, and evicted families stand unsheltered, their furniture and meager belongings around them. Police and bailiffs are often gathered around, preparing themselves and their tools or smoking pipes after the event. The stilled action necessitated by slow exposure times gives a quality of artifice to the scenes: victims and violators, the law and the unlawful, curious and sympathetic onlookers, often united in posing for the camera if little else. For Gonne, who had campaigned against evictions and used lantern slides in her talks,[45] such images exposed the brutality and hypocrisy of British rule and the blinkered views of those who supported it. They showed both oppression and resistance. They were records of the policing powers of government authority as administered by Dublin Castle, but also of the organization of rent protests across much of the countryside.

FIG 16
Robert French/W M Lawrence—'Eviction scene,' 1886–90.

FIG 15
Robert French/W M Lawrence—'Eviction scene,' 1886–90.

FIG 12
Robert French/W M Lawrence—'Eviction of Michael Connell,' 1886–90.

FIG 14
Robert French/W M Lawrence—'The battering ram has done its work,' 1886–90.

FIG 11
Robert French/W M Lawrence—'T. Birmingham's house, Moyasta, County Clare, with Battering Ram and soldiers outside,' 1886–90.

FIG 13
Robert French/W M Lawrence—'Mathias Magrath's house, Moyasta, County Clare, after destruction by the Battering Ram,' 1886–90.

FIG 17
The Vale of Ovoca, 1899.

The lantern slides were also evidence of the power and violence of the law brought to bear against *buildings*—as homes, as barricaded forts defending family life, and as the property of landlords and thus the means of a collective violence against working-class rural life. But even (and perhaps especially) with their roofs burned, walls battered, and windows broken in, they now held inescapable resonances with the Georgian houses in Rutland Square itself. So an element of mimicry was carried over from the march to the slide projections. Buildings were again the targets, but the contrast was now a visual one. Replication of the image activated the politics of displacement. If one body of residents was banished from their homes, another set of homes was to be claimed for the nationalist cause by projecting those rural homes onto them. Following from this, if one group of people (bailiffs and police) were the agents of the colonial state, of sovereign and disciplinary power, then another group of people (the demonstrators) became the audience and active agents in a theater of displacement.

The rural had been made newly dialectical. The cottage was, of course, already a cliché in Ireland's political symbology. If for Gonne it signaled poverty and misrule, for others it implied the good life and landscape ornaments of tourism. FIG 17 In Ireland, as in England, the cottage was one of those prime markers of the picturesque and the pastoral, a framing of human habitation as part of the natural order.[46] In the 1840s it had become fraught with pressing political questions: Who owned it? Why was it abandoned? Was its decline evidence of an unbearable distress? As successive famines racked the countryside in the late nineteenth century, the cottage was the focus of relief and improvement, of state and philanthropic attention. Curiously, just as the cottage had become a pejorative it also evolved into a new symbol of national longing, a locus for romantic urbanites of an older, more authentic form of life in contrast to the overcrowded city as the place of the administered imperial world. Gonne's longing for national resurgence was guided by a wistful conjuring of the "land of Ireland ... [as] powerfully alive and invisibly peopled" and by hashish-driven collaborations with Yeats evoking that mystical fantasy.[47] Fintan Cullen has argued that Gonne had something else in mind for her images and that the "domestic environment as defined by broken walls and a disturbed hearth" could only be "an unhomely home" or a "mass unhoming."[48] There is much to this, even if the tinge of Freudian haunting does not register the contemporary violence of the images, both the brutality of what they witness and their brutality as records. And in Rutland Square there was also their situated effect as projections.

A century later the artist Krysztof Wodiczko used images similarly projected onto buildings and public statues, making counter-monuments through temporary interventions onto the urban facades of New York. Wodiczko's work was often about housing and redevelopment; the buildings onto which he projected his images were not just surfaces but themselves the sites of proprietorial conflict. His images deliberately worked at undermining or dissolving the boundaries of institutions and social structures that seemed embodied in the hard surfaces of architecture; they exposed the disavowals of social conflict endemic to the urban landscape, temporarily remaking it as what has been called an 'architecture of the evicted.'[49] In 1985, at a peak moment in campaigning against nuclear weapons, Wodiczko translated his strategy into commentary on the monuments of imperialism in London with an American missile overlaid onto Nelson's Column. FIG 18 Following Wodiczko's lead, we can understand that the siting of the 1897 magic lantern display, from one window onto a screen within a Georgian square, was as much the issue as the content of the images.

FIG 18
Krzystof Wodiczko, 'City Projections,' commissioned and produced by Artangel, August 1985.

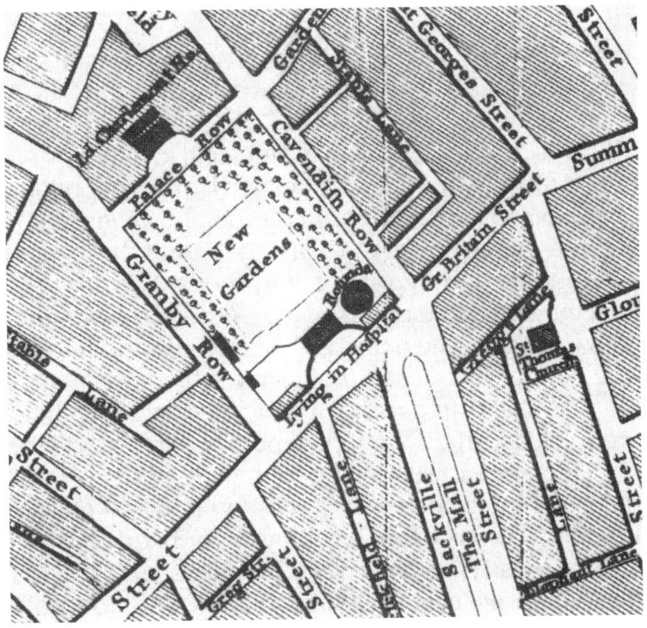

FIG 19
The Lying-in Hospital, the Rotunda and Gardens in 1780.

Cottages, in the context of Gonne's images, should thus be related to the place where they were projected. They were used to shock as a form of public agitprop, a coordination of actions and images marking a specific event at a specific time and place. They implied that the Plan of Campaign and the previous Land War (1879–82) were connected with the urban campaign to come. Gonne favored such architectural juxtapositions, contrasting the "broken thatch ... [and] shaky boards" of the cottages with "Her Majesty's hotels."[50] The demonstrators came to Rutland Square in solidarity with Gonne's agenda, not to be entertained but to have their convictions reinforced. The lantern slides were projected several times "across the wide east side of Rutland Square, a distance of perhaps forty feet," their images probably between ten and fifteen feet wide.[51] The technology enabled them to be projected outdoors, and displays had been used previously in Britain and Ireland for political agitation and public information, often in public spaces.[52] Yet it would be hard to find any other location where the specifics were quite so crucial to the effect. The Rutland Square display straddled its public space, claiming it and creating a spectacle—with cheers and groans at certain points in the display.[53] It was an obstruction but also a reclamation, an overlaying of one world onto another.

Rutland Square was in social and political transition in the 1890s, and the counterdemonstrators showed as much understanding of this in their slide projections as they had shown earlier of the circuit of official memorials in their march.[54] The name of the square was coming under nationalist pressure, as with Sackville Street, and would later be changed to Parnell Square. Its choice as the location for the magic-lantern display was related to this shifting of political affiliations, and the campaign to have its name changed was part of this tipping moment. In the eighteenth century the square was a nexus of Anglo-Irish gentility, with a nearby mall for promenades. The form of the square had been testament to Ascendancy mythology about nature as a fantasyland. Its central pleasure gardens had been placed at the back of the Rotunda Hospital, as a place where charitable consciences were rewarded with an area for conspicuous display and spectacle.[55] FIG 19

By the end of the nineteenth century the square had growing status as a headquarters for Irish nationalists and for the sharp ideological differences of its occupants. In 1897 there could be found not just the obviously nationalist National Club but also the obviously loyalist Orange Hall (whose Jubilee decorations, we're told, were a "conspicuous object in the darkness" on the night of June 22).[56] A little further south, around Nelson's Pillar, were shops and restaurants well known as meeting places for radicals. The Gaelic League, established in a room on Lower Sackville Street in 1893, was moved in 1901 to a house in Upper Sackville Street. A little to the east was the house on North Great Georges Street that Gonne rented for Inghinidhe na hÉireann ("The Daughters of Ireland"), her feminist-nationalist women's organization.[57] The grand Georgian mansions in and around this area had by then mostly declined and housed slum tenements so that a mix of bohemian, feminist, and nationalist subcultures was sewn into the cultural geography of a once-aristocratic but now increasingly proletarian area of Dublin. A century before Wodiczko, Gonne was challenging a rigid divide or dualism, in her case of the city and country. She did so in precisely the location where the compartmental reading of each domain had become actively problematized by new spatial and social relationships.

This setting mattered greatly then in terms of how the relation between city and country, which had reached a carefully framed balance under the Ascendancy, was now in a state of constant crisis. The relation between rural and urban poverty had been prominent in the great National Land League rally in Dublin in 1880, but without the same exploitation of its comparably poignant location, that great rus in urbe, Phoenix Park.[58] The projection of the magic-lantern slides in Rutland Square was a staging of images of rural conflict within a site of tamed rurality—an urban landscape representing the pleasures of nature. Casting images of lack and violence into the grand Ascendancy-created townscape of the square, the projection led viewers toward the injustices elsewhere, such as the enclosures and land-ownings of the Irish countryside, but also inward to the phenomenal and overlapping structures of power around them. The urban-rural divide was made permeable, specifically through exposure of the representational violence done by the disavowal of rural conditions in the Rotunda gardens.

Although it was unplanned by Gonne and Connolly, and certainly uncontrolled by them, the third part of the program of resistance was rioting. If the loyalist reports of Jubilee events in the *Irish Times* are anything to go by, we would know nothing of the counterdemonstrations and only about the riots, and then in an entirely negative light.[59] By contrast, if we relied on the nationalist media, we would view the riots as a relatively mild affair in which counterdemonstrators exercised self-control and the police as well the loyalist Trinity College students were equally at fault.[60] Beyond destruction or righteous disorder, the riots were a continuation of the counterdemonstrations by other means, and there seemed to be a sense and even a sensibility to them.

If rioting is an expression of corporeal alienation from political process, then violence toward architecture is one of its paradigms. Isobel Armstrong has argued suggestively that the breaking of glass during the Birmingham Bull Ring riots of 1830 and in those leading up to the 1832 Reform Act was exactly this: "[The crowds] affirmed something about the specificity of their own experiences as well as, or through, shattering glass."[61] In such protests the breaking of glass had a visceral excitement; it was a release that demonstrated that a facade could be cracked, penetrated, and defenestrated. Glass breaking thus could be seen to constitute a form of architectural criticism. Similarly, there is no doubt that the 1897 riots were discriminating: the Dublin glass breakers projected their frustrated nationalist expression onto the facades and physicality of the city. Despite the loyalist media's attempt to diagnose a "glass-breaking epidemic,"[62] as if such things were symptomatic merely of passing social ill health, the immediate cause of the outbreak was the police charge in Rutland Square. And if we are to believe Gonne, the riots had a clear target: "£2,000 worth of plate glass in every shop with Jubilee decorations was smashed that night."[63] FIG 20

The windows of Orange Hall (next to the National Club) and most houses on the east side of Rutland Square were broken.[64] Windows in the Bank of Ireland and the offices of the Mutual Life Assurance Company were smashed. Henry and Mary Streets seemed to have borne the brunt of this, with windows broken in "the houses which displayed flags."[65] The businesses Todd, Burns & Co. and Arnott & Co. were particular targets; the latter was a new large department store noted for "magnificent windows on its ground floor." FIG 21 These windows, we are told, "were of the very finest class of glass, and the money value of the property destroyed is exceedingly great."[66] Todd, Burns & Co, a dealer in leather and fur goods, had just announced its summer sales with the catchphrase "See our windows," claiming the shop as central to Dublin life and its windows as a necessary part of it.[67] In the *Irish Times*, one journalist described how it had been "simply riddled with stones. The windows must have been subjected to a perfect fusillade, as in some cases whole masses of glass are simply cut out clean by a circle of holes. Ten great windows in this house have been destroyed."[68] By itemizing the size, cost, location, and pattern of the breakage the article not only confirmed the wreckers' accuracy of aim and rightness of target but also conveyed the visceral pleasures of glass breaking as a complementary act to that of display. Buildings may not be easily busted or ruined, but windows can be punctured, punctuated, can promise a differently spangled effect—this is the article's subtext. Whether this was as "premeditated" as the *Irish Times* asserted is unlikely, but what is certainly true is the accuracy of the attacks.[69]

If there was a tradition of signaling loyalty by illumination, then disloyalty was newly signaled by the reconfiguration of the urban and architectural order, however temporary, and the cathartic act of breaking through transparencies.[70] Another element brought out by the *Irish Times* report is how the extensive panes of late Victorian commercial plate glass had become a target. The interesting thing here is that neither the glass's modernity, which was not inherently identified with empire, nor its commercialism were targets in themselves; after all, shopkeepers would change their political allegiance to suit their economic interests. Rather it was the signaling of loyalty that was the target. If glass and light formed a conjoint medium, they were linked only temporarily around loyalty: commercialism would change its feather. Anti-imperialism was not in this case anti-modernism.[71]

As much as the counterdemonstrators sought historical resonances for their actions, the events of 1897 need not be measured by those of 1916. There was certainly no desire by Connolly in 1897 to develop violent forms of nationalism. After 1910 there would be great upheavals in Irish politics that were unimagined in 1897.[72] But Yeats's "long gestation" was also a period when Dublin became "a place of world importance for a brief time."[73] The year 1897 was the near height of what has been called Irish "demo" politics, when pressure, agitation, and rhetoric were the means adopted by nationalists outside the Irish Parliamentary Party.[74] It led into a year of counterdemonstrations when the centenary of the 1798 rebellion was celebrated in 1898. Yet 1897 also marked the turn of political agitation from countryside to city, although this turn is usually claimed to have happened in 1916.[75] The counterdemonstrations of June 1897 did not take military form, as they did in 1916–21, and they were much less explosive. In the later conflicts the major administrative and architectural monuments of British rule became as much symbolic targets for capture and violence as nodal points for communications and governance. Thus the 1897 demonstrations marked a moment of transition in Ireland between the largely rural-based resistance of the rest of the century and the urban crises of the early twentieth.[76]

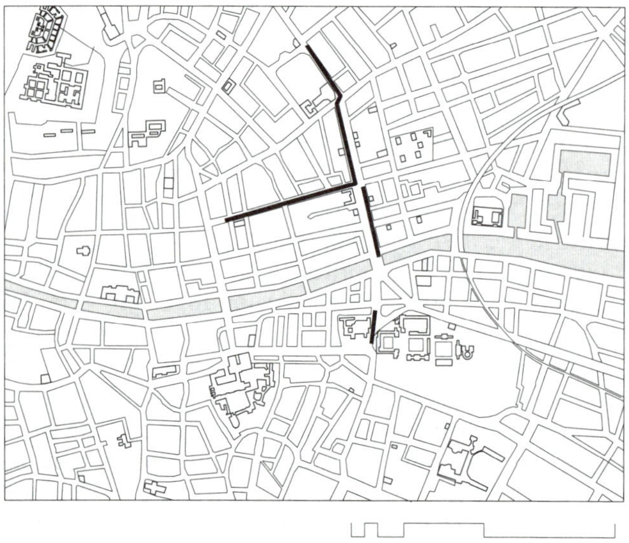

FIG 20
Streets marked represent areas of anti-Jubilee rioting.

FIG 21
Arnott and Co. Department Store, from *The World Illustrated—First Series, Beautiful Ireland*, Dublin: Irish Times, 1899.

This shift of the primary site of resistance is inscribed into the demonstrations; it might be seen as belated acknowledgment of Dublin's considerable demographic changes during the nineteenth century, as poor rural populations moved into the city. For nationalists, nevertheless, this was the city that still spoke "of the foreigner and the foreigner's power," whose planning was not "best suited to represent the country."[77]

What remains the most interesting aspect of these events is the different forms that protest took—some imaginative, some destructive—and the various ways it related to Dublin as a space of colonialism. As such, the anti-Jubilee movement demonstrates the inadequacy of distinctions between what has recently been called "visible politics" (studies of buildings where power is materialized) and "spatialized power" (architecture as a system of knowledge).[78] The police that baton-charged the nationalist demonstrators enacted a forcefully visible politics of sovereign power (in Michel Foucault's lexicon). But this same police force also included among their regular duties the collection of agricultural statistics, census work, the serving of poor-law election notices, customs duty, weights and measures inspection, factory inspection, the enforcement of extensive new laws governing fishing and liquor sales, and a registry of prostitutes.[79] Similarly, the images of eviction might seem a classic example of biopower, tied to the policing acts they depict, but at the same time they reveal the limits of analysis only along these lines. We have an inadequate knowledge of such images if we miss not only their capturing of a crude form of resistance, but also their dynamic re-deployment within a show staged by Gonne. She and the demonstrators appropriated the images and deployed them dialectically in relation to the city itself and as part of a largely choreographed script of urban colonial contestation. There is agency and affect in the anti-Jubilee: architecture received distractedly, architecture as mere frame, but also still architecture as symbol, cause, and target.

1 Dell Upton, *Another City: Urban Life and Urban Spaces in the New American Republic* (New Haven and London: Yale University Press, 2008), 14 and chapter 2 title.
2 Georges Bataille, "Architecture," in *Rethinking Architecture: A Reader in Cultural Theory*, ed. Neil Leach (New York and London: Routledge, 1997), 21. Bataille defined architecture as the physiognomy of a society's authority and understood events such as the storming of the Bastille as ways of transgressing against the very nature of architecture.
3 Catulle Mendès, *Les 73 Journées de la Commune* (Paris: Lachaud, 1897), as quoted in Kristin Ross, *The Emergence of Social Space: Rimbaud and the Paris Commune* (Minneapolis: University of Minnesota Press, 1988), 8.
4 The destruction of the great Anglo-Irish estates or "big houses" in these conflicts is still more a mythology than something that has been closely documented and analyzed. Using a journalistic source, Bevan gives the figure as two hundred houses, or ten percent of the total. See Robert Bevan, *The Destruction of Memory: Architecture at War* (London: Reaktion, 2006), 67.
5 All of these buildings were restored after the formation of the Free State, in 1921, and attained increased significance as important monuments in the Dublin cityscape including, in the case of the General Post Office, an official shrine to the Easter 1916 Rising.
6 See Robert C. Young, *Postcolonialism: An Historical Introduction* (Oxford: Blackwell, 2001), 303–7.
7 See, for instance, *Weekly Freeman*, June 26, 1897.
8 W. B. Yeats, "Nobel Lecture" (1923) https://www.nobelprize.org/nobel_prizes/literature/laureates/1923/yeats-lecture.html (accessed March 28, 2018).
9 *Irish Daily Independent*, June 23, 1897; James H. Murphy, *Abject Loyalty: Nationalism and Monarchy in Ireland During the Reign of Queen Victoria* (Cork, Ireland: Cork University Press, 2001), 27. According to one report, the nationalist city hall even flew a black flag bearing a skull and crossbones.
10 *Weekly Freeman*, June 26, 1897. Signaling loyalty by lighting windows had some history. In Dublin in 1828, for instance, campaigners for Catholic emancipation mobilized a mass demonstration in which people placed lighted candles in their windows. Isobel Armstrong, *Victorian Glassworlds: Glass Culture and the Imagination 1830–1880* (Oxford, UK: Oxford University Press, 2008), 66. This form of demonstration might be understood in relation to the tradition of loyal citizens illuminating their windows on patriotic occasions. E. P. Thompson, *The Making of the English Working Class* (Harmondsworth, UK: Penguin, 1968), 76.
11 These details come from *Freeman's Journal* (June 22, 1897) and are supported by reports in *United Ireland* (June 26, 1897).
12 *Illustrated London News*, June 26, 1897.
13 *Freeman's Journal*, June 22 and 23, 1897.
14 *Irish Times*, June 22, 1897; *Freeman's Journal*, June 22, 1897.
15 *Irish Daily Independent*, June 21, 1897; see also June 22, 1897.
16 *Irish Daily Independent*, June 21, 1897.
17 See Maud Gonne MacBride, *A Servant of the Queen: Reminiscences* (Gerrards Cross, UK: Colin Smythe, 1994), 215–18.
18 On the 1898 centenary celebrations, see T. J. O'Keefe, "The 1898 Efforts to Celebrate the United Irishmen: The '98 Centennial," *Eire/Ireland* 23, no. 2, (1988): 51–73.
19 R. F. Foster, "Remembering 1798," in *The Irish Story: Telling Tales and Making It Up in Ireland* (London: Penguin, 2001), 211–34.
20 *Freeman's Journal*, June 21, 1897. Gonne's letter also appeared in the *Irish Daily Independent*, June 21, 1897. In its report on a visit by a group of representatives of the '98 Centenary Committee, *United Ireland* made no mention of their passage being blocked. *United Ireland*, June 26, 1897.
21 See *Glasgow Herald*, June 23, 1897.
22 See also *United Ireland*, June 19, 1897, which reports that the gravesite of Wolfe Tone, in Bodenstown, is savored for its "ruined walls."
23 On the controversial attendance of Dublin's Lord Mayor, see *Freeman's Journal*, June 26, 1897. On

demonstrations of loyalty see *The Graphic*, June 26, 1897. On events in London, see *The Graphic*, June 26, 1897; *Illustrated London News*, June 12, 1897.

24 As quoted in *Aberdeen Weekly Journal*, June 24, 1897.

25 *United Ireland*, June 19, 1897.

26 *Daily Chronicle*, as reported in *Freeman's Journal*, June 23, 1897.

27 There were anti-Jubilee protests in India, and they made a similar point: that rural crisis was caused by imperial misrule. Mike Davis, *Late Victorian Holocausts: El Niño Famines and the Making of the Third World* (London: Verso, 2002), 150–52.

28 The night before an anti-Jubilee meeting was held in Foster Place, with speeches by Connolly and Gonne. Gonne's speech dwelt on the Jubilee decorations, particularly the insulting decoration of the Bank of Ireland/Parliament House. She encouraged a boycott of the shops that had Jubilee decorations and repeated her account of being barred from visiting nationalist graves on Decoration Day. *Irish Daily Independent*, June 22, 1897.

29 Michael F. J. McCarthy, *Five Years in Ireland 1895–1900* (London and Dublin: Simpkin, Marshall, Hamilton, 1902), 263.

30 Maud Gonne, "Le Martyre de l'Irlande," *Le Journal des Voyages*, November 28, 1897: 402; *Freeman's Journal*, June 23, 1897; *United Ireland*, June 26, 1897.

31 *Freeman's Journal*, June 23, 1897.

32 *Freeman's Journal*, June 23, 1897.

33 Yeats's and Gonne's accounts differ in some respects. For Yeats's account, see Anna MacBride White and A. Norman Jeffares, eds., *The Gonne-Yeats Letters, 1893–1938: Always Your Friend* (London: Pimlico, 1993), 72.

34 R. F. Foster, *Vivid Faces: The Revolutionary Generation in Ireland 1890–1923* (London: Allen Lane, 2014), 78. There had been a recent nationalist parody of official protocol during the Queen's previous Jubilee. In 1888 two Liberal supporters of Home Rule were invited to Dublin, taken on a processional route, and given the freedom of the city, echoing the loyalist events of the previous year's Jubilee celebrations. Murphy, *Abject Loyalty*, 258–9. Gonne's high awareness of the London events is shown in "Le Martyre," 402. See also *Irish Times*, June 22, 1997; *Freeman's Journal*, June 22, 1897.

35 Gonne, "Le Martyre," 402; Gonne MacBride, *A Servant*, 216.

36 *Freeman's Journal*, June 23, 1897.

37 *Freeman's Journal*, June 23, 1897.

38 Gonne MacBride, *A Servant*, 216.

39 Gonne MacBride, *A Servant*, 217. According to one report, a similar coffin appeared (or reappeared) at the display in Rutland Square. *Irish Daily Independent*, June 23, 1897.

40 *Weekly Freeman*, June 26, 1897; Gonne, "Le Martyre," 402. For attacks on the William III statue, see Yvonne Whelan, *Reinventing Modern Dublin: Streetscape, Iconography, and the Politics of Identity* (Dublin: University College Dublin Press, 2003), 38–9.

41 Whelan, *Reinventing Modern Dublin*, 101–3.

42 *Weekly Freeman*, June 26, 1897. Other sources suggest the reverse arrangement, with the projector in a window of the club. Gonne MacBride, *A Servant*, 215.

43 Gonne, "Le Martyre," 402. The historical scenes included "Cromwell's massacre at Drogheda" and "Sarsfield's defense at Limerick." *Irish Daily Independent*, June 23, 1897.

44 Fintan Cullen, "Marketing National Sentiment: Lantern Slides of Evictions in Late Nineteenth-Century Ireland," *History Workshop Journal* 54 (2002): 162–79. Gonne had already used the slides for lectures in support of the Plan of Campaign and reproduced some in the *Journal des Voyages*.

45 Cullen, "Marketing," 168.

46 This and the following comments in this paragraph are based on Brian P. Kennedy, "The Traditional Irish Thatched House: Image and Reality, 1793–1993," in *Visualizing Ireland: National Identity and the Pictorial Tradition*, ed. Adele M. Dalsimer (London: Faber and Faber, 1993), 164–79.

47 Margaret Ward, *Maud Gonne: A Life* (London: Pandora, 1990), 42.

48 Cullen, "Marketing," 170.

49 Maud Gonne, "The Evicted Tenants" (1899), in *Maud Gonne's Irish Nationalist Writings 1895–1946*, ed. Karen Steele (Dublin and Portland, Oregon: Irish Academic Press, 2004), 129.

50 Maud Gonne, "The Evicted Tenants" (1899), in ed. Karen Steele, 129.

51 Cullen, "Marketing," 165.

52 Cullen, "Marketing," 167.

53 *Irish Daily Independent*, June 23, 1997.

54 Richard Killeen, *Historical Atlas of Dublin* (Dublin: Gill & Macmillan, 2009), 144.

55 Gary A. Boyd, *Dublin 1745–1922: Hospitals, Spectacle, and Vice* (Dublin: Four Courts Press, 2006), 46–56.

56 *United Ireland*, June 26, 1897.

57 Foster, *Vivid Faces*, 8.

58 David Dickson, *Dublin: The Making of a Capital City* (London: Profile, 2014), 381.

59 *Irish Times*, June 23, 1997.

60 *Weekly Freeman*, June 26, 1897. The *Irish Daily Independent* gave a detailed account that did not stint on the brutality of the police or imply that it was directly responsible for the riots. *Irish Daily Independent*, June 23, 1897. Reports in the newspaper were rather similar to those on the 2011 riots in Britain, a predictable manifestation of already formed positions.

61 Armstrong, *Victorian Glassworlds*, 62.

62 *Irish Daily Independent*, June 23, 1897.

63 Gonne MacBride, *A Servant*, 218.

64 *Freeman's Journal*, June 23, 1897; *Irish Times*, June 23, 1897; *Weekly Freeman*, June 26, 1897.

65 *Freeman's Journal*, June 23, 1897.

66 *Irish Times*, June 23, 1997.

67 See advertisement in *Irish Daily Independent*, June 19, 1897.

68 *Irish Times*, June 23, 1997.

69 Although some damage to nationalist houses was noted, see *Irish Times*, June 23, 1897.

70 The riots were debated in Parliament and questions about the role of the police were recorded in Hansard. *Freeman's Journal*, June 26, 1897.

71 Armstrong, *Victorian Glassworlds*, 12. See also Clare Pettitt, "Poetics and Perspectives," *Journal of Victorian Culture* 14 (Spring 2009): 108–9.

72 See R. F. Foster, *Modern Ireland 1600–1972* (London: Penguin, 1989), 459–61.

73 F. S. L. Lyons, *Culture and Anarchy in Ireland 1890–1939* (Oxford, UK: Clarendon Press, 1979), 27.

74 Foster, *Irish Story*, 221.

75 Most recently, Clair Wills, *Dublin 1916: The Siege of the GPO* (London: Profile, 2010), 2.

76 James Kincaid, *Postcolonial Dublin: Imperial Legacies and the Built Environment* (London and Minneapolis: University of Minnesota Press, 2006), 6–7; Mark Crinson, "Georgianism and the Tenements, Dublin 1908–1926," *Art History*, 29 (September 2006): 625–59.

77 John McBride in 1924 and the *United Irishman* in 1902, as quoted in Kincaid, *Postcolonial Dublin*, 74–5.

78 Jiat-Hwee Chang, "Building a Colonial Technoscientific Network: Tropical Architecture, Building Science, and the Politics of Decolonization," in *Third World Modernism: Architecture, Development, and Identity*, ed. Duanfang Lu (London and New York: Routledge, 2010), 211–35, esp. 229; Stephen Legg, *Spaces of Colonialism: Delhi's Urban Governmentalities* (Malden, Massachusetts: Blackwell, 2007).

79 Charles Townshend, *Political Violence in Ireland: Government and Resistance Since 1848* (Oxford: Clarendon Press, 1983), 70.

Late to the After Party: Neo-Geo Architecture

Hans Tursack

In the exhibition *44 Low-resolution houses* at the Princeton University School of Architecture this past fall, Michael Meredith offered "low-resolution" as a term to describe certain contemporary practices that privilege orthographic projection, primitives, flatness, and simple geometric games in their design processes.[1] The display in the main gallery of the exhibition showed forty-four models of houses in white paper at a uniform architectural scale, rendering the designs as geometric cicada-shells of real and imagined projects. Stripped of all but the most essential detail, and without any significant indications of site, these "low-resolution" architectures were presented as an argument for a design language of subtle combinations and manipulations of cubes, cylinders, cones, and prisms. If the work demonstrated a keen awareness of the past overall, the cross-section of low-resolution houses presented in the exhibition also expressed a wide range of theoretical stances and adopted different attitudes towards modernist and post-modern precedents. While some projects spoke to smooth historical continuities, i.e. neo-modernism and neo-pop, others appeared more like critical ruptures, i.e. low-resolution as a reaction to first wave digital excess. In my own design practice, as well as in my contribution to the exhibition, I suggest "neo-geometric" as another sub-genre of contemporary, low-resolution architecture.

The neo-geometric in architecture pirates the visual and conceptual strategies, defined by a group of artists working in the 1980s in New York often described under the heading of "neo-geometric" or "neo-geo," that reactivate elements from minimalism, pop-art, and hard-edge abstraction through the lens of structuralist and post-structuralist theory and commodity capitalism. I identify in neo-geo art a novel method for dealing with "dyschronia,"[2] the term used by Mark Fisher to describe a pervasive feeling that the past perpetually leaks into the present—an aesthetic theme that haunts cultural production today especially architecture and visual art. What follows is a brief and impressionistic account of the emergence of neo-geo art, and a loose diagram for a possible neo-geometric architecture that extrapolates generative spatial concepts from the formal innovations of neo-geo artists Ashley Bickerton, Peter Halley, Jonathan Lasker and Haim Steinbach. Examining the work of neo-geo artists, and using their particular application of artificial color fields, graphic figures, industrial design sensibility, primitive geometries, as well as their references to science fiction, infrastructure or ecological peril, it is possible to identify methods for dealing the cards of modernism again. In this brief sketch, I want to offer the neo-geometric both as a set of operations, but also as a finer-grained category within the larger umbrella of low-resolution work. For those operating within a geometric tradition that favors the manipulation of base elements—primitives, grids, color fields, two-dimensional figures—the neo-geometric provides a model for communing with disciplinary history that is capable of avoiding naive rehearsals, apathetic distance, and melancholic memorials to the past. FIG 1

Frozen Monuments

Although it had been hailed as the kernel of the visual arts

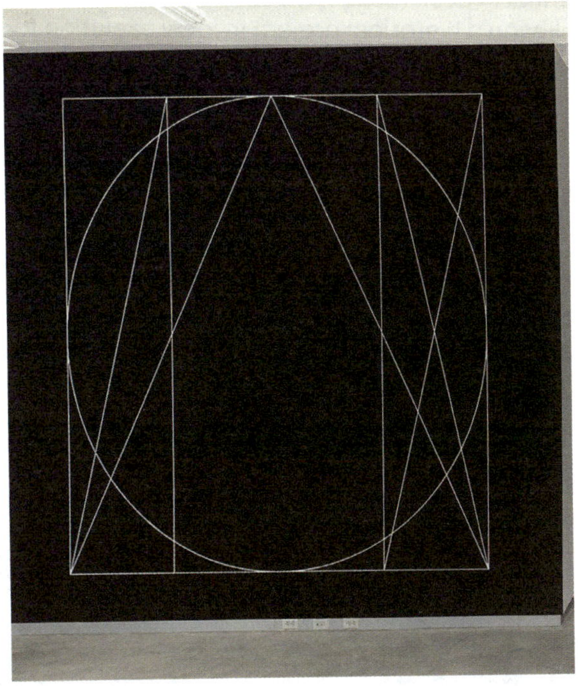

FIG 2
Sol LeWitt, Wall Drawing 295, October 1976.

FIG 1
Hans Tursack, Desert House, 2017.

in the early twentieth century, and considered key to an ontological equivalence between painting and architecture, geometric abstraction suffered several distinct deaths during the post-war period. The semantic sterilization of abstraction in the 1960s and 1970s was nearly as dramatic as earlier claims, by pre-war utopic revolutionaries and mystics, that geometry held the promise of a universal language and was the representational code for a new social order. The catastrophic failure of the collective project of abstraction occurred across several crisis movements. In minimalist sculpture, this was epitomized by the gray, featureless columns of Robert Morris and the Beckettian cages of Sol LeWitt, FIG 2 work which in both cases imagined mute volumes and irrational composition-machines suspended in a macabre limbo.[3] In post-minimal sculpture, the architecturally scaled figures used by Richard Serra and Alice Aycock developed a phenomenologically grounded geometric order marked by precarity, and violent images of heavy industry and danger. Geometric expression suffered parallel deaths in architectural avant-gardes in the 60s and 70s, for example in Peter Eisenman's experiments with the nihilistic automatization of the formal codes established by Giuseppe Terragni,[4] in John Hejduk's arcane syntheses (or cleaning-up) of Frank Lloyd Wright, Mies van der Rohe and Le Corbusier, and in Hiromi Fujii's existential rhetoric of emptiness and loss of meaning realized through manic, destabilized grid-games.[5]

In the final decades of the twentieth century some felt that the grave of modernism was not nearly deep enough, and there was still work to be done on dismantling its geometric hubris. This accounts for the various strands of deconstruction in architecture, the pursuit of base materialism or anti-form, and the formless in sculpture. Others went into a kind of religious mourning and made solemn, reverent homages to dying language, i.e. Raimund Abraham's archaic, concrete poetics, Massimo Scolari and his drawings of dream-visions and floating primitives, Robert Mangold's shaped color field canvases with lyrical ellipsoid figures, Donald Judd and the late works he produced in Marfa, Texas. In the 1980s and the approaching millennium, the contention that modernist master narratives would shortly arrive at a full stop provided those looking for running room with an ostensibly limited domain: that is, for those visual practices based in modernist experimentation, predicated on the use of simple geometric forms, colors, and the primary elements of composition, the strategies and operations looked limited. By the end of the 1970s conceptual positions of mourning, obscurantism, nostalgia, belated attack or, more likely, wholesale indifference, were apparently all that was left to occupy.

Enter mixed-media sculptors Ashley Bickerton, Haim Steinbach, Jeff Koons, Sherrie Levine and painter Peter Halley; these are some of the artists who begin making another kind of geometric work in the 1980s in New York under headings such as *neo-conceptualism*, *simulationism*, and *neo-geo*. Neo-geo art presented a cool, surgically precise redeployment of the earlier geometric abstraction, but one that was playfully corrupted by references to popular culture, commerce, and developing information technologies. FIG 3 Peter Halley developed super-sized images of offset squares using Day-Glo fluorescent paint colors overlaying Josef Albers with technical reference to architectural plans. Haim Steinbach built shelves for Nike shoes and lava-lamps that appeared like a mix of Donald Judd and Anne Truitt laced with IKEA. Ashley Bickerton freely combined the visual languages of Larry Bell and Donald Judd with earlier, prewar, abstraction, and integrated darker overtones of science fiction futures and environmental apocalypse. Abstraction as redefined by the neo-geos—and others within the East Village scene like Jonathan Lasker—became an artificial, synthetic, visual language, consciously self-sited within a new matrix of art historical citations. Some contemporary critics decried neo-geo art as empty sign-play that subjected previous art to cryogenic preservation. Hal Foster, for example, declared the work as "static signs that then stood as if out of time."[6] Viewed as an immersive acceleration of previous art, however, neo-geo work seemed to suggest that living in the end of time—or working after the end of history—had its advantages, so neo-geo developed with a sense of over-caffeinated enthusiasm for a cohort of references. Under a surface of commercial finishes, neon color, decals, and pop-minimalism, an intensive rhetorical strategy was determined to come to terms with the art of the past—recent criticism has described the work as "intertextual."[7] The collective production of Bickerton, Steinbach and Halley, as well as Koons, Levine and others, carved out a theoretical and visual territory for the further development of abstraction, or perhaps its prolonged spectral afterlife.

As an architect looking for extra-disciplinary conceptual models, I view the particular cultural abstraction developed by neo-geo artists as an unfinished project. Neo-geo art implies the possibility for a new subset within a contemporary architectural design field dominated by a struggle to reconcile itself with the death of formalism as a master narrative. Just as the neo-geo artists recast the minimalist "specific object,"[8] and cross-pollinated representational and non-referential codes, so too might contemporary architects selectively reanimate modern and postmodern formalism. In this sense, a project like MOS Architects' *House No. 13 House Parts Collected* (2018) can be interpreted as a neo-geometric exercise that produces a hyperreality from a carefully calibrated historical pastiche. *House No. 13* is almost certainly a callback of Japanese new-wave architecture, for example, the *Toy Block House* series (1979–84) by Takefumi Aida comes to mind. However, the project images of the *House No. 13* depict a physical model washed by Lasker-esque hues. A color field background nods to the office's more extreme use of color in their software experiments, and the house structure's siding is etched with CAD hatches, similar to Peter Halley paintings that develop a new semiotics from their combinations of acrylic paint and Roll-a-Tex, the paint texture normally intended for application as a building interior finish. The presentation photograph of *House No. 13* by MOS FIG 4 also shows kitsch detritus of suburban life in the form of the planters and garden tools that litter the scene. The many house projects by MOS over the last decade similarly constitute a research of postwar movements, like European neo-rationalism, while bleaching out their melancholy and metaphysics. They tune the neo-rationalists to the speed of a digital remaster. In this sense, MOS suggests a movement towards the generative potential in over-realizing, doubling down, and dramatically amplifying a historical project in low-resolution formal experimentation. The MOS model photography imagines *House No. 13* as a Takefumi Aida-like exercise seen through the lens of a Nintendo game—that is, *House No. 13* is something like a special 'level' of a video game environment, a game that exceeds the limits of recitation.[9] The massing of the MOS images takes Aida's playful geometric sensibility a step further by adding artificial color, CAD hatches, domestic bric-a-brac, and notes of surrealism to the equation so that *House No. 13* can be seen as a MOS reinterpretation of Takefumi Aida. According to the neo-geometric formula, the aesthetic sum is more than its sampled parts.

FIG 4
MOS Architects, *House No. 13 House Parts Collected*, 2018.

FIG 3
Peter Halley, White Cell, 1989.

FIG 5
Jonathan Lasker, *Pleasures of Cognition*, 2019.

Synthetic Color as Form

One of the most contested formalist narratives in recent histories of architecture—as well as one of the most generative—is the exchange between abstract painting and architecture. As early as 1918, members of the *De Stijl* movement declared hard-edged, geometric abstraction as the base element of a new, universal visual language, utilizing fluid transition between small, intimately scaled panel-paintings of grids, squares, and rectangles rendered in primary colors, i.e. Piet Mondrian, and moving screens, floors, and walls in chromatic, architectural spaces, i.e. Gerrit Rietveld. In modernisms beyond *De Stijl*, architects had great difficulty in assimilating color into any formal grammar other than as a secondary, decorative applique or in pop signage that was ironic or kitschy. A tenet of a neo-geometric architecture, then, would be a return to the project of a graphic and spatial equivalency, in which the serious but abstract coloration of *De Stijl* would be reconciled with pop art and architecture. The genealogy of this marriage would combine sculptors and artists of high modernism like Anne Truitt, Donald Judd and his mature era of painting-sculpture hybrids, and John McCracken—or other west-coast minimalists—with an architectural history that would likely include Robert Slutzky and his spatial collaborations, Michael Bell and his early houses, Robert Venturi on the pop side of the divide, for example, in his *Lieb House* of 1969, and even Michael Graves, in the *Schulman House* era of 1976. Extending a "perfect coincidence between the basic elements of painting,"[10] to this other possible coincidence between painting and architectural form, the Day-Glo, Atari palette of Peter Halley, and the neon-sherbet color fields of Jonathan Lasker FIG 5 find approximations and three-dimensional equalities articulated comparatively in the chunky grids of Zago Architecture and even in the architecturally-scaled art installations of Alex Da Corte.

In *A New Federal Project* (2016) by Zago Architecture sited in metro Detroit, FIG 6 park-scaled swathes of the urban grid are rendered in electric, yellow-green fields littered with Lasker-esque graphic scribbles; building masses are wrapped with multi-layered, misregistered color-screens that produce indeterminate edge conditions reminiscent of Mark Rothko's aqueous rectangles. *A New Federal Project* absorbs lessons from pop-art, op-art, and color field painting and sets them within a conversation about architectural ideas of abstract, volumetric figuration, and posture. In Alex Da Corte's *Lightning* (2015–16) FIG 7 these ideas are expanded to the scale of a domestic interior. *Lightning* reads like an American, suburban house exploded where room-scaled zones are laid out in a large, industrial museum. Each separate area—room, lawn, or facade fragment—is demarcated using littered arrangements of neon lighting, colorful carpets, monochrome painted walls, and luminescent commercial products with surface decals. In one of *Lightning*'s vignettes, a cherry-red Coca-Cola mini-fridge spills its guts onto a blue carpet in front of an orange and blue billiard table painted to match both the floor and the artificial lighting. Through its immaculate detail, sparse placement of colorful objects, and compositional sensitivity, Da Corte's zoning recalls Tom Wesselmann, Ellsworth Kelly, and David Lynch, all rendered through a new color field created by the neon wash lighting suspended at ceiling-height that perfectly aligns to the perimeter of the blue carpet outlines on the floor below. Clearly the color choices of both Zago and Da Corte are inspired by computer screenshots and smartphones rather than typical modernist observations drawn from nature or heavy industry. In both instances, the works produce architecture-specific effects that employ what media theorist Carolyn L. Kane calls "algorithmic color" or, artificial, computationally generated hues that are the result of "the mathematical intensification and transformation of perception in the *age of algorithmic optimization*."[11] In neo-geometric architecture, the primary agents in the production of form are artificial, algorithmic color-fields and graphic figures in two dimensional shapes. These painterly agents are as primary to neo-geo as figure-ground, solid-void and point-line-plane relationships were to modernists of art and architecture.

Product Design and Structural Ornament

The sculptural practices of Haim Steinbach and Ashley Bickerton—as well as the early Jeff Koons—literalize a process in which artistic practices dealing with abstract painting or the minimalist object and the fetishistic detailing of industrial design are conflated—consider Donald Judd, Ad Reinhardt or Tony Smith's *Die* (1962) and the designs of computer shells, for example. Bickerton's "wall contemplation units," and Steinbach's plastic-laminated shelves bring the austere, frontally-oriented, wall-mounted pieces of Judd

FIG 6
Zago Architecture, A New Federal Project, 2016.

into the hyperbolic, overly detailed realm of high-tech athletic apparel, automotive design and electronics. Following the example of Bickerton and Steinbach, one of the tenets of a neo-geometric formalism would be simplicity in the overall massing of a piece—i.e. cube, sphere, pyramid, grid—coupled with the excessive detailing of structure, assemblies, and surfaces. In his recent work *Water Vector 1* (2017), FIG 8 Ashley Bickerton makes a callback to his own earlier works of the 1980s and produces essentially a minimalist box—it could be one of the units in Judd's *Untitled (88-31 Bernstein)* (1988) or Larry Bell's *20" Untitled (Tom Messer Cube)* (1969)—that integrates the straps, snaps, handles, exposed hardware and graphic logos characteristic of performance outerwear brands like Helly Hansen and Arc'teryx. The work blends images of utility—metal handles and trim—and performance—textile coverings or the semi-abstract alphabet-symbol-logos that decal its facade—with the unitary gestalt of a geometric primitive.

FIG 8
Ashley Bickerton. Water Vector 1, 2017.

FIG 7
Alex Da Corte, *Free Roses*, installation view, Massachusetts Museum of Contemporary Art, North Adams, Massachusetts, 2016.

An architectural complement to Bickerton and Steinbach would similarly fuse minimal form, pop detailing, logo-elements, and structure-as-ornament. In attempting to create my own architectural analogue for a piece like Bickerton's *Water Vector 1*, the early experiments of British high-tech design provided inspiration, i.e. the Hopkins House by Hopkins Architects (1976). The visualities of the pop-assemblies in British high-tech architecture resound with similar arrangements of fasteners, tension cable systems, and hanging hardware to those found in Bickerton's sculptural vocabulary, although with Bickerton they are made to utilize all the ambiguities of redundancy. Considered as a proto-architectural gesture, *Water Vector 1* resembles an early Richard Rogers in miniature, for example the *Patscentre* (1982–85) in Princeton, NJ. In my *Summer House* (2019) FIG 9—just as in the *Hopkins House* by Hopkins Architects (1976)—structural members and assemblies serve an emphatically graphic role. In the *Hopkins House*, the bright, blue steel of the structural grid and staircase use load-bearing elements as a foil for three-dimensional linear compositions. A similar celebration of structure-as-graphic is produced in a parallel projection by Common Accounts for the project *Three Ordinary Funerals* (2017). FIG 10 The drawing shows a Memphis-speckled white lattice frame and printed textiles against a neon-green ground. The dot-pattern applied to the structure of *Three Ordinary Funerals* was inspired by the decorative interiors of Josef Hoffmann and the late-career work of Michael Graves—after Graves became fully postmodern-commercial.[12] However, the strong abstract-figure of this structural skeleton maintains allusions to Sol LeWitt, while the textile-elements refer in turn to the work of Daniel Buren. Interface aesthetics are another source of reference for the Common Accounts drawing; the use of logos, decals, and text in *Three Ordinary Funerals* speaks to Steinbach and Bickerton. Younger neo-geo inflected artists, like Alex Da Corte, as well as Magali Reus, similarly relish a sense of transgressive movement between both the geometric primitives in minimalist sculpture and high-modernist painting respectively, as well as between these uses for primitives and the graphics of consumer products, for example the ecstatic celebrations of detail that one might find in premium line, limited, edition athletic wear.

Sci-fi Futures

In his (now) infamous essay *The Crisis in Geometry* (1984), Peter Halley examines Robert Smithson's late freehand drawings, describing them as "hellish island environments, bristling with fortifications and littered with smoking and flaming instruments of death, most of which are formed out of simple geometric shapes like cones, cylinders, and cubes."[13] In Smithson's work, Halley encountered an exemplar of culturally-charged geometric thinking, where images of dark, apocalyptic, science-fiction revealed another, unconscious, impulse latent in abstraction below the surface of either pure "opticality" or pre-linguistic, phenomenological "presence." In an essay titled "Entropy and the New Monuments" (1966) (surely a precursor to Halley's *Crisis*) Smithson conflated minimalist and high-modernist sculpture with images of apocalypse and time travel: "The works of many of these artists celebrate what Flavin calls 'inactive history' or what the physicist calls 'entropy' or 'energy-drain.' They bring to mind the Ice Age rather than the Golden Age..."[14] If the geometric imaginary of the twentieth century was haunted by industrial destruction and ecological ruin—think abandoned highways and drill grounds referenced in Tony Smith's narration of his journey on the unfinished New Jersey Turnpike—then neo-geo art externalized this haunted imaginary.[15]

Halley's own paintings can be read as circuit boards, civic building plans, prison diagrams, or screenshots from traffic-control room interfaces. Bickerton's practice exhibits a similar paranoia in works like his *Anthroposphere #2* (1990) where Judd's wall-mounted works and Smithson's *Enantiomorphic Chambers* (1965) return as an atmosphere-controlled time capsule for trash detailed in the manner of the spaceship refinery from Ridley Scott's *Alien* (1979).[16] The neo-geo proposes that geometry is both a non-referential abstract signifier and a malign industrial and information-processing infrastructure. It is perhaps unsurprising then that object-oriented-ontology and ecology theorist Timothy Morton has viewed Steinbach's work as a visual analogue to his theoretical writings.[17] A final note for the development

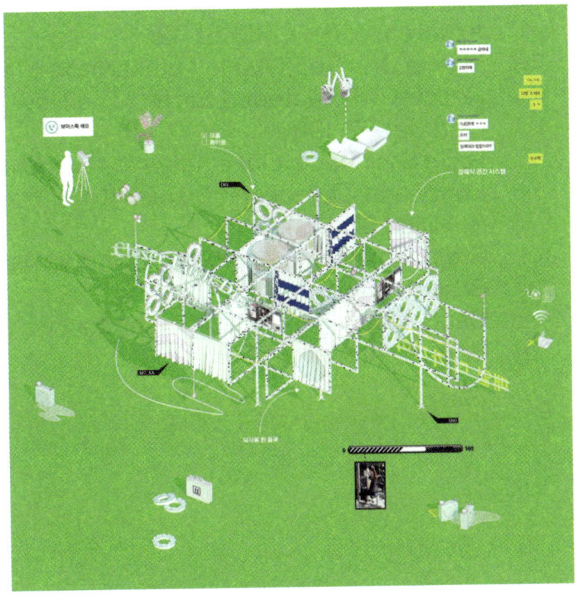

FIG 10
Common Accounts, Three Ordinary Funerals, 2017.

of a neo-geo sensibility in architecture, then, would be a thematic celebration of commercially manufactured objects, synthetic materials and infrastructural (life-support) systems. Meditating on the ecological takeaway from Steinbach's work, Morton writes: "In order to have that [ecological awareness], you have to attune to things, allow things to influence you, tell you how to use them, how to keep them safe."[18] FIG 11 Here, the architectural thematization of the materiality of the human body proposed by Common Accounts can serve as an example—so too the younger materially-focused art practices like Reus, Antoine Catala and Alisa Bareboym. In one of my own projects entitled *Graphic Fields*, I present a park-scaled proposal for an artificial landscape etched in low-relief with systems to support the growth of exotic plant life. FIG 12 In this proposal, Bickerton-like specimen-vitrines, artificial lighting, generators, and data collection/energy management units are arrayed in cells reminiscent of Halley's urban diagrams. The neo-geometric formula uses geometry to accumulate associations with science fiction, urban infrastructures, crystallography, extreme environmental conditions, and terraformed landscapes.

Running Room

Contemplating the Deconstructionist theories of Paul De Man, neo-geo historian Amy L. Brandt writes, "Modernity therefore recurrently fluctuates between remembrance of past events and the obliteration of their historical weight."[19] If the neo-geometric can be used as a term in the contemporary landscape of low-resolution architectural production, it should be less as a description of a style than as a marker for a precise position within a spatial field of disciplinary anchor-points and cultural references. The neo-geometric embraces and celebrates post-postmodern (or neo-post-modern) stasis as a "suspended eternity,"[20] and relishes in each precision recombination and permutation, procedures Jacques Derrida describes as "textual grafting."[21] Beyond mere citation games, this grafting is coupled with a euphoric over-subscription to previous strategies. Far from taking an

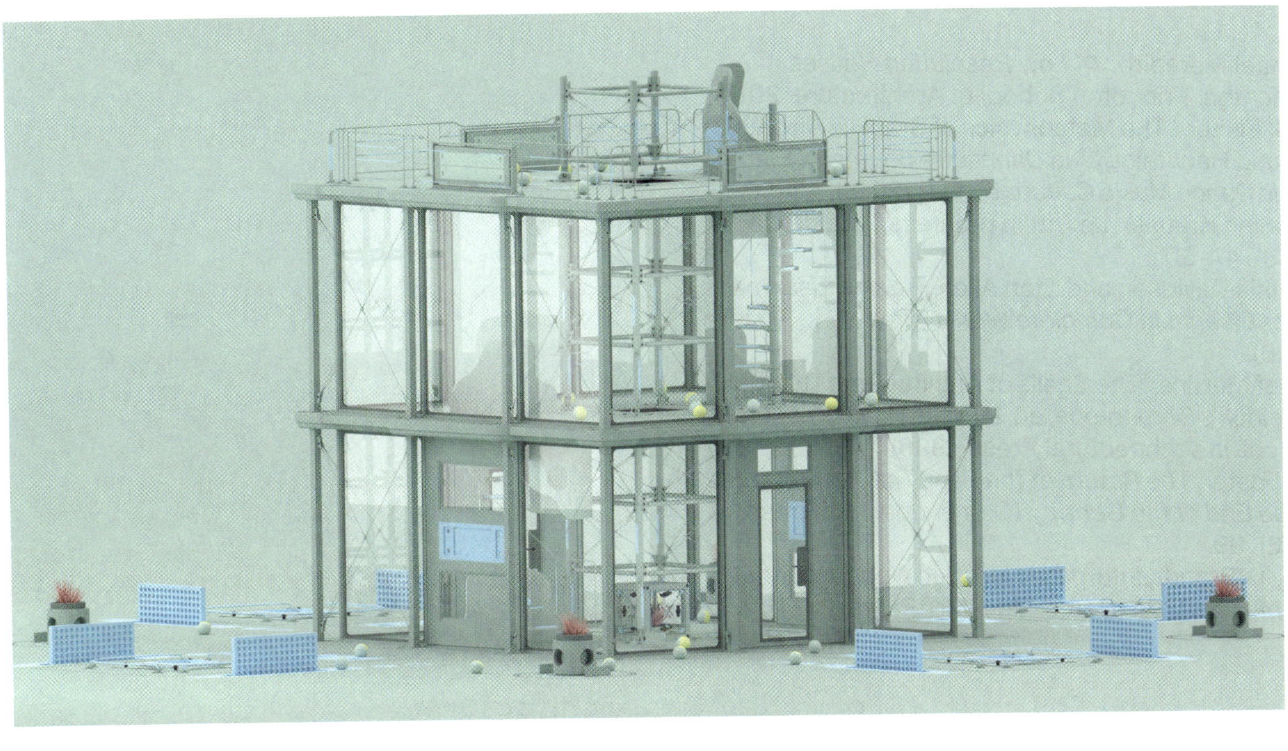

FIG 9
Hans Tursack. Summer House, 2019.

ironic distance, Halley's paintings are more vibrant than his color field predecessors. Neo-geometric architecture reanimates the modernist conversation between color and form through the lens of the digital screen. It employs structures and assemblies as ornament in the manner of luxury product design and concurrently adopts a capacity to speak of issues in ecological philosophy regarding human capacities to empathize with anonymous materials and commercially-produced objects. Not to be mistaken with some kind of recipe for novel form (can one even imagine such a manifesto at this point?) the neo-geometric is merely a micro-strategy for elbowing out a bit of space to operate in the weathered arena of abstract formalism. It is an optimistic method for coping with the present, already too crowded with static images of the past.

FIG 12
Hans Tursack. Graphic Fields (Composition V), 2015.

FIG 11
Haim Steinbach, Untitled (dog chew, ball, fins), 2017, Plastic laminated wood shelf; Kong rubber dog chew; Kong rubber dog ball; 3 George Greenough Design fiberglass surfboard fins, 26 5/8 × 46 × 14 1/2 in. (67.6 × 116.8 × 36.8 cm).

1 Michael Meredith, *44 Low Resolution Houses* (Princeton: Princeton School of Architecture, 2018).
2 Mark Fisher, "The Metaphysics of Crackle: Afrofuturism and Hauntology," in *Dancecult: Journal of Electronic Dance Music Culture* 5, no. 2 (2013), 42–55.
3 Rosalind Krauss, "LeWitt in progress," in *October* 6 (1978), 47–60.
4 Cynthia Davidson and Stan Allen, *Tracing Eisenman: Peter Eisenman Complete Works* (New York: Rizzoli, 2006).
5 Detlef Mertins,"The Shells of Architectural Thought." in *Hejduk's Chronotope*, ed. Michael Hays (Princeton: Princeton Architectural Press, 1996).
6 Hal Foster, *The Return of the Real: The Avant-garde at the End of the Century* (Cambridge: MIT Press, 1996), 99.
7 Amy L. Brandt, *Interplay: Neo-Geo Neoconceptual Art of the 1980s* (Cambridge: MIT Press, 2014).
8 Donald Judd, "Specific Objects" in *Donald Judd: Early Work, 1955–1968*, ed. Thomas Kellein (New York: Distributed Art Publishers, Inc, 2002).
9 Artist-theorist Hito Steyerl suggests the gamer's reset button as an alternative to such "reenactments" that may be relevant in the context of a Neo-Geometric architecture: "...play is also about the improvised creation of new, common rules. So reenactment is scrapped in favor of gaming moving towards play...". See, Hito Steyerl, *Duty Free Art: Art in the Age of Planetary Civil War* (New York: Verso Books, 2017).
10 Yve Alan Bois, *Painting as Model* (Cambridge: MIT Press, 1993), 116.
11 Carolyn L. Kane, *Chromatic algorithms: Synthetic color, computer art, and aesthetics after code.* (Chicago: University of Chicago Press, 2014), 215.
12 Conversations with the architects.
13 Peter Halley, "The Crisis in Geometry and the Current State of Geometric Art," *Arts Magazine* 58, no. 10 (1984), 111–115.
14 Robert Smithson, "Entropy And The New Monuments," in *Robert Smithson: the collected writings*, ed. Jack Flam (Berkley and Los Angeles: University of California Press, 1996).
15 Samuel Wagstaff Jr, "Talking with Tony Smith," *Artforum* 5, no. 4 (1966), 19.
16 Michel Brenson, "Ashley Bickerton's Pleas to Rescue a Threatened Earth," The New York Times, October 27, 1989.
17 Haim Steinbach, *Once Again the World Is Flat: Haim Steinbach: Object and Display* (New York: Gregory R. Miller, 2015).
18 Steinbach, *Once Again the World Is Flat*, 393.
19 Brandt, *Interplay*, 48
20 Baudrillard, Jean. *America* (London: Verso, 2010),131.
21 Brandt, *Interplay*, 56.

The Construction of Soviet Culture: From Mass Spectacle to Synthetic Theater

Anna Bokov

In 1926 El Lissitzky was commissioned to design a stage set for *I Want a Child* [*Khochu rebenka*], by Sergey Tretyakov, to be performed at the Meyerhold Theater in Moscow. The play was produced by Vsevolod Meyerhold (1874–1940), the legendary avant-garde theater director known for an experimental system of stage movement referred to as "biomechanics," developed immediately following the October Revolution in 1918. It took nearly four years for Meyerhold to secure censorship approval for the play. Despite his official involvement in cultural policy at the highest level in the 1920s, the play's controversial content prevented it from being produced. *I Want a Child* explored the sexual and social challenges faced by Milda, a fiercely independent Soviet agronomist who decided to have a child on her own, outside of traditional family bounds. Meyerhold envisioned the play as a real-time dialogue between actors and spectators: the latter could "join" the performance at any moment, which required not only a radically different directorial approach but also an entirely new architectural setting. "What kind of theater do we envisage for the presentation of the new spectacle?" he wondered. "First of all, we must remove the boxes and abolish seating in tiers."[1] Meyerhold declared, "The only design suitable for a performance created by the combined efforts of actors and spectators is the amphitheater, where there is no division of the audience into separate classes dependent on social standing and financial resources."[2]

Originally trained as an actor in the studios of Konstantin Stanislavsky and Vladimir Nemirovich-Danchenko, Meyerhold developed his biomechanics as a critique of the Stanislavsky system, which was based on empathy and psychological authenticity. FIG 1 Meyerhold's system drew upon the concepts of William James regarding the primacy of physical over emotional reactions, Vladimir Bekhterev on conditioned reflexes and Frederick Winslow Taylor on the scientific organization of labor.[3] Taylor's theory included the notion of a worker's "economy of physical energy," achieved by reducing unnecessary movements, developing a rhythm and locating the center of gravity. Actors were required to develop their physical apparatus, the body, in a process interpreted by Meyerhold as "conserving expressive means ... guaranteeing the accuracy of movements."[4] Taylor's biomechanics, according to Meyerhold, "sought to establish the laws of an actor's movement on a stage" by developing a system of exercises on the basis of human behavior. It treated actors as anonymous functions in the collective fabric of a play rather than as individuals, recalling the notion of "mass ornament" described by critic and sociologist Siegfried Kracauer in 1927:

> Although the masses give rise to the ornament, they are not involved in thinking it through. As linear as it may be, there is no line that extends from the small sections of the mass to the entire figure. The ornament resembles aerial photographs of landscapes and cities in that it does not emerge out of the interior of the given conditions, but rather appears above them. Actors likewise never grasp the stage setting in its totality, yet they consciously take part in its construction.[5]

Biomechanics relied on expressive body language and the

"elementary laws of reflexes" rather than elaborate stage and costume design to communicate the act.[6] According to Meyerhold, "If the actor remains on the bare stage, the greatness of the theater stays with him."[7] This emphasis on bodily movement was manifest in the new intention for stage: constructions [*konstruktsii*] rather than scenic decorations [*dekoratsii*].

The constructions for stage, designed by avant-garde artists such as Lyubov Popova and Varvara Stepanova, functioned as utilitarian apparatuses for activating the spectacle and, more importantly, for engaging the spectator masses. Describing Popova's stage set for *Magnanimous Cuckold* [*Velikodushnyy rogonosets*] Meyerhold wrote:

> We wanted to lay this foundation for a new kind of theatrical action, which does not require any illusory scenery or complex props but utilizes the basic improvised objects and transitions from a play done with professional actors to a free game with workers during their time off.[8]

As an active member of the Bolshevik Party in 1918 and the head of the theater division of the Commissariat of Education (*Narkompros*) from 1920, Meyerhold formulated his radical views in a program titled Theatrical October [*Teatral'niyy Oktyabr'*].[9] This manifesto called for reforming the traditional "counter-revolutionary" theater and proposed ways of politicizing it based on the gains of the October Revolution. Convinced that the social revolution would lead to a theatrical one, Meyerhold advocated for the complete destruction of the old art and the creation on its ruins of a fundamentally new one. Theater was to become a

FIG 1
Vsevolod Meyerhold, Biomechanics. Actor Training Workshop, 1920s.

FIG 2
El Lissitzky working on a stage design of Sergei Tretyakov's Play *I Want a Child* (1926–1930) in the Meyerhold Theater, 1929.

"means of political agitation and propaganda" in the revolutionary struggle, while the stage was to turn into a political tribune. Meyerhold outlined five principles for constructing a "true people's theater": 1) Unification of the audience and stage in one space (removal of the stage box); 2) Axonometric perception of the spectacle (amphitheater); 3) Experience of action by a viewer from three sides (spatial development of a spectacle onstage-stadium); 4) Introduction of all service elements into the composition of the auditorium (actors' cabin, technical part, orchestra); 5) Stage access for the mechanical transport and demonstration.[10]

Meyerhold used real technology in his plays—motorcycles, cars, machine guns, and even an agricultural combine. In one of the early plays, performed during the civil war, Red Army soldiers marched through the stage with their banners while reports from the front were announced throughout the performance. Meyerhold continued the development of this radical typology with a team of young Constructivist architects who designed the new theater building in the 1930s. Sadly the director did not live to see his new theater open, in the fall of 1940. He was arrested and executed just months before by the very regime he so passionately helped envision and materialize.

Lissitzky's design for the Meyerhold production of *I Want a Child* sought to transform the theatrical space itself according to the principles of Theatrical October. Trained as an architect, he approached the challenge by developing a prototype for an entirely new theater. Lissitzky proposed to reconfigure the entire interior of the theater building in the center of Moscow granted to Meyerhold by the Soviet government in 1920.[11] A photograph shows the designer inside a model of what would typically be the backstage, in this case a seating area. FIG 2 The project eliminated the proscenium—the partition between stage and auditorium—to transform the traditional separation between audience and performance. What was formerly a proscenium was wrapped around an elliptically shaped seating area. The ribbon strip carried the slogan "A healthy child is the future builder of socialism"—an effective way to communicate the message of the play. The design eroded the barrier between the action onstage and the backstage functions, effectively folding the mechanics of the play and its audience into the play itself.

Thus both the screenplay and form of the performance pursued the singular goal of imagining a particular instance of a future social order. A key question in this ambitious task was how properly to shape the future human, a subject of impassioned discussion in Soviet society. The unabashedly materialistic stance assumed by the authorities presupposed that human nature—and the environment at large—could be consciously reshaped, an idea adopted by scientists, educators, and writers as well as artists and architects. The creation of a "new Soviet man" [*novyy sovetskiy chelovek*] and a "new Soviet woman," what Leon Trotsky referred to as a "higher social biological type ... or a superman," was not simply about the making of a new type of individual but an integral part of constructing a new "we"—a single unified Soviet nation.[12] Lissitzky interpreted this "truly proletarian" concept of a new superhuman turned new nation quite literally by merging the faces of a man and a woman in his 1929 poster *Russische Ausstellung*.[13] FIG 3

Architecture and design were seen as vehicles for articulating the proletarian concept of "we" by shaping a new social order through spatial and visual means. Although at first glance spatial arrangement of Lissitzky's project might seem reminiscent of the Roman amphitheater, it differed from it in its treatment of actors and audience by its multiple stage configurations and its direct engagement of the audience in an active participation as part of the performance. In the context of early Soviet period, the inclusion of spectators in mass spectacle (*massovyy akt*)—which typically included a reenactment of October revolution—was believed to indoctrinate or "convert" them into a revolutionary culture.[14]

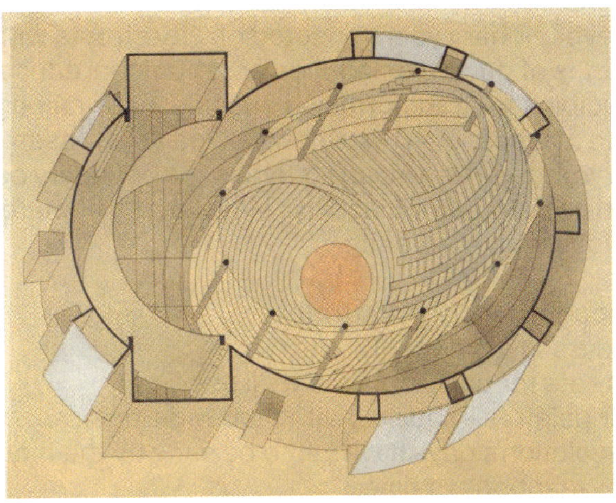

FIG 4
Design for a total theater by Walter Gropius, 1926.

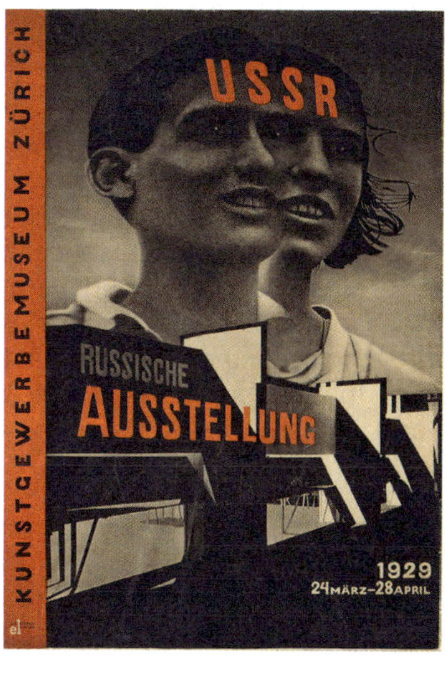

FIG 3
El Lissitzky poster for USSR Russian Exhibition, 1929.

Political conditioning through active participation of the spectators—in this case the proletarian masses—was an objective that Meyerhold actively pursued. He further formulated a detailed program for a new type of theater fit for mass spectacle starting in 1927.[15] He believed that the new typology required a "close collaboration between director and architect" similar to the relationship between the Bauhaus director, architect Walter Gropius, and the Berlin theater director Erwin Piscator. FIG 4 In 1926 Gropius developed a design for a "synthetic"—or as he called it, "total"—theater for Piscator, who was notorious for his left-wing political views and "commitment to the Russian Revolution."[16] As director of the People's Theatre [*Volksbühne*] during the Weimer Republic, Piscator had staged works by Maxim Gorky and Leo Tolstoy in the early 1920s. Like those of Meyerhold, his plays were treated as a means of political propaganda and carried a clear leftist agenda. To achieve his goals Piscator used a variety of artistic and technological devices, from film projections to mechanized sets, something that no doubt inspired Gropius, who wrote:

> The contemporary theater architect should set himself the aim to create a great keyboard for light and space, so objective and adaptable in character that it would respond to any imaginable vision of a stage director; a flexible building, capable of transforming and refreshing the mind by its spatial impact alone.[17]

Like Meyerhold, Gropius felt that a modern stage and theater embodying these new interpretations of theatrical space was still to be created. The Bauhaus director was familiar with the contemporary needs of the theater through his experience at the school. The Bauhaus theater workshop became known under the leadership of Oskar Schlemmer, a multimedia artist and theater director who created radical theatrical performances such the Triadic Ballet. Schlemmer saw the theater as fundamental for its role in transcending reality and constructing a world of illusion—an embodiment of the Bauhaus ideal:

> It is natural that the aims of the Bauhaus—to seek the union of the artistic ideal with the craftsmanlike practicality by thoroughly investigating the creative elements and to understand in all its ramifications the essence of *der Bau*, creative construction. ... For, like the concept of Bau itself, the stage is an orchestral complex which comes about only through the cooperation of many different forces. It is the union of the most heterogeneous assortment of creative elements. Not the least of its functions is to serve the metaphysical needs of man by constructing a world of illusion and by creating the transcendental on the basis of the rational.[18]

Theatrical performance has long been one of the main laboratories for advancing a new art form most closely resembling the idea of a "total work of art," or *Gesamtkunstwerk*. Combining the use of various media—music, dance, painting, architectural and costume design—it was the perfect context for employing principles of "the essence of der Bau" or "creative construction." Schlemmer wrote:

> If the aims of the Bauhaus are also the aims of our stage, it is natural that the following elements should

> be of first and foremost importance to us: *space* as a part of the larger total complex, building [Bau]. The art of the stage is a spatial art, a fact which is bound to become clearer and clearer in the future. The stage, including the auditorium, is above all an architectonic-spatial organism where all things happening to it and within it exist in a spatially conditioned relationship.[19]

Schlemmer described the "present" theater as an evolution of the two traditional types of theatrical organization: the first, a central arena "on which the play unfolds itself three-dimensionally while the spectators crowd around concentrically," and the second, a classic stage form of the Greek proscenium theater, "with its protruding platform around which the audience is seated in concentric half-circles." Eventually this open proscenium moved away the spectator, to be "finally pulled back altogether behind a curtain to form today's deep stage which dominates our present theater."[20]

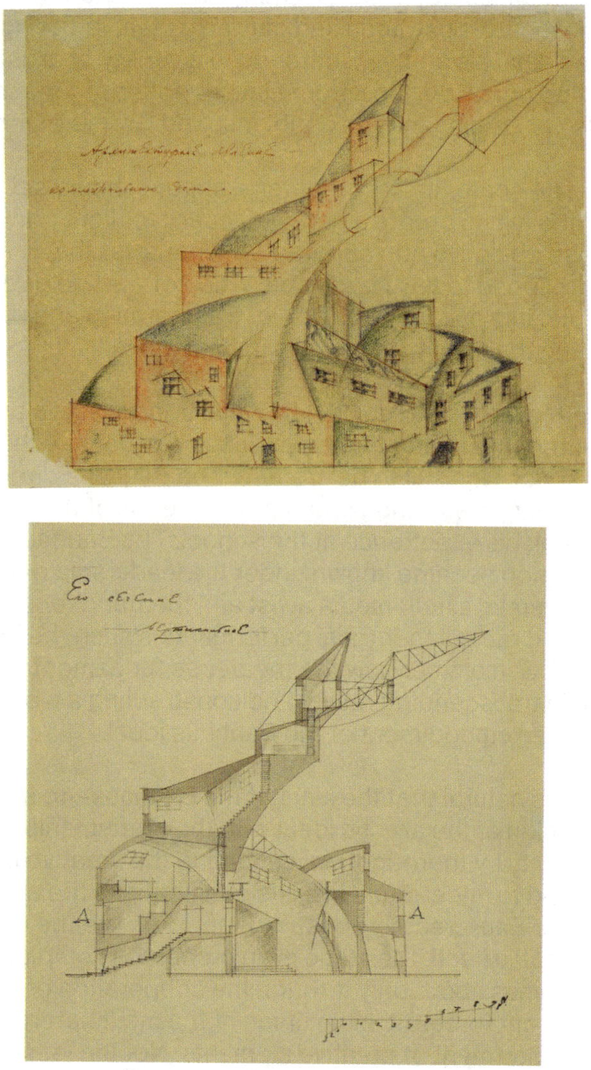

FIG 6
Nikolay Ladovsky, Communal House, 1919.

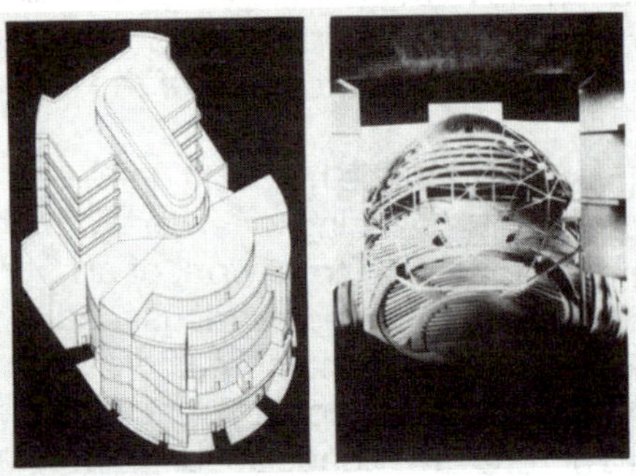

FIG 5
Design for a total theater by Walter Gropius, 1926. Walter Gropius & Oskar Schlemmer, *Die Bühne im Bauhaus*, 1924, 25.

Gropius conceived of this building as an "instrument so flexible that a director can employ any one of the three stage forms by the use of simple, ingenious mechanisms." This instrument could be used for diverse kinds of performances: "drama, opera, film, and dance; for choral or instrumental music; for sports events or assemblies," as well as conventional plays.[21] FIG 5

An element common to the theater projects of Lissitzky and Gropius is the elliptical form—a cross between the O-shape of the Roman amphitheater and the U-shape of the Greek theater. They also incorporated aspects of the "present theater," a building type that originated in an urban setting, where a town plaza served as the stage and surrounding buildings hosted the audience and where often the facade of a municipal building acted as a backdrop, as in Siena, Italy, for example. Through their synthetic designs Gropius and Lissitzky sought to create the antithesis to the class-segregated theater in the form of a democratic space with a flexible stage that combined properties found in both Greek and Roman theaters. Their flexible configurations offered new modes of engaging the spectators and actors, making the audience an integral part of the play.

The goal of Cultural Revolution was to erase the boundary between spectators and actors, between illiterate masses and intellectual elites. Leftist artists urged everyone to "immediately come out and with their skilled brushes illuminate, color the sides, foreheads, chests of cities, railroad stations."[22] Revolution pushed the crowds onto the streets and turned the city itself into a stage for artistic experimentation that no longer belonged to the elite but became an "art of the commune."[23] The mass spectacles of the first post-revolutionary years enacted on city streets with thousands of people functioned as agitational education, as "crucibles for transforming consciousness among the illiterate masses."[24] Art was now viewed as an essential part of everyday life—as a means to erase the boundary between old and new eras. Poet Vladimir Mayakovsky captured this ubiquitous mood brilliantly:

> Enough of half-penny truths!
> Old trash from your hearts erase!
> Streets for paint-brushes we'll use,
> our palettes—squares with their wide-open space.
> Revolution's days have yet to be sung by the thousand-
>   year book of time.
> Into the streets, the crowds among,
> futurists, drummers, masters of rhyme![25]

According to Alexander Bogdanov, the mastermind behind the Proletkult movement, every work of art reflected the ideology of a particular class and was not applicable to another.[26] "Art is one of the ideologies of class, an element of class consciousness," he wrote. "Hence it is an organizational form of the class life, a way of unifying and bringing cohesion to class forces."[27] It was through art, or to be precise by "throwing away the art of the past" and creating new forms of art, that the proletariat was to create "its own culture" and ultimately is own "empire"—one building at a time.[28]

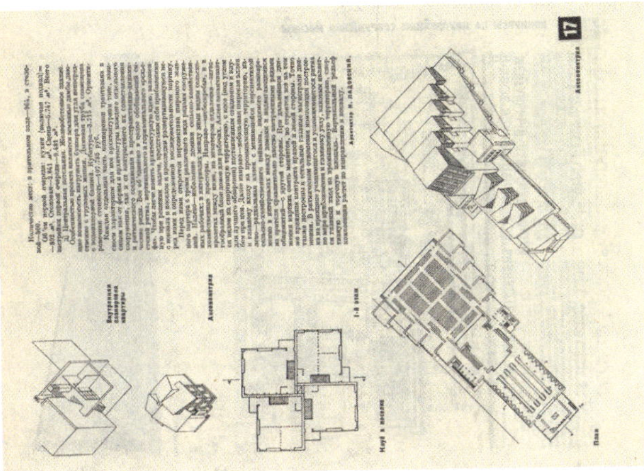

FIG 7
Nikolay Ladovsky, Workers' Club for Kostino (1927) (top). *Stroitelstvo Moskvy*, no. 7, 1929.

A fundamental theme in Soviet architecture and urbanism was designing assembly spaces that could facilitate the mass spectacles. Tatlin's Monument to the Third International, designed in 1919, initiated the decade long exploration for the symbol for the young Soviet nation.[29] Projects by Tatlin's contemporaries, members of Zhivskulptarkh (an acronym for the commission of Painterly and Sculptural-Architectural Synthesis), architect Nikolay Ladovsky, sculptor Boris Korolev, and artist Alexander Rodchenko developed proposals for a collective project "Temple of Communication of the Peoples" in 1919–1920. All of them, including Tatlin, were faculty at Vkhutemas—the Soviet counterpart to the Bauhaus.[30] Zhivskulptarkh's proposals, similarly to the Monument to the Third International, deployed what was considered the "best expression of our spirit," dynamic spiraling form.[31] FIG 6

Lenin's death in January 1924 marked another phase in the development of the assembly typology, now recast as a memorial in addition to its primary "congregational" function. Lenin was now seen as an "extrahistorical" figure, someone who belonged to a "different order of humanity" personifying the Revolution itself.[32] The mass spectacles following Lenin's death, in particular those commemorating the tenth anniversary of October in 1927, represented the complex course of history through "hyperbolizing" one figure, Lenin.[33] This dual vision, for an assembly building as a memorial on the one hand, and a site for mass spectacle on the other, manifested a dichotomy inherent in the typology. The search for a monumental structure symbolizing the proletariat was resolved by the end of the decade with the three-stage international competition for the Palace of Soviets—featuring a monumental figure of Lenin.[34]

The principle function of a building for mass assembly was to "conduct" Soviet ideology in a more "condensed" way. The term "social conductors and condensers of socialist culture" [*provodniki i kondensatory sotsialisticheskoy kul'tury*] was coined by Constructivist architects in the late 1920s and popularized on an international level in the 1970s by historian Anatole Kopp.[35] The idea of a condenser was that society would function in an analogous way to electricity: its revolutionary current would get "intensified" via its transmission through the charge carriers of modern architecture. Constructivists juxtaposed the new architecture with buildings such as the "speculative tenement house," the private residence, or the "gentlemen's club," all products of "pre-revolutionary social, technical, and economic circumstances."[36] They advocated for a "new social type" that would resolve the "question of impact on the user (ideological, emotional impact, and so on)."[37] This notion of social condenser applied to a range of building types—"communal housing, workers' clubs, palaces of labor, administrative buildings, and factories"—but it was ultimately manifested in a new building type known as the workers' club.[38] When first introduced, the workers' club was intended to challenge the origins of clubs as social institutions accessible only to the elite, and therefore it was perceived as a provocative proposition. Ultimately these "condensers" were instrumental for a larger social-engineering project that would forge a proletarian age. The club's spatial organization would condition new social behavior through a series of orchestrated collective experiences.

While workers' clubs were not theaters, they included a theatrical component—typically an auditorium with a stage, used for meetings, lectures and performances. Nikolay Ladovsky, leader of a competing movement in Soviet architecture called Rationalism, produced one of the more interesting solutions for a workers' club stage in his proposal for the Kostino labor commune [*trudkommuna*] in 1927. FIG 7 In his project the stage is positioned as a hinge between the auditorium and the dining hall, allowing it to operate simultaneously in both spaces with spectators on both sides. The plan is organized along a central axis in a telescoping configuration with staggered chambers, which could be used as rehearsal spaces, and movable walls flanking the main auditorium. A stepped volume on the auditorium side reflects the sawtooth roof of the dining room. Ladovsky's flexible organizational solution allowed for a wide range of activities, from more customary performances to processional events such as marches or mass celebrations.[39]

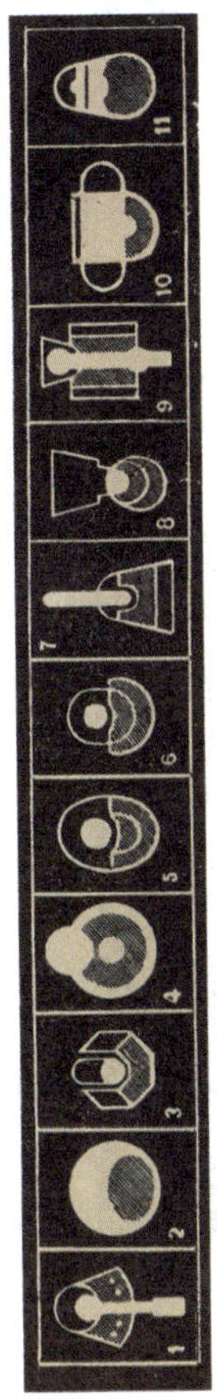

FIG 8
Georgy Krutikov, analysis of stage configurations for Synthetic Theater, 1930. *Soviet Architecture*, No.1, 1932.

Meyerhold's radical approach to theater design was symptomatic of the revolutionary dictum that the theatrical act should engage the audience as active participants. Thus, it aimed to educate, agitate, and ultimately empower the masses. This approach generated new public space typologies that explored the agency of architecture in reorganizing modes of social interaction and political engagement. Such was an objective of the national competition for a Synthetic Theater [*Sinteticheskiy Teatr*] for Sverdlovsk (now Yekaterinburg), a city in the Ural Mountains, held in 1930. Among the eleven participants there were representatives of both Constructivist and Rationalist camps. The teams included members of Constructivist OSA (acronym for *Organizatsiya Sovremennykh Arkhitektorov*, translated as Organization of Contemporary Architects), Rationalist Asnova (acronym for *Assotsiatsia Novykh Arkhitektorov*, translated as Association of New Architects) and ARU (acronym for *Assotsiatsia Arkhitektorov-Urbabanistov*, translated as Association of Architects-Urbanists). The project by Constructivist architect Moisei Ginzburg was awarded first prize.

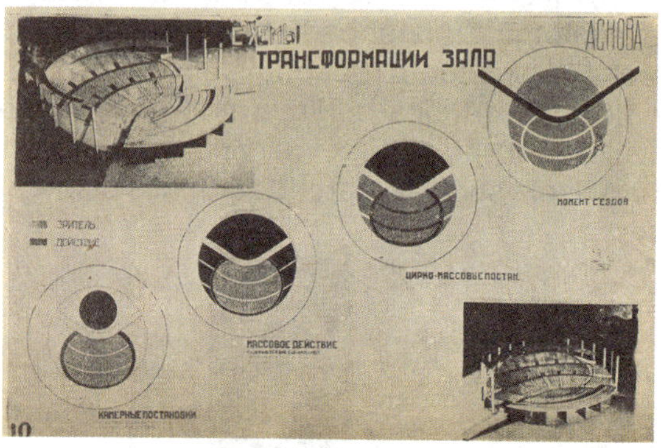

FIG 9
Asnova team: Zalesskaya, Korzhev, Prokhorova, Turkus. Competition entry for Synthetic Theater, 1930. *Soviet Architecture*, No. 1, 1932.

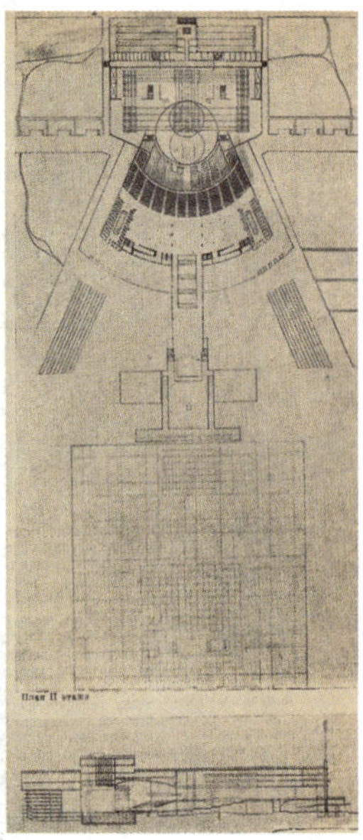

FIG 12
Nikolay Ladovsky, competition entry for Synthetic Theater, Sverdlovsk, 1930.

FIG 11
Nikolay Ladovsky, competition entry for Synthetic Theater, Sverdlovsk, 1930.

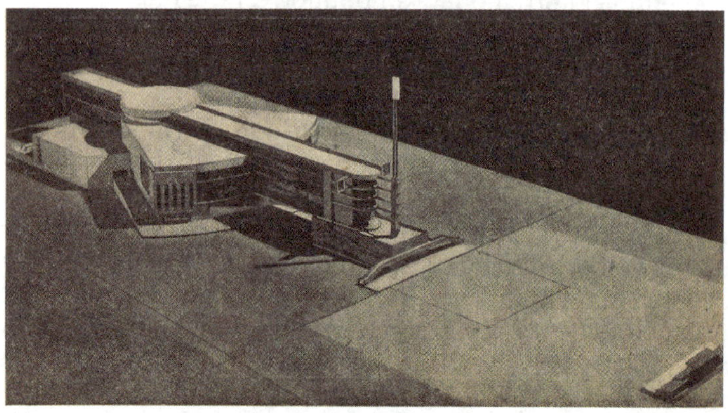

FIG 10
ARU team: Krutikov, Lavrov, Popov (bottom). Competition entry for Synthetic Theatre.

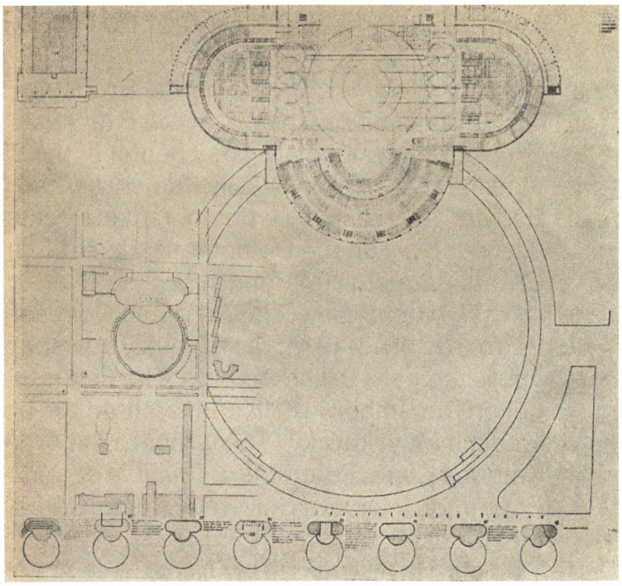

FIG 12
Nikolay Ladovsky, competition entry for Synthetic Theater, Sverdlovsk, 1930.

All of the competition entries addressed the relationship between the stage and the auditorium and proposed the transformation scenarios for the auditorium hall into different types of venue. In his analysis of the projects, architect Georgy Krutikov—a former student of Ladovsky and a graduate of Vkhutemas —made a comparative chart of the stage and seating configurations.[40] FIG 8 The project by the Asnova team was the most radical in that regard, offering the most flexible solutions for the relationship between stage and auditorium in theater performances, mass spectacles, circuses, and congressional assemblies. The stage wrapped around the seating so that the audience was placed in the center of the theater. FIG 9 ARU's design combined the theater typology with that of a tribune. The symmetrical complex intended to draw crowds in via its axial "arm," which functioned as an extension of the stage projected into the city. FIG 10 In most of the proposals the open space in front of the theater was as important as the interior. The programs of Ladovsky and Asnova initiated the theater in the outdoor plaza, similar to classical and baroque masterpieces such as Saint Peter's Square, by Bernini, and ensembles of Roman villas. The role reversal between theater and plaza recalled Bakhtin's idea of a "profane" plaza in front of a sacred edifice, interpreted as an inversion of a cathedral. He assigned primary importance to the plaza as a space for mass celebrations where all participants are both spectators and actors. This new paradigm of an anti-cathedral, where everyone was indoctrinated with a mass identity espoused by Communism, was instrumental in the creation of the proletarian culture. FIG 11, 12

FIG 14
Karo Alabyan, Vladimir Simbirtsev, Red Army Theatre (Teatr Krasnoy Armii), Moscow, 1934–1940.

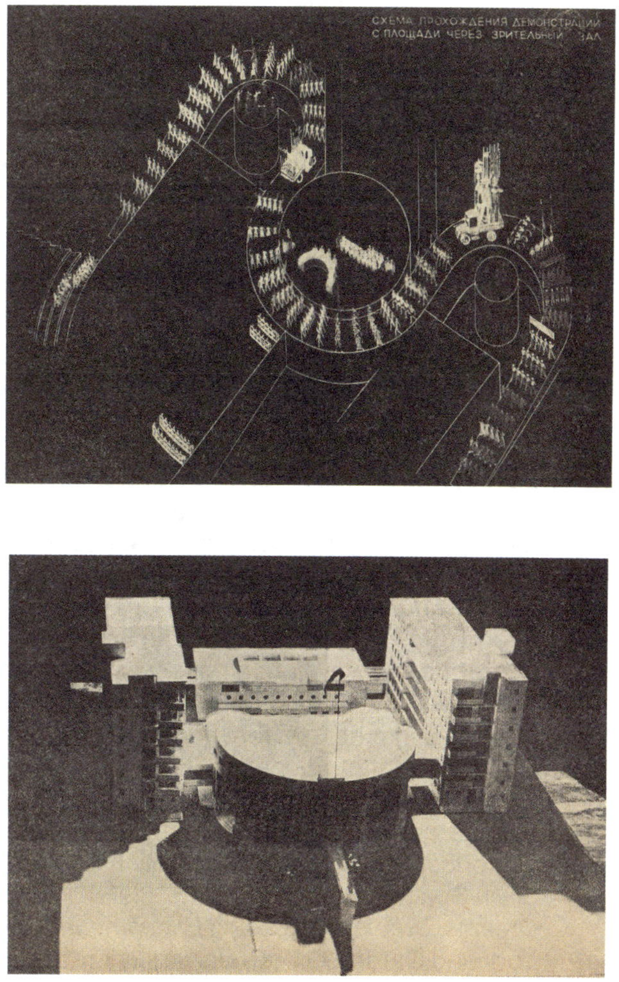

FIG 13
Gevorg Kochar, Mikael Mazmanyan, Palace of Labor and Culture, Scheme of movement through the auditorium (top), Yerevan. *Soviet Architecture*, No. 1, 1932.

Although a Synthetic Theater was never built in Sverdlovsk, it was widely publicized and its design ideas influenced multiple other projects, including the Theater for Mass Spectacle in Novosibirsk (1931) by architects Aleksandr Grinberg and Mikhail Kurilko; the Red Army Theater in Moscow (1930), completed in 1940 and shaped as a five-point star, by architects Karo Alabyan and Vladimir Simbirtsev; and the Palace of Labor and Culture in Yerevan (1931) by Gevorg Kochar and Mikael Mazmanyan. FIG 13 Civic demonstrations and military parades were incorporated into theatrical performances and at the outset of World War II military troops marched through the stage of the Red Army Theater on their way to the front lines, truly merging "art into life." FIG 14

1 Vsevolod Meyerhold, "The Reconstruction of the Theatre" (1927), in *Meyerhold on Theatre*, trans. and ed. Edward Braun (London: Methuen, 1998).
2 Meyerhold, "Reconstruction."
3 Vsevolod Meyerhold, "Actor of the Future and Biomechanics" (first presented in 1922).
4 Vsevolod Meyerhold [V. E. Mejerhol'd], *Stat'I, Pis'ma, Rechi, Besedy* [Articles, Letters, Speeches, Conversations], vol. 2 (Moscow: Iskusstvo, 1968), 488; my translation. Unless otherwise noted, all translations are my own.
5 Siegfried Kracauer, *The Mass Ornament: Weimar Essays* (1927), trans. and ed. Thomas Y. Levin (Cambridge, MA; London, England: Harvard University Press, 1995), 75.
6 P. A. Markov, *The Soviet Theatre* (London: Victor Gollancz, 1934).
7 N. A. Gorchakov, *The Theater in Soviet Russia* (New York: Columbia University Press, 1957), 201.
8 Vsevolod Meyerhold, "Velikodushnyy rogonosets" [Magnanimous Cuckold] (1922), in David Zolotnitskiy, *Budni i prazdniki teatral'nogo Oktyabrya* (Leningrad: Iskusstvo, 1978), 22.
9 Vsevolod Meyerhold, "Printsipy Teatralnogo Oktyabrya" [Principles of Theatrical October] (1920), in Selim Khan-Magomedov, *El Lissitzky* (Moscow: Russkiy Avangard, 2011).
10 Meyerhold, "Printsipy."
11 Meyerhold's State Theater [*Gosudarstvennyy teatr imeni Meyyerkhol'da*] was housed in the former "Zor" Theater, at Triumfalnaya ploschad (Mayakovsky square), in central Moscow, 1920–38. The building was demolished and a new one designed by Constructivist architects Mikhail Barkhin and Sergey Vakhtangov started construction in 1938. After Meyerhold's arrest and execution in 1940, the theater building was completed (although reduced in scope) and repurposed as the Tchaikovsky Concert Hall [*Kontsertnyy zal imeni Chaykovskogo*].
12 Leon Trotsky, "Revolutionary and Socialist Art," in *Literature and Revolution* (Moscow: Izdatel'stvo Krasnaya Nov', Glavpolitprosvet, 1923).
13 Anatoly Lunacharsky, first head of the People's Commissariat of Education [Narkompros] and mastermind behind the Soviet higher educational system, postulated that "if there is truly a proletarian concept, it is the word 'we.'" Richard Stites, "Utopia in Space: City and Building," in *Revolutionary Dreams: Utopian Vision and Experimental Life* (New York and Oxford: Oxford University Press, 1991).
14 Katerina Clark, *Petersburg, Crucible of Cultural Revolution* (Harvard University Press: Cambridge, MA; London, England, 1995), 243, 248.
15 Khan-Magomedov, *El Lissitzky*. Vsevolod Meyerhold eventually published the program in the brochure "Rekonstruktsiya teatra" [Reconstruction of Theater], 1929–30.
16 John Willett, introduction to *Erwin Piscator, 1893–1966: An Exhibition by the Archiv der Akademie der Künste Berlin, in cooperation with the Goethe Institute*, ed. Walter Huder (London: Methuen, 1978).
17 Walter Gropius, introduction to *The Theater of the Bauhaus*, ed. Walter Gropius and Arthur Wensinger, trans. Arthur Wensinger (Middletown, CT: Wesleyan University Press, 1961).
18 Oskar Schlemmer, *Theater at the Bauhaus* (1925), https://thecharnelhouse.org/2013/07/20/theater-buhne/.
19 Oskar Schlemmer, *Theater at the Bauhaus*.
20 Oskar Schlemmer, *Theater at the Bauhaus*.
21 Gropius, Introduction to The Theater of the Bauhaus.
22 Vladimir Mayakovsky, Vasily Kamensky, and David Burlyuk, "Dekret No. 1 o demokratizatsii iskusstva" [Decree No. 1 on the Democratization of Art], *Gazeta futuristov* (March 1918).
23 *Iskusstvo Kommuny* (The Art of the Commune) Petrograd, 1918–1919 was a weekly newspaper, published by IZO Narkompros. The first issue came out on December 7, 1918 and featured the poem by Vladimir Mayakovsky "The Order to the Art Army."
24 Katerina Clark, *Petersburg, Crucible of Cultural Revolution* (Harvard University Press: Cambridge, MA; London, England, 1995), 243.
25 Vladimir Mayakovsky, "An Order to the Art Army," in *Iskusstvo Kommuny* [Art of the Commune] (1918). (Moscow: Khudozhestvennaya Literatura, 1955–61).
26 Proletkult is an abbreviation for Proletarian Culture.
27 Alexander Bogdanov, *O proletarskoy kul'ture 1904–1924* [On Proletarian Culture 1904–1924] (Leningrad and Moscow: Kniga, 1924), 105.
28 "Throw away the art of the past" [*Iskusstvo proshlogo—na svalku*] was a famous revolutionary Proletkult slogan from 1919.
29 Zhivskulptarkh acronym for *Zhivopis', Skul'ptura, Arkhitektura*, translated as Commission for Painterly and Sculptural-Architectural Synthesis, an organization that was active between spring 1919 and fall 1920 in Moscow. Zhivskulptarkh was established to investigate an architectonic synthesis of spatial arts. It was the first avant-garde organization to proclaim architecture its central activity. Originally it was Sinskulptarkh (Sculptural-Architectural Synthesis), at the end of 1919 was reformed as Zhivskulptarkh.
30 Vkhutemas Russian: Вхутемас—acronym for Высшие художественно-технические мастерские (*Vysshiye Khudozhestvenno-Tekhnicheskiye Masterskiye*), translated as Higher Artistic and Technical Studios. Vkhutemas was an interdisciplinary design school founded in 1920 in Moscow, Russia, on the basis of the First and Second Svomas (Free State Art Studios)—former crafts school and fine arts college. In 1927 Vkhutemas was renamed *Vkhutein*, an acronym for Высший художественно-технический институт (*Vysshiy Khudozhestvenno-Tekhnicheskiy Institut*), translated as Higher Artistic and Technical Institute.
31 Nikolay Punin, *Pamyatnik III Internatsionala* [Monument to the III International], Petersburg: Izdanie Otdela Izobrazitelnykh Iskusstv, 1920. Author's translation.
32 Katerina Clark, *Petersburg, Crucible of Cultural Revolution* (Harvard University Press: Cambridge, MA; London, England, 1995), 248.
33 Katerina Clark, 248.

34 Katerina Clark, 248. Quote from S. Gres, "Plan velikikh rabot: Film A.Rooma," *Rit*, no. 19 (April 6, 1930), 12.

35 Anatole Kopp, *Ville et révolution: Architecture et urbanisme soviétiques des années vingt* (1967) [Town and Revolution: Soviet Architecture and City Planning, 1917–1935], trans. Thomas E. Burton (New York: George Braziller, 1970), 94.

36 Gan and Ginzburg, "Rezolutsiya", 94.

37 Gan and Ginzburg, "Rezolutsiya", 94.

38 Alexey Gan and Moisey Ginzburg, eds., "Rezolutsiya po dokladam ideologicheskoy sektsii OSA" [Resolution on the Reports of the Ideological Section of the OSA], *Sovremennaya Arkhitektura* [Modern Architecture] 3 (1928): 78.

39 Nikolay Ladovsky, "Proekt planirovki trudkommuny Kostino," [Planning of labor commune Kostino] *Stroitelstvo Moskvy* [Construction of Moscow] 7 (1929): 17.

40 Georgy Krutikov, Bolshoy syntetichesky teatr v Sverdlovske [Big Synthetic Theater in Sverdlovsk] *Sovetskaya Architektura* [Soviet Architecture] 1 (1932): 73.

Christian Art in Kerala Between Saint Thomas and Saint Peter

Cristina Osswald

Christian communities existed in southern India well ahead of Vasco da Gama's anchoring in Calicut, in 1498. Commonly known as Saint Thomas Christians, or simply Thomas Christians, these communities have a demonstrated presence in India from the fourth-century. Thomas Christians trace their origin to the conversion activity of Thomas the Apostle (circa 50AD–72AD) and they claim to keep the Apostle's tomb in Meliapor, or Mylapore (Chennai). At Portuguese arrival Thomas Christian communities inhabited an area extending from Cranganore (Kodungallur), on the west coast in what is now Kerala, south to Kochi, Kollam, and Travancore, and north along the Coromandel Coast to Chennai, in the region of Tamil Nadu. Since the majority of Indian Christians lived in a hilly region around Kochi, the Portuguese referred to them as Hill Christians (*Cristãos da Serra*).[1]

Conversion, or "reduction" (*redução*), was the Padroado Português do Oriente's principal task. In a scheme that lasted centuries, formalized by Pope Leo X in 1514, the Portuguese king was chief authority for Roman Catholic missionary activity within the geographic area under his political rule.[2] Upon first contact in 1502, the Portuguese initiated a policy to convert Thomas Christians to the 'Church of Peter', *i. e.*, to Roman Catholicism, a campaign that strengthened toward the end of the sixteenth century. In 1599 a synod was convened in Diamper (Udayamperoor) with the sole aim of subjugating the Hill Christians.[3] This was informed by observations made during a visit to Hill Christian communities led by the Archbishop of Goa Aleixo de Menezes two years previously.[4] The Indian Christians opposed this imposition of Western political-religious tradition. On January 3, 1653, Thomas Christians in Mattancherry, Kochi, broke away from Portuguese religious rule and swore to stop obeying the "Franks" (the Portuguese) and the "Paulists" (the Jesuits). This revolt, commonly known as the Bent's Oath (*Koonan Kurishu*), led to the division of the Thomas Christians into Syrian Catholic and Syrian Orthodox.[5] The Portuguese interlude in South India was relatively brief. It ended with the successive conquest of Portuguese settlements in Malabar by the Dutch, who conquered Pulicapat in 1605, Pallipuram Fort and Kollam in 1661, Cranganore in 1662, and eventually Kochi in 1663. The Dutch Calvinists eventually expelled the Portuguese and the Catholic priests.[6]

While there are distinct differences between the churches of the Indian Christians and the Catholics, the Portuguese influence on architectural and artistic production in Kerala during the sixteenth and seventeenth centuries led to distinctive interchanges. Throughout this period the complex vectors of the strategic application of architecture, along with its confrontations and adaptations among conflicting ideological systems, can be discussed in terms of the Kerala churches across three main coordinates: the distinct qualities of Indian Thomas Christian architecture, iconography, and ritual; the politics of the early Portuguese Catholic commissions in Kerala; and the mutual adaptation between different Christian faiths, each with distinct ceremonial forms and spatial models.

A South Indian legend says that Thomas the Apostle founded seven and a half churches in India: the half was a chapel.[7] The sixth-century text *Christian Topography*, attributed to Cosmas Indicopleustes, a sixth century Greek *traveler* in the Indian Ocean region, reports that Indian Christians had many churches.[8] In Sunil Edward's 2005 study of pre-Portuguese Kerala church architecture, he dates the oldest remaining structures to the late fourteenth century, the earliest to 1399 in Kallooppara.[9]

By the time the Portuguese arrived, Kerala Christians had more than one hundred churches. The Europeans noticed close similarities between these churches and Hindu temples: "built in the style of the temples," their main architectural and decorative features were similar to "houses of the idols."[10]

This native Christian religion had developed in relative isolation, and its artistic and religious traditions diverged in fundamental ways from those of the European Catholic Church. Pre-Portuguese Christian churches in Kerala followed the principles of *Vastu shastra*, the Hindu architectural design system. In the selection of a location for the construction of new temples and churches, ecological criteria such as the existence of wind and clean water are considered.[11] The architectural compound was to be surrounded by an area used for processions and purifying rituals, according to Hindu *tirtha*, the conception of sacred space as a place of passage or progression of the faithful to perfection.[12]

Walls in laterite still enclose many old Christian churches and Hindu temples, forming courts with processional and purifying functions.[13] Many, such as the St. George Forane Church, in Aruvithura (Erattupetta), were built of bamboo with thatched roofs, following ancestral South Indian tradition.[14] Before the arrival of the Portuguese, the interiors and exteriors of many Indian Christian churches were built of laterite that was left exposed rather than plastered.[15]

By the late fifteenth century a new typology demonstrated a plain facade and a projected tile roof, permitting the monsoon rain to flow easily, typified in the churches of Karthiyapalli and Thiruvithancode.[16] Most commonly, as in Kunnamkulam, a *mukha-mandapam* or *shala* (entrance porch supported by pillars and built partly in wood) or a *padippura* (gateway) led to temples and churches.[17] FIG 1 The *deepa-stambham* (oil lamp) in granite or wood still exists in front of both types of building. The raising of the *kodimaram* (flag staff or mast) during religious ceremonies is still a characteristic feature of Kerala churches. Traditionally Thomas Christian churches didn't have bells. A system of sticks hanging by two ropes called the faithful to mass.

The structures were longitudinal in plan, with two main interior zones separated by an arch: the *hykala* (derived from the Syrian word *hykalo*, which means temple), the nave or main hall for congregations; and the *madhaba* (from the Syrian word for sacrifice, *dabaha*), the chancel or altar area. FIG 2 The *madhaba* is an elevated sanctuary reached by a small staircase of two or three steps. It forms a square two-story tower-like building with a pyramidal roof higher than that of the *hykala*. This is the most important distinguishing feature of Thomas Christian churches: the Christian *madhaba*, as with the Hindu *shikara*, is the divine place linking earth to heaven. FIG 3

Some *madhabas*, such as the one in the Old Syrian Church in Chengannur, have a separate canopy roof just over the altar. As in Jain and Hindu temples, the heights of the roofs over the different sacred areas indicate their varying degrees of sacredness. The *madhaba* is accordingly the highest element, while the *mukha-mandapam* is at the lowest level.[19] The *cepo*, a spring where the faithful throw offerings, is another element without a counterpart in European ecclesiastical space.[20]

Thomas Christian churches differed further from Catholic churches in terms of their small presence. According to António de Gouveia, for example, the church of Diamper "was so narrow and low, that scarcely was it possible to raise the Most Holy Sacrament at the altar."[21] As in Hindu temples, the interiors of Thomas churches were dark, often with no windows at all, and they sometimes had an additional

FIG 2
High Altar of St. Maryan Syrian-Orthodox church of Thumpamon, District of Thiruvalla, South Kottayam, Kerala.

FIG 1
Church of Saint Mathew, Kunnamkulam, District of Thrissur, Kerala.

FIG 3
Interior of Saint Thomas Church of Thiruvithancode, Nagercoil, Kerala.

row of aisle columns.[22] There were often only three openings in church interiors: a door on the western end and two along the longer sides. In addition to natural light entering through the doors, churches were illuminated by a *nila-vilakku* (floor lamp) or a *thookku-vilakku* (hanging lamp). Early-sixteenth-century churches might also have a granite oil lamp affixed to the wall.[23]

The interiors of Indian churches were devoid of statues and other imagery. At the beginning of the sixteenth century the Portuguese Dominicans observed that crosses were the only liturgical item adorning the church interior and roof.[24] FIG 4 The *Jornada de Arcebispo de Goa Frey Aleixo de Menezes* transmitted the complaint that the churches were often very dirty and that the cross was the only adornment.[25]

Thomas Christians, on the other hand, wondered why Christian churches would have sculptures since they believed that Thomas the Apostle had forbidden them inside of churches.[26] This adoption of bare walls and ceilings has been not been explained satisfactorily by current research. It contrasts sharply with an essentially oriental idiom of decorative profusion influenced by *horror vacui*.

The Syrian influence on Kerala ecclesiastical architecture was limited to churches dedicated to Syrian martyr saints Mar Prodh and Mar Sapor and the presence of the Persian cross. Nine extant examples of these crosses have self-contained iconography with inscription in Pahlavi, the 3rd–6th-century Middle Persian language of the Sassanids, sometimes substituted by an imitation script.[27] FIG 5 The placement of the Persian cross in front of or inside the church or on the roof was a clear feature that distinguished a Thomas Christian church from a Kerala Hindu temple.

FIG 5
Old cross of the Thomas Christians. Side altar of the Holy Virgin Mary Church of Valiyapally, Kottayam, Kerala.

FIG 4
Detail of the angel of the socle of the cross. Church of Holy Mary of Thippinuttuzha, Cochin.

The impact of the Catholic presence on Kerala architecture was twofold: while the territorial and military expansion of the Portuguese was accompanied by the construction of new churches following a radically different program, alterations were also made to the Thomas Christian churches. The church of St. Francis (now St. Antony) was a Portuguese commission constructed in Kochi between 1505 and 1515, and the first European-style church built in India. FIG 6 Jordanus Catellanis, a Latin Christian, who was responsible for the building of St. Francis, implemented in the building certain features proper to the Indian churches, such as a distinct lack of interior images and sculptures.[28] As Spanish Jesuit father António Monserrate wrote in 1579:

> Their [Thomas Christians'] churches, of which there are still many, were built in the same manner as the houses of the idols of these parts. The present Archbishop sees to it that they are built in our style.[29]

This passage notes the policy of tabula rasa in church art and architecture followed under the Padroado. Catholic authorities attempted to consciously replace the traditional indigenous style of church architecture of South India with a European church archetype. That Catholic churches were different to Thomas Christian churches, both structurally and ceremonially, was inferred immediately from the imposing facades of the former in contrast to the simple, bare appearance of the latter. A huge door, or *aana vathil* (elephant door), is a Western Catholic feature.[30]

Two main categories of facade were introduced under the Padroado in Kerala: The oldest typology dates to the late sixteenth century and follows the Manueline style (a late Gothic style that developed in Portugal under King Manuel I, who ruled between 1495 and 1521, and which spread overseas to regions under Portuguese rule or influence), exemplified in the doorways of St. Anthony, in Kochi, and Our Lady of Hope, in Mattancherry, and the window frameworks and columns of Our Lady of the Hope, in Vypeen. FIG 7A, 7B Other facades have simple arched windows. Side towers were often built adjacent to either the churches or the dormitories, as can been seen at the church at Vypeen.[31] Another type of facade illustrates a Mannerist paradigm introduced in the late sixteenth century in a prototype that was essentially developed in Goa.

FIG 6
Facade of Saint Francis Church, Kochi.

FIG 7B
Late-Manueline doorway of the Our Lady of Hope Church, Vypeen, Cochin.

FIG 7A
Late-Manueline doorway of the Our Lady of Hope Church, Vypeen, Cochin.

The Franciscans, who were in continuous conflict with the Jesuits over control of the conversion of Thomas Christians, favored the use of facades with Manueline elements until as late as the seventeenth century. Their churches were also flanked by towers. By contrast, the Jesuits were at the forefront in introducing an Italian Mannerist style—*modo al romano*—in Asia. Jesuit Goan churches ranked among the first such buildings constructed in Asia and represent the powerful capacities of the Mannerist language, in turn providing a favored model for later churches within and beyond Goa. The first use of engaged columns of pilasters and the tympanum design in windows and doors was in India, at Kerala churches such as St. Mary's Forane Church in Kaduthuruthy and the old St. Paul's in Goa (1560–72).[32] FIG 8

Jesuit church facades were marked by details such as linear treatments and sharp rectilinear sections, arched doorways flanked by coupled columns, and *oculi*. The alternation of pilasters and arched windows and the use of the Corinthian order are conventions probably related to the diffusion among the missionaries of treatises by Italian architects such as Giacomo da Vignola and Sebastiano Serlio. Particularly enlightening is the following letter, dated 1567:

> Due to the fact that we are here so far away from the things of art, I dare to ask you for two books, one on perspective and another on doors, that have been compiled by Vignola, the architect of St. Peter; and also rooms of stucco houses, of which many are already in engravings.[33]

The decorative grammar of these Mannerist church facades comprises a vocabulary in strong molding work via pilasters, columns, pediments, friezes, and fan-shaped alettes with radiating striations. FIG 9 Conch-shell volutes framing the gable are a Lombard-Venetian motif first employed by Mauro Codussi in the Chiesa di San Michele in Isola (1469–78) and imported to India on the facade of the Jesuit Basilica of the Bom Jesus, in Goa. It is worth noting that features such as the treatment of the facade, double columns, and the alternation between rectangular and circular forms were appropriated in turn by the later Dutch church builders.

Kerala catholic church architecture contributed to a fervent religious life with frequent ceremonies. Under the Padroado, many people received the sacraments of confession and Eucharist.[34] The churches had to be large enough to host the crowds on special holidays and saint days. The first Catholic churches had carved wooden balconies for priests.[35] The conversion of Thomas Christians to the law of Peter pursued under Portuguese rule was symbolized by the introduction of particular features in older churches. The king of Portugal John III (João III) sent bells to be installed in former Thomas Christian churches. The Synod of Diamper required the replacement of sticks with bells, housed in new steeples constructed alongside churches. Belfries were attached to the main facades to one side of the nave walls or built as separate bell towers, as still seen in the Holy Ghost Forane Church, in Muttuchira. Kottayam. In accordance with the biblical decree of John 1:5 ("God is light"), Catholic authorities were very concerned about the interior darkness of Indian indigenous churches, and the assembly of Diamper decreed that windows be opened into the clerestories.[36]

FIG 9
Main facade of the Church of Saint Thomas of Palai, District of Kottayam, Kerala.

FIG 8
Ruins of the façade of the second church of Old Saint Paul, Goa.

The churches built by agents of the Padroado were single-nave two-story buildings with windows on the first floor. The structures were greater in width and height than the early churches commissioned by local Christians to accommodate the new architectural elements and liturgical equipment. A triumphal arch separated the nave from the high altar. A church plan comprising a high chapel flanked by two side chapels was favored.[37]

Baptismal fonts were used in Kerala churches prior to the arrival of the Portuguese, but they were not always permanent. For that reason, the assembly at Diamper ordered permanent baptismal fonts installed in all churches as soon as possible.[38] As in the Church of Our Lady of Life, in Mattancherry, they were made of materials such as plastered and painted laterite.[39]

The application of reason through the power of words was inherent to the conversion of the public to Tridentine Catholicism and was thus transposed to missionary contexts overseas. Applying this mandate to church architecture, the Synod of Diamper determined that a pulpit be built in all churches with the physical capacity.[40] An imposing wood pulpit, or *pushpam*, reaching a height of two to three meters was thus a fundamental fixture marking church interiors. Moreover, elaborately carved wood altarpieces were gilded or polychromatic and set in a superstructure of varying levels.

> Whereas almost all the churches of this diocese are without *retables*, which was the effect of their being governed by Nestorian vicars who do not allow of the healthful use of sacred images, therefore the Synod orders that the first pious work done out of the church's alms, after that of the Baptismal font, would be the *retables* that will be done according to their patron saint, and the directions of the prelate, who shall always be consulted about every picture.[41]

This extract of the Diamper Synod's decree illustrates the relevance of altars, altarpieces, and retables, as interpreted by the Council of Trent on the sacredness of relics and images of divine figures. For the Catholics, likenesses of sacred figures and events have above all a representative value as incarnations of the divine or saintly nature of the subject they portray.

The oldest altarpieces extant in Kerala manifest a late Mannerist language. The compositions often show cherubs and soldier figures supporting ornaments of twisted grapevines, corn, wheat, or acanthus leaves. The flora species they depicted, also found in the décor of other Indian Catholic churches, were native to Europe and not grown in India.

FIG 10
Side gallery of the Saint Augustine's Forane Church of Ramapuram. District of Kottoyam, Kerala.

Padroado missionaries ordered the painting of exquisite fresco cycles in churches such as St. George Orthodox Church, in Cheppad; St. Mary's Jacobite Syrian Cathedral, in Piravom; St. George Orthodox Church, in Paliakkara; the Mor Sabor and Afroth Jacobite Syrian Orthodox Cathedral, in Akaparambu; and the impressive St. Anthony's Forane Church, in Ollur. Accompanied by oil paintings and carved wooden and ivory sculptures.[42]

The accommodation strategy in Kerala describes the process of adapting European church architecture to local climatic conditions. This adaptive process generated, in turn, new and innovative alterations to imported archetypes. This process is in many ways separate to the program for the alteration of St Thomas churches. New Roman Catholic churches were built or rebuilt; one of the older local churches in Palur was repurposed. In these constructions the local architecture, Thomas Christian and Hindu, was suggested in both structural and decorative aspects. Churches might have loggias or open galleries with roofs supported by columns to provide vital air circulation in humid and extremely hot areas. FIG 10 Elaborately embellished rectilinear facades correspond to the Indian predilection for *horror vacui*. The conch-shell volutes on vernacular church facades recall the decorative Indian spinning wheels (*chakra*).[43]

The cross of the Holy Ghost Forane Church in Muttuchira, erected in 1528 (prior to the Portuguese exploration of the area), is one of the oldest known examples of an open-air granite cross. In 1599 Archbishop De Menezes inaugurated another open-air cross, in front of the Church of Our Lady, in Kaduthuruthy.[44] FIG 11 The origin of this type of cross—which rises up to twelve meters high and contains an oil lamp—is both important and relatively obscure. A distinctive feature of Indo-Portuguese Christian art and architecture, the open-air cross bears affinities with the offering altar in Hindu temples (*balikkal pura*). Reflecting motifs from Thomas Christian material culture, they normally have quadrangular bases topped by circular lotus-shaped surfaces. FIG 12 Like the Hindu altars, the crosses might be placed at the entrance to the inner precincts.

Most Kerala churches have a vaulted roof over the high chapel, recalling a popular element of sixteenth- and seventeenth-century Indo-Portuguese churches as well as Syrian Christian architecture and the Buddhist *viharas*.[45] At the end of the sixteenth century a distinction was made between Catholic churches for the lower castes and those for former Saint Thomas Christians, who were historically members of the elite, alongside Brahmins.[46] Indeed, church design and architecture reflected the highly stratified local caste system. When no separate churches existed for different social groups, either separate buildings or sections of the church were arranged.[47] More elaborate Thomas Christian churches could have three naves in their plans.

Churches of elite communities were distinguished with coffered stone or wooden barrel-vaulted ceilings in chapels, as well as richer decoration expressed in bas-reliefs combining European and Asian iconographies on the facades.[48] Kerala indigenous architecture further reflects gender differentiation: a screen separated the front area of churches, intended for men, from the rear, where women were to worship. Some churches had separate entrances for men and women.[49]

Christian crosses, altarpieces, pulpits, and baptismal basins in South India borrow a great number of iconographic elements from the Asian context. The bases of pulpits were usually carved in the shape of an elephant's trunk. Peacocks, lions, monkeys, and lotus flowers frequently decorated early modern stone and wood sculpture in the Catholic churches. The representations of angels are analogous to Christian depictions of angels in Persia and figures in Buddhist temples. FIG 13 Facades often have side panels bearing exotic dragons, an allusion to the myth of Vritra and the healing potential of the first waters.[50]

There were various reasons for such crossovers, and the Europeans absolved local traditions and rituals both voluntarily and involuntarily. The long distances, the existence of well-developed building traditions and artistic castes, and the chronic scarcity of European materials and techniques forced the Catholic Church to appropriate local methods of construction in South India. In the early 1560s Pope V permitted the Thomas Christians to keep some particular, if relatively unimportant, customs while accommodations to the local context were imposed on Roman Catholics.[51] During his visit Menezes ordered the bells of the church in Moothedath to be transferred from the belfry due to complaints Hindus made about their ringing.[52] In 1619 the Indian Christians destroyed a church built by the Portuguese in Cranganore because its style differed from that of their own churches.[53] In 1601 Jesuit missionary and architect Jacome Fenizio mentioned the local superstition according to which the destruction of churches would be the cause of misfortunes:

FIG 12
Detail of the Monumental Cross at St. Mary's Church, Kaduthuruthy, District of Kottoyam, Kerala.

FIG 11
Monumental cross at the St. Mary's Church, Kaduthuruthy, District of Kottayam, Kerala, and which was inaugurated by D. Aleixo de Menezes in 1599.

FIG 13
Detail of the angel in the socle of the cross at the Church of Our Lady of Trippunittuzha, outskirts of Kochi.

> The stone church which I began two years ago [at Palayoor] had risen to the height of windows. At this stage, no one would dare to pull down the old wooden building, fearing to be struck down by sudden death: it stood surrounded by the walls of new erection, but after I prayed and removed their timidity, the old structure was pulled down, and the new building stood out in such fine proportions that the Hindus, the Mohammedans, and the Jews flocked to see it.[54]

In 1548 the Jesuits settled in Kochi near the Vettukad church Madre de Deus (Mother of God). This marked the beginning of Jesuit missionary activity among the Thomas Christians in South India. Assigned to the Jesuits by the king of Portugal, Madre De Deus developed into a college and the primary departure point for missionaries working among the Hill Christians. Jesuit residences and colleges contributed to the shaping of local architecture and devotion. Jesuit settlements extended across a larger region than the others and were more strategically located. As early as 1549 the Jesuits had a college in Coulão (Kollam), an important seaport and pepper-trading center on the banks of Ashtamudi Lake.[55] They were responsible for principal shrines such as the Chinnamalai, or Little Mount, venerated as the place of Saint Thomas's martyrdom. Moreover, they had churches in important settlements of Thomas Christians such as Alangad and Vaipicota, near Cranganore.[56]

Jesuit enterprise in Thomas Christian communities expanded rapidly. In 1565 the order ran only one church, Our Lady of Assumption, in Mampally, south of Kollam.[57] By 1571 priests held mass in nineteen churches in the area.[58] Jesuit missionary activity intensified with the establishment in 1578 of a residence later transformed into the College of the Holy Cross, in Vaipicota (Pallipuram), on the northern part of Vypeen Island not far from Kudangallur, an important settlement of Thomas Christians.[59] By the early seventeenth century the Jesuits operated three schools to instruct the children of Thomas Christians: College of the Mother of God at Kochi, College of the Holy Cross at Vaipicota, the ecclesiastical center of Thomas Christians, and College of the Savior at Kollam.[60]

The success of the Jesuit endeavor was due largely to their ability to bring about favorable legislation and attract generous patronage. Phillip II of Portugal determined in 1610 that only priests acquainted with local languages should lead churches.[61] This policy benefited the Jesuits, who were, together with the Franciscans, the most reputed experts of Indian languages. The Jesuits had a monopoly on the conversion of the Hill Christians until 1628, when the king of Portugal authorized the Dominicans to build a church at Kaduthuruthy.[62] The Jesuits also profited from their good relationship with Indian authorities: In a letter written in 1600, Nicolau Pimenta enumerated a series of benefits the king of Purakkad had bestowed upon the Jesuits, including permission to build churches and set up crosses and belfries in areas they chose.[63]

As in other missionary areas such as Paraguay and Brazil, the Jesuit principle *non cantat* gave way to local recognition of the usefulness of music. Thus, priests meeting at the First Congregation for the Province of India in 1575 decided to keep music in the churches since it was thought to be particularly helpful in the conversion of indigenous people.[64] Accordingly the internal arrangement of churches like St. Mary's in Kochi and St. John the Baptist in Paravur were modified to include choirs.[65]

The Jesuits shared the discourse of magnificence favored by the Padroado. The Dutch followers of Baldaeaus were astonished by the "lofty steeple" of the Jesuit church in Kochi and the "stately chapels and steeples" adorning their church in Nagapattinam.[66] The Jesuits paid great attention to the external aspects of cult, filling churches with religious paraphernalia such as sacred statues and pictures. In 1550 Jesuit priest Mateus Dias asked the king of Portugal to send ornaments, clothing, chalices, bells, retables, and other objects necessary for the cult. The *Annual Letter* of 1597 for India reports that the shrines kept by the Jesuits among Saint Thomas Christians had been decorated with great care.[68] Similarly, according to the *Annual Letter* of 1600, the church of the College of Kochi was enriched with two new retables and the choir was embellished with exquisite woodwork.[69]

The Kerala Thomas Christian community had a sophisticated religious identity, expressed in a holistic artistic and architectural legacy. From the late sixteenth century Portuguese authorities reinforced their policy to subjugate the community to the Roman Papacy, and their presence brought considerable changes to Thomas Christian art. Working under the Padroado, the Catholic Church largely succeeded in replacing Thomas Christian architecture and art with an alien ecclesiastical style, *i.e.* a Roman Catholic language. FIG 13 At the same time, Catholic art in Kerala was indigenized, and the Jesuits led this complex process. Along with the Franciscans, they contributed decisively to the introduction of Kerala Thomas Christian church artistic traditions into the globalized conception of religious art and architecture in the early modern era.

1 Matthias Mundadan, *History of Christianity in India, from the Beginning Up to the Middle of the 16th century* (Bangalore: Theological Publications in India, 1982).

2 Roland Jacques, *De Castro Marim à Faifo: Naissance et développement du Padroado portugais d'Orient des origines à 1659* (Lisbon: Fundação Calouste Gulbenkian, 1999). This work remains the most comprehensive analysis of the political-ecclesiastical system of Padroado.

3 The proceedings of the Diamper Synod were first published in Coimbra in 1606. This paper uses the latest Portuguese version: J. O. Bragança, ed., "O sínodo de Diamper," *Didaskalia* 14 (1984): 247–61.

4 Augustinian friar António de Gouveia compiled a detailed description of that visit in 1599. A first edition in Portuguese was published in 1606. The English version from 2003 is referenced in this work. See António de Gouveia, *Jornada of Dom Aleixo de Menezes: A Portuguese Account of the Sixteenth-Century Malabar*, trans. Pius Malekandathil (Kochi: LRC Publications, 2003).

5 Dyron B. Daughrity, "The Indianness of Christianity: The Task of Re-imagination," in *Re-imagining South Asian Religions: Essays in Honour of Professors Harold G. Coward and Ronald W. Neufeldt*, ed. Pashaura Singh and Michael Hawley (Leiden: Brill, 2013), 245–69.

6 This occurred in Maliankara (near Kodungallur), Kottakaavu (North Paravur), Palayur (near Chavakad, Trichur district), Niranan (near Thiruvalla), Kollam (Karikkoni Kollam), Kokkamangalam (near Vaikkom), Nilakkal (or Chayal, near Shabarimala), and Thiruvithamcode, respectively. See Charles Borges, "India," in *The Blackwell Companion to Catholicism*, ed. James Buckley, Frederick Bauerschmid, and Trent Pomplun (Malden, UK: Blackwell, 2007), 114.

7 Paul Thomas, *Churches in India* (New Delhi: Ministry of Information and Broadcasting. Government of India, 1990), 13.

8 John McCrindle, trans., *The Christian Topography of Cosmas, an Egyptian Monk* (Cambridge, UK: Cambridge University Press, 2010), 120.

9 Sunil Edward, "A Study of Indigenous Church Architecture of Kerala State" (PhD diss., Indian Institute of Technology Roorkee, 2005), 299.

10 Sumam Panjikaran and Ranee Maria Vedamuthu, "An Evaluation of Spatial Organization of the Church Architecture of Kerala during the Sixteenth to Seventeenth Centuries," *Journal of the Institution of Engineers India Series* 94 (May 2013): 125.

11 Gouveia, *Jornada of Dom Aleixo de Menezes*, 29–30.

12 George Mitchell, *The Hindu Temple: An Introduction to Its Meaning and Forms* (Chicago: University of Chicago Press, 1977), 82.

13 Edward, "Indigenous Church Architecture," 214–62.

14 Andrew Athappilly, "Thomas Christian Architecture," in *The St. Thomas Christian Encyclopaedia of India*, vol. 2, ed. George Menachery and Edward René Hambye (Trichur, India: St. Thomas Christian Encyclopaedia of India, 1973), 441–42.

15 Sunil Edward, "A Prelude to the Study of Indigenous, Pre-European Church Architecture of Kerala," *Creative Space* 1.2 (January 2014): 167.

16 Edward, "Indigenous Church Architecture," 85, 284.

17 Edward, "Indigenous Church Architecture," 110.

18 Helder Carita, *Arquitectura Indo-Portuguesa: na região de Cochim e Kerala* (Lisbon: Transbooks, 2008), 157–58.

19 Edward, "Indigenous Church Architecture," 269, 280, 286, 303.

20 Gouveia, *Jornada of Dom Aleixo de Menezes*, 299.

21 Gouveia, *Jornada of Dom Aleixo de Menezes*, 34.

22 Andrews Athappilly, "Thomas Christian Architecture," 437.
23 Edward, "Indigenous Church Architecture," 191, 209.
24 As noted by Ines Zupanov, *Missionary Tropics: The Catholic Frontier in India (16th–17th Centuries)* (Ann Arbor, MI: University of Michigan Press, 2005), 97. For Zupanov's reference see Gaspar Corrêa, *Lendas da India* (Lisbon: Na Typographia da Academia Real das Sciencias, 1858).
25 Gouveia, *Jornada of Dom Aleixo de Menezes*, 244.
26 "Letter of Álvaro Penteado to the King of Portugal, between 1515 and 1518," *Documentação para a história das missões do padroado português do Oriente: Índia (1499–1522)*, vol. 1, ed. Isabel Murta Pina and Adriano Moreira Pina José da Silva Rego (Lisbon: Fundação Oriente and Comissão Nacional para a Comemoração dos Descobrimentos Portugueses, 1991), 176.
27 Istvan Perczel, "Monuments of Indian Christian Art: Problems of Genres, Dating, and Context," in *Christianity in Asia: Sacred Art and Visual Splendour*, ed. Pedro de Moura Carvalho et. al. (Singapore: Asian Civilisations Museum, 2016), 45.
28 Panjikaran and Vedamuthu, "An Evaluation," 126.
29 "Letter of Father António Monserrate SJ to General Everard Mercurian, Cochi, the 12 January 1579," *Documenta Indica (1577–1580)*, vol. 2, ed. Josef Wicki (Rome: Institutum Historicum Societatis Iesu, 1950), 518.
30 Edward, "Indigenous Church Architecture," 193.
31 José Manuel Fernandes, "Vestígios do Manuelino na arquitectura religiosa de influência portuguesa na Índia: Malabar, Coromandel, Goa," *Oceanos* 19/20 (September–December 1994): 136–38.
32 Falk Reitz, "The Western Facade of St Mary's Church (Martha Mariam Forane Church) in Kaduthuruthi (Kottayam Dt., Kerala)," *Berliner Indologische Studien* 13/14 (Berlin: Verlag für Orientalische Fachpublikationen, 2000), 420–22.
33 "Letter of Martin Ochoa to General Francisco Borja, December 12, 1567", *Documenta Indica (1566–1569)*, vol. 7 (Rome: Institutum Historicum Societatis Iesu, 1962), 409.
34 The artistic evidence and the sources consulted for this paper don't permit the author to infer the popularity of confessionals in the form of wooden structures in Tridentine church interiors in South India. Nevertheless, she is committed to continuing research on the subject.
35 Edward, "Indigenous Church Architecture," 86, 213.
36 Diamper Synod, *Action VIII: The Reform of Ecclesiastic Matters*, decree 28, 422.
37 Helder Carita, "Arquitectura Indo-Portuguesa na Região do Sul da Índia e o impacto da arte dos cristãos de São Tomé da Índia na formação de tipologias e linguagens na arquitectura colonial," in *A arte no mundo português no sécs. XVI, XVII e XVIII, V. Colóquio Luso-Brasileiro de História de Arte*, ed. Francisco Lameiras (Faro, Portugal: Universidade Do Algarve, 2005), 50.
38 Diamper Synod, *Action IV: Doctrine of the Holy Baptism and Confirmation*, decree 19, 324–26.
39 Panjikaran and Vedamuthu, "An Evaluation," 129.
40 Diamper Synod, *Action VIII, The Reform of Ecclesiastic Matters*, decree 29, 422.
41 Diamper Synod, *Action VIII, The Reform of Ecclesiastic Matters*, decree 29, 422.zzz
42 Carita, *Arquitectura Indo-Portuguesa*, 179.
43 Carita, *Arquitectura Indo-Portuguesa*, 168.
44 Carita, *Arquitectura Indo-Portuguesa*, 70.
45 Edward, "Indigenous Church Architecture," 71.
46 David Mosse, *The Saint in the Banyan Tree: Christianity and Caste Society in India* (Berkeley: University of California Press, 2012), 4.
47 K. T. Mathewkutty, "The Synod of Diamper and Its Aftereffects on the Socio-Cultural Life of the St. Thomas Christians of India during the 17th century AD" (PhD diss., University of Mysore, 2003), 55, 272.
48 Carita, *Arquitectura Indo-Portuguesa*, 201.
49 Edward, "Indigenous Church Architecture," 196–97.
50 Helder Carita, "Religious Architecture: Malabar/Kerala," in *Portuguese Architecture around the World, Architecture and Urbanism, Asia and Oceania*, ed. José Mattoso et. al. (Lisbon: Fundação Calouste Gulbenkian, 2011), 348.
51 "Francisco Dionisio, Rector of the Jesuit college of Vaipicota to General Everard Mercurian, Cochin," January 2, 1578, in *Documenta Indica (1577–1580)*, vol. 11 (Rome: Institutum Historicum Societatis Iesu, 1970), 64–65.
52 Gouveia, *Jornada of Dom Aleixo de Menezes*, 365.
53 Domenico S. J. Ferroli, *The Jesuits in Malabar*, vol. 1 (Bangalore: Bangalore Press, 1939), 355.
54 "Annual Letter for the Province of India 1601", Archivum Romanum Societatis Iesu, Rome, Italy, GOA 55, Fol. 206.
55 Sebastião Gonçalves, "Primeira parte da História dos Religiosos das Companhia de Jesus," in *História da Companhia de Jesus no Oriente (1560–1570)*, vol. 1, ed. Josef Wicki (Coimbra, Portugal: Atlântida, 1957), 296.
56 Gouveia, *Jornada of Dom Aleixo de Menezes*, 136.
57 "Letter of André Fernandes to Father Nunes Barreto, January 1565", *Documenta Indica (1567–1569)*, vol. 7 (Rome: Institutum Historicum Societatis Iesu, 1962), 447, note 5.
58 "Catalogue of the churches, places, and number of Christians between Coulon and Comorin Coast, Quilon, 7 January 1571," in *Documenta Indica (1569–1573)*, vol. 8 (Rome: Institutum Romanum Socieatis Iesu, 1964), 122–23.
59 Ines Zupanov, "'One Civility, But Multiple Religions': Jesuit Mission among St. Thomas Christians in India (16th–17th Centuries)," *Journal of Early Modern History* 9 (January 2005): 302–3.
60 Sebastião Gonçalves, "Primeira parte da História dos Religiosos das Companhia de Jesus," in *História da Companhia de Jesus no Oriente (1560–1570)*, vol. 3, ed. Josef Wicki (Coimbra, Portugal: Atlântida, 1962), 307.
61 "Royal Law of the 25th February 1610," in *Documentos remetidos da India ou livro das Monções*, vol. 1, ed. R. A. Bulhão Pato (Lisbon: Academia Real das Sciências 1880, 359.
62 Domenico Ferroli, *The Jesuits in Malabar*, vol. 1 (Bangalore, India: King, 1951), 363.

63 "Letter of the Jesuit Visitor of India Father Nicolau Pimenta da Companhia to General Claudia Acquaviva, Goa, the 1th December of 1600," *Cartas que o Padre Nicolao Pimenta da Companhia de Jesu Visitador nas partes do Oriente da mesma companhia, escreveo ao Géral della à 26. de Nove[m]bro do ano de 1599. & ao 1. de Dezembro de 600. nas quaes entre algu[m]as cousas notaveis & curiosas q[ue] conta de diversos reinos, relata o sucesso da insigne victoria q[ue] Andre Furtado de Mendoça alcãçou do Cunhale grande perseguidor da Fee & Christãdade da India & cruel inimigo daquelle estado* (Lisbon: Pedro Craesbeck, 1602, 82.

64 Cristina Osswald, *Written in Stone: Jesuit Buildings in Goa and Their Artistic and Architectural Features* (Goa, India, Porto, Portugal and Pamplona, Spain: Goa 1556 and Golden Heart Emporium Bookshop / Universidade do Porto and Universidad de Navarra, 2013), 262.

65 Gasparo Balbi, *Viaggio nelle Indie Orientali* (Venice: Apresso Camillo Borgominieri, 1590), 86.

66 Phillipus Baldaeus, "A True and Exact Description of the Most Celebrated East-India Coasts of Malabar and Coromandel; as Also of the Isle of Ceylon," in *A Collection of Voyages and Travels*, vol. 2, ed. Awnsham Churchill (London: A. and J. Churchill, 1704), 165.

67 "Letter of Father Mateus Dias to the King of Portugal," December 22, 1550", *Documentação para a história das missões do padroado português do Oriente: Índia (1499–1522)*, vol. 4, ed. Isabel Murta Pina and Adriano Moreira Pina José da Silva Rego (Lisbon: Fundação Oriente and Comissão Nacional para a Comemoração dos Descobrimentos Portugueses, 1992) 478.

68 "Annual Letter for the Province of India (1597)," *Documenta Indica (1595–1597)*, ed. vol. 18 (Rome: Institutum Historicum Socieatatis Iesu, 1988), 919.

69 "Annual Letter for the Province of India (1600)", Archivum Romanum Societatis Iesu, Rome, Italy, GOA 55, Fol. 39.

Building and Resistance in Barbados

Emily Mann

March 31, 2018

It is Saturday afternoon on Easter weekend and, as on most days in the small, palm-fringed island of Barbados in the eastern Caribbean, hundreds of people are on the beach. Children are busy with buckets and spades, adults are lazing on sun loungers, and roaming vendors are touting their wares. Not everyone has come to soak up the high-season sun or make a sale, however. Indeed, the skies are ominously overcast—and yet, despite impending showers, scores of islanders have gathered to draw a line in the sand and have their voices heard. One voice rising above the rest is that of the crown-winning calypsonian and government-appointed cultural ambassador Anthony "The Mighty Gabby" Carter who, armed with his guitar, leads the protest along the length of the beach to the tune of a renowned resistance song he first performed in 1982. The calypso sound is typically up-tempo, seemingly carefree, but the title—"Jack (Dah Beach is Mine)"—announces the political message and stirs the sleepy coastal strip into contested space. Gabby recites, in biting Barbadian creole:

> Jack doan want me to bade on my beach
> Jack tell dem to keep me outta reach
> Jack tell dem, I would never make de grade dey
> Strengthen security and build barricade ...

The song, created a decade and a half after Barbados gained independence from Britain in 1966, was "a reaction to an action," as Gabby put it; a counterattack to a statement by Jack Dear, a corporate lawyer then serving as chair of the Barbados Tourist Board, that hoteliers and other coastal land-owners had the right to develop their properties down to the high water line.[1] For Gabby and others, this signaled the privatization and segregation of the beloved beaches where they grew up bathing, a denial of their birthright. Gigging in a hotel one evening, Gabby was asked by a white woman to "play some local music." Jack Dear was at the same hotel that night and so the song was sparked. The lyrical repetition of "Jack" through the song rendered his name a symbol of oppression: "I want Jack to know that dah beach belong ta we," Gabby retorted. It was a matter not simply of access, but also of identity. Gabby conjured the beach as the root of his very being with the graphic line "My navel string buried right here," whereas "a touris' one could be anywhere."

For a song written as an act of resistance, it is fitting that the recording was made in a studio that the legendary Guyanese-British musician Eddy Grant had recently built in Barbados on the site of a former slave plantation. It was from the same plantation, moreover, that the African-born slave Bussa reputedly led the largest rebellion in the island's history on Easter Sunday, 1816.[2] Deemed as negative publicity for the tourism industry, the song was banned from Barbados national radio, which if anything guaranteed its popularity. "Tourism vital, I can't deny," Gabby acknowledged in the song, "But can't mean more than I and I." The insistent "I and I" at once conveyed Rasta consciousness (outer and inner self) and asserted the united force of the collective "you and me"—that is, "we." Gabby was giving expression to many people's resentment, fear and willingness to fight. The song was a hit. A silver plaque displayed on the wall of Grant's Ice Records office celebrates sales of 20,000 copies, a higher figure than achieved by any earlier record in Barbados history.[3]

Gabby never imagined that four decades later, aged 70, he would still be singing "Dah beach belong ta we!" in protest. In all those years, the song has lost none of its relevance. Its assertion of islanders' rights to the space of the beach perhaps has more resonance than ever. Barbados beaches may be proclaimed public, or at least publicly accessible, but since the 1980s they have been increasingly policed and the presence of local residents restricted or controlled, especially if their activities have been deemed to disturb the comfort and enjoyment of tourists.[4] A combination of coastal development driven by tourism and coastal erosion hastened by climate change has diminished stretches of beach and exacerbated tensions between property-owners and local beach-users. The protest on March 31, 2018, FIG 1 was a response to action taken by management at the Crane resort on the south coast, which was bought by the Canadian entrepreneur Paul Doyle in 1988 and transformed from an 18-room historic hotel to a 265-room (and still growing) luxury complex. In early March, the hotel management had taken beach chairs belonging to independent vendors and locked them in a container. This confiscation-cum-eviction caused an outcry, to which the owner responded by arguing the vendors were unfairly conducting business on his land, and by calling on the government to proceed with a 'rehabilitation' project to expand the beach (using imported sand and protective boulders) and thus reduce future encroachment on his property and his profits.[5]

As the Barbadian historian Tara Inniss has noted, whether the chairs are set up by hoteliers or vendors, their spread across the island's beaches has formed an unhealthy barricade between private and public property; they are a "land grab" that infringes on local people's freedom to use the beach.[6] Yet, in its pitting of expat white property-owner—and predominantly white vacationers whose business he was claiming for himself—against local black workers, the Crane chair controversy brought to the surface deeper and wider feelings of injustice about the tourist industry, and its semblance of a modern plantation system in Barbados and beyond.[7] Just as the Trinidad-born writer V. S. Naipaul starkly observed in his independence-era travelogue *The Middle Passage* (1962) that the Caribbean countries opening up to tourism were "selling themselves into a new slavery," Gabby promoted his 2018 protest with the declaration: "The tourism industry as practised in the Caribbean is an upgrade of the slave trade."[8]

The continuities of the plantation economy that Norwell Harrigan observed in the development of tourism in the mid-1970s still resound—foreign ownership, expatriate or local elite management, and black workers.[9] Tourism reigns much as sugar did in a single-crop economy; the tourist has supplanted the cane as king.[10] The sand churned up by Gabby's protest march among the sun loungers drew attention to how the continuity of past segregation and subjugation in the service economy of the present is most visually perceptible and physically felt on the beach. Such is the contested character of the space that even the meaning of the word "beach" is disputed here, with interpretations as fluid as the high water mark itself. The debates surrounding its definition underline how the coastal zone has become, to borrow Polly Pattullo's phrase, "a function of the tourist industry," as it once was of the sugar industry, rather than "an intrinsic part of local life."[11] The hotel owner's description of the beaches of Barbados as "the island's most important natural resource" cannot help but carry, in the context of the island's colonial history, the threat of their exploitation for external benefit—hence Gabby's insistence that "the first grain of sand belongs to us."[12] He warns the Easter 2018 protest is just "the beginning of a war," but the battle lines have long been drawn along these golden shores, and the barricades are merely taking a new form.

July 1, 1631

Five weeks and five days after departing Weymouth, on England's south coast, the crew of the *Alexander* caught sight of land—so "low and hard to finde" that many ships missed it completely—and came to anchor in Carlisle Bay, a crescent-shaped natural harbor in the southwest of Barbados named for the colonial proprietor James Hay, 1st Earl of Carlisle.[13] The ship carried sixteen large guns to guard its great timber walls and mast, along with four squadrons of musketeers marshaled and trained to fight. It was a floating fort, or a sailing citadel, which unusually

FIG 2
A Topographicall Description and Admeasurement of the Yland of Barbados in the West Indyaes from Richard Ligon, *A True and Exact History of the Island of Barbados* (London, 1657).

FIG 1
Poster for "Dah Beach Belong Ta We" protest, March 31, 2018.

favorable conditions had helped "glide over the face" of the ocean rather than "rudely plough it upp."[14] Thanking God for the providentially smooth voyage was the expedition's leader Sir Henry Colt, a wealthy Essex landowner on a mission to establish a new estate on the island of St Christopher (St Kitts), located around 300 miles to the northwest.[15] During the couple of weeks that the *Alexander* lay over at Barbados, loading fustic wood and tobacco, Colt explored the English settlement—which had now been under way for almost five years—and made notes in his journal.

Observing the productive soil and climate, Colt described in detail the abundant variety of trees, plants and animal life, all of which pleased him so much he wished the island were "my owne & thus seated in any part of Europe."[16] Only sloth and negligence could cause the inhabitants of such a place to suffer want, he declared—the problem being that he judged the settlers dangerously prone to both. The drunken quarrels and evasion of work were a serious concern, but it was the lack of security that literally kept Colt awake at night. "Wher your assembly for armes?" he begged. "Whatt places have you for defence?" So weak did he perceive the land to be against an enemy, such as the Spanish who loomed large in his fears, that he believed himself "in greater securitye in our shipp," despite finding himself its only guard. By mid-July, he left "this land of discord" with no small relief.[17] On arrival in St Kitts, Colt pitched up a tent by the beach, this flimsy temporary home at least located reassuringly close to the "old fort."[18]

The construction of coastal fortifications during the first decade of settlement in Barbados was hindered by divisions and disgruntlements that stemmed from a conflict over the colonial proprietorship between the Earl of Carlisle and another claimant, Sir William Courteen, and were exacerbated by Carlisle's laissez-faire attitude to his possession. Richard Ligon, an English royalist who lived in exile on the island between 1647 and 1650, observed that one particular fort designed to command the whole of Carlisle Bay was in the process of being pulled down and rebuilt, having been found "most pernicious" and "not of strength to defend it self."[19] On the map included in Ligon's *True and Exact History of the Island of Barbados,* FIG 2 first published in 1657, there are no signs of forts. The only defense appears to be a row of guns either side of the bay, which would have proved about as effective as the imported camels seen decorating the map inland. The colony's security had been so neglected by the Earl of Carlisle, Ligon wrote, that its planters refused to call him "proprietor."[20]

The new defenses under construction from the late 1640s consisted of a chain of coastal forts, batteries, platforms and earthworks, a linear system similar to that which the governor of Barbados from 1640 to 1650, Philip Bell, had previously overseen as governor of the shortlived colony of Providence Island (the forts there having warded off the Spanish once but not for long). The line of defenses in Barbados incorporated, as Ligon described it, a combination of "trenches, and rampiers, with pallisadoes, hornworks, curtains, and counter-scarps" and "a very good Fortification of standing wood round about the Island near the Sea."[21] The "Lines," along with the forts and batteries, are marked on the map printed in John Oldmixon's 1708 history of *The British Empire in America.* FIG 3 They pick up on the shoreline where the crosses surrounding the coast stop—the crosses "signifying rocks under water" which served as a natural barricade. By means of ramparts and reefs, the island appeared encircled. A young George Washington, visiting the island from 1751 to 1752, remarked on the "large Intrenchments cast up wherever its possible for an Enemy to Land" and concluded Barbados was "one intire fortification."[22] Timber and sand defenses were bolstered by stone where extra strength was required, and the trenches, once dug, were planted with cacti and thorns. By their nature, great parts of these defenses were impermanent and demanded a constant process of renewal and repair. They functioned, in effect, like scaffolding around which the colony was steadily built.[23]

By keeping the coast a continual construction site, the Barbados authorities were upholding the Dutch jurist Hugo Grotius's argument that "Building is a kind of occupation" at the same time as defying his claim that the sea was free because it could not be built on.[24] The construction site extended not just inland through plantations and planters' houses—the latter "built in the manner of fortifications" against the threat of rebellions by the indentured and enslaved labor force—but also into the surrounding waters via the slave economy's infrastructure of wharves, platforms and ships.[25] Regardless that the actual effectiveness of these defenses was largely illusory, as much on land as on water, the colonists sought to construct an *image* of dominance, and this image of dominance served as a form of defense.

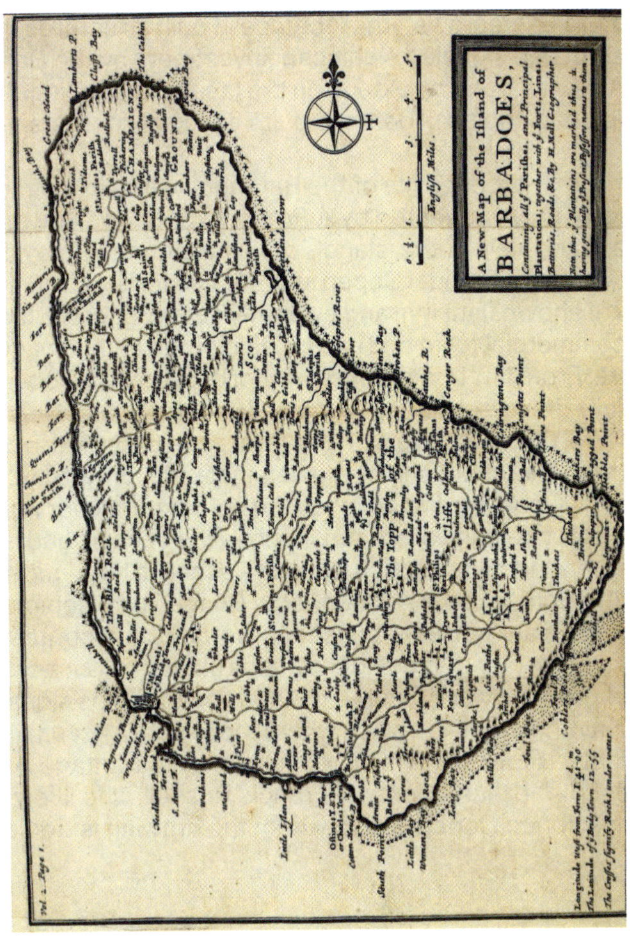

FIG 3
Herman Moll, *A New Map of the Island of Barbadoes*, from John Oldmixon, *The British Empire in America*, 2 vols (London, 1708), II, 1.

FIG 4
A Prospect of Bridge Town, drawn by Samuel Copen in 1695 and engraved by J. Kip.

The colonial settlers in Barbados also sought to assert a certain independence. After Barbados was taken under the British Crown's control in the 1660s, funds for building and maintaining fortifications and other public works were supposed to be made available through taxes imposed by the restored King Charles II, namely a four-and-a-half per cent duty on commodities exported. However, islanders complained that they never saw any of this money again. Mounting requests from Whitehall officials for information about the number and condition of the forts made them a serious bone of contention. In 1680, Governor Jonathan Atkins reported that artillery was mounted at fifteen stone fortifications along the coast, the construction of which had, he said, cost the islanders "a great deal of money."[26] In 1695, Governor Francis Russell recorded twenty-two different structures, and by the mid-1740s that number doubled.[27] Despite complaints of poor maintenance and scarcity of ammunition—without which the forts stood as mere scarecrows—the increase in built structures on the shoreline signaled significant investment by the Barbados Assembly, and by extension the local elite's willingness to expend capital in defense of its financial interests.

The productivity of the Barbados elite's investment is forcefully suggested by *A Prospect of Bridge Town*, FIG 4 a grand view of the island's principal port drawn by the resident artist Samuel Copen in 1695. The forts of Carlisle Bay are shown flanking, and evidently supporting, the thriving commercial town and harbor delineated at the image's centre. From left to right (roughly north to south), Copen carefully drew and named James, Willoughby's and Needham's forts, the latter two with platforms and batteries in between them. Merchant ships also dominate the foreground and are shown coming and going on the horizon at the far right, while the gentle cultivated landscape in the background is dotted with windmills. At each level, the scene is busy, moving, industrious. Even if *A Prospect of Bridge Town* depicts where "riches are gotten"—to use the words of one contemporary pamphleteer defending Barbados planters from accusations of profligacy and luxury—the flags on the ships signal clearly that England is the place where those riches accumulate, and that it is England "which reaps the sole advantage and interest of the plantations."[28] Francis Russell, who likely commissioned Copen and to whom the drawing is dedicated as "Captain General and Chief Governor" (see the cartouche top right), was himself considerably invested in the business of sending wealth abroad from the island and planned extensive improvements to the wharves for the benefit of trade.

It is significant that apart from the wharfs, where barrels and "Wheelers stones to build" represent trade and its future development, the forts are the only built features identified in the print. In 1695, the same year that Copen drew his *Prospect*, Governor Russell sent to London a comprehensive report on the island's defenses in which he stressed the importance of being seen to fortify: "had not the French known of my reinforcing" of the forts, he wrote, "I dare swear that we should have had them here."[29] And of all the forts, he explained to the Lords of Trade and Plantations the year before, Needham's "is of the greatest consequence to us."[30] That Needham's Fort was only slowly and sporadically called Charles Fort by the islanders, since being renamed for the restored king in the 1660s, gives a sense of their historical attachment to the place. The reason for this fort's 'great consequence' is made clear in Copen's *Prospect*. Its depiction at the end of an exaggeratedly narrow peninsula (known as Needham's Point) emphasizes the strategic situation, which offered superb visibility and command both across Carlisle Bay and along the island's south coast. "Should we lose Needham's Fort," Russell wrote, "we could not save the town from being bombarded or the shipping in Carlisle Bay from being burnt."[31] He worried that Needham's Fort itself could be commanded by two rocky hills within a radius of a mile. One of these would be the "proper site for a citadel," he conjectured, expressing incredulity "that one has never been built in an Island which contains 50,000 negroes, always plotting to cut the white men's throats."[32]

Governor Russell's desire to put Barbados into "such a state of defence as to give any enemy a warm reception" was clearly intensified by the memory of a slave conspiracy that had been discovered and suppressed in the autumn of 1692.[33] The timing of the rebellion was planned to take advantage of weakened military defences on the island amid war with France. In the climax of their insurrectionary plot, the rebels intended to enlist four or five Irish men to gain access to Needham's Fort and get the lower-rank soldiers drunk, then to open the gates to a group waiting outside the defences. Having conquered Needham's Fort, the rebels reportedly planned to use its guns to destroy all the ships in the harbor and burn large parts of the town. After the plot was revealed, hundreds of enslaved peoples were rounded up and a great number of them condemned; many "were Hang'd, and a great many Burn'd," according to one contemporary who arrived on the island in the aftermath. "And, (for a Terror to others,) there are now seven Hanging in Chains, alive, and so Starving to Death."[34]

After white fears of a further insurrection in 1701 and the outbreak of the war of the Spanish succession the same year, a citadel was soon under construction on a hill overlooking Needham's Fort, as Russell had hoped. Yet St Ann's Castle, as it would be named for the new queen of England, was never completed as originally designed. The royal engineer who was consulted on the project, Christian Lilly, instead regarded Needham's Fort as "one of the chief bulwarks of this Island" and of "great usefulness" at small cost—if only the local authorities would follow his renovation proposals. As indicated by a plan dated 1748, FIG 5 Charles Fort was strengthened in the eighteenth century, with the original timber and earth structures turned to stone and bolstered by new outer defenses. The heavy construction was the burden of the same people whose enslavement the building served to enforce, and who imagined overrunning it at their peril. Charles Fort retained a symbolic significance well beyond its original military use, literally so as a signal station in the mid-nineteenth century. By the early twentieth century, it was declared a "historic site" worthy of preservation as a fort originating from "a very early time," a building with the distinction of having preserved the colony.[35]

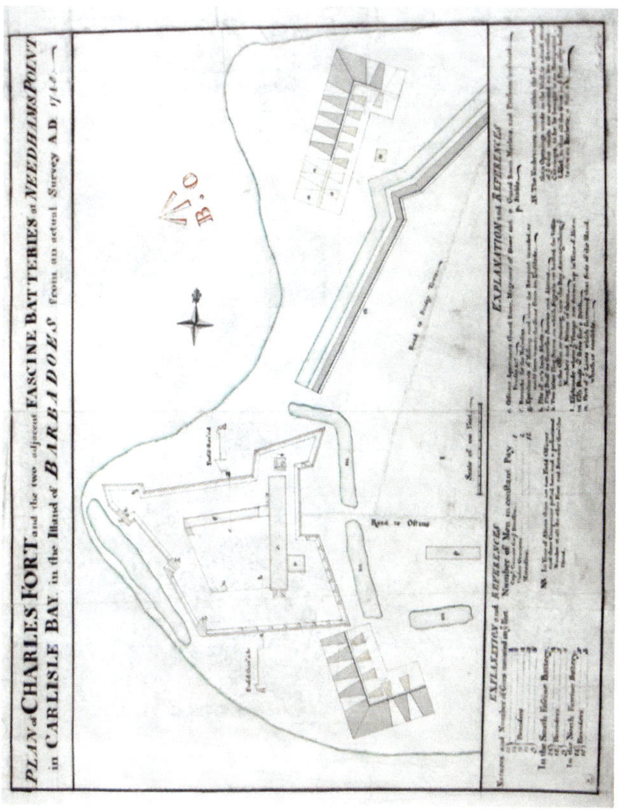

FIG 5
Plan of Charles Fort and the Two Adjacent Fascine Batteries at Needhams Point in Carlisle Bay in Barbadoes from an Actual Survey A.D. 1748.

SUNDAY ADVOCATE

BARBADOS HILTON

THE BARBADOS HILTON TAKES GREAT PRIDE IN ANNOUNCING ITS OPENING SIMULTANEOUSLY WITH THE INDEPENDENCE OF BARBADOS. THE ADVANCEMENT OF TOURISM AND PROSPERITY FOR THE ISLAND WILL BE ITS AIM.

FIG 7
Barbados *Sunday Advocate*, Hilton supplement, November 27, 1966.

SUPPLEMENT
SUNDAY NEWS
NOVEMBER 27, 1966

BARBADOS HILTON

FIG 6
Barbados *Sunday News*, Hilton supplement, November 27, 1966.

November 30, 1966

Shortly before midnight on the eve of independence in Barbados, a 50,000-strong crowd gathered on the parade ground of the garrison that had grown around St Ann's Castle from the late eighteenth century, some clambering up onto rooftops and into trees. In the dark and driving rain, they came to witness and celebrate a long-awaited shift in power, marked by the lowering of the Union Jack and hoisting of the new nation's flag: a sea-and-sun-inspired striped design of ultramarine and gold, with a broken trident at its center symbolizing the break from British rule. An unseasonal downpour could not dampen spirits as the crowd applauded their prime minister, Errol Walton Barrow, ushering in this "very proud moment in the history of the people of Barbados."[36]

Two days earlier, sponsored supplements in local newspapers FIG 6, 7 put their own spin on the momentous events by announcing the opening of the Barbados Hilton —"A New Hotel in a New Nation"—situated just down the hill from the garrison on Needham's Point peninsula, where the remains of Charles Fort still stood.[37] The five-story, 158-room hotel, designed by the New York-based architects Warner Burns Toan and Lunde (WBTL), was a striking construction of locally produced precast concrete, native coral stone and imported plate glass, distinguished in particular by the series of barrel-vaulted duplex suites with adjoining solariums rolling like a wave across its rooftop. FIG 8–10 The visual spectacle, even when reduced to the size of a postage stamp for a commemorative independence issue, FIG 11 persuasively sold the building as a sign of the new nation's modernity, fashionability and future prosperity. "Hilton: the name which means Barbados has arrived," one headline declared.[38] The Hilton International management expressed "great pride in announcing its opening simultaneously with the independence of Barbados," a coincidence that was advertised with a hint of providentialism ("it is very fitting") but was calculatingly strategic.[39] As one commentator put it, the hotel was "almost forced open while workers were still installing basic fittings and furnishings in bedrooms, and before the pool was filled," to ensure it would provide the setting for lavish independence celebrations including a state dinner.[40] Hilton had much at stake, in both the location and the timing of this latest addition to its "family" of hotels, and it went deeper than business.[41]

The Barbados Hilton was the latest link in a global chain: the seventeenth hotel constructed by Hilton International (a subsidiary of the Hilton Hotel Corporation founded to expand its mainland business overseas) and the thirty-eighth to be operated by the firm, its seventh in the Caribbean. The first Hilton International opened in San Juan, Puerto Rico, in 1949, the same year that the US colony gained its first democratically elected governor, and three years before it was granted commonwealth status. The coincidence of these events demonstrates that each new Hilton intervention "engaged politics at the highest level."[42] The hotel empire's leader, Conrad N. Hilton, had already dreamed of playing a role on a worldwide stage—stirred by the notion that "if business didn't cross frontiers, armies would"—when the US State Department (as Hilton told it in his autobiography) "suggested that the Hilton organization could make a substantial contribution to the government program of Foreign Aid by establishing American-operated hotels in important world cities."[43] Armed with the slogan "World Peace Through International Trade and Travel," and upgrading the Hilton Hotel Corporation motto from "Across the Nation" to "Around the World," Hilton International embarked on what an advertisement in the US *Foreign Service Journal* of May 1958 heralded as "the largest world-wide expansion in history."[44] Locations added to the hotel chain were "key spots" targeted "Because there is a job to be done there"—a job that, in Conrad Hilton's view, satellites and H-bombs could not do. His hotels would far more effectively "work as an offensive to destroy Communism across the world" through industrial assistance rather than military aid.[45] "An integral part of my dream," Hilton wrote in 1957, "was to show the countries most exposed to communism the other side of the coin—the fruits of the free world."[46]

FIG 9
Postcard showing aerial view of the Barbados Hilton on Needham's Point following its completion in 1966. The colonial defenses (to left of hotel) are revealed by the aerial view.

FIG 8
Postcard showing the entrance front of the Barbados Hilton, opened 1966.

FIG 11
Barbados independence postage stamp illustrating the Hilton Hotel.

FIG 10
Postcard showing the Barbados Hilton poolside, and the Old Lighthouse.

Hence the high-tech Modernist Hilton hotels rising in cities such as Istanbul (1955), Berlin (1958), Cairo (1959) and Baghdad, which was planned but halted in 1959. The threat that communism posed to Conrad Hilton's (and the American) dream was underlined by events in Cuba. The Havana Hilton, which opened in 1958 with heavy security, including marksmen on nearby rooftops, was occupied by the revolutionary leadership within months, then nationalized, and renamed the Habana Libre in June 1960.[47] It was a serious blow to Hilton's "offensive" in the wider Caribbean—a terrestrial paradise that Hilton had envisioned himself "discovering" like a modern-day Christopher Columbus—when the Soviet embassy subsequently moved in.[48]

The front page of the Barbados *Advocate* on the day of independence indicated the shift in political influence and direction made possible by the end of colonial rule. In a prominent side column and beneath a graphic of the new national flag, the *Advocate* reported that "The Soviet Union has declared its recognition of Barbados as an independent and sovereign state" and, moreover, that the premier of the People's Republic of China, Zhou Enlai, wished Barbados "new successes in [the] cause of combating imperialism, colonialism and neo-colonialism, safeguarding national independence and building their own country."[49] Conrad Hilton believed that helping Barbados build, both physically and economically, through a "business fellowship" would successfully sell the superiority of American values and practices and stop any swing from the capitalist to communist camp. "Our Hilton house flag is one small flag of freedom which is being waved defiantly against Communism exactly as Lenin predicted," he wrote.[50] On a map in his office, he charted his corporation's global expansion—red flags stood for hotels in operation, blue for those under construction and already contracted for, and green for others projected over the next five years—and delighted in the flags of Hilton National and International "flying gaily across the world."[51] In a newly independent nation eager to bring down an old imperial flag, it is understandable that the newspaper correspondent who noted three tall flagpoles outside the entrance of the Barbados Hilton, ready to fly the American and Hilton flags alongside the Barbadian, quickly and emphatically added: "but the feeling of the Barbados Hilton is **Barbadian** [bold original]."[52]

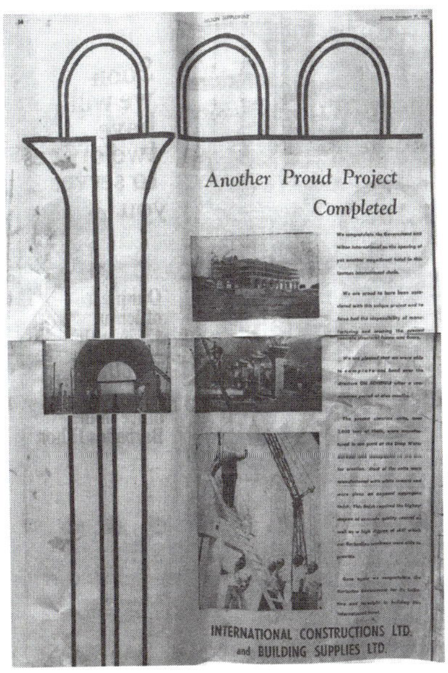
Another Proud Project

Completed

INTERNATIONAL CONSTRUCTIONS LTD. and BUILDING SUPPLIES LTD.

FIG 12
Back-page advertorial for International Constructions in the Barbados *Sunday Advocate*, Hilton supplement, November 27, 1966.

FIG 13
The naturally air-conditioned central atrium of the Barbados Hilton as opened in 1966, from a promotional leaflet.

What was Barbadian, then, about the Barbados Hilton? The design was American, the construction company was British, but the materials and labor were predominantly Bajan.[53] Advertorials heralded the local source and production of the principal parts: the concrete frame and floors, proudly manufactured at the Deep Water Harbour (Bridgetown's port, itself recently constructed on the other side of Carlisle Bay) and the aggregate finish produced by highly skilled Barbadian workmen FIG 12; the coral stone infill intended to reflect the color of the Caribbean sun; the roof well-waterproofed against tropical rain by Barbados Mastic Company; and the "native-made" fans, fixtures, furniture, fabrics and finish materials, from wrought iron railings to place mats woven of Barbados straw. Seating was cushioned in the colors of the new national flag, and walls decorated with local art. The building was even oriented so its main interior spaces—a five-story lushly planted atrium and the terrace café FIG 13—were naturally air-conditioned by the cooling trade winds passing through louvered shutters. The indigenous materials blended with a local atmosphere. "There is a friendly Bajan spirit at the Barbados Hilton," one reporter remarked.[54] The hotel was, in fact, locally owned. Following the model devised for the first international Hilton, the Caribe in Puerto Rico, the cost of construction was financed by public funds through the Barbados Development Board, acting for the government. As Dennis Merrill explains, Conrad Hilton "had a knack for structuring deals in which host country investors put up the bulk of the investment," thereby minimizing his own company's liability and risk.[55] Hilton International operated the hotel, supplied the working capital and retained one-third of the profits, the rest going to the Barbados government in rent. The crucial importance of local political support in realizing the new hotel is expressed in a letter from Conrad Hilton to Errol Barrow following its opening, in which he thanked the Barbadian premier for his "unstinting support of our project."[56] He continued: "I think the Barbados Hilton is one of the most beautiful hotels I have ever seen, and it will greatly contribute to the well-being of your beautiful country."

NEWS/

In the blink of an eye...

Blast leaves pile of rubble

FIG 14
The Barbados *Daily Nation*'s double-page report on the demolition of the original Barbados Hilton on October 24, 1999.

The strong local accent of the Barbados Hilton made it seem less of a "little America," as Conrad Hilton saw each new hotel, and was likely a response by the architects Warner Burns Toan and Lunde to criticism of the Caribe, for which Warner-Leeds Associates acted as consultants but where their influence was seen to predominate.[57] According to *Architectural Forum*, "Visitors who search for uniquely native character in this building will not find much of it;" there is "comparatively little that is Puerto Rican."[58] On the contrary, the hotel had "the color, texture, and finish demanded by Americans off to the semi-tropics."[59] The foreign styling encouraged interpretations of the hotel as a sellout to foreigners, rather than the "friendly center" of shared peace and profit that Hilton hoped people would see.[60] The wider tourist industry's image problem in the Caribbean was encapsulated in 1966 by the first director of tourism in Jamaica, where the 1950s Arawak Hotel, named for the island's indigenous people, had in 1963 been taken over and renamed the Jamaica Hilton. The "biggest problem we are facing isn't 'selling' Jamaica to the tourist," the director remarked, "but 'selling' tourists to the Jamaicans," many of whom saw tourism as a new form of imperialism.[61]

In Barbados, the advertorials stressed to readers that the new hotel was "the Hilton with a difference." For critics, this one was "worth a visit just for its architecture" and the island's "only good 20th century building."[62] The manufacture and marketing of the Barbados Hilton were formulated to foster a local sense of agency and attachment to both building and brand; to make Barbadians feel invested, economically and emotionally. The strategy's success is testified by the islanders' mass turnout to witness the hotel's demolition in 1999 to make way for a far larger replacement. Newspaper coverage of the historic implosion FIG 14 describes how "excited and in some cases overzealous locals and tourists rushed toward Needham's Point for any available vantage point," and dozens of boats bobbed in the bay.[63] Short and spectacular, the building's destruction by 800 detonations was also a moment of shock and sadness at the loss of the island's most renowned hotel and a symbol, through their joint inception, of national independence.[64]

Yet the "majestic" and "imposing structure," as commentators described it in 1966, was not received unanimously or uncritically as a benign force. While Conrad Hilton resisted the mantle of invader, "intent upon siphoning back all profits to the United States," one article tracing his company's spread remarked (beneath the subheading "*Invasion*"): "That Hilton has invaded the Caribbean seems an understatement."[65] The owners of Buccaneer Bay Hotel, which opened on the west coast of Barbados just two months after the Hilton, pitched their beach resort as courageous local resistance against corporate foreign competition. In direct dialogue with the Hilton advertorials, a newspaper piece began by emphasizing that the two-story 22-room Buccaneer Bay Hotel was "the first hotel on the west coast of Barbados to be owned entirely by Barbadians... The hotel was built in just over eight months by Barbadian labour; it is staffed almost entirely by Barbadians, and much of the furniture in the hotel was built locally."[66] It was suggested that the hotel would revitalize "a popular spot [...] used by many a Barbadian in the old days," and "Local patronage is welcomed."[67] The clearest riposte to the Hilton—and hint of wider animosity towards the American outsider—came in a four-line verse heading the principal advert:

> *... Big confusion today*
> *Buccaneer has come to Payne's Bay!*
> *Michael [Whittaker, the hotel manager] now running the show*
> *Conrad has had to go!!*[68]

Conrad Hilton had indeed jetted in and out again after a hectic schedule of events simultaneously celebrating the birth of his hotel and the nation, including a two-minute ribbon-cutting speech he had to have written for him being "not familiar enough with Barbados to know what I should say."[69] Nonetheless, through ceremonies and news coverage, Hilton had aligned himself closely with the Prime Minister in the public eye—an advertorial "Who's Who" of "The men who made the Barbados Hilton possible" positioned Premier Barrow ("A man of many parts") only slightly above Hilton himself ("Builder of an empire")—and had entrenched his hotel in the environmental and economic landscape.[70] As with all Hilton hotels, the site secured for the Barbados Hilton was a prime spot, highly prized for the same reasons it was heavily protected by English settlers in the seventeenth century: "anywhere you are in the Barbados Hilton you see the sea ... [it is] all around you," one reporter noted breathlessly; "the Barbados Hilton has captured the sea."[71]

But the site now had "historic value" too.[72] The hotel rose amid the remains of the colonial defenses, FIG 9 a flagship hotel founded on flagship fort. The sea-mossed old fortress walls, cannons and dungeons were kept intact and preserved "so that they will be there forever," as the reviewer Ann Zimmerman put it.[73] Zimmerman also noted how the building's plantation references—coral stone and dark wooden louvers—gave "a strange feeling of the past coming alive." As she saw it, "Nothing jars the sensitivities," but it was a contradictory building that sought to project the island's modernity and postcolonial future while evoking its militarized, oppressed past.

Through its explicit quotations from the past, the Barbados Hilton was arguably an early example of post-modern design, though one that was "largely unsung in the architectural press of the time."[74] The architects Warner Burns Toan and Lunde sent a team to study the history of the island and its architecture, and the resulting design (largely the creation, according to partner Frithjof Lunde, of project associate Bernard Ehrlich's imagination) was "patterned after the dramatic arches which characterized the island's old military garrisons."[75] Inside, function rooms were named the Savannah Room and the Garrison Room, and the major eatery was the Fort Charles Grill, "a pentagonal design, dramatized by the wrought iron grilled gun post windows with the black cast iron table bases lending emphasis to the fortress theme." The entrance to the Flambeau Bar, meanwhile, was centered between "two of the four fortress towers which form the corners of the structure."[76] As one marketing leaflet boasted, "the motif of the old fort, and its native coral limestone (used throughout Barbados for three centuries) permeate our hotel."[77] Another eulogized how the hotel "recaptures the old fort's flavor."[78] The fort-inspired structure, fused with tropical plantings both in the internal atrium lobby and in the surrounding grounds (the landscaping was begun before the building, in 1964), fed growing touristic desires for heritage as well as the exotic environment, all within the confines of the beach resort's own boundaries. With a well-tended oasis and historic monument always in their gaze, guests were in effect fortified against the need to venture inland or delve deeper into the island's past. Its nature and history were here tamed, pacified, packaged, commoditized.

Marketing copy selling the concept of old colonial comfort and a sense of belonging to predominantly white western elites—"The minute you arrive here, you'll believe that it's 'Your Club'"—follow uncomfortably from the image of a black female model in white lace and red beads on the leaflet's front cover. As Annabel Wharton has shown, Hilton hotels made a habit of drawing on past structures of power to inscribe their own images of strength and superiority.[79] Elsewhere in the Caribbean, the Caribe Hilton in Puerto Rico (opened 1958) occupied a plot of land in San Juan adjacent to San Gerónimo Fort, built under Spanish colonial rule and then occupied by the US navy. A brochure illustration FIG 15 situates the Modernist hotel—its logo a series of castellated towers—against the fortified setting. The Curacao Hilton (opened 1967) was conceived as "a self-contained resort surrounded by fort-like walls in the style of the country's ancient fortresses and designed to give [...] a feeling of privacy and intimacy." Privacy, intimacy, serenity, seclusion, security: the Barbados Hilton's occupation of space was designed for the benefit of some to the exclusion of others. A leaflet in the architect's archive lures visitors with the promise of a "private, 1000-foot-long beach." In thick black pen the word "private" has been ruled out, and a later printing included the correction, but the presumptions and desires inherent in the word remain.

FIG 15
Opening brochure of the Havana Hilton, 1958.

FIG 17
Barbados *Sunday Sun* supplement, December 4, 2006, celebrating 50 years.

FIG 16
Entrance of the new Barbados Hilton with Barbadian, US and corporate flags, June 2017.

May 14, 2018

Ten days ahead of the general election on May 24, and after months of secrecy surrounding the sale of the Barbados Hilton to the British real estate investor London and Regional Properties, the island's parliamentary opposition leader Mia Mottley threatened mass protests by thousands of her supporters if the planned transaction was not delayed and put up for discussion by the new government.[80] Mottley won the election and halted the deal, which was opposed not just because the sale price fell well below the property's valuation, but because the hotel, now lying within the UNESCO World Heritage Site (as designated in 2011), was "a state asset with sentimental values for Barbadians because it was acquired at the same time as independence."[81] When the hotel that was opened to such ceremony in 1966 was reduced to rubble in 1999, many islanders saw for the first time the beauty of the space left behind and wanted it saved for the people. Today, keeping the asset public seems the best they can hope for.[82]

The new 350-room Barbados Hilton, designed by the same firm as the 1966 hotel (now known as WBTL Architects) and opened in 2005, followed core principles of the original: to maximize the visitors' commanding views of the sea, to provide access to the historic fort, and to create a "tropical ambience" in the heavily landscaped grounds (see the entrance, with the same flags, in FIG 16).[83] New and old Hiltons were aligned on the front page of a Hilton-sponsored newspaper supplement celebrating 50 years of the hotel in Barbados alongside the island's independence. FIG 17 Economic factors have encouraged the hotel (vastly bigger and therefore more vulnerable in downturn) to address and open itself up to local people in new ways—it is now a place, as one local visitor put it, "where Bajans who have only ever served can go to be served."[84] It nonetheless still presides over the beach, standing as a cornerstone of the gated fortress of luxury hotels, condos and private villas that today hog the island's Caribbean coastline where colonial fortifications and plantations once stood. Sun loungers now line up in place of long-range guns. Perhaps, as the Mighty Gabby warned, the war has only just begun.

1 Jack Dear was commenting on the new National Conservation Commission Act, which established a licensing regime for beach vendors. His speech stressed the restraints on enterprising locals that had been introduced by the new law. See Christine Toppin-Allahar, "'*De Beach Belong to We!*' Socio-economic Disparity and Islanders' Rights of Access to the Coast in a Tourist Paradise," *Oñati Socio-legal Series* 5, no. 1 (2015): 298–317. On the origins of Gabby's song, see his discography, accessed September 10, 2018, http://www.icerecords.com/artists/artists-gabby.html.

2 See Hilary Beckles, "The Slave-Drivers' War: Bussa and the 1816 Barbados Slave Rebellion," *Boletín de Estudios Latinoamericanos y del Caribe* 39 (1985): 85–110. Evidence relating to the revolt and Bussa's role (also his origins) has recently been reassessed by Lilian McNaught in "The 1816 Barbados Slave Revolt" (Masters diss., University of Exeter, 2017), accessed September 10, 2018, https://ore.exeter.ac.uk/repository/bitstream/handle/10871/31536/McNaughtL_TPC.pdf.

3 Debbie Jacob, "No Eclipse for the Mighty Gabby," *Caribbean Beat*, no. 7 (Autumn 1993), accessed September 10, 2018, https://www.caribbean-beat.com/issue-7/no-eclipse-mighty-gabby#axzz5Rx47wu9s. The song can be heard on YouTube, accessed September 10, 2018, https://www.youtube.com/watch?v=gTbGkop7mss. On the radicalism and impact of "Jack" and other calypso songs by Gabby and contemporaries, see Curwen Best, *The Popular Music and Entertainment Culture of Barbados: Pathways to Digital Culture* (Lanham, MD: Scarecrow Press, 2012), 65–88 (esp. 73–75).

4 Krista A. Thompson, *An Eye for the Tropics: Tourism, Photography, and Framing the Caribbean Picturesque* (Durham, NC: Duke University Press, 2007), 328.

5 For news of the protest see, for example, Katrina King, "The Mighty Gabby Leads Scores in Protest against the Crane," *Barbados Today*, March 31, 2018, https://barbadostoday.bb/2018/03/31/the-mighty-gabby-leads-scores-in-protest/; footage at https://www.youtube.com/watch?v=-4x0c6tXU4U; Maria Bradshaw, "Doyle's Solution: Develop Crane Beach," *Nation News*, March 24, 2018, http://www.nationnews.com/nationnews/news/141592/doyle-solution-develop-crane-beach. All accessed September 10, 2018.

6 Tara A. Inniss, "The Beach Belong to We," *Barbados Underground*, accessed September 10, 2018, https://barbadosunderground.net/2018/03/30/the-beach-belong-to-we/.

7 The risk that local workers would take on the role of "field labourers on the modern plantation of the tourist industry" was discussed by the Barbadian scholar Elliott Parris in 1983, cited by Graham M. S. Dann and Robert B. Potter in "Supplanting the Planters: Hawking Heritage in Barbados," *International Journal of Hospitality and Tourism Administration* 2, no. 3–4 (2001): 51–84 (56).

8 V. S. Naipaul, *The Middle Passage* (London: André Deutsch, 1962; Picador, 2011), 198. For others who have taken a similar line, including Frantz Fanon, see Polly Pattullo, *Last Resorts: The Cost of Tourism in the Caribbean* (London: Latin American Bureau, 2005), 81–83. Gabby released a statement on his Facebook page @MightyGabby on March 31, 2018.

9 Norwell Harrigan, "The Legacy of Caribbean History and Tourism," *Annals of Tourism Research* 2, no. 1 (September/October 1974): 13–25 (20).

10 For the latest figures showing tourism's centrality in the island's economy (predicted to grow over the next decade), see https://www.wttc.org/-/media/files/reports/economic-impact-research/countries-2018/barbados2018.pdf (accessed September 23, 2018).

11 For discussion on the definition of the beach see https://barbadosunderground.net/2018/04/08/the-caswell-franklyn-column-that-beach-is-not-mine/?relatedposts_hit=1&relatedposts_origin=58128&relatedposts_position=2 (accessed September 10, 2018). Pattullo, *Last Resorts*, 76.

12 King, "The Mighty Gabby Leads Scores in Protest."

13 The manuscript account of the voyage cited here is in Cambridge University Library, MSS Mm. 3, 9. It is transcribed and annotated by J. Edward Hutson in *The Voyage of Sir Henry Colt to the Islands of Barbados and St Christopher* (St Michael, Barbados: Barbados National Trust, 2002): for quotation here, see i. The manuscript is also printed in V. T. Harlow, ed., *Colonising Expeditions to the West Indies and Guiana, 1623–1667* (London: Hakluyt Society, 1925), 54–102.

14 *Voyage of Sir Henry Colt*, 3, vii.

15 *Voyage of Sir Henry Colt*, 12.

16 *Voyage of Sir Henry Colt*, 17.

17 *Voyage of Sir Henry Colt*, 18, 22.

18 *Voyage of Sir Henry Colt*, 34.

19 Richard Ligon, *A True and Exact History of the Island of Barbadoes*, 2nd edn (London: Peter Parker and Thomas Guy, 1673), 100.

20 Ligon, *True and Exact History*, 100.

21 Ligon, *True and Exact History*, 100.

22 George Washington, *The Daily Journal of Major George Washington, in 1751–2, Kept While on a Tour from Virginia to the Island of Barbadoes*, ed. J. M. Toner (Albany, NY: Joel Munsell's Sons, 1892), 62.

23 The idea of fortification as scaffold in the colonization process is drawn from Philip Levy, "A New Look at an Old Wall: Indians, Englishmen, Landscape, and the 1634 Palisade at Middle Plantation," *Virginia Magazine of History and Biography* 112, no. 3 (2004): 226–65.

24 Hugo Grotius, *The Free Sea*, trans. Richard Hakluyt, ed. David Armitage (Indianapolis: Liberty Fund, 2004), 27. *Mare Liberum*, published anonymously in 1609 and translated into English by Hakluyt sometime before his death in 1616, was contested by John Selden in *Mare Clausum* (1635), which argued that England's jurisdiction extended to all waters surrounding the isles.

25 On houses with "Lines, Bulwarks, and Bastions," see Ligon, *True and Exact History*, 29.

26 Jonathan Atkins to William Blathwayt, April 1, 1680, *Calendar of State Papers, Colonial* [hereafter *CSPC*], accessed August 20, 2018, http://www.british-history.ac.uk/report.aspx?compid=70001.

27 Francis Russell to the Lords of Trade and Plantations, August 25, 1695, *CSPC*, accessed August 20, 2018, http://www.british-history.ac.uk/report.aspx?compid=70823.

28 *A State of the Present Condition of the Island of Barbadoes* (London: Thomas Northcott, 1698), 4.

29 Russell to the Lords of Trade, August 25, 1695.

30 Russell to the Lords of Trade, September 25, 1694, *CSPC*, accessed November 26, 2018, http://www.british-history.ac.uk/cal-state-papers/colonial/america-west-indies/vol14/pp354-366.

31 Russell to the Lords of Trade, September 25, 1694.

32 Russell to the Lords of Trade, September 25, 1694.

33 Jerome S. Handler, "Slave Revolts and Conspiracies in Seventeenth-Century Barbados," *Nieuwe West-Indische Gids/New West Indian Guide* 56, no. 1/2 (1982): 5–42 (see esp. 22–29).

34 *A Brief, But Most True Relation of the Late Barbarous and Bloody Plot of the Negro's in the Island of Barbados on Friday the 21 of October, 1692* (London: Printed for George Croom, 1693).

35 "The Historic Sites and Buildings of Barbados: The Report of the Committee Appointed to Enquire into the Present Condition of Historic Sites etc, in Barbados and to Report What Steps Should be Taken for their Preservation," June 10, 1910, printed in *The Journal of the Barbados Museum and Historical Society* 1, no. 1 (1933): 16–32, esp. 18. The editor noted that no action had been taken between 1910 and 1933.

36 Barrow cited by Tony Vanterpool, "Barbados is Independent," Barbados *Advocate*, November 30, 1966, 1.

37 "Hilton Hotel: A New Hotel in a New Nation," Barbados *Sunday News*, Hilton supplement, November 27, 1966, 4.

38 Ann Zimmerman, "Hilton: The Name Which Means Barbados Has Arrived," Barbados *Sunday News*, Hilton supplement, November 27, 1966, 3.

39 "Barbados Hilton Has Many New Features!," Barbados *Sunday Advocate*, Hilton supplement, November 27, 1966, 4; see also the front page (FIG 7).

40 Account of independence celebrations in *The Bajan*, January 1967, cited by Albert Brandford, "Rain, fanfare at Savannah," Barbados *Daily Nation*, November 30, 2011.

41 "Barbados Joins the Family," Barbados *Sunday Advocate*, Hilton supplement, November 27, 1966, 3.

42 Annabel Wharton, *Building the Cold War: Hilton International Hotels and Modern Architecture* (Chicago, IL: Chicago University Press, 2001), 4. On the coincidence, see Richard Rosa, "Governing Tourism: Representation, Domination and Freedom in Puerto Rico: 1949," *Global South* 6, no. 1 (2012): 87–97.

43 Conrad N. Hilton, *Be My Guest* (1957; New York: Fireside, 1994), 232–33.

44 Hilton, *Be My Guest*, 234. US *Foreign Service Journal* (May 1958), 2.

45 "The President's Corner," *Hiltonitems*, May 1958, 1.

46 Hilton, *Be My Guest*, 237.

47 Dennis Merrill, *Negotiating Paradise: US Tourism and Empire in Twentieth-Century Latin America* (Chapel Hill, NC: University of North Carolina Press), 142.

48 In his oration at the opening of his Havana hotel, Conrad Hilton commented: "To say that Christopher Columbus was a world traveler must be something of an understatement. I am very happy today that four hundred and sixty six years later Hilton hotels has discovered Cuba" (cited by Merrill, *Negotiating Paradise*, 141).

49 "Russia Recognises Bimshire," Barbados *Advocate*, November 30, 1966, 1.

50 Hilton, *Be My Guest*, 262.

51 Hilton, *Be My Guest*, 261.

52 Zimmerman, "Hilton: The Name Which Means Barbados Has Arrived," 4. The trio of flags (US Stars and Stripes at the centre) remain at the entrance of the new Barbados Hilton: see FIG 16.

53 The London-based construction company, Token, had worked on the London Hilton on Park Lane, which opened in 1963.

54 Zimmerman, "Hilton: The Name Which Means Barbados Has Arrived," 3.

55 Merrill, *Negotiating Paradise*, 126.

56 Hilton to Barrow, December 12, 1966, Hilton Hotel Archive, Houston, TX.

57 Hilton, *Be My Guest*, 265.

58 *Architectural Forum*, March 1950, 97, cited by Merrill, *Negotiating Paradise*, 198–99.

59 *Architectural Forum*, March 1950, 97.

60 Merrill, *Negotiating Paradise*, 197. Hilton, *Be My Guest*, 265.

61 John Pringle cited by Frank Fonda Taylor, *To Hell With Paradise: A History of the Jamaican Tourist Industry* (Pittsburgh, PA: University of Pittsburgh Press, 1993), 169.

62 "Barbados Hilton Has Many New Features!", Barbados *Sunday Advocate*, Hilton supplement, November 27, 1966, 4. "Resort Hotel Forms Own Environment," reprinted from *Architectural Record*, April 1968.

63 Mike King, "In the Blink of an Eye...," Barbados *Daily Nation*, October 25, 1999.

64 Interviews conducted in Barbados, June 2017. The public response is consistent with the "astonishingly enthusiastic reception of Hilton hotels" that Wharton found in Istanbul, Cairo, Athens, Tel Aviv and Berlin, in contrast to Hilton projects in London, Rome and Florence (*Building the Cold War*, 4).

65 Hilton, *Be My Guest*, 267. "Hilton Spreads in the Carib Area," Barbados *Sunday Advocate*, Hilton supplement, November 27, 1966, 4.

66 "U-Shaped Hotel is Owned by Barbadians," Barbados *Advocate*, February 10, 1967, 7.

67 "Built on a Popular Spot," Barbados *Advocate*, February 10, 1967, 8. The encouragement of local patronage appears in the advert on the previous page.

68 Barbados *Advocate*, February 10, 1967, 7.

69 Hilton to Curt R. Strand, vice-president of Hilton International, October 19, 1966, Hilton Hotel Archive, Houston TX.

70 Barbados *Sunday News*, Hilton supplement, November 27, 1966, 5.

71 "Barbados Hilton Has Many New Features!", Barbados *Sunday Advocate*, Hilton supplement, November 27, 1966, 4.

72 "Barbados Hilton Has Many New Features!", Barbados *Sunday Advocate*, Hilton supplement, November 27, 1966, 4.

73 Zimmerman, "Hilton: The Name Which Means Barbados Has Arrived," 3.

74 "Bernard Erlich: Obituary," *New York Times*, August 9, 2009.

75 "Erlich: Obituary." "Telling the Story of the Barbados Hilton," Barbados *Sunday News*, Hilton supplement, November 27, 1966.

76 "Telling the Story of the Barbados Hilton," Barbados *Sunday News*, Hilton supplement, November 27, 1966.

77 Hilton International promotional leaflet, Charles Warner archive, Columbia University, New York.

78 Hilton International promotional leaflet, Charles Warner archive, Columbia University, New York.

79 Wharton, *Building the Cold War*.

80 George Alleyne, "Barbados Hilton Hotel Sale Halted Amid Opposition," May 14, 2018, accessed November 20, 2018, https://www.caribbeanlifenews.com/stories/2018/5/2018-05-25-ga-barbados-hilton-sale-halted-cl.html.

81 Alleyne, "Barbados Hilton Hotel Sale Halted."

82 From interviews, June 2017.

83 Website of WBTL Architects, accessed November 30, 2018, http://wbtl-llp.com/bhh-b8.html.

84 Quotation from interviews, June 2017.

Pavilions and Tents: Pietro della Valle's Mobile Architecture

Matteo Burioni

On May 27, 1615, Roman patrician Pietro della Valle saw a vast gathering of Ottoman troops near Constantinople.[1] The traveler described a city of tents and recorded his observations of an intricate layout. Four years later he similarly described a large pavilion erected by the Persian *shah* for a festive gathering of the main officers and commanders serving in the war against the Ottomans. The complex ceremonial use of these tent cities was noteworthy; the Safavid and Ottoman encampments reminded della Valle of the sprawling military encampments in Europe. During the Thirty Years' War the European continent saw extraordinarily large military encampments with shops, entertainment districts, batteries of artillery, and fortifications. These provisional settlements brought large revenues via an elaborate economy of war. Sometimes the economic functions of these settlements were more important than their military aims. The use of tents in military camps was an ancient custom. Military camps comprised of tents and pavilions are distinctly recorded in ancient Rome. Architectural theorist Andrea Palladio illustrated the layout of these Roman ephemeral cities in his sixteenth-century commentary on Julius Caesar.[2] If the association between tents and war was an old one, it was also still very much alive in Europe, the Near East, and Asia. The mobility of the camp was a token of movement, military might, and conquest. Early modern tents and pavilions are of perishable textile material and their preservation presents several challenges, leading to a considerable loss. Because of their very ephemerality and materiality, many of these textile structures and mobile cities can only be reconstructed from textual and visual descriptions. Some of them, in whole or part, have been preserved in museum collections as trophies of war or as part of princely heritage. FIG 1, 2

FIG 2
Roundel with hunting scenes (possibly decoration for a tent ceiling), Persian, Safavid Dynasty, 1520–1550, 99,4 × 97,8 cm..

FIG 1
Ceiling and lateral covering of a three-pole tent, 17,95 m × 7,8 m × 5,6 m, Ottoman, 17th century.

The conjunction of culture and settlement, of civilization and cities, reached back as far as Herodotus, who saw fit to praise the Scythians as unconquerable because they had neither cities nor walls; they brought their houses with them already assembled.[3] Roman historian Ammianus Marcellinus wrote of the unstable nature of the nomad's life: "None of their offspring, when asked, can tell you where he comes from, since he was conceived in one place, born far from there, and brought up still farther away."[4] For Greek and Roman historians mobility signified a primitive and uncivilized culture, and thus the Scythian pavilion was an emblem of a barbaric and unstable life.[5] The difficulty of locating the Scythians, the absence of settlements and consequentially of cities, established their culture as the antithesis of Greek civilization. Indeed it was precisely the unstable nature of nomadic life that meant it lacked culture. Tents were associated with the primitive beginnings of humankind. If life in a tent was considered dirty, poor, and unbecoming, the primitive hut, as simple and rude as it was, could be conceived as the beginning of architecture. But life in a tent could not be construed as the beginning of a succession that led to monumental architecture.

According to Judeo-Christian tradition, Jewish patriarchs moved around the desert in textile homes. Biblical examples engendered a way for Franciscan missionaries of the thirteenth century to understand the tents and pavilions of the Mongol rulers.[6]

> Their homes are circular made in the form of tents. ... Above they have a round window from where light comes in and where the smoke from the fire that is always burning can come out. The walls and roof are covered with felt.[7]

FIG 3
Unknown engraver after an unknown draftsman, Portrait of Pietro della Valle, Geneva 1674.

This description is from the *History of the Mongols*, by John of Plano Carpini, a Franciscan missionary sent by Pope Innocent IV. Another Franciscan, William of Rubruk, visited the Mongol lands as an envoy of King Louis IX of France. He remarked that some of the tents were so large that the carts had to be pulled by twenty-two oxen arranged in two lines of eleven each. This cart's drawbar was as long as the mast of a ship. A man standing at the entrance of the tent loaded onto the cart would guide the oxen.[8] Rubruk equated the cart with a ship, evoking mobile homes of considerable sophistication. The tents described by the Franciscans countered an idea about architecture contemporary to them: structures did not necessarily need to be constructed of stone or be stable to be monumental. These descriptions by the Franciscan missionaries challenged fundamental assumptions about architecture, building materials, and human settlements. The Mongols used tents not only in time of war but as domestic housing. The luxury and sheer size of the Mongol pavilions made moving them an admirable feat. They were monumental, even if they contradicted conventional standards of architecture and stability.

The tradition of architectural theory going back to Vitruvius honored stability (*firmitas*) as one of the fundamental requirements of architecture.[9] An ephemeral mobile home did not count as architecture. Tents were used for war, hunting, parties, and city pageantry, but they could never be thought of as real homes. The idea that tents were magnificent signs of a ruler's power defied common sensibility. But the Franciscan missionaries were nonetheless awed by the military might of the Mongols and their devastating conquests in Eastern Europe, events which conveyed a newly compelling perspective on nomadic life. The ancient Jewish and Islamic culture of tents played a predominant role in della Valle's understanding of the tradition of mobile architecture.

Travelers like della Valle were crucial in opening up a discussion about architecture that presented a more nuanced picture of world traditions.[10] At the beginning of the nineteenth century Antoine Chrysostôme Quatrèmere de Quincy expressed the elementary insight that architecture "has not been invented by one people alone."[11] He was persuaded that building was universal to all times and to all people.[12] Quatrèmere de Quincy proposed a theoretical approach to architectural history that is highly relevant to thinking about della Valle. The architecture of the world could be divided into three distinct traditions identified in three primordial building types: the cave, the hut, and the tent.[13] These three types were connected to three different societies: the cave to hunters, the hut to peasants, and the tent to nomadic shepherds.[14] Quatrèmere de Quincy's insight was that architecture has a plurality of principles producing a set of consequences.[15] della Valle can be considered to have paved the way for these theoretical developments.

Pietro della Valle's Publications

A series of interconnected developments defined the early seventeenth century as a crucial phase for the global penetration of exchange networks, and coincided with challenges to paradigms of art, history, and architecture.

FIG 4
Unknown engraver after an unknown draftsman, Portrait of Sitti Maani Gioerida, Geneva 1674. Courtesy of the Research Library, The Getty Research Institute.

These processes of exchange were in a state of active formation during the years 1614 to 1626, during which the Roman patrician Pietro della Valle made an extensive journey through Turkey, to Persia and India. FIG 3 Examples of this include: the exhibition organized by Jesuit Athanasius Kircher in his museum at the *Collegio Romano*. Kircher, younger in age than Pietro della Valle, combined natural philosophical, linguistic, and archaeological materials into a concept of universal knowledge. Furthermore, crises, wars, famines, and cold waves were encountered during this period in multiple regions across the world, and the Thirty Years' War raged. The Jesuit method of "accommodation" flourished, and was adopted by figures including Alessandro Valignano in Japan, Matteo Ricci in China, and Roberto Nobili in India. This method saw Europeans adopt local rites, customs, and attire, and integrate them actively into the practice of Christianity in order to be taken seriously during missionary field-work, and decisively promoted the exchange of knowledge through their position of trust.[16]

In 1614 Pietro della Valle left Venice for Istanbul, where he remained one year as a guest of the French ambassador. From the capital of the Ottoman Empire, he traveled through Alexandria, Cairo, Jerusalem, Damascus, Aleppo, and Baghdad. He remained the longest in Safavid Persia, which he explored extensively from 1617 to 1621. In 1621, he departed from Isfahan and traveled via Shiraz to India, where he reached Surat and Ahmedabad in the Mughal Empire and Goa. He stayed six months in the capital of Portuguese India, describing the festive processions for the canonization of Francis Xavier while there. From Goa, he made a side trip to Ikkeri. In 1624, he sailed from Goa and returned to Rome in March 1626. The event that established his lasting fame, however, was della Valle's marriage to an Eastern Rite Christian woman from Baghdad, Sitti Maani Gioerida FIG 4 with whom he lived for four years at the court of Abbas I in Isfahan. Pietro della Valle decided to return to Rome when his wife died in childbirth.[17]

Della Valle's journey to the East made him a leading expert in Asian languages, art objects, architecture, and natural history.[18] Before he began his trip in 1614, he moved in a circle of natural philosophers and literary figures in Naples.[19] His correspondence, primarily with Mario Schipano, was published in 1650 across four volumes.[20] Translations in French, Dutch, German, and English followed in the seventeenth century; the Dutch and German editions are illustrated extensively with engravings. The letters della Valle wrote were edited for publication in the volumes, and had been sent from abroad to Naples. Some have been preserved in the *Archivio Segreto Vaticano*. Pietro della Valle also kept a travel diary. The manuscript of the travel writing is held in the archive of the *Società Geografica Italiana* (Italian Geographic Society).[21] Long before the travel account was published his letters circulated in Rome, as demonstrated by the numerous copies still preserved.[22] Della Valle did not leave this to chance; he had his servant make copies and sent the long accounts simultaneously to several recipients in Naples and Rome.[23] He deliberately wrote to people in scientific, literary, and artistic networks, strategically disseminating his accounts to achieve maximum publicity for his journey. Thus it is misleading to consider the four-volume published travel account as the sole aim of his writing.[24] Composed in epistolary form, it circulated widely as individual letters, and as a collection of letters. The explorer constantly added to his "Journeys" in the form of correspondence and other writings. and the countries he visited and the things he saw were described primarily through first person encounter.[25]

A letter from Mario Schipano to della Valle dated April 1616 demonstrates that the traveler's reports caused quite a stir in Naples and Rome:

> I have lost the desire to eat and drink when I think about what could happen to you on such a long journey among barbarian peoples and traversing so many countries. ... Your letter was therefore rightly so long. It was a comfort to read, first, the certain news that you are in good health, second, that you have gotten past these thieving Arabs and these unhappy deserts without problems or danger, and third, your remarkable successes with the mummies, the pyramids, on Mt. Sinai, and at the Red Sea. I rejoiced about this not only with the closest friends, but also informed many knowledgeable people, who seem to have a prerogative; among these was Signore Fabio Colonna, Signore Imperato, and Signore Stigliola, who have congratulated you on the faithful and detailed reports, and are burning with desire to see the strange things that you will send. ... [H]ere your letters are as eagerly awaited as the jubilee year of the popes.[26]

The letters required one to two years to reach Rome or Naples and were then in great public demand, with numerous copies made. At a certain point della Valle wrote that he considered taking up residence permanently at the court of Abbas I in Persia. He pondered establishing a Catholic quarter in Isfahan that would boast a new St.

Peter's and Capitoline complex bearing the name *Nuova Roma di Oriente* (New Rome of the Orient). A draft letter rich in fantasy addressed to the Roman senate informs us about this thoroughly utopian project, mentioned also in the letters and in the printed travel account, although the senate no longer played any real role at the time.[27] This gesture suggests that della Valle considered the Orient as a utopian projection allowing him to air political grievances in Italy, and he declared he was no longer simply Roman but a citizen of the world:

> All the more, since I consider myself a citizen of the world and not just of Rome, since I have made the entire world my native land with my efforts ... my acts should not be judged only by four impassioned people who live in a little corner of Rome, but rather by all nations.[28]

The manuscript letters and travel diary reveal a voice unimpaired by censorship. Pietro della Valle stayed with Christian missionaries in the cities, whose networks he used for travel logistics, accommodations, letters of recommendation, and financial transactions; after his return della Valle supported the missionaries with his best efforts.[29] In a censured passage of text he compared the Shiite shrine near Baghdad to the Franciscan monastery of La Verna in Tuscany, which dated to the order's founder.[30] Political and intellectual unease about developments in Europe as well as the enthusiasm unleashed by the reports at home apparently motivated him to take the significant risk in a journey to Persia. A small book on Abbas I published by della Valle shortly after his return home, in 1628, demonstrates that Persia served as the antithesis of the politics of princes in the Italian peninsula.[31] It could not be published in Rome because of the Inquisition, so he had it produced in Venice.

Della Valle considered the Orient to be a place where one would gladly settle as well as the source of scientific discoveries of the most varied kinds. He became so familiar with these places, languages, people, and objects that he returned to Rome transformed and endeavored to devise strategies for connecting these new experiences with his identity as a Roman patrician. The textualization of the "journeys"—whether printed or unprinted—played a central role since it allowed for biography and topography to be imaginatively intertwined and della Valle's self-image to appear in the light of experiences and adventures in other places.

The Pavilion as Mobile Architecture

During his travels della Valle encountered multiplicity of tents and pavilions. He lived himself in such a pavilion, utilized as a mobile home that offered him and his companions a comfortable lodging on long journeys. His habituation to the amenities offered by the pavilion went so far that he considered their accommodation substantially better than "our Italian inns" "*nostre hosterie d'Italia*".[32] On the dates of December 4th and 15th, 1618, della Valle made a record of the expenses for a big pavilion he acquired.[33] It was shipped in September 14, 1625, from Constantinople to Rome.[34] The pavilion was mentioned in a postmortem inventory from 1652 as still extant in the collection stored in his Roman house.[35] Traveling through the desert in a pavilion engendered sympathy with the nomadic Arabs, and he praised the advantages of living a life free of rulers or feudal lords.

At first della Valle undervalued and dismissed the nomadic Turks and Arabs. When he encountered a Turkish woman from a nomadic tribe who wore "Turkish simple garments," he expected to be in contact with "a women of the fields," someone with neither house nor property. After a while he was surprised to hear her speak civilized Turkish and that she was the owner of five hundred sheep. Her tribe's pavilions were made of a "certain rough material" dissimilar to the black tents of the Arabs.[36] On December 5, 1616, della Valle visited "many black tents from Nomadic Arabs" gathered like a village.[37] Although these differed from the pavilions, he described them as "a mobile village of tents" and admired "in their poorest of lives a sweet freedom."[38] della Valle added a long passage distinguishing pavilions from tents:

> There is a great difference between these two names, tent and pavilion, even if often in writing they get confused and one name is used for the other. A pavilion is round and supported by only one pole in the middle, which results in a dome. If it has an oblong shape it will be supported by two or more poles, and each pole will result in a dome reaching from the top to the ground. These pavilions are made of two or three layers of coarse fabric ... to protect from rain and from the outside. ... The simple ones are white in the interior or from just one color. ... [T]he beautiful ones are made out of thousands of colors, putting together these fabrics like a wonderful embroidery. Such is my pavilion that I call the Ladies Pavilion. There are much more magnificent ones with silk on the inside with similar decorations made with satin, with velvet and textiles, with gold as I described in my Diary. ... May they be rich or poor, big or small, made out of linen or coarser fabric in the case of the Turks, or made out of felt in the case of the Tartars as a protection against snowfall and cold, the shape of all these pavilions is round. ... The tents however, which can also be rich or poor, made out of different textiles, big or small, ... have an oblong shape and are of much lesser height than the pavilions.[39]

Della Valle observed the workmanship and use of pavilions and tents to understand their value in nomadic contexts as well as in military camps and courtly entertainment. On May 27, 1615, he visited a vast military camp of Ottoman forces near Constantinople.[40] He was surprised to see that they used neither fences nor trenches, nor any other defensive walls, although part of the camp was secured by artillery connected by a chain to prevent an attack by cavalry. What struck his imagination was the size and beauty of the Ottoman pasha's pavilion, worth the considerable sum of 16,000 Venetian *zecchini*. The principal quality of these immense pavilions, according to della Valle, was that their size and workmanship overwhelmed the beholder.

No book or fantastic tale della Valle had ever read, not even the incredible descriptions by poet Torquato Tasso in *Gerusalemme Liberata* (Jerusalem Delivered), approached a faithful account of experience of the magnificent temporary lodgings of the Ottoman pasha. A three-part structure consisted of a large central pavilion served by a smaller entrance pavilion. Within a textile fence, an outside area was situated reserved for the court and smaller tents of the wives and servants. The interior of the main tent was uniformly red and decorated with a columned portico.[41] A road flanked by high golden poles, as big as one of the main arteries of Naples, led from the entrance pavilion to the pasha's dwelling.[42]

During the war against the Ottomans, Shah Abbas erected a large pavilion for a festive gathering of his court and military commanders. On July 30, 1618, della Valle and the prior of Carmelites in Isfahan were invited to attend. The gallery-like structure was covered with felt to protect against the hot sun as well as the cold and rain.[43] The pavilion was open on one side to afford a view of the whole countryside. Only two big poles supported the structure, one at each end, along with a series of wooden arches.[44] Although tents were used for festive gatherings, hunting, and military encampments in Europe, the mobile homes of nomadic peoples were dismissed as an unfamiliar phenomenon. Yet della Valle took this mobile architecture seriously, admiring equally the princely pavilions and the functional tents of the nomadic population. As he bought such a pavilion and traveled with it for long periods of time, the importance he accorded to his mobile home is acknowledged by his bringing it back home to Rome.

The Antiquity of Others, The Arch of Khosrow in Ctesiphon and The Dust of Babel

In a letter dated 23 December 1616 sent from Baghdad to Naples, which evidences substantial editing, an interpretation of a building is set out. Pietro della Valle writes that he wanted to "see certain antique sites [...] attributed to Nebuchadnezzar and therefore [...] considered part of ancient Babylon."[45] Della Valle travelled directly from Baghdad to this location, finding "ruins of a temple, of which it is said, it is the one in which Nebuchadnezzar had the statue worshiped, which is mentioned so often in the Holy Scriptures."[46] The site was named "*Soleimàn Pac*," which translates, as della Valle described to "Soleiman World," or to be more precise, it originated with a certain Soleiman, whom they consider saintly and because of his holiness is called 'world' and lays buried in a nearby mosque [next to the] ruins of a temple. The place is named after a nearby Shiite shrine "Salman Pak."[47] della Valle describes the encounter of the ruins in detail:

> Is actually true, I will check when I get a chance. I will be content with reporting only what I saw. It is a large structure built entirely out of bricks and good mortar, with huge towering walls, the facade of which faces east. This facade is covered from top to bottom with a thousand ornaments of the same bricks, and is 114 of my paces long. The structure apparently had three naves like our churches, of which only the central one is still standing [...]. It does not have a large portal in the middle, as is customary for us, but instead the entire central nave stands open, as high and wide as it is, so that one can see into the interior of the building from outside. Therefore, the peasants here call it "the arch," since it in fact looks like an enormous [triumphal] arch with its large vault open to the front.[48]

Refusing to believe the account of locals who referred to the structure at *Soleimàn Pac* as "the arch," della Valle's basis for such incredulity was the fact that the locals were "uneducated." To della Valle, the structure seemed to better resemble a monumental relic of an Old Testament temple, and he very clearly let this interpretation flavor his description of the building. Later, della Valle recounts that "the Mohammedans gave the building an Arabic name and called it *Aivan Kesra* or *Atrio dei Cesari* since it was built by kings [...], whom they elevated to emperors, and in Persian history [it is] called Ctesiphon."[49] Such incredulity was perhaps not justified since the word "arch," originates in the Persian "Taq-e Kesra" which, translated, means "Arch of Khosrow." After encountering the site at *Soleman Pac*, della Valle noted the need to rewrite his report chapter entirely, since he took the view the building had nothing to do with Nebuchadnezzar but instead was better identified with Ctesiphon, according to the statements of the Persian historians.

From his time spent in Rome, della Valle was intimately familiar with the practice that buildings could carry several names and different identifications, and that even apparently incorrect attributions often contained a certain grain of truth. Pietro della Valle saw the archaeological sites of Persia through the lens of a Roman, and with an interpretation shaped by the ancient architectural monuments in his native city. In Rome, the history of a building's use, and public perception of its use, was reflected in the material form of the buildings as much as it embodied in the stories to which it was linked. The Shiite shrine could have reminded della Valle of pilgrimage churches, which were often constructed near ancient buildings. Pietro della Valle had his accompanying artist make a drawing of the Arch of Khosrow, a drawing that was located in his collection in Rome.[50] FIG 5

The multiple identification of the building at *Soleman Pac* was connected with multiple systems of reference. If it really was to be identified as the Temple of Nebuchadnezzar, the site would have had an exceptional significance for Christian archaeology and would have been a sensational find. As "*Taq-e Kesra*" or the "Arch of Khosrow," the building simply existed beyond della Valle's topographical imagination; and because of his lack of information, he could not link it to any of his own tales. From the hall open to the front of the structure, della Valle retrospectively derived and willfully legitimized the building form as an *Iwan*, an important element of mosque architecture. In Ctesiphon, della Valle confronted a site that had been a touchstone for buildings across the Near East and Asia since the eighth century; he invoked the *topoi* of architectural panegyrics.

After a stay in Baghdad, Pietro della Valle headed for the place at which he had been told the remains of the Tower of Babel would be found, and described his journey thus:

> On 23 November 1616, we left our quarters early [...] and traveled through barren regions and after a while, there was no more vegetation. The earth was entirely

> white, as from rubbed lime from old buildings. One hour before midday, we arrived in Babel, after we could already see it from afar as we left our bivouac in the morning. It seemed to us like a mountain in this flat plain [...], we pitched our pavilion tent directly beneath Babel, in order to stay for a while and to observe it from all sides.[51]

As for the assumed location in which the Tower Babel would be found, della Valle derived it from inquiries he made in Baghdad—apparently the ruins were known there. Many travelers before della Valle had identified the massive ziggurat of *Aqar Quf*, also near Baghdad, as the famous tower—Cesare Federici and Giuseppe Balbi for example.[52] The *Epitome Geographicum* of the geographer Filippo Ferrari from 1605—a remarkable book constantly consulted by della Valle on his journey, practically an early modern version of Google Earth—listed Babylon under the location of Baghdad. Pietro della Valle had heard of the site "*Tel Babyl*" which the Jewish traveler from Spain, Benjamin of Tudela, had already described in the eleventh century as the location of the Tower of Babel.[53] On approach, della Valle now sighted a shapeless hill with a dilapidated building:

> I saw a massive building of one piece, unequal and with crevices at many points, showing many misshapen and confusing forms, which are regularly found in ruined buildings. The height that one can still see today corresponds more or less to a respectable house in Rome, like my own. Today one sees it projecting only slightly above the foundations. [...] I wandered around the rise, went everywhere, and found neither stairs nor rooms nor similar things. Only a massive block of a building [...]. At some points, one finds caves, but one sees that people who traveled through the region dug them out in the modern age. The building material is particularly remarkable. They are all white bricks of raw earth. There are also a few red bricks [...], these, however, are rare. These bricks were not joined with lime, but with fragile earth, and layers of straw were placed between the bricks, similar to those that we use for our roofs [...]. I will bring a few of these bricks along and show them to curious antiquaries, since they are lovely antiquities.[54]

It is not easy to determine the exact location Pietro della Valle visited. Perhaps it was the site that today is known as the "Summer Palace of Nebuchadnezzar." Another possibility would be that he was in Borsippa (*Birs Nimrud*), an ancient Babylonian city around 20 kilometers away.[55] The fact that virtually nothing remained of what was once the highest building in human history led della Valle to be skeptical of the identification of the site with the Tower Babel; he puzzled that so few remains could be seen "of such a building."[56] In a letter written in 1616, these doubts were argued over several pages. In the published travel account, however, della Valle removed all critical undertones and enthusiastically confirmed the identification of the location with the Tower of Babel, the building remains with the Kingdom of Babylon and the tower with King Nimrod, via diverse quotes and many pieces of evidence. Athanasius Kircher extensively quoted the della Valle account in his 1679 book *Turris Babel, sive Archontologia*, published in Amsterdam; Kircher also had two views of the ruins of Babylon engraved based on two drawings from della Valle's collection.[57] FIG 6

In these two examples, the intertwining of biography and geography occurs not only at the level of larger spaces and groups, but also in the respective biographical tale, its phrasing, and narrative shaping. With the description of the discovery of the Tower of Babel, Pietro della Valle invented a building account that seemed to make the site archaeologically comprehensible for the first time.

FIG 6
Unknown engraver after Jan Lucasz. Van Hasselt, View of the Ruins of the Tower of Babel.

FIG 5
Unknown engraver after Jan Lucasz. Van Hasselt, View of the Arch of Khosrow in Ctesiphon, Amsterdam 1679.

FIG 7
Coin with the seated Jahangir and the sun, Mughal dynasty, 1605–1627. Gold, diameter: 21mm.

Pietro della Valle and the Global Baroque

Pope Urban VIII named della Valle honorary chamberlain and an advisor to the recently founded *Congregatio de Propaganda Fide* (Congregation for the Propagation of Faith) upon his return to Italy. Thereafter, della Valle maintained an active correspondence with the secretary of the missionary congregation, Francesco Ingoli, requesting his advice on various dealings.[58] Della Valle provided the impetus for the newly founded mission of the Theatines to Georgia and fostered numerous contacts with missionaries, diplomats, and foreign visitors.[59] He also maintained contact with the family of his first wife in Persia, who informed him regularly of news regarding children and weddings.[60] He corresponded with Sebastian Tengnagel, the imperial librarian in Vienna, Nicolas-Claude Fabri de Peiresc, in Aix-en-Provence, and Jesuit scholar Athanasius Kircher.[61] Even before his departure he was a member of the *Accademia degli Umoristi* (Academy of the Humorists) in Rome, and he became an active member again, and for a period even the "Prince," or head, of the academy.[62]

Pietro della Valle's close friend Francesco Crescenzi was a painter and, like his brothers Giacomo, Pietro Paolo, and Giovanni Battista, had the best connections within literary, artistic, and antiquarian circles. The Crescenzi brothers played a decisive role in all aspects of the logistics of della Valle's journey.[63] Through a series of contacts among the circles of the noble Barberini family, della Valle became friends with philosopher Tommaso Campanella. A few members of the Accademia dei Lincei (Lincean Academy), a science academy, corresponded with him, and Federico Cesi considered granting him membership.[64] While he was still in Goa, della Valle sent Persian scholar and astronomer Zayn al-Din al-Lari an explanation of the newest astronomical theories of Tycho Brahe, Johannes Kepler, and Galileo Galilei.[65] He supported music theorist Giovanni Battista Doni and wrote texts on music theory himself.[66] The famous antiquary and influential art theorist Giovan Pietro Bellori wrote a biography of della Valle in 1662.[67]

FIG 8
Scenes from 'Encampment in the Desert.' Eighteen Songs of a Nomad Flute: The Story of Lady Wenji, early 15th century, Unidentified Artist. Public Domain.

Della Valle housed a collection of books, mummies, and exotic objects in his palace, which became one of the attractions of Rome.[68] The key facts of this collection are well known.[69] One of his mummy masks ended up in the Egyptian Museum and Papyrus Collection in Berlin through Bellori.[70] Two mummies are held in the collection of the *Staatliche Kunstsammlung*, Dresden.[71] The descendants of della Valle left the Islamic manuscripts to the Vatican Library in the early eighteenth century.[72] Della Valle's collection included three mummies, an extensive group of textiles, drawings of Babel, Ctesiphon, and Constantinople, numerous botanical and geological specimens, several paintings, small idols, weapons, books with Chinese characters, bricks from Babel, and the large travel tent.[73] Among the currency and medals he collected were coins of Mughal ruler Jahangir with representations of the sun.[74] FIG 7

On a sheet of paper, della Valle wrote the name of god in in fifteenth languages he was able to read and write. The Latin "deus" was written next to the Hebrew "jahwe" and the Arabic "allah" demonstrating the way della Valle understood the different names of god to be many different perspectives on a similar concept. This approach resembles the method of "accommodation" used by the Jesuits, in which they adapted and integrated rites and costumes into Christianity as a missionary strategy. With this mindset della Valle conceived the architecture and settlements he encountered. Cultural exchange promoted by travelers and intellectuals such as della Valle led to increasing consciousness of the built heritage of the world, and his revelations served to add tents and pavilions to this expansive perspective. This challenged a vision of architecture still very much shaped by the idea of stability dating back to Roman antiquity. Pietro della Valle tried to overcome the dismissal and denigration of nomadic life while exploring the tradition of mobile architecture. FIG 8 For him these structures seemed to be part of a human culture encompassing the entire globe. Pietro della Valle pursued this decidedly utopian project with an impressive tenacity despite the turmoil of the Thirty Years' War. The utopian characteristics of such a definition are clear when it is considered the extents to which della Valle's definition of human culture pushed the limits set by the Inquisition and Christian missions even though it was precisely these Christian missionary networks that provided logistical support for his journey.

1 For the date see Archivio Segreto Vaticano (ASV), Archivio della Valle-Del Bufalo, busta 51, fasc. 4, fol. 147r [Pietro della Valle to Mario Schipano, from Costantinople, June 13, 1615]. On the Islamic traditions of tents and pavilions see Peter A. Andrews, *Felt Tents and Pavilions: The Nomadic Tradition and Its Interaction with Princely Tentage*, 2 vols. (London: Melisende, 1999); Bernard O' Kane, From Tents to Pavilions: Royal Mobility and Persian Palace Design, in: Ars Orientalis, 23, 1993, 249–268; David J. Roxburgh, Ruy González de Clavijo's narrative of courtly life and ceremony in Timur's Samarquand, in: Palmira Brunett, (ed.) The "book" of travels, (Leiden: Brill, 2009), 113–158.

2 Julius Caesar, *I commentari di C. Giulio Cesare: con le figure in rame de gli alloggiamenti, de' fatti d'arme, delle circonvallationi delle città, & di molte altre cose notabili descritte in essi* (Venice: De Franceschi, 1575). For architectural theory see Alina Payne, *The Architectural Treatise in the Italian Renaissance: Architectural Invention, Ornament, and Literary Culture* (Cambridge, UK: Cambridge University Press, 1999).

3 Herodotus, trans. Aubrey de Sélincourt revised by John Marincola, *The Histories*, (London: Penguin, 2003), 255 (IV, 46).

4 Ammianus Marcellinus, History, 31, 2, 10. Ammianus Marcellinus, trans. John C. Rolfe, *History*, (Cambridge, MA: Harvard University Press), 387 (XXXI, 2, 10).

5 François Hartog, *The Mirror of Herodotus: The Representation of the Other* (Berkeley and Los Angeles: University of California Press, 1988), 3–33.

6 *Sinica Franciscana, Itinera et relationes fratrum minorum saeculi XIII et XIV*, vol. 1, ed. Anastasius von den Wyngaert (Rome: Collegium S. Bonaventurae, 1929). For a history of subsequent editions of the texts by the Franciscan missionaries see Armand d'Avezac, *Relation des Mongols ou Tartares par le Frère Jean du Plan de Carpin* (Paris:Librarie Géographique de Arthus-Bertrand, 1838), 3–53. For the manuscripts of the text see *Sinica Franciscana*, xxiii.

7 *Sinica Franciscana*, vol. I, 35.

8 *Sinica Franciscana*, vol. I, 172–73.

9 Vitruvius, trans. Frank Granger, *On Architecture*, vol. 1, (Cambridge, MA: Harvard University Press, 1931), 34–35 (I, 3, 2).

10 See also Gülru Necipoğlu and Alina Payne, eds., *Histories of Ornament: From Global to Local* (Princeton, NJ: Princeton University Press, 2016).

11 Antoine-Chrysostome Quatrèmere de Quincy, *De l'Architecture Ègyptienne* (Paris: Chez Barrois l'aîné et Fils, 1803), 12. See Sylvia Lavin, *Quatremère de Quincy and the Invention of a Modern Language of Architecture* (Cambridge, MA: MIT Press, 1992), 62–101.

12 Quatrèmere de Quincy, *L'Architecture* Ègyptienne, 11–12.

13 Quatrèmere de Quincy, *L'Architecture* Ègyptienne, 226.

14 Quatrèmere de Quincy, *L'Architecture* Ègyptienne, 16–17.

15 Quatrèmere de Quincy, *L'Architecture* Ègyptienne, 17.

16 Ines G. Zupanov, *Disputed Mission. Jesuit Experiments and Brahmanical Knowledge in Seventeenth-Century India*. New Dehli: Oxford University Press, 1999.

17 He had her preserved and returned to Italy via India, then buried her in the family tomb in Santa Maria in Ara Coeli.

18 See Ignazio Ciampi, *Della vita e delle opere di Pietro della Valle il Pellegrino: monografia illustrata con nuovi documenti* (Rome: Barbèra, 1880); Roberto Almagià, "Per una conoscenza più completa della figura e dell'opera di Pietro della Valle," *Atti dell'Accademia Nazionale dei Lincei, Classe di Scienza Morali* 6 (1951): 375–81; Raffaella Salvante, *Il "Pellegrino" in Oriente: La Turchia di Pietro della Valle (1614–1617)* (Florence: Edizioni Polistampa,

1997); Pietro della Valle, *In Viaggio per l'Oriente: Le Mummie, Babilonia, Persepoli*, ed. Antonio Invernizzi (Alessandria, Italy: Edizione dell'Orso, 2001). See also Joan Pau Rubiés, *Travel and Ethnology in the Renaissance: South India through European Eyes, 1250–1625* (Cambridge, UK: Cambridge University Press, 2000), 353–78.

19 A complete critical edition of della Valle's letters, diary, and the travel account does not yet exist. Excerpts from the travel account and diary are found in della Valle, *Viaggio per l'Oriente* (note 18); the letters from Turkey are edited in Chiara Cardini, ed., *La Porta d'Oriente. Lettere di Pietro della Valle: Istanbul 1614* (Rome: Città Nuova, 2001). For some letters from Persia see Pietro della Valle, *Viaggi: La Persia*, ed. Franco Gaeta and Laurence Lockhart (Rome: Istituto Poligrafico dello Stato–Libreria dello Stato, 1972). Important manuscript material is available in the appendices to Ciampi, *Della Vita*, 155–90, note 18; and Salvante, *Il Pellegrino*, 319–97, note 18.

20 The travel account was published in Rome in four volumes, from 1650 to 1663 (Pietro della Valle, *Viaggi di Pietro della Valle il Pellegrino* (vol. 1: Mascardi, 1650; vol. 2: Biagio Deversin, 1658; vol. 3: Biagio Deversin, 1658; vol. 4: Biagio Deversin and Felice Cesaretti, 1663). Deversin reissued the first volume in 1662 with a biography by Giovan Pietro Bellori. Further Italian editions were published in Venice, by Baglioni (1661, 1667, 1681–87), and in Bologna, by Longhi (1672, 1677). A Dutch edition by Jan Hendriksz appeared in Amsterdam in six volumes, from 1664 to 1666; an English translation by John Macock in London, in 1665; a French translation by Jacques Clouzier in Paris, in four volumes, from 1661 to 1664; and a German translation by Johann Hermann Widerhold in Geneva, in four volumes, in 1674.

21 Biblioteca Apostolica Vaticana (BAV), Ottob. Lat., fol. 1-260r, as well as the eight-volume manuscript of the Società Geografica Italiana. A printed facsimile of the latter exists in a limited edition, see Pietro della Valle, De' Viaggi di Pietro della Valle il Pellegrino. Ed. Carla Masetti. 8 vols. (Rome, Società Geografica Italiana, 2011).

22 Copies are found in the Archivio della Valle del Bufalo, in BAV, Ott. Lat. 3383 and 3384, and in Barb. Lat. 5206.

23 On the deliberate practice of making copies see BAV, Ottob. Lat. 3383, fol. 25r-26v; Salvante, *Il Pellegrino*, 342, note 18.

24 Previous research limited to the printed accounts failed to recognize the complexity of the practice of travel writing. See Salvante, *Il Pellegrino*; Giovanna Rabitti, "Stratigrafia testimoniale e strategie compositive nei Viaggi di Pietro della Valle," in della Valle, *De' Viaggi*, vol. 8, 51–117, note 21.

25 On travel accounts see Sanjay Subrahmanyam and Muẓaffar ʿĀlam, *Indo-Persian Travels in the Age of Discoveries: 1400–1800* (Cambridge, UK: Cambridge University Press, 2007); and Giancarlo Casale, *The Ottoman Age of Exploration* (Oxford, UK: Oxford University Press, 2010). See also Gülru Necipoğlu, *The Age of Sinan: Architectural Culture in the Ottoman Empire* (London: Reaktion Books, 2005); Sheila R. Canby, ed., *Shah ʿAbbas: The Remaking of Iran* (London: British Museum Press, 2009); and Ebba Koch, *The Complete Taj Mahal and the Riverfront Gardens of Agra* (London: Thames & Hudson, 2012).

26 ASV, Archivio della Valle-Del Bufalo, busta 51, fasc. 5, fol. 210r-212r, Mario Schipano to Pietro della Valle, April 23, 1616 [translation by author]. If not otherwise noted, all translations are by the author.

27 BAV, Ottob. Lat. 3382, fol. 293r-294v.

28 ASV, Archivio della Valle-Del Bufalo, busta 52, fol. 166v, Pietro della Valle to Angelo Crescenzi, June 14, 1629.

29 With a message from Giacomo Crescenzi, Abbot of Sant'Eutizio, dated October 7, 1620, from Rome Pietro della Valle received five letters of recommendation that were addressed to the eminent clergy in Goa to facilitate his journey to India. ASV, Archivo della Valle-Del Bufalo, busta 51, fol. 240v.

30 ASV, Archivio della Valle-Del Bufalo, busta 51, fol. 246v.

31 Pietro della Valle, *Abbas Re di Persia: Un Patrizio Romano alla Corte dello Scià nel Primo '600*, ed. Antonio Invernizzi (Turin: Zamorani, 2004).

32 Della Valle, *Viaggi di Pietro della Valle*, vol. 1, 711, note 26.

33 ASV, Archivio della Valle-Del Bufalo, busta 190, fol. 27r [December 4, 1618].

34 ASV, Archivio della Valle-Del Bufalo, busta 37, fol. 151r [September 14, 1615].

35 ASV, Archivio della Valle-Del Bufalo, busta 63, fol. 534r [September 14, 1615].

36 Della Valle, *Viaggi*, vol. 1, 657, note 26.

37 BAV, Ottob. Lat. 3382, fol. 56r [December 5, 1616].

38 Della Valle, *Viaggi*, vol. 1, 740, note 26.

39 BAV, Ottob. Lat. 3382, fol. 56r-56v [December 5, 1616].

40 For the date see ASV, Archivio della Valle-Del Bufalo, busta 51, fasc. 4, fol. 147r [Pietro della Valle to Mario Schipano, from Costantinople, June 13, 1615]. Della Valle, *Viaggi*, vol. 1, 238, note 26.

41 For a treatment of Ottoman tents and decorations see Nurhan Atasoy, *Otag-I Hümayun: the Ottoman Imperial Tent Complex* (Istanbul: Aygaz, 2000), cat. no. 126, 262–63.

42 Della Valle, *Viaggi*, vol. 1, 241, note 26.

43 Della Valle, *Viaggi*, vol. 2, 358, note 26.

44 BAV, Ottob. Lat. 3382, fol. 106v [July 30, 1618].

45 ASV, Archivio della Valle-Del Bufalo, busta 51, fol. 253r, Pietro della Valle to Mario Schipano, 23.12.1616. The earlier version of the report is cited here, which is still easy to recognize underneath numerous cancellations and additions.

46 ASV, Archivio della Valle-Del Bufalo, busta 51, fol. 253v, Pietro della Valle to Mario Schipano, 23.12.1616.

47 ASV, Archivio della Valle-Del Bufalo, busta 51, fol. 253v, Pietro della Valle to Mario Schipano, 23.12.1616.

48 ASV, Archivio della Valle-Del Bufalo, busta 51, fol. 253v-254r, Pietro della Valle to Mario Schipano, 23.12.1616.

49 ASV, Archivio della Valle-Del Bufalo, busta 51, fol. 253r, Pietro della Valle to Mario Schipano, 23.12.1616. This sentence is a part of the later edited version of the letter.

50 The drawing, which has yet to be rediscovered, was located in the collection ASV, Archivo della Valle-Del Bufalo, busta 92, f. 132r. An engraving after the drawing was published by Kircher: Athanasius Kircher, *Athanasii Kircheri Turris Babel sive Archontologia*. (Amsterdam: Janssonio-Waesbergiana, 1679), 99.

51 BAV, Cod. Ottob. Lat. 3382, fol. 51v; Pietro della Valle, *In viaggio per l'Oriente*, 136–137, note 18.

52 Cesare Federici, *Viaggi di C. Federici e G. Balbi alle Indie Orientali*. Ed. Olga Pinto. (Rome: Libreria dello Stato, 1962), 5 and 96.

53 According to Pietro della Valle's list of books he read, in 1639 he consulted the edition printed in Leiden in 1633. See ASV, Archivo della Valle-Del Bufalo, busta 92, fol. 39r.

54 BAV, Cod. Ottob. Lat. 3382, fol. 51v; della Valle, *Oriente*, ed. Invernizzi, 137–139, note 18.

55 On this, see Antonio Invernizzi, "Die ersten Reisenden". In: Moritz Wullen / Joachin Marzahn (ed.), *Babylon: Mythos & Wahrheit*. 2 vols., vol. 2. (Munich: Hirmer, 2008), 53–56.

56 ASV, Archivio della Valle-Del Bufalo, busta 51, fasc. 5, fol. 252r.

57 Kircher, *Athanasii Kircheri*, 94, note 50. For the inventory, see ASV, Archivo della Valle-Del Bufalo, busta 92, f. 132r.

58 On his biography see to date Claudia Micocci and Stefano La Via, "Pietro della Valle," *Dizionario Biografico degli Italiani*, 84 Bde., Bd. 37 (Rome: Istituto della Enciclopedia Italiana, 1960–2015), 764–71. Ingoli is often mentioned in the diary as well as the letters. della Valle was consulted, for instance, regarding the visit of the prince of Ethiopia in 1633. ASV, Archivo della Valle-Del Bufalo, busta 186, fol. 16r.

59 BAV, Barb. Lat. 5181.

60 ASV, Archivio della Valle-Del Bufalo, busta 53, fol. 11r (1636); busta 53, fol. 62r (1639).

61 On Sebastian Tengnagel, who suggested having the travel report printed in Germany to circumvent the Inquisition, see ASV, Archivo della Valle-Del Bufalo, busta 52, fols. 175r (8.9.1629). On Peiresc, Kircher, and Morin see Peter N. Miller, "A Philologist, a Traveller and an Antiquary Rediscover the Samaritans in Seventeenth-Century Paris, Rome, and Aix: Jean Morin, Pietro della Valle and N. C. Fabri de Peiresc," in *Gelehrsamkeit als Praxis: Arbeitsweisen, Funktionen, Grenzbereiche*, ed. Helmut Zedelmaier and Martin Mulsow (Tübingen: De Gruyter, 2001), 123–46; Peter N. Miller, "Copts and Scholars: Kircher in Peiresc's Republic of Letters," in *Athanasius Kircher: the last man who knew everything*, ed. Paula Findlen (New York: Routledge, 2004), 133–48.

62 The letters to Gasparo Salviani and his lecture about the journey to the academy are found in BAV, Barb. Lat. 5206.

63 The letters to Francesco Crescenzi are found in BAV, Ottob. Lat. 3383, and are partially transcribed in Salvante, *Il Pellegrino*, 319–81, note 18.

64 Salvante, *Il Pellegrino*, 45–46, note 18.

65 See Avner Ben-Zaken, "From Naples to Goa and Back: A Secretive Galilean Messenger and a Radical Hermeneutist," *History of Science* 47 (2009): 147–74.

66 Martin Kirnbauer, *Vieltönige Musik: Spielarten chromatischer und enharmonischer Musik in Rom in der ersten Häfte des 17. Jahrhunderts* (Basel: Schwabe, 2013), 119–46.

67 Giovan Pietro Bellori, "Vita di Pietro della Valle il Pellegrino," in Pietro della Valle, *Viaggi di Pietro della Valle il Pellegrino descritti da lui medesimo in Lettere familiari all'erudito*. Published in Rome at the expense of Biagio Deversin, endorsed by the queen, 1662. (Rome: Biagio Deversin, 1662).

68 Giovan Pietro Bellori, *Nota delli Musei, Librerie, Galerie et Ornamenti di Statue e Pitture ne' Palazzi, nelle Case e ne' Giardini di Roma* (Rome: Biagio Deversin, 1664), 55.

69 See Archivio di Stato di Roma, Notai dell'A. C., vol. 6484, c. 309r, 8.8.1652, published in Francesco Barbieri, "Pietro della Valle: The Esthèr Oratorio (1639) and Other Experiments in the 'Stylus Metabolicus': With New Documents on Triharmonic Instruments," *Recercare* 19 (2007): 73–124, 106–9. For an almost identical inventory see ASV, Archivio della Valle-Del Bufalo, busta 63, fasc. 42, ff. 531r-536v (8.8.1652). On this (without the inventory in the Vatican) together with the inventory of the estate of Nicolò Francesco della Valle of 8.8.1708, see Kathleen Wren Christian, "Mummies, Scimitars, and a Lost Crucifixion by Domenichino: The Collections of Pietro and Nicolò Francesco della Valle in Seventeenth-Century Rome," in *Renaissance Studies in Honor of Joseph Connors*, ed. Machtelt Israëls and Louis A. Waldman, vol. 1 (Milan: Officina Libraria, 2013), 591–96.

70 Mummy mask, third century AD (height 55 cm), Berlin, Staatliche Museen, Ägyptische Museum und Papyrussammlung, inv. 813. Evelina Borea and Lucilla de Lachenal, eds., *L'Idea del Bello: Viaggio per Roma nel Seicento con Giovan Pietro Bellori*, vol. 2 (Rome: De Luca, 2000), cat. no. 51, 521–22 (Gabriella Scandone Matthiae). See also Pietro della Valle's mention in a letter to Athanasius Kircher, in ASV, Archivio della Valle-Del Bufalo, busta 53, fol. 51v (6.7.1638).

71 Dresden, Staatliche Kunstsammlungen, Skulpturensammlung, Aeg. 777 and 778. See Wren Christian, "Mummies, Scimitars," 594–95.

72 The manuscripts came to the Vatican Library in 1718: Ettore Rossi, *Elenco dei Manoscritti Persiani della Biblioteca Vaticana* (Vatican City: Biblioteca Apostolica Vaticana, 1948), 12–13.

73 Several unpublished lists that are substantially more detailed than the inventories of his estate have been preserved. See, for example, ASV, Archivio della Valle-Del Bufalo, busta 92, fol. 125r-135v.

74 BAV, Barb. Lat. 5206, f. 112v.

Lines of Infrastructural Control in Plantation Jamaica

Hayden Bassett

> By the vast improvement of the roads within these few years, the carriage of goods and merchandise in general is managed with the half number of horses formerly required; [...] Improvements in agriculture have kept pace with those of trade, and every article of produce has grown more valuable. Knowledge and arts have made their way through these channels to the remotest and most uncivilized parts of the kingdom. [...] It seems as if the whole island had been suddenly animated, while the flux and reflux is carried on without impediment by innumerable currents from the heart to the extremities, and from these again to the center of motion. The many excellent roads, already formed, are the vital principle which has infused all these symptoms of vigour, agility, and health, into the whole mass, and roused it into active life.[1]
> —Edward Long, *The History of Jamaica*

By the early eighteenth century an elaborate system of roads connected every Jamaican plantation to the sea. For the planter-elite, sugar, rum, and cattle needed to be moved from plantation to coast, or internally between plantations, safely and rapidly in order to secure a profit. During the first quarter of the eighteenth century, shipping to the sea was relatively easy since most plantations occupied the rich alluvial grounds of the island's coast. In these cases individual plantations typically operated their own wharfs, shipping commodities directly from their coastal estates. By the mid-eighteenth century, as more land patents were granted and larger tracts of land were subdivided, plantation settlement moved from flat coastal landholdings to the semi-mountainous interior.[2] Lacking coastal property, these plantations relied increasingly upon the emerging urban form for the island: the port town. Interior planters commissioned surveyors and engineers to construct connections to the nearest port employing enslaved labor; in most cases this simply required a connection to the nearest existing road. The numerous interior plantations created a system of roads that traversed the entire island and, by 1790, any given Jamaican plantation was connected to each other by way of road. FIG 1

This landscape was not simply a utilitarian construction. Rather, as I will argue, this was a highly socialized infrastructure of control that mediated the movement of enslaved and other subjugated people beyond and between plantation boundaries. Jamaican roads will be theorized as physical infrastructures of planter control and as sites of negotiated power under three headings: Crossroads and Walls, Runaways and Maroons, Roads and Revolt. A reading of these complementary components taken together will render a new context for the eighteenth and nineteenth century roadways of Jamaica: broadly integral to the functions of British rule, road networks comprised an infrastructure of movement in Jamaica understood from both the position of the road builder and the experience of the road traveler. As an architectural expression, an aggregation of planning intentions, and a fulcrum of imperial logistics, this interpretative approach will reveal the roads of empires as sites of both social "reiteration" and "disruption."[3]

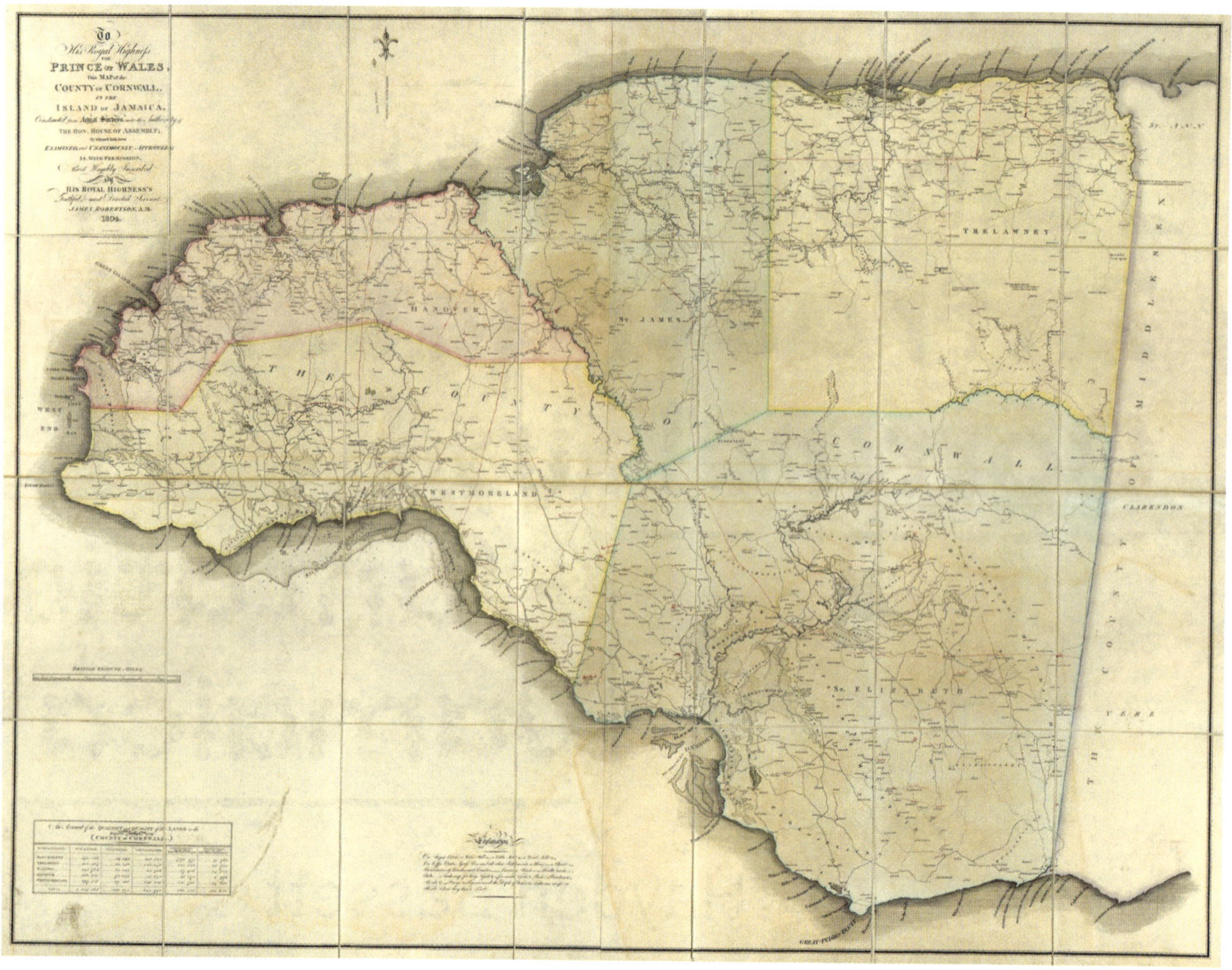

FIG 1
Roads of northeastern Jamaica, as recorded 1804 by James Robertson.

In 2012 the journal *Mobilities* published a special issue entitled "Roads and Anthropology" with theoretically diverse articles by a range of scholars focusing on different geographies united by a common conceptualization of roads, largely from the viewpoint of the ethnographic present.[4] To activate deeper histories, one can look to the infrastructure of earlier movement to map the *flow* of long dead bodies in motion as well as the implications and motivations of interruptions, "frictions," and "turbulence" in the far from smooth *flow* of human mobility.[5] In the documentary records of many colonial settings, "frictions" in the flow of movement are recoverable through survey records, period maps, travelers' accounts, militia archives, and other records of inequalities and conflicts in motion. As eighteenth century Jamaican planter Byran Edwards notes in his history of the British colonies, "Let it not be forgotten, however, that I have had to conduct my readers through a path—not strewed with roses, but—perplexed with briars, and hitherto almost untrodden."[6] While largely a metaphor for historiography, it is equally true in the literal sense.

The changes taking place in Jamaican roads align with those of the British port town generally. The port town grew in global significance as a site of exchange over the course of the eighteenth century and acquired an increasingly urban character. Organized in a grid of streets and alleys, it promoted movement that was concentrated, channeled, and paced. Carried aboard mules and ox-driven carts, barrels of goods from Caribbean plantations such as sugar, rum, and coffee flowed out of the port while imports arrived upon ships, livestock, carts, and upon the arms and heads of enslaved laborers, supporting both formal and informal markets. The Jamaican port also became the point of "seasoning"—the marketing and sale of human cargo prior to marching it to nearby plantations.[7] By the third quarter of the eighteenth century the port became the established seat of government, with troops and colonial administrators taking council and quarters in dedicated buildings within town limits. Officers, troops, and appointed officials moved from parish to parish through port towns that acquired the status of parish capitals. By the 1780s and 90s post offices emerged in major ports to circulate mail outbound in packet ships and internally along roads on the backs of mules.[8] The movement of goods, correspondence, and people became central to island commerce and sociability. Port towns became the centers of gravity for movement along a rapidly growing road network that attracted, channeled, and distributed people and commodities in seemingly unequal ways. As described through the eyes of one Jamaican planter:

> The different wharfs are now a scene of bustle and confusion: the boats passing to and from the different shipping, the wains that are continually clattering along the roads, the noise of the cartmen, the cracking of their whips, and the strings of negroes that are seen passing and repassing upon a variety of avocations; and, last of all, the groups of white people whom curiosity, friendship, or trade, assemble together; afford an agreeable scene of tumult and variety, to which the hurry and confusion of the attending wagons and carts, with the disorder of the cattle, the drivers, and the boys, do not a little contribute.[9]

Although Jamaica had indeed become "animated" by the late eighteenth century, this movement was far from continuous and smooth. Each developing form of movement in the port town gave shape to a physical infrastructure created to connect plantations, ports, landlocked communities, and outlying resources. Segments of road were intentional, though as a network while any given route between two or more places was piecemeal, varied and chosen from a range of options.

Planters commissioned road segments in different ways, for different purposes, and for the most part without centralized regulations. When regulations were passed, such as the establishment of "waywardens" to maintain existing roads, they typically supported the financial and social interests of the road-building planter elite. Such was the case for Jamaica's "public" roads in the late eighteenth and early nineteenth centuries. After a series of proclamations by the Assembly of Jamaica,[10] "public" roads became privately constructed and maintained. Many individual road segments achieved this status after connections to existing roads were established. As a result, transportation taxes were simply redistributed back to plantations and used to maintain a network of roads that was publicly accessible yet largely instrumental to private gain. This gave plantation investors and proprietors considerable control over the design of the island's internal movement, including how people moved to, through and around and what material things they moved in relation to.

Roads were thoroughly contextual: a road moved through a plantation, others to a plantation, and others around a plantation. In this way the particular form and place of connectivity for road segments was motivated by private enterprise, proprietary ideas of movement, and even individual forms of control. Roads could be directed to key buildings that displayed a planter's wealth, often serving as surrogate representations of absentee or resident proprietors. Road segments could equally navigate terrain that concealed certain aspects of the plantation system to abolitionist writers, government officials, tax collectors, missionaries, and other traveling spectators. In some cases, as described in *The Jamaica Planter's Guide*, many of the island's roads had "no other apparent view but to excite the attention of the traveler."[11]

The network of roadways among Jamaica's plantations serves as key evidence for the changing ways in which life in the eighteenth and nineteenth centuries was "animated" through orchestrated movement. Intentions, influences, and consequences of terrestrial connections were varied, and entangled social and economic practices were combined in complex ways. Together this form of material influence provided the literal ground for controlling movement for some and negotiating this control for others.

Between the eighteenth and nineteenth centuries Jamaica's enslaved population grew, from 173,000 in 1760 to 276,000 in 1790 and more than 354,000 by 1808, far outnumbering the small white planter and managerial class.[12] Thus plantation owners designed infrastructure and exercised independent oversight of its construction to extend control through the built environment. Archaeologist James Delle has suggested that the houses of the overseers had strategic viewsheds to and from work areas, and villages allowed a small managerial class to use surveillance, fear, and self-discipline to exert control.[13] Yet stepping beyond the plantation boundaries, where enslaved people frequently traveled, this narrative requires one to look to the roads themselves.

The movement of enslaved people beyond plantation confines was frequent, for both official and illicit reasons. For enslaved individuals whose occupations required travel or those attending weekly markets in port towns, movement along the island's roads was by foot over long distances limited to single days and occasionally nights.[14] In the case of northern Jamaica's Good Hope estate, archaeological and historical evidence from the plantation's villages suggests that enslaved laborers made weekly fourteen-mile trips (seven miles each way) to the coastal market in Falmouth. These individuals loaded their heads and arms with surplus goods from their personal provision grounds to sell or barter. Before evening they made the return trip, entirely uphill, carrying purchased or traded items back to Good Hope. While travel to this market was permitted, and indeed, encouraged by planters to promote self-sufficiency, laborers also made personal visits to relatives and events on neighboring plantations.[15] As historian Justin Roberts observed, "Planters recognized that their estates were part of a 'neighborhood' of plantations" and "there was little a planter could do to prevent nighttime and Sunday journeys around the neighborhood."[16] While little could be done to contain this movement, management of the roadways allowed planters to manipulate the direction, quality, and experience of the physical and perceptual dimensions of movement.

In this regard movement beyond the plantation boundaries appears to have been as controlled as movement within, although in different ways. Early descriptions of the fieldstone walls bordering most eighteenth and nineteenth century roads in Jamaica indicate their confining function. Travelers commonly found "penguin" (Bromelia penguin), a sharp bush, planted atop roadside stone walls, fences, and hedges to "prevent intruders, whether bipeds or quadrupeds."[17] As frequently described in plantation recommendation guides,[18] this prickly relative to the pineapple functioned like barbed wire, FIG 2 serving as a means for keeping people on the roads, out of fields, and off of subversive paths. In port towns, broken bottle glass FIG 3 was mortared atop walls, keeping people to the visible streetscapes and away from lots, yards, and cemeteries.

Roadways, even in close proximity, separated as much as they connected. Movement was channeled to specific destinations, and there were few opportunities to deviate without the threat of bodily injury. Limiting mobility through material infrastructures channeled and distributed the population in ways that equated social position with particular conduits of movement.

Bernard Herman describes similar conditions in South Carolina: "As people moved through [...] the plantation countryside, they encountered an array of landscape experiences that both affirmed and contested social relation-

FIG 4
Engraving, dated 1823, depicting bodies and severed heads of enslaved laborers positioned at crossroads between plantations.

ships within the larger community."[19] Accounts of travelers and planters in Jamaica suggest that fear remained a constant instrument in these in-between spaces.[20] Intersections became predictable points of interaction through which individuals traveling upon a network of roads had to pass. After brutally executing an enslaved laborer for attempting to run away in 1764, Jamaican overseer Thomas Thistlewood recorded in his diary that he severed the individual's head and "put it upon a pole and stuck it up just at the angle of the road in the home pasture."[21] In the design of "paths of observation" for road traffic,[22] the severed head—as anthropologist Rocio Magaña suggests in terms of similar contemporary displays along the U.S.-Mexico border[23]—served not as social "disruption" but as "reiteration." Such reiterative practices were the case not only for human remains displayed along roads FIG 4 but also for the formation of walls, prohibitive glass and vegetation, and other mechanisms limiting movement to prescribed paths of travel to, from, and through an imperial society.

In some cases roads were avoided, yet for the most part, by the late eighteenth century, they were unavoidable. A mosaic of roadways and intervals (areas between sugarcane fields) blanketed the island with countless linear viewsheds and visibly prominent intersections. Runaway ads published in the major newspapers of each parish reveal that many enslaved individuals were apprehended on or near roads and vulnerable intersections. The physical descriptions within these ads records the methods planters used to identify runaways and reflects the brutal strategy to visually index previous runaway attempts. Cropped ears or noses and skin brands were commonly used to physically mark captured runaways and discourage others.

Such was the case for an individual captured in 1792 and described in Jamaica's *Cornwall Chronicle* as "SCIPIO, an Eboe Bruchee, new Negro, marked THARP."[24] Enslaved

FIG 3
Broken 18th-century bottle glass mortared into the tops of the Jewish cemetery of Falmouth, Jamaica.

FIG 2
Early-19th century drawing of "penguin," by British botanist John Lindley. The sharp bush, native to Jamaica, was planted atop roadside walls to keep travelers from deviating from formal roads.

by John Tharp of Good Hope, Scipio covered considerable ground before his capture along the roads of neighboring St. James Parish. Traveling west along the border of the Cockpit Country jungle, Scipio likely was seeking the location of the Maroon communities who had escaped enslavement and formed autonomous societies deep in the island's secluded interior. For Scipio and countless others captured along Jamaica's more accessible roadways, the Maroons were far too removed from areas accessible by road.

Jamaica's Maroon communities were fundamentally unconnected to each other. Accounts suggest that northern Jamaica's Maroons traveled on foot through gullies, discreet paths, and other subtle conduits, avoiding roads frequented by European planters and militia. These modes of movement are difficult to trace, but recent research by historians has shed light on the value of tracing the related spaces and actions. In the innovative project "Slave Revolt in Jamaica, 1760–1761," historian Vincent Brown mapped the sequence of events surrounding the largest slave insurrection of the British colonies in the eighteenth century. He inscribes skirmishes, sightings, responses, and firsthand accounts onto physical landscapes "to discern some of their strategic aims and to observe the tactical dynamics of slave insurrection and counter-revolt."[25] Using this method to follow the movements of Maroons in late-eighteenth century Jamaica reveals much about alternative mobility throughout the island.

In many ways Maroon communities carved out their own infrastructures, in stark contrast to British modes of travel. Writing in 1796, planter Byran Edwards observed:

> The place called the Cockpits before mentioned could be reached only by a path down a steep rock 150 feet in almost perpendicular height. Strange as it may appear, this obstacle was surmounted by the Maroons without difficulty. Habituated to employ naked feet with singular effect, in climbing up trees and precipices, they had acquired a dexterity in the practice, which to British troops was altogether astonishing and wholly inimitable.[26]

In his historical overview of the Maroons of Jamaica, Richard Price suggests that "paths leading to the villages were carefully disguised, and much use was made of false trails replete with dangerous booby traps."[27] Attempting to access the Jamaican Maroon town of Nanny, one early-eighteenth century soldier found "the only path leading to their town [...] steep, rocky, and difficult, and not wide enough to admit the passage of two persons abreast."[28] As with planters nearer to the coast, control of movement via physical infrastructure—however discreet—allowed Jamaica's Maroons to manipulate the mobility of the "other" in strategic ways.

FIG 5
"The Maroons in Ambush on the Dromilly Estate in the Parish of Trelawney, Jamaica, 1801" by F. C. Bourgoin.

This inaccessibility to English travelers gave Maroon communities considerable autonomy and power, which culminated in two major Maroon Wars in the 1730s and '90s. In the latter, known as the Second Maroon War, roadways played a significant and decisive role. Describing British soldiers' attempts to locate Maroon paths, Robert Renny noted, "Confidential Negroes, called Black-shot, Mulattoes, and Indians [...] were added to the regular troops [...] and were of great service in tracing the haunts of the Maroons, and in discovering their settlements and provision-grounds."[29] When questioned on his use of dogs in the Second Maroon War, William Cobbett describes their use for "tracing the footsteps, and discovering the haunts of the Maroons."[30] By all accounts from the early 1790s, the movements of Jamaica's Maroon communities were far from controllable since British authorities lacked the knowledge and ability to navigate the intentionally deceptive and complex infrastructures of Maroon roads.

Reporting on Jamaica in 1795, London based publication *Foreign Intelligence* noted "The Commander in Chief [Gen. Walpole] having obtained the most correct information of every road, tract, and path, leading to the Maroon Town, conceived the idea of blockading them in their own country."[31] Several months later Jamaica's militia commandeered upward of one thousand enslaved laborers from nearby plantations to construct a system of roads to and around the same Maroon communities.[32] The island's militia used these roads to transport infantry and supplies while besieging Maroon towns by cutting off access to nearby springs and provision grounds. After a stalemate, reported as a British victory, Jamaica's Maroons were given property rights to their community lands under the stipulation that they construct and maintain roads to their settlements. Following the construction of several roads, however, Maroon community leaders were "sentenced to transportation" and exiled to Nova Scotia.[33]

In the years following the 1796 truce, Maroon conflicts in Jamaica resurfaced occasionally. Parties of militia were frequently sent out to Maroon territory using the roads constructed after the treaty. By this time Maroon soldiers had redefined their guerrilla warfare to focus on the new-found predictability of British movement the very roads they were forced to build. Roads became the front lines of warfare where Maroon soldiers ambushed British militia during their marches to the interior. An 1801 painting by F. C. Bourgoin, commissioned by General Walpole, illustrates the Maroon roadside warfare tactics. FIG 5 This strategy included scattering British soldiers from the roads into the forest, losing them in rough and unfamiliar territory, where they died of wounds, exhaustion, exposure, thirst, or "fever" [malaria].[34] In an ironic turn of events, the visibility of roads became central to the Maroon defensive and thus the primary obstacle to British militia marches into the interior.

In his early-nineteenth-century *History of the Maroons*, Robert Dallas observed, "On the approach of the troops, the Maroons retreated within the defile [narrow gorge], and remained on a position where, unseen themselves, they could observe the motions of the body acting against them."[35] Whereas the formal battle march of the British along interior roads was linear, visible, and predictable, Maroon movements were fast, disorienting, and incomprehensible to British soldiers. This perplexity is captured vividly in the proceedings of the 1796 Assembly of Jamaica:

> With amazing agility they ran, or rather rolled, through their various firings and evolutions. ... They fire stooping almost to the very ground; and no sooner is the piece discharged, than they throw themselves into a thousand antic gestures, and tumble over and over, so as to be continually shifting their place; the intention of which is to elude the shot, as well as to deceive the aim of their adversaries, which their nimble and almost instantaneous change of position renders extremely uncertain.[36]

In warfare, Jamaica's Maroons traveled not upon but across, around, and over roads in tactical ways. Their asymmetrical appropriation of roads removed the advantage of the British in numbers and caused the road traveler to fear what British road building sought to overcome: invisibility and unpredictability.

As British officers and Maroon leaders fought for sovereignty over the island's deep interior, the roads became something fundamentally different for travelers. For Jamaica's colonial administration the Maroon roads were instruments of political integration through connectivity and accessibility. For the Maroon communities they provided visibility of the movements of the British political authority and facilitated continued resistance to political integration.

By the 1820s, on the eve of emancipation, British road building had reached nearly every nook and cranny of the island. Tollgates, guardhouses, walls, and neighborhood patrols monitored virtually all activity on rural roads and urban streets. Police and road patrols were established in many of the major ports, and a system of written permission for any enslaved laborer traveling upon the island's roads was enforced through confinement, torture, and bail paid by their owner.[37] By this time roads had become not only violent landscapes of control but symbols of planter authority integral to the economic and social interests of Jamaica's plantocracy. This is shown in Adolphe Duperly's 1833 lithograph 'The Rebels Destroying the Road; and Reading Wharf in Flames' depicting Jamaica's Christmas Rebellion. The artist records the destruction of the main road leading to Montego Bay, one of the island's largest ports, by a large and highly organized group of enslaved laborers. FIG 6 This new depiction of an 1824 painting underscores the meaningful implications of such an act to contemporary British observers and of this image Tim Barringer has observed: "Rebels are portrayed as attacking the means of distribution rather than the actual process of cultivation."[38] FIG 7

Yet the framing of this strategy fails to recognize the more fundamental damage achieved by the widespread destruction of Jamaica's roads. It was not simply an attack on the logistics and economics of a finely tuned mechanical process; it was the physical disruption of the infrastructural network that controlled the island's landscape through limited mobility, if not sheer immobility. This control of movement significantly restricted enslaved individuals and households from engaging with the dispersed communities throughout the region.

FIG 6
"Montego Bay from Reading Hill, 1824" from *A picturesque tour of the island of Jamaica* by J. Hakewill.

FIG 7
Adolphe Duperly, "A View of Montego Bay; Taken from Reading Hill; The Rebels destroying the Road; and Reading Wharf in flames, Jamaica," 1833.

Speaking to colonial administrators and Jamaican planters in the 1770s, Edward Long emphatically entreated the enforcement of "any measure, which may bring the roads used for carriage of produce to market, into as perfect a condition as possible; for these are the main springs, which give motion, and due regularity, to every other part of their commercial machine."[39] Long's machine metaphor suggests an empire of moving parts rather than stationary buildings and fields. These components extended beyond plantations and port towns to the connective tissue between them. The roads were far more than an effective means of carrying produce and other commodities.

As discussed, Jamaican roads historically limited the options of movement more than they facilitated it. As large-scale infrastructural investments, they allowed a small managerial class to orchestrate the movements of the island's massive enslaved population. Yet as illustrated in the subversive actions of Maroon communities, in particular the Christmas Revolt, enslaved people exercised strategies for moving around, appropriating, and in some cases destroying this infrastructure of control. In this way roads became sites of social "reiteration" and "disruption,"[40] processes that were experienced or exercised through movement.

By highlighting the role of roadways in subjugation and colonization, it is my objective to augment a growing body of scholarship that implicates the design of infrastructures of movement in promoting inequality and control. Control over the organization of communities was as much a material as an interpersonal interaction between imperial subjects and subjugators. As a concrete construction of control across time and space, roads were not simply utilitarian modes of transport but also means of physical, political, and social manipulation of human and material movement.

1 Edward Long, *The History of Jamaica. Or, General Survey of the Antient and Modern State of That Island* (London: T. Lowndes, 1774), 465–66.

2 See Barry Higman, "The Spatial Economy of Jamaican Sugar Plantations: Cartographic Evidence from the Eighteenth and Nineteenth Centuries," *Journal of Historical Geography* 13 (1987): 17–39; and *Jamaica Surveyed: Plantation Maps and Plans of the Eighteenth and Nineteenth Centuries* (Kingston: University of the West Indies Press, 2001).

3 These ideas of social iteration and disruption were developed in Rocío Magaña,"Dead Bodies," in *A Companion to the Anthropology of the Body and Embodiment* (Hoboken, NJ: Wiley-Blackwell, 2011), 157–71. These two notions were developed to understand the practices of the Mexican cartel along pathways for crossing the U.S.–Mexico border.

4 *Mobilities 7* (2012): Dimitris Dalakoglou, "The Road from Capitalism to Capitalism: Infrastructures of (Post)Socialism in Albania," 571–86; Dimitris Dalakoglou and Penny Harvey, "Roads and Anthropology: Ethnographic Perspectives on Space, Time, and (Im)Mobility," 459–65; Penny Harvey and Hannah Knox, "The Enchantments of Infrastructure," 521–36; Richard Kernaghan, "Furrows and Walls, or the Legal Topography of a Frontier Road in Peru," 501–20; Gabriel Klaeger, "Rush and Relax: The Rhythms and Speeds of Touting Perishable Products on a Ghanaian Roadside," 537–54; Morten Nielsen, "Roadside Inventions: Making Time and Money Work at a Road Construction Site in Mozambique," 467–80; Morten Pedersen and Mikkel Bunkenborg, "Roads that Separate: Sino-Mongolian Relations in the Inner Asian Desert," 555–69.

5 These authors use various terms to describe the social variation of physical movement throughout the world. For further discussion on the politics of differential movement, see Michelle Lelièvre and Maureen Marshall, "Because Life Itself Is But Motion: Toward an Anthropology of Mobility," *Anthropological Theory* 15 (2015): 434–71. For discussion on the "frictions" of human mobility, see Allison Truitt, "On the Back of a Motorbike," Journal of the American Ethnological Society 35, Issue 1 (Feb 2008); 3–19. For further discussion on "turbulence" in the "flow" of human movement, see Stuart Rockefeller, "Flow," *Current Anthropology* 52 (2011): 557–78.

6 Bryan Edwards, *The History, Civil and Commercial, of the British Colonies in the West Indies* (London: John Stockdale, 1793), 149.

7 Louis P. Nelson, *Architecture and Empire in Jamaica* (New Haven, CT: Yale University Press, 2016).

8 Barry Higman, *Plantation Jamaica 1750–1850: Capital and Control in a Colonial Economy* (Kingston: University of the West Indies Press, 2005).

9 William Beckford, *A Descriptive Account of the Island of Jamaica: In Two Volumes* (London: T. and J. Egerton, 1790), 320.

10 Francis Hanson, William Wood, and Bryan Edwards, *The Laws of Jamaica: Comprehending All the Acts in Force, Passed between the Thirty-Third Year of the Reign of King George the Third and the Thirty-Ninth Year of the Reign of King George the Third, Inclusive* (Kingston: A. Aikman, 1811).

11 Thomas Roughley, *The Jamaica Planter's Guide; Or, A System for Planting and Managing a Sugar Estate, or Other Plantations in That Island, and throughout the British West Indies in General* (London: Longman, Hurst, Rees, Orme, and Brown, 1823), 258.

12 Justin Roberts, *Slavery and the Enlightenment in the British Atlantic, 1750–1807* (Cambridge, UK: Cambridge University Press, 2013), 15.

13 For a discussion of Foucault's Panopticon model considered in the siting of plantation overseer houses, see James Delle, *An Archaeology of Social Space: Analyzing Coffee Plantations in Jamaica's Blue Mountains* (New York: Plenum, 1998); *The Colonial Caribbean: Landscapes of Power in Jamaica's Plantation System* (Cambridge, UK: Cambridge University Press: 2014); "The Landscapes of Class Negotiation on Coffee Plantations in the Blue Mountains of Jamaica: 1790–1850," *Historical Archaeology* 33 (1999): 136–58; "The Habitus of Jamaican Plantation Landscapes," *Out of Many, One People: The Historical Archaeology of Colonial Jamaica*, ed. James A. Delle, Mark W. Hauser, and Douglas Armstrong (Tuscaloosa, AL: University of Alabama Press, 2011), 122–43.

14 Mark W. Hauser, *An Archaeology of Black Markets: Local Ceramics and Economies in Eighteenth-Century Jamaica* (Gainesville, FL: University Press of Florida, 2008).

15 Frederick Smith and Hayden Bassett, "The Role of Caves and Gullies in Escape, Mobility, and the Creation of Community Networks Among Enslaved Peoples of Barbados," in *Archaeologies of Slavery and Freedom in the Caribbean: Exploring the Spaces in Between*, ed. Lynsey A. Bates, John M. Chenoweth, and James A. Delle (Gainesville, FL: University Press of Florida, 2016): 31–48.

16 Roberts, *Slavery and the Enlightenment*, 266.

17 Philodinus Scotus, *Reminiscences of a Scottish Gentleman Commencing in 1787* (London: A. Hall, 1861), 176–77.

18 For period discussion of the use of roadside "penguin" fences, see William Beckford, *A Descriptive Account* (London: printed for T. and J. Egerton 1790), 167; James Stewart, *An Account of Jamaica: And Its Inhabitants* (London: Longman, Hurst, Rees and Orme, 1809), 81; and Cynric R. Williams, *A Tour Through the Island of Jamaica: From the Western to the Eastern End in the Year 1823* (London: Hunt and Clarke, 1827), 343.

19 Bernard Herman, "The Embedded Landscapes of the Charleston Single House, 1780–1820," *Perspectives in Vernacular Architecture* 7 (1997): 43.

20 For further discussion on the visual practices of intimidation in plantation landscapes, see Nelson, *Architecture and Empire*.

21 Douglas Hall, *In Miserable Slavery: Thomas Thistlewood in Jamaica, 1750–86* (Kingston: University of the West Indies Press, 1999), 30.

22 For discussion of the design and experience of "paths of observation," see Timothy Ingold, *Perception of the Environment: Essays in Livelihood, Dwelling, and Skill* (London: Psychology Press, 2000), 229.

23 Magaña, "Dead Bodies," 157–71.

24 Douglas B. Chambers, "Jamaica Runaway Slaves: 18th Century," in Douglas B. Chambers, *Documenting Runaway Slaves* (Gainsville: University of Florida Digital Library of the Caribbean, 2013), *accessed March 31, 2014, http://ufdc.ufl.edu/AA00021144/00001

25 Vincent Brown, "Slave Revolt in Jamaica: A Cartographic Narrative, 1760–1761," Harvard University, 2012, March 28, 2014. http://revolt.axismaps.com/project.html.

26 Bryan Edwards, *The Proceedings of the Governor and Assembly of Jamaica: In Regard to the Maroon Negroes* (London: J. Stockdale, 1796), xxiv.

27 Richard Price, *Maroon Societies: Rebel Slave Communities in the Americas* (Baltimore, MD: John Hopkins University Press, 1996), 6.

28 Long, History of Jamaica, 340.

29 Robert Renny, *An History of Jamaica: With Observations on the Climate, Scenery, Trade, Productions, Negroes, Slave Trade, Diseases of Europeans, Customs, Manners, And Dispositions of the Inhabitants* (London: J. Cawthorn, 1807), 56.

30 William Cobbett, *Cobbett's Parliamentary History of England from the Norman Conquest in 1066, to the Year 1803* (London: Bagshaw, 1818), 929.

31 Alexander Lindsay Balcarras, "General Orders: Montego Bay, Headquarters, Vaughn's Field, Aug. 15," in *The Scots Magazine; or General Repository of Literature, History, and Politics* (Edinburgh: Alex. Chapman and Co, 1795), 958.

32 Edwards, *Proceedings*, 59.

33 Hanson et al., *Laws of Jamaica*, 167.

34 Long, *History of Jamaica*; Scotus, *Reminiscences*, 210.

35 Robert C. Dallas, *The History of the Maroons, from Their Origin to the Establishment of Their Chief Tribe at Sierra Leone* (London: T. N. Longman and O. Rees, 1803), 188.

36 Edwards, *Proceedings*, xxxiii.

37 Hanson et al., *Laws of Jamaica*.

38 Timothy Barringer, Gillian Forrester, and Bárbaro Martinez-Ruiz, *Art and Emancipation in Jamaica: Isaac Mendes Belisario and His Worlds* (New Haven, CT: Yale University Press, 2007), 356–57.

39 Long, *History of Jamaica*, 482.

40 Magaña, "Dead Bodies," 164.

Extracts from a Conversation with **Kimberly D. Bowes:** Reprise on the Villa Romana at Piazza Armerina

The site of the Villa Romana at Piazza Armerina is economically tied, above all, to North Africa, this much is now clear. The mosaics of the Villa themselves are entirely about ideas of empire as collection, and the heterogeneity of the collection as an encyclopaedic sense of everything that empire imagines. These ideas explain why we would encounter a perfectly detailed copy of the Circus Maximus in Rome in the mosaic floor of a bathhouse in the middle of nowhere in Sicily. I think of the Villa Romana at Piazza Armerina as standing for an idea of empire as cosmopolis, empire as collection. If such an agency means one thing in Rome, it means quite another in Sicily. Archaeologists have sourced the precious marbles from the *aula* from all over the world. It reflects a very typical Roman obsession with geology, as though taking a little bit of the rock of everywhere is the same thing as actually controlling that real estate. FIG 1 And if you're in a villa in Sicily doing this, it makes very plain that what is actually at stake is economics and the control of labour and people.

Our research project relating to the Villa Romana at Piazza Armerina began from an investigation of what was supposed to be the estate village of Piazza Armerina—a town called Philosophiana. At this site, we found an urban-like entity with a grid plan, baths and its own internal quasi-urban logic. The ceramics from this agro-town were overwhelmingly from North Africa. Such massive quantities of North African *amphorae* only increase after Rome loses control of North Africa to the Vandals. As other scholars have also suggested, the contacts between Rome and North Africa only increase after the political disconnect.

What I think is really interesting is the way in which the senatorial elite of the Villa Romana at Piazza Armerina are no longer the same senators of the early empire who were largely Rome-based and who did bureaucratic things only sporadically.[1] The senators of later empire often have their hands really dirty in the actual mechanisms of running the empire. The bureaucratic elite and the senatorial elite, in some ways, become one. A place like Piazza Armerina is not simply a statement about what it means to be elite, but it is also is very much a statement about what it means to be a part of the engine of the state. A geopolitical shift in terms of centers and peripheries is perhaps better understood here as a new redefinition of "center." There are broad implications for the former center, namely Italy. Exactly at the time Piazza Armerina is built, Italy has to pay taxes. That is a huge change. It is almost as though Italy itself becomes a colony. Having previously been the center exempt from this kind of extraction and oppression that goes along with it, now it is subject to the same things that it has subjected everywhere else to for hundreds of years. Piazza Armerina, I have argued, is a direct product of that. Because now, suddenly, Italian territory has to produce, and produce quite urgently, and it becomes a real center of bureaucratic attention. I was interested in this moment in which the economic engine of the empire becomes realigned. Italy has a new role, which it hadn't assumed for hundreds of years. And with the loss of Egypt to feed Constantinople the new capital, suddenly Rome has to find a new source of food, and that source is Sicily and Southern Italy above all.

If the architecture of the Villa Romana at Piazza Armerina sits outside of the canon of Roman architecture that's perhaps also because of the chronology. It's too late, it's too Sicilian. Similarly, it's also much less considered actually as an architecture but rather a group of mosaics. FIG 2 The volumetric figure of the house is becoming increasingly apparent now, in part due to the big restoration campaigns ongoing there. The periodization issue is important: Late antique architecture eclipses the canon, except for maybe the Basilica of Maxentius and Constantine and there only because it informs Christian architecture. The domestic architecture of this period is completely off the radar. Piazza Armerina is further off the radar because it doesn't fit well into contemporary domestic architectural trends. It has no real predecessors for its plan, and no real successors. The closest thing it looks like is Hadrian's villa, but the Villa Romana at Piazza Armerina is tiny in comparison to that precedent. But these factors are also in part to do with the archaeological expectations of domestic architecture. There is a general sense that archaeology doesn't want a house to reflect any kind of individual agency. Domestic buildings are meant to represent "society." And, if domestic buildings aren't held to represent society, then they just represent the idiosyncrasies of the person who designed them or built them—they fail to do "history."

Ultimately, architecture in the context of "the house" is often more than anything the product of an individual person and their interaction with the architect. It embodies the collision between an individual and design. While we're happy to think about architects exerting meaning in certain contexts, we find it problematic for houses in the past. Because it means this stuff can't be used to do history because you can't excavate that kind of individuality. What is wonderful about Piazza Armerina is that it is so marvellously idiosyncratic. It had to be the collaboration between someone with a very specific idea, and a set of designers and builders who realised it. Whether the emphasis is on one agent or the other in the final built outcome we can't know.

What we think was likely to have taken place at the time was that family units were actually communicating through their houses. Several designs can be seen which are clearly in conversation with one another. Such groupings emerge in tiny little micro-regional pockets with distances small enough that you can imagine the inhabitants visiting each other. We have evidence that these rural elites exchanged letters, even shipped plans around to each other as part of this ritual of friendship. Individuals would write letters, but those letters would be accompanied by building plans. One family would actually write by letter to another, "well, what do you think, I've done this thing." Then, there would be a long piece of excurses that describes the thing that you've done. No one, of course, has done enough work in Sicily to know if this building has a conversation partner. And if, in fact, the owner of the Villa at Piazza Armerina is in conversation with another villa nearby we haven't found yet. It is entirely possible too.

No one had ever looked at the landscape around Piazza Armerina prior to our research there. The Villa had been seen mostly through its mosaics, not really as an economic entity. FIG 3 What we found is, that at the moment or even just before this Villa is expanded to its current form, intense new landscape activity coincides. The number of sites increase, large sites, small sites, and huge numbers of agricultural entities throughout the landscape. The Villa and its condition in the broader landscape must be related. The Villa is founded probably to control and ultimately to store the products of that landscape. And indeed, a fundamental part of the design of the Villa at Piazza Armerina is the inclusion of huge warehouses to store the products of the land which are then shipped off on a huge long-distance inland route which connected Agrigento and Catania. The produce, probably grain, is then loaded on ships and shipped off to Rome. The Villa at Piazza Armerina is one piece of the cog of that broad machine.

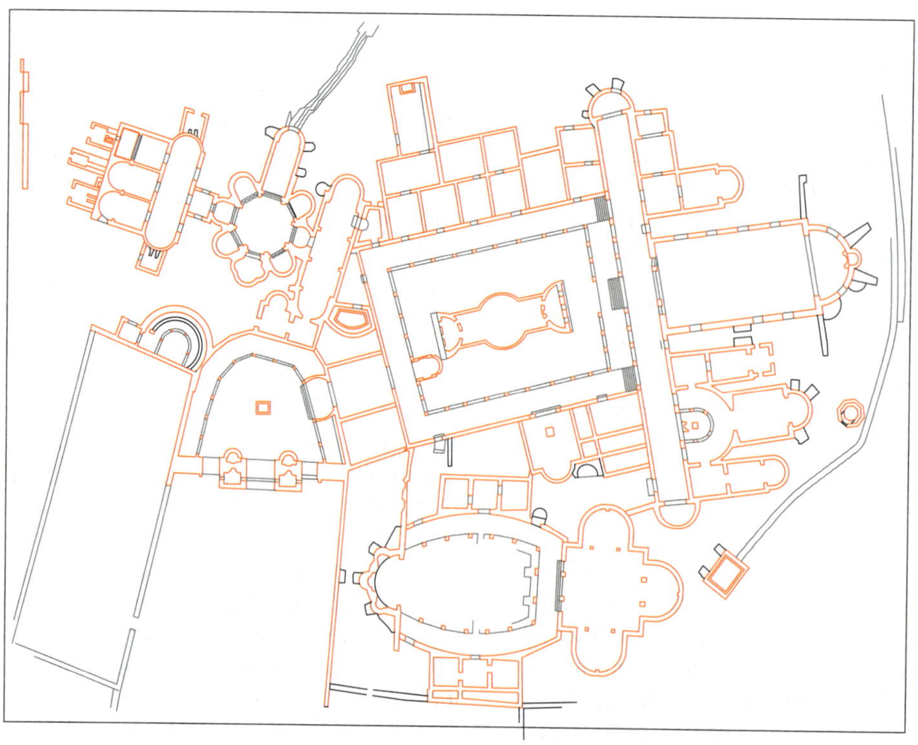

FIG 1
Apse drawing by Patrizio Pensabene and Enrico Gallocchio.

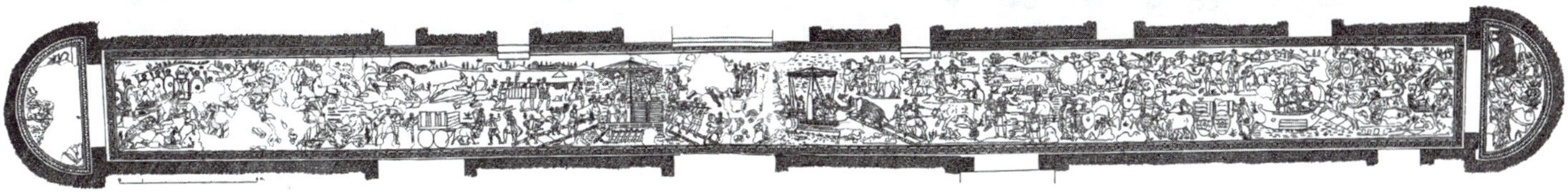

FIG 4 Villa Romana at Piazza Armerina, Plan.

We have a really hard time imagining the house generally as an instrument of bureaucracy. Such a concept doesn't sit alongside the idea of an opulent private home. In a modern American context, it is hard to reckon with the particular overlap of the private realm and the state that occurred in antiquity. These are two entities which for Americans occupy so very different hermeneutic spheres, which is why constructs about the late empire as a privatisation of power are ubiquitous. But power is always private in the Roman world. The Roman state is purely the private extended. Piazza Armerina is just the late antique manifestation of the same thing—a house that has become an arm of the state. Roman ideas of commemoration are very different. Consider the way in which Romans and modern American presidents commemorate their term of office—a Presidential library. This would have been inconceivable to a Roman. President Trump had the idea that his presidency will be commemorated with a golf course, or by something on his golf course. This would have made perfect sense to a Roman. Because the ideas of landscape and of commemoration go very tightly together. Romans very often built their tombs on their royal estates. Because this was a representation of your private self and your public self, mixed.

FIG 3 Mosaic from the Villa Romana at Piazza Armerina.

FIG 2 Mosaic from the Villa Romana at Piazza Armerina.

In terms of the internal comparison of the Villa at Piazza Armerina to the first century CE house, it is important to note that even most late Roman houses do not have the qualities of the Villa at Piazza Armerina. Everyone wants to fit the Villa at Piazza Armerina with some kind of ideal of the late antique house. But most late antique houses are on some kind of continuum with the Pompeian house. Piazza Armerina has no particular relationship with anything. While the Pompeian house and its successors are a phenomenological architecture meant to be experienced in space, I've argued that the Villa at Piazza Armerina is a noetic architecture, that is, an architecture meant to be understood in plan. In many cases the rooms are so big that their actual spatial qualities can only be appreciated in plan because when you're in them you can't actually sense their form. Take the large bi-apsidal hall with the Great Hunt mosaic, for example. Here, you can't actually feel you're in a bi-apsoidal hall when you're in it, it's too big. FIG 4 Its only when you look at it in plan that you can see it. Consider also the obsessive proliferation of the apse at Piazza Armerina as well—in the baths, in the dining spaces. This too is a design aspect that must be intended to be appreciated in plan.

This is a condensed extract of a conversation recorded on March 12, 2018, between Charlotte Algie and Kimberly D. Bowes.

1 See the research of Jon Weisweiler, for example: Weisweiler, J., *Making Masters, Making Subjects: Imperial Ideology and Memory Policy in the Early Roman Empire and in the Later Roman State* (Los Angeles: J. Paul Getty Museum, 2015).; Weisweiler, J. "The Price of Integration: State and Élite in Symmachus' Correspondence," in *Staatlichkeit und Staatswerdung in Spätantike und Früher Neuzeit*, eds. Peter Eich, Sebastian Schmidt-Hofner and Christian Wieland (Heidelberg: Universitätsverlag Winter, 2011).; Weisweiler, J., 'Inscribing Imperial Power: Letters from Emperors in Late-Antique Rome' in *Historische Erinnerung im städtischen Raum: Rom in der Spätantike*, eds. Ralph Behrwald und Christian Witschel (Stuttgart: Franz Steiner Verlag, 2010).

Other Methods

Yasmin Vobis & Aaron Forrest

Disegno, meaning drawing or design, has held a privileged role in Western art and architecture since the time of the Renaissance. In the sixteenth century text *The Lives of the Artists*, the Renaissance painter and historian Giorgio Vasari characterized a fundamental split in artistic production between two distinct modes, *disegno* (drawing) and *colore* (color). Vasari heralded *disegno* as "the animating principle of all creative processes."[1] He associated it with his native Tuscan tradition of hardlining as well as with the tradition of the preparatory drawing as exemplified by the artist and architect Michelangelo.[2] In opposition to this was *colore*, which Vasari linked to the working methods of Venetian painters such as Titian, whose paintings are structured by vibrant fields of color and atmospheric tone. Over time, *disegno* became associated in Italian arts with Apollonian rationalism in clear contrast to *colore* and its Dionysian excesses apparently founded in intuition and a lack of control. Not surprisingly, *disegno* has been taken up as the primary mode of architectural design ever since.

The role of the line drawing in architecture cannot be overstated. Recent histories of Italian architecture have been almost uniformly framed by treatises that analyze buildings through the lens of *disegno*: plan diagrams and black-and-white photographs in publications by Colin Rowe, Rudolf Wittkower, John Summerson, Robert Venturi are a few such examples. Orthographic projection, including both plan and section, was developed as a technique of abstraction, scrubbing subjects clean of color as well as contingency, irregularity, and atmosphere. The line drawing—following *disegno*—stresses form, space, geometry and structure as the primary *loci* of architecture.

Architects today are expert manipulators of lines and increasingly complex virtual geometries. But when it comes to color there is little to say. Color, when used at all, is typically understood as an applied surface treatment, subservient to form. However, when viewed through a contemporary lens, each half of Vasari's dichotomy appears to promise a different spatial conception: *disegno* promises the hard-lined, geometrically defined space based on projective apparatuses; *colore* on the other hand, suggests a tonal approach rooted in aerial perspective that deals directly with regions and gradients, fields and potential environments. By considering *colore* in conjunction with *disegno*, fresh possibilities arise for both the analysis and design of architecture.

Polychrome Atmospheres

There are two notable exceptions in the modern history of architectural drawing to the disciplinary lopsidedness described above; the early nineteenth century controversies over polychromy, and certain early Renaissance dead-ends in the history of perspective. Both of these exceptions offer alternative approaches to the opposition between *disegno* and *colore*. That is, they are cases which specifically suggest a method of reading *disegno* through *colore*, and vice-versa. Not surprisingly, both historical examples bind together issues of representation as well as the production of new built works.

Because the bleached monuments of antiquity elicited a classical ideal, color has been eyed with suspicion by architects in the modern era. The monuments of antiquity suggested a blankness and severity of decorum that inspired white marble reconstructions in the Renaissance and, later, in the era of Neoclassicism. Knowledge of ancient polychromy—multiple colors applied to works of sculpture or architecture—has existed at least since the seventeenth century, but it was not until the rise of archaeology as a discipline in the nineteenth century and the associated uncovering of new excavations with remnant color traces, that the body of evidence became overwhelmingly clear. This, in turn, precipitated a crisis for architects.[3] Ancient Roman and Greek architecture was not white. It was probably garishly colorful—to the point of hedonism—in a way that had been previously unimaginable. Tempers at the time ran hot, and even early proponents of polychromy such as Quatremère de Quincy quickly realized that archaeological reasoning would lead to a monstrosity that jeopardized the timelessness of the classical ideal, and that placed color at the forefront of architectural debate.[4]

Among the archeologist-architects embroiled in this debate were Jacques Ignace Hittorff, Gottfried Semper, Owen Jones, and Henri Labrouste, who set off on their Grand Tours to southern Europe, redrawing the ancient monuments and attempting to reframe the discipline. Hittorff, Semper, Jones and Labrouste were among those who showed that the works of the ancients demanded a contemporary reimagination, and that ancient architecture was not static or timeless, but rather that its received interpretation was just as unstable as the paints applied to it. The architectural problem that the trace evidence of color fomented, that "ancient polychromy had to be imagined,"[5] also became a creative opening for certain architects. The fragments of color brought the contemporary obsessions into contrast and allowed a reinvigorated classicism to be imagined. The drawings of these Grand Tour travelers inhabit a space between documentation and projection as partial ruins are reimagined into active, vibrant spaces full of life and color. The imaginative methods that were developed to produce the drawings were subsequently applied to the design of new civic architectures for the modern city.

Perhaps the most-well known and controversial drawings of the polychromic revival are Henri Labrouste's restorations of Paestum, completed in 1830 while he was

FIG 1
Henri Labrouste, *House of the Tragic Poet in Pompeii*, a perspective view from the atrium, 1825–30.

FIG 2
Owen Jones and Jules Goury, "Court of the Fish-pond," chromolithograph from the volume *Plans, Elevations, Sections & Details of the Alhambra*, 1842.

a *pensionnaire* at the French Academy in Rome. FIG 1 Infusing the ruins with washes of vibrant color, Labrouste's Paestum went against the canons of the French Academy and the principles of neoclassicism writ large. There is evidence that Labrouste made use of the camera lucida for his studies of ancient structures,[6] and it was perhaps his optical relationship to the evidence, rather than a metric one, that would allow him to introduce materiality, light, color and atmosphere into his studies. It is no wonder that his later work seized upon this uncovered potential of *colore*. In his Bibliothèque Nationale, Labrouste imagined the reading room as a virtual garden, with integrated environmental paintings and a cloud-like ceiling structure broken apart by light.

Owen Jones's and Jules Goury's travel studies developed this atmospheric approach further. Jones' landmark publication on the Alhambra which grew out of these studies, was remarkable not only for its unusual subject matter at the time, which looked further afield from the accepted canon of Greece and Rome to the Islamic world.[7] FIG 2 The study was also notable for the particular representational techniques Jones employed to present the Alhambra as a major monument through plans, sections and detail drawings. Going beyond romanticized views of the building complex, Jones described the forms and colors of the Alhambra with painstaking precision, showing both the optical effects and the detail of their technical underpinnings.

To disseminate his drawings in color, Jones made use of early techniques of chromolithography.[8] Lacking government support, Jones published the Alhambra drawings by subscription over roughly a decade, from 1836 to 1845. His initial work with a professional printer proved unsatisfactory: "when my work was printed at the printers, a most horrid waste of time, paper and consequently money, took place."[9] As a result, Jones set up a press and hired printers in his own atelier so that he could directly supervise the process, eventually printing the volumes himself at great financial cost. While chromolithography was still in its infancy, the new setup allowed Jones to experiment over many years, in particular with the registration of the separate plates—sometimes up to seven—and the chemical interaction of the inks, paper and printing surface. Jones used both zinc and stone printing surfaces in order to find the more reliable surface that would allow multiple prints without a loss in fidelity. The desire to incorporate gold for a heightened illusory effect—such as those seen in medieval illuminated manuscripts—led Jones to experiment with printing varnish on the page and sprinkling it with gold dust. He instituted a painstaking, laboratory-like process, through which he developed a reproduction technique phenomenal enough to match the ambition of the Alhambra study itself. This is evident in the experimentation visible across the consecutive volumes printed throughout the decade. Nevertheless, it was this obsessive spirit that allowed Jones to help set the early standards for chromolithography.[10]

One remarkable aspect of the chromolithographs in the Alhambra study is that their incredible detail was produced through multiple, separate layers of colors. The layers of color are pure *colore*: rather than infills of forms described primarily with outlines—as was the case for Labrouste. The drawings are made of flat, overlaid, translucent fields of tone. These flat patterns nevertheless result in intricate surfaces that leap off the page through their painterly opticality: their layering, blending, and interactions of color capture the surreal atmosphere of the Alhambra simultaneous with its geometry.

These fascinations with color and atmosphere bore fruit when Jones set to work on the project for the interior decoration of the Crystal Palace in 1851, developing a painting scheme for the Crystal Palace's iron structure that consisted of narrow, alternating stripes of primary colors and white. Jones's intent was to produce an "atmosphere in bloom."[11] FIG 3 Stripes of red, yellow, and blue, separated by white, were positioned based on their relative optical advancement. The result was "the slow passage from vivid colour outlining the forms of the elements in the foreground to an atmospheric, vibrant white...as the hues mixed in the distance."[12]

FIG 3
William Deane Butler and Edmund Walker, 'Owen Jones's decoration of the transept of the Great Exhibition,' 1850.

Interestingly, Jones saw this as a way of increasing the perceived volume of the Crystal Palace's prominent 'Great Exhibition Hall' spaces.[13] By the time the Crystal Palace painting was complete, Jones had fully embraced the implications of architectural polychromy, with "its tendency to be the vehicle of the expression of a vast luminous indefiniteness."[14]

Correspondences between Jones's study of the Alhambra and his later architecture are striking. They demonstrate one way to understand the agency of architectural representation tailored to an interest in color, and its attendant implications for buildings. Seen together, projects like Labrouste's *Bibliotheque Nationale* and Jones' Crystal Palace extend early fascinations with polychromy into a rich moment of integration between structure, space, and color.

Heads in the Clouds

At stake in the *disegno* versus *colore* dichotomy is not simply the inclusion or exclusion of coloration in architecture, but rather the ubiquity of delineation as the unchallenged framework for design production. The reliance on edges for the description of surfaces and volumes, and on linear constructs for perspective and parallel projection, determine that lines organize virtually everything for architects—via their incredible yet unspoken efficiency and abstraction. *Colore* promises an alternate paradigm: a tonal approach based on fields, rather than outlines.

Robin Evans points to the germination of such an approach in his essay "Piero's Heads" that looks to Piero della Francesca's fifteenth century treatise *De prospective pingendi* (On the Perspective of PAINTING) and in particular to the third section of the text in which Piero describes his use of the "Other Method." This outlines a way for painters to deal with the unruly objects in the world, i.e. the objects other than buildings and man-made artifacts that resist perspectival constructions based in the principles of Euclidean geometry.[15] In discussing early Renaissance perspective, Evans recognizes that "there was a perspective construction for architecture, and a [different] perspective construction for heads."[16] This latter construction is of interest here, and not only for the way in which it vastly expanded the types of objects that could be precisely described with drawings. Piero's Other Method, as interpreted by Evans, is curious in that it involves the mapping of points taken from irregular surfaces directly onto a picture plane. FIG 4 Rather than reducing objects to contour edges that can neatly snap into a projective armature, the Other Method samples point geometries directly from an object's surface, thereby resulting in the "dissolution of surfaces into constellations of dots."[17] Measuring local relationships without the geometric armature produced by vanishing points, it is significant that the origination of overall form lies in the mapping of points and not lines. Whereas lines can summarize whole areas by mapping key features, a point method treats each piece of information as discrete and constructs features via a process of building up the many pieces of information. The Other Method even-handedly samples what is there and implies relationships through accumulation and juxtaposition rather than abstract rule sets.

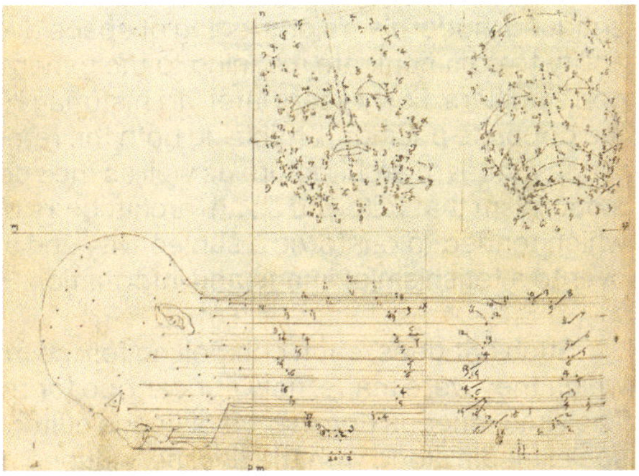

FIG 4
Studies of heads from Piero della Francesca's *De prospectiva pingendi*, Book 3, c. 1474.

It goes without saying that the Other Method is much less efficient. Questions of resolution and computation time—or hand-plotting, in Piero's case—quickly come into play. There is no doubt that even Piero della Francesca recognized the tediousness of his technique. His drawings of heads dissolve into sparse point clouds and are further scaffolded by annotations and construction lines overlaid to keep track of information. In the end, he reverts to contour line drawing for the outlines of main features to make sense of his data. Perhaps due to the difficulty of the approach, as well as the perceived overwrought appearance of the figures in his resulting paintings, according to Evans, the Other Method was largely ignored by Piero's contemporaries.

What the Other Method promised, however, was an ability to map irregular and complex surfaces, thereby potentially expanding the canon of objects that could be precisely described. Moreover, the capacity to draw more than just hard-edged boundaries opens territories that are far less definite without sacrificing precision. Information is sampled from all over surfaces not just the edges, and thereby also allows for a description of the surface itself which might otherwise be left blank in a hardline drafting technique. The Other Method allows the draftsman to draw surfaces and spaces in terms of their perceptible qualities, which might include the interaction of color, pattern, and form, as well as ambient phenomena such as light, shadow, and atmosphere.

This method for a drawing is even more sophisticated if we begin to understand Piero's work as a low-resolution, primitive virtual model of a head. He sets up his drawings as a set of related proto-orthographic projections. From these he employs a process akin to auxiliary projection—a technique not developed fully until the nineteenth century—to produce a potentially infinite series of views. Piero's studies of turned heads are thus developed from two other orthographic projections and he organizes information for a virtual point cloud model of a head through multiple projections on paper so that the model can be turned and tumbled in space as needed. Piero della Francesca's Other Method points to a concept of drawing that is less a static, singular projection, than it is a modeling of space in three dimensions. This brings attention to a particular combination of attributes necessary for the description of surface qualities and forms in three dimensions and leads to a way of drawing space and surface qualities, including color, simultaneously.

Precise Atmospheres

Owen Jones and Piero della Francesca—both iconoclasts—proposed alternatives to the dominance of *disegno* in their respective eras. The current moment, simultaneously dominated by parametric design methods on the one hand and dimensionless, 'post-digital' collage methods on the other, suggests the urgency of a contemporary alternative. Working with photogrammetry drawing techniques that contain information about space and color simultaneously, we have recently begun to see the possibility of a third position in this debate. Photogrammetry treats *disegno* and *colore* as dialectic rather than as a duality, and as such suggests a contemporary Other Method for reimagining the terms on which contemporary architectural production is based.

The technique of photogrammetry uses photographs taken from complementary positions to model complex three-dimensional real-world forms. FIG 5 It has historically been used to survey facades, as well as produce topographic maps from aerial photographs using stereo-plotters.[18] The method in use today uses software to compare digital photographs and compute point coordinates in a digital modeling environment. Relying on the camera as a simple perspective-machine, spatial coordinates and RGB values are combined to produce digital point cloud models that connect color and space in a form of spatial pointillism. While such models are most often used as an intermediary step towards mesh or surface models, the raw output of the process is more provocative, producing navigable, colorful point clouds.

Photogrammetry presents the possibility of creating a dialectic between *disegno* and *colore* in architectural representation. In a point cloud environment, *colore*, i.e. color and tone, is the protagonist, while *disegno*, i.e. linework and geometry, is merely inferred from the color clouds presenting an inversion of the typical draftsman's approach to delineating architecture. Such models produce information about color, light and surfaces in three dimensions, transporting the hardline drafting work from the deduction of line-based rulesets into the rendering of precise atmospheres.

Recently, throughout 2017, we used this technique to scan thirty-two building interiors in Italy.[19] The buildings were selected to constitute a spectrum of the varied uses of color in the architecture of antiquity to the Baroque era. Across the selection of buildings, the use of color began to reveal a more complex and subtle set of interactions of color and space than anticipated. Color, we found, could reinforce building geometries through close alignment; alternatively, it could run past corners, obscuring the formal definition transcribed so clearly by plans and sections. And while the bulk of the scans focus on fresco and mosaic surfaces, scans of the seemingly colorless white interiors of the Baroque period provided new readings of spaces that had up until now been represented stripped of color and other contingencies.

In their comprehensive clarity, the point cloud drawings illuminate a lacuna within architectural and art historical narratives of the subject buildings, namely that a representation of the interplay between architectural form and surface treatments provides a more challenging reading than either on its own. The pairing of geometric coordinates with color data forces a simultaneous reading of sets of content that have hitherto rested comfortably within their respective domains. Rather than reinforce accepted narratives, the point clouds upend architectural-historical narratives, and suggest a possible reevaluation of the works themselves as well as some of our disciplinary assumptions.

Likewise, the drawings suggest an alternative method for developing representations of existing buildings, but also for thinking through the limitations of contemporary architectural production and for anticipating new ways of seeing and making architecture. More specifically, they propose a means of rethinking the dominance of the line-as-generator in architectural design, as well as the fixed and sometimes stale relationship between surface and volume—or image and structure—in buildings themselves. Indeed, the very three-dimensionalization of the image that is distinguished in the photogrammetry point cloud models implies a new mode of architectural realism whereby image and space are valued as co-equal elements, and are placed in structured simultaneity rather than left in abstract isolation.

The drawings display mechanisms by which we might reevaluate the often uncomfortable relationship that has existed between image and form in architecture since the Renaissance. During this period, architectural discourse has ping-ponged back and forth between—typically brief—movements that embrace the role of color, tone and image in architecture, and those that attempt to eradicate it. In just the last half century alone, we have seen this full cycle repeat itself at least once. In *Learning from Las Vegas*, Denise Scott Brown, Robert Venturi, and Steven Izenour famously critiqued modernism's privileging of space over buildings' ability to communicate meaning to the general public via pop signifiers. Forty years later, art historian Hal Foster took the opposite position, criticizing both the referential basis for postmodern architecture as well as the spectacular neo-modernism that followed as an "architecture of obfuscation, which tended to reinforce a subjectivity and society given over to a fetishism of image and information."[20]

Such critiques, each compelling for the moment in which they were made, now appear ripe for reevaluation. The simultaneous dominance of image culture based in social media along with the decline in phenomenological discourse presage the possibility that there is more to be found in the contemporary dialectic between image and space than from either one individually. The point-cloud drawings suggest a new position amidst these supposed binaries, staking out an unlikely common ground between Mies van der Rohe and Venturi-Scott Brown. The images suggest the possibility of imagining surface and structure, image and space, in dialogue, and offer new territory for architectural design based in an ambiguous tonality rather than hardline oppositions. The methods of their construction imply buildings that construct ambivalent atmospheres rather than definite objects, and an architecture that can take on a complex reality without sacrificing a clear aesthetic agenda. But in order to do so, it must begin with—rather than merely result in—images. It is an architecture constructed from points rather than lines.

Point Clouds

The Basilica di San Vitale is well-known among art historians and architects alike, but the readings of the space of the church have typically been isolated endeavors. FIG 6 Art historians have tended to focus on the elaborate mosaics and their communication of early Christian narratives via photographic close-ups.[21] Architecture historians, on the other hand, have repeatedly reproduced its octagonal plan as an alternative to the standard basilica form, heralding its centralized, spiraling earthenware dome as a fusion of Byzantine and local traditions.[22] However, San Vitale is a complex three-dimensional construct, and when one sees the surface details precisely mapped onto the building

FIG 6
Reflected Ceiling Plan of the Basilica di San Vitale, Ravenna (521–547 CE). Drawing by author.

FIG 5
Point Cloud Model of the Basilica di San Vitale, Ravenna. Drawing by author.

FIG 7
Point Cloud Model of Santa Costanza, Rome (4th century CE). Drawing by author.

FIG 8
Reflected ceiling plan of the Basilica Papale di San Francesco d'Assisi (1228–1253 CE). Drawing by author.

FIG 9
Reflected ceiling plan of the Cattedrale Metropolitana di Santa Maria Assunta, Napoli (4th–19th century). Drawing by author.

geometry, it makes evident the ways in which surface scaffolds geometry and vice versa. The interior represents a complex color atmosphere, where the verticality of the section, the openings below the dome, and the vaulting of the perimeter all dramatize light and shadow. The colorful surface mosaics reflect and refract light to create an ambiguity of space, and the powerful emotive effect of the mosaics is in turn heightened by this context.

The cloud-like photogrammetric scan of Santa Costanza, an early Christian mausoleum relates building geometry to the delicate late Roman mosaics on the ambulatory vaults and apses. FIG 7 One of the ceiling mosaics shows plants, animals, and objects set on a white ground, recalling ancient floor mosaics depicting 'unswept floors.' In a radical reorientation, when we look up, we seem to be looking down. Walls, floors and ceilings do not yet have a predetermined representational status. It is not yet a given that the wall becomes the site for depicting the horizon, the floor for the ground, and the ceiling for the sky. Furthermore, another significant aspect of the scans that becomes evident here is their reversibility. The axonometric seems to be looking from the outside in, yet what we are seeing is the interior surface. The scans are skin deep, capturing only the perceptible interior surface, without any poché or wall thickness. At the same time, the points of the scans are isotropic—that is, visible from any direction—and they resist falling along a perfect theoretical surface. Instead, they form an uncertain cloud, a color-space probability rather than a geometrical certainty. The spaces become re-read as mere skins, which strip the buildings of their weight and recast them as projects that belong firmly to the 21st century.

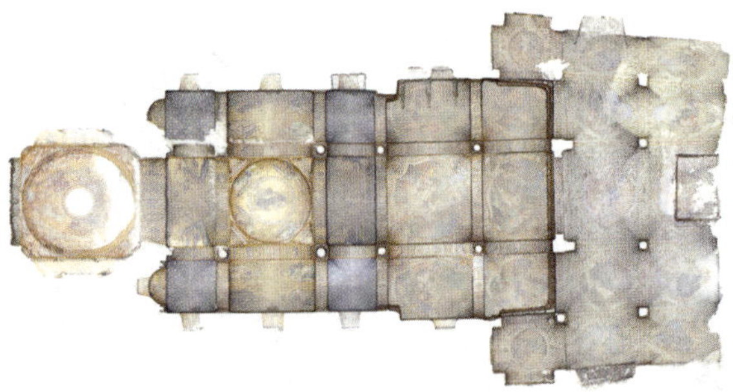

FIG 11
Reflected ceiling plan of the Santa Maria dell'Ammiraglio (La Martorana), Palermo (12th–18th centuries). Drawing by author.

FIG 10
Reflected ceiling plan of the Duomo di Siena (Santa Maria Assunta), Siena (13th century). Drawing by author.

FIG 12
Reflected ceiling plan of the Mausoleo di Galla Placidia, Ravenna (5th century). Drawing by author.

The Basilica d'Assisi is an exploration of spatial and temporal expansion through painting. FIG 8 Both the Upper and Lower basilicas are relentlessly covered in late medieval frescoes and other surface ornamentation. The frescoes are set on the walls as well as the curved ribbed vaults above to form a continuous, complex, colorful, all-encompassing surface. This skin resists quick glances and an overall comprehension: the onslaught of visual detail on every surface is overwhelming. Our gaze moves more slowly, to absorb all of the surface details, and even longer to piece together the many episodes of the life of St. Francis on display over the various spaces of the complex. The collaborative effort of the many authors of the frescoes, including Giotto, among others, proliferates minutiae over a vast, architectural space. Zooming in progressively on the scan we can go from reading the overall organization to individual narrative frames. Several stages of details are revealed in a powers-of-ten like fashion, that would otherwise be impossible to discern from a simple plan or photograph.

Photogrammetric scans thrive on geometric irregularities. In fact, making a scan of a perfectly even, smooth, flat white surface is incredibly difficult because the technique relies on differences in contrast and coloration. As such, this technique is well-suited to map the concatenated complexities and idiosyncrasies of some of the larger interiors that have been built over many centuries, such as the cathedrals of Naples and Siena, and La Martorana in Palermo. For example, the Duomo di Siena has an interior that is mat-like, a growth of vaulted bays defined by heavy columns, and interrupted only by the hexagonal dome and the campanile, around which the other geometries skew to adapt. FIG 10 It becomes clear that the expression of a perfectly shaped cross plan is less important than the construction of a vast atmosphere; in this case an overwhelmingly dark blue one, as the walls and columns are covered in alternating bluish-black and white travertine stripes, and the ceiling is continuously frescoed with a dark blue starry sky.

Likewise, the scans of the cathedrals in Siena and Naples show us how buildings grow incrementally over many centuries, foregrounding an interest in creating spatial connections through coloration rather than perfectly planned geometries. The construction of Santa Maria dell'Ammiraglio (La Martorana) began in Palermo in the twelfth century following a compact, cross-in-square plan, to which a larger forehall, dome and campanile were added in the sixteenth and eighteenth centuries. While these spaces feel unified in experience, the reflected ceiling plan of La Martorana lays bare an incremental construction, revealing the subtle changes in the geometry and surface decoration that occur at each stage. FIG 11 In Naples, the reflected ceiling plan of the Cattedrale Metropolitana di Santa Maria Assunta also reveals the ad-hoc ways in which it was built. The complex began at the tip with the colorful Battistero di San Giovanni in Fonte with its refined mosaics from the fourth century, and grew along increasingly larger, perpendicular axes until the nineteenth century. As such, the reflected ceiling plans of the digital models reveal both the organization of the complex and the surface ornamentation. FIG 9 They are simultaneously measurable, preserving distance and proportions, and atmospheric, capturing color and light. They productively flatten these vast buildings onto the two-dimensional page, collapsing space, structure, and ornamentation into a single view. At the same time, photogrammetry makes apparent the incredible handmade quality of these buildings. With their documentary spirit, they depict every feature: the inconsistencies of lighting, the warps of materials, dirty colors, and the messiness of construction.

The Mausoleo di Galla Placida in Ravenna takes the logic of colore to an extreme. Every surface of its vaulted ceiling and walls are covered with small tesserae (tile) in an all-encompassing mosaic. FIG 12 The tiles are made from glass, not stone, and are set onto curved surfaces, so that any movement through the space makes them sparkle. As a result, the surfaces are difficult to gauge and seem to be constantly shifting, making perception of geometry unstable. Color here leaps from the walls, liberated from the flattened realm of surfaces, to become a spatial condition. The building is a color environment to the point of distraction. So much so that a deviation from the orthogonal in plan, which had been indiscernible in person, was revealed when reviewing the photogrammetric scan.[23] Most published plans of the mausoleum fail to note this skew, an omission which clearly demonstrates the way that orthographic constructions normalize buildings through representational conventions. We know that the scan is correct because despite the overall skew, the applied mosaic cruciform at the center of the ceiling—the image—remains perfectly perpendicular in the scan. Along with its misshapen dome, we can deduce that imperfections in building geometry were made irrelevant in the face of overwhelming color on every surface. This tendency signals a shift in the intent of the builders: not an obsession with the perfect, rational geometry, but the construction of an atmosphere.

Like many buildings in Matera, the church of Madonna delle Virtù is carved directly out from the side of a mountain, an architecture which turns a mass of the rock into a seamless surface and a volume to be inhabited. FIG 13 Although the church interior was originally frescoed, the majority of what is now visible is the surface of the soft tufa limestone from which this church was carved. The unmasked, monolithic mass of stone creates a seamless interior with subtle gradations. It is impossible to talk about joints or lines in this building—the framework of *disegno* simply does not

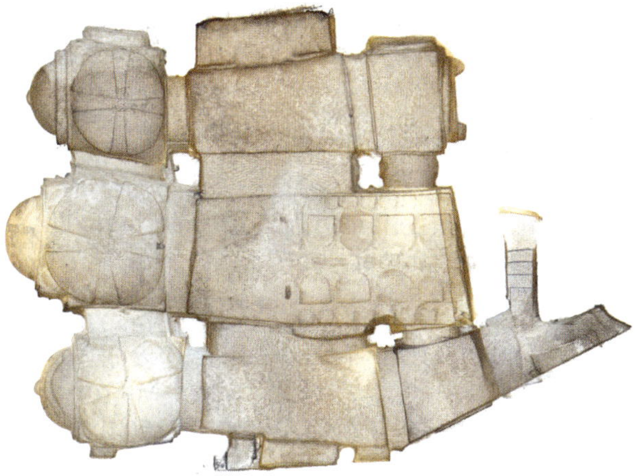

FIG 13
Reflected ceiling plan of the Chiesa di Madonna delle Virtù, Matera (10th–11th century). Drawing by author.

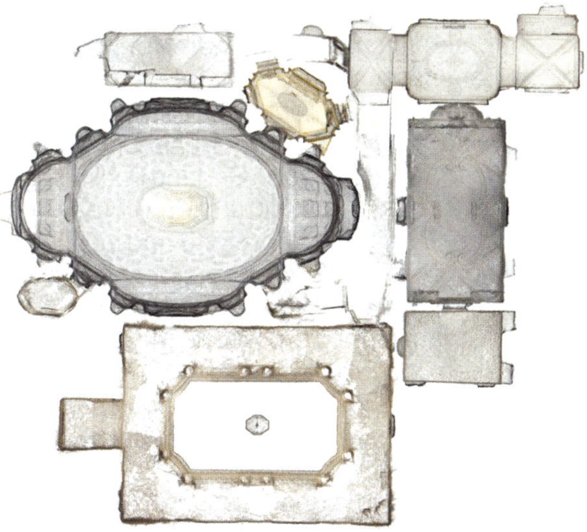

FIG 14
Reflected ceiling plan of the San Carlo alle Quattro Fontane, Rome (1634–1646). Drawing by author.

apply. What becomes clear with the scan of the Matera church is the strangeness of this type of subtractive architecture: the translation and approximation of the typical basilica plan with its three naves and gabled timber roof into an alternate material and method.[24] The scan captures the church's irregularities: its lack of rational geometries, as well as the subtle coloration of its surfaces and lighting. The church of Madonna delle Virtù is a building that was conceived without drawing and thus an architecture without a projective apparatus. Resisting rationalization, the irreducible nature of its form and color can only be represented by a sampling process like photogrammetry.

The church of San Carlo alle Quattro Fontane in Rome provides an example of a work of Baroque architecture that has been so carefully studied in terms of its dominant geometrical innovation that the sophistication of the complex as a whole has often been neglected. FIG 14 Academic interest in the dome above the nave, which takes its geometry from the elliptical floor plan, clearly shown in Borromini's own belabored drawings, has been revived in recent years due to its seemingly parametric basis and totalizing consistency, forming an unexpected precedent for contemporary trends in digital architectural practice. The drawings which we produced of Borromini's complex reveal an architect's careful consideration of a sequence of interconnected spaces, each shaped according to function and the contingencies of the site. The reflected ceiling plan shows that the dome above the nave is not the only vault, but rather the culmination of a thematic interest in vaults generally that plays itself out across the building. Each space within the cluster has a unique vault form, from the lunette vault in the sacristy to the "pinched squinch" vault in the refectory anteroom to the softened groin vaults in the cloister. Despite their apparent whiteness, each vault is illuminated in a distinct manner. Taken together, the ceilings of San Carlo can be understood as a series of studies that relate ceiling form, color, and light, and, via these mechanisms, Borromini himself as a deft manipulator of atmosphere.

1 Giorgio Vasari, *The Lives of the Artists Volume 1* (New York: Penguin Books, 1987).
2 A recent show in 2017 at the Metropolitan Museum of Art in New York memorialized this with the show's title, "Michelangelo: Divine Draftsman and Designer."
3 Cecilie Brons, "Transmission and Transformation: Ancient Polychromy in an Architectural Context," Carlsberg Fondet, Accessed January 9, 2018, http://www.carlsbergfondet.dk/da/Forskningsaktiviteter/Forskningsprojekter/Andre-forskningsprojekter/Transmission-and-Transformation-Ancient-Polychromy-in-an-Architectural-Context.
4 David van Zanten, *The Architectural Polychromy of the 1830s*, (New York: Garland Publishing, Inc. 1977), 7.
5 van Zanten, *Architectural Polychromy*, 6.
6 Barry Bergdoll, "Labrouste and Italy" in *Henri Labrouste: Structure Brought to Light*, eds. Corinne Bélier, Barry Bergdoll, and Marc Le Cœur (New York: Museum of Modern Art, 2012), 59.
7 Owen Jones and Jules Goury, *Plans, Elevations, Sections, and Details of the Alhambra: From Drawings Taken on the Spot in 1834* (London: Owen Jones, 1842–45).
8 André Tavares describes the relationship between Jones's *Alhambra* publication, the development of chromolithography, and his later design for the interior of the Crystal Palace in "Colorful Crossroads: From Paper to the Crystal Palace" in André Tavares, *The Anatomy of the Architectural Book* (Montreal: Canadian Center for Architecture, 2016).
9 Kathryn Ferry, "Printing the Alhambra: Owen Jones and Chromolithography" in *Architectural History* 46 (2003), 177.
10 David van Zanten, "Architectural Polychromy: Life in Architecture," in *The Beaux-Arts and Nineteenth Century French Architecture*, ed. Robin Middleton, (Cambridge, MA: MIT Press), 211.
11 van Zanten, "Architectural Polychromy: Life in Architecture," 213.
12 van Zanten, "Architectural Polychromy: Life in Architecture," 213.
13 David van Zanten, *The Architectural Polychromy of the 1830s*, (New York: Garland Publishing, Inc. 1977), 258.
14 van Zanten, *The Architectural Polychromy of the 1830s*, 269.
15 Robin Evans, "Piero's Heads" in *The Projective Cast: Architecture and Its Three Geometries*, (Cambridge, MA: MIT Press, 1995).
16 Evans, *The Projective Cast: Architecture and Its Three Geometries*, 123.
17 Evans, *The Projective Cast: Architecture and Its Three Geometries*, 151.
18 "Photogrammetry," Wikipedia, accessed January 4, 2018, https://en.wikipedia.org/wiki/Photogrammetry.
19 The scans formed Yasmin Vobis' project *Color Space* as a Fellow at the American Academy in Rome in 2017. Her research was made generously possible through the Founders/ Arnold W. Brunner/ Katherine Edwards Gordon Rome Prize in Architecture.
20 Hal Foster, *The Art-Architecture Complex*. (New York: Verso, 2011), 129. The chapter expands upon the argument made in Foster's remarkably prescient essay "Illuminated Space, Embodied Structure" from a Richard Gluckman monograph a decade earlier.
21 See E.H. Gombrich, *The Story of Art* (London: Phaidon Press Limited, 2000), 135.
22 Cyril Mango, *Byzantine Architecture* (New York: Rizzoli, 1985), 76–79.
23 It is possible that the plan skew is a result of the mausoleum having been originally built as a chapel connected to the Chiesa di Santa Croce, and each of its principal axes was aligned with a different part of the church complex.
24 The scan of the church in Matera was a collaborative effort between Yasmin Vobis and Joseph Williams, a fellow in art history at the American Academy in Rome in 2017.

Joseph Urban's Mar-a-Lago

John Loring

> The new art is a fusion of the pictorial with the dramatic. It demands not only new designers of scenery, but new stage managers who understand how to train actors in speech, gesture and movement, harmonizing with the scenery.
> —Joseph Urban, 1913[1]

The Austrian designer and architect Joseph Urban arrived in the United States of America in March 1911 in Boston, Massachusetts. His Atlantic crossing was instigated by the contract he had been offered and had accepted, to assume the position of the artistic director of the Boston Opera, but Urban's earliest design works in the United States had already been designed and realized in some seven years prior. In 1904 Urban executed his design of the Hagenbund exhibit at the Louisiana Purchase Exhibition in St. Louis, Missouri, one small section of the Austrian Pavilion complex combined under the overarching thematic "Sceneries and People of Austria." For his Hagenbund design, Joseph Urban won a grand prize, and the St. Louis Exhibition Gold Medal.[2] FIG 1 The Peter Behrens-designed Pavilion of the German Empire was nearby.[3] After the success of the Louisiana Purchase Exhibition project, Joseph Urban remained in Vienna despite commissions offered in the United States, and devoted himself to a prolific practice encompassing architecture, furniture design, stage design and book illustration. He developed an expanded repertoire of built work across the world which included villas, city apartments and public spaces.[4]

It was in this intervening period—after the first U.S. works in St. Louis and before his departure from Vienna—that Urban's debut as a set designer occurred.[5] Joseph Urban had designed public events such as the design and stage management of the 1899 Vienna *Ringstrasse* parade for the Golden Jubilee of the Austro-Hungarian Emperor Franz Joseph, which Urban worked on together with artist Oskar Kokoschka.[6] FIG 2 But the pivot into the theatre was initiated by a commission for the comedy *Zwischenspiel*, three acts by Arthur Schnitzler; Urban developed the scene design in 1906 and the production took place the same year. This was followed by a stage commission for the design of the sets for Parts I & II of Goethe's *Faust*, performed in 1906 at the *Burgtheatre* with the costumes designed by Urban's noted brother in law Heinrich Lefler. Twenty-three further stage productions were realized by Joseph Urban in Europe before World War I, work for which there regrettably remains little visual evidence. The last of these European set designs was developed in 1911—also a joint commission between Urban and Lefler—for three productions with the Boston Opera Company to be performed in Milan. It was while in Paris, for discussions about one of these three Milan productions, *Pelleas et Mélisande*, with the composer Claude Debussy and the Boston Opera's Director Henry Russell, that Russell personally offered Urban the role of artistic director of the Boston Opera, instigating his Spring 1911 Atlantic crossing.

About Urban's work in the United States theatre, it can be said that he took everything he learned and assimilated from the golden age of Viennese art, with all its eclecticism, and applied it to the stage with an unparalleled brilliance.

FIG 1
Joseph Urban design for the Hagenbund Winter Exhibition in Vienna, 1904. *The International Studio* 22 (1904), 265–268.

Urban thoroughly mastered the New Stagecraft explored by contemporary and leading Russian, Swiss, German and English set and costume designers. Until Urban's arrival, however, American stagecraft remained in a primitive phase; rows of footlights characteristically still illuminated two-dimensional painted drops. As described by theatre critic Kenneth Macgowan in *Century Magazine* in January 1914, the opening of Urban's production of *Pelleas et Melisande* for the Boston Opera on the January 10, 1912 "changed everything."[7] Macgowan continues: "Urban's lavish use of color—the intense blues and the sapphire-blue skies he loved in Egypt—his opulent and diffused lighting that for the first time eliminated footlights revolutionized stage design... (This vision) was made of strange, shadowed and sun-flecked glimpses of wood and fountain, grotto and castle, vivid and varied color..... His scenery and costumes and lights have given the productions of this opera-house music a distinction which they could never have obtained through their singing and acting alone."[8] FIG 3, 4

By way of introducing some of the technical aspects of Urban's innovations in theatre, of particular importance is his use of "*pointillage*," a method well already known and debated within fields of art production by 1906 when Urban began his work in Theatre. Kenneth Macgowan provides some contemporary notes of his encounter with Urban's unique use of this technique for the theatre, noting: "...It is the secret of his living colors that makes his walls look like something besides flapping canvas. Unlike the conventional scene-painter, [Urban] does not try to make a coating of glutinous paint and some shreds of canvas look like rock or air. He follows the modern artist, daubs a fleck of color here, another there, and achieves a total effect that is as suggestive of reality as is any painting by Monet, and hence in the same degree beautiful. And the many flecks of mingled color carry all the prismatic glory of natural light."[9] As Macgown describes, the theatrical surface was revolutionized by Urban. Instead of flat blocks of uniformly pigmented liquid paint filling in a drawn scene, the scenic backdrop developed by Urban used multitudes of layered applications of thinly sprayed plumes of paint, flecked into a quasi-pixelation logic whereby only from the distance of the theatrical viewer would the surface take on the desired uniform hue.

FIG 4
Drawing for the set of the Boston Opera production of the Wolfgang Amadeus Mozart opera *Don Giovanni*, 1913. The production opened on February 7, 1913.

FIG 3
Drawing for the set of the Boston Opera production of *Louise*, December 18,1912. Opera by Gustave Charpentier, conducted by André Caplet with Louise Edvina as Louise.

FIG 2
Pavilion designed by Joseph Urban the 1908 Jubilee of Emperor Franz Joseph II in Vienna. The reviewing stand for the Emperor design is topped by the figure of a crown.

FIG 5
Joseph Urban, Sketch of scene design for Tales of Hoffman, Boston Opera, 1912.

A further equally important, though less noted, architectural feature of Urban's technique for the stage is the use of portals and platforms. FIG 5 Contemporaneously, Macgown noted this: "The portals which Boston first saw in 'The Tales of Hoffmann,' are a characteristic new convention. They are narrow walls set at right angles to the footlights, framing in the sides of the stage, and connected at the top by a strip of the same width. The portals proper, at the sides, narrow the huge stage space of our opera-houses to navigable proportions. The horizontal strip at the top rids us of the worst convention of our theater, the "sky borders," or parallel strips of cloth used to represent the sky and to hide the rafters. It brings down the sight-line to the top of the cycloramic back-drop. The other purpose of the portals is more curious. They are both a new proscenium and a part of the scene. They replace the old glaring frame of gold and red draperies, and they enter into the design of the setting."[10] Thus the use of portals in the Urban stage sets both complemented and framed his harmonization of color, painted scenery and lighting, via a means to spatially sample and direct the eye to exclusive portions of surface. Under Urban's leadership, the American Theatre in Boston became an intensifying center of global innovation in set coloration and lighting design.

Urban evidently enjoyed phenomenal critical success in Boston. The critic Henry Taylor Parker reviewed Joseph Urban's first production for the Boston Opera, *The Tales of Hoffmann*, in November 1912 for *The Boston Evening Transcript*, and described Urban's production as "a revolution in the setting and lighting of the American stage."[11] But Urban returned to Europe as part of the Boston Opera's tour of performances at the Théâtre des Champs-Élysées in May and June 1914. When World War I broke out in August 1914, he was stranded and forced to flee back to America via Naples. The Boston Opera thereafter also shuttered in September 1914 because of the war. Thus, Urban relocated to New York at the request of George C. Tayler, of Tayler & Liebler and Co., for an engagement to design Edward Sheldon's script for the *The Garden of Paradise*, a play based on Hans Christian Andersen's *The Little Mermaid*. This performance opened on November 28, 1914 in New York. There, Joseph Urban began producing designs for the Metropolitan Opera, New York, and his total of fifty-three designs in this role deserve particular note. For a 1920 production of *Parsifal* performed in English at the Metropolitan Opera, Urban designed sets and costumes including a sacred grove. FIG 6, 7 While in New York, Urban sustained delirious levels of realized work in theatre in increasingly vivid, evocative and multi-dimensional media. FIG 8–10 His practice extended from theatrical sets and costumes into commissions for several designed interiors and furniture, among others.

By 1915 Urban ultimately, and famously, assumed a position as the director of the Ziegfeld Folies. He produced over twenty scene designs for the stage with Florence Ziegfeld for the revues and performances at the New Amsterdam and Century Theatres and the New Ziegfeld Theatre at 54th Street and 6th Avenue in New York City.[12] In addition, he designed the beautiful murals in oil paint that decorated the interior of the New Ziegfeld theatre itself.[13] FIG 11 Of the Ziegfeld productions Urban describes, in a self-authored pamphlet published in 1929 entitled *Theatre*, his intention was to create a "modern playhouse for modern musical shows" in which "the keynote of such a theater must be its brilliance."[14] With Ziegfeld, Urban further developed his use of comprehensive ensembles of set and costume. FIG 12, 13 Via his association with Ziegfeld, Urban also became involved, around 1920, with early progressive experimentation in film set design at the studios of William Randolph Hearst's Cosmopolitan Pictures. With Hearst, Urban designed settings that included work for the nascent medium of early silent film, such as *Little Old New York* (1923) and *When Knighthood Was in Flower* (1922). FIG 14 It was in these latter roles that Joseph Urban was drawn increasingly into those social circles where a contemporary taste for humid vacation villas in the American south was developing.

FIG 7
Joseph Urban set design for Edward Sheldon's *Garden of Paradise*. Glade Scene. Play in nine scenes by based on *The Little Mermaid* by Hans Christian Andersen, directed by O. P. Heggie, produced by Liebler and Co. at the Park Theater. 17 performances. The production premiered November 28, 1914.

FIG 6
Holy Woods, *Parsifal*, Metropolitan Opera, 1920.

FIG 8
Joseph Urban scene design for a Klingsor's garden, *Parsifal*, Metropolitan Opera New York, Premiere February 19, 1920.

Between 1914 and 1926 Joseph Urban received a series of engagements to work in Florida. Urban's previous work for Emperor Franz Joseph of Austria certainly would have adequately prepared him for such clientele. Derek Ostergard has also noted that: "...apart from his facility to design in a variety of idioms which often constituted antagonistic schools of thought, one of the great accomplishments of Urban's life was that he quickly came to understand the complexities of the American marketplace which, in many ways, reflected the diversity of the Vienna he had known in his early professional life."[15]

Of Joseph Urban's Florida works, Mar-a-Lago requires an introduction through specificities of its siting. FIG 15 The large property on which the house sits is accessed from Ocean Boulevard, the premiere residential axis of Palm Beach. Vehicular traffic is terraced above the ocean shore to the east, but below the residences to the west a passage bridges secretly under the road. The house was itself named, in Spanish, after this very connection between Sea—the Atlantic Ocean—and Lake—Lake Worth. Atop these siting connections, Mar-a-Lago is the beachfront archetype of Palm Beach and the prized local real estate model. The beach itself is not an enclosed water edge, although the natural exclusivity is provided by other soft limits to pedestrian proximity. Today, and from the outset, the house elevated the apex of luxury in the realms of private leisure.

Joseph Urban's architectural stage and film sets had attracted the attention of many potential clients, among them Addison Mizner, the creator of the 1920s Mediterranean Renaissance Revival style in Palm Beach—and Mizner's patron, Paris Singer, the heir to the sewing machine fortune. In 1918 Singer hired Mizner to build the Everglades Club at the west end of Worth Avenue. This was followed by palatial homes designed by Mizner in the same style for Palm Beach social leaders including the Stotesburys, the Munns and the Biddles. Urban's career in Palm Beach was jump started by Singer who hired him to refurbish the Everglades Club, where he drew the attention of Anthony J. Drexel Biddle Jr, the 27-year-old Philadelphia and Palm Beach millionaire, socialite sportsman, later career diplomat, and husband of tobacco heiress Mary Duke. It was Anthony Biddle who later commissioned Joseph Urban to design the Bath and Tennis Club. FIG 16

The Florida development boom was at its peak by 1926 when Joseph Urban first met his client, the then Mrs. E.F. Hutton, later Marjorie Merriweather Post, in Palm Beach. Heiress to her father Charles William Post's cereal company, Postum Cereals, founded in 1895, Marjorie Merriweather Post was the wealthiest woman in the United States upon inheriting a fortune of $250 million. The house at Palm Beach was built for her and her second husband Edward Francis Hutton, financier and founder of the investment firm E.F. Hutton & Co—who became chairman in Post Cereals, diversifying the company, acquiring Birdseye, and forming General Foods Corporation. It was Anthony J. Drexel Biddle Jr., a local society leader, who first introduced Marjorie Merriweather Post to Joseph Urban for the purpose of seeking the approval of neighbor Merriweather Post for his proposed Bath & Tennis Club to be built adjacent to her property. Biddle arranged a luncheon to introduce Urban and Post. At this meeting, Urban so charmed his hostess that not only did she approve Biddle's plans for the new club but she also commissioned Urban to redesign and redecorate her own house. The Bath and Tennis Club project would be remodeled to harmonize with her home.[16]

Upon meeting Urban, Marjorie Merriweather Post was already underway with the development of own house at the Palm Beach site, having commissioned Princeton-trained architect Marion Sims Wyeth to produce its design. Sims Wyeth was immediately replaced with Joseph Urban after Merriweather Post's first introduction to the Austrian. The far less adventurous conceptualization by Sims Wyeth had fallen short of the young and party-loving Marjorie Merriweather Post's expectations for a pleasure palace. It is important to note the fact of the change in architectural authors mid-project. It explains a sense of superimposed order. The house embodies and reflects modifications to the Sims Wyeth scheme undertaken by Urban. Urban's changes are substantial, but aspects of the Sims Wyeth organization remain the basis of Mar-a-Lago today. Wyeth was a New York native who, after graduating from Princeton in 1910, studied for four years in Paris at *L'Ecole des Beaux Arts*. The array of varied and differentiated rooms, and a relatively disordered experience in the plan of the house, are at least two of the factors that can be understood as resulting from the hybrid authorship of the house. FIG 17A, B

What is also fundamental to keep in mind is the broader setting of the house, that is, its location in Palm Beach, a place simply never intended to be a focus for serious architectural thought. It is a setting, on the contrary, that was established precisely with the ambition of pure abandon. A place outside metropolitan life and manners was intended both socially and architecturally at Palm Beach. Within the flux of an already temporary season, Palm Beach was an outlet for pure frivolity. It was and remains a rich and very social playground.

FIG 9
Joseph Urban scene design for a Klingsor's garden, *Parsifal*, Metropolitan Opera New York, Premiere February 19, 1920.

FIG 13
Set model for Act II, Scene I, Jungle scene for the 1931 Ziegfeld Follies. The New York Times critic Brooks Atkinson praised "the quiet amplitude of Mr. Urban's scenery, the lustre of the lighting, the depth of the spectacles."

FIG 12
Set design of the New York skyline seen from Central Park. This was the backdrop for the finale of the Ziegfeld Follies of 1931 starring Ruth Etting and Helen Morgan. The skyline includes the just completed Empire State Building.

FIG 11
Joseph Urban, Murals at the New Ziegfeld Theatre.

FIG 10
Design for an Oriental city with an 'Urban Blue' sky, labelled "Orpheum Circuit 1925."

FIG 16
Joseph Urban, Drawing for the proposed Bath and Tennis Club, 1924.

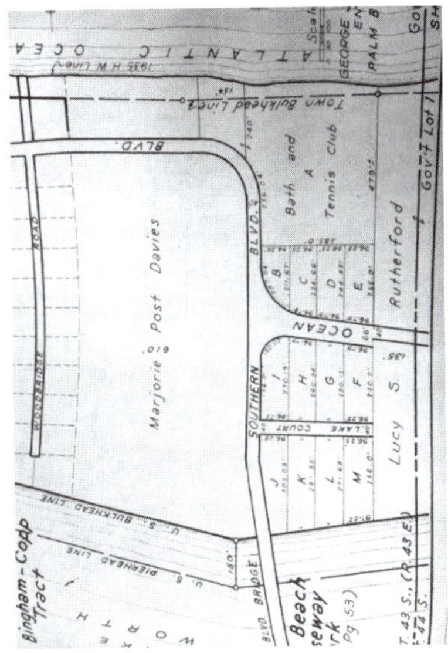

FIG 15
West Palm Beach Florida Atlas, 1935. Survey showing Marjorie Post Davies property and Bath and Tennis Club, and shore line. Weber and Brockway civil Engineers.

FIG 14
Joseph Urban photographed directing the production of *When Knighthood Was in Flower* (1922), Cosmopolitan Pictures.

These factors among others played a part in determining that Mar-a-Lago remains little understood in and of itself as architecture. It is undeniable, however, that Mar-a-Lago remains the most dramatic, integrated and significant example from this climate in the development of the first half of the twentieth century in Palm Beach. The house is truly in keeping with the character of its locality: it is a house considered as stage. FIG 18 The key entertaining spaces of the house are simply devised as an ensemble of diverse and highly differentiated stage sets. FIG 19–25 The house is a space, therefore, where interiors are also absolutely discontinuous with exteriors. To experience Mar-a-Lago is to experience a space where, from room to room, a visitor moves from one stage set to another. From volume to volume, the décor changes drastically, dramatically. The house is intended to feel, as you move through the building, as though you move from one act of a play to another—

from one operatic number to the next. Yet, there's no real logic between one number and the next in this musical revue, nor any sequence—there is not meant to be. Rather, the space deeply values that precise element sustained in the house's composition: surprise. A vast space is placed next to a compressed space. Things contract and expand, from bigger to smaller. It is really like falling down the rabbit hole. The plan is on no real grid or alignment but fans out from the principle of a roughly semi-circular geometry. Yet the real anchoring element is a vertical line in the form of the sudden insertion of a tower placed unambiguously within the home's center, although the entrance to this tower remains secret and concealed.

The exterior form at Mar-a-Lago is primarily defined by this tower as a visible profile, rather than by any point inside or near the house. FIG 26 The nursery of Mar-a-Lago is a sizeable room, larger than many bedrooms and, unusually, the nursery is aggregated within a complex of central public living rooms. There were reasons for it being located as such; the nursery could be protected. Merriweather Post was deeply concerned about the safety of the child, her granddaughter Dina, and had reason for concern about kidnapping. The room was built to allow her security detail to see the nursery and clearly distinguish if anyone should approach anywhere near it. Yet, all this doesn't entirely explain why suddenly this nursery is a piece of the building that sits just slightly out, projected in space. It is named on an early plan as "Baby House." Within, the art-nouveau/werkstatte interior is an organizational situation that would be novel to even to the respective conventions of Palm Beach. FIG 27

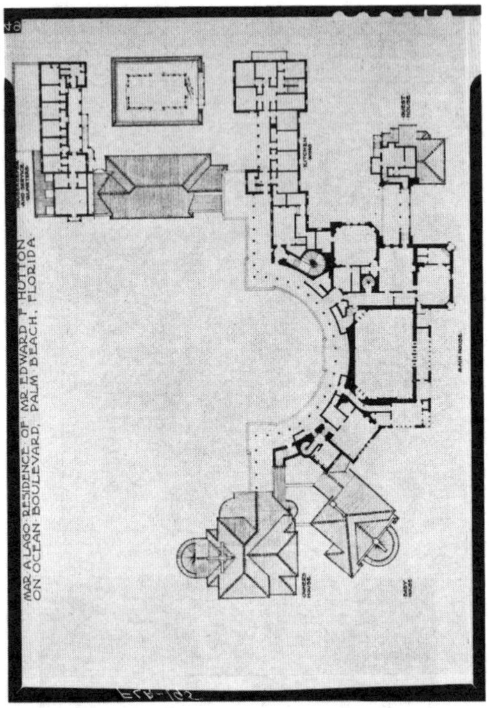

FIG 17B
Historic American Buildings Survey, Original drawing of the second floor plan 'Mar-a-Lago.' Photocopy of plate from Irvin L. Scott, *The American Architect* (June 20, 1928), 798.

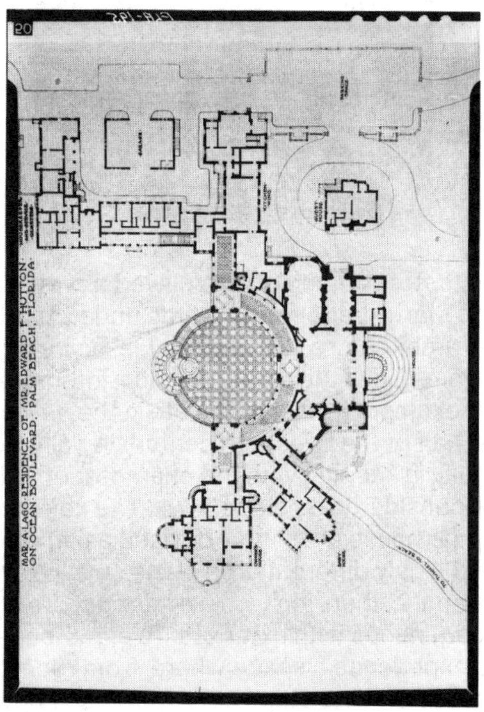

FIG 17A
Historic American Buildings Survey, Original drawing of the ground floor plan 'Mar-a-Lago.' Photocopy of plate from Irvin L. Scott, *The American Architect* (June 20, 1928), 798.

FIG 20
General View of Entrance Hall Toward Living Room Mar-a-Lago.

FIG 19
General view of living room of Mar-a-Lago looking Southwest.

FIG 18
House in Palm Beach, Joseph Urban Architect, Whitehead ed, *Pencil Points An Illustrated Monthly Journal for the Drafting Room* 11 (1927), 652.

FIG 21
Main entrance door of Mar-a-Lago.

FIG 22
View in Dining Room of Mar-a-Lago from the North.

FIG 23
View from entrance hall into living room through main doors Mar-a-Lago.

FIG 24
View from entrance hall into living room through main doors Mar-a-Lago.

FIG 25
Hooded fireplace on south wall of living room, Mar-a-Lago.

FIG 26
General view of east elevation Mar-a-Lago.

FIG 27
The nursery at Mar-a-Lago, Photograph by Jim Fairman.

FIG 28
Joseph Urban, Original Colour Charts for the "Century of Progress" Fair Chicago 1933.

If we could, then, fill the intentional lacuna and speculate an architectural theory for Palm Beach, it might be that Mar-a-Lago is the very first experiment which asks: could we have a playfulness that would lighten up modernism but that has nothing to do with modernism? This much can be asserted in light of the fact that it is undeniable that Joseph Urban understood the principles of modernism entirely. He won the New School Competition in New York over second-placed Frank Lloyd Wright. Moreover, Joseph Urban's New School interior demonstrated an incredible competence within dogmas of modernism. He deployed a squared proportion and a simple reduced surface. But even there, Urban insisted on the extensive use of color on the exterior of buildings. It is often forgotten that color was such an integral and original part of modernism. In this regard, Urban's vast use of color in his design for the Chicago "Century of Progress" Exhibition (1933) also deserves discussion. In this scheme, twenty-eight distinct colors were specified and constituted a parsimonious range with which the Exhibit would be painted. FIG 28 Urban designed distinct color arrangements for each building which, according to the promotional pamphlet for the exhibition, created "an expanse of beauty never seen anywhere."[17] With controlled means, Urban specified specific paint products from the Valdura product range, so that flat color was applied to steel and aluminum building surfaces throughout the Chicago fair. FIG 29–33

Later postmodernists such as Michael Graves found ways to re-integrate color as an attempt at humor and play. It is somewhat forgotten now that in modernism you could already—very early on in fact—introduce wit and charm and playfulness, which postmodernists did in a reactionary way some years later. Urban had already shown, in appropriate settings, the capacity of modernism to introduce theatrical playfulness into large and extensive pieces of architecture via his design at The New School. The extensive use of color in massive American buildings predated post-modernism and was absolutely spearheaded by Urban's work. Urban and his role in Mar-a-Lago should be understood in this way: the architect was at the center of the most important American figures, a challenger to Frank Lloyd Wright for commissions, a collaborator and friend of Raymond Hood and Wallace Harrison. Joseph Urban engaged in intellectual discussion with a cohort who were creating the most important American buildings of that period. Yet, he retained a wit and gregariousness. Why did he construct these maverick buildings in Palm Beach when he was doing other very serious things?

Joseph Urban did not write anything particular about Mar-a-Lago or what he was doing there. After receiving the commission to design the project, he sent directly for Franz Barwig, his sculptor and early collaborator who had been prominent in Vienna in the Secession period. The beautiful sculpted macaws and monkeys at Mar-a-Lago are the artistic product of Barwig and his dialogue with Urban, although the sculptor seldom receives acknowledgement or discussion. FIG 34, 35 Other stone sculptures at Mar-a-Lago feature animals and are nestled and concealed in proscenium arches at the interior and exterior. FIG 36, 37 In all of Urban's architectural projects, the interiors were completely coordinated: tables, chairs, curtains; floor tiles, wallpaper and painted decor; lighting fixtures, utensils, and appliances were all designed specifically for an individual space. Urban relied on the good and major collaborators who worked on Mar-a-Lago with him. And, undeniably, their details added tremendously to the amusing theatrical effect. There has always been a theatrical, operatic quality to Urban's designs, and these new residential commissions were absolutely no exception. They embody a cross-pollination of his innovative theatrical principles. This is evident when considering that a Joseph Urban rendering of the oceanside façade of the Bath and Tennis Club could equally serve as stage set visualization for an opera such as Pietro Mascagni's *Cavalleria Rusticana*. Palm Beach was a playground in which citizenry were only looking to entertain and to be entertained. Urban's works not only fulfilled this demand but added depth and dimension to Palm Beach.

FIG 33
Joseph Urban, Rainbow City for the "Century of Progress" Fair Chicago 1933.

FIG 37
Eagle figurines on roof soffit of Mar-a-Lago, Franz Barwig sculptor.

FIG 36
Male figurines on capitals of porte cochere at Mar-a-Lago, Franz Barwig sculptor.

FIG 35
Detail of swan fountain spout Mar-a-Lago, Franz Barwig sculptor.

FIG 34
Monkey pendant window to womens' cloak room of Mar-a-Lago, Franz Barwig sculptor.

1 Cited in Arnold Aronson, Looking into the Abyss: Essays on Scenography, Joseph Urban quote from the Sunday Leader, on a typed manuscript in Columbia Rare Books Library Joseph Urban Collection, cat. box 34, file 5.

2 A widespread misidentification attributes the Hoffman interior of the Austrian Exhibit at the 1904 World's Fair to Joseph Urban. According to recent research, no actual photograph Urban's gold medal winning design from St Louis exists, although another Hagenbund Exhibit designed by Urban soon after likely has some resemblance to the design. See Aurora Wilson McClain, "Meeting in St. Louis: American encounters with nascent European modernisms at the 1904 Louisiana Purchase Exposition," (PhD Dissertation, The University of Texas at Austin, 2015).

3 But one example of the range of encounters with European modernism that occurred at the 1904 World's Fair. See Aurora Wilson McClain, "Meeting in St. Louis: American encounters with nascent European modernisms at the 1904 Louisiana Purchase Exposition," (PhD Dissertation, The University of Texas at Austin, 2015).

4 John Loring, Joseph Urban (New York: Harry N. Abrams, Inc., 2010), 25.

5 Loring, *Joseph Urban*, 26.

6 Kirk Varnedoe, *Vienna 1900: art, architecture & design*, (New York: The Museum of Modern Art, 1986), 238. by New York Graphic Society

7 Kenneth MacGowan, "The New Stage-Craft in America," *Century Magazine*, January 1914, 414–421.

8 Kenneth MacGowan, "The New Stage-Craft," 414–421.

9 Kenneth MacGowan, "The New Stage-Craft," 414–421.

10 Kenneth MacGowan, "The New Stage-Craft," 414–421.

11 Henry T. Parker, "The Opera Outdoes Itself…'The Tales of Hoffman' Produced as Never Before in America," *Boston Evening Transcript*, November 26, 1912.

12 Loring, *Joseph Urban*, 112.

13 Cooper Hewitt Museum, The Jazz Age: American Style in the 1920's. Photograph Courtesy of The Collection of Richard H. Driehaus, Chicago and the Cooper Hewitt Museum.

14 Joseph Urban, *Theatres*, (New York: New York, Theatre Arts, inc., 1929). Courtesy of the Cooper Hewitt Museum Collection.

15 Derek E. Ostergard, "Assimilation and Eclecticism: The Architecture of Joseph Urban" Arnold Aronson, Derek E. Ostergard, and Matthew Wilson Smith eds., *Architect of Dreams The Theatrical Vision of Joseph Urban* (New York: Wallach Art Gallery Columbia University, 2000), 44.

16 Loring, *Joseph Urban*, 45.

17 Chicago World's Fair Advertising Brochure "Progress in Industrial Color and Protection at "A Century of Progress," 1933. These drawings have been cited by others including Cheryl Ganz, The 1933 Chicago World's Fair: A Century of Progress, (Urbana: University of Illinois Press, 2008).

The Epic of Gilgamesh and the Political Symbolism of the Periphery

Mark Jarzombek

> No "local centre," no "pattern of transformation" could function if, through a series of sequences, it did not eventually enter into an over-all strategy. And inversely, no strategy could achieve comprehensive effects if it did not gain support from precise and tenuous relations serving, not as its point of application or final outcomes, but as its prop and anchor point.
> —Michel Foucault, *History of Sexuality*[1]

Announcements from the U.S. President are given from a lectern in a briefing room with a prominent oval plaque behind it that features a frontal representation of the White House. The plaque is more than just a locational sign. It is an object in which the realities of power, representation, institutionality and speech are collapsed. Already the ancient Egyptians would have been familiar with such a practice. The word *pharaoh*, which means 'great house,' referred not just to the king but also to the palace of the king, and its earliest cartouche represented the palace gate as if speech emanated from the gate.[2] Parallel to such speculations, the cedar tree of ancient Mesopotamia can be considered another such spatial—and speaking—figure. I use as my evidence *The Epic of Gilgamesh*—about which there has been little discussion in the tradition of the architectural treatise. In *The Epic of Gilgamesh*, the cedar tree's conquest, destruction and reconstitution into architecture—both as an exhibited symbol and as lumber for the temple gates—brings to light the imaginary of the city as not just a place bounded by walls and filled with palaces and temples, but also as a place that depends upon the dangerous far-off periphery—in mythology and in representation—as a demonstration of power beyond the palace and outside the city walls.

If a definition of empire is as an aggregate of different regional identities fused into a single political entity, it is also true that empires often sustain a center versus periphery dynamic. What we see described in *The Epic of Gilgamesh*, through the context of the cedar, is perhaps the beginnings of such an awareness. Unlike the Egyptian palace or the White House which both speak from the center outward, the Mesopotamian tree-cult in *The Epic of Gilgamesh* describes something of a greater organizational complexity. The cedar is not just an item with religious significance about which much has been written, but a symbol of alienation and reconstitution since cedars can *only* be acquired through risky military action in areas far from the city. Furthermore, as a living member of the spirit world the cedar tree 'speaks,' in both a primary and a secondary sense, about the complex status of periphery as a subject of the center. FIG 1

In *The Epic of Gilgamesh*, Enkidu, a forest dweller, and Gilgamesh, king of Uruk, plan their assault on the forest in meticulous detail.[3] FIG 2 The initial decision to make the journey had not been easy, and the long march from the treeless marshes of Mesopotamia to the forested mountains of Lebanon (or so it is generally presumed)[4] had been stressful, especially since the two heroes were aware that a fearsome deity protected the forest:

> He is a power without rest, Humbaba, whose voice is

> the Deluge. His speech is the inferno, and his breath is death. He can hear the movements of the forest at a double hour. Who would venture into his forest? Adad is the first, but Humbaba is the second. None among even the Igigi would oppose him, to keep safe the cedar forest, for Enlil has decreed him to be a seven-fold terror.[5]

After a prolonged struggle Gilgamesh and Enkidu succeed in defeating Humbaba:

> Enkidu opened his mouth to speak, saying unto Gilgamesh: "Thou hast felled the guardian of the forest by thy strength alone. Nothing can bring dishonor unto thee. Therefore, flatten the Forest of Cedar!"[6]

Their aim, however, had been not only to the defeat of the deity but also to fell the forest for lumber. An armed group had accompanied the pair from Uruk, presumably to first assist in the conquest, and then afterwards to help extract and transport the wood:

> To the sons of his city who accompanied him [Gilgamesh said], "Cut down the branches, bundle them up, Lay them at the foot of the mountain."[7]

One of the trees was set aside so that Enkidu could build a huge temple door:

> Find for me a tall cedar whose tip touches the sky. I shall fashion from it a door as broad as the length of a reed, which shall have no pivot but instead shall sit within the door jamb.[8]

FIG 2
The Epic of Gilgamesh Tablet V. Old Babylonian period, 2003–1595 BCE, Mesopotamia, Iraq.

FIG 1
Sacred Yew grove at the top of Taebaek Mountain, destroyed to make way for a South Korea Winter Olympics 2018 Ski Run.

FIG 3
An altar site in the sacred forest, Seifa Utak, Okinawa, Japan.

Enkidu and Gilgamesh placed the door on a raft, piloting the vessel down the Euphrates to the Temple of Enlil, in Nippur. Enlil was a supreme deity of the Mesopotamian pantheon responsible for granting kingship, and the warriors had hoped to receive such a blessing in return for dedicating the door as an offering. It made sense since, apart from the altar, the enormous gates of a temple, as the symbolic threshold between sacred and divine, were the next most important element of the building. Later, in the first Century BCE, the Assyrian ruler Tiglath-Pileser III would record a similar description of the gates to his capital city of Nimrud in Upper Mesopotamia, as follows:

> Double doors of cedar and pine, which bestow (great) pleasure on those who enter them (and) whose fragrance wafts into the heart, I overlaid with strips of shining silver alloy and [gold alloy] and set them up in the gateways.

Heaven itself was deemed to have gates, and Shamash, the Mesopotamian sun god, was the gatekeeper.[10] Shamash is described as "he who [draws back] the bolt of the heavens, who opens wide the doors of the earth."[11] But things did not go as planned; Enlil, surprisingly, rejects the door. Later in *The Epic of Gilgamesh*, Enkidu—embittered and on the verge of death—speaks to the door "as though it were a man," speculating that maybe he should have offered it to the temple of Shamash at Sippar (Ebabbara) instead:

> Had I but known how you would reward mine effort, I would have used my axe to cut you down and set you adrift as a raft to Ebabbara to place you as portal to the temple of Shamash, who heard my words and gave me my weapon. O, door, if I raised thee, might I also destroy thee? May some king who follows me burn with hatred for thee, or remove my name from thy wood, and install his own.[12]

Yet the problem may not have been the temple to which the door was dedicated, but the fundamental act of cutting the tree. In one of *The Epic of Gilgamesh* fragments, the cutting was described as nothing less than "murdering the cedar," pointing to the fundamental tension underlying the enterprise.[13]

At the beginning of the story, Enkidu is portrayed as living alone in a forest and as "a murderous fellow from the midst of the wild."[14]

He knew not the land and the inhabitants thereof; he was clothed with garments as the god of the field. With gazelles he ate herbs, with the beasts he slaked his thirst, with the creatures of the water his heart rejoiced.[15]

But Enkidu is not simply a wild man. He should be understood as a mythologized "First Society" person, perhaps a member of a forest tribe the likes of which were still relatively common throughout Asia before the advent of the modern world.[16] A recently discovered text suggests that in his youth Enkidu had spent time with Humbaba, implying that Enkidu's origins might have been in that very forest and that Humbaba, when he heard of the young man's arrival, even assumed that Enkidu was merely returning home.[17] Humbaba is also clearly not an isolated deity but also functions as a mythological personification of the forest temple that was sacred to local villagers. Why else would the two warriors travel a thousand kilometers with a cadre of well-armed soldiers if not to defeat the chiefdom that would have typically protected such a temple? But the important outstanding question posed by *The Epic of Gilgamesh* is, why is Enkidu, a man who came from and truly belonged to the forest, portrayed as deciding to turn against his own sacred domain so fiercely?

The question that first needs to be answered is, what exactly is the nature of a sacred forest? Despite the abundant scholarly writing on the epic as an archaeological or historical text, there has been notably little discussion about the sacred forest as a spatial or architectural concept.[18]

It is generally thought that sacred forests originated in the time following the introduction of agriculture: as land was opened for fields, certain areas were ritualistically designated as special. Today there are so few of these places left that we could be forgiven for failing to adequately place them in the registers of history, but for millennia sacred forests were an established part of societies throughout Europe, Asia, and Africa.[19] In some cases groves encompass a large territory, and in others they are just a few trees. The Celts possessed hundreds of such groves, as did the people of Germania, whose rituals were described by Tacitus, the Roman historian of the first century CE:

> Their holy places are woods and groves, and they apply the names of deities to that hidden presence which is seen only by the eye of reverence. ... They carry with them into the fight certain figures and emblems taken from their sacred groves.[20]

Sacred forests were associated with rain and thunder deities as well as divination. In terms of the interrelationship between agricultural deities and groves there was both relative autonomy and a special kind of mutual dependence. Agricultural deities reigned supreme in the fields, but ancestral and fertility deities needed forests and groves. Groves also served political purposes through their links to land tenure, moral order, and political legitimacy. A grove of Diana near Rome provided a safe place for rival communities to meet.[21] The tweeting of the birds, the rustling of the leaves, and the activities of animals were all taken seriously as oracular pronouncements. The grove as a whole was considered even to speak in some cases. For example, Cicero recounted how not long after a battle with the Gauls a voice issued from the sacred grove of Vesta, at the base of the Palatine Hill: "The walls and gates must be repaired: unless this is done, the city will be taken."[22]

The community of Malshegu, in the Northern Region of Ghana, has a sacred grove that houses the deity Kpalevorgu, where all forms of farming and grazing are prohibited. Only the priests and their aides have regular access to pray to the god on the community's behalf. Others are permitted entry only during biannual rituals honoring Kpalevorgu or on other special occasions with advance consent of the priest and village leaders.[23] Groves are the abodes of the ancestors of local elites and thus central to the identity of the neighboring community. The relation between the grove and ancestor cults is so foundational that the death of an elder or chief is usually communicated to the people as "a great tree has fallen."[24] Some villages in Madagascar differentiate between ancestor-burial forests and those where spirits reside.[25] Communities in Rajasthan respect sacred groves, called *oran*, in honor of a local deity. A recent survey of chiefdoms in the Moyamba District of Sierra Leone showed that of 392 sacred groves over half are dedicated to women and a third to men, with others devoted to fetal burials or mythical deities.[26] On the island of Okinawa sacred forests, called *utaki*, are usually associated with villages positioned to the south of the grove. FIG 3 It is believed that when a woman dies her spirit goes back to the *utaki* and is transferred to a granddaughter, so the forest is a medium of contact between generations.[27]

Stated plainly, sacred groves are never simply components of nature. Despite their perceived wildness, they are institutions that control ancestry, marriage, puberty, and the cycles of agriculture. Monitored and tended, they have active and important roles in village and urban rituals. Ancient Greek groves (*alsos*, plural *alse*) were linked to towns by wide paths allowing for festivals to pass back and forth on ritual days.[28] In other words, groves were located at one end of a spatial, urban, and spiritual continuum with the urban temple at the other. The two, grove and temple, were held in an evident and necessary tension maintained through cultural traditions in the form of rituals and taboos. In the villages of southern India, according to John Freeman, the grove and temple are seen as functioning together: "They take their food here [in the city-temple] and take their rest there [in the grove]."[29]

FIG 4
Ise Shrine Naiku, 1953.

FIG 6
Ise Shrine Naiku, 1953. Source Wikimedia commons, Rekishi-Japan.

Entering groves is a risky act even in the best of circumstances, since groves defend themselves through psychological warfare. The Romans had a phrase to describe it, *mysterium tremendum*, a terrifying shake that the deities can transmit to humans. Indeed, though Gilgamesh starts off unafraid of the voice of the forest, Enkidu is predictably nervous. He knows that "to enter his forest is to be seized by shaking," and, during the journey to the forest, Gilgamesh has a series of three dreams in which the spirit world of the forest tries to warn him off:

> Why art my muscles trembling? Enkidu, my friend, I have had a dream. The dream that I dreamed was very terrible; in the valleys between the mountains we were walking. A great mountain fell down upon us.[30]

Despite the risks, the warriors would have known that it was not impossible to remove trees. Permission would have to be granted not just by the priests but also by the tree itself.[31] Spirits would have to be consulted, omens interpreted, blessings made, and offerings given. In Ghana in former times, before any big tree was cut, a libation was poured for the gods to ask for their blessing and guidance so that no bad omen would befall the community.[32] In Japan, even today, the trees that are felled to construct the Ise Grand Shrine have to be asked their permission. FIG 4–6 The elaborate rituals are part of *Yamaguchi-Sai* ("mountain entrancing ceremony"). Cato the Elder, writing on Roman agriculture in the second century BCE, recounts a special ritual used by the husbandman when cutting down a tree for timber:

FIG 5
The 62nd "Shikinen Sengu Ceremony" of the Japanese Imperial family: people of Ise transport wood for new sanctuary via Isuzu River.

> A pig is to be sacrificed, and the following prayer uttered: "Whether thou be god or goddess to whom this grove is dedicated, as it is thy right to receive a sacrifice of a pig for the thinning of this sacred grove, and to this intent, whether I or one at my bidding do it, may it be rightly done. To this end, in offering this pig to thee I humbly beg that thou wilt be gracious and merciful to me, to my house and household, and to my children. Wilt thou deign to receive this pig which I offer thee to this end."[33]

Destruction without the proper supplication carried grave consequences. In the ninth century in Kishmar Persia, a tree of particular beauty was dedicated to Zoroaster at the site of a significant pilgrimage cult where Persian notables gathered for a few days every year to worship. Caliph Al-Mutawakkil had the tree felled and cut into pieces despite the warnings of his close friends that it would bode ill. He was murdered before the 1,300 camels carrying the cypress pieces reached Baghdad.[34] A similar story revolves around Erysichthon, a Thessalian king who chopped down the sacred grove of the goddess Demeter to build himself a feast hall. As described eloquently by Hesiod, one huge oak covered with votive wreaths was so intimidating that Erysichthon's men refused to cut it down, so he grabbed an ax and cut it down himself, killing a dryad in the process. The tree nymph cursed Erysichthon and he was soon inflicted with insatiable hunger, driving him to exhaust his riches and finally, in abject poverty, devour his own flesh:

> I am a nymph, most dear to Ceres,
> under the surface of this wood,
> who prophesy to you, as I die,
> that punishment will follow blood:
> out of my ruin, the only good.[35]

Even today the power of these groves is not to be trifled with. In Java, the tree spirits Gendruwo and Wewe, male and female deities respectively, if not properly respected, can make one become ill or go insane.[36] At the Mawphlang Sacred Forest in north India, FIG 7 large warning signs spell out the proper course of behavior for the unsuspecting visitor. FIG 8

Enkidu thus knows full well that one cannot just take an ax to a tree, as Humbaba reminds him: "If any mortal, Enkidu, knows the rules of my forest, it is you. You know that this is my place, and that I am the forest's guarding." Even Gilgamesh knows the importance of protocol. It is told how on the march he goes to a nearby mountaintop, pours a sacrificial meal into a hole, and says: "Mountain, bring a dream unto me! Let me see dream-visions, O Shamash." But when his dream turns out to be more of a nightmare, Enkidu steps up and misinterprets it:

> Enkidu heard this dream and said to him: "My friend, this dream is favorable, for it tells us that we shall triumph over Humbaba. The mountain which thou sawest in thy dream is Humbaba. The dream foretells that we shall kill Humbaba and dispatch his corpse to the wasteland. Come morning Shamash shall send us a favorable omen."[37]

FIG 7
The sacred groves of Meghalaya, West Bengal.

It is impossible to miss Enkidu's deception since he repeats it in various ways for all three dreams. And in the end, after Enkidu had turned the tide of the battle leading to the destruction of Humbaba, the great deity Enlil even inquires:

> "Why have you acted so?" asks the god, "Why, by what is done his name [Humbaba] is destroyed from the earth! You should have seated him before you, You should have given him food from your food, You should have given him drink from your drink."[38]

And indeed they should have, for it is the failure to have acted properly that leads to Enlil's rejection of the door.

The refusal to perform the usual supplications and the subsequent violence toward the forest, and its related temple protectors, was not the foolhardy act of two young men. It was purposeful. Grove destruction was a well-known way to defeat an enemy and was used repeatedly throughout history.[39] In the Bible (Exodus 34:13) Moses was told by none other than Jahwe, "Ye shall destroy their altars, break their images, and cut down their groves." Julius Caesar systematically destroyed the sacred groves of the Gauls to force them into the embrace of Roman deities. When his army came to one particular grove, Caesar seized an ax and began to chop at a tree. To offset the nervousness of the soldiers, he promised to absorb any guilt they may subsequently experience into his own person: *iam ne quis uestrum dubitet subuertere siluam/credite me fecisse nefas* ("Now let none of you hesitate to fell the wood. [You should] believe that I [alone] have committed the unspeakable crime.") Similarly, when the Roman general Gaius Suetonius Paulinus wanted to wipe out the resistance of the Welsh tribes, he went to the sacred island of Mon (today known as Anglesey) to massacre the druids and burn the sacred groves.[40] The aim was simple: to disenfranchise locals from their attachment to place and ancestors. It was the first step toward pacification since the destruction of the forest meant that those who held it sacred were now essentially homeless. As was true throughout the tribal world, without a connection to ancestors, a person's future is that of a slave, whether in real terms or in cognitive terms, and this can extend to an entire clan or village.

In Europe, the destruction of scared groves was a key element in Christianization. So thorough were the Christians that few groves have survived. One that did survive, however, is the Forest of Sainte-Baume, which according to ancient sources was inhabited by the goddess of fertility.[41] Another is Mount Ślęża, in Poland, which was apparently dedicated to a sun deity by the Celts and Vandals. The Old Slavic holiday Kupala Night was reportedly celebrated on the mountain with bonfires called Sobótki into the eleventh century. The hagiographers of Saint Boniface record the destruction of sacred woods in the Anglo-Saxon mission to convert the Germanic parts of the Frankish Empire during the eighth century. FIG 9 As recounted by Willibald in *The Life of St. Boniface*:

> Now many of the Hessians who at that time [the year 723] had acknowledged the Catholic faith were confirmed by the grace of the Holy Spirit and received the laying-on of hands. But others, not yet strong in the spirit, refused to accept the pure teachings of the Church in their entirety. Moreover, some continued secretly, others openly, to offer sacrifices to trees and springs, to inspect the entrails of victims; some practiced divination, legerdemain and incantations; some turned their attention to auguries, auspices and other sacrificial rites; whilst others, of a more reasonable character, forsook all the profane practices of heathenism and committed none of these crimes. With the counsel and advice of the latter persons, Boniface in their presence attempted to cut down, at a place called Gaesmere, a certain oak of extraordinary size called by the pagans of olden times the Oak of Donar. Taking his courage in his hands (for a great crowd of pagans stood by watching and bitterly cursing in their hearts the enemy of the gods), he cut the first notch. But when he had made a superficial cut, suddenly the oak's vast bulk, shaken by a mighty blast of wind from above, crashed to the ground shivering its topmost branches

FIG 8
Entrance to the sacred forest near Mawphlang, India.

> into fragments in its fall. As if by the express will of God (for the brethren present had done nothing to cause it) the oak burst asunder into four parts, each part having a trunk of equal length. At the sight of this extraordinary spectacle the heathens who had been cursing ceased to revile and began, on the contrary, to believe and bless the Lord. Thereupon the holy bishop took counsel with the brethren, built an oratory from the timber of the oak and dedicated it to St. Peter the Apostle.[42]

Although the text describes that Boniface was killed by bandits, the attackers were more likely members of a pagan resistance movement. Nonetheless, his death made Boniface into a Christian martyr and saint.[43] The history of the decommissioning of ancient groves is not yet over. The ongoing Christianization of Africa and Asia has resulted in the destruction of numerous "heathen" forest shrines.[44] Urban development has also come into conflict with forests and groves in these contexts.

Returning to *The Epic of Gilgamesh*, we can see the larger implications in the destruction of the forest, namely in the severance of regional and village elites from their power bases to make them subservient to new urban-based realities.[45] Some scholars still refer to Enkidu as a hero who wins fame but dies early, yet from another point of view he was just the opposite, a traitor to his people and ancestors, as Humbaba clearly points out in his dying breath:[46]

> Enkidu, thou art the spawn of the fish, a man who knoweth no father, the hatchling of a turtle, who suckled not his mother's milk. In thy youth, I saw and watched thee, though I did not go over unto thee ... in my belly. Traitor! Thou bringest before me Gilgamesh and standeth before me as warrior and stranger.[47]

By understanding the sacred forest as a type of institution and its destruction as a geopolitical act rather than one of youthful heroism and folly, we can see that *The Epic of Gilgamesh* is at its most schematic the struggle between what we might call "organized" religion practiced in city temples and the ancient world of village animism with its emphasis on mountains, springs, and groves.

The first-century BCE bronze bands that decorated the hinges on the huge cedar gates of the Temple of Mamu at Imgur-Enlil, in Balawat, Iraq show the aftermath of the conquest of Syrian mountain tribes by the Assyrians. FIG 10 One band depicts the conquered people dutifully offering goods to the new Assyrian overlords; another part shows soldiers carrying logs, clearly a prized possession, on special harnesses over rough wooded terrain. In all likelihood these logs came from a sacred forest controlled by the town. They may also be the very logs used to make the gate of the Temple of Mamu.

FIG 9
Johann Andreas Herrlein, Martyrium des heiligen Bonifatius, 1778. Katholische Kirchengemeinde Mariae Himmelfahrt, Sinntal-Sannerz.

The historical and ideological distinctions between urban temple and remote village, in Mesopotamia at least, emerged under the Ubaid culture (4,500–3,600 BCE), credited with developing the shift to urban temples. This also reflected a shift in geography: from the ninth millennium BCE onward villages grew on the slopes overlooking the rivers and valleys, and by the fifth millennium BCE constituted a network extending from the Levant to the northern edge of the still largely unpopulated Iraqi marshes. Though often called the Fertile Crescent, the name is a falsification of late-nineteenth-century archaeology.[48] The arid slopes were ideal, however, for wheat and barley that could thrive in relatively low-nutrient environments. Settlements rarely exceeded two hundred people, with each village most certainly having its own sacred grove or spring somewhere in the nearby hills. The marshes farther south could not support a complex village life—there was no stone, no lumber, no metal, and a limited supply of dry land for cattle. Over time various groups entered into the marshes to take advantage of what was missing from the thousands of years of agricultural development in Mesopotamia: fertile soil. Archaeologists identify these groups as the Ubaid and the later Sumerians. Their success in agriculture and gardening led to the rapid intensification of economic trade and, of course, to the first cities, all of which forms the backdrop of *The Epic of Gilgamesh*. Indeed its opening is an eloquent advertisement for the city:

> Of Uruk, its great rampart he [Gilgamesh] built, and the wall of the sacred Eanna temple, the holy sanctuary. Behold the outer walls which gleam with the brilliance of copper; see the inner wall which none might rival. Touch the threshold stone—it is from ancient days. Goest thou into the Eanna temple, yea, the dwelling place of Ishtar, the like of which no subsequent king or living man might equal. Ascend and walk about on the wall of Uruk, inspect the corner-stone, and examine its brick-work, whether its wall is not made of burned brick, and its foundation laid by the Seven Sages. One third for city, one third for garden, one third for field, and a precinct for the temple of Ishtar. These parts and the precinct comprise Uruk.[49]

By the time of Sargon in the twenty-third century BCE—more or less when the first Gilgamesh stories were conceived—the wealth of the city and its temples depended primarily on commercial expansion, supported in part by an administrative and military apparatus.[50] However, the ancient hill villages did not just disappear. What changed was their status. Villages were no longer at the formative upper end of cultural life but at a lower, subservient register, with a familiar status to that of today. Similarly, people left the villages, whether unwillingly as slaves or willingly to become devotees of an urban temple, working in the fields or in various capacities within the structure of the temple economy. There are parallels in this to the premodern temple-cities of South India, where the temples are something like agro-corporations ruled over by priests with ceremonial fanfare. It was not just agricultural labor that was required but everything from weavers, cooks, and pot makers to musicians and dancers. As the Mesopotamian temples became more powerful, villages came to be assigned special tasks relating to the ever more expansive needs of the city, if they were not outright depopulated.

One of the primary material needs of the developing cities was lumber—for buildings, kilns, metalwork, and so on. Deforestation was compounded by erosion accompanying the rapid proliferation of goat herding. The effect on the landscape was devastating, attested to also by the fact that Enkidu and Gilgamesh had to cross seven mountains to locate a satisfactory forest. The wanderers even came upon a place described in the text as "Land of the cut-down Erin (Cedar)-trees." The scarcity of suitable trees only enhanced their mythological and geo-political status.[51] It also meant that by the third millennium BCE forested peripheral territories had become a source of wealth. Gold and copper are better known as luxury commodities today, but wood was certainly on this list during the third millennium BCE. The problem was that unlike metal, which could be brought to urban centers, the procurement of wood inevitably required territorial conquest. Wood from residual sacred groves would have had a particularly special place. As a *living* entity, its inner spirit could be ceremoniously reembodied through the civilizing forces of carpentry into the form of architecture. Once the sacred tree becomes sawed, planed, and assembled into a temple gate, it is reincarnated as a symbol of the power of the temple and city. The legitimacy of urban deities was at stake in this effort, for rulers were expected to build and dedicate temples as a sign of their potency, meaning that the acquisition of roofing beams and doors became a symbolic extension of power.[52] Showing off things that came from remote places, either through conquest or trade, was to become a trope of Near Eastern kingship, later exotic animals were added to the list.[53] The cedar tree, however, was of a different order. For early Mesopotamian cities, foreign conquest and the acquisition of lumber were symbolically intertwined.

The Epic of Gilgamesh thus revolves around the temple not just as the prime consumer of sacred lumber but also as the urban replacement of the distant mountain. The temple of Enlil was known as *é-kur*, or "mountain house," implying that in the flat plains of the marsh the man-made temple had to supplant the ancient natural residences of the gods for it to succeed. In India, every *shikhara* (Sanskrit for "mountain peak") of a Hindu temple replicates the sacred mountain and places the deity within the urban realm and its expectations and demands. For the city to serve as a theocentric space, the architectural mountain has to proclaim its symbolically compressed superiority over the real thing. This means that the temple gates represent not just the distinction between sacred and profane but also a liminal space between the spirit world of the remote grove and that of the urban temple. The temple consumes the ancient forest as an index of its supremacy.

This is indicated in a stone-carved frieze showing the Sumerian king Ur-Nammu standing before the seated deity Enlil, the very same whose temple received Gilgamesh's doors. FIG 11 Between the two figures is a cedar tree, sitting in a huge pot into which Ur-Nammu pours water. As the trophy of a distant conquest, the tree is more than an image of primitive devotion—it symbolizes a complex set of risk-related actions. Most importantly it evidences the existence of the far-off tributary kingdoms that supplied various types of goods, including slaves. There is another dimension to Enlil that should not be ignored. The deity may have been the god of wind, air, earth, and storms, but he also invented the mattock (the pickax) which he gave to humans so they could clear land to build cities.[54] In the band just below the seated deity, we see a man carrying just such a mattock on his shoulder, making the link between the mattock and the deity unmistakable. Researchers have even argued that here the deity is giving Ur-Nammu instructions on how to build temples.[55]

FIG 11
Stela of Ur-Namu, 3rd Century BCE, 97 cm × 72.5 cm.

FIG 10
Fragments of Hinge Bands from Balawat Gate.

FIG 13
Cypress Tree Relief, Apadana Staircase, Persepolis, Iran. Photograph by Peter von Gaza, 1999.

FIG 12
Apadana staircase, Persepolis, Iran.

A century later, when the Assyrians portrayed cedars being boated down the Euphrates for their palaces and gardens, it was not just in celebration of their newfound wealth but also a reenactment of Gilgamesh. Defeating the Levantine kingdoms may have been important to the Assyrian kingdom was in the human dimension but defeating "Humbaba"—for Gilgamesh was certainly known to them—was likely still not an insignificant aspect of regional political interrelationships. The same is true for the cedars and cypresses that feature so prominently on the grand staircase leading to the Apadana portico at Persepolis, built during the fifth century BCE. FIG 12 Much scholarly discussion of the steps focuses on the people and animals depicted on the walls rather than on representation of the artificially made world-mountain-forest in the background that was meant to replace the distant world-mountain it signifies. FIG 13 The Apadana trees are set in rows on fourteen terraces, with two rows of trees to a terrace; at the apex there is a winged solar disk inside a fenced enclosure. There is no evidence that such a huge, terraced mountain was ever built, but it was certainly imagined. Ascending the stairs was at the same time ascending the man-made mountain. Those who ascended would have all likely understood what was implied in the symbolism of an architectural reforestation.

Did Gilgamesh's raiding party similarly travel many hundreds of kilometers in the pursuit of sacred logs and the associated contingent of slaves as a testament to the capacity—or perhaps ambition—of a city to extend its power into the farther reaches of an interior? If that were the case, the story would only be about Gilgamesh. Instead it is Enkidu who leads the operation. Does this mean that Enkidu was a type of middleman, or more likely a local highland chieftain who turned against his mountain brethren? After all, the local chiefdoms that protected the remaining areas of arboreal wealth probably made their living by harvesting the wood for export. Humbaba even pleads with the warriors to allow him to cut and prepare the wood himself, an offer that is rejected by Enkidu, leading Enlil to refuse the door.[56]

The interpretation of this essay suggests that Enkidu was no hapless primitive "wild man" of the forest, but a tribal mountain warrior who sought out an alliance with urban elites as a way to control the lucrative economy in timber and slaves. Situations like this were common and have been recorded even in modern times.[57] Enkidu was perhaps a traitor from the very start, bringing to the city in his very persona the imaginary of a far-off grove that would lure Gilgamesh into becoming the "muscle" in their alliance. That may explain why Enkidu strikes the first blow when he sees Gilgamesh trying to negotiate a deal with Humbaba rather going after the trees in a more direct fashion—the cedars little more than a cover for actions behind the scenes. How then do we interpret the miscalculation between Nippur and Sippar? Since Mesopotamian deities were closely allied with cities, it is quite possible that Enkidu somehow misunderstood the nature of the alliance. We cannot speculate further without added insights into the murky zone of such implied contestation.

Sumerian scholars largely accept the proposition that events recounted in Sumerian epics may have some form of historical basis.[58] I am not making such a claim specifically, but if we add historical and anthropological evidence about sacred forests to the discussion, we begin to recognize a possible framework for the story as much about buildings or sites as it is about trees that serve as a vital element in the newly forming urban imaginary. In ancient Mesopotamian visual culture we often see the colonized subject offering tribute to authorities interpreted as a symbol of passivity, or at least acquiescence. But as the bearer of divine meaning translated and transplanted into the materiality of architecture, the tree—as seen by the urban elites—served a more important purpose as the spiritual embodiment of the geopolitics of remoteness and the refashioning of power.

In a place where an empire is constructed upon narratives of heroic action, the transposition of the forest from the natural to the man-made environment demands a real and simultaneously a mythological conquest of the tribal world, represented by the destruction of forests and its assimilation into urban architecture.[59] Scholars drawing on literary and archaeological evidence have tended to study Mesopotamia from the perspective of the city. For example, we know quite a bit about Assyrian urbanism since the annals describe founding cities, constructing canals, planting orchards, opening quarries, and resettling conquered populations. The Assyrian state also inscribed their identity on rock reliefs and stelae in symbolically charged foreign landscapes to incorporate them into narratives of the empire. Though the periphery is spatially as such, when encountered in histories of conquest and imperial imaginaries, I argue that early Mesopotamian contexts described a tribal periphery with a narrative and architectural "voice" that reverberates, however mythologically, in the form of the cedar from the sacred forest. In its simplest terms, the act of defiling the sacred forest and celebrating the predictable "wrath of the gods" was a method to demonstrate the domestication of the hill tribes. The city's conquest of the periphery is thus not just a consequence of territorial claims or the need for security and resources, it is part of the substantiation of a "civilizing" imaginary.

Geopolitics articulates itself variously through texts, actions, and strategies but also through architecture. In a sense, every Mesopotamian temple embodies this strategy of violence and replacement. In taming the tree—placing it in a pot, planting it on an artificial mountain, sawing it into lumber for a temple gate, or even representing it in a story inscribed into a clay tablet—a reading backward in time and space is required to find everything it implies. *The Epic of Gilgamesh* is a story not only about humans and deities but also about the changing and contested nature of the tree as the material unit and figural embodiment of power beyond the city walls and the power inherent in the alien world of tribality. And the great cedar forest is quite likely the earliest symbolic abstraction of this geopolitical contestation in history.

1 Michel Foucault, *The History of Sexuality*, Vol 1 (New York: Pantheon Books, 1981), 99.

2 See Ogden Goelet, *Two Aspects of the Royal Palace in the Egyptian Old Kingdom*, Dissertation, (Columbia University, 1983). David P. Silverman, "Divinity and Deities in Ancient Egypt," *Religion in Ancient Egypt: Gods, Myths, and Personal Practice*, Edited by Byron E. Shafer (Ithaca: Cornell University Press, 1991), 59.

3 Enkidu is a slave in the earliest versions of *The Epic of Gilgamesh*; later he is identified as a companion. See John R. Maier, *Gilgamesh and the Great Goddess of Uruk*, https://digitalcommons.brockport.edu/sunybeb/4, 295.

4 In older versions of the story, the forest seems to be located to the east of Uruk, in Elam (now Iran), while in later accounts it is located to the far north and west of Uruk. See Maier, *Gilgamesh and the Great Goddess*, 157.

5 Epic of Gilgamesh/William Muss-Arnolt/Tablet II, https://en.wikisource.org/wiki/Epic_of_Gilgamesh/William_Muss-Arnolt.

6 Epic of Gilgamesh/William Muss-Arnolt/Tablet V,.

7 J. Hansman, "Gilgamesh, Humbaba, and the Land of the Erin-Trees," *Iraq* 38 (Spring 1976): 23–35.

8 Epic of Gilgamesh/William Muss-Arnolt/Tablet V.

9 Hayim Tadmor, *The Inscriptions of Tiglath-Pileser, King of Assyria*, ed. Hayim Tadmor (Jerusalem: Israel Academy of Sciences and Humanities, 1994), 173–5, lines 28–9.

10 Richard David Barnett, introduction to *The Balawat Gates of Ashurnasirpal II*, ed. John E. Curtis and Nigel Tallis (London: British Museum Press, 2008), 4.

11 William G. Lambert, *Babylonian Wisdom Literature* (Oxford, UK: Oxford University Press, 1960), 137.

12 Epic of Gilgamesh/William Muss-Arnolt/Tablet VII.

13 Aaron Shaffer, "Gilgamesh, the Cedar Forest, and Mesopotamian History," *Journal of the American Oriental Society* 103 (January/March 1983): 307–13.

14 Andrew R. George, *The Babylonian Gilgamesh Epic*, vol. 1 (Oxford, UK: Oxford University Press, 2003), 549.

15 Epic of Gilgamesh/William Muss-Arnolt/Tablet VII.

16 Such characters pop up in a range of ancient texts, even the Bible, but the Enkidu story is particularly important since it is the first recorded account of the encounter between an aboriginal and a self-proclaimed "civilization." Gregory Mobley has pointed out that Enkidu is the oldest extant literary representative of the wild man. This characterization appears to be an innovation of the Old Babylonian version of *Gilgamesh* since in the earlier Sumerian versions Enkidu was merely a colorless servant and companion. See Gregory Mobley, "The Wild Man in the Bible and the Ancient Near East," *Journal of Biblical Literature* 116 (Summer 1997): 217–33.

17 Farouk N. H. Al-Rawi and Andrew R. George, "Back to the Cedar Forest: The Beginning and End of Tablet V of the Standard Babylonian Epic of Gilgamesh," *Journal of Cuneiform Studies* 66 (2014): 69–90.

18 A great amount of scholarly effort has been dedicated to determining the location of the forest. Suggested places range from Elam (to the east of Babylonia), the mountains of North Syria and southern Turkey, and of course Lebanon.

19 See Vykintas Vaitkevičius, "The Sacred Groves of the Balts: Lost History and Modern Research," *Electronic Journal of Folklore* 42 (2009).

20 Tacitus, *The Agricola and the Germania*, translated by H. Mattingly (London: Penguin Books, 1970), p. 107.

21 C. M. C. Green, *Roman Religion and the Cult of Diana at Aricia* (Cambridge, UK: Cambridge University Press, 2007), 90.

22 Marcus Tullius Cicero and David Wardle, *Cicero on Divination: De Divinatione*, 1.45.101 (Oxford, UK: Clarendon Press, 2006).

23 See Clements Dorm-Adzobu, Okyeame Ampadu-Agyei, and Peter G. Veit, *Religious Beliefs and Environmental Protection: The Malshegu Sacred Grove in Northern Ghana* (Washington, DC: World Resources Institute, 1991).

24 George J. S. Dei, "A Forest Beyond the Trees: Tree Cutting in Rural Ghana," *Human Ecology* 20 (March 1992): 57–88.

25 Maria Tengö, Kristin Johansson, Fanambinantsoa Rakotondrasoa, Jakob Lundberg, Jean-Aimé Andriamaherilala, Jean-Aimé Rakotoarisoa, and Thomas Elmqvist, "Taboos and Forest Governance: Informal Protection of Hot Spot Dry Forest in Southern Madagascar," *Ambio* 36 (December 2007): 683–91.

26 Miguel Pinedo-Vasquez and Christine Padoch, "Sacred Groves in Africa: Forest Patches in Transition," in *Forest Patches in Tropical Landscapes*, ed. John Schelhas and Russell S. Greenberg (Washington, DC: Island Press, 1996), 309.

27 Asato Eiko, "Okinawan Identity and Resistance to Militarization and Maldevelopment," in *Islands of Discontent: Okinawan Responses to Japanese and American Power*, ed. Laura Hein and Mark Selden (Lanham, MD: Rowman & Littlefield, 2003), 238.

28 See Pierre Bonnechere, "The Place of the Sacred Grove (Alsos) in the Mantic Rituals of Greece; The Example of the Alsos of Trophonios (Boeotia)," in *Sacred Gardens and Landscapes: Ritual and Agency*, ed. Michel Conan (Cambridge, MA: Harvard University Press, 2007), 17–42.

29 John Richard Freeman, "Gods, Groves, and the Culture of Nature in Kerala," *Modern Asian Studies* 33 (May 1999): 257–302.

30 Epic of Gilgamesh/ William Muss-Arnolt/Tablet IV.

31 Sacred groves in ancient Greece and Rome were protected by strict regulations against violation. See Darice Elizabeth Birge, *Sacred Groves in the Ancient Greek World* (PhD diss., University of California Berkeley, 1982).

32 Dei, "A Forest," 72. See also Bruce A. Byers, Robert N. Cunliffe, and Andrew T. Hudak, "Linking the Conservation of Culture and Nature: A Case Study of Sacred Forests in Zimbabwe," *Human Ecology* 29 (June 2001): 187–218.

33 Cato and Varro, *On Agriculture*, Loeb Classical Library 283, trans. W. D. Cooper and Harrison Boyd Ash (Cambridge, MA: Harvard University Press, 1934).

34 "Cypresses," *Encyclopaedia Iranica*, vol. 6, fasc. 5, 505–8.

35 Ovid, *Metamorphoses* VIII, 738–78. Translated by A.S. Kline (Ann Arbor MI: Borders Classics, 2004), 146.

36 Peter Boomgaard, "Sacred Trees and Haunted Forests in Indonesia," *Asian Perceptions of Nature: A Critical Approach*, ed. Ole Bruun and Arne Kalland (London: Routledge, 1995), 51. Among the Iban in Indonesia, anyone wanting to fell trees within such a site had to perform proper ritual offerings. Farming on or near such land was said to result in illness for the family. See Reed L. Wadley and Carol J. Pierce Colfer, "Sacred Forest, Hunting, and Conservation in West Kalimantan, Indonesia," *Human Ecology* 32 (June 2004): 313–38.

37 Epic of Gilgamesh/ William Muss-Arnolt/Tablet IV.

38 Quoted in Aaron Shaffer, "Gilgamesh, the Cedar Forest, and Mesopotamian History," *Journal of the American Oriental Society* 103 (January/March 1983): 307–13.

39 See Danica M. Anderson, Jan Salick, and Robert K. Moseley, "Conserving the Sacred Medicine Mountains: A Vegetation Analysis of Tibetan Sacred Sites in Northwest Yunnan, *Biodiversity & Conservation* 14 (December 2005): 3065–91.

40 Tacitus, *Annals*, Loeb Classical Library 322, trans. John Jackson (Cambridge, MA: Harvard University Press, 1937), 14.29–14:33.

41 In the town of Fritzlar, not far from the church he built, there is a statue of Boniface standing on a tree stump holding a giant ax in one hand and a model of the church in the other. This representation could easily be emulated in the thousands around the world. See Linda Kay Davidson and David Martin Gitlitz, *Pilgrimage: From the Ganges to Graceland, an Encyclopedia*, vol. 1 (Santa Barbara, CA: ABC-CLIO, 2002), 562.

42 Willibald, *The Life of Boniface*, trans. George Washington Robinson, (Cambridge: Harvard University Press, 1916.

43 Ancient cults of tree worship have occasionally been converted into the worship or adoration of saints and prophets in Christianity and Islam. See Amots Dafni, "The Supernatural Characters and Powers of Sacred Trees in the Holy Land," *Journal of Ethnobiology and Ethnomedicine* 2 (2007), https://www.ncbi.nlm.nih.gov/pmc/articles/PMC1820775/.

44 Henry Kam Kah, *The Sacred Forest: Gender and Matriliny in the Laimbwe History (Cameroon), c. 1750–2001* (Vienna: LIT Verlag, 2015), 11. See Ronaldo Lidorio, *Unafraid of the Sacred Forest: The Birth of a Church in an African Tribe* (Fearn, UK: Christian Focus, 2007).

45 It is astonishing that the geopolitical implication of the sacred forest's destruction has rarely been raised. Even in Michael Williams's book *Deforesting the Earth* there is not a single mention of deforestation as a ritual act.

46 See Hope Nash Wolff, "Gilgamesh, Enkidu, and the Heroic Life," *Journal of the American Oriental Society* 89 (April–June 1969): 392–98.

47 Epic of Gilgamesh/ William Muss-Arnolt/Tablet V.

48 Archaeologist James Henry Breasted popularized the term *fertile crescent*, beginning with the books *Outlines of European History* (1914) and *Ancient Times: A History of the Early World* (1916). Today scholars tend to shy away from that term since Mesopotamia, with the exception of the marshes, was not technically fertile.

49 Epic of Gilgamesh/ William Muss-Arnolt/Tablet I.

50 Christophe Wall-Romana, "An Areal Location of Agade," *Journal of Near Eastern Studies* 49 (July 1990): 205–45.

51 Hansman, "Gilgamesh," 24.

52 Sacred trees existed within the city itself of course, as the opening of the epic implies, but they were planted in gardens not designed for harvesting lumber.

53 See discussion of early Iron Age Assyrian king Tiglath-Pileser I (Tukulti-āpil-ešarra) in Ömür Harmanşah, "Beyond Aššur: New Cities and the Assyrian Politics of Landscape," *Bulletin of the American Schools of Oriental Research* (February 2012), 53–77.

54 Samuel Noah Kramer, *Sumerian Mythology: A Study of Spiritual and Literary Achievement in the Third Millennium B.C.* (Philadelphia, PA: University of Pennsylvania Press, 1961), 51–53.

55 Samuel Noah Kramer, *Sumerian Mythology: A Study of Spiritual and Literary Achievement in the Third Millennium B.C.* (Philadelphia, PA: University of Pennsylvania Press, 1961), 51–53.

56 Epic of Gilgamesh/William Muss-Arnolt/Tablet V.

57 John Richard Freeman, "Gods, Groves, and the Culture of Nature in Kerala," *Modern Asian Studies* 33 (May 1999): 257–302.

58 Some argue that Enkidu represents an invading foreigner from a primitive culture. See Henry F. Lutz, "The Sumerian and Anthropology," *American Anthropologist, New Series* 29 (April 1927): 202–9. See also Samuel Noah Kramer, *History Begins at Sumer* (London: Doubleday, 1960), 275.

59 See Harmanşah, "Beyond Aššur", 53–77.

Empire of the Senseless

Edward Mitchell

> The witchcraft of sleep divides with the truth the empire of our lives.
> —Ralph Waldo Emerson, "Demonology."[1]

> But before all this, in the very beginning of things, the universe was organized; and all that man has done in society, in the church, in business, and all that he ever can do in the centuries to come, can never bring to pass so complete a form of organization, so vast a trust, so centralized a form of control, as passes before our eyes in each twenty-four hours of our lives as we contemplate that all-including system of perfect organization called the Universe. It does not require a very vivid imagination to picture the waste, the destruction, the chaos, that would follow if there were not perfect organization, perfect cooperation, perfect regulation, perfect control in the affairs of the universe. How could we live, for example, if there were constant competition between day and night or a constant struggle for supremacy between the seasons? Does any one, for a moment, think that he would prefer such a condition to the cooperation that now exists through all the affairs of the universe?
> —George W. Perkins, "Keep the Corporation or Kill It."[2]

Wrigley's chewing gum; spray paint; the dishwasher; the Automatic Continuous Clothing Closure; the spinning Ferris wheel; Tesla's illuminated wireless vacuum tubes; the rotating egg of Columbus; wind up rabbits that hopped; a silver encrusted toilet; the telautograph; moving sidewalks; a perfume fountain spraying out a different scent every day; shredded wheat; and Cracker Jack: The 1893 Chicago World's Fair was named the "World's Columbian Exposition" in its celebration of the fifth century of America's "discovery" and displayed a churning menagerie of inventions, a flotsam and jetsam of new consumer products and scientific wonders on a tidal wave of future visions. The forty-four acres of floor space contained in the Manufactures and Liberal Arts Building at the Columbian Exposition referred, hypothetically, to the contents of the entire world, displaying: "tens of thousands of things that need not be enumerated."[3] Providing a visual form for a de-natured America, the Chicago World's Fair grounds were a testimonial to a faith in planning to govern the laissez-faire development that characterized Chicago's rapid growth. And it was his attendance at the World's Columbian Exposition that inspired King Camp Gillette, the inventor of the disposable razor, to develop his project for a social utopian trust.

In three books written over three decades, King Camp Gillette elaborated a sweeping treatise on the power of capital to self-organize. The text of *Human Drift* (1894), subtitled *The United Intelligence vs. Competition*, was conjured up by Gillette in a hotel room in Scranton, Pennsylvania and described the formation and logistics of his concept for "the United Company." Gillette would expand this proposal in his *World Corporation*, published as an excerpt in periodical format in 1907 and as a first edition in 1910. Gillette extended the thesis in *People's Corporation* published in 1923. Each of these iterations describes a vast commercial monopoly acting as a purifying filter to displace the waste and inefficiencies of a competitive, market-driven economy. Across each publication, Gillette built and developed the scheme of a "World Corporation" as a logic of motivated individuals who drift towards a physical consensus by means of mass consumption. In the "World Corporation," any ideological differences amongst populations were usurped not by force but by a voluntary surrender to the native intelligence of the market. Monopoly, Gillette wrote, was an inevitability: "Open competition must logically result in final control."[4]

Each of the three Gillette publications coincided with a distinct period of fiscal crisis: *Human Drift* posed as a solution to the Panic of 1893 and anticipated the period of corporate mergers;[5] *World Corporation* was published in first edition during 1910 at the start of the 1910–11 Panic,[6] but was penned amidst the 1907 fiscal crisis; *People's Corporation* (1924), co-authored with Upton Sinclair, responded to the 1920–1921 Depression. The Boston-based inventor and acolyte Melvin Linwood Severy published two extended commentaries on these books, entitled *Industrial Solution* (1903) and *Gillette's Social Redemption* (1907) respectively. The latter was a 783-page tome of case studies and statistical evidence in support of Gillette's proposal.

Concurrent with these writing endeavors, Gillette's iconic razor business grew rapidly. Founded ten years after his visit to the Columbian Exposition, the business expanded from inaugural annual sales of 51 razor sets and 168 blades in 1903 to 90,000 razor sets and 12 million blades by 1904.[7] The articulation of Gillette's utopian visions is ostensibly incongruous with the more widely-known razor blade endeavor. If the razor was disposable, Gillette's utopian visions predicted a permanent center. As noted by Kenneth Frampton however, the emergence of cycles of rapid obsolescence in consumer goods and the possibility for the rapid amortization of construction components were two themes that coincided historically.[8] Frampton observes the eradicated distinction between *meubles* and *immeubles*, or merchandise and buildings, whereby both the "freestanding, high-rise megaliths of the modern city" and the safety razor became discrete but correlated forms.[9] According to this view, the razor and the metropolis were, for Gillette, both *meubles* and therefore served as equivalent instruments of idealization—the razor because it was disposable and the city of skyscrapers because of its contingent assembly was dependent on market forces that all but guaranteed its replacement.[10] Both city and commodity were, moreover, independent from indigenous economies that relied on natural resources as the source or location. Such a newly indistinct logic of product and building demonstrated a strong capacity to undo the concept of place and property on which the political constructs of the early nineteenth century were based.

The Human Drift

Established social constructs, such as those first envisioned in Thomas More's California-based Utopia, suddenly ceased to be either relevant or practiced. More's vision of an Arcadian England, figuratively reached by a world spinning backwards in time, had screeched to a halt. The western territories had been settled, absorbed and networked, by telegraph and then rail. This occurred at a cost however—the destabilization of the national economy. In his 1893 paper, read to the American Historical Association close to the Exposition fairgrounds, the historian Frederic Turner announced this as a cultural shift.[11] His essay "The Significance of the Frontier in American History" theorized the western lands as a relief valve to urban tensions, and established a dominant myth of cultural studies for several decades. For Turner, "frontier" constituted the crest of a churning surf of civilization as it washed up against an uncivilized wilderness. By the 1896 presidential election, three years later, the need to exploit or colonize foreign markets to stabilize production and capital had become topical and contentious. The conquest of overseas territories sparked major political debate between the agrarian Democratic party and the progressive, pro-business Republican party. The only possible remaining westward motion was to cross the Pacific to reach distant shores and discover new trinkets for emerging consumer cultures. The same exotic islands exhibited at the White City's *Midway Plaisance* remained, as yet, unspoiled by the mounds of discarded dreams and desires, which one could read as the material traces of the *Human Drift*. In the mid-1890s, it was still possible to set shore on some tropical island without stepping into a wad of chewing gum.

Commercial consolidation during the Great Merger Movement was a vehicle of a new political era and followed the collapse of William Jennings Bryan's Populist Revolt. Railroads were the most important corporations post-war, but widespread corruption and waste were contributory to the 1873 and 1893 panics. Gillette's vision of a single corporation governing price fluctuations was intended to eliminate economic instability. Individual business owners, acting in partnerships, still retained dominance in the nineteenth century market. Corporations provided the necessary credit, insurance, and transportation for such enterprises. While corporate organizations, as well as fraternal and mortgage communities, sometimes had local or regional membership, the financial structures that underwrote and managed risk were, often, statistical clusters displaced from another origin. The new statistical communities could be made up of properties or individuals disconnected from and anonymous to one another. Risk followed the logic of actuarial tables, not geographic boundaries. Another change to the concept of insurance, now unrelated to place, was its new association with the human body itself, calculated by assessment of age, health history, or occupation. Unlike the earlier agrarian utopias these new assemblages were virtual—it mattered *where* you were, as much as it did *who* you were in these virtual clusters. Such nomadic fiscal "communities" unconstrained by proximity, were, of course, abstractions.

The corporate paternalism expressed in Gillette's writings was not an isolated phenomenon. George Perkins, the noted businessman and leader of the Progressive movement, had referred to William Jennings Bryan's rear guard Peoples Party as "wicked' and likened it to "the firing on Sumter" (i.e. the bombardment on Fort Sumter which started the American Civil War).[12] Walter Lippman, a cofounder of the New York Socialist party with Gillette co-author Upton Sinclair, in his book *Drift and Mastery: An Attempt to Diagnose the Current Unrest*, later called William Jennings Bryan the Don Quixote of American politics, accusing him of moving in a world that no longer existed.[13] Dudley Wooten,

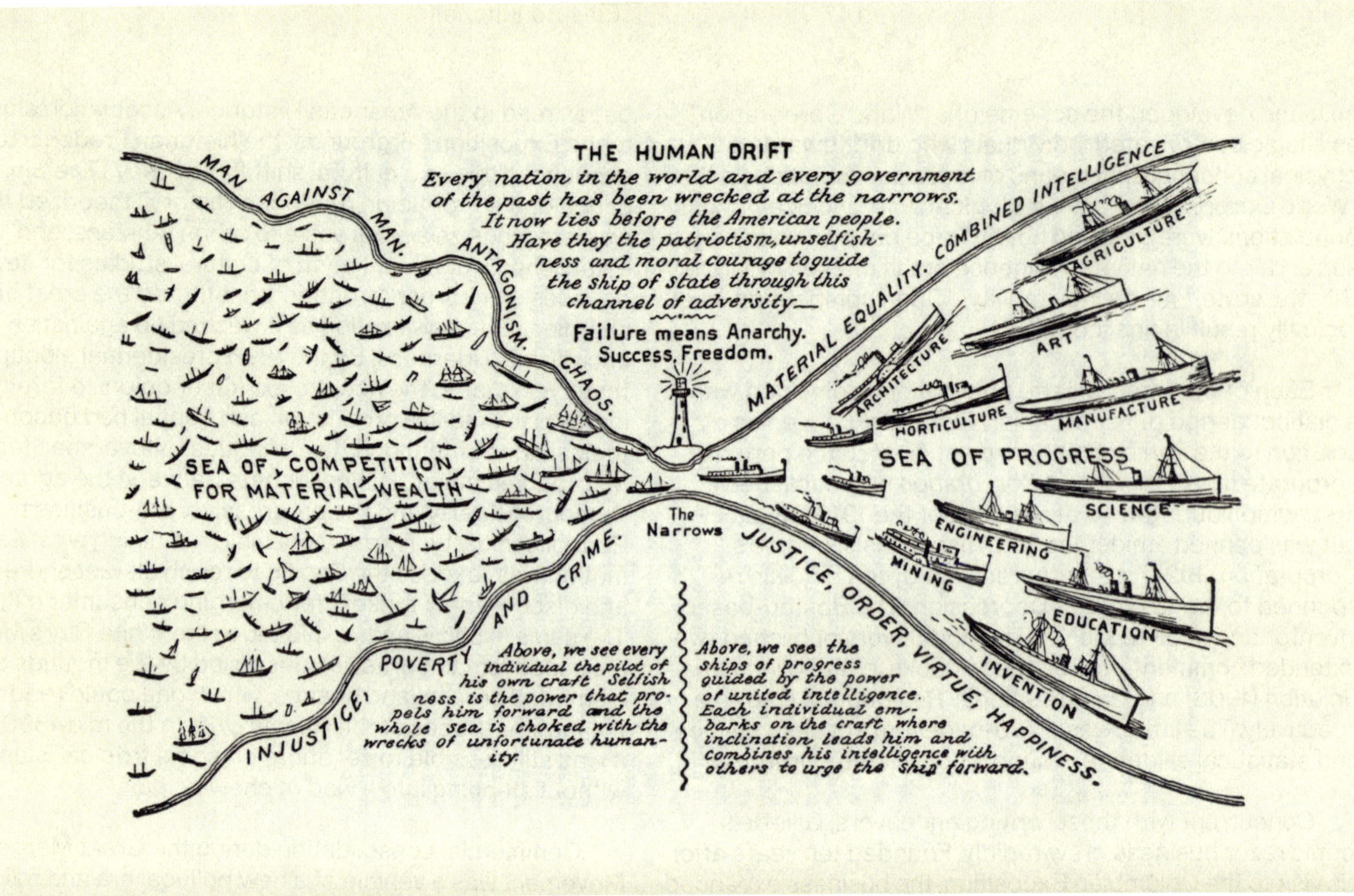

FIG 1
From Human Drift by King Camp Gillette (1894).

a Texas Democrat, still saw corporations as a threat to the "sovereignty of individual manhood" claiming industrialization had produced an "artificial person" via the corporation. Rather than a free form of personhood this, the corporation was, according to Wooten, a new form of indenture "imposed upon the toil and talents of seventy million of American citizens by syndicated wealth..."[14] Although joint stock companies were critical in the establishment of the original colonies, they were a forbidden formation for colonial Americans themselves. After the Revolution corporations were linked with the state and ostensibly worked in the public interest, playing important roles in the building of early infrastructure in the United States from Jamestown to Lowell.

While the shifts from Jeffersonian to corporate structures were contested, the national center for political and architectural debate also shifted to Gillette's birthplace of Chicago. Larger-scale manufacturing and agricultural businesses supervened on the traditionally-scaled political unit of the farm in and around Chicago during Gillette's early life. He saw the farm—an axiom of economy and of place—being absorbed in the new commercial dimension, becoming increasingly vestigial in relation to the political theory and identity that it had both founded and been foundational to.[15] The loss of the farm unit coincided with the emergence of new descriptions of an American public as untethered and directionless. But this "drift", both for Gillette and cultural figures like Walt Whitman and Louis Sullivan, also brought redemptive values. Drift, or oceanic feelings, is symptomatic in the literature of the latter half of the 19th century. This literature often implies a nascent supra-natural order whereby the psychology of a sovereign individual was threatened by an emerging primitive form in the modern consumer, and in which oceans, tides, and floods could also describe the extensive space of great western migrations over the vast plains of grasses. Whitman imagined drift as an ecstatic possibility for rebirth:

> Forth from the war emerging, a book I have made.
> The words of my book are nothing, the drift of it is everything.[16]

In contrast to Whitman's romantic wandering across the fertile western landscape, Gillette imagined a giant corporate center as an anchor on the Great Lakes. The patented inventions exhibited at the Columbian Exhibition's White City exhibit appeared to a businessman like Gillette as the catalysts of a new man-made Eden. For Gillette, mobility was facilitated by commodities and cities, rather than attributed to any capacity of the self, as could describe an attitude such as Whitman's. Thus the movements of people in the *Human Drift* were shown in an image depicting a flotilla of small ships, drifting towards the narrows of the present and re-emerging as large ocean liners formed by justice, order, virtue, happiness. FIG 1 These ocean liners anticipate in some ways Le Corbusier's "Eyes That Do Not See" discussion.[17] In *Human Drift*, the liners are made by Gillette to metamorphose into giant skyscrapers, becoming islands of refuge in a vast commercial sea. Products rather than people circulated within this great urban center. The conjuring of consumer brands would elicit the incantatory magic that Whitman claimed for the names of native places.

Cast into this sea of consumer gifts, Gillette wrote *Human Drift* as a self-described member of the "nomadic fraternity" of the business world, a travelling salesman, like the great French *utopianist* Charles Fourier.[18] Both Fourier and Gillette were drifters in the world of commodities and worked to stabilize and direct the same cultural and economic flows through architecture. If Chicago was urban headquarters to the nation's largest commodities trading operation until the 1890s, it was also unplanned—subject to and object of laissez-faire development. As such, Chicago was itself a physical consequence of drift. Architect Louis Sullivan was captivated by the idea of drift which he recorded in a letter to Whitman:

> My dear and honoured Walt Whitman:—
> It is less than a year ago that I made your acquaintance so to speak, quite by accident, searching among the shelves of a bookstore.
> I was attracted by the curious title "Leaves of Grass," opened the book at random, and my eyes met the lines of "Elemental Drifts"[19]

The World's Columbian Exhibition, designed by architects John Wellborn Root and Daniel Burnham together with landscape architect Frederick Law Olmsted, offered a politics and an architecture of control that contrasted strongly with the views of Chicago architect Louis Sullivan, who favored an individuated and expressive idiom. The Columbian Exhibition, to Sullivan, proposed to set American architecture back "for half a century from its date, if not longer."[20] His objection was more architectural than political. The neo-classical styling and the organizational logic of the Columbian Exhibition's White City plan was both decorative and compositional, motivated by *Beaux Arts* principles rather than market driven pragmatics. Despite his objections to Root's White City, Sullivan's is in other ways indebted to Root's design approach. For example, Root, viewed the tall office as a building type that should by its "mass and proportion convey in some elemental sense an idea of the great, stable, conserving forces of modern civilization:"[21]

> Since, therefore, buildings are the largest things made by man, a deviation in them from this universal law is the most elemental of mistakes, increasing in enormity as the building considered increases in size. Both in this and other respects many things may be pardoned to a little house, or one without public significance, which become un- pardonable in a larger or more important building.[22]

Although in a moment of Whitmanesque reverie, Sullivan had metaphorically tied the skyscraper to the organic growth of the prairie, his approach to the office tower, compared to Root, is utilitarian:

> Only in rare instances does the plan or floor arrangement of the tall office building take on an aesthetic value, and this usually when the lighting court is external or becomes an internal feature of great importance."[23]

Colin Rowe—in 1976, a century later—recounted a story of the critic and journalist Montgomery Schuyler who, when asked by a Chicago architect what the outcome would be if an architect were to elaborate urban requirements, declared: "why the word would be passed around and he would never get another one to do. No, we never try tricks on our businessman, they are too wide awake."[24] For Rowe, "the Chicago structural revolution therefore was the result of a certain combination, of ruthless open-mindedness and imaginative salesmanship. Accordingly, on Sullivan's admission, the architects of Chicago "did not demand the frame; it was presented to them."[25] Rowe elaborates:[26]

> "Sullivan was primarily an architect of commercial buildings; and of all buildings, the office block is obviously that without the need of any but the minimum of planning. It requires elementary circulations and a well lit floor area; but apart from these, it neither can nor should present any spatial elaboration. Thus, the unobstructed evenly lit floor and the indefinite number of floors which it permitted, recommend the steel frame to the architects of Chicago as the answer to a practical dilemma. These structures make no compromise with the observer; they are neither capricious nor urbane and they display an authenticity so complete that we are disposed to accept them as facts of nature, as geological manifestations rather than as architectural achievements."[27]

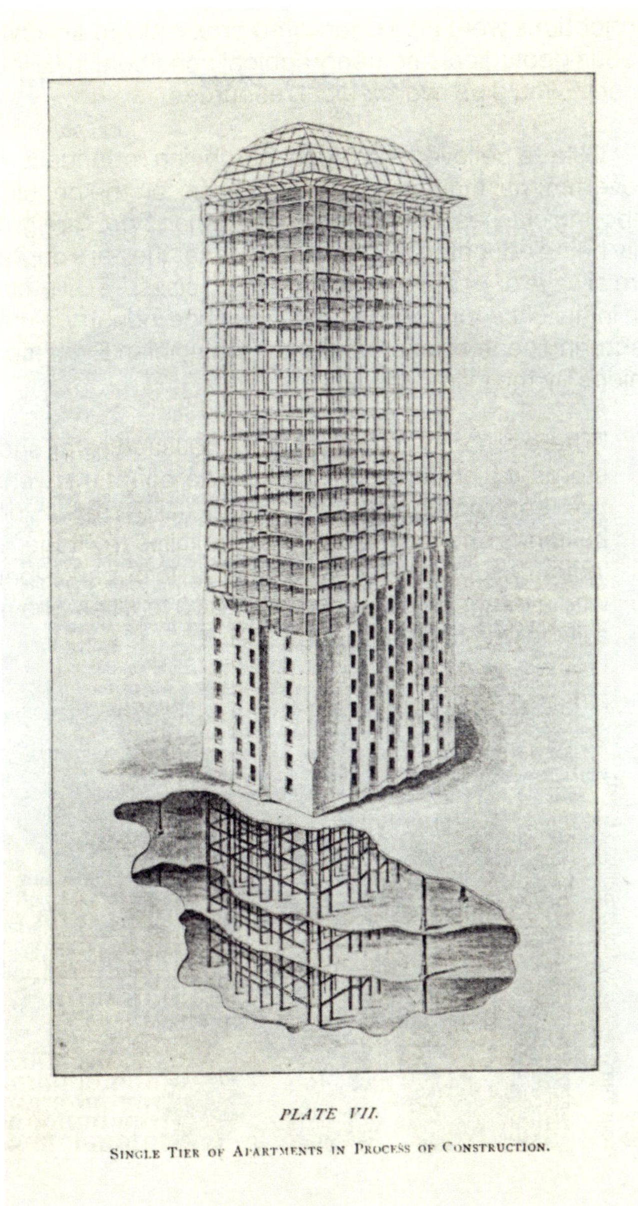

FIG 2
Plate VII from Human Drift by King Camp Gillette (1894).

FIG 2 King Camp Gillette proposed a city of towers for the large central city in *Human Drift*, to be named "Metropolis." His schematic idea was aligned with Louis Sullivan's approach, that is, one in which towers are presented as evidence of the logical outcome of a rationalized market for the production and exchange of commodities.[28] But, like Root and Sullivan, Gillette answered to corporate needs rather than grass roots populism. The illustrations that accompany Gillette's proposal in *Human Drift* were not vastly different from Louis Sullivan's drawings for a city of tiered skyscrapers, published during 1891 in *The Graphic*.[29] FIG 3 Gillette's idea of a city that would house an entire national population was at once, following Rowe, both practical and a grand form of "salesmanship."[30]

Contemporary with *Human Drift*, the idea that a large central city might develop in the middle of the country was surprisingly not an altogether far-fetched notion among civic boosters and *utopianists*. William Gilpin, who served as the first governor of the Territory of Colorado from 1861–1862, subscribed to the Prussian geographer Alexander von Humboldt's racist theory that great civilizations clustered around a global band at a mean annual isotherm of 50 degrees Fahrenheit and projected a world city, *Centropolis*, that would emerge near Kansas City. Other boosters often estimated that the region around their own constituencies would be the location for a city.[31] This cohort of utopian projections were also often sited proximally to an advantageous geological and geographical condition; in Gillette's case it would be hydrological resources.

Gillette believed that costs of running redundant local governments manifested as a direct tax on the people. The laboring classes, Gillette writes in *Human Drift*, "are gradually being educated to a knowledge that they are dupes, and are always dupes, of a non-producing class."[32] Gillette made an initial case for consolidating the shoe industry, a manufacturing sector described at the Columbian Exhibition as "hides by the mile":

> "There are... upward of 25,000 thousand retail shoe stores, which, if placed side by side, counting twenty-five feet front to the store...would make a solid block of buildings one hundred and fifteen miles frontage." That industry supports 100,000 clerks and book-keepers who average $500 per year; 25,000 families who make a living retailing these shoes."[33]

FIG 3
From *The Graphic* by Louis Sullivan (1891).

Consolidation would reconfigure the entire manufacturing system of the United States into a select few companies located in a single large manufacturing center, and industrial integration would eliminate waste of raw material supply. Populations would naturally "drift" toward the area where goods would be cheaper and this would form the Metropolis.[34] The cost of maintaining multiple retail branches and attending staff, Gillette continued, was a "frightful aggregate of waste."[35] The redundancy of stores was multiplied by a diverse range of ancillary costs.[36] According to Gillette, "the lack of power to regulate supply and demand... is in part, the cause of periods of depression and failure."[37] Unlike farming, corporate operations and failures could not be associated with natural or divine causes. A poor crop, insect infestation, disease, harsh winters and other mishaps could be attributable to forces outside of human control, but market shortages, plant shut downs, and obsolescence were human-induced maladies that challenged any claims to rationality in the market. Instead the perfection of commodities would, Gillette claimed, allow society to arrive at stasis and equilibrium. If a company could control the shoe industry with $200 million in capital, every industry could be consolidated, so Gillette claimed. In *Human Drift*, this was expected to destroy some industries, like the advertising companies and the travelling salesmen—Gillette's own former livelihood.[38] Gillette's Metropolis was an urban scheme where physical and fiscal consolidation was fully intended to be catalyzed entirely by commercial forces, as opposed to linking to a notion of western migratory patterns.[39]

Metropolis was also a scheme designed to be hydroelectrically powered by Niagara Falls. Two to three hundred of Gillette's manufacturing establishments would be located in one center at Niagara Falls, utilizing hydro-electric power. Though initially only producing non-perishable groceries and necessary clothing—i.e. shoes, hosiery, underwear, white goods, dress goods, furnishing goods and outer garments—further factories would follow in separate locations to make no more than one product each. Gillette projected one such factory to produce flour, at a volume of 50,000 barrels of a day. Each such factory building would be fire proofed, with numerous elevators large enough to lift and load a freight car to any floor in order to minimize the handling of material. This scheme as a whole was called the "United Company."[40]

From the Niagara manufacturing center, the finished products in Metropolis would be distributed to one hundred United Company stores located in one hundred of the largest metropolitan cities—including New York City with a population of two million people, and Elmira, New York, a town of forty thousand people. The aggregate population of the one hundred cities was 16 million people. Including their respective suburbs, this meant the United Company served roughly one-third of the United States population. Gillette predicted that the relatively low cost of goods in urban centers would exponentially catalyze even more drift to the urban cores.[41]

It is important to emphasize that, despite the grandiosity of this scheme, Gillette saw the United Company as a realistic proposition: It was meant to be evolutionary not revolutionary. The Company would not rely on any federal consolidation of business, nor existing plant infrastructure, but rather it would instead work hermetically and independently as a mega-corporation. After utilizing $700 million in capital to control the clothing and grocery trade, thereby marginalizing all existing secondary businesses, centralized control would naturally and efficiently destroy smaller cities. In *Human Drift*, Gillette portended the demise of smaller regional centers including Elmira, New York; Quincy, Illinois; Council Bluff, Iowa; Youngstown, Ohio; Holyoke, Massachusetts and St. Joseph, Missouri. His projection was only contradicted by the handful of small cities that survived: Little Rock, Arkansas; Elizabeth, New Jersey; and Norfolk, Virginia—these became significant ports or future corporate centers.

Trusts, Gillette asserted, already caused drift. Perfection of products would happen naturally, and altruism would prevent price gouging. Gillette added that the Armour Company, one of the largest meat packers, could control shoe manufacturing immediately—simply by taking control of the hide market, then turning hides to leather, and finally to shoes. Gillette asks: "What is the use of legislation against syndicates, trusts, and controlling corporations?"[42] Consolidation would also enable cost saving by a seventy-five percent reduction in the cost of power. With one facility, rather than two hundred, the number of machines and the cost of repairs would reduce by one third. By adopting three shifts of eight hours per day the number of buildings would reduce. Three hundred coffee and spice mills relocated into one building—two-hundred feet by five-hundred feet, or ten stories high—would incur a saving of fifty percent in manual labor, and seventy-five percent in salesmen, teamsters, horses, office help, and book-keepers. Twenty-five percent of the reduction in power use would be achieved via a seventy-five percent reduction in coal usage, which, in turn would reduce railroad labor and cars required to carry the coal, which would reduce the labor for producing the railroad car, and so on. The system-based efficiency measure was not only advantageous to cost. By eradicating competition and its boom and bust cycles it also offered stability, avoiding the problems of the depression Gillette had recently witnessed.[43]

Anticipating big box retail centers of a century later, the warehouses Gillette described in *Human Drift* would have urban proportion and would be contiguous with railroads. Almost directly quoting from John Wellborn Root's playbook, the Gillette warehouses would be constructed of an iron framework with plain brick walls with iron joists and brick floors. All doors and shelving would be fabricated by sheet iron. Sample rooms—at a one to one hundred ratio of rooms to people—would be located in urban cores. These rooms would hold no stock but would transmit orders to the distribution centers by telephone and telegraph. Deliveries would be made daily by company truck to sectors of the city at regular intervals, as often as once per hour. No one in the warehouses would have to wait more than two hours to have their order filled. The financing of each distribution center, and the share of the costs of the manufacturing center, would adhere to a controlled ratio, population number to urban center. At a cost of five dollars per head for goods in the store, plus five dollars per head for aggregate cost for building the distribution centers, the total of ten dollars per person came to a total capital investment of $200 million required to develop Gillette's retail infrastructure as a whole. Accordingly, by Gillette's estimate the Niagara plant would cost less than $500 million including stock making a total investment of $700 million for the network entire. United States federal railroad infrastructure by comparison was supposedly capitalized at twenty times that amount. The United Company's financing would be cash only; no credit would be offered. Executive officers would manage the manufacturing centers. Daily transactions and cash received would be transmitted to the central office. The United Company would produce its own paper, do its own printing and manufacture all packaging.[44]

Like other contemporary advocates of monopoly, Gillette asserted that economic progress would not benefit the wealthy. Enlightened, altruistic industrialists such as Thomas Edison, he claimed, did not work solely for profit but for fame and renown.[45] From wealth human suffering was born; the gain of one is at the loss of another; greed had filled the prisons; the adulteration of food products was caused by competition; war was a sign that, like the brute, man still hunted in packs, and nation was pitted against nation; despite progress in labor saving devices, resulting fiscal gains had not been passed down to the laborers as they were in worse position in 1893 than twenty years earlier; one soap is really no better than another; any benefit from variety in the market was illusionary. All of these claims were declared by Gillette in *Human Drift*.[46]

Like-minded monopolists had put forward the proposition that competitive markets enslaved individuals, subjecting them to shifts in the market. As the argument went, under the current system the small businessman and wage laborer worked in arbitrary service to competition. Money, in a monopolistic system, would ultimately reach equilibrium then resolve itself to its simplest form and pass out of existence within fifty years. Would anyone take advantage of such control? Would workers, supplied with every want, take advantage of the corporate welfare system? With every want fulfilled, would this be abuse? Gillette asserted that the progressive system would set the mind above the struggle for material wealth, "just as a child does not abuse the love and confidence of his parents."[47]

In order to finance this hypothetical United Company, Gillette estimated the need of nominal capital at one thousand million dollars divided into one thousand million shares, "By the People—For the People."[48] The mega-monopoly would then issue non-dividend bearing stock—bonded so as not to induce a demand for increase of the profits of the Company beyond a set fixed interest charge for the initial investment. Issues of the stock were to be sold in ten $100 million dollar increments. The first issues would produce a six-percent return, then five percent, then four percent, and all subsequent issues at a three percent maximum return. The low price of stock, set at one dollar, allowed all citizens to contribute to the financing of the United Company.[49]

During the development of the United Company, and via its absorption of fields of production, the centralization of manufacturing would cause massive unemployment.[50]

But the underemployed, Gillette figured, would build the great Metropolis. If war was the inevitable outcome of competition, corporate cooperation would be the great counter example. The Civil War, said Gillette, "employed" three million men for destruction, so five million would be employed for the construction of the new Metropolis.[51] In this new egalitarian society, "Women should count the same as men."[52] As for the wealthy, Gillette warns: "you may be happy and secure in your position to-day, you may be one of the unfortunates of society to-morrow..."[53] Only the United Company can assure the common welfare.

Niagara Falls, with an elevation change of three hundred thirty feet, had enormous power capacity, and would provide not only energy but also the necessary source of fresh water for Metropolis. FIG 4 The falls would be divided into ten drops of thirty feet of head in order to supply a steady source of 10 million horsepower. The savings in coal used for steam generation at a cost of fifteen dollars per unit of horsepower meant a net gain of $1.5 billion per year. Water would be taken from the elevation of Lake Erie and discharged as waste into Lake Ontario, requiring twenty-five miles of pipe in parallel connecting the two lakes in the western section of Metropolis. The city would have a perfect sewage system, perfect water distribution, cold air distribution for refrigeration, central heating, mass transit, and the latest in electric telephonic communication.[54]

Metropolis's pedestrian street-level section resembled other late nineteenth century architectural fantasies; John Wellborn Root's Rookery is one obvious referent. Like actual urban projects such as Boston's Back Bay, the entire city of Metropolis was to be built *above* the existing ground plane, requiring no excavation. The base of the city formed a honeycomb of chambers supported by a colossal steel framework, protected by facings of glass or glazed tile inside and out. The infrastructure consisted of three levels—the lowest twenty-five feet high for building systems, the middle twenty-five feet for transport, and the upper a fifty feet high pedestrian passage between buildings. The raised system facilitated defect identification and made repairs and service more efficient. The steel and glass platform would be laid twenty-five feet above the web of public services, so the new effective ground plane of the city would turn into a hovering transparent floor. Like the Columbian Exhibition, the transport and building levels in Metropolis would be tiled in white with colored borders. Like the "Arabian Nights" exhibit at the Columbian Exhibition, the pavement would be tile and glass in subdued color. The upper chamber would have changing colors and "artificial parks topped above the upper platforms with domes of colored glass in beautiful designs, its urns of flowers, and beautiful works of art and statuary, would make it an endless gallery of loveliness."[55]

The citizens of Metropolis would live in apartment houses free of housekeeping. Twenty-four thousand apartment buildings holding twenty-five thousand people each would be required. Carefully dimensioned buildings—six hundred feet in diameter and twenty-five stories high—would have eighteen apartment wings on each level. Each wing contained a parlor (20' × 25'), a library (17' × 15'), a music room (17' × 15') with four adjoining suites of rooms, a sitting room (15' × 20'), bedroom (15' × 20') and bath (10' × 12'). FIG 5

The shape of the apartment type was probably more rhetorical than practical; it resembled a huge cog right down to the tapering of the apartment edges.[56] In the apartment layout the bedrooms do not receive much light, but Gillette allowed that the floor plans would vary. Automatic machinery could be adapted for tile manufacturing so that the materials were modular and repeatable, and so would become cheaper than plaster. With upward of one hundred million rooms required in the Metropolis, the scale of the industry would produce price efficiency. All windows would face away from the building with the space between arms of building at about forty-five feet towards the exterior of the wing tapering to eighteen feet at the inner ring. A ten-foot corridor landing circumscribed the central space with metal connecting walls. Like other radical schemes for housing around the turn of the century, there were no individual kitchens.[57]

At the center of the apartment buildings was a glass-domed interior court—four hundred feet in diameter. It sheltered a dining room—two hundred feet in diameter and roughly nine stories tall. Food preparation occurred in central kitchens—six hundred feet in diameter, woven into the urban grid. There would be four thousand kitchens for the twenty-four-thousand apartment houses. Major deliveries, for example one annual supply of grain, would be dispatched to the four thousand food service buildings while other non-perishable items were delivered on a rotating schedule servicing twelve to fourteen buildings per day. Goods from emporiums would be selected "without money and without price."[58] As Gillette saw it, without any financial transaction there would be no incentive to hoard. The agricultural system would be rationalized and optimized for ideal crop production.[59] Gillette developed a sample of the detailed site plan matrix.[60] FIG 6

FIG 4
Niagara Falls

FIG 6
Plate I from *Human Drift* by King Camp Gillette (1894).

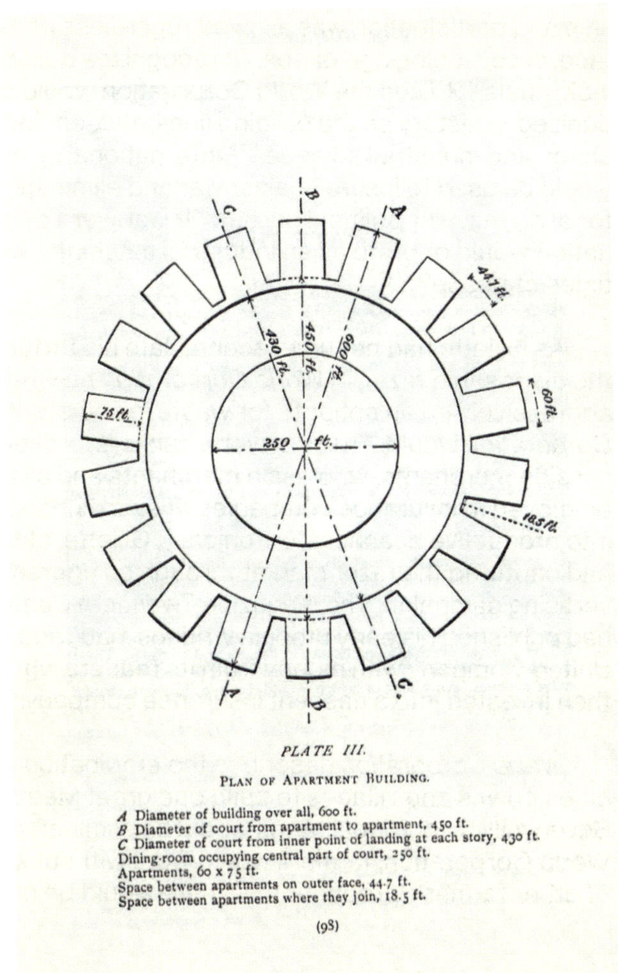

FIG 5
Plate III from *Human Drift* by King Camp Gillette (1894)

According to this plan, an artificial lawn of one hundred fifty feet in length surrounds a glass and porcelain network of walkways of one hundred fifty feet wide. The remaining traffic islands are covered in glass domes that give light to the walkways. FIG 7 These domed areas provide a total of 36,000 conservatories, in a city of 60 million people. A Bureau of Horticulture would therefore need to be established for the city of Metropolis, employing about one percent of the population—or 500,000 people—to plant trees, shrubs and flowers. Flowers would bloom all year. Trees and urns of flowers would also be distributed at regular intervals along both sides and through the center of every walkway on both the upper and middle platforms. Any anticipated increase in population would simply generate an expansion for the Metropolis urban grid; In *Human Drift*, Gillette anticipated a five to ten percent population growth and thus projected a building campaign set in advance of this increase. Gillette's plan demanded a total of 30–40,000 buildings: "Like the heart of a sentient being the city would pulsate with life through its millions of arteries of copper and steel, and stand a living, breathing monument of man's combined and highest intelligence."[61] Though the buildings were shown as repetitive structures, Gillette thought that each would be the subject of a competition between architects and submitted to the Bureau of Architecture which would then pass on labor and award credit. This would "make architecture, in all its details, one of the most fascinating scientific studies, and would result in an endless variety of beautiful designs, both in exterior and interior finish of buildings."[62]

In *Human Drift*, Gillette extrapolated that after twenty-five years of operation ninety percent of the citizens of Metropolis greater than forty years in age would be gone, so any large cultural changes would then be more acceptable to younger generations.[63] Employees over the age of forty would work in one of the bureaus for five to ten years with recognition of merit marked on their permanent record. Bureaus would manage systems of education, agriculture, architecture, manufacture, distribution, labor, transportation, electrical engineering, with multiple subdivisions designating technical parts of each bureau. A Bureau of Vital Statistics would be responsible for a record that Gillette named a Birth Number, effectively similar to the current Social Security system that included name and gender, date of birth, name of the father and mother, marital status, name of spouse, children, and a photograph of the individual updated every fifth year. The Birth Record would also hold a Life Record of key achievements, date of death and an obituary. The Bureau would effectively become a database of the entire history of Metropolis.

Gillette's vision, outlandish as though it may appear, was in keeping with the rise of the corporate welfare advocated by many of the captains of industry. Gerald Stanley Lee, a Congregational clergyman and author, wrote a self-published book in 1908 entitled *Inspired Millionaires: An Interpretation of America*.[64] In it he set rules for the new breed of millionaires. "One can hardly go anywhere in the United States the last few years," Lee joked, "without seeing millionaires standing in rows."[65] Lee saw monopoly as a perfection of service, an "art form" at its cultural apogee. The problem of socialism was that everyone was being a socialist for someone else, he wrote, but the monopolist would be the better socialist: "The special function of the millionaire is that he is inventing people."[66] Lee described:

> Someone is going to loom up in America and do a factory yet that will rank with Shakespeare's *Hamlet*, Homer's *Iliad*, and the Sixtieth Chapter of Isaiah... It will not need to have great columns in front to seem beautiful to us, and it will not need Gothic windows to seem like a church, and it will be filled, all day long as we go by, with the whirl of the wheels in it, and the whirl of the wheels will be the chant of the people in it.[67]

The prognostications of a new age fostered by the transparent network of corporate mergers had genuine prophets in the field of business and politics. In a lecture entitled "Modern Corporation" given at Columbia University in 1907, George Walbridge Perkins, Sr.—a Hanna associate—made his own grandiose comparisons likening the ordering of the universe to a possible nation governed by corporations.[68] Like Gillette, Perkins saw himself as a benevolent manager of the interests of his stock holders and workers, guiding them towards an era of co-operation and control. Perkins wanted games of chance further reduced. In another address, also in 1906, Perkins claimed that the "modern corporation" would lead to a "form of socialism of the highest order" while preserving the "right of private property."[69] Perkins' corporate socialism was markedly different from actual socialism. For Perkins, the Great Merger Movement was emancipatory. Fortunes were made and lost in the nineteenth century seemingly out of thin air. Gillette's biography was a case in point: After losing his family wealth in the Chicago Great Fire, he made his personal fortune on the perfection of the disposable razor.

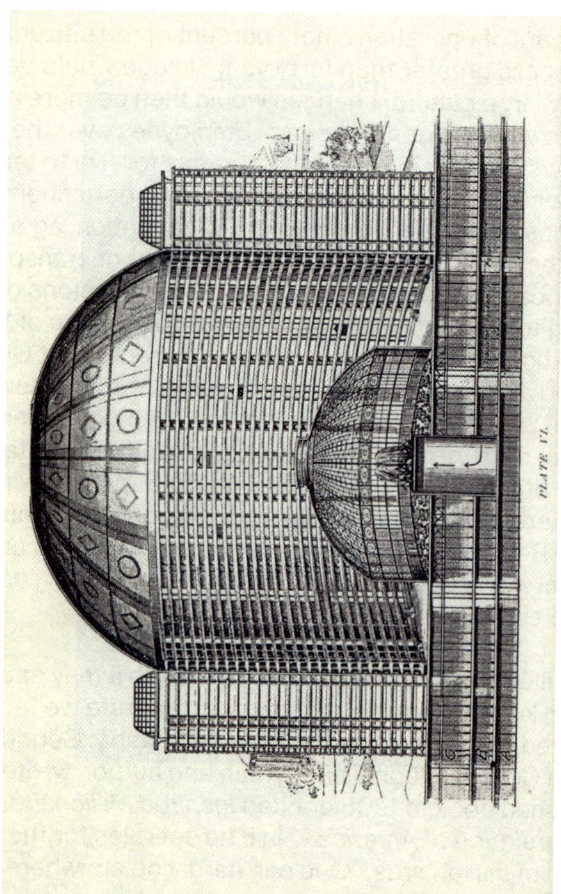

FIG 7
Plate VI from *Human Drift* by King Camp Gillette (1894)

World Corporation

King Camp Gillette's second book *World Corporation* (1910) kept many of the same premises as *Human Drift* but added in the actual incorporation of a United Company, and legal paperwork for incorporation was filed in Arizona on June 8, 1910. In writing *World Corporation*, Gillette provided a detailed account of the stock company and described the jobs eliminated by the "drift" towards corporate socialism. The company directors of the United Company, as described in *World Corporation*, consisted of Gillette as President and Treasurer; Boston Attorney Edward S. Crockett as Vice President and Secretary; and Charles A. Gaines, Gillette's brother-in-law, listed as an unspecified director. Edward Crockett's law offices at No 6. Beacon Street, Boston, Massachusetts, operated as the address of the corporation. Once again Corporate America provided a beacon: "World Corporation is like US Steel Corp., stripped of stockholders and extended to infinity, and combining in one vast organization for people."[70]

The organization and by-laws of the United Corporation were similar to that outlined in *Human Drift*. The Arizona articles of incorporation stipulated the issuing of common shares at one dollar each with certification in twenty and fifty share blocks, and drew up the organization of the Board of Directors.[71] Representatives to the World Corporation Congress would be named by every chapter from one of its ten board members. The total of indebtedness of each chapter would not exceed two thirds of the capitol stock.

With the development of an arms race in Europe, *World Corporation* anticipated national competition and the impending war. Gillette declared that the United Company would not recognize nations or divisions of people. Citizenship and participation was allowed regardless of nationality, race, creed, color, age or sex: "It recognizes dollars, not individuals."[72] Thus the World Corporation would be recognized in history as the dividing line between "industrial chaos and industrial science."[73] International investment would be used to insure against war and eliminate the need for army, navy or political parties: "If war were declared the nation would operate as an industrial machine—why not in times of peace?"[74]

As Gillette had begun to accumulate his fortune with the disposable razor, in *World Corporation* he writes more aggressively on an antidote for waste in society. *World Corporation* would: "Turn lawyers, bankers, brokers, commission merchants, wholesale merchants and all those employed in insurance companies of every kind and nature into productive channels."[75] Ironically, Gillette, at the time, had captured the razor market through an aggressive advertising campaign. The magazine *Twentieth Century*, which had published his early utopian writings, had tried to finance United Company with money from its readers which was then invested into a nascent insurance company.[76]

World Corporation describes the eradication of 50,000 cities, towns and villages to build one great Metropolis. Seven million individual farms would be eliminated. In the World Corporation, farmers would work without knowledge of other farmer's production.[77] There would be no more need for unnecessary industries including government, law, insurance, merchants, and advertising.[78] Gillette frequently anticipates contemporary theories and practices of modern food production. Gillette claimed that twenty-five to fifty manufacturing industries in the grocery trade might control retail distribution throughout the US, a prediction which accurately corresponds the market condition today in which Walmart controls fourteen percent of the U.S grocery trade, Kroger has a nine percent market share, and where the top twenty chains control roughly sixty-four percent of all American grocery services.[79]

The physical publication of *World Corporation* was less elaborately illustrated than *Human Drift*. While Gillette re-used some drawings from the prior book, *World Corporation* describes buildings that are comparatively modest in size, and that contain only ten thousand people as opposed to twenty-five thousand people. In contrast, the built structures in *World Corporation* increase in number to ten thousand buildings total, for a population of one hundred million people. The descriptions Gillette provides of the structures in World Corporation suggests they are modelled on the New Municipal Building in New York City, designed by McKim Mead & White (later renamed the Manhattan Municipal Building), a 926,000 square foot office complex.[80] The Municipal Building was then the fourth tallest building in the world, and thus a primary case study for consolidation. It brought together New York City's five boroughs and organized them into one great bureaucracy in a single building that featured the first subway entrance at its base. Though the borough of Manhattan was wealthy at that time, Brooklyn was nearly bankrupt and running out of water. Consolidation was actively posed via the Municipal Building as a solution to problems of the outer boroughs, while providing access to available real estate by networking the city. A white-tiled plaza arcade appears in the Municipal Building, resembling the infrastructural base envisioned in the original United Company buildings.

Instead of the grid pattern proposed in *Human Drift*, Gillette configures a radiating plan for World Corporation with the center marked by a great edifice for city administration, a building that was to house each division of industry, a "World Corporate Congress." This urban circle's center point was hypothetically to be located in the actual city of Buffalo, New York, and circumscribed by a forty-mile radius that extended to the outskirts of present day Rochester, New York. An inner circle would house a range of new institutions, for Chemical Laboratories and Technical and Experimental Science and Research. A surrounding ring of manufacturing industries would include a circle of warehouses, education buildings, art buildings, museums, and nurseries. The outer ring would contain homes.

An ambitious schedule for the project is established by Gillette in *World Corporation*. If the buildings were erected as steel and reinforced concrete structures without embellishment, Gillette surmises that a thousand homes could be built for one hundred million people in ten years: building above ground would save a year in constructing the foundations, the additional labor required could be tabulated by comparing the roughly five thousand workmen needed to build the Municipal Building. The technology that had been used in the construction of the Municipal Building borrowed from bridge construction and involved the use of hot rivets to assemble the steel work. Accordingly, Gillette proposes that five million workers per year could build the housing for Metropolis while another five million would be required during the same ten-year period to build the urban infrastructure, municipal buildings and manufacturing centers. All workers deemed underemployed would be paid in World Corporation stocks.

Other utopian plans, like Charles Caryl's New Era Model City of 1897, depicted a radiating circular urban form.[81] Caryl's large circular civic plan housed five million people in ten square miles with large rings of apartment blocks, glass covered atriums and several rings of parks. Caryl's plan was, in summary, both more military and socially hierarchical than Gillette's conception and lacked the elaborate fiscal and political logic.

Closer in spirit to Gillette's skyscraper city was Edgar Chambless's *Roadtown* of 1910—a linear city or a skyscraper turned on its side. Chambless' own precedent is Arturo Soria y Mata's Linear city plan of 1882, which serves in turn as a possible inspiration for Le Corbusier's *Plan Obus* of 1933, as well as several Soviet linear cities. The Soviets saw the Soria y Mata's linear scheme as an equitable division of land appropriate for a communist state. Chambless was no communist, dedicating his book, with no degree of irony, to "J. Pierpont Morgan, a *straight* player in a crooked game" who held the securities of the Central Railroad of Georgia, which for Chambless, "made me *suffer* first and then made me think."[82] Chambless envisioned a magnificent two-story linear phalanstery, housing a thousand people per mile, built using Thomas Edison's patent for concrete housing with a linear rail line imbedded in its basement, and a grand boulevard on its roof for promenading or roller skating. Like Gillette, Chambless believed his vision was a logical outcome—that is, a nation built on both the logic and the power of corporations.

The People's Corporation

Gillette's third and final book, *The People's Corporation* (1923), was edited by Sinclair Lewis and dedicated 'To Mankind.' It was more politically strident, and its tone was more urgent, perhaps heightened by the devastating effects of the First World War and widening economic disparity. It opened with a quote from Jean-Jacques Rousseau:

> The first person who, having enclosed a piece of ground, took thought to declare,"This is mine," and found people simple enough to believe him, was the true founder of civil society. How many crimes, wars, murders, how much misery and horror would have been spared the human race if someone tearing down the pickets and filling up the ditch, had cried out to his fellows, "Beware of listening to this imposter; you are lost if you forget that the land belong to none and its fruits to all."[83]

This returns to some aspects of John Locke. But, in Rousseau's telling, civil society, and its origins in private property, was the root cause of misery. Gillette calculated that income in the form of dividends, profits, interest, and business savings for all industries in 1918 amounted to over $27 billion, or nearly half of the $60 billion output of these industries.[84] Gillette cites the National Bureau of Economic Research "Income in the United States, Vol. II, pp. 240, 242 Of every dollar $0.55 goes to labor, $0.45 to shareholders, owners and investors" and "If that latter group were to emigrate to some new territory they could absorb half the industries and control all the labor of the United States.[85]

> "With this income they could import labor and purchase materials and build themselves a paradise in the country of their adoption." "The paradise of profits is here in this very year of 1924. It is the Fifth Avenues, Sheridan Roads, Newports, Bar Harbors, Trouvilles, Mayfairs, Monte Carlos, and the thousands of beautiful palaces, private estates, mountain and seaside homes, built and maintained by means of unearned income derived from capital investment of one sort or another."

The idle would be forced to work. The "busy-ness class" was not just the corporate millionaires but all the bankers, brokers, and money lenders; clerks in stores; commercial travelers; decorators, drapers, and window dressers; floorwalkers, foremen and overseers; inspectors, gaugers, and samplers; proprietors, officials, and managers in warehouses; retail dealers; salesmen and saleswomen; wholesale dealers, exporters, and importers; insurance agents and officials totaling 4,242,979 people in trade.[86] Furthermore, eliminating those jobs involved in transportation, 690,027 jobs to be precise, left a population of 3,552,952 individuals who, Gillette claimed, were "engaged in this totally useless occupation of handling goods without adding one iota to their value."[87]

All such jobs, as Gillette well knew, "*persuade* people to buy" and census figures do not include those in advertising who also employ printers, lithographers, paper makers, and office labor and pays millions of dollars for space. Gillette cited the 1920 census which listed 122,519 lawyers, judges and justices who he also viewed as expendable in *The People's Corporation* due to the reduction in crime and lawsuits:[88] "95% of crimes are due to the "acquisitive impulse", he said. Eliminating crime would shrink law enforcement; a half million federal and a half million state level government jobs were not productive nor were professors and students in advertising, insurance classes, and law schools, and so on. With these 1.5 million state-sector unproductive jobs added to the 3,675,471 in the commercial sector, a total of over five million individuals were engaged in non-productive work (or, one in every eight individuals in the United States population in 1921, excluding the unemployed which stood between 5.5 and 6.5 million). In other words, Gillette argued, of his contemporaneous United States: "very conservatively... our machine [the factory] is twelve and one half percent inefficient."[89]

Just as the Civil War was a waste of man power and money, the First World War only magnified Gillette's convictions. Germany went to war to increase its markets, but one seventh of the German citizens who went to war died, and twice as many were wounded. Debt from the war, Gillette predicted, would not be paid off for generations. Productive capacity was lost in the previous ten years through war and preparation for war—twenty-five percent of productive capacity to be precise, a number higher in central Europe. After the war, England alone had 5,000,000 unemployed, one quarter of its working population.[90]

Although these were harbingers of the coming Depression, larger cities like Philadelphia had been able to survive due to the diversity of trades. The unnecessary duplication of some 30,000 smaller cities and towns however, particularly those that rely on only one or two industries, was costing the economy. Wilkes-Barre, Pennsylvania, near the town in which Gillette wrote his first book, was doubly devastated in the early twentieth century: first by the Japanese earthquake that cut off silk supply to its garment industry, next by coal strikes in 1923 that severed its retail market. A city of 66,000 was run on the wage income of only 7,000 workers.

Waste was not occurring at an industrial scale, but also occurred on the farm. As Gillette described, in the United States there were more than 7 million individual farms each with an average of five people per farm, some 35 million farm workers total. From a central agency, that 35 million could be restructured into a workforce of 5 million.[91] Extrapolating those figures to Kansas, a case where size increases due to farm production but where towns themselves do nothing, 409,596 workers support a population of 1.75 million, that is, some eighty-seven-and-a-half percent of the workforce engage in productive labor. Assuming that fifty percent of this group will be inefficient due to lack of coordination, this leaves 43.75 percent of the citizens as productive workers. A quarter of the overall population lost to war further reduces that number to a thirty-four percent productive capacity. Coupled with a fifty percent loss in agriculture due to the idle class, an estimate of seventy percent inefficiency seemed to Gillette to be a modest estimation, because if one was to include losses due to transportation and scattered settlement patterns this figure would be conservative.[92]

Wages in Gillette's new economy would not be paid in money but via labor credits, a method proposed by mid-century reformists like Robert Owen and later by Josiah Warren who had run the Cincinnati Time Store on labor credits, a system like that advocated by Henry Olerich. For Gillette, labor credits would represent total cost of production, and to balance the books *The People's Corporation* would adjust its prices for service and products so that the total value of the commodity stock would match the total labor credits on the books. Margins of difference could be wiped out in readjustment in the following fiscal year.

Living conditions in *The People's Corporation* were again modelled on modern precedents and escalated to a colossal scale. With the comparison that half of all New Yorkers lived in apartments, Gillette predicted a future with no more than three or four great cities, and where the apartment building would be the preferred typology. The buildings in People's Corporation operated like the best hotels. They were surrounded by gardens and housed up to 100,000 inhabitants per building, four times larger than the schemes in *World Corporation* or *Human Drift*. Up to fifty stories tall, the building design commissions would be awarded by competition in Gillette's People's Corporation, as per the Chicago Tribune Competition.

Food supplies would be allocated by the Food Bureau, which would oversee agricultural production and ensure each citizen would pay a standardized cost. Meal tickets would be issued at the beginning of the year, to record where food was served in *The People's Corporation*. The cost of food supplies would be set at a cumulative total of one tenth of all labor costs. Clothing costs would also be determined by labor and adjusted so that total returns are about one twentieth of total labor. The remaining labor income would purchase services and luxury goods, furniture, decorative arts, entertainment and travel. Under the perfection of the centralized organization of The People's Corporation, a laborer could produce in five years all of his or her needs for a seventy-year lifetime.

Rather envisioning People's Corporation as a place that would be realized via an emergent consumer logic, King Camp Gillette—and Upton Sinclair—proposed another logic for the formation of the city, in this case comprised of three explicit steps. The first step was the formation of shareholders into Associate Units, and Associate Unit representatives into a People's Corporate Congress. The central organization of the People's Corporate Congress would be established in Washington, DC, to work with Associate Units within labor organizations, educational associations, engineering and architectural associations, agricultural and grange associations, professional and art organizations, employees of transportation and industrial corporations, and any other cooperative associations. The Associate Units would elect appointed representatives; labor or trade groups that are alike in different states could combine and have options to appoint representatives. The Corporate Congress would be an enlarged board of directors composed of varying individuals. Each member would be provided only one vote. Term limits would be set by members. The second step was a system of collective deposits from Associate Units into a Treasury of the People's Corporation, a fund to be invested in industrial securities and the ownership of properties. Monies deposited would be remitted daily to the Treasurer of the People's Corporation, less five percent of the total sum to meet withdrawals deposits made by Associate Units to the People's Corporation. All deposits to the Treasury of the People's Corporation would be used to purchase securities of industries and profits issued in the form of dividends would be paid quarterly. The third step proposed the rapid takeover of properties by the Government. The Government could purchase People's Corporation stock as seen fit, but the goal was to replace speculative investors with industrialists who would stabilize the stock value. Anyone could sell their stock to People's Corporation. Every dollar—less two-and-a-half percent—would be used to purchase securities of other industries. By accumulating this vast fund, the People's Corporation could systematically acquire one industry after another, major industries first, followed by minor. For the dividends paid out every three months, all notes issued were to be based on labor value rather than gold.

King Camp Gillette believed the year 1923 was the last great "fork in the road." The Progressive Party, and its platform of enthusiastic support for corporate socialism, declined in popularity during the early decades of the twentieth century. It was revived somewhat after market instability caused the Great Depression and ushered in President Franklin D. Roosevelt's social programs that came to structure the modern social safety net. Like other visionaries, George W. Perkins would die of a nervous breakdown in 1920. Gillette lost most of his razor blade fortune in the Crash of 1929.

"Did the Generic City start in America?" asks Rem Koolhaas. Like the Generic City, one could say of Metropolis: "It is a place of weak and distended sensations, few and far between emotions."[93] The Generic City "hovers around the 15 million mark"; Metropolis builds out to 60 million, the Generic City is fractal; Metropolis is a repeating pattern, in the Generic City: "...the skyscraper looks as if it will be the final, definitive typology... It can exist anywhere... it makes no difference anymore. The towers stand alone together; they are spaced so that they don't interact. Density in isolation is the ideal";[94] Metropolis is made up of 24,000 towers, distinctly set apart. In the Generic City "The only activity is shopping.... The same spaces inundated with other programs—libraries, baths, universities—would be terrific; we would be awed by their grandeur"; In Metropolis, work is underrepresented. Its major activities are dining and shopping at large retail centers. In the Generic City, hotels are now containers that, in the expansion and completeness of their facilities, make all other buildings redundant; Metropolis's buildings have all the modern conveniences. In the Generic City "51% of volume consists of atrium." A Metropolis atrium is thirty-five percent of a building volume. Which is to say that, like the Generic City, void spaces are the essential building blocks.

Gillette's Metropolis aspires—at maximum efficiency—to be a dull and repetitive experience. What are our visions of cities, after all, if not defined by redundancy and inefficiency? "Bankers, brokers, and money lenders; clerks in stores; commercial travelers; decorators, drapers, and window dressers; floorwalkers, foreman and overseers; inspectors, gaugers, and samplers; proprietors, officials, and managers in warehouses; retail dealers; salesmen and saleswomen; wholesale dealers, exporters, and importers; insurance agents":[95] all of these roles and functions are eliminated in Metropolis.

But as Koolhaas has noted, postmodernism entails a world where "the colonial seems the only inexhaustible source of the authentic." And so, despite the massive scale of many developments and the radical changes still being made to cities and economies, one can still hear architects and designers both conservative and progressive referring to the vacated rhetoric of 'place' as the motivation for design fundamentally dictated by massive financial algorithms and software geared toward managed design technique.

In Gillette's thirty-year publishing career, we see a future in the rearview mirror. We understand his need—our need—to stabilize the circulation of commodities, to lock them down, to slow their exchange, to consolidate them into a coherent buzzing hive, to give them, in short, an architecture.

FIG 8
From *Human Drift* by King Camp Gillette (1894)

Just as Gillette must have mentally taken note of the goods he saw at the World's Fair, then catalogued, shipped and stored them in the hundred great warehouses he envisioned across the United States, Gillette also removed each item in turn from those same shelves, distributed them equitably into the closets and wardrobes and end tables of the parlors, libraries, and sitting rooms of each apartment, eighteen apartments per floor, twenty-three floors per building, in upwards of twenty-five thousand more-or-less identical structures. He may also have been both overwhelmed by the magnitude of this empire and blanched at its numbing, repetitive banality. In Gillette's schemes, we make sense of the cacophony of merchandise and the ecstasy of consumption, by the ways these are wed to the heroic boredom of the actuarial science that underwrites the enterprise of World Corporation. The barbaric inequities of capital in the late nineteenth century, and the deadpan projections and aspirations for radical new civilizations of visionaries such as Gillette, suggest a possibility of Utopia that may have disappeared in the conquests of "spatial politics." FIG 8

In fact, New England Factories bosses encountered a reality whereby, just as Gillette had stated "carefully managed proportions of workers from different national backgrounds in each workshop and each mine proved to be a powerful formula of command. The linguistic, cultural, and ethnic differences within each work force were stabilizing because they could be used as a weapon to combat worker organization. It was in the bosses' interest that the melting pot not dissolve identities and that each ethnic group continue to live in a separate community maintaining differences."[96] Identity thus appears as a principled goal of radical politics, but can also be used against those same causes as institutions and disciplines evolve. "Subjectivity is a constant social progress of generation." "One of the central and most common theses of the institutional analyses proposed by modern social theory is that subjectivity is not pre-given and original but at least to some degree formed in the field of social forces." Hardt and Negri have described: "institutions provide above all a discrete place (the home, the chapel, the classroom, the shop floor) where the production of subjectivity is enacted. The various institutions of modern society should be viewed as an archipelago of factories of subjectivity."[97] Under empire, the first condition holds but the second condition—the place—is no longer definitive—"inside and outside are becoming indistinguishable."[98]

As described by Ron Suskind, an official of the George W. Bush administration, possibly Karl Rove, lay claim to the same didactic ground that once could be claimed against the nostalgic, nineteenth century Populists. This time he targeted "the real":

> The aide said that guys like me were 'in what we call the reality-based community,' which he defined as people who 'believe that solutions emerge from your judicious study of discernible reality.' [...] 'That's not the way the world really works anymore,' he continued. '....when we act, we create our own reality. And while you're studying that reality—judiciously, as you will—we'll act again, creating other new realities, which you can study too, and that's how things will sort out. We're history's actors... and you, all of you, will be left to just study what we do.'[99]

In contrast to such of formlessness, Gillette's territory is hierarchical. The contemporary Metropolis, after a period of dynamic aggregation, portends of a final, architectural solution. What exactly was the new American identity entailed in Gillette's vision of incorporation and management? Like other corporate utopias, Gillette's new identity could be defined as an inevitable drive towards the average. The most radical kernel of Gillette's Metropolis is its depiction of what it meant to be an "American" and the evolution from the Enlightenment project of liberty to the economics of neo-liberty. If America had, by 1907, lost both the proper rights and the property rights of sovereignty that established the Enlightenment project, the nation could no longer continue to be defined by origin, family, or occupation. Instead, in Gillette's new and efficiently organized regime, American individuals were defined by what they bought.

We are all travelling salesman.

1 Ralph Waldo Emerson, "Demonology", in *The Complete Works 10: Lectures and Biographical Sketches*, 1904, at www.bartleby.com. Accessed 03/06/2012. Part of a summary from a course of ten lectures on Human Life, given by Emerson in Boston in the winter of 1838–39—"Demonology" was the last. In 1877 it was published in the *North American Review*. Much of the matter was drawn from his journals of 1837 and 1838.

2 George W. Perkins, "Keep the Corporation or Kill It," in Appleton Magazine, Col. XI, January–June 1908 originally given as a lecture entitled, *The Modern Corporation*, 1907.

3 Benjamin Cummings Truman and Thomas Witherall Palmer, *History of the World's Fair; Being a Complete Description of the World's Columbia Exposition from its Inception*, (Chicago: Mammoth Publishing, 1893), 211.

4 King Camp Gillette, *Human Drift* (New York: New Era Publishing, 1894), 5.

5 Severy was the inventor of musical instruments such as the 'choralcelo,' a hybrid electronic and electro-acoustic instrument conceived as a commercial high-end domestic organ and the earlier prototype the 'vocalcelo' which will be discussed later. Severy also had included patents for printing presses, solar heating systems, a camera, and fluid drives and was the author of several works of fiction.

6 Excerpts were first published in the journal of public affairs, *National Magazine*, in 1906.

7 Robert Neer, "Where the World Learns to Shave", https://www.thecrimson.com/article/1985/12/12/where-the-world-learns-to-shave/.

8 Kenneth Frampton, "The Status of Man and the Status of His Objects: A Reading of the Human Condition" in *Architecture Theory Since 1968*, (Cambridge, Massachusetts MIT Press, 1998), 370.

9 Frampton, "The Status of Man," 370.

10 Frampton, "The Status of Man," 370.

11 For a more extensive discussion of the legacy and misconceptions that developed from Turner's essay see Walter Rundell, Jr.'s "Concepts of the 'Frontier' and the 'West," in *Arizona and the West* 1, no. 1 (Spring 1959), 13–41, at http://www.jstor.org/stable/40166911. Accessed 03/06/2012.

12 From "Personal Scrapbooks," GWPP; Perkins to Mrs. D.P. Kingsley, July 10, 1896, Letterbooks, GWPP as cited in Jonathan Levy, *Freaks of Fortune: The Emerging World of Capitalism and Risk in America* (Cambridge, Massachusetts: Harvard University Press, 2014), 277.

13 Walter Lippman, *Drift and Mastery: An Attempt to Diagnose the Current Unrest* (Madison, WI: University of Wisconsin Press, 1914), 129.

14 Chicago Conference on Trusts; Speeches, debates, resolutions, list of delegates, committees, etc. (Chicago: Civic Federation of Chicago, 1899), 43–49 as cited in Levy, *Freaks of Fortune*, 278.

15 In Edward Bellamy's *Looking Backwards* of 1888, that crisis comes to a head. *Looking Backwards* was the most important of dozens of utopian novels of the late 1880s and early 1890s, becoming the third bestselling novel of that century. The plot centers on the tales of the future as told by a timer traveler who comes to a rural hotel. In one chapter the son of a farmer articulates the problems of the present. He challenges the other summer hotel guests from the city who claim that without tourism the local economy could never survive. The young man retorts that it is the very practices of the elite urban class, namely their excessive and harsh lending policies, which have forced his family into bankruptcy.

16 Walt Whitman, 'Shut Not Your Doors', Leaves of Grass, 1900.

17 See Le Corbusier, "Eyes That Do Not See...," in *Toward an Architecture*, trans. John Goodman (London: Frances Lincoln Ltd., 2008 [1923]), 145–92.

18 Gillette had recently begun working for the Crown Cork and Seal Company, now Crown Holdings Incorporated. The company, founded in 1892 in Philadelphia, had patented a sealing device for beverages and currently claims to manufacture one out of five beverage cans and one out three food cans internationally. Ibid, 217.

19 From a letter written on letterhead from the office of Adler & Sullivan, Architects, February 3, 1887. https://whitmanarchive.org/biography/correspondence/tei/loc.04753.html.

20 Manfredo Tafuri's remarks on Sullivan's drawing of a city of skyscrapers to an extent undermines the true differences, architecturally speaking, between Sullivan's vision and Burnham's planned development. *The Graphic*, December 19,1891. See Manfredo Tafuri, *Architecture and Utopia: Design and Capitalist Development* (Cambridge: MIT Press, 1976), 47. Gillette's Metropolis is in some way and amalgam of both large-scale economic organization with the repetitive blocks of Sullivan's skyscrapers.

21 Harriet Monroe, *John Wellborn Root; a Study of his Life and Work* (Boston: Houghton, Mifflin, 1896), 106.

22 Monroe, *John Wellborn Root*, 81.

23 Louis Sullivan, "The Tall Office Building Artistically Considered," *Lippicott's Monthly Magazine*, March 1896, 404.

24 Colin Rowe, "The Chicago Frame," in *The Mathematic of the Ideal Villa and Other Essays*, Cambridge, Massachusetts: The MIT Press, 1976), 98. Rowe is quoting from Montgomery Schuyler's "A Critique of the Works of Adler and Sullivan," *Architectural Record*, February (1896).

25 Rowe, "The Chicago Frame," 98.

26 Rowe, "The Chicago Frame," 103.

27 Rowe, "The Chicago Frame," 98.

28 "The passion to sell is the impelling power in American life. Manufacturing is subsidiary and adventitious. But selling must be based on a semblance of service—the satisfaction of a need. The need was there, the capacity to satisfy was there, but contact was not there. Then came the flash of imagination which saw the single thing. The trick was turned; and there swiftly came into being something new under the sun. For the true steel-frame structure stands unique in the flowing of man and his works; a brilliant material example of man's capacity to satisfy his needs through the exercise of his natural powers. The tall steel-frame structure may have its aspects of beneficence; but so long as a man may say: "I shall do as I please with my own," it presents opposite aspects of social menace and danger. For such is the complexity, the complication, the intricacy of modern feudal society; such is its neurasthenia, its hyperesthesia, its precarious instability, that not a move may be made in any one of its manifold activities, according to its code, without creating risk and danger in its wake; as will be, further on, elaborated" Louis Sullivan, *Autobiography of an Idea*, (New York: Dover, 1956), 312–313.

29 Louis Sullivan, "The High Building Question," *Graphic*, December 19, 1891. Reprinted in Donald Hoffman, "The Setback Skyscraper City of 1891: An Unknown

Essay by Louis H. Sullivan," *Journal of the Society of Architectural Historians* 29, no. 2 (1970), 181–187.

30 Rowe, "The Chicago Frame," 98.

31 For a brief discussion see William Cronon, *Nature's Metropolis: Chicago and the Great West*, (New York and London: W.W. Norton and Company, 1991), 38.

32 Gillette, *Human Drift*, 12.

33 Gillette, *Human Drift*, 12.

34 This concept, later theorized as Central Place Theory, is verified by observation that as industries became more interconnected as the network of interrelated parts industries formed, the greater balance of industry in the United States gravitated to a belt stretching from the Great Lakes to the East Coast. See also Paul Krugman, "Increasing Returns and Economic Geography" *The Journal of Political Economics*, Volume 99, Issue 3 (June 1991), 483–499.

35 "repair of the plant of warehouses, jobbing houses, retail stores which demands employment of quarries, machine shops, planning mills, glass factories, the additional tribute to insurance and banking industries—lawyers, brokers, commission merchants, agents and middleman." Gillette, *Human Drift*, 12.

36 Gillette, *Human Drift*, 7.

37 Gillette, *Human Drift*, 7.

38 Gillette, *Human Drift*, 15.

39 Other treatises of the great central city include J. W. Scott, *Toledo, future great city of the world as envisaged almost a century ago*, Blade Printing and Paper Co.; Scott, *A presentation of causes tending to fix the position of the future great city of the world in the central plain of North America: ... On the great lakes*, (Toledo, Blade Print), 1876; L.U. Reavis, *St. Louis, Future Great City of the World*, (St. Louis: Gray and Baker Company, 1875); S.H. Goodin, "Cincinnati—It's Destiny," in *Sketches and Statistics of Cincinnati*, (Cincinnati: W.H. Moore & Co, 1851); Daniel Drake, *Natural and Statistical View of Cincinnati and Miami County*, (Cincinnati: Looker and Wallace, 1815).

40 Gillette, *Human Drift*, 23.

41 Gillette's tabulation roughly matches the same population listed as urban in the 1990 census. Compare the 1990 census where 75% of the U.S. population lives in urban centers. Gillette's table of cities listed on pg. 24–25. https://www.census.gov/geo/reference/urban-rural.html.

42 Gillette, *Human Drift*, 23.

43 Gillette, *Human Drift*, 41.

44 Gillette, *Human Drift*, 41.

45 Gillette, *Human Drift*, 32.

46 Gillette, *Human Drift*, 32.

47 Gillette, *Human Drift*. 49.

48 Gillette, *World Corporation*, 57.

49 Gillette, *Human Drift*, 22.

50 Gillette, *Human Drift*, 46.

51 Gillette, *Human Drift*, 46.

52 Gillette, *Human Drift*, 47.

53 Gillette, *Human Drift*, 47.

54 Gillette, *Human Drift*, 91.

55 Gillette, *Human Drift*, 93.

56 Given Gillette's close association with Melvin Linwood Severy it is tempting to see the plans as further evidence of a tendency to see all social relationships transformed into the form of a vast mechanical device. Severy's choralcelo, for instance, a hybrid electronic and electro-acoustic instrument used recorded sounds that were printed on magnetic spectrograms or as endless loops on rotating wheels and transmitted by a variable magnetic pulse that would activate a speaker membrane. The choralcelo was a smaller version of the telharmonium, a seven ton apparatus constructed in a mill building in Holyoke, Massachusetts and then shipped to the Telharmonic Hall and installed in the basement of a hotel at 39th and Broadway and its sounds which could also be transmitted by telephone, were sent into the hotel lobby like an early form of Muzak. While these are, at best, coincidences, the period has numerous examples of such devices which despite the colossal nature of their physical manifestations are prototypes for transforming then present reality into more ephemeral constructs. Metropolis, therefore, might be understood as an overwrought and overdetermined physical construct of what became the essential data-driven algorithms of our contemporary Empire.

57 Dolores Hayden describes in detail how the kitchenless plan evolves during this period in *The Grand Domestic Revolution*, (Cambridge, Massachusetts: The MIT Press, 1982).

58 Gillette, *Human Drift*, 111.

59 See "Climate by Numbers: Can a tech firm help farmers survive global warming?" by Michael Specter *New Yorker*, (November 11, 2013).

60 The drawing resembled similar patterns for classically-inspired Renaissance ceilings, most notably the woodcuts from Sebastiano Serlio's architectural treatise *Regole generali di architecttura* of 1537.

61 Gillette, *Human Drift*, 112.

62 Gillette, *Human Drift*, 92–92.

63 Gillette, *Human Drift*, 119.

64 Gerald Stanley Lee, "Edgar Chambless and his Runaway Town," *Forum. XLI*, no. 1 (January, 1911): 94–96.

65 Gerald Stanley Lee, *Inspired Millionaires: A Forecast*, (Holyoake, Massachusetts: Mount Tom Press, 1908), 205.

66 Lee, *Inspired Millionaires*, 217.

67 Lee, *Inspired Millionaires*, 226.

68 George W. Perkins, "Keep the Corporation or Kill It," *Appleton Magazine* XI, January-June 1908 originally given as a lecture entitled, "The Modern Corporation," 1907.

69 Levy, *Freaks of Fortune*, 265.

70 Gillette, *World Corporation*, 196.

71 Gillette, *World Corporation*, 9.

72 Gillette, *World Corporation*, 43.

73 Gillette, *World Corporation*, 41–46.

74 Gillette, *World Corporation*, 151.

75 Gillette, *World Corporation*, 151.

76 Russell Adams, *The Man and His Wonderful Shaving Device*, (Boston and Toronto: Little Brown and Company, 1978), 5.

77 Gillette, 147.

78 Gillette, *World Corporation*, 143.

79 https://www.statista.com/statistics/818602/online-and-offline-grocery-market-share-of-leading-grocery-retailers-us/.

80 Gillette, *The People's Corporation*, (New York: Boni and Liveright, 1924), 227.
81 Charles w. Caryl, *New Era: Presenting the Plans for The New Era Union To Help Develop and Utilize the Best Resources of this Country*. (Denver: Charles. W. Caryl, 1897).
82 Edgar Chambless, *Roadtown*, (New York: Roadtown Press, 1910) v.
83 Gillette, *The People's Corporation*, vii.
84 Gillette, *The People's Corporation*, 35–37.
85 Gillette, *The People's Corporation*, 35–37.
86 Gillette, *The People's Corporation*, 42–43.
87 Gillette, *The People's Corporation*, 42–43.
88 Gillette, *The People's Corporation*, 50.
89 Gillette, *The People's Corporation*, 50.
90 Gillette, *The People's Corporation*, 93.
91 Gillette, *The People's Corporation*, 107.
92 Gillette, *The People's Corporation*, 113–114.
93 Rem Koolhaas, "The Generic City" in *S, M, L, XL*, (New York: The Monacelli Press, 1995), 1253.
94 Koolhaas, "The Generic City", 1253.
95 Gillette, *People's Corporation*, 42–43.
96 Gillette, *People's Corporation*, 210.
97 Michael Hardt and Antonio Negri, *Empire*, (Cambridge, Massachusetts: Harvard University Press, 2001), 195–196.
98 Hardt and Negri, *Empire*, 195–196.
99 Ron Suskind, "Faith, Certainty and the Presidency of George W. Bush." *The New York Times Magazine*, (October 17, 2004). https://www.nytimes.com/2004/10/17/magazine/faith-certainty-and-the-presidency-of-george-w-bush.html.

WB-01
Z-7536

ELITE
ELITE

CUSTOMS

HANUMAN
LAKSHMAN

LUX cozi
SUNO TOH APNE DIL KI

Thums Up

Happy Durga Puja!

ADMISSION GOING ON NOW

WB-19
C-3475
asianpaints

প্রভাত
ঢাকুরিয়া, কলকাতা-৩১
প্রভাতসংঘ

14TFL-23A
L-23B
L-2
JB

VIDEOCON

DANGER

Abodes of the Goddess

Tapati Guha-Thakurta

The city of Kolkata turns into a frenetic site of fabrications and simulations as the season of the autumn festival approaches. In all corners of the city, elaborate bamboo armatures begin to emerge in open parks and empty plots, and within narrow alleys or slightly broader roads where they often unapologetically block the passage of people and vehicles. Stacks of bamboo poles—stored in neighbourhood corners throughout the year—are supplemented with fresh stock and brought back into circulation. Work begins on tying them together again into a mesh of vertical, horizontal and diagonal poles. In the coming weeks, these bamboo awnings are covered bit-by-bit with plywood sheets and plaster, then embellished with decorations in a variety of materials, including wood, metal, terracotta, polystyrene and fibreglass, to be transformed into a mind-boggling variety of architectural edifices. Inside of each structure the buffalo-demon slaying goddess Durga will appear, along with her family entourage, as she arrives for her annual week-long sojourn on earth. During the days and nights of the festival, these temporary abodes of the goddess become ritually sanctified as spaces for both worship and display, in which liturgical ritual spills into rituals of mass touring and viewing.

While the Durga Puja is the grandest festival of Bengal and is celebrated by Bengalis throughout the globe, the city of Kolkata offers the biggest transformations in scale and appearance. And Kolkata is the location where these transformations of the festival can best be charted—from precincts of exclusive aristocratic homes to spaces of expanding communities, neighbourhoods and public grounds, and from the latter half of the eighteenth century to the beginning of the middle of the twentieth century. The colonial and postcolonial eras of the city are the settings for the changing communitarian and public life of the Durga Pujas. Their contexts lay the measure, on the one hand, for the ostentation, extravaganza and spectacle that marks the different phases of the festival, and, on the other hand, for the new artistic dispensations and aspirations that mark out its contemporary career.

This essay builds itself around the relationship between the city of Kolkata and the festival that lends it its most powerful cultural branding. In the contemporary metropolis, as in its historical counterpart, the community Durga Pujas—those organised by local clubs—map the geographical spread and the socio-spatial graph of both older and newer neighbourhoods in Kolkata. Concurrently, the Durga Pujas hold up a vibrant mirror to the creative and commercial economy of the city, with its curious mix of craft and capital, labour and leisure, artistic flourish and visual clutter. There is a continuous overlap of the everyday and the exceptional, as 'festival time' becomes inextricable from the ordinary time and pace of the city. Whether via the plethora of visual and material productions or the frenzies of mass spectators, and their touring and photography, the blends of affect and excess that characterise all aspects of the Durga Pujas leave a lasting resonance within the broader life of the city.

Out of the myriad image complexes that constitute the urban logic of Kolkata's Durga Pujas, this essay focusses on these temporary edifices—locally termed *pandals*. Pandals constitute the most spectacular corpus in the festival productions. Laying out a conceptual framework for this particular form of festival architecture and the functions it performs, the essay moves along three lines of analysis, each of which weave together the exhibitionary worlds of the festival with its range of skills and styles of making: firstly, to dissect the ephemeral seasonal cityscape and identify some of the main genres of Durga Puja productions, their changing orientations and their interwoven strands of creative practice; secondly, to consider the ways in which these Puja *pandals* produce an imaginary festival topography that sprouts out of the inhabited spaces of the city and rests thickly within its built fabric, continuously blurring the boundaries between the actual and the illusory, the real and the fabricated; thirdly, to delve into the local art of *pandal*-making in an attempt to generate the profiles of its largely anonymous work-force and the assemblage of labour, expertise, materials and design resources that sustain the trade of decorator firms and pavilion designers. FIG 1

Not just perceived as spectacle and simulacra, the festival *pandals* are considered a colloquial form of architecture, with a self-contained economy of accumulation, redistribution and recycling. The new artistic dispensation of the contemporary festival is a theme that runs through all sections of the essay. The entry of new categories of designers, the shaping of a new festival aesthetic and the emergence of new genres of 'art-Pujas' and 'theme-Pujas' have been my key concerns in conceptualizing a specifically contemporary, artistic history of this urban festival.[1] This essay uses the central object of the Puja *pandal* to interrogate the tenuous locations of 'art' within this arena of production and viewership. One of its main aims is to lay open the claims of art in this field both as a set of insistent projections and as a set of incomplete formations.

FIG 2
Mohammed Ali Park Puja pandal under construction, 2007.

FIG 1
Puja pavilion construction, Nalin Sarkar Street, 2010.

Let me begin with explaining why I choose the term 'tableau' to refer to the kinds of architectural ensembles that the festival places on display throughout the city. FIG 2 The term 'tableau,' which has dictionary definitions ranging from a "picturesque presentation" to the "putting up of structures, objects and still or moving figures to represent a scene," usefully approximates the form of a stage-set or a coordinated exhibit layout. It defines the way in which the goddess and her family are central, still, figures around which the larger setting of the *pandal* pavilion and its decor unfold. The animation of this divine entourage, and the flow of spectators in and out of the simulated setting, can be seen to give the Durga Puja 'tableau' the qualities of a 'living picture.' FIG 3 With the Durga Pujas of the Kolkata, the term 'tableau' takes on the element of a full-blown live exhibitionary space, marking it as one that belongs less to the worlds of art exhibition and more to the world of theatre, pageants, floats and parades, fairground shows and pavilions, models possessing an embedded connotation of temporary and popular display.

As a mode of production, the term 'tableau' lends itself well to the architecture of Puja *pandals*, in terms of the portable and dismountable nature of Puja constructions. It speaks directly, as the writer Amit Chaudhuri puts it, to the language of craftsmanship which implies "a quality of tactility, of 'madeness'... the instinct to shape and touch things, to impart intimacy to materials."[2] A vast variety of materials are indeed put to use within these fabrications. The 'tableau' speaks equally to what the architectural historian Swati Chattopadhyay has termed "fungibility," or "infinite inter-changeability" that, between everyday space and make-believe touring sites, catapults viewers into journeys across the nation and the globe.[3] In the context of the new forms of 'art' Puja, the term 'tableau' is also used in conscious distinction to the term 'installation,' which is derived from a very different international history of critical art practice and a distinctly separate milieu of curators and critics, art exhibitions and art viewership. In playing one term against the other, what is called into question, however, is the separateness of these two areas of contemporary public art, and the mutual exclusivity of their practitioners and publics. What emerges during the Durga Pujas are new spaces of the production and viewing of public art, ones for which the category of 'installation art' remains inappositely lodged and repeatedly dissolves into the alternative popular ambience of a 'tableau.' FIG 4

If we were to regard 'simulation' as forming a constitutive core of today's Puja productions, then another term, 'simulacrum,' suggests itself for thinking about this entire range of fabrications. In this term, we can refer to Jean Baudrillard's radical sense of a process that leads to the displacement and erasure of the real: "the liquidation of all referentials."[4] Or, we could situate it as the creation of a 'hyper-real' that is capable of "substituting signs of the real for the real itself."[5] The physical act of making and replicating, a gathering of materials and objects to create artifices that stand on their own ground and take on promiscuous independent lives, can be equated to what Baudrillard calls "the panic of material production," or "the panic stricken production of the real and the referential."[6] In the context of the Durga Pujas, this translates to a frenzy of architectural and spatial simulations, where the term 'simulacrum' thus refers not just to the final production but to all the labour, material and processes that go into the assemblage. A 'simulacrum' expands from single edifice into a broader architectural and archaeological complex in which landscaped theme parks and recreated sets of village life and culture also appear. It is with the central notion of the replica as 'simulacra' that this next section looks at the layering of the older and newer forms of Puja tableaux that transform the entire city into a large exhibitionary site, or a spectatorial complex.

Genres and Forms

During the ten days of the festival, Kolkata stands transformed into an ephemeral fantasy land—make-believe palaces, fortresses, temples and pagodas and replicas of monuments are drawn from over India and the world, as well as archaeological sites, theme parks and folk-art villages. The specialty of the Durga Puja has been, for decades now, the production of spectacles, with effects that revolve around the creation of huge architectural replicas and elaborate light bulb illuminations. Many kinds of structure, global and local, historical and mythical, ancient and modern, can be, and continue to be, transplanted on to the most congested parts of the city, without any sense of irony or incongruity. Alongside the nation's own historical monuments, an ever-widening range of world monuments have entered the repertoire of the *pandal* makers—the Trevi Fountain of Rome in Khidipur, the Kremlin in Baghbazar, the Sphinx of Luxor in Lake Terrace, the façade of the Paris Opera House. FIG 5 Typical of Durga Puja has been the looseness of the remakes, and the randomness of the mix of structures that vie for attention in overgrown spaces. Equally important is an irrepressible taste for the cosmopolitan and contemporary—a model of the gigantic wreck of the Titanic was dreamt up by a Salt Lake Puja in 1998, the year of the release of the block-buster film, and a model of the Columbia Space Shuttle was envisioned in 2003, the year of its crash, and a Hogwarts Castle of the Harry Potter stories made an extremely popular display in 2007, when it was commissioned from a local *pandal* maker. FIG 6 Anything, it seems, can go in the field of Puja *pandals*.

FIG 3
Sapami morning Puja inside the Behala Club pavilion, 2008.

FIG 5
Remake of the Paris Opera House, Salt Lake, 2009.

FIG 4
Touring crowds mill around a worshipped goddess, Badamtala Ashar Sangha Puja, 2008.

It is the unapologetic catholicity of this representational field that became the hallmark of the secular mass identity of the Durga Pujas—just as its opening up brought to charges of desacralization and trivialization. The late 1990s to early 2000s coincided with important shifts in Puja tableaux, propelling an internal metamorphosis of the festival from a 'low' to a 'high' culture profile. With different cultural tastes and artistic identities furrowing the social space of festivity, worlds of make-believe began to turn into coordinated spaces of art and craft viewing. The practice of "*Pandal*-hopping"[7] began to shift into the guise of 'theme park' touring, whereby viewing encompassed an entire archaeological complex or an integrated package of the architecture, sculpture, handicrafts, dances and food of a region. New points of pride in these Puja tableaux came to hinge on the research and scholarship that went into their making, and on the exactitude and faithfulness to the original structures that were being simulated.

On Architectural Replicas

Architectural replicas have long stood as a prime attraction of festival tourism in Kolkata's Durga Puja. The replicas offer a passage from older to newer practices of *pandal* making, connecting and separating out the work of the decorator firms from new designer groups, and facilitating both freestyle remake Pujas as well as exact reproductions of national and world monuments. For the decorator firms who assemble palace or temple edifices, their claims to emulate the Akshardham temple of Gujarat or the Satya Sai Baba temple in Karnataka carry no attendant burdens

FIG 7
Bishnupur temple replica, Bagha Jatin colony Puja, 2004.

FIG 6
Harry Potter Castle, FD Block Puja Salt Lake, 2007.

FIG 8
Dipak Ghosh, Jaisalmer Temple replica, Lake Town, 2007.

of authentication. Neither for viewers nor for creators do tests exist for the historical or representational fidelity of the replica. The copy prides itself on its local accretions and excesses. However, the desire for a conscious departure from such constructions caused a different genre of laboriously reconstructed architectural replicas to begin to be produced by new groups of amateur and professional designers of Durga Pujas. A faithful recreation of an eighteenth-century terracotta temple of Bishnupur inside a small lower middle-class colony in the deep south of Kolkata during the festival of 2004—the work of a local resident and club member, Tapas Kharati—provides an exemplary instance of the labour and research that marks this new form of architectural replica. The *pandal* was a deft compression of the original scale of the Bishnupur temple into a forty-seven feet high and thirty feet wide structure that could fit the smaller availability of space in the Kolkata site, a local park. FIG 7 A blue enamel sign modelled on the Archaeological Survey of India site placards, with information in Bengali on the date and style of the original Bishnupur temple, added further play on authenticity, even as it competed for attention with a range other sponsorship banners and festival competition paraphernalia.

The intensity of work and the scale of material fabrications become key points of consideration, here. What propels the need to produce thousands of minutely modelled and baked terracotta panels, such as those created by Tapas Kharati for his temple replica, that have no life beyond the week of the festival? What calls for the investment in a durable medium instead of the standard bamboo and plywood, cloth and plaster *pandals*? The answer to these questions lies in the belief that the replica, however brief its existence, will rival the original in the artistry and workmanship of its makers. If we invoke the notion of simulacra, here, it would not be in its dictionary meanings of "deceptive substitute" or "mere pretence," but in the sense of a parallel creation that wishes in no way to deceive viewers with the false claim of being original but, rather, to simulate in a small way the art and labour that went into its making. This explains the new emphasis in making not on quick and random improvisations but on painstaking assemblage of objects and materials, and on the detailing of form and design.

It is in the work of designer Dipak Ghosh that we are introduced to the greatest fidelity in the work of reproduction. In his *pandal* designs, displayed in a variety of different festival neighbourhoods over the past two decades, Ghosh utilizes the highest order of workmanship in carved interiors and exteriors of *pandal* structures. He also uses the widest repertoire of historical architecture from different parts of India. Exact 1:1 replicas became his forte, requiring a close perusal of the original monuments through site visits, photographs and books, and sometimes a nearly year-long timeframe of conception and execution. FIG 8 Panel-by-panel, Ghosh *pandals* would be fabricated off-site in temporary workshops prior to assembly at the Puja location, a few

FIG 9
Dipak Ghosh, Details of a sculpted panel, Khiching temple replica, 2007.

FIG 11
Recreation of a Ghana village, Behala Sahajatri Puja, 2004.

FIG 12
Gateway into the recreated Ghana village, Behala Sahajatri Puja, 2004.

FIG 10
Rajasthan fort and palace complex, Surushi Sangha Puja, 2004.

weeks before the festival.[8] Ghosh's specialty was the utilization of the light packing material polystyrene to recreate the look of marble and various hues of stone, and to reproduce within it the intricacies of architectural decoration. The fineness of architectural ornamentation both governed his choice of subject matter and nurtured the artistic claims of Ghosh reproductions alongside their originals. FIG 9 Over different festival seasons, the Ghosh productions came to include: a life-size replica of a Rajasthani fort and palace complex in New Alipore in 2004, FIG 10 a Mukteshwar temple of Bhuvaneshwar at Mudiali in 2005, a restored Kinchakeswari temple of Khiching at Pratapaditya Road in 2008, a carved wooden palace from Padmanabhapuram, Kerala in 2008, a Nepalese temple at Monoharpukur Road in 2009, and a Sanchi Stupa in Jodhpur Park in 2011. It was fascinating to travel in time and location via these remakes. Each neighbourhood lent its own quality to the viewing of these monumental structures and the savouring of their decorative workmanship, with the designer exercising his own judgements about what kinds of replicas went best with the spaces and tastes of a locality.

On Theme Parks and Displays of World Cultures

In the exhibitionary world of Durga Pujas, the architectural replica continually leads the viewer from single monuments to larger archaeological complexes and theme parks, also from different states of India into other exotic countries of the globe. The national seamlessly expands into the transnational. From a 'mini-India' laid out for touring in Kolkata, crowds are also invited to mingle with other world civilizations in these same spaces, as a vernacular global imaginary fuels desires of travel in the festival. The 'theme park' as a form takes on an elasticity that allows it to lodge itself in the middle of streets and tiny corner parks or unfold over a domain of enclosed open ground in the city. It can accommodate varying orders of authenticity and similitude and engage viewers in different frames of credibility and artistic appeal. It can effortlessly conduct viewers from a tableau featuring art, architecture, crafts and performing arts of the different states of India presented at Suruchi Sangha Puja of New Alipore each year. Shifts occur from faithful reproductions of African villages and tribal art complexes to an Inca archaeological site in other neighbourhoods of the city, each aimed at momentarily transporting a different geographic location. They entice viewers to step in, see and wonder, but equally to learn and know about the original structures and sites in distant locations.

Some Puja locations become a repeating site of these 'theme parks.' Puja organisers often issue a widely advertised promise of a 'package tour' of a region of India, so that, for instance, the Suruchi Sangha grounds in New Alipore can have elephants and backwaters, camels and sand-dunes, or terraced hills and gurgling hill streams alongside temple and palace architecture, laid out over different seasons among a created topography of Kerala, Rajasthan, or Himachal Pradesh. There is also a reverse pattern that emerges in this festival topography, for example, where a particular template of an African tribal complex begins to proliferate over consecutive years across diverse neighbourhoods with each instance following a common trail even as the work of different designers with their own distinctive aesthetics. A good example of this theme park model was a remake of a Ghanaian village with brightly painted and decorated thatched huts that on the grounds of the Sahajatri Club Puja of Behala. FIG 11 This design presented a wonderful example of the way a densely inhabited neighbourhood space—a small empty plot between rows of houses—could be effectively transformed into an imaginary village site from distant Ghana, in which viewers entered through a striking painted gateway FIG 12 into a meandering complex of huts to read about the region of Sirigu in Ghana and view the recreated local tradition of wall decorations made by Sirigu poor peasant women. The main intention of the designer at Sahajatri Club in Behala—one of the many art college trained artists coming into this vocation—was to highlight the aesthetic and creativity of womenfolk that alleviated the acute poverty of village life.[9] And it also fell to one of the new generation idol makers to produce a Durga iconography that blended with the ambience of this African village.

In recent years, the transnational imaginaries of the contemporary festival have revelled in a primitivist aesthetic, in the art-historical sense of the term with its compelling modernist overtones. These deep engagements with world antiquity, art and civilization often springs out of obscure, non-elite neighbourhoods of the city, and this is fully in keeping with the social trajectory of 'theme' Pujas and their designer's profiles and publics. It underlines the insistently local strains of the dialogue with the global that occurs in these neighbourhoods. This is evident in the decision of a group of young local artists to profile the art of the ancient Inca civilization in a Puja sited in the small plot at 41 Pally Puja, Haridebpur, in 2007. FIG 13 Their choices specifically rival a display at a neighbouring Puja focussing on the Indus Valley civilization. FIG 14 Using the internet as their main source material, the artists at 41 Pally produced relief carvings of Inca motifs on material simulating granite stone slabs or grafted onto Peruvian textile designs, and fresco panels painted around the carvings according to imagery found online.

The fact that the designers, club members and the viewing crowds have never visited these distant sites does not detract from the credibility of these reconstructions. In the age of the internet, a globally accessible pool of information and downloadable images of world art and monuments comes to the aid of all these new groups of Puja designers. It also allows the older variety of decorator firms to recreate a Harry Potter castle, Paris Opera, or an Egyptian Sphinx. An important point to emphasise here is the undiminished local élan that spills over from the fabrication of Indian temples and craft villages into a 'world civilisation' sensibility, which is expressed in tableau that recreate African, Inca or Egyptian art. In these make-believe sites, an exotic global frame of reference occupies a similar footing as that of the nation's own art, architectural and craft heritages.

On Craft and Folk-Art Villages

A contrast occurs in another prevalent type that permeates the contemporary wave of 'theme' Pujas. Alongside the colloquial-global, colloquial-ethnic forms are deepening engagement with the many rural and tribal art forms of India and Bengal. The global paradigm coincides with a complimentary passion for the intensely local. While local talent can stage world cultures, simulating the skills of the makers of African totem poles or the relief sculptures of the ancient Incas without in any way diminishing the effectiveness of the copy, conversely, the featuring of Indian village and tribal arts has always required the authenticating inputs of persons and products from their original locations. This is where the compulsions of copying and improvisation give way to a preoccupation with the salvage of endangered local art forms and concern for disappearing communities of folk artists. Here, the figure of the craftsperson or tribal artist becomes the vital marker of authenticity, and a premium is placed by Puja designers on transporting craft and folk communities from distant areas to perform their skills and produce their wares on site. The presence of these practitioners in the preparation stages of Puja design was crucial to achieving the making of 'genuine' Santhal, Masan, Naga or Gond villages in the heart of Kolkata, and to achieving true association of a Madhubani painting or Orissa *patachitras* in terms of the specific village milieu in which they originate. FIG 15 In Durga Puja, concerns of Puja organizers and designers about extinction of tribal art forms are utilized as an occasion for promoting and rejuvenating these disappearing traditions.[10]

Durga Puja has long provided seasonal employment to various groups of artisanal labour, ranging from those who load, mix and knead alluvial clay for the making of images of deities to those who erect the bamboo and plywood framework of *pandals*, or work on its outer plaster, polystyrene or fibreglass decorations. Yet there are other groups: those who may paint the background arch of the goddess group (the *chaalchitra*), those who make different kinds of ornaments and weapons, those who toil at transporting the images from workshops to *pandals* and from there to the immersion banks. More recently, folk artists from various pockets of the country joined the skilled and unskilled, rural or semi-urban labour force, to bring a touch of both the exotic and organic to the Durga Puja productions. At these sites, groups find themselves in varying hierarchical relations with the rest of the work force, and a key person often coordinates between the making of the set and the organising Puja clubs.

Craft villages and folk-art complexes have evolved along two broad models. In one type, art school trained designers like Amar Sarka—who pioneered this genre—emphasise hands-on involvement with craft techniques and design innovations brought about by collaboration with the rural work force. In the other type, a designer, like Gopal

FIG 14
Recreation of the Indus Valley civilization, Paschim Putiary, 2007.

FIG 13
Recreation of an Inca archaeological site, Haridebpur, 2007.

FIG 15
Godhna Madhubani artist at work, Abasar Puja, Bhowanipore, 2008.

FIG 17
A Gond art village, Behala Club Puja, 2006.

FIG 16
Tribal art goddess group, Behala Tapoban Club, 2004.

Poddar, operates more in the role of an impresario, mobilising folk artists and overseers from all over India to work on a series of craft complexes in different Puja locations, handling multiple commissions and folk-art traditions in a single season. The rapid proliferation of these types of craft paradigms across the city's Durga Puja tableaux is a phenomenon integrally linked to the more general escalating visibility of handicrafts and folk arts in the public life of contemporary India.[11] The increase of urban tastes for 'folklore' in Kolkata can be tracked by the year-round circuit of government-sponsored craft fairs, and the parallel trend of locally organized 'folk' food, dance and music festivals in various neighbourhoods. The burgeoning fashion of 'folk-art' Durga Pujas in Kolkata has ridden this wave for more than a decade now. During this time we have seen the thatched and storied structure of the Bengali mud hut emerging as a favourite form of *pandal* architecture, and the template of the small village cluster, its halls decorated with tribal art, repeating itself across the whole city. FIG 16, 17 We could argue that these villages cropping up throughout Kolkata transcend their artificiality via a grounding in the authenticity of the folk communities and art-forms that they profile, which make 'folk' the central trope of a new design aesthetic. Village sites play a critical role, not merely in staging the pristine aura of folk traditions but also in aesthetically transmuting their motifs and styles into a vocabulary of urban design.

Heterotopias and Time Travels

Old or new style replica, authentic historical architecture or perfectly simulated craft village; there is no doing away with the inescapable thinness of simulated sites. We enter these spaces with the full awareness of their location in the everyday space of the city of Kolkata and the special event of the Durga Puja. The fragility and impermanence of these structures is also apparent, in the shared understanding that the illusions in bamboo, plywood, plaster, polystyrene or fiberglass will soon disappear. Yet it is also clear that knowledge of such impermanence seldom diminishes the seduction of the travels in space and time that Pujas induce. *Pandals* become analogous to fungible borders and borderlands in their ability to slip out of the material and metaphoric and also to lay hold of both."[12] In this sense, both a simulated archaeological site and a richly decorated folk art pavilion in the midst of a Kolkata street perform effects through the materiality of the fabrications and their simultaneous ability to move beyond material structures, and into metaphors of other imagined sites.

Durga Puja is a time of the year in the city when the familiar becomes newly unfamiliar, when one willfully loses oneself in the maze of streets and *paras* [neighborhoods].[13] The incongruity of *pandal* structures curiously dovetails with the organic connections to the spaces in which they sprout. It becomes impossible in this milieu to separate the actual from the fabricated. A Puja tableau at Kalighat replicates the crumbling façade of an old mansion such that the pandal is barely distinguishable from the ramshackle building behind it, a Puja at Bosepukur adopts a standard two-story neighborhood house form but as an old home with interior precincts where the worship of the goddess takes place. In the contemporary Kolkata, where new buildings flaunt the strangest mix of ornamental architectural styles, and in a festival where even public toilets are made to simulate the Sydney Opera House, it is hard to determine where the representational world of the Puja ends and where the outside world begins.

The lines of distinction between the artificial and the real continuously dissolve—perhaps a fundamental condition of the object worlds of modernity, of a society of commodity where the real can only be apprehended as part of an endless regime of illusions and representations. This is what Timothy Mitchell conceptualized as 'world-as-exhibition' or, a world organized and grasped in such a way that one is continually required to serve as a spectator.[14] The festival scape of twenty-first century Kolkata, however, defies simple corollary with the late nineteenth-century sequence of World Exhibitions that Mitchell analyses. In Kolkata, Durga Puja begins not as the city of arcades, departmental stores and ordered vistas, i.e. nineteenth-century Paris, but as a city of dark alleys, decaying neighborhoods and crowded streets. In Durga Puja, every step outside the simulated displays returns spectators to a different order of the everyday city before they move on, to other fabricated sites that they keep entering and exiting at every point of touring.

In a landmark essay entitled *The Heterotopias of Puja's Calcutta*, the sociologist Pradip Bose analyzed the exhibitionary world of the city's Durga Pujas.[15] Drawing on Michel Foucault's notion of 'heterotopias,' he asks how we can designate these temporarily fabricated spaces in the city and the illusions they create? Utopias, as Foucault explains, are purely imaginary worlds, "sites with no real place" or "fundamentally unreal spaces" that have an inverted analogy with the real space of society. Heterotopias are, by contrast, something like alternative spaces or counter sites, in which all the real sites that can be found in a culture are "simultaneously represented, contested and inverted."[16] The city's Puja productions can be seen to effectively lend themselves to Foucault's third defining principle of heterotopias—a capacity for juxtaposing several imaginary sites that are in themselves incongruous and incompatible. They also invite us to think of the fourth principle of heterotopias, which Foucault terms "heterochronies," that involves a radical disjunction a sense of linear everyday time. Unlike the accumulation of time in the heterotopias of museums or libraries "in which time never stops building up and topping its own summit," the heterotopia of the Kolkata Pujas is linked to a contrary mode: "time in its most fleeting, transitory, precarious aspect, to time in the mode of the festival."[17]

We have seen how the Kolkata of the festival offers innumerable instances of a mélange of multiple emplacements, where time and history are indiscriminately collapsed and the whole country and the world can be randomly brought home to local spectators. The leaps across space and time are often concentrated within a traversable zone of the city. This was the case, for instance, when viewers moved backward in history from the site of a late medieval palace of the Deccan—embellished with real and simulated *bidri* ornamentation—to two separate sites of the ancient Inca and Indus Valley civilizations, all within the space of the neighborhoods of Putiary and Haridebpur, and in the Puja festival interiors that connected Tollygunge and Behala in the deep south of the city. The new genres of 'art' and 'craft' never entirely displace older styles—architectural remakes or gimmicky tableaux. In the Pujas of 2007, the multiple layering of artistic and spectatorial preferences was best seen in the various Puja tableaux in Salt Lake. On the one hand, the taste for the global and the spectacular found its newest attraction in a remake of Harry Potter's castle at Hogwarts which, after becoming embroiled in last-minute copyright controversy with the production company of JK Rowling, gained even greater publicity and became the biggest crowd-puller of the season.[18] On the other hand, the taste for regional ethnic-chic echoed across a series of elegantly designed craft and rural art ensembles across the township, each featuring a different local craft form There is something on offer, then, every season, for all tastes and types of viewers. However, a unique characteristic of this city-wide display is the impossibility of keeping apart multiple strands of spectatorial interests or maintaining any firmly sealed circles of aesthetic distinction.

The Unsung Art of the *Pandal* Makers

It is in this context of deep entanglements between older and newer genres of Puja productions, and in the collapsing boundaries between artist and artisan in this sphere of work, that I return to the art of *pandal* constructions. The *pandal*, despite its ubiquity and its multiple functional capacities, remains a grossly understudied object in the field of festival art. No historian or ethnographer, journalist or photographer has invested the same order of attention in the material, work processes and styles of *pandal* making. The literature and information on pandal making is paltry, especially in comparison to the range of writing that exists on the complementary art of the creation of the images of the goddess—work that centres around the city's founding hub of clay idol making at Kumartuli. Like the sculpting of clay images, *pandal* making too is a unique kind of 'urban folk art' [*nagariklokshilpa*] born and nurtured in the streets of the city, and has the same umbilical connection with the history of the public festival.[20] The temporary street-side fabrications of the *pandals* came of age in the same years that the first public community Pujas emerged in open places at the north and south of the city. And the intensities of artistry and intricacy in the *pandals* can be mapped alongside a broadly similar chronology as the innovations that the clay modellers brought about in the appearance of the goddess group over the course of the twentieth century.[21]

While there is a longer history of making of open-air pavilions for public rituals and ceremonies using local construction material of bamboo, plywood strips, rope and cloth, the specific forms that the *pandal* takes on for the festival are clearly propelled by the spectacular genres of public Pujas of the past five or six decades. The etymology of the word *pandal* is itself something of a mystery, with its apparent roots not in Bengali, Hindi or English but in the Tamil language, where it refers to a temporarily constructed marquee for housing a deity and hosting ritual events and celebrations. It remains to be researched as to why and when the term begins to circulate in common Bengali parlance.[22] How it comes to supplant another equivalent term, *mandap*, which comes to us more directly from the architectural space and terminology of the Hindu temple, and translates as a covered, semi-enclosed site for worship, feasting, and congregation is another open question. The *chandi-mandap* or the *tulsi-mandap* are common features of the open courtyards of rural Bengali temples and homes. However, the Durga Puja, when it came to be hosted in the mansions of aristocratic and wealthy households of Bengal, was given a place not in a temple-style *mandap* but in the grand architectural setting of the *thakur-dalan*, a western-style arched and colonnaded altar, often with elaborately sculpted facades, that overlooked the open courtyard at the centre of the house. FIG 18 An associated form of temporary construction for festivities is the *shamiana*: This term is in wide usage in other parts of India, and connotes a large covered area with a decorative cloth and canvas canopy set up for weddings and other social ceremonies. The Durga Puja *pandal* form in Bengal emerged as a structure somewhere in between the traditional ritual space of the *mandap* and the modern secular public space of the *shamiana*.

If clay constitutes the essence of idol making in Bengal,

then bamboo, as we have seen, forms the primary material of *pandal* making. Drawing on the traditional techniques of bamboo and mud house construction in rural Bengal, all *pandals* use an awning of bamboo poles as their core frame planted in shallow holes in the ground, with vertical, horizontal and cross bars tied together for structural stability, and thin wooden battens—the material is locally paraphrased as *batam*—introduced as reinforcements over the bamboo frame. From the tying of bamboo poles together with jute ropes or cloth strips, to the elaborate cladding of the frame with stretched cloth, wooden planks, or synthetic material like plaster, ornamented polystyrene or fibre, *pandal* construction has relied upon a well-honed set of local skills to create these giant dismountable edifices. Despite recent attempts by the Ministry of Steel to promote the use of light steel and aluminium, claiming it to be a less cumbersome and more durable material for construction, *pandal* makers have refused to part with bamboo. FIG 19 Its value lies in its being not just a cheaper resource but also a more versatile and reusable building medium, as Swati Chattopadhyay explains:

> "The bamboo structure signifies (the) dual attribute of infinite interchangeability and specific articulation. It is in this sense doubly fungible. Its short life span on a site (and this is where it differs from house construction with bamboo) makes it possible for this duality to be maintained... (T)he construction of Puja venues is a process of creating a fungible infrastructure from materials and space that are highly capacious. In this process, venue and landscape are not distinct; one is the entrée to the other. In creating a venue, it enthusiastically projects connections—physical, social, sensorial—to constitute itself as landscape."[23]

FIG 19 Temple replica pandal under construction at Ekdalia, 2007.

FIG 18 Thakur dalan, or courtyard columned altar, Dorjipara Mitra family Puja, 2017.

The idea of "infinite interchangeability" can be applied to the multiple public purposes that these temporary spaces simultaneously serve during the days and nights of the festival—as ritual devotional space, as social communitarian space, or as spaces of touring, viewing and wonderment. It can also be used to think of how the single term, Puja *pandal*, stands to connote an extraordinary range of fabricated structures—from a standardized segmented covered pavilion to massive replicas of archaeological sites and architectural monuments, recreated villages or conceptual installations. Just as each phase of sculpting and finishing clay Durga image is laden with ritual and devotional significance, the labour of assembling material and part by part construction of the physical space of the Puja *pandal* may also be seen to produce its own layers of feeling and affect, in terms of the bringing together the producers and viewers.

As a form of architecture, Puja *pandal* making pulls in two important directions. On the one hand, this key area of festival work continually opens the city out into its rural hinterland. Through the supply of large consignments of bamboo, plywood, jute and coir and the main pool of seasonal labour, traditional *pandal* making remains the most important mode through which rural and suburban Bengal impacts the festival city of Kolkata, especially as work, in the past decades, has passed largely into the hands of suburban decorators, mainly from small district towns. On the other hand, this is also the area of work that has seen the greatest shifts in material, medium and design conception, and has brought into the fray new teams of pavilion and set designers. *Pandals*, as we have seen, have moved from being single fabricated structures to elaborate open air theme parks and simulated touring complexes. Historically, it is also in the sphere of fabrications that one can trace antecedents of the figure of the local Durga Puja 'designer' who would lend his professional skills in interior or film to the work of the decorator firm, which had by the mid twentieth century taken over making Puja *pandals*. Undoubtedly, the trade of the *pandal* makers came to play an early and important role in the transformation of the festival into an exhibitionary spectacle. As the scope of the goddess' temporary abode came to be dramatically expanded from a functional cloth, plywood and bamboo shelter into ornamental pavilions and giant architectural replicas, these *pandal* makers could also lay the first claims to 'theme' productions in the field.

Only a few of those Kolkata locals recalling the histories of *pandal* making can hark back to a time when cloth, wooden planks (batam) and bamboo poles prevailed as the primary ingredients of construction. Decorators developed a fine craft of ornamentation of the structure, using pleated cloth and intricate thread-work patterns supported by bamboo armatures on flat or spire-roofed structures. The *pandals*, as a contemporary Puja designer explained, had a tautly stretched and framed two-dimensional look.[24] FIG 20 From the 1980s, the trend of gigantic architectural replicas began, bringing depth, height and three-dimensionality to these pavilions. These developments involved new structural mastery alongside skills of constructing surface and body decoration. Many of the *pandal* makers in the 1980's continued to rely on cloth, *batam* and bamboo as their main construction material. Their novelties were distinguished

FIG 21
Pandal maker Amiya Sahoo of Medinipur holding a model, Ekdalia Evergreen Puja, 2007.

FIG 20
Example of an older style of pandal with stretched and pleated cloth, Kumartuli, 2008.

by the uses of pure white or specially dyed fabric to create the look of marble, sandstone, gold leaf or terracotta.[25] A break in this pattern, appearing from the late 1990s and early 2000s, was the replacement of cloth with new construction materials, such as plaster of Paris, polystyrene, wood and fibreglass, and the entry onto the scene of professional interior and set design personnel with their own small production units who began beating out decorator firms for contracts. As film and television set design labour began to invade the field of Pujas, new hierarchies consolidated through these workers and the styles they conceived. Decorator firms and their craft of *pandal* making was never phased out in this changing scenario, but they had to increasingly contend with the domination of the field by a different breed of art-school trained designers, many of whom continued to use the same rural labour pool in setting up the bamboo and *batam* scaffoldings and to turn to the same trends of simulating sites and monuments.

A key figure at the helm of the traditional work of *pandal*-making is the *sardar*, who takes on the standing of a head 'artist' able to plot out a structural elevation from a photograph, controlling an enlargement of scale in the design, internal scaffolding and the outer details of a standing structure.[26] These skills have been, and continue to be, the pride of this artisanal trade: the ability of an experienced work-hand in these units to do the work of a structural engineer, the techniques to translate a photograph of a building into an elevation at scale, and the aptitude to develop a massing form that meets the standards of a professional architect. The practice continues today, with many of the suburban decorator firms preparing a small model of the *pandal* architecture in plywood or polystyrene in order to secure the approval of the respective Puja committee.[27] Many of these artistic units have also developed a long-term informal working contract with prominent Kolkata Pujas, who continue with their preference for old-style architectural pavilions.

An interview with Amiya Kumar Sahoo provided a brief glimpse into the present workings of the trade thus described. Sahoo is the owner of the firm *Ma Mongola Decorators* based in the town of Dantan, West Medinipur and has been making the pandal for the Ekdalia Evergreen Puja since the mid 2000s. FIG 21 Sahoo described the scopes of artistry and design within his work, and the unresolved equations that throw open the rifts between *pandal*-makers and new categories of artists and designers who deploy their skills to execute their own new tableaux. The seasonal work force that Sahoo employs changes each year, as with most of decorator enterprises. In 2011, the entire group Sahoo worked within was from a single village in West Medinipur: the head-*mistri*, also from the same village, said there were over one hundred families there who were skilled in this work of *pandal* construction. The decorator firms often combine seasonal farming, and separate year-round contracts for wedding *pandals*, with the demand for Puja *pandal* work, which peaks during the extended festival season that stretches from Vishwakarma Puja in mid-September to Jagaddhatri Puja in early November. During this period, each member of the workforce earned around thirty to forty thousand rupees [430 to 570 US] for their combined labour during the festival, payment which included work on several *pandal* constructions in Kolkata, and suburban towns around it, over these months. Depending on the scale of these constructions and the time frames for their completion, decorator teams divide into groups of fifteen to thirty workers who simultaneously operate at different *pandal* sites in the city and districts during the Pujas. Just as the labour team changes, as workers constantly seek out new proprietors who give them more lucrative contracts each season, the expert figure of the *sardar* also rotates constantly between different decorator units.[28]

At the head of Sahoo's team in 2011 was *sardar* Durga Charan Mishra (a.k.a. Jota). Jota was entitled to the highest rate of pay in the unit, as he had been working for thirteen years in the *pandal*-making profession with different Medinipur firms. His affluence, he said, came from the family business of road-construction contracting, which was looked after mainly by his brother. His own passion lay in politics—he had been for some years with the Trinamool Congress—and with designing *pandals*, work that he assumed with verve only during the Puja months. Working largely, he said, from his own designs, Jota has a clear standing in this trade as a '*shilpi*' [artist] and 'engineer', who confidently puts scale and form to any concept that is required to be made into a *pandal*.[29] In 2011, Jota found himself in the novel enterprise of working for an a German installation artist, Gregor Schneider, at the Ekdalia Evergreen Club where he was in charge of visualizing and erecting Schneider's avant-garde concept of a vertically rising street tarmac. In bringing his ideas of public installation art into Kolkata's biggest public street festival, a crucial aspect of Schneider's venture was his wish to have "his design completely executed by local artisans using locally available materials so that the *collaborative* nature of the construction becomes apparent to all visitors."[30] Thus, Schneider came to meet Jota, the head of the suburban *pandal*-making team from Medinipur some months before. As Schneider drawings and designs went back and forth between Germany, via Max Mueller Bhavan in Kolkata, various local models began to emerge of this curious 'German *Pandal*."

In keeping with Schneider's intentions, it could well be posited that the local expertise of a figure like Jota and the skills of the traditional *pandal*-making labour of Bengal were in fact the key agents that brought this project to fruition. But the myth of this avowed 'collaboration' was rapidly dispelled, with tensions and incomprehension mounting at both ends as the work on site began. And it was hardly surprising that the contributions of Jota and his team—however heavily relied upon by Schneider and the local coordinators of his project—remained side-lined in the publicity surrounding the opening of the 'Germany in India' venture at the Ekdalia Puja.[31] Not that this made a huge difference to Jota in his career or aspirations. Relishing the new attention that this venture with a German artist brought while it lasted, Jota remained secure in his status and sense of esteem within his own trade. A figure like Jota seldom gets transformed into the figure of the Puja 'designer' in the new festival setting.

Neither social mobility, nor artistic ambitions—agencies that are demonstratively capable of making 'artists' out of the new generations in the idol-making trade—seem to be at work within these groups of *pandal* makers and their head *sardars*. The figure of the 'artist' is hard to find within the ranks of pandal makers and sardars, even as several of the decorator firms refer to the 'artists' who provide them with a major component of Puja design and visualisation. The ecclectism of skills and the capacity to do all types of work in the field are what seem to unite the 'artist' in this milieu with the *pandal* decorator who draws on his design and sculpting skills. The thin line of distinction between film set designers, artists, visualisers and the more conventional peri-urban workforce continue to dissolve, as the *pandal*-making trade today constantly diversifies and 'moves with the times.' The *pandal*-making work continues to expand from a repertoire of spectacular architectural and archaeological complexes to elaborate craft displays, and experimental installation art. FIG 22, 23

FIG 22
Tree shaped installation, Lake Youth Corner Puja, Mudiali, 2007.

To end, let me return to the motif with which I started the essay. The transient bamboo and ply armatures that announce the beginnings of the festival are also the main residues that linger, marking the end of the Pujas and the next sphase of dismantling, recycling and reuses. Where we began is also where we trail off. As the mega-event of the Durga Pujas ends, and the festival of other gods and goddess unfold over the coming months, the inner skeletal frameworks, portions of decorated facades and sculptural assortments await sales and recirculation among decorator firms, as well as organisers of the Kali and Jagaddhatri Pujas of the city and the suburbs. At times, an occasional striking remnant is left standing on streets and parks, involuntarily serving as a form of public art until its dismantling. FIG 24 At other times, after Durga Puja, the pandal structure is often retained by a club for Kali Puja, that follows a fortnight later. It is pertinent to recall how the single term, Puja *pandal*, connotes an extraordinary range of fabricated structures, from a standardized segmented covered pavilion, to a massive replica of an architectural monument, from recreated villages to conceptual installation.

In this sense, 'theme' Puja productions, whatever the genre, are essentially *pandals* in their core anatomy, with basic scaffolding holding "an iterative capacity that maximizes the variety of possible forms."[32] This formulation has a double edge: If it shows up the *pandal* as a generic fabricated form, a foundational unit of labour, skill and material that serves as the infrastructure beneath the entire urban spectacle of Kolkata Durga Puja, then it also underlines the way the term *pandal* functions as the great leveller between the work of the decorator firms and those of new-age designers. The transience of the *pandal* structure is also what continually mitigates the prestige, prerogatives and permanence of art.

Even the most ambitious and artistic of festival productions, we find, can seldom secure a future as collectible works of art. Their artistic credentials quickly drain away with the end of the Durga Puja. As public grounds need to be cleared, each of these productions dissemble as mere *pandals*—works whose ownership remains not with the artists but with the organising clubs who pay for their labour and material. Stripped and dismantled, Durga Puja *pandals*, in part or whole, must find new reuses in other festivals and events. In tandem with the layers of materials, skill and labour that constitute its making, the dissembling of Durga Puja occurs as a similarly complex mobilization of labour and movement of objects—movement from one festival site to another, from Kolkata into different suburban towns, from open streets into artist's studios, decorator's workshops, club backyards, private homes and lawns, or an odd boutique or public ground tucked away in a corner of the city where the remnants lie in wait of other uses. These concluding acts of dispersal extend in time from a few days at the original *pandal* location to weeks and months across these other sites of use, disuse, display or storage. With no strict demarcation of their ritual lives in the first place, the afterlives of these structures are premised on loose spreads and residues, on their propensity to disaggregate and reappear in different times and spaces.

FIG 24
Remnant from a Puja tableau designed by Bhabatosh Sutar, Bhowanipur, 2010.

FIG 23
Bhabatosh Sutar, Installation with the goddess's hands and buffalo head of the demon, Rajdanga Naba Uday Sangha Puja, 2010.

1 See Tapati Guha-Thakurta, *In the Name of the Goddess; The Durga Pujas of Contemporary Kolkata* (New Delhi: Primus Books, 2015).

2 Amit Chaudhuri, *Calcutta: Two Years in the City* (New Delhi: Penguin, 2013), 243.

3 Swati Chattopadhyay, "Fungible Geographies" in *Unlearning the City: Infrastructure in a New Optical Field* (Minneapolis: University of Minnesota Press, 2012), 228–229.

4 Jean Baudrillard, "Simulacra and Simulations," in *Selected Writings*, ed. Mark Poster, (Stanford: Stanford University Press, 1988), 167.

5 Baudrillard, "Simulacra and Simulations," 167.

6 Baudrillard, "Simulacra and Simulations," 171.

7 The practice of '*pandal*-hopping' (indicating crowds of spectators moving with determination and direction from one Puja *pandal* to the next) is quintessentially local and specific to the city's Durga Pujas. "Where pandal-hopping is way of life for five days every year," *The Telegraph, Metro*, Calcutta, September 28, 2009.

8 Dipak Ghosh's work and career are tracked through several interviews taken with him over successive seasons at different Puja sites—at the Jodhpur Park Puja on 25 September 2003; at the Suruchi Sangha Puja, New Alipore, on 4 October 2004 and on 21 September 2006; and at the 95 Pally Puja, Jodhpur Park and the Tridhara Sammillani Puja, Monoharpukur Road, on 8 September 2009.

9 Interview with the designer of this Ghana village complex, Partha Chowdhury, at the Behala Sahajtri Puja the following year, 6 October 2005.

10 The compelling urge to salvage various tribal and folk art forms, by profiling both the practitioners and their arts, holds together the work of an entire gamut of older and younger Puja designers, such as from Amar Sarkar, Subodh Ray, Gopal Poddar, Kamaldeep Dhar, Nirmal Malik, Tamal Krishna Goswami or Anirban Das.

11 Among recent writings that lay out the historical colonial and nationalist antecedents of this trend, see, Abigail McGowan, *Crafting the Nation in Colonial India*; and Rituparna Basu, *The Rediscovery of Folk Art and Crafts in Bengal: Reappraisal of a Twentieth Century Endeavour* (unpublished Ph.D. diss, Department of History, Calcutta University, 2008). An important essay that highlights the new configuration of this trend in post-Independence India is Paul Greenough, 'Nation, Economy and Tradition Displayed: The Indian Crafts Museum, New Delhi," in Carol A. Breckenridge, ed., *Consuming Modernity: Public Culture in Contemporary India* (Delhi: Oxford University Press, 1996).

12 Swati Chattopadhyay, *Unlearning the City*, 228–229. Chattopadhyay quotes from Mary Prat Brady, "The Fungibility of Borders," *Nepantla: Views from the South* 1, No. 1, (2000), 170–191.

13 The heading of a Bengali newspaper article aptly captures the spirit of these Puja tour, Debashish Bhattacharya, "*Chena Rastaye Hariye Jawar Din*" ("Days when one gets lost in known streets"), Anandabazar Patrika Bengali News, September 29, 1987.

14 Timothy Mitchell, "The World as Exhibition," in *Comparative Studies in History and Society* 31, no. 9 (1989).Reprinted as "Orientalism and the Exhibitionary Complex," in *The Art of Art History: A Critical Anthology*, ed. Donald Preziosi, (Oxford: Oxford University Press, 1998), 460–461.

15 The original Bengali essay, titled "*Pujor Kolkatar Bikolpolok*," was published in *Baromas*, Sharadiya, 1997. The English translation by Manas Ray appears in Amit Chaudhuri ed., *Memory's Gold: Writings on Calcutta* (New Delhi: Penguin/Viking, 2008), 291–304.

16 Michel Foucault, "Of Other Spaces," trans. Jay Miskoweic, *Diacritics* 16, No. 1 (Spring 1986), 22–27. The text is based on a lecture given by Foucault in 1967, posthumously published in the French, "Des Espaces Autres," *Architecture-Mouvement-Continuite* no. 5, (October 1984), 46–49.

17 Foucault, "Of Other Spaces," 25–26.

18 "Summons for Potter Pandal," and "Pandal wins reprieve," in *The Telegraph, Metro*, Calcutta, October 11 and 13, 2007. The paradox of the copyright violation charges brought by Penguin India, as the distributor of Harry Potter books in India, against the Durga Puja remake. The pyrrhic triumph of the local copy over Penguin's charges is dealt with in my article, "Conceits of the Copy: Travelling Replicas in Colonial and Postcolonial India," in *New Cultural Histories of India: Materiality and Practices*, eds. Partha Chatterjee, Tapati Guha-Thakurta and Bodhisattva Kar (New Delhi: Oxford University Press, 2014).

19 Along with my own interviews with the idol-makers of Kumartuli, my information on the past and present history of the place drew on three dissertations: (i)

Beth Goldblatt, *The Image Makers of Kumartuli: The Transformation of a Caste-based Industry in a Slum Quarter of Calcutta* (Ph.D. thesis submitted at the Faculty of Economic and Social Studies, University of Manchester, UK., April 1979) (ii) Geir Heierstad, *Images of Kumartuli Kumars—The Image Makers of Kolkata: Changing Notions of Caste and Modernity during the last century* (Ph.D. dissertation submitted at the Department of Cultural Studies and Oriental Languages, University of Oslo, June 2008) (iii) Moumita Sen, *Enframing Kumartuli; A Study in Space, Practice and Images* (M.Phil. diss. Jadavpur University and the Centre for Studies in Social Sciences, Calcutta, June 2011). An earlier foundational sociology of the art of clay modelling, tracing Kumartuli's ancestry to the older settlement at Krishnanagar can be found in, Sudhir Chakrabarty, *Krishnanagarer Mrtishilpa o Mrtishilpi Samaj* (Kolkata: K.P.Bagchi and CSSSC, 1985). This text has extensively cited both Geir Heierstad's and Moumita Sen's theses.

20 The term '*nagarik lok shilpa*' was specifically used by the Puja designer, Tamal Krishna Goswami, in recounting the history of the art of pandal making and designing, during an interview with him at the Selimpur Puja on September 3, 2007. More generally too, the idea of the 'urban folk' is now seen to find its best resonance, expression and promotion in the production economies of Kolkata's contemporary Durga Puja. On this theme, see, Jawhar Sircar, "A festival and more," *The Telegraph*, Calcutta, October 17, 2010.

21 This is described in Anita Agnihotri, *Kolkatar Protimashilpira* (Kolkata: Ananda Publishers, 2001). It is also discussed at length in Guha-Thakurta, *In the Name of the Goddess*, 161–174.

22 The colloquial term is still nowhere to be found in the standard Bengali dictionary, like the Samsad *Bengali-English dictionary*, 2nd ed. (Kolkata: Sahitya Samsad, 1989). This dictionary even makes room for English usages in Bengali like 'paddle' and 'packet.'

23 Chattopadhyay, "Fungible Geographies," 235.

24 Interview with Tamal Krishna Goswami, Selimpur Puja, September 3, 2007.

25 Interview with Ranadhir Dhar, pavilion designer, Adi Ballygunge Puja Club, September 5, 2007.

26 So, for instance, a newspaper report (*The Telegraph*, Calcutta, 24 September 1990) mentions a *pandal* decorator, Subol Chandra Sardar, taking on the construction of a replica of the Hawa Mahal of Jaipur based on a photograph. It is unusual for *pandal* decorators to be identified by names, and the surname Sardar in this case places the person as the headman of the construction unit.

27 Interview with *pandal* makers Anjan Pal of Pal Decorators of Shantipur, Nadia, at College Square Puja, September 13, 2006.

28 Interview with Kalipada Raut and Dulal Roy at Ekdalia, Gariahat. September 5, 2011. Roy and Gariahat were part of the Danton *pandal*-making workforce of the Ekdalia Evergreen Club's collaborative Puja venture with German installation artist, Gregor Schneider in 2011.

29 Interview with Durga Charan Misra (Jota), at the Ekdalia Evergreen Puja, September 20, 2011.

30 The press-kit brochure, *Infinite Opportunities—Germany in India*, 2011–2012, was circulated by Max Mueller Bhavan, Kolkata on this 2011 'collaboration' between Gregor Schneider and the *pandal* makers of Medinipur at the Ekdalia Evergreen Puja. Schneider's project was called "*It's all Rheydt, Kolkata, 2011.*" He sought to transplant a street from his German hometown, Rheydt, into a Kolkata *pandal*.

31 No one from this local *pandal*-making team, not even the *sardar*, Jota, was anywhere to be seen nor was their contribution ever mentioned at the mega launch of the Ekdalia Evergreen Puja on October 2, 2011. The Chief Minister, Mamata Banerjee, inaugurated the Puja against a podium of German delegates accompanying the artist Gregor Schneider. The opening was presided over by the club president, Subrata Mukherjee.

32 Chattopadhyay, "Fungible Geographies," 331.

Fabricating Community and Public Space in Kolkata's Durga Puja

Swati Chattopadhyay

The inauguration of a 1.2 km-long painted floor design—*alpona*—on Lake Road, Kolkata, announced the 2017 Durga Puja celebrations of Samajsebi Sangha, a neighborhood club in the southern part of the city. The large brightly colored floral motifs, hand-painted on asphalt, struck a lively contrast in this street lined with mid-twentieth century Art Deco and modernist residences. Executed in twelve hours, the *alpona* responded to the urban scale and functioned as a welcome rug stretching from a major cross-street, Sarat Bose Road, to the puja venue. It became a non-invasive yet bold claim to public space and community.[1]

Durga Puja—worship of the goddess Durga—is the biggest festival in West Bengal, and its capital city, Kolkata. Durga Puja has a diasporic presence and is celebrated in hundreds of locations outside India. The form, style and scale of the celebration in Kolkata, however, are exceptional. Every autumn more than two thousand puja *pandals* occupy streets, parks and vacant lots, and transform the city into a pulsating celebratory venue.[2]

The *pandal* in its simplest form is a temporary tent-like structure that uses tarpaulin and colored fabric on bamboo frame to provide shelter at outdoor events. The *pandals* constructed to host the Durga Puja are elaborate renditions of this modest vernacular form, and are central to the transformation of the city during the festivities into a spectacle of art and design. Durga Puja is frequently compared to the Rio carnival. It may be argued that both the spatial unfolding and the temporal elaboration of Durga Puja produce a larger cultural footprint than the Rio carnival. But whether it is a bigger deal than the Rio carnival is besides the point. My concern is with the kind of cultural footprint the festival in Kolkata produces.

Durga Puja is socially transformative. Considered important for vertically connecting the caste community in Bengal for four centuries, this Hindu religious festival has been nurtured on a substantial dose of secular investment in the last two hundred odd years to garner a broader appeal. A major revenue generator for artisans and entrepreneurs, Durga Puja connects rural West Bengal and provincial towns with the metropolis and its suburbs in myriad ways. The connections have become transformative not least because Durga Puja has become a haunt for global corporate capital. Demand for design talent has made it possible for once-obscure rural artists and craftspeople to become financially successful. Formally trained artists and designers now vie with the farmer-turned-artists for laurels by designing the most spectacular deity and pavilion.[3] Yet, this is not quite Guy Debord's society of the spectacle: "autonomous movement of the non-living."[4] Corporate capital is not the cause of the transformation we see at present. All evidence suggests that this is very much a home-grown, locally based enterprise that now invites and partners with global corporate capital in a very specific sense. Durga Puja with its innovative designs and large number of visitors makes it appealing for marketing products. This has been a pattern for few decades now. More recently, however, Durga Puja's entanglement with capital has changed. A decade ago, as the scale of Durga Puja expanded, newspaper editorials routinely bemoaned the "waste" of time and labor occasioned by the festival and its popular "excess."[5] There is very little of that sentiment in the media today, as what was considered "waste" and "excess" even a decade ago is now recognized as an opportunity and a sign of home-grown enterprise. This change in attitude suggests a larger transformation taking place, and thus as urban event and community practice, the new contours of the festival deserve a close reading.

The *alpona* on Lake Road is thus a good place to start. *Alpona* is the Bengali traditional art of creating intricate designs on the floor, particularly during Hindu religious and social rituals. Made by hand, using a small piece of cloth rather than a paint brush, these rice-paste designs are the brethren of *rangolis* which are wet or dry color designs, executed in distinctive regional styles in various parts of the Indian subcontinent. The art of women folk and deeply tied to the well-being of the household, these designs mark space as auspicious and sacred. In the *alpona*-turned-street art, the traditional scale, color and design are all changed. The *alpona* executed in vivid enamel paint by about four hundred art school students is a magnified—upscaled—version of a traditional *alpona*. The enlarged scale of design seeks to address the dimension of the street, and as a visual medium it is best appreciated from an aerial vantage. The "stunning artwork was unveiled" by a Bengali film superstar on Mahalaya, a week prior to the commencement of the five-day puja festivities.[6] As the Samajsebi Sangha *alpona* circulated in global media, it exceeded the puja design plans of a single club to represent the 2017 Durga Puja in Kolkata and with it the city at large.[7]

The media celebrated the artwork as the "longest" *alpona*, noting that the Chief Minister would inaugurate the Samajsebi Durga Puja.[8] Whether experienced in person—where one is, after all, invited to step on it—or as a global media feast, the Samajsebi *alpona* is symptomatic of the formal transformation of a regional religious and cultural celebration into a dazzling art scene, and a new site for cultural and political aspirations. Up-scaling in the form of the "biggest," "longest," "costliest" design, as well as the desire for scale-jumping to achieve global legibility, increasingly describe Durga Puja as spatial phenomenon.

Just as *alpona*-as-art had moved beyond the confines of a domestic craft a century ago under the aegis of the Santiniketan School of Art, experimentation with the image of the goddess and her entourage and the designs of *pandals* have received the imprimatur of well-known artists at least since the mid-twentieth century.[9] The changes in the design of pavilions and the deities, alongside the involvement of corporate capital and its new political import, however, have seen two major shifts in the last two decades.

The first is the introduction of "theme puja" in the mid-1990s. This new conceptualization of the puja in terms of a secular theme produces a directed reading of the art of the *pandal* and idols. Impelled to innovate by the lure of corporate awards and global legibility, the designs of the pavilions have seen a further conceptual shift in the last five years. Recent descriptions of Durga Puja by artists, organizers, and critics now borrow terms from global contemporary art: *pandal* designers refer to themselves as "curators" and the *pandals* as art and environmental installations.[10] Some designers flatly reject the premise of a "theme puja" ("puja itself is a theme"[11]) or of the puja as an "art" event. "There are plenty of exhibition spaces for that," quips artist Rono Banerjee, affirming the uniqueness of the artistic environment of puja that requires neither comparison nor translation of ideas from contemporary art in India or elsewhere.[12] Such differing self-descriptions and attributions of value speak to the diverse imaginations of art, space, and community that animate Durga Puja and defines its heterogeneous topography.

There are several issues here: the global aspiration and imagination of Durga Puja, the event as a springboard for artists and its emergence as a prime art venue, the negotiation of competing values—economic, cultural, social, religious—to form new communities, and the capacity of Durga Puja to redefine urban space. I am particularly interested in the relation between public space and the imagination and fabrication of community at the intersection of multiple axes of production and consumption, infrastructure, and habitation. These axes produce an urban palimpsest rich with investment, affect, and imagination. The spatial knots created by the convergence of people, practices, and material culture in the days leading up to and during the festival leave spatial traces after the temporary puja pavilions are dismantled. Such layered confluence of material relations reveals the existence of overlapping communities, even if the goals of these communities are not always aligned.

In this article I discuss the process through which these communities emerge and coalesce using as case studies the 2017 *pandal* designs of two clubs: Badamtala Ashar Sangha and Kumartuli Sarbojanin. Both these *pandals* occupy street space and thus provide some common points that aid comparison. Bamboo is the primary building material in these pavilions. A traditional material choice in many ways, it is, however, deployed entirely differently to generate two distinct thematic statements and visions of community.

Organization

Durga Puja's emergence as an urban phenomenon can be dated to the mid-eighteenth century when wealthy Bengali landlords and merchants in the capital of British Bengal, Calcutta (Kolkata), took to celebrating Durga Puja in an ostentatious manner. Celebrated in the public courtyards of elite mansions, Durga Puja created a city geography that highlighted the location and prestige of about two dozen elite families. This geography of elite houses during Durga Puja would be challenged with the popularization of the *sarbojanin* puja, or puja open to all. The *sarobjanin* puja emerged in 1911, breaking out of the caste community and self-consciously embracing the entire neighborhood as a community, irrespective of caste, class, rank and even religion. Nurtured in the milieu of anti-colonial nationalism, the *sarbojanin* Durga Puja had at its very inception a pronounced attachment to secular political goals.[14] The community pujas of today, feeding on neighborhood identity, often organized by local clubs, are successors of these early twentieth-century *sarbojanin* pujas.

The number of community pujas in Kolkata increased significantly by the mid-twentieth century. While the city recovered from the trauma of the 1947 Partition and the attendant pressure of in-migration, community pujas came to be viewed as mechanisms for consolidating a fractured community. The Samajsebi Sangha Durga Puja has the distinction of having eminent scholars—historian Jadunath Sarkar, astrophysicist Meghnad Saha, and writer Leela Ray—among its founders. The members of this neighborhood-based social organization, formed to provide relief to the people in the wake of the 1946 Hindu-Muslim riots, decided to host a Durga Puja as a universal message of community.[15] In the next few decades, these community pujas, often allied with a strong social commitment, became important sites for cultural and artistic practices as a premise for celebration. Samajsebi Sangha's Durga Puja was renowned for the artistry of the Durga image, created by Ramesh Pal, as well as the ambiance of the venue in which classical music was played.[16]

Since the 1950s the number of pujas in Kolkata have increased ten-fold, far outpacing population growth, even if we take the expansion of the city limits into consideration. The budgets of these pujas have correspondingly increased. Only since the mid-1990s, however, the demand for theme pujas have impelled neighborhood puja committees to raise large sums of money from corporate sponsors. While corporate sponsorship can be traced back to the 1960s at least, the volume of corporate capital that has supported these celebrations in the last two decades runs into crores of rupees. The phenomenon we witness today—elaborately designed pavilions and deities vying for attention and awards, twenty-four-hour *pandal*-hopping for five days, global media coverage of the festivities—is rooted in the desire of puja organizers to compete with and locate themselves among the top fifty to one hundred pujas.[17]

The overwhelming reason for moving from a traditional puja to a theme puja is attracting a large crowd. Large viewership garners media attention and makes the neighborhood legible in the puja landscape of the city. Many of the pujas in the suburbs of the city, languishing in the shadow of well-known, elite, city pujas, have sought innovation in order to lure spectators.[18] The tally of visitors (which is published in a popular daily), corporate sponsorship, and celebrity recognition go hand in hand.[19] It is remarkable that for many puja organizers the goal is to attract such numbers of visitors that would create a problem of crowd control. This desire for the unruly urban experience is not merely a craving for excitement, but an attempt to acquire the agency to shape urban presence—to become "law-givers" for a few days. Large crowds that require the cordoning off of paths at the entrance and exit of the puja venue, and the presence of an army of volunteers and the police, signal the venue's arrival as one of the top pujas in the city.[20] If the large crowds bring recognition to the neighborhood and its puja, the policing role confers visibility and legitimacy to those who otherwise find themselves on the fringes of society.

With the visitor count an indicator of popularity, the winning of awards is the mark of success. Artists are hired with the expectation that the monetary investment in their artwork would result in awards. The frequent comparison between winning the top puja awards and sports victories—India's international cricket victories, in particular—gives a sense of the kind of pride and name-recognition that is at stake.[21] The new competitive dimension, akin to corporate sponsorship of sports events, is the primary mode by which corporate capital lodges itself in a religious and cultural event to turn it into a giant advertisement, a spectacle for corporate publicity.

There are three caveats here. First, of the two thousand odd community pujas in the city, perhaps no more than twenty-five percent are themed.[22] Second, what constitutes a theme puja remains fluid, and many puja committees do not aspire to having renowned artists design their *pandals* and deities, either by inclination or necessity. Rather they trust their local neighborhood talent to produce a coherent aesthetic statement. Third, the entry of corporate capital remains uneven and heterogeneous.

Among the puja committees aspiring to host a noteworthy theme puja, there is a wide range of expectations and financial capacities. Some of these puja committees are satisfied with a reasonable budget of two-to-five lakh rupees, and work with local talent, local decorators and electricians to stage their theme puja.[23] One organizer of a puja in a suburban neighborhood pointed out that they consider it unconscionable to spend millions of rupees for a five-day festival when sixty-five percent of the population of the neighborhood belongs to the lower-middle class. Eschewing celebrity presence, the suburban Behala Buroshibtala Janakalyan Sangha takes pride in hosting a "common-man's puja," arguing that success can be measured in non-monetary attributes: innovation within a modest budget, commitment to immediate community, and promotion of goodwill through hospitality.[24]

The mega-budget pujas spend from fifty lakhs to several crores.[25] They unabashedly acknowledge that for such a big-budget event they need a political leader in their camp capable of strong-arming corporate sponsors.[26] The cost of the 2017 Mahishmati Palace *pandal* design inspired by the movie, *Bahubali*, was reported to be one and a half crores, and the jewelry of the deities alone was worth more than ten crores. Fashion designer Agni Mitra Paul created the clothing of the deities of the Santosh Mitra Square puja, in a *pandal* styled after the Buckingham Palace. The gold couture of the gods and goddesses, worth crores, was sponsored by a well-known jewelry business in Kolkata.[27]

When a community puja makes a mark on the map of the city, its puja organizers become major power brokers. Not surprisingly, the organizers have also begun to self-consciously articulate their motivations for embracing theme pujas and their commitment to their community and the culture of Durga Puja. Organizing a puja requires the acumen of managing a large budget and multiple constituencies, including local leaders, volunteers, artists, laborers, contractors, caterers, subscribers, sponsors, city authorities, the police, fire marshal, as well as the competition judges.[28] Puja organizers become spokespeople for their community. Indeed, Durga Puja in the last two decades has produced its own legendary organizers.[29] It is noteworthy that awards are given not only for artistry, environmental and social commitment of the pujas, but also to the top organizers.[30]

Stories about personal financial sacrifice abound, including the one about mortgaging one's house for the sake of a community puja. Some organizers feel puja management is a personal responsibility akin to a familial duty. The principal patron of the Kashi Bose Lane puja offered his large house for the puja preparations and ensured that the obscure puja would become a celebrated festival site. A family that owns decorating and catering businesses supplies not only the materials for the *pandal* but also the food for the festivities that feeds the neighborhood in Narkeldanga, suggesting that "someone has to hold the puja together."[31] Others feel it is a way of giving back to the neighborhood community that has nurtured them. While the organizing is not limited to the Bengali community, it is clearly viewed as an investment in the local neighborhood, with a supra-local purchase. Global media attention brings its own rewards in terms of future sponsors and the ability of both artists and organizers to jump scale from humble surroundings to achieve national and international reputations.

A recognition of collective interest has induced organizers to move beyond the fierce competitive spirit of puja awards and create the Forum for Durgapuja (FFD), a voluntary association of Durga Puja committees. The FFD, with a membership of over three hundred puja associations, functions as a support group, shares information, represents the puja committees, and lobbies on their behalf. The need for an organizational umbrella for multiple neighborhoods and community pujas has grafted a certain formality on an informal organizing process, while acknowledging that Durga Puja has become a sufficiently complex management phenomenon that demands a new level of organizational infrastructure.[32]

There is a palpable tension between the local puja organizers' desire to make their neighborhood puja a prominent community event and the need to yield the limelight to powerful politicians and celebrities, who may not be from the neighborhood but who sponsor pujas and act as "brand-ambassadors" for their chosen puja as a career move. While left politicians have generally stayed away from puja sponsorship, several current politicians from center and center-right parties have honed their organizational skills by acting as puja organizers.[33] Others from the municipal and state levels are eager to get into the organizing fray as they view the experience of managing a Durga Puja, and the associated social connections, as crucial to creating a prominent political profile and shaping voting constituencies. Such constituencies need not be local, and the imagination of a larger public—a larger political community—is always implicit in the assumption of Durga Puja as a platform for constructing or bolstering one's political profile.

Geography

The competing visions of community that constitute Durga Puja find a common core in the spatial construction of the puja venue. The production process itself is spatially dispersed and temporally sequenced, connecting various existing communities across significant distances and socio-economic scales. Much of the prefabrication of parts comprising the decorative ensemble of the *pandal* and deity is conducted in the suburbs or provincial towns. Most of the laborers who construct the *pandals* come from the provinces as well. The movement of labor, commodities, and money produces spaces that congeal and thin out in keeping with the different stages of the production process.

If Durga Puja celebrations have always been about shaping communities ideologically, culturally and spatially, the goals of the various constituencies who participate in Durga Puja today have through their discrepant notions and parameters of community produced new geographies. The expanded time-sense of Durga Puja in the last two decades has powerfully contributed toward this phenomenon.

Theme pujas have in a fundamental sense changed the temporality of Durga Puja. Traditionally, planning for the autumn festival began about mid-year. Idol-makers started preparing in summer, and puja committees would meet in August to make plans and commission the idols. *Pandal* making started a week prior to the beginning of festivities, and lighting was installed along with last-minute decorative touches on the evening of *sashti*, the first day of the puja. On *dashami*, the concluding day of the puja, the idols were immersed in a nearby body of water. Now, artists for theme pujas are commissioned even before the previous year's Durga Puja concludes, thus making the planning process and fund-raising a year-long affair. By February, artists have sourced their materials and sketched out their design plans. Pre-fabricated parts of the *pandal* are being produced in workshops scattered across the city and provinces. *Pandal* construction begins two to three months prior to the commencement of the festival, when the municipality allows puja committees to occupy public space while the venue takes shape. Pavilions remain on the site for a week or so after the conclusion of the festivities, in the process of being dismantled. This duration of about three months produces recognizable spatial knots in the city fabric.

Durational imagination of Durga Puja has changed in other ways as well. Some Durga images are not immersed at the conclusion of the festivities as tradition dictates. Instead they are housed in museums as art works, thus extending their "life-span." Others regret that no plan for "preserving" these works of art is in place. Some theme *pandals* are sold and thus recycled partly or wholly to other puja committees for Kali Puja, the next major religious event in the calendar, while others are bought by organizations quite far removed from the city and reinstalled to serve entirely different purposes, often as more permanent structures.

Durga Puja as a source of media attention has introduced the phenomenon of puja "inauguration." It is not uncommon for temple high priests and celebrities from very different fields—film, sports, and media—to share the ribbon-cutting stage at Durga Puja *pandals*.[34] To be contrary, the puja organizers of Buroshibtala Sarbojanin opted for a municipal janitor to inaugurate its puja, thus affirming the working-class foundation of its community. Inaugurating a puja prior to the ritual commencement of the religious ceremony which is fixed by the lunar calendar, however, inserts a new secular temporality that fundamentally alters the time-sense and meaning of Durga Puja as a seasonal community event. With this change in the temporality of puja comes a spatial shuffling as well, fostering new spatial imaginations and ideas of community.

Historically, the performance of Durga Puja in Kolkata has had a tight correspondence with the *para* or neighborhood. The thick space of people, practice, and material culture that fosters the festival has traditionally been given concrete shape by the physical space of the *para* seen as a collectivity. An area roughly a mile square, the *para* is an easily walkable space and a zone with which its residents learn to identify. The idea of the *para* in the city goes back to the eighteenth century. Despite being overlaid by new administrative jurisdictions such as the *thana* for policing purposes and the ward for administrative purposes, the *para* retained, against all odds, an experiential validity well into the late twentieth century. The kind of community intimacy and belonging that the *para* encouraged was self-contained. A sense of neighborhood interiority crystallized as several generations of each family chose to live there and call that locality their home. In an otherwise alienating city, the para provided face-to-face connection and recognition. Durga Puja in the twentieth century was one mode of affirming the togetherness of the *para*.[35]

In the last three decades this understanding of the *para* has undergone a recalibration. In the sprawling middle- and lower-middle class suburbs of the city, Durga Puja has become an instrument for affirming a *para* in the proper sense of the term, suggestive of their desire for upward mobility and recognition. Who would know the location of Buroshibtala, if it were not for the fame of its Durga Puja? Discussing the success of their five-year old theme puja, organizer Robin Mondal said in a 2013 interview: "Our *bustee* (slum) pujo had (sic) gone global."[36] His remark indicates that to successfully cohere as a community requires acknowledgement in the larger urban community, and lower-middle class and poor neighborhoods achieve this recognition by means that are different from the well-off city-center neighborhoods. In the "traditional" and elite/middle-class *paras* of the city proper this mode of conceptualizing community and neighborhood has been under pressure because of outmigration of younger generations in search of better economic opportunities. The upscale version of Durga Puja undertaken in such neighborhoods is in some ways compensatory. Thus Durga Puja either attempts to graft an identity, and a sense of pride, to an existing neighborhood and its thin sense of community, or it fills a gap in a thinning community, created by the loss of generational togetherness.

As many would argue, this process of upscaling exacerbates the loss of public intimacy that defines a *para*. This argument becomes apparent in some of the well-known pujas in middle- and upper-middle-class neighborhoods in the city proper, where theme pujas attracting large crowds have become contentious. Massive numbers of spectators rob residents of the intimacy of the *para* and the ability to participate fully in the festivities. The space of the *para* reconfigured to accommodate the indiscriminate presence of "outsiders" erodes existing neighborhood identity and conviviality. Not everyone agrees with this assessment, however, suggesting that what is at stake is not the irredeemable dilution of community, but the new contours it now occupies.

The impact of new forces—corporate capital, population influxes, politics, and artistic practices—enhances and generates layers of spatial possibility beyond that defined by the older configuration of the *para*. For one, the businesses in any given locality of a puja, particularly grocery stores, tea shops, and restaurants, augmented by a host of pop-up food and art/crafts stalls, are bound to see an increase in sales during the five days of festivities. Some temporary food stalls linger to become fixtures in the neighborhood. The creation of the *pandal*, more elaborate than ever, generates new sets of spatial patterns, some of which leave traces in the neighborhood, even after it is dismantled. The fame of a puja venue such as that of Ekdalia Evergreen, a grand puja ensemble occupying the same street location every year, might become a fixed reference for giving street directions, even when it is not actually there. People remember a locality by the impression cast by its Durga Puja. The event marks the *para* in tangible and intangible ways.

Since the early twentieth century, the center of neighborhood conviviality has been a local sports club, library, and often a vocational training center organized by community members. This pattern continues to this day. As community nuclei of the *para* these facilities are often attached to open or semi-open spaces such as parks and vacant lots that might be suitable for *pandal* construction. Usually the adjoining street space is incorporated, and in situations where parks or vacant lots are not available, a suitable street location is adopted for pandal construction. Building a *pandal* on the street changes the conventional use of street space and sidewalk, and alters traffic patterns. Such appropriation of public space requires permission from the municipality and approval of neighbors directly affected by the construction.

A few examples of what constitute these changes in urban space will make this point clear. The bamboo structures of the *pandal* rest on shallow footings. As in post-hole construction, six- to eight-inch holes are dug in the ground (often in the street itself) and bamboo poles are inserted to create vertical supports. In large pavilions intermittent *sal* timber posts are used to reinforce the bamboo structure. The rectangular frame of the enclosure is created by horizontally placed bamboo poles that are tied to the verticals at the base, at waist height, and at the top where the pitched roof meets the posts. The longest poles are used for the roof ridges and are left untrimmed beyond the overhang. Their ends are tied to the metal structure of a nearby building—exposed beams, arches, columns, even wrought iron railings of verandahs—for stability. This necessitates the *pandal*'s location and orientation to be in keeping with the building line and urban form of the street. Its location must also consider local traffic patterns and be suitable for drawing electrical connections. Consideration of vehicular access is important for construction materials to be brought to the site, as well as the selective closure of streets that would take place during the festivities. On a thirty-foot wide street, a ten-foot egress for vehicles is allowed, and on forty-foot wide streets a twenty-foot passage for two vehicles is usually left open. For *pandals* occupying a green island in the center of an intersection, one of the streets might be blocked to vehicular traffic during the festivities. In such cases, and in narrow lanes adopted for *pandals*, the sidewalk is left open for pedestrian traffic. Police and fire marshals must approve the structure of the pavilion for structural safety and access for emergency vehicles.

Such appropriation of space is premised upon two already existing shared views on public space in the city.[37] First, the understanding of the street as a space of movement as well as habitation anticipates the use of outdoor space as living space, even in fairly crowded streets. Second, the claim of the puja committees on shared public space is one of accommodation, acknowledging the fact that these spatial interventions cause significant disruption of everyday routines.

Viewing and Spectating

The roles of spectators and organizers of theme pujas are mutually supportive. While all *pandals* articulate a space of worship, gathering, and celebration, theme *pandals* add to it a dimension of spectatorship that augments the practice of viewing by those who are culturally attuned to the practice of Durga Puja as a five-day festival. Since all seeing is culturally grounded, let me explain the specificities here.

By culturally attuned viewing of Durga Puja I mean knowing, in a nominal sense at least, that ritual installation of the deity does not mean putting the idol on a platform, but instituting alterity and supernatural "life" in the material form of the idol (*pran pratistha*) at the beginning of the five-day duration of the puja on *sashti*. It means knowing that the last day, *dashami*, is marked by the goddess's victory over the demon-god; it is also the day of her "departure" when the life instituted in her material form is let go. That life is put to rest by immersing and shattering the image in water, and yet that "departure" is merely a distancing that already anticipates a return. The colloquialization of that anticipation as a crowd chant during the immersion of the deity on *dashami*—"*asche bachar abar hobe*," [coming year (it will) again happen]—is an activation of the tacit knowledge that the goddess will arrive again the following year, and that there will be another material form in which the "same" life will be instituted. It means to presume the possibility of alterity in the sameness of return. The emergence of the supernatural resides in the ephemeral installation/manifestation of the goddess and her entourage. To view the goddess is to presuppose all of this in a cultural sense that does not require one to be devout.[38]

I am making a distinction between this cultural sense of viewing that links looking at the goddess with an extended field of practice and performance, and *darshan* as the Hindu devotee's gaze at a deity/venerable person. *Darshan* is premised on the idea that to see and "be seen" by the deity is a form of worship, that is capable of producing a singular relationship between the viewer and the deity, without foreclosing the possibility of devotional affect when viewed as part of a collectivity. The devotional gaze may very well accompany a cultural sense of viewing the goddess, expressed in the colloquial as "*thakur dekhte jawoa*" (to go to see the goddess) that entails dressing up and going around from *pandal* to *pandal* with friends and family to appreciate the beauty and artistry of the images and installations. Much has been written about the secularization of *darshan* as adoration (as in the fandom of film stars or gazing at religious objects in art museums), but I am adhering to the idea of *darshan* as the gaze of the devotee to make room for other modes of seeing that presume alterity in a culturally received sense.[39] It is this latter, more ordinary, more capacious sense of viewing as "*thakur dekha*" (seeing the goddess)—a realm in which the distinction between secular and sacred does not hold much sway—on which theme pujas attempt to cast an impress.

The sense of wonder and awe that theme *pandals* seek to invoke in the spectator is primarily about the pleasure of looking as part of a larger viewing community. The process of coming to view the *pandal* from other parts of the city and from distant villages and provincial towns, and then standing in line to participate in the collective experience of wonderment, critique and image production—photographs, videos, and selfies—makes the spectator essential to the fabrication of the theme event. There is no reason to assume that such secular spectating and devotional gazing are at cross purposes. Rather I assume that these intersect in patterns of irreducible heterogeneity.

The desire on the part of puja organizers to engage this spectating community operates on the assumption that the viewer must be immersed in a novel puja environment. The role of art here is meant to be experientially unique and ideally transformative. This transformation is intended to move beyond the religious-cultural ambiance created by a puja *pandal* in the century-long tradition of constructing a venue, which by its very nature is immersive. The worship of the goddess at defined durations in the morning and evening produces a deeply multi-sensorial experience involving the warmth and fragrance of lamps, incense, floral and food offerings, and the auditory environment produced by *mantras*, ritual sounds, and music. In other words, the puja *pandal* as a micro-environment has always been immersive, affirming the puja venue as an exceptional space within the everyday urban fabric. So if the goal of the theme *pandals* is to produce a novel environment, how does it augment this immersive experience?

The most ambitious theme *pandals* enhance these cultural practices by creating environments that are visually stunning and synesthetic. In terms of structure, the frontal engagement with the traditional *pandal* façade and its thin section have been replaced in recent theme pujas with structures that encourage visual engagement with its formal content. Whereas the traditional puja *pandal* was primarily a shelter against the weather and a fairly simple replication of the *thakur-dalan* form of elite mansions, these newly styled pavilions draw attention to themselves.[40] It is possible to see much of these new designs as elaborations of the decorative touches that have made the traditional puja *pandal* a festive space, but there is a certain structural and therefore creative autonomy incited by the modulation of surfaces assembled with unusual materials or in a novel manner.[41] These experiments with material, color, and assemblage, re-mark the traditional *pandal* with new concepts and intentions. Akin to literary world building, it assembles a spatial experience to tell a story. This push for novelty of form has meant a fundamental change in the approach to *pandal* design.

From 1995 to 2005, *pandal* themes incorporated unusual building materials—the more unusual the better. This included clay cups, sugarcane fiber, date-palm fans, aluminum foil, and patently absurd use of materials such as pea-nut shells, dry lentil dumplings, and chow-mien noodles. *Pandals* simulating or recreating contemporary and historical sites such as the Golden Temple of Amritsar, the Sanchi Stupa, the Cathedral of Notre Dame, the Meenakshi Temple, Big Ben, Disneyland, and more recently, Buckingham Palace—the possibilities are seemingly endless—have been crowd pleasers. So are recreations of various building types (North Indian temple, Roman church, Buddhist temple), and entire regions (Sundarbans, Rajasthan, Kashmir), that appeal explicitly to the touristic imagination. These simulations often go hand in hand with the demonstration of an associated art form, such as the Mughal miniature, or *kalamkari*, or performance traditions such as *chau*, *bhadu*, *baul*. These themes are frequently aligned with social commentary on contemporary issues such as deindustrialization, environmental degradation, global warming, water pollution, women's rights, feticide, etc. Concept-based themes that foray into free association are only contingently linked to the material construction of the *pandal*: "Nostalgia," "Dreams," "Wandering Alone," "Puja Songs," "Rabindranath's Letters." The relation between a theme, as in a subject that guides the ambiance of a particular place (e.g. "Disneyland"), and a concept as an abstract idea (e.g. "nostalgia") that requires material articulation through installation, is often not clear. Concept-based designs have garnered a certain cachet in the last five years or so, as designers attempt to find a closer connection between the novel articulation of materials and a larger idea, either expressive (production of a surrealist landscape for "Dreams") or didactic (suggesting the loss of immediate community in a digital era in "Wandering Alone"). Some of the most carefully designed *pandals* assume the need to coordinate the *pandal* design, the design of the idols, the lighting, and music to create a coherent environment.

In 2017, the designs exhibited this whole gamut of "theme" responses. Gauranga Kuila, well-known for delivering theme *pandals* created visually stunning ceiling designs made of little more than fabric, wire and paper at Tridhara Sammilani and Mudiali Club. FIG 1, 2 Subrata Chakrabarty's surface modulation using spray-painted bubble wrap on walls and color glass hangings from the ceiling in the Abasar *pandal* was a variation on this idea. FIG 3 The effect of depth created by the layers of folded fabric and a limited set of motifs in sync with the lighting design generated the primary ambiance within which the themes of these settings were elaborated. Some *pandal* designs, however, sought to move beyond such brilliant decorative treatment and craft virtuosity that viewers have come to expect and admire.

Badamtala Ashar Sangha's designers, Purnendu Dey and Snehasish Maity, represented the theme "Pashimi Haowa" (Westerly Wind) by reproducing not one building but a whole iconic skyline. Sponsored by tourism agency Global Enterprises, a private education company JIS, and the US Consulate in Kolkata, the concept of the "West" was thematized here in a projection of New York City. An arc of skyscrapers designed to create the canyon effect of New York City streets, punctuated by a Frank Gehry design-inspired pavilion that housed the goddess and her entourage, constituted the puja environment. Built of paper and fabric mounted on bamboo scaffolds, the panels representing the skyline ambiance were literally skin-deep. The illusion of surface, color and lighting invited the viewer to a fabulous experience.

Constructed on a thirty-foot wide street, lined with mid-rise houses, FIG 4 the design responded to the site in an imaginative recreation of urban space. Abandoning the idea of an enclosed rectangular puja space for the deity and an adjacent stage for cultural events, Ashar Sangha's designers opted for an open-to-sky enclosure within which a few spaces were roofed. Unlike the typical puja *pandal* there was no façade here. The vacant lot next to the street housed the pavilion with the deity, while the street was remodeled as a new passage.

The approach to the venue was lined with corporate advertisements in the usual manner, and the visitor moved underneath a gateway sporting the Indian and U.S. national flags on its marquee, signaling a political-cultural alliance. The banal entry to the site from the south did not presage the surprise in store. Beyond the gateway, the tall scaffolds burst into view, surrounding the visitor on three sides with a skyscraper skyline in hues of pink and blue. FIG 5 The Flatiron Building flanked the left and directed attention to the bold

FIG 1
Mudiali Club Durgapuja *pandal* ceiling, 2017.

FIG 2
Tridhara Sammilani Durgapuja *pandal* ceiling, 2017.

curves of the Gehry-inspired pavilion housing the deity. A host of skyscrapers including the Empire State Building, the Seagram Building, and One World Trade Center jostled for space in a skyline that was recognizable as American through its sheer iconic redundancy. The aluminum panels that simulated the polished titanium of Gehry's signature buildings reflected the color of the adjacent skyscrapers in a mesmerizing visual feast.

The deities were almost hidden in the cave-like pavilion, their outfits highlighted in pink and blue resonating the colors of the constructed skyline. The choice of colors, as if a hint from fashion designer Sabyasachi's palette, was critical in extending the fantasy setting when extended to the *pandal* shell. No such color ever played so tantalizingly on the titanium shells of Gehry's buildings. In the morning and at dusk the design responded beautifully to Kolkata's rain-refracted autumn light. At night the back-lit paper-covered fenestration of the panel ensemble created a veritable theatrical setting. Yet the play between pastel colors and neon lights induced a romanticism that is found neither in the everyday urban setting of New York nor in Kolkata.

The experience of walking past the pavilion underneath a passage, which doubled as a platform to hoist the faux skyscrapers, bled into the ordinary festive street space of the city populated by street vendors and food stalls. A scaled down "Brooklyn Bridge," resting on a three-story townhouse at one end, created a recognizable illusion. Only upon observing the juxtaposition between the plywood bridge and the town house or noticing the trees on the sidewalk did one become cognizant of the degree to which this was a momentary play on scale. FIG 6 The effectiveness of the formal arrangement of the skyscraper skyline, treated as a large-scale folded building model, resided in two factors: the height of the bamboo scaffolds rising to one hundred feet, and the sense of depth created by the folded panels producing the illusion of a distant skyline.

FIG 5
Nigh-time view of skyscraper skyline of Badamtala Ashar Sangha Durga Puja pandal, 2017.

FIG 4
Site of Badamtala Ashar Sangha Durgapuja, 2017.

FIG 3
Abasar Durgapuja *pandal* detail, 2017.

The Ashar Sangha puja venue created a fantastic fragment of New York in Kolkata, striking a homology between the two former colonial cities and a premise for conversation, as if the audacity of this illusory cityscape was necessary to parlay on politics and culture. The *pandal* acted as a mediating form between the two cities, exceeding its role as a copy or a simulation to become a re-making of the older idea of the *pandal* in line with a new set of desires. Not the copy, but the illusion stood on its own merits.

The formal organization of Ashar Sangha's venue exploded the idea of a *pandal* as traditionally conceived, bringing out its role as an urban infill while producing a new dialogue about competition, alliance, and difference. Unlike the typical *pandal*, here the scaffolds were treated as one would advertisement billboards. Rather than the building becoming an advertisement (as with corporate architecture), the advertisement became a building-illusion. The sponsors' advertisements that populated the space just outside the venue was given a different scalar and material turn in the *pandal* to momentarily obscure the site itself. The reveals—for example, the junction where the plywood bridge form met the townhouse—were not failures to sustain the illusion, but keen signals of the daring of the implausible fabrication. The artists' and the neighborhood's capacity to inhabit-by-invoking a distant cityscape declared their global disposition and desire. In the double movement of forces and counterforces, the site presented local agents working in partnership with distant agencies, representing various interests, and inhabiting the space of global corporate capital, all folded outside in.

This *doubleness* was also evident in the spatial ordering. After all, it was the background of faux skyscrapers and not the foreground with the Gehry-esque pavilion, that was the prime effect of the space. In a clear acknowledgement that the *pandal* design is of independent value in this clamor for visitor and media attention, the iconicity of the surrounding environs superseded the place of worship. There is another way of seeing this background-foreground distinction, however. The pavilion housing the object of worship was built at the scale of the neighborhood, for the people in the neighborhood to offer worship at ritual moments (it was cordoned off from the main passage), while the rest of the structure—the background—served to offset the smaller curved form of the pavilion. The skyscraper skyline modeled a distant world, a visual delight to be appreciated from afar by those visitors who would not be offering puja, and thus have no direct investment in the locality.

Canonicity

If Ashar Sangha offered a global community and internationality as its address and concern, Parimal Paul, the designer of Kumartuli Sarbojanin, made a claim for the long lineage of artisans who craft the puja idols, offering that tradition as canonic. Erected on a busy street, a stone's throw from the lanes and by-lanes of Kumartuli (literally, potter's locality), the *pandal* at Kumartuli Sarbojanin served as a localized homage to the great masters of the art. Its insistence on framing the locality as a new venue of concern in many ways made this design ensemble entirely different from the spatial models and construction techniques adopted at Ashar Sangha. Paul's global claims rode on something more close at hand, an artistic lineage that has only recently found global recognition. It was about inserting the local community and its creative history and potential in a new narrative of Durga Puja as a global enterprise. In honoring the past and present practitioners of the art of idol-making, the *pandal* validated the future turn in their practice.

The display process through which the concept "Sraddhanjali" (homage) was elaborated is noteworthy. The spatial idioms of street, pedestrian lane, studio, and art gallery were combined in the *pandal* as a novel recreation of the workshops that line the pedestrian lanes partly shaded with the roof overhangs in Kumartuli. The work-in-progress messiness evident in the studio-workshops of Kumartuli was here simulated with a formal elaboration that sought to highlight and make explicit the process of making idols. This involved exposed surfaces and materials left intentionally "untidy." At the same time, the *pandal* quite literally enshrined the names of the master artisans and their labor as so many crafted utterances, framed and enigmatic. In so doing it gave a particular kind of legibility to the artisanal community in the larger milieu of Durga Puja. The concept, as articulated, made the artisanal community the theme itself, and the *pandal* a series of statements about craft, art, and community.

FIG 6
Pandal connection with adjacent town house; Badamtala Ashar Sangha Durgapuja, 2017.

FIG 7
Kathamo as sculpture, Kumartuli Sarbojanin Durgapuja, 2017.

The bamboo-frame *pandal* structure consisted of two distinct levels. A raised platform through which the visitor approached the deity was enclosed in walls of extruded aluminum sheets and rough exposed brickwork that supported a collage of different materials and decorative motifs. At the end of the pavilion, the space of the deity was raised on a mezzanine, creating an egress underneath the deity's platform. The unfolding of the decorative program, as one moved across the linear space of the pavilion, was an explication of the entire process of production, from the names of the ingredients that went into the crafting of the clay images, and the equipment at work in the delivery and installation of the deity. The conventional linear spatial organization was interrupted by the narrative experience of the "gallery" that favored episodic instantiations. The visitor was required to work through a process of recognition, encountering the images, materials, motifs, and texts as layered sign systems.

At the entrance the wooden frame (*kathamo*) that supports an idol was represented as a repetitive module. FIG 7 Variously wrapped in red, white and black fabric, a sculptural form constructed of these modules "descended" from the tree on the sidewalk, thus "attaching" the venue to the site. Still ahead a door led from the *pandal* directly onto the side street where the daily market continued unimpeded. FIG 8 The connections and openings were meant to create attentive links between the temporally bound ritual event space and that of daily inhabitation and work in that locality. Still ahead on the left of the gallery, a deity covered in plastic sheet was placed on a tempo (small truck) next to a clay female figure—a roadside goddess with a third eye and a headdress in her hand—connecting the neglected figure of the (crafts)woman-as-goddess to the exalted goddess worshipped at the head of the spatial sequence. The plastic covered deity representing the modest-dimensioned Durga idols of yesteryear and their conventionally stylized iconography was placed as a necessary side-note to the main attraction, thus instigating multiple plays on time and space.

The Durga image concluding the spatial sequence was large and unconventional. Designed as a dynamic form at the moment of her killing the demon-god Mahishasur (not after the deed is done, as the traditional iconography demands), the goddess did not look straight on. FIG 9 A goddess about to throw her weapon, she looked up at the the magically empowered form-shifting demon-god emerging from the ceiling, his head hanging upside down (perhaps the demon-god in his *avatar* or incarnation as Mahisashur displayed in a literalization of *avatarana* or descent). To complete the moment of witnessing the slaying of evil, the viewer must take in the ceiling and surrounding environs as an integral part of the experience of seeing. The walls next to the goddess featuring a geometric composition of square fenestration hinted at the physical site of elite venues—of a street lined with contemporary residential buildings. Thus framed, the space of worship was presented as a work-in-progress, the deities being installed by laborers. The time of installation and the time of ritual intersected dramatically to enchant the viewer into thinking about the labor that enabled the event. The eye was enticed to wander toward and away from the deity, from the product to the process, from the goddess to the makers in a new canon formation. But here the goddess did not "look back" to meet the gaze of the worshipper: she was not amenable to the tradition of *darshan*.

Just as the anonymous laborer became part of the tableau as a present continuous—his labor made explicit and honored as he installs the images—so did the past and present practitioners of the art of clay modeling, the *pratima shilpis*. Names of the renowned practitioners appeared in gilt frames, referencing the oil-portraits in older mansions. The busts of *pratima shilpis* provided a figurative counterpart to the inscribed names, lending a certain redundancy to the canonization process. The gilt-framed names and busts as commemorative gestures articulated a genealogy of artisanal greatness, but in so doing they did something significant to the process of idol-making itself: the idol-makers were turned into idols (in the colloquial sense), as worthy of recognition and honor.

FIG 8
Kumartuli Sarbojanin Durgapuja pandal with door leading to side street, 2017.

All the names in the gilt frames were of male artists. The work and fame of these artists and many like them have for the longest time been crucially dependent on the laborers in the workshop, both women and men. The project of making a great craft tradition legible as art, in a surreptitious way, elevated the well-known male practitioners using a process by which art traditions have historically detached themselves from craft traditions.[42]

The construction of the pavilion and the materials used in the pavilion were statements on the relation between art and craft, artisan and artist, the past and the present. Bamboo of ordinary *muli* variety was left exposed but painted black. FIG 8 Although the bamboo poles were nailed to one another, red ribbon ties were used at the structural joints to provide color contrast while referring to the older method of tying bamboo. Traditionally, bamboo poles would be secured with coconut coir ropes of a shade darker perhaps than the bamboo itself. In the last five years or so, synthetic umbrella fabric has replaced these coir ropes because it is easier to handle and just as strong. If the red-ribbon ties signaled a conceptual distance from these common methods of construction, the distinctive red checker pattern of the *gamcha* (a thin woven cotton towel) used as ties in key locations, lent a vernacular touch. *Gamcha* serves many everyday functions—as cloth for wiping and body covering, and ready-at-hand fabric for making bundles to carry small loads—but do not have sufficient strength to be used as structural ties. Thus the displacement of traditional methods of constructing *pandals* and the artful re-citation of vernacularity posed its very redefinition as "Art."

The interior surfaces at the entrance, assembled in a patchwork of colored pieces of corrugated aluminum sheets against rustic brick walls, might have been a reference to the expedient use of such materials in constructing roadside sheds for a variety of purposes. These also registered the manner in which the studio-workshops of Kumartuli are built: colorful stretches of *saree* and *gamcha* that cover the bamboo, masonry, and corrugated aluminum surfaces of the workshops served here as stylized references to their architectonics. The names of the esoteric ingredients and processes used in the traditional crafting of deities—at least thirty-four different vernacular terms served as decorative-didactics—affirmed the plebian language of the craft tradition. Most visitors, if they read Bengali, would be able to read the words, but their actual application might elude the uninitiated. Suspended paint brushes, mini square palettes, and paint-dripped glass beakers admitting the introduction of new colors, techniques and methods connected the improvised ties and fabric patches with a re-description of the idol-making "cottage" industry.

Like many of the newer generation of *pratima-shilpis*, the designer himself is formally trained in an art school, and bridges the two worlds of art practice and ideology. The artisanal community that is the subject of Paul's meditation is part of an extended network of craftspeople, most of whom are on a precarious economic footing. One bad season could push them deeply into debt. Only a few among them have made it to the big leagues, so to speak, and acquired name recognition. The design, in honoring these men, spoke of the possibility of an upward mobility that refused to

FIG 9
Durga image, Kumartuli Sarbojanin Durgapuja, 2017.

accept the vernacular crafts tradition as belonging to the past. The language of practice as an art-vernacular registered difference and a desire to be grounded in the local community. Visitors were encouraged to see the vernacular craft tradition in renewed terms as the *pandal* design posited imaginative connections in space and time. Perhaps a reflexive positioning of the artisanal community in relation to a new breed of designers who have assumed prominence in the puja milieu but are not grounded in this artisanal lineage, the pavilion, and its claim to art was also a story of becoming. The open-ended nature of the design, relying more on a concept than a theme, claimed recognition for a community yet to come.

Coda

With some notable exceptions, the desire of many of the artists and critics to see the design of theme *pandals* as contemporary installation or environmental art may be likened to Parimal Paul's effort to gain legibility in a global landscape. Yet the positing of theme pujas as art installations construes the history of Durga Puja as teleological sequence of craft becoming art, where "art" is understood to be a self-explanatory higher order achievement. The desire to distance oneself from the older tradition—when the *pandal* was just a *pandal* in the hand of decorators—arbitrarily denies the artistry of the former. One of the important stakes in calling theme pujas fine art is the demand for documenting and preserving, and effectively conferring upon them the status of museum work. In so doing theme artists not only practice their own obsolescence but are unmindful of the impact that their work has as ephemeral construction.

The *alpona* of the Samajsebi Sangha with which I began this article was meant to last a month; hundreds of thousands of footfalls and the rains during the pujas limited its life to the duration of the festival, as it should be. *Alpona* is, after all, ephemeral art *par excellence*. A long life robs it of the virtue of renewability and future design virtuosity, of expectation of another festival. The memory of a former propels the expectation of the one yet to come. It is through such memory strands that ephemeral artworks such as the *alpona* or a *pandal* contribute to the fabrication of community as thick space. It demonstrates altogether new possibilities of a site, leaving a few traces around which other built structures gather permanence, even after the flows of

FIG 10
Alpona next to the Samajsebi Sangha pandal at the end of the festivities, 2017.

people, labor and commodities thin out. FIG 10 It is in this that the contemporary Durga Puja exceeds its role as figured by corporate capital.

Various constituencies—artists, organizers, municipal authorities, vendors and visitors—find their own niche in this advertising arena-in-the-making in a double movement of forces and counterforces. Corporate capital attempts to locate points of entry in a pre-existing spatiotemporal mode thus casting an impress on the city, and local agents attempt to shape the changing contours of the cityscape according to their interests. These forces and counterforces, "serve each other citations, summoning each other to appear," and create what Jacques Derrida might have described as the effect of the principle of contamination, a "parasitical economy .... a sort of participation without belonging, a taking part in without being part of, without having membership of a set."[43] The effect created by these movements appears as dynamic folds in the cityscape that obliterates clear boundaries between inner-outer in terms of the temporality of the Durga Puja, the space of the *para*, and the event as performance. It leaves uneven traces and the possibility of alterity. As an event, Durga Puja works as a precipitative moment for a sedimentation of meaning in this continual process of fabricating community.

1 "Street art paves for piety," *The Telegraph*, September 20, 2017. https://www.telegraphindia.com/1170920/jsp/calcutta/story_174096.jsp. "Durga Puja 2017: 400 Bengalis create longest street rangoli in Kolkata," *Deccan Chronicle*, September 19, 2017. https://www.deccanchronicle.com/lifestyle/viral-and-trending/190917/durga-puja-2017-400-bengalis-create-longest-street-rangoli-in-kolkata.html
2 The puja is based on the lunar calendar and thus the dates are different every year.
3 Rajeshwari Sharma, "Behind the Scenes of Bengal's Stunning Pandals: Meet the Farmers Who Are the Real Artists!" *The Better India*, September 27, 2017, https://www.thebetterindia.com/116629/bengals-farmers-behind-kolkatas-stunning-durga-puja-pandals/

4 Guy Debord, *The Society of the Spectacle*, trans. by Donald Nicholson-Smith (1967, New York: Zone Books, 1995), 12.

5 The number of pujas have almost doubled in the last decade, or perhaps there is a more accurate count now in addition to the increase in numbers. For a discussion of "waste" of time and the festival's entanglement with capital, see Anjan Ghosh, "Spaces of Recognition: Puja and Power in Contemporary Kolkata," *Journal of South African Studies* 26, no 2 (2000): 289–99; Swati Chattopadhyay, "Fungible Geographies," *Unlearning the City: Infrastructure in a New Optical Field* (Minneapolis: University of Minnesota Press, 2012).

6 Technically, Mahalaya begins the ten-day duration of the great conflict between the goddess Durga and the demon-god Mahisasur. In Bengal Durga is celebrated as a warrior, but also as a mother who comes to her natal home in the company of her children, Saraswati, Lakshmi, Kartick and Ganesh. The sixth day she arrives at her mother's house and she departs on the tenth day. These are the five days of prayer and offering that constitute Durga Puja.

7 "400 Bengalis create longest street rangoli in Kolkata," *India Tribune*, September 19, 2017. https://indiatribune.com/400-bengalis-create-longest-street-rangoli-in-kolkata/

8 "Durga Puja 2017: Kolkata streets decorated with the longest alpana," *Indian Express*, September 20, 2017. http://indianexpress.com/article/lifestyle/art-and-culture/durga-puja-2017-kolkata-streets-decorated-with-longest-alpona-4851324. It is useful to note that the Chief Minister of West Bengal, Mamata Banerjee has herself tried her hand in designing the Bakulbagan Durga Puja *pandal* in 2010.

9 For the introduction of new motifs, material, color and enlarged scale of *alpona* introduced by Nandalal Bose in Santiniketan, see Anukana Khastagir and Gauri Bhanja's articles in Pranati Mukhopadhyay, ed. *Rabindra Bhavana: Nandalal Sankhya* (Calcutta: Tagore Research Institute, 1984).

10 Susanto Pal, who trained as an artist, and has worked as a costume designer as well as set designer for Bengali films, namely by Rituparno Ghosh, bemoans the inability of the puja organizers to "get the big picture" and the failed opportunities for "branding." See "Best Durga Pujas 2013," http://durgapuja.trisyscom.com/

11 Conversation with Rono Banerjee, "Best Durga Pujas 2013," http://durgapuja.trisyscom.com.

12 Interview with Rono Banerjee, "Art and Business of Durgapuja," https://www.youtube.com/watch?v=eX6iIVXxM4s.

13 Chattopadhyay, "Fungible Geographies."

14 The first *sarbojanin pujas* were Shyampukur Adi Sarbonjanin Puja, 1911; Sikdarbagan Sabojanin Durgatsov, 1913; Banathakurtala Mandir, Linton Street, 1916; Bagbazar Sarbojanin (Nebubagan Barowari), 1919; Simla Byamsamiti, 1926; Hatibagan Sarbojanin, 1934.

15 "Samajsebi Sangha," in Samrat Chattopadhyay, ed. *Kolkatar Durgapujor Galpo Salpo* (Kolkata: Serena Publications, 2016), 149–52. I thank Sanjeet Chowdhury for this source.

16 Chattopadhyay, *Kolkatar Durgapujor Galpo*, 151.

17 While theme pujas are no more than two decades old, *pandal*-hopping has been popular since the 1950s. The phenomenon of best puja awards started in 1985 with the Asian Paints awards. Durga Puja guides have been published since the 1970s. A 1985 puja guide published in a Bengali daily sought to provide information in the top 100 pujas in the city.

18 The narrative of Santoshpur Lake Palli's organizers makes interesting reading. See Somnath Das, "Santoshpur—Gali theke rajpath," in Chattopadhyay, ed. *Kolkatar Durgapujor Galpo*, 25–29. A common theme is feeling slighted directly or indirectly at the well-known pujas, and being spurred on to create a competing puja venue.

19 One hundred thousand visitors each day during the five-day puja is considered the benchmark of popularity.

20 Debdoot Ghosh-Thakur, "Chhera patay amulya dhan," in Chattopadhyay, ed. *Kolkatar Durgapujor* Galpo, 8.

21 Das, "Santoshpur," 25.

22 The Forum for Durgapuja (FFD) listed 368 puja associations in 2016. These puja associations share a commitment to theme-puja, and it is safe to assume that another 400 pujas that are not members of FFD embrace a theme for their pujas. Chattopadhyay, ed. *Kolkatar Durgapujor Galpo*, 190.

23 A club founded in 1980 on Nepal Bhattacharya Lane, in the middle/lower-middle class neighborhood of Kalighat, began its first puja in 1986 with a budget of 15,000 rupees. Between 2005 and 2016 its budget for theme puja rose from 1.5 to 4.10 lakhs. Chattopadhyay, ed. *Kolkatar Durgapujor Galpo*, 190.

24 Conversation with Robin Mandal, 2013. Best Durga Pujas 2013," http://durgapuja.trisyscom.com.

25 In the Indian numbering system, one lakh is one hundred thousand and one crore is ten million.

26 Chattopadhyay, "Galpo holeo satyi," in *Kolkatar Durgapujor Galpo*, 62.

27 Senco Jewellers was the sponsor. While it is fairly common for permanent idols in households and temples to have silver and gold jewelry, this is a new phenomenon for temporary deities.

28 Dinesh Jaiswal, "Wellington Nagaril Kalyan Samiti," in Chattopadhyay, ed. *Kolkatar Durgapujor Galpo*, 129. All puja committees give the responsibility for managing the budget to a trained professional, typically also a member of the organizing committee. Since these pujas do rely on neighborhood subscription and feel accountable to the local constituency, an account of the expenses and balances is delivered to the subscribers in the form of a brochure at the conclusion of the puja.

29 Piyali Basu Chattopadhyay, "Chhak bhangader dinalipi," in Chattopadhyay, ed. *Kolkatar Durgapujor Galpo*, 42–54; Partha Chattopadhyay, "Bharatchakra," in Chattopadhyay, ed. *Kolkatar Durgapujor Galpo*, 107.

30 The Saharer Shera Puja Sangathak (SSPS) award began in 2010. Basu Chattopadhyay, "Chhak bhangaader dinalipi," 42.

31 Ghosh-Thakur, "Chhera patay amulya dhan," 7.

32 Chattopadhyay, "Galpo holeyo satyi," 57–58; and Ghosh-Thakur, "Chhera patay amulya dhan," 67–69.

57–58, 67–69. PPA—*Puja Pagolder Adda*, a WhatsApp group, is considered the heart of puja organizers.

33 Several pujas that have become synonymous with political figures, including Ekdalia Evergreen with Subrata Mukherjee. For the controversy over left politicians asking the event to be called "sharadotsav" (autumn festival) as opposed to Durgotsav (Durga festival) see Tapati Guha-Thakurta, *In the Name of the Goddess: the Durga Pujas of Contemporary Kolkata* (Delhi: Primus Books, 2015).

34 Guha-Thakurta, *In the Name of the Goddess*, 147.

35 For more on this see Swati Chattopadhyay, "Telling Stories," *Representing Calcutta: Modernity, Nationalism and the Colonial Uncanny* (London: Routledge, 2005).

36 Conversation with Robin Mandal, 2013. Best Durga Pujas 2013," http://durgapuja.trisyscom.com.

37 For more discussion on this see Chattopadhyay, *Unlearning the City*, Ch.7; and "Ephemeral Architecture: Toward Radical Contingency," in Swati Chattopadhyay and Jeremy White, eds. *Critical Approaches to Contemporary Architecture* (New York: Taylor & Francis, 2019), 138–160.

38 See Gayatri Chakravorty Spivak's explanation of the *dvaita* sense of viewing, "Moving Devi," in Vidya Dehehia, ed. *Devi* (Ahmedabad: Mapin Publishing, 1999).

39 Shalini Kakar, "'Starring' Madhuri as Durga: The Madhuri Dixit Temple and the Performative Fan Bhakti of Pappu Sardar," *Journal of Hindu Studies* 3, no. 9 (December, 2009); Madhava Prasad, "Fan Bhakti and Subaltern Sovereignty: Enthusiasm and Indian Politics," *Economic and Political Weekly* 44, no. 29 (July 2009); Tapati Guha-Thakurta, *Monuments, Objects, Histories: Institutions of Art and Colonial and Post-colonial India* (New York: Columbia University Press, 2004).

40 See my explanation of this formal translation in Chattopadhyay, "Fungible Geographies."

41 For more on this see Guha-Thakurta, *In the Name of the Goddess*.

42 For an analysis of the transition from craft to art in the professionalization of architecture see Dell Upton, "Architecture History as Landscape History?" *Journal of Architectural Education* 44, no 4 (Aug 1991): 195–199.

43 Jacques Derrida, "The Law of Genre," trans. Avital Ronell, *Critical Inquiry* 7, no. 1 (Autumn 1980), 58–59.

The American Architect on a Cosmic Stage

Bryan E. Norwood

> The inquiry is often made, what architecture must a nation, situated as ours is, adopt? It has no indigenous architecture; it is not, therefore, a matter of religion with us, but a matter of taste. We may and must have all the architectures of the world, but we may ennoble them all by an attention to truth.
> —Minard Lafever[1]

In New Orleans in 1819 one of the founding fathers of the American architectural profession, 64-year-old Benjamin Henry Latrobe, recalled when a Lutheran minister almost convinced him as a teenager that the greatest epistemic sin was not to believe in the wrong doctrine but to be indifferent altogether to matters of faith.[2] Yet reflecting back in the pages of his journal, the sexagenarian Latrobe observed, "Thus far it appears to me that every reasonable and benevolent man must be an Indifferentist."[3] The sincere option for the enlightened humanist was to withhold belief.

Latrobe was one of the first in the United States to call for the principled formation of an architectural profession delimited by pedigree and exclusivity and that would mediate between builder and client.[4] For Latrobe and fellow enlightenment adherent and amateur architect Thomas Jefferson, architecture had secular foundations and could agnostically serve political and civil life.[5] Their outlook was echoed by other architects, including several members of the short-lived American Institution of Architects (1836) such as the craftsman-turned-architect Minard Lafever, who contrasted the real contingency of architectural taste with the absoluteness of religion. Taste was contingent for the American architect, Lafever said, because he was freed from the confines of indigeneity and faith. FIG 1

The agnostic early American architect thus could understand himself as unburdened by the confines of absolutes, and in particular of Old World tradition and place. The lightness of being that characterized his indifferentism was not, however, achieved by overcoming architectural order altogether. Rather it was an achievement of what Frederick Jackson Turner would later famously label the frontier thesis, of an enlightened and progressive individualism close enough to primitivism to be unburdened by the weight of the immediate past.[6] Adherence to the architectural frontier thesis, to an unburdened self-determinism, raises the question of what exactly one must profess in order to be an architect. How can "profession" arise out of indifference? Put a bit paradoxically, is there an indigeneity of the nonindigenous? Put a bit grandly, is there a faith of the faithless?[7]

The formation of the architectural profession in the nineteenth century has largely been understood as a secular pursuit of authority and class, but the agnostic perspective was not the only way into a definition of architectural identity in the early republic, nor was it the most prevalent. A set of Protestant religious sentiments that I will call "republican theology," as defined by Benjamin T. Lynerd, crossed the architect's first baptism with a second: the profession of architecture with the profession of religious faith.[8] Republican theology was developed by a host of American intellectuals, and it had profound influence a number of early republican architects. It was a credo that sought to reconcile the concept of limited government based on a social contract with a Christian moral imperative. Crossing strains of theology, philosophy, and political theory, republican theology emphasized individual self-improvement and citizen responsibility for national sanctification.

I turn my attention to this belief structure because it deeply affected how early professional architects framed their practice as having universal, world-historical foundations and responsibilities. An answer to the question of the faith of the faithless may be formed by considering its intellectual proximity to the faith of the faithful. The influence of republican theology can be seen most clearly in the employment of architectural history to distinguish and anchor professional pedigree in the early American republic. In this context design was never merely a matter of arbitrary taste or practicality, nor were its civic responsibilities merely contractual. Architecture's purpose was rooted in a progressive grand narrative, a divinely organized cosmic drama in which the United States of America was a key player. Individual and national sanctification was part of global progress. In describing republican theology, Lynerd argues that its continued influence can be seen in the American exceptionalism and fusion of libertarianism and traditional morality that mark the civil religion of large segments of evangelical Christianity.[9] I will conclude by suggesting that an interrogation of this worldview and its attendant epistemology, metaphysics, and historiography matters for architecture because it is inscribed into the contemporary institutional structure of the profession and its educational system.

FIG 1
Frontispiece from Edward Shaw, *The Modern Architect, or Every Carpenter His Own Master* (Boston: Dayton and Wentworth, 1854).

Thomas Ustick Walter's Two Bodies

Our exemplar for the influence of republican theology on architecture will be Thomas Ustick Walter (1804–1887), who began independent architectural practice in 1830, obtaining his most important early commission, the expansive and expensive Girard College for Orphans, two years later. His architectural education started at William Strickland's office in Philadelphia in 1819, followed by study at the Franklin Institute, also in the city. Walter gained national fame after winning the Girard College architectural competition.[10] In 1840, four years after participating in the founding of the American Institution of Architects, he was appointed professor of architecture at the Franklin Institute, where he gave a series of lectures on the technical aspects of building. The following year he delivered his "Lectures on Architecture" for the first time, treating the discipline as a fine art that could be understood through an ethno-nationalistic history of style and taste.[11] Walter would go on to serve as Architect of the Capitol (1851–65) and to help reincarnate the American Institute of Architects in 1856, serving first as vice president and then as president (1877–87). FIG 2

Throughout his career Walter consistently defended a conception of the profession in harmony with Latrobe's principles. In 1871, for example, he refused a request to submit plans for a library at Princeton College, informing the committee that he could not participate in a situation in which "all mankind is invited to send in plans" without compromising his professional "fidelity."[12] He argued that an architect's drawings are not equivalent to the sketches of amateurs; they are products of real labor, valuable on their own regardless of whether they result in something built.[13] Walter made a key move in defining the unique status of the professional: "Princeton college wants but *one* Architect, and if he is well skilled in his profession he requires no outside aid whatever." The singular body of the professional architect stood in for the professional body as an individual that represented the collective whole.

But Walter had a second body. The year before professing to be an architect, he publicly professed to be a Christian when he was baptized in the Schuylkill River.[14] As a Baptist, a Protestant denomination that like many others was rapidly expanding in membership, Walter believed that this purification in water was not an act of salvation but a public declaration of commitment to the church.[15] Walter was as devoted to this Christian body as he was to the architectural profession.[16] Beginning at the E Street Baptist Church in 1854, while serving as Architect of the Capitol, Walter taught a Sunday school class for young men, and he continued after his relocation to the Philadelphia suburbs in 1865 until 1872.[17] "The Sunday school," he wrote in one of his lessons, "is the church in action."[18] It is in his extensive collection of lessons that we find Walter's theories of humanity and history, and of how and why his two bodies—architectural and Christian—should act. FIG 3

For the voices of republican theology, voluntary civil bodies were seen as key to taking worldly action at a scale situated between personal improvement and national progress.[19] Walter's second body, the church, was the archetypal version of a voluntary institution, but it was viewed as a unique player in the cosmic drama because of its divine calling. The church was separated from the carnality of the world through the privilege of salvation, which it was also to diffuse to the world. Paraphrasing a Presbyterian publication, Walter declared that any collective body called together for a purpose is a kind of church in the sense of the ancient ecclesia (Greek: ἐκκλησία).[20] Thus his professional body was also an ecclesia, and architectural practice a calling. Assembled together through education, experience, and exams, professional architects were to use their privileged position to diffuse goodness throughout the world.

There were, however, practical tensions between Walter's professional and Christian bodies, as described in his 1871 letter to the Princeton College committee:

> My high regard for you, and the attachments of friendship, and of Christian fellowship that exists between us, led me, at first, to entertain the thought of complying with the circular; but, upon reflection I found that I could not do so without going contrary to all my teachings—public and private; to my obligations to the profession to which I belong, and to my own self respect.[21]

As a Christian Walter was dedicated to self-sacrifice in the promotion of collective virtue, while his profession obliged him to acknowledge his work as expert labor exercised over time and converted into money. Resolving the tension between his two collective bodies—church and architectural profession—required a particular form of universalization: history, understood as a divinely directed progressive narrative, would hold these two bodies together.

Global Historical Consciousness and Nonindigenous Progress

Although composed of localized congregations of individuals, according to Walter's theology the church was globally united through the calling to salvation of all. This abstract imperative that all should be justified and sanctified by God organized a universal history that positioned the local church within a narrative that extended from the creation of the world through Israel (sometimes referred to as the "Jewish church" in this discourse) to the United States, and forward toward a utopic millenarian future.[22]

The authority and purpose of Walter's collective professional body was, if properly oriented by history, also ultimately global. This global legitimization through a *longue durée* was not unusual. National politics often drew legitimization from an extended historical scale, and, as sociologist Magali Sarfatti Larson notes, deep historical continuity "is deliberately sought in the attempts by organized professions to give themselves a culture with roots in a classic past."[23] But for architectural voices like Walter's this past was not only classical but also divine. The precursor to the United States was not only Greece but also Israel.[24] Studying architectural history was thus understood as a way of discovering classical order as well as glimpsing the structure of the divinely-directed cosmic drama instructing the individual how to improve and sanctify themselves, their nation, and the world.

Into the grand narrative of architecture, much of it lifted from British sources, Walter plotted and justified the American experiment, from colonization to westward expansion,

FIG 2
Thomas U. Walter, Girard College, Philadelphia, PA, 1835.

FIG 3
The Baptisterion on the Schuykill, Frontispiece from Morgan Edwards, *Materials Towards a History of the American Baptists* (Philadelphia: Joseph Crushank and Isaac Collins, 1770).

as part of a divine narrative in which the United States was the chosen forefront—the new spiritual Israel. He was not alone in this historiographical exercise. The vision of America as a divinely destined nation and the guiding light of historical development was a recurrent theme of republican theology. In 1783 Yale president Ezra Stiles famously called the United States "God's American Israel," and this idea of America as a spiritual Israel would be repeated as often as civic American architecture repeated classical forms in an attempt to shape a national domestic order.[25] There were certainly variations on how the future was projected, but the pervasive idea of a key American role in this progress set the nation on the cosmic stage where architectural improvement was enacted. For Walter and other Protestants this meant finding a collective spiritual direction. Thus it is no surprise that the first professional exams proposed by the American Institution of Architects in 1837 began with architectural history.[26]

Walter accounted for architectural history through a fundamental dualism and a narrative of progress. Emulating methods of what the Scottish philosopher Dugald Stewart called "conjectural history"—a kind of speculative history that employed a metaphysical understanding of human nature to project a grand narrative—Walter bound the conditions of dualism and progress together through an anthropology of human imperfection and a theology of divine perfection.[27] Architecture began in the wake of an original loss. In the uncompromised conditions of the garden of Eden, humans and nature knew no enmity.[28] It was with the Fall that humans were expelled from this harmony and forced "to build the first habitation" as protection against the elements.[29] Although compromised by sin, a divine "ray of immortality" allowed humanity to unite material action and "the heaven-born power of thought."[30]

The dualism of the human condition was mirrored by an architectural dualism (one repeated in many other architectural histories of the time). In the first paragraphs of his *Lectures*, Walter said:

> Architecture possesses a twofold character. —As far as it relates to our physical comforts it is simply a *useful* art; —in this relation it is usually so designated; but in its *adornments* it is, in an eminent degree, an imaginative art; —In this relation it is called a fine art.[31]

To clarify this division of physical comfort and intellectual pleasure, he described his philosophical anthropology by appealing to a common point of comparison:

> Man is distinguished from the brute creation by his progressive faculties;—the Beaver builds his dam, and the bird his nest far better than we could do it; but they build as they did in Eden, while the course of man is onward—always unsatisfied with past attainments—always pressing on to higher, and still higher achievements in human knowledge.[32]

Architectural progress was not predicated on a backward-looking desire to returning to prelapsarian Eden, where dwelling was provided by nature. The Fall severed humanity from that idealized unity, and thus progress aimed at lifting the spirit over nature's limitations.[33] The useful art of building was, without a doubt, as old as the "first wants of our race," and the form of primitive dwelling derived directly from the "fabrics of the brute creation."[34] But architecture in its higher form, understood as a fine art, exceeded this mere necessity through a recursive, symbolic re-presentation of necessity.[35] Progress was structured by a dualism in which the constraints of one side, the material, were to be exceeded by the other, the spiritual.

A metaphysics characterizing human progress as uplifting the spirit over the repetitions of the organic body (while not eliminating this body) cohered with a view of the profession as a practice elevated above mere craft. Walter's lament that the builder's body all too often dominated architecture was not only practical or financial—it was a complaint about metaphysical order. When the builder was in control, the machine drove the spirit rather than the other way around.[36]

In the narrative Walter first outlined at the Franklin Institute, the development of an architectural practice that exceeded the prefiguration of mere building out of need was first concretely developed in the Egyptian "science" of architecture.[37] The order discovered along the Nile was picked up by other nations and transported by the Israelites in their escape from enslavement to Greece, where it was perfected. This ethno-nationalistic narrative was also one of progressive whitening, as Walter laid out a racial account of progress from blackness to whiteness in Sunday school lessons on the biblical Curse of Ham.[38] However, what the Greeks made elegant was compromised in the luxurious decadence of Rome. And although a new principle of Christian unity was discovered in the forms of the Gothic period (Walter credits this epoch with the discovery of a particular architectural way of representing sublimity), classicism was recovered (but often bastardized) from the fifteenth century onward. Developing an account of European architecture that saw its failures as rooted in popery and monarchy—in the glorification of man over God and republican simplicity—Walter positioned declensionist narratives as parts of an overall global progress, a march in which the United States had taken up the torch.

The coherence of American architecture hinged on history, on the proleptic appearance of an architectural past within which the purportedly nonindigenous architectural profession forming in the United States continuously progressed.[39] In his first address as president of the AIA in 1877, Walter described a constant and cumulative "innate feeling of irresistible progress" that characterized the civilization and architecture of the United States.[40]

Fitting the United States into a global architectural narrative presented a problem during the early republic, particularly if one relied on texts written by European architects and historians, which often understood the Americas as outside of the Western lineage of progress, doomed to primitivism and degeneracy by its climate and geography. Arguments for the robust nature of past civilizations—the Aztecs in particular—were thus particularly important for American enlightenment intellectuals.[41] These Americans experienced, as Cornel West notes, a double consciousness of being both American and European, and this dialectic problematized global accounts of architecture written from the colonial frontier.[42] Robert Cary Long, Jr. one of Walter's allies in the early republican development of historical architectural discourse, argued that a progressive narrative had also played out in the Americas.[43] But this progressive past did not bind the American empire to the remains of indigeneity. The process of internal colonization was legitimized through characterizing contemporary native people as mere savages—poor reflections of a once great people. Thus the architectural traces of the indigenous past were construed as evidence of an isolated, primitive territory primed for architectural progress.

American architecture's burden was light, disconnected as it was from both the proximate indigenous past of its territory and the legacies of the European monarchies from which its body politic had fled. Its past was much deeper: a *longue durée* of progress oriented by a divine plot. While the immediate future of progress was certainly national advancement, republican theology shaped the national future toward a utopic *millennialism*, a set of eschatological beliefs that imagined a coming dominion of Christianity on Earth.[44]

The progress of American architectural practice was thus conditioned not as dependent primarily on proximate tradition but rather on distant origins and millenarian futures. Non-indigeneity could be characterized by a position between the republican simplicity of ideal Grecian rootedness and the religious flight of the Israelites toward a promised land. The frontier was conceived as an empty field for the nonindigenous collection of all possibilities to freely progress.

The Project of Taste

The relation between individual and collective presented challenges for both religious and secular bodies. How did Protestants relate personal improvement to national and global progress? And how were individual architectural practices and designs related to the overall progressive narrative of architectural history? A connection for the Christian was secured through the local church, a civil body that could, guided by divine directive, mediate and take definable moral action at a scale between individual and nation. Architects, however, were faced with the challenge of defining a medium and orientation that would drive their collective professional practices. This became a particularly acute problem for the indifferentist who, like Lafever, juxtaposed the grounds of religion and taste: while the former was absolute, and thus provided an epistemic ground, the latter was absolutely contingent. If taste is groundless, how could it ground a practice?

One response to the contingency of architectural taste was to secure a secular foundation for architecture. As Horst Bredekamp argues in *The Lure of Antiquity and the Cult of the Machine*, fine art was disconnected from utilitarian technology by eighteenth-century writers, such as Johann Joachim Winckelmann, who posited fine art as a medium for orienting humanity toward nature and politics.[45] The enlightenment projects of Jefferson and Latrobe followed this line of thought to a large extent. For them the choice of style was entwined in what it could do for civic life, and classicism was by association an embodiment of the "republican simplicity" that they saw as the destiny of the United States. In 1810 Latrobe compared the formation of taste to a national language and promoted republican simplicity through an alignment of Grecian arts with individual freedom.[46]

In this view architecture belonged to a nationalistic project. As Lafever wrote, "It has been justly observed that the public at large has a claim over the architecture of a country."[47] Architecture is "a common property, in as much as it involves the national taste and character." The architect did not have a right to invention independent of the nation because the root of architectural taste was the need to embody republicanism and to orient the body politic.[48] Architectural form embodied the relationship between individual and collective by finding something material—the nation—on which architecture as a fine art could be contingent.

In contrast, Walter's response to this contingency resolved the dialectic of religion and taste by imbuing the medium through which the professional architect worked with divine roots: republican theology rather than a-theological republicanism. Understanding taste as an effect of the ray of immortality conveyed by the human soul transformed the distinction between functional and fine arts into two types: lower and higher. While providing for the basic material needs of human life was a requirement for architecture, meeting the spiritual needs of a fallen creation that pursued the divine, although always imperfectly and incompletely, was a higher calling. The latter vocation was guided by the universalizing historical narrative through which the project of American nationalism was aimed at the sanctification of the globe. Thus architecture embodied a historical relationship between individual and divine drama as much as individual and nation.

The immediate recommendations of these two approaches varied only in degree. Christianity was threaded through the metaphysics and epistemology of indifferentism in the early American republic, and ultimately the prescriptions for the individual and nation given by Jefferson and Latrobe's republicanism and by Walter's republican theology were similar. Taste, both divine and worldly, was largely understood through the lens of associationism, shaped by the intense influence of Scottish Enlightenment philosophy and political theory on early American intellectuals. In the associationist model, form and meaning were related through repeated alignments rather than absolute necessity.[49] Architecture mattered as a moral and political technology.[50] Architecture's higher calling was to produce ornamental excess over and above mere building in order to encourage the progress of national sanctification. Although this view was not unique in architectural discourse, it is striking how the views of Walter and Latrobe converge in situating judgments of meaningful association in a philosophical anthropology intertwined with a particular view of history. Personal improvement and national progress were understood as aspects of the same metaphysics. Control of the political technology of architecture required a practitioner aware of the associated ethical responsibilities, which were formulated in turn through knowledge of progressive architectural history.

Enlightenment and material progress as supposedly experienced in American architecture were deeply bound up with religion—Yankee ingenuity was likewise Yankee faith. The educated white gentlemanly body of Walter, or any other member of the American Institution of Architects, acted as a particular standing in for a universal, a subject who existed in the world and through knowledge of history understood and participated in cosmic order. This body's supposedly nonindigenous status obscured its particular indigeneity by claiming a view of history's grand narrative.

Republican theology's inscription of the white Protestant gentleman's experience as a form of transcendental subjectivity is key. Walter's form of explicit religious argument would fade from architectural discourse after the Civil War within the context of the first university-based architecture programs. Yet the focus on history as a form of justification remained, and the structure of that history remained deeply theological and progressive. Even a cursory pass through the history textbooks used in the first full-fledged architecture schools established at American universities reveals a similar narrative structure. For example, Columbia architectural history professor A. D. F. Hamlin's *Textbook of the History of Architecture* (1896) mirrors the racial and ethno-nationalistic narrative and the dualistic metaphysics of these earlier American histories, as does the extensively used *A History of Architecture on the Comparative Method* (1896), by English architectural historian Sir Banister Fletcher.[51]

The Hegelian architectural histories of the twentieth century, which unlike Hegel (but exactly like Walter) did not see architecture as an art that had been passed by in Spirit's advancement, likewise told a story of universal progress. The narrative of architectural salvation is present, for example, in Sigfried Giedion's *Space, Time, and Architecture* (1941). And in the later emergence of the tradition of architectural phenomenology, there remains a markedly Christian set of universalizing commitments to grand historical narratives, to the restoration of human wholeness, and to a conception of architecture's ethical agency.[52] To acknowledge the traces of republican theology in these histories is to recognize the ways in which our supposedly secular conception of architecture remains inscribed with the religious. And to see these traces is to begin to understand how the presentation of the professional as nonindigenous is one of the most deeply indigenous and imperial acts.[53]

1 Minard Lafever, *The Architectural Instructor: Containing a History of Architecture from the Earliest Ages to the Present Time* (New York: G. P. Putnam & Co., 1856), 15.

2 Benjamin Henry Latrobe, *The Journals of Benjamin Henry Latrobe, 1799–1820: From Philadelphia to New Orleans*, eds. Edward C. Carter II, John C. Van Horne, and Lee W. Formwalt, vol. 3 (New Haven, CT: Yale University Press, 1980), 225–30.

3 Latrobe, *Journals*, 226.

4 See Mary N. Woods, *From Craft to Profession: The Practice of Architecture in Nineteenth-Century America* (Berkeley, CA: University of California Press, 1999), 9–26.

5 Following Caroline Winterer, I write "enlightenment" in lowercase; see Caroline Winterer, *American Enlightenments: Pursuing Happiness in the Age of Reason* (New Haven, CT: Yale University Press, 2016).

6 Frederick Jackson Turner, "The Significance of the Frontier in American History," in *Proceedings of the Forty-First Annual Meeting of the State Historical Society of Wisconsin* (Madison, WI: State Historical Society of Wisconsin, 1894).

7 I think here, indirectly, of Simon Critchley, *The Faith of the Faithless: Experiments in Political Theology* (London and New York: Verso Books, 2012).

8 Benjamin T. Lynerd, *Republican Theology: The Civil Religion of American Evangelicals* (Oxford, UK: Oxford University Press, 2014). Republican theology intersected three traditions of thought. The first was a moderation of traditional Calvinist theology, which preached the absolute depravity of human beings and their complete dependence on God for

salvation and sanctified daily living in the corrupt world. Moderate Calvinism restrained the extent of depravity and softened the division of the holy God and fallen humanity's worldly existence, thus attempting to uphold divine providence while emphasizing personal responsibility for self-improvement; see Donald Harvey Meyer, *The Instructed Conscience: The Shaping of the American National Ethic* (Philadelphia: University of Pennsylvania Press, 1972), 15. This moderation overlapped well with republican political theory, which tasked the individual as a citizen with the sanctification of the nation. Human agency was not passive nor was religion apolitical. Improvement was both personal and collective, and the model of political theory and history was Whiggish. As Mark Noll puts it, "America's main Calvinist theologians, especially in the North, were never Whig to uniform or identical degrees, but as even brief attention to major figures can show, they were nonetheless all still Whig theologians." Mark A. Noll, *America's God: From Jonathan Edwards to Abraham Lincoln* (Oxford, UK: Oxford University Press, 2002), 313. These religious and political commitments were crossed with the epistemology and theory of mind of Scottish Enlightenment philosophy, which emphasized universal conditions of good and common sense. Thus republican theology organized a set of beliefs around the idea that a divinely-inspired good sense could guide the nation chosen to play an exceptional, progressive historical role.

9 See Lynerd, *Republican Theology*, 1–16, 114.

10 See Bruce Laverty, Michael J. Lewis, and Michele Taillon Taylor, eds., *Monument to Philanthropy: The Design and Building of Girard College, 1832–1848* (Philadelphia: Girard College, 1998).

11 While the notes for his 1840 lectures appear to be lost, at least one of Walter's articles in the *Journal of the Franklin Institute* (*JFI*) is an extract from this first set of lectures: "On Glass as Applied to Architecture—Extract from a Lecture on the Architecture of the Middle Ages, Delivered before the Franklin Institute, by T. U. WALTER, Professor of Architecture, December 10, 1840," *Journal of the Franklin Institute* 1, no. 4 (April 1841): 266–67. Walter published several other articles in the JFI in 1841 that may also be developed from this series, including "Architecture" (January 1841), "Street Architecture" (February 1841), "The Orders" (April 1841), and "On Chromatics as Pertaining to Architecture" (July 1841). See Jeffrey A. Cohen, "Building a Discipline: Early Institutional Settings for Architectural Education in Philadelphia, 1804–1890," *Journal of the Society of Architectural Historians* 53, no. 2 (1994): 153–54; Jhennifer A. Amundson, "'Vast Avenues to Knowledge': Thomas Ustick Walter's Books," in *American Architects and Their Books, 1840–1915*, ed. Kenneth Hafertepe and James F. O'Gorman (Amherst, MA: University of Massachusetts Press, 2007), 63–94.

12 Walter to Welling, March 9, 1871, Thomas Ustick Walter Letterbooks, Thomas U. Walter Collection, The Athenaeum of Philadelphia (WTU).

13 This argument was echoed in Walter's eleventh annual address to the AIA, when he said that only private, select competitions should exist; Box 20, Folder 286, WTU. It also echoes an 1866 letter sent in response to an open competition for the design of the War Office, which was signed by a number of architects, including Walter; Upjohn et al. to Brevet Lt. Col. T. J. Treadwell et al., December 6, 1866, Box 3, Folder 29, WTU.

14 See the two-page biography of Walter in William Cathcart, ed., *The Baptist Encyclopaedia: A Dictionary of the Doctrines, Ordinances ... of the General History of the Baptist Denomination in All Lands* (Philadelphia: L. H. Everts, 1883), 1207–8.

15 "The Church," Acts 1, February 19, 1860, Box 21, Folder 315, WTU. Walter writes that "the church visible consists of baptized believers in Christ, and of none others."

16 Walter's church in Philadelphia prior to moving to Washington, D.C., was the Spruce Street Baptist Church. After his time in D.C., Walter moved to Germantown, an area that had begun to develop as one of Philadelphia's first suburbs in the 1830s. His later churches were 2nd Baptist Church of Germantown and Memorial Baptist Church of Mt. Pleasant. Walter's diaries record attending these three churches plus the E Street Baptist Church in Washington, D.C. regularly, but he mentions attending services at others, such as the 2nd Church Southwark and the Arch St. Church in Philadelphia and the 13th Street Baptist and Calvary Baptist Churches in Washington, D.C. He also refers to the 2nd Baptist Church of Germantown as Upsall Street Baptist Church (today spelled Upsal). See the 1837–87 diaries in Boxes 25–31, WTU. In Germantown and Mt. Pleasant, Walter also served as a deacon. See Cathcart, *The Baptist Encyclopaedia*, 1208.

17 Sunday school was one of the many means of institution building that took shape in American Protestant churches in the first decades of the nineteenth century, and it was a valuable tool in a church's arsenal for using knowledge to create moral and material order. See Anne M. Boylan, *Sunday School: The Formation of an American Institution, 1790–1880* (New Haven, CT: Yale University Press, 1988). Sunday school already was a well-established tradition Philadelphia when Walter began teaching. In 1791 Benjamin Rush and others in Philadelphia founded the "Sunday School Society." Robert H. Abzug, *Cosmos Crumbling: American Reform and the Religious Imagination* (New York: Oxford University Press, 1994), 39.

18 "The Secrets of a Sunday-School Teacher's Success," January 21, 1868, Box 21, Folder 307, WTU.

19 As famed preacher Lyman Beecher said in an 1803 sermon, evidence confirms the "belief of the practicability of suppressing vice, by means of societies instituted for that purpose." Lyman Beecher, *The Practicability of Suppressing Vice, by Means of Societies Instituted for That Purpose* (New London, CT: Samuel Green, 1804), 10. See also Francis Wayland, *The Elements of Moral Science* (Cambridge, MA: Belknap Press of Harvard University Press, 1963), 308.

20 "The Church," Acts I, February 9, 1860, Box 21, Folder 315, WTU. Parts of this lesson are copied and paraphrased from multiple sources, including the entry on "church" in the Presbyterian *Bible Dictionary for the Use of Bible Classes, Schools and Families*, 3rd ed. (Philadelphia: Presbyterian Board of Publication, 1851), 102–3. Also, Albert Barnes, *Notes, Explanatory and Practical, on the Acts of the Apostles, Designed for Bible Class and Sunday-Schools*, 2nd ed. (New York: Leavitt Lord & Co., 1835). See also, Lynerd, *Republican Theology: The Civil Religion of American Evangelicals*, 94–98. Lyman Beecher, for example, declared the church "a society incorporated by the God of heaven with specific chartered privileges" whose purpose was quasi-architectural: "each church is a body corporate for the exclusive purpose of promoting the benevolent designs of the Most High God." Lyman Beecher, *The Design, Rights, and Duties of Local Churches* (Andover: Flagg and Gould, 1819), 5. In this sermon, a historical grand narrative is traced from the initial patriarchy of priesthood and a single body of human beings, to the break from the pastoral into agricultural and commercial states and the formation of multiple people groups and nations (in which the Jews were unique), and finally to the present Christian age of the church. See also Gerhard Kittel, ed., *Theological Dictionary of the New Testament*, vol. 3 (Grand Rapids, MI: Eerdmans, 1965), 500–536. As Karl Ludwig Schmidt points out in Kittel, the word *ekklesia* has cultic and political origins and meant: "Those who are summoned and called together by the herald." But this Christian cult is one that desires to be distinct from all others and stands against the entire world, including "the so-called religious world" of false religions.

21 Walter to Welling, March 9, 1871, WTU.

22 See Beecher, *Design*; Robert Cary Long, *The Ancient Architecture of America, Its Historical Value and Parallelism of Development with the Architecture of the Old World* (New York: Bartlett & Welford, 1849), 12.

23 Magali Sarfatti Larson, *The Rise of Professionalism: Monopolies of Competence and Sheltered Markets* (New Brunswick, NJ: Transaction Publishers, 2012).

24 Abzug, *Cosmos Crumbling*; Jonathan D. Sassi, *A Republic of Righteousness: The Public Christianity of the Post-Revolutionary New England Clergy* (Oxford, UK: Oxford University Press, 2001), 4.

25 Jefferson famously insisted on this particular architectural associationism in the early American republic. Richard Guy Wilson, "Thomas Jefferson's Classical Architecture: An American Agenda," in *Thomas Jefferson, the Classical World, and Early America*, ed. Peter S. Onuf and Nicholas Cole (Charlottesville, VA: University of Virginia Press, 2011), 99–127. The relation between Greece and Rome for early American architects and writers on architecture was complicated. While having many positive qualities, such as robustness and scale, Rome was also viewed as brought down by the excesses of luxury. Republican simplicity, as it was often described, was seen as better embodied by Grecian restraint and order. See Thomas Ustick Walter, *Thomas U. Walter: The Lectures on Architecture, 1841–53*, ed. Jhennifer A. Amundson (Philadelphia: Athenaeum of Philadelphia, 2006), 139.

26 See *Constitution and By-Laws of the American Institution of Architects* (Philadelphia: Lydia R. Bailey, 1837). Reprinted in Louisa Hall, "Artificer to Architect in America" (PhD diss., Radcliffe College, 1954).

27 Aaron Garrett, "Anthropology: The 'Original' of Human Nature," in *The Cambridge Companion to the Scottish Enlightenment*, ed. Alexander Broadie (Cambridge, UK: Cambridge University Press, 2003), 89.

28 "The Creation," June 16, 1872, Box 22, Folder 341, WTU; see also "The Creation," June 23, 1872, Box 22, Folder 342; "The Creation," November 30, 1856, Box 23, Folder 407; and "The Creation," November 29, 1957, Box 23, Folder 436. Walter appeals to Milton's description of these origins: "it was a place / Chos'n by the sovran planter, when he fram'd / All things to man's delightful use." John Milton, *Paradise Lost*, ed. Barbara K. Lewalski (Malden, UK: Wiley-Blackwell, 2007), 126, ln. 690. See also the reference to this section in Louisa C. Tuthill, *History of Architecture, from the Earliest Times; Its Present Condition in Europe and the United States; with a Biography of Eminent Architects, and a Glossary of Architectural Terms* (Philadelphia: Lindsay and Blakiston, 1848), 18; Louisa C. Tuthill, *Architecture. Part I. Ancient Architecture* (New Haven, CT: Hezekiah Howe, 1831), 4. Walter often cites Milton as one of the few works of fiction he approved. See Walter, *Lectures*, 195–96. On his invocation of Milton in the discussion of Creation and the Fall, see "The Fall," Gen. 2:8, 9, 15–17; 3:1–6, January 29, 1965, Box 21, folder 300 and "Effects of the Fall," December 17, 1854, Box 22, Folder 360, WTU.

29 Edward Said describes Milton as characterizing the postlapsarian beginnings of language in much the same way: "Human discourse, like Paradise Lost, lives with the memory of origins long since violently cut off from it: having begun, discourse can never recover its origins in the unity and unspoken Word of God's Being." Edward W. Said, *Beginnings: Intention and Method* (New York: Columbia University Press, 1975), 280.

30 Walter, *Lectures*, 35. Walter borrowed this phrase from Lord Byron's description of Apollo Belvedere in *Childe Harold's Pilgrimage*, Canto IV, stanza CLXII.

31 Walter, *Lectures*, 33–34.

32 "The Creation," Box 23, Folder 407, WTU. This description is very similar to the one Walter used in his lectures, Walter, *Lectures*, 34–35. The comparison of human architecture to the works of birds and beavers was a recurrent theme in nineteenth century architectural discourse.

33 Like God making the world a residence fit for humans, humanity's progress was tied to work. As Max Weber describes the last lines of *Paradise Lost*, one feels a "powerful expression of the Puritan's serious attention to this world, his acceptance of his life in the world as a task." Max Weber, *The Protestant Ethic and the Spirit of Capitalism*, trans. Talcott Parsons (London: Routledge, 1992), 47.

34 Walter, *Lectures*, 34–35.

35 A useful (and telling) account of just this sort of re-presentation is developed in Karsten Harries, *The Ethical Function of Architecture* (Cambridge, MA: MIT Press, 1998), 118ff.

36 Walter's Journal 1834–36, Box 19, Folder 263, WTU.

37 Walter, *Lectures*, 34.

38 "Landing from the Ark," Gen. 8:15–22 and 9:1–16, July 14, 1867, Box 21, Folder 303, WTU. However, by this account the Egyptians were not of the same blackness as the descendants of Canaan, who were destined for enslavement. I will develop a detailed reading of racialization, racism, and white supremacy in the narratives of architectural history in the early American republic in forthcoming publications.

39 See Robert A. Nisbet, *History of the Idea of Progress* (New York: Basic Books, 1980); Reinhart Koselleck, *Futures Past: On the Semantics of Historical Time* (New York: Columbia University Press, 2004); Tom F. Peters, *Building the Nineteenth Century* (Cambridge, MA: MIT Press, 1996), 26ff; Sigfried Giedion, *Mechanization Takes Command: A Contribution to Anonymous History* (New York: Oxford University Press, 1948), 717.

40 Address to the eleventh annual convention of the American Institute of Architects, Box 20, Folder 286, WTU. Having been a key member of the American Institution of Architects, Walter was again a key player in the AIA's formation, roughly two decades after the first attempt had fizzled out. The revived professional body first met in 1857 at the office of Richard Morris Hunt, who had who worked in Walter's office upon his return from the École des Beaux-Arts in 1855, while Walter was serving as the fourth Architect of the Capitol. Marcus Whiffen and Frederick Koeper, *American Architecture: Volume 2, 1860–1976* (Cambridge, MA: MIT Press, 1983), *xiii*.

41 Winterer, *American Enlightenments*.

42 See Cornel West, "Race and Modernity," in *The Cornel West Reader* (New York: Basic Civitas Books, 1999), 55–86.

43 Long, *Ancient Architecture*.

44 Nisbet, *History*, 197–206.

45 Horst Bredekamp, *The Lure of Antiquity and the Cult of the Machine: The Kunstkammer and the Evolution of Nature, Art, and Technology* (Princeton, NJ: Markus Wiener Publishers, 1995), 94ff.

46 Benjamin Henry Latrobe, *The Correspondence and Miscellaneous Papers of Benjamin Henry Latrobe* (New Haven, CT: Yale University Press, 1984), 65–91.

47 Lafever, *Architectural Instructor*, 16.

48 See Dell Upton, "Architectural History or Landscape History?," *Journal of Architectural Education* 44, no. 4 (1991): 195–99.

49 Lafever, for example, cites Archibald Alison to this effect soon after the initial quote in this paper. On the influence of Scottish Enlightenment thought, see Daniel N. Robinson, "The Scottish Enlightenment and the American Founding," *The Monist* 90, no. 2 (2007): 170–81; Terence Martin, *The Instructed Vision: Scottish Common Sense Philosophy and the Origins of American Fiction* (Bloomington, IN: Indiana University Press, 1961); Benjamin W. Redekop, "Reid's Influence in Britain, Germany, France, and America," in *The Cambridge Companion to Thomas Reid*, eds. Terence Cuneo and René van Woudenberg (Cambridge, UK: Cambridge University Press, 2004), 313–40; Meyer, *Instructed Conscience*.

50 As Jeffry Morrison points out, we can see many similarities between Jefferson and the more religiously devout, like John Witherspoon, because they shared a moral anthropology that is deeply indebted to Scottish Enlightenment thought. Jeffry H. Morrison, *John Witherspoon and the Founding of the American Republic* (Notre Dame, IN: University of Notre Dame Press, 2005), 51–62.

51 On Banister Fletcher, see Gülsüm Baydar Nalbantoglu, "Toward Postcolonial Openings: Rereading Sir Banister Fletcher's 'History of Architecture,'" *Assemblage* 35 (April 1998): 6–17.

52 See Jorge Otero-Pailos, *Architecture's Historical Turn: Phenomenology and the Rise of the Postmodern* (Minneapolis: University of Minnesota Press, 2010); Benjamin M. Roth, "The Abetment of Nihilism: Architectural Phenomenology's Ethical Project," ed. Bryan E. Norwood, *Log* 42 (Winter/Spring 2018): 127–35.

53 I would like to thank Azra Dawood, Aleksandr Bierig, and Lisa Haber-Thomson for their helpful comments on earlier drafts of this essay. I would also like to acknowledge the support of the Charles E. Peterson Senior Fellowship from the Athenaeum of Philadelphia, and in particular the assistance of Bruce Laverty, curator of architecture, in the research that led to this essay.

War, Visuality and the Militarized City

Zahra Malkani & Shahana Rajani

In the years since 9/11, Pakistan's largest city has been increasingly both represented and constituted as a key site in the global War On Terror: Karachi has been delimited by security analysts as an epicenter of terrorism in the twenty-first century and as "a distinctive battlefield."[1] It is described in international media as one of the most dangerous cities in the world. Violence permeates from and extends beyond the city boundaries, imbricating it within a larger geography of networked conflict, and marking it as one of the key sites across the globe rendered exceptional since the onset of the War on Terror. As a reflection of this new gaze, Karachi has been subject to immense transformation, shaped and structured increasingly in the interests and vision of an accelerating militarism, never more so than in the years following the launch of the paramilitary Karachi Operation in 2013: "a concerted campaign against lawlessness and terrorism in the city."[2] This essay explores the multidimensional and multilayered geography of militarization that has recently emerged in, and transformed, the fabric of Karachi.

Much has been written about the urbanization of warfare and both the causes and consequences of such processes. Stephen Graham argues that "contemporary warfare and terror now largely boils down to contests over the spaces, symbols, meanings, support systems or power structures of cities and urban regions. As a result, war, terrorism and cities are redefining each other in complex... ways."[3] In fact, war and the city have always been intimately entangled and mutually constitutive. Urban form as we know it today emerged through a history of militarism in which cities have always acted as agents.[4] The ever-present potentiality of political violence and warfare is therefore inscribed and woven into the fabric of the city by its very design. However, the global scale of contemporary warfare represents a shift where "cities are no longer the bounded fortified spaces of old, but rather spaces of multiple networks and internal boundaries which simultaneously demand and defy fortification and defence."[5]

Urban militarization today refers not simply to the placement of military entities and activities in urban space but to a situation in which warfare permeates urban life. It refers to the establishment and entrenchment of borders across the surface of the city and to the ways these processes become a contemporary way of life. This essay attempts to understand the "wider geographical imprint of militarism and military activities."[6] In Karachi, we take into account the ways in which space, discourse, visuality and social relations have been structured and mobilized in service of the "everywhere war" that has increasingly come to saturate and shape life in the city.[7] We look not only at the spatial geography of militarization, but at the ways in which the project of boundless war has come to shape the wider landscape of civilian spheres of life, paying particular attention to the representational and discursive strategies.

Much of the violence of the Karachi Operation unfolds at the peripheries of the city in spaces discursively produced by the state, law-enforcement and media as "no-go zones"—a term that demarcates spaces so rife with violence that they cannot be entered. These spaces are inhabited largely by Pashtun refugee and indigenous Sindhi and Baloch populations and have become proxy sites in the War on Terror. Communities are policed and surveilled for the purported potentiality of insurgents in devastating cycles of raids, resettlement, and ruination. The violence surrounding these transformations is both obscured and upheld by a discursive and visual regime dedicated to the legitimization of war. For a city so deeply imbricated in contemporary discussions surrounding war, geopolitics and security, it is important to question the different ways in which Karachi is being reimagined in popular representations at this moment. Therefore, we study the ways in which modern war visuality plays an essential role in sanitizing the escalating imperial and state-sanctioned violence, and activating the city as a whole in service of it.

Discourse, visuality and processes of 'development' are also a key configuration here. Development is deeply entangled with, and constitutive of, the processes of militarization and securitization across the city. Urban development has always been a militaristic process, couched in militaristic language and geared towards militaristic ends. The military-development nexus in Karachi spans a vast range of projects and processes, from military-backed real estate and infrastructural development to a new imperial aid infrastructure couched in 'Countering Violent Extremism' (CVE) discourse that is saturating and re-structuring the art, culture and education spheres. To fully understand the geography of violence in Karachi we explore multiple manifestations of this nexus: a real estate mega-project, literature festivals and public art interventions.

Military and Land Accumulation

Constituted in 1959 to patrol and protect the border areas of the newly formed nation-state of Pakistan, the paramilitary Pakistan Rangers police a domain that grows as borders become diffused and dispersed, no longer confined to the outer limits of territories. First called into Karachi in 1989 to restore law and order on the politically charged campus of Karachi University, the Rangers have remained in the city ever since. Over the past decade, their jurisdiction has expanded exponentially, and their powers have extended to combating terrorism as Karachi was a focal point in the national and international War on Terror. As the border patrol fortifies, restructures and securitizes the city, the city borders have been drawn and redrawn. New borders crop up every day, functioning in turn as a key technology for the annihilation of landscapes and ecologies. New securitized infrastructures emerge through which the border patrol is able to apply unprecedented intensity to their methods of policing and surveillance of populations.

"The violence in Karachi is related to its land,"[8] architect Perween Rehman said in a 2011 interview, two years before she was killed on the streets of the city by unknown assailants. Perween Rehman had been working with the NGO Orangi Pilot Project, and much of her practice involved mapping and advocating for the legalization of informal settlements inhabited by indigenous and refugee communities at risk of dispossession due to public and private development schemes. Interviewed at a time when hysteria and media coverage around violence in the city was escalating, Rehman highlighted the centrality of land to the many forms of conflict in Karachi. Perween Rehman's words and work, and her subsequent murder just months prior to the launch of the Karachi Operation, highlight the stakes of land accumulation and development in Karachi. In the years since the onset of the Karachi Operation, these processes become evermore brazen and militarized.

The interests of Pakistani military in land accumulation in Karachi have long been recognized and predate the Karachi Operation. While exact data regarding military land holdings is difficult to obtain, it is most comprehensively discussed in Ayesha Siddiqa's banned book, *Military Inc.* (2005). In a chapter titled "The New Land Barons," Siddiqa states: "The Pakistani military is one of the biggest landowners in the country. As a single group, the armed forces own more land than any other institution or group. The military controls about 11.58 million acres... [and] unlike any other state institution, the armed forces have the capacity to convert the usage of state land from official purposes to private ones. In addition, they are the only state organization that has institutionalized the acquisition of state land for distribution amongst the members of their fraternity."[9]

In Karachi, military land holdings primarily consist of vast expanses of cantonment land, or housing schemes generated by military subsidiaries that usually take the form of securitized enclaves built on questionably acquired land. The military justifies its land acquisitions based on the inherited colonial tradition of granting land to military personnel, or the need for housing for the families of 'martyrs,' or, as Siddiqa describes, "the greater logic of the nation paying the price for its military's social security." Siddiqa argues "land is acquired not just for capital accumulation, but also to exhibit the military's authority and power in relation to other stakeholders such as the landed-feudal class and the masses."[10]

In the years since the Karachi Operation, military-backed housing schemes have multiplied. The Defence Housing Authority City (DHA City) and Bahria Town Karachi are two important examples. Both developments are located in Gadap Town, a neighborhood at the northwestern peripheries of Karachi formerly inhabited by indigenous and refugee communities. Land in these communities was used for agriculture, and primary livelihoods were structured around this use. Militarization has thus aided a violent annihilation in the restructuring of these city outskirts for high-yield real estate. The securitized enclaves and gated communities that have emerged on this land, built by the military and subsidiaries, serve to further divide, surveil and police the city. Paul Virilio has argued, in *City of Panic*, that securitized enclaves and gated communities serve as a tactic to further immerse the city in a new militarized aesthetic, they create forms and structures of living that divide and fragment any sense of an urban community fabric.[11] Such transformations in the urban landscape serve to further entrench the Karachi populace in a state of total war.

The Pakistan Rangers have inscribed and fully immersed themselves into the city's diverse spaces in other diverse ways. Since 1999, the Rangers have been using the historic heritage building called Jinnah Courts, in the city center, as their headquarters—a structure that once served as a hostel for law students. In 2015, it was reported by the newspaper *Pakistan Today* that the Rangers were running a construction business on the premises of Karachi University, the city's largest public university.[12] The same year, another daily newspaper, *Dawn*, reported that Rangers personnel had moved into the centrally located Radio Pakistan building that housed the archives of Pakistan's historical radio broadcast network.[13] Since 2013, Karachi has also seen a proliferation of paramilitary checkpoints throughout the city, and multiple concrete structures painted in camouflage and adorned with slogans and army propaganda. Posters and billboards supporting the military have popped up in every neighborhood, radically transforming the visuality of the city with increasingly ubiquitous military presence. As Giroux suggests, notions of community are now organized not only around flag-waving displays of patriotism, but also around collective fears and militarization of public space and visual culture.[14]

Terror Maps and Militarized Visualities

Modern war-visuality plays an essential role in sanitizing and selling military violence, as well as turning the citizenry into participants of war. In the months prior to the launch of the Karachi Operation, a series of maps were produced and circulated in leading English newspapers. These maps played a crucial role in building public support for the operation: they reproduced an imperial visuality that, alongside media discourse, presented a city teeming with violence. Crafting 'red zones' and 'no-go zones,' the new borders marked across the city conjured visions of danger, terror and insurgency. Through press briefings and media reports, the narrative of the *ghairmehfooz* (insecure) city was created and enforced, where living spaces were reduced to sites of "sneaking terrorist attacks."[15] Barely known but vividly imagined, certain neighborhoods and ethnic communities entered the public imaginary through maps in phantasmic form. As colors bled from map to city, a 'red zone' became indisputable truth.

Counterinsurgency in the post 9/11 era, as Nicholas Mirzoeff argues, deploys itself as a visualized field to produce legitimacy.[16] Geographic visualization has become an important military tactic through which counterinsurgency seeks to render a culture in its own image. In this explicitly cultural war, the discursive practice of visuality comes to have new and material consequences for the social and spatial fabric of the city. As Judith Butler argues, the apparatus of military violence has become so closely entangled with that of visualization that "there is no way to separate, under present historical conditions, the material reality of war from those representational regimes through which it operates and which rationalize its own operation."[17]

Six months prior to the launch of the Karachi Operation, in March 2013, *The Express Tribune* published a story entitled "Where law enforcers fear to tread: The entry fee for these spots of Karachi may be your life." It featured a map that visualized no-go zones of the city.[18] Thirteen complete no-go zones were presented, marked in red, and twenty-nine partial no-go zones were marked in orange. The article explained that since the Kalosha II Operation in South Waziristan in 2004, Karachi has seen an increasing influx of Mehsud tribesmen. Embedded in this influx are "Taliban militants who have settled in Pakhtun-dominated areas in the city and have established an iron grip in these neighbourhoods." Quoting the Deputy Superintendent of Police Qamar Ahmed, the article warned that if left unchecked, these no-go areas would proliferate.

This report and map were key evidence in an ongoing *suo motu* case in the Pakistan Supreme Court that addressed the issue of increased violence and killings in Karachi. Since the case began in October 2011, law enforcement agencies had been adamantly denying the existence of no-go areas. During the hearing on March 29, 2013, Chief Justice Iftikhar Muhammad Chaudhry included the *Express Tribune* map and report as part of the proceedings and ordered both the Director General of Rangers and the Inspector General of Sindh Police to testify in response. In the following week, the police submitted a report to the court which, for the first time, admitted the presence of no-go zones in Karachi. "So, you've admitted the newspaper's report is correct," said Justice Khilji Arif Hussain, referring to the special report and map. "Yes," replied IG Baloch.[19] These exchanges illustrate the productive power of the map in creating certain truth claims about the city. Once mapped as objective truth, the no-go zone became an irrefutable reality. This unveiling has since become central to the public imaginary of Karachi.

The frequency with which such maps were circulated in the media prior to and during the Karachi Operation helped to create and intensify panic around Karachi's imagined descent into terror and violence. Routine visualizations of a lawless and volatile city were used to assert the need for intense security measures. These maps, while claiming to "open up" and make the city transparent, also worked to 'close down' urban space under an intensified regime of surveillance and violent military control.[20] The scientificity of the map, which allowed these visualizations to be consumed as objective and truthful representation, became an important means through which the paramilitary began to assert its command over the battle space, or the "urban jungle," of Karachi.[21] Derek Gregory similarly argues that such maps produced and sustained a militarized visuality that was integral to the US invasion of Iraq. These public displays "worked to stabilize the city, visually, imaginatively and rhetorically," into an ordered, coherent totality.[22] While urban war is constantly fluid and in the process of construction, a map resolves the city into a single definite picture, becoming a sovereign map. The no-go zones became those "dark, labrynthine, structureless places that needed to be unveiled for the production of order through scientific, planning and military technologies."[23]

Chad Harris argues that those maps that visualize the abstract realm of 'battlespace' "detect objects and people, but also produce both objects on the ground and surveillant subjects."[24] Visual representations form a dangerous feedback loop where security paradigms that depend on abstractions of terror derive power partly from the concrete images that abstractions purport to explain. Jordan Crandall calls this conjuring a mode of "armed seeing." Through the illusion of the no-go zone and the specter of terrorism, a military colonizes the entire city, unleashing violence "not only on the side which is redlined, but also upon the side that is protected [through] a mechanism of control in relation to an exterior danger produced for that purpose."[25] In this process, the city becomes a limitless battlespace, or a battlescape, what Gregory calls an "everywhere war."[26] The Karachi Operation similarly unleashes a boundless and unending process of militarization in which everything becomes a site of permanent war—a limitless battlespace with no edges and no end.

These visuals worked in tandem with the post 9/11 global security, development and media discourse. In September 2012, *Al Jazeera* published an interactive map titled "Karachi's Killing Fields." This was perhaps the first terror map of Karachi, published six months before the *Express Tribune* map. It provided readers with detailed instructions on how to use the map:

> Our interactive illustrates homicide data for the years 2011 and 2012, broken down by police station, letting you explore a map of the city's violence... The default view shows you the city's most dangerous districts. To get deeper into the data, click on the arrow in the top right corner. From there, you can explore the Detailed Homicide Data tab, which will show you all of the city's police stations, as well as administrative and electoral maps of the city.[27]

In this map, dangerous districts appeared as 'default.' They were depicted as a natural, intrinsic part of Karachi's urban landscape which was defined in the article's by-line as "the world's most dangerous megacity." The prompt to explore the city is similar to the frequently invoked metaphor of 'walking through maps' and these instructions worked to virtually erase the distinction between the city and its representation.[28] The format of the interactive map produced a compelling spatial vector of terrorism framed through the lens of objectivity and scientific data. However, in the process, these maps flattened and effaced the three-dimensional social space of the city, staging it for global consumption.

Karachi's portrayal as a ruined and repellent city, under siege, is not a neutral act of representing the city as it is. These maps are not disinterested presentations of statistical information, but rather reflect the desires and fears of their authors and audience. They are highly politicized representations that exemplify the persisting relations of a cultural colonialism, produced through the performance of imaginative geographies. Through a series of spatializations, these representational constructions fold distance into difference. Edward Said argued that imaginative geographies work by multiplying partitions and enclosures that serve to demarcate 'the same' from 'the other' while also constructing and calibrating a gap between them by "designating in one's mind a familiar space that is ours and an unfamiliar space beyond ours which is theirs."[29] The differences and distances that constitute imaginative geographies are set in motion and made meaningful through cultural practices. These representational regimes are reflective of a global world order, as Graham argues, in which contemporary reality is split into the civilization of the rich, modern north and the separate global south, characterized by backwardness, danger, pathology and anarchy.[30]

Over the past decade, Karachi has been described with increasing authority as a "failed and feral" city in global security and media discourse: Richard Norton, in a 2003 paper for the *Naval War College Review*, devised a taxonomy of "feral cities," encouraging readers to:

> Imagine a great metropolis covering hundreds of square miles. Once a vital component in a national economy, this sprawling urban environment is now a vast collection of blighted buildings, an immense petri dish of both ancient and new diseases, a territory where the rule of law has long been replaced by near anarchy... Yet this city would still be globally connected. It would possess at least a modicum of commercial linkages, and some of its inhabitants would have access to the world's most modern communication and computing technologies. It would, in effect, be a feral city.[31]

Norton claims that while such cities have been routinely imagined in apocalyptic movies and science-fiction genres, these imaginations have now become reality: While "cities have descended into savagery in the past," feral cities "will pose security threats on a scale hitherto not encountered."[32] Norton constantly uses biomedical terms to describe these challenges. He warns that "the toxic environment" of a feral city poses uniquely severe threats—it is "a 'petri dish' of deadly virulent epidemics and dangerous terrorist activities."[33] Disease and terrorism are used interchangeably to render the city as a pathological space. Norton's discussion illustrates the ways in which counter-insurgency and military strategy are envisioned as a surgical practice. Norton continues the use of medicalized language to propose a diagnostic tool to assess the 'health' of cities. In it, measurements representing a healthy city are green, those that would suggest cause for concern are yellow, and those that indicate danger are red. He explains that "the picture of a city that emerges is a mosaic, and like an artist's mosaic it can be expected to contain more than one colour."[34]

The *Express Tribune* map takes its cue from these discourses to produce a similar medical diagnosis of the city. Just like an x-ray scan of the body, maps of red zones and hotspots become irrefutable depictions of the health of the city. The *Express Tribune* report furthered this medical analogy by describing red zones as "cancer" spreading through the city.[35] General Raheel Sharif has also frequently described terrorism as a cancer that needs to be rooted out from Pakistan. By describing terrorism in these terms, military operations are likened to surgeons cutting out cancerous tissue. In visualizing the no-go zone, militaries practice a capacity to fragment the body of the city, and isolate and target a tumor.[36] Rational-scientific means become inseparable from a series of truth claims about the danger posed by a target. Military violence appears intrinsically therapeutic and abstract, another bloody surgical reality of an operation enacted on human lives.

Enforcing the no-go zone

The Pakistan Rangers launched the second phase of the Karachi Operation in 2015 with a special mandate to "police, surveil and secure" the "vast suburbs of Karachi."[37]

Inhabited largely by Pashtun refugee and indigenous Sindhi and Baloch populations, certain neighborhoods were systematically shrouded in darkness and mystery through the discourse of the no-go zone. Home to large populations of refugees from the war-torn northern regions of Pakistan—where a series of military operations since 9/11 have displaced millions—these refugee settlements are brutally policed and surveilled and have become proxy sites for the War on Terror. The Karachi Operation equipped the paramilitary with special powers of prosecution and investigation, utilising the 1997 Anti Terrorism Act (ATA). This included the power to seize property, the power to arrest without warrant, and the power to fire upon and use force as deemed necessary. In 2014, the Protection of Pakistan Act and amendments to the ATA expanded state impunity—Rangers could detain suspects without cause for up to ninety days. This legally enabled the paramilitary to use greater of violence than before.[38]

The peripheries of the city, neighborhoods such as Gadap and Malir, are also chosen sites for 'encounters'—the term used for the now almost daily processes by which citizens disappear. Unofficial reports record that between 2013 and 2017, four-hundred and forty four refugees from the Federally Administered Tribal Areas were killed in 'encounter killings' in Karachi.[39] The newspaper *Dawn* reports:

> According to police records, Malir saw 195 police encounters from January to October 2012, in which 18 people were killed and 276 arrested; the ratio of deaths to arrests—the 'kill rate'—was 6.5 per cent. Between February to June 2013, the kill rate was 17.6pc. In 2014, after the operation began, there were 186 encounters, in which 152 people died and 192 were arrested—the kill rate a whopping 79pc. Last year, there were 93 encounters resulting in 110 deaths and 89 arrests. That translates to the number of arrests falling 23pc below the number of people killed.[40]

Gadap and Malir emerge as favored sites for these activities, as a long-serving police official reports: "Men are airlifted from as far away as Fata[41] and brought here for [Karachi law enforcement] to dispatch."[42] In the no-go zones of Gadap and Malir, borders of citizenship are constantly made and remade. New borders are enforced by the Karachi Operation and serve to limit movement, access and visibility. The no-go zones are sites of containment, enclosure and opacity. Border lines displace indigenous and refugee neighborhoods such as Gadap by redrawing them as outside of national territory, in shadowlands where anything and everything can be and is done. Feldman explains that "the ubiquity of borders create flexible biopolitical zones, capable of traversing the globe, in which certain subjects are invited to occupy categories of life and wield power over the lives of others, while others are banished from sociality to the point of death."[43] The configuration of life-in-death "constitutes the kernel of the raciality of the War on Terror." Although Feldman is describing the exceptional site of the "Af-Pak" frontier, this argument holds true for the no-go zones of Karachi.

Drawing on Junaid Rana, Feldman explores how the production of national fear at the local everyday level is a practice, expanded through the creation of specific demonized figures.[44] Certain bodies are racialized not only in relation to terror but also in relation to certain ideas of illegality and criminality that are historically associated with racialized populations. The conceptual linkage relies on the logic of fungibility in which a number of objects, things and ideas are conflated into a particular racial figure—from the criminal to the illegal alien to the security threat to the terrorist.[45]

The Karachi Operation depends on this comparative racialization where Pashtun populations are suffused with the potential of terror through the rhetoric of illegality and criminality. The act of migration becomes a suspect activity in which particular kinds of labor and informal economies are deemed part of underground and illicit activities. Here refugee populations are constantly imagined as inherently linked to suspicious activity.

These biopolitical frontiers draw upon and re-enact older colonial violence that legitimates the production of racialized targets through a rubric of threat, fear, and terror. These frameworks invoke practices that mark the colonized body as irredeemably savage, wild, other. The Sindhi/Baloch native and the Pashtun refugee bear markers of criminality and illegality, that are rendered spectacularly visible in the emerging borderlands of Karachi.

Imagining landscapes of development

The violence of securitization infiltrates neighborhoods and communities hand in hand with processes of urban development and place annihilation. Stefan Kipfer and Kanishka Goonewardena argue that urbicidal violence is heavily shaped by the political economies of imperialism and the geographical dynamics of colonization: "The production of colonized space necessarily involves multiple scales of urban erasure."[46] To understand the spatial relations underscoring the War on Terror as a new imperialism, we must engage with the changing relations between colonization, imperialism and urbanization. Integral to the War on Terror and its urban militarization are various acts of urban erasure, securitization, and reconstruction. Here, military geographies and technologies, connected to predatory capital flows, also function as key drivers of neoliberal globalization.

The Karachi Operation is testament to the increasingly militarized nature of real estate accumulation and development. As mentioned, two of the largest real estate development projects, DHA City and Bahria Town Karachi, each sited over more than twenty-thousand acres of land, are located in Gadap—one of the first neighborhoods to be cordoned off and cast as a no-go zone in the Karachi Operation. FIG 1 The bordering up, securitization, devastation, appropriation and development of spaces that had previously been identified as no-go zones, all demonstrate the ways in which the Karachi Operation is closely linked to real estate and the War on Terror: "the new military urbanism's wars ... now operate to fuel capital accumulation through the global city system."[47] Across the city, securitization has paved the way for privatization and gentrification—transforming lands that were previously common into global capital. In Karachi's vast suburbs, under the guise of an operation targeted at terrorists, the military has been "clearing new space for the exigencies of global-city formation, neoliberal production, or as urban tabula rasa necessary for the most profitable bubbles of real estate speculation."[48]

The transformation of indigenous Sindhi and Baloch settlements into spaces of exception and destruction is in keeping with a long history of urban warfare in Karachi, entailed by planned annihilation of indigenous space to make room for a modern, orderly urbanity. The 'global cities' that Bahria Town and DHA City are building in Gadap give form to aspirations for western-style development, but also require the complete erasure of the forms and visualities of life specific to Gadap indigenous community and ecology. There is a colonial history to both this devastation-by-urban-planning, and the abjection of the native and of nature that allows such unspeakable violence to be committed. Achille Mbembe writes:

> In the eyes of the conqueror, *savage life* is just another form of *animal life*, a horrifying experience, something alien beyond imagination or comprehension. In fact, according to Arendt, what makes the savages different from other human beings is less the color of their skin than the fear that they behave like a part of nature, that they treat nature as their undisputed master. Nature thus remains, in all its majesty, an overwhelming reality compared to which they appear to be phantoms, unreal and ghostlike. The savages are, as it were, "natural" human beings who lack the specifically human character, the specifically human reality, "so that when European men massacred them they somehow were not aware that they had committed murder."[49]

Place annihilation, the creation of "death-worlds,"[50] accompanies the vilification and demonization of indigenous and refugee communities. As Karachi's landscapes are gouged with the violence of raids, 'encounters', land-grabs and resource extraction, entire community histories are erased to create blank slates upon which a new Pakistani urban modernity can be built. This restructuring is made possible and sustained as much by cultural technologies of representation as by more obvious and brutal modes of conquest.

The development sector utilizes and builds upon the militarized visuality of no-go zones to legitimize urban expansion and expropriation at the city's outskirts. Malik Riaz, the CEO of Bahria Town, proudly claimed that Gadap had been the habitat of drug peddlers and criminals prior to his

FIG 1
Entrance to Bahria Town, Karachi.

FIG 2
Screenshot from Bahria Town Karachi advertisement.

leadership of the development (he made these claims in an on-going case in the Pakistan Supreme Court regarding the illegal acquisition of lands by Bahria Town). He further explained to the court "how barren lands had been converted into a modern, developed city by planting over ten million trees, constructing one of the largest mosques in the world, building schools, colleges, hospitals, golf courses and dancing fountains, and providing other amenities."[51] Bahria Town's promotional video similarly envisions Gadap as a barren and wild landscape, with a voiceover that describes the location before Bahria Town's development as "*ghairabad, banjar aur ghairmehfooz*" (uninhabited, barren and insecure).[52] FIG 2 The force of this image, evoking Gadap as a barren wasteland, constitutes an erasure not only of the communities that currently live there but also of centuries of place-making practices and indigenous settlement that mark its landscapes.

The rendering of Gadap as a blank space continues the colonial myth of a no man's land, dry dusty paths and thorny bushes waiting to be ordered and made productive.[53] This visuality continually erases indigenous rights, creating frontiers of wild and empty spaces, where 'discovering' land and resources remains to be made possible. The Karachi Operation and development projects like Bahria Town are two sides of the same frontier-making project, as Anna Tsing explains: "built from historical models of European conquest, frontiers create wildness so that some and not others may reap its rewards."[54] This imagined wildness turns everything visible into threat. Unruly subjects exist in unruly landscapes. Development and security intertwine, as fear and threat are embedded in, and are byproducts of, the process of securing new frontiers.

Stephen Graham argues that "place annihilation is utterly intrinsic to both urban modernity, and modern urbanism and planning."[55] Much of the spaces constituted as no-go zones, such as Gadap and Malir, previously constituted the 'greenbelt' of Karachi. Water was abundant, in wells and from rainfed rivers that emerged on its ranges in monsoon seasons. The Karachi Development Plan of 1975–1985 termed Gadap as "the fruit basket of Karachi" and envisioned that eighty-five percent of the city's agricultural needs would come from this region.[56] Today however, Gadap's lands can barely sustain fodder.

Over the past decades, Gadap has undergone a systematic and sustained ruination. The place annihilation of Gadap has been a drawn out project—not only conducted through military violence but also through environmental violence. *Dawn* reports that the law enforcement agencies in Gadap are also responsible for unleashing environmental destruction in the region through sand mining. Interlinkages between ecological devastation and securitization can be seen clearly in the case of Rao Anwar, an infamous law enforcement officer known widely as the 'encounter specialist' for his strong-arm, extra-judicial tactics. In Gadap, Anwar was known for threatening, abducting and torturing villagers, coercing them sell their ancestral lands to Bahria Town or other developers. Lesser known was Anwar's stake in sand mining, a lucrative business.[57]

The systematic desertification of Gadap has largely taken place through the long project of sand mining, which has dried rivers and debilitated agriculture in these areas. As early as the 1970s, when the military first became involved in developing land as real estate, topsoil from cultivable lands in Gadap was illegally lifted for construction purposes, leading to soil erosion, water depletion and environmental degradation. As sand mining laid waste to fertile landscapes and ecologies, debilitating the livelihoods of the local population, it also created a landscape ripe for the discursive projections of "*banjar, ghairabad aur ghairmehfooz*" (uninhabited, barren and insecure).

Cast as simultaneously barren and insecure, Gadap's ruined landscapes were now available for militarized development. Indigenous communities faced a double dispossession, robbed of their livelihoods, and then their physical lands. In this sense Gadap is a testament to the intersection of militarization, environmental devastation and land development in Karachi.

Local ecologies such as rivers, wells, agricultural land are ripped apart in no-go zones. Roads, walls, barriers, checkpoints and prime real estate are instituted in their place. In these transformations, infrastructure becomes a tactical measure. Wide, new roads cut through these landscapes, with grand promises of modernity, accessibility, surveillance and profit. The borders of the no-go zone give way to gated community as security and development intertwine, naturalizing each other's conquering, settling and colonizing processes.

Warfare in the terrains of culture

The daily violence of urbanization processes, in which military visualities are increasingly imprinted into the built environment and public discourse, determines life in the city as increasingly a military-development nexus. Boundaries between global and civil war, citizen and combatant, start to blur as the global War on Terror is increasingly invoked in contestations over the city, its spaces, history and future. All citizens are imagined as potential fighters or threats and "all terrain [becomes] the site of battle."[58]

The culture sphere, too, is activated as a site of combat. If representational strategies are essential to the militarization project, it is through these practices that military entities build support for their activities, and create a pervasive sense of fear, panic and warfare. Woodward argues that these activities too, are:

> geographically constituted, in that they require and draw upon the resources (material or discursive) of spaces and places, environments and landscapes, in order to come into being...Furthermore, these military geographies also have a far wider imprint than armed conflict, marking and shaping places and spaces far distant from the points of military engagement...they impinge upon other geographies, of production, reproduction, circulation, exchange and representation, of material entities and discursive constructions.[59]

Much of this work is done directly by the military's media wing, Inter-Services Public Relations. Over the past few years, the cultural and education sphere of Karachi has been engaged through the language of 'Countering Violent Extremism,' CVE. The Chief of Army Staff General Qamar Javed Bajwa, in a speech given at a seminar titled "Role of the Youth in Rejecting Extremism" in May 2017, made clear that the first line of defence for Pakistan is indeed media houses and educational institutions.[60] He elaborated, "having defeated terrorism physically, now [terrorists'] deceitful message and narrative must also be defeated." That is, the enemy must be decisively defeated not only in battle but also in ideology. Here the university and media—both key sites of knowledge and cultural production—are cast as the new battlegrounds of counterterrorism. Therefore it is unsurprising to see the Pakistan army's renewed interest in these sites of knowledge-production to acculturate citizens to the proliferation of violence and control.[61] These practices normalize the boundless process of militarization, of both the urban landscape and realms of culture, collapsing the distinction between military and civilian binaries. An increasingly militarized culture is geared towards the production of values that support the pervasive surveillance and securitization under the guise of an unlimited war against terrorism.

These narratives have been patronized not only by the Pakistani military but by a larger, global network. A new imperialist aid infrastructure emerged post-War On Terror, siphoning money into the cultural and education spheres under the discursive framework of countering violent extremism. This triggered an unprecedented growth in literature festivals, public art projects and educational endeavors all of which propagate the same narrative about the need to activate civil society and the citizenry of Pakistan in service of the war against terror. This boom coincided with dramatic and brutal growth in the policing and surveillance of cultural spaces and educational institutions by the Pakistan military.[62]

One collaboration that has been widely covered in the media took place between the fine art department at the Indus Valley School of Art and Architecture, one of the country's leading art schools, and the Karachi Youth Initiative (KYI)—a local 'funnel' organization for USAID, part of USAID's CVE (Countering Violent Extremism) stream that was established to sidestep the growing skepticism and fears amongst local organizations about accepting USAID money. The project set out to cover supposedly rampant 'hate graffiti' in Karachi by replacing it with aesthetically pleasing imagery. FIG 3 'Reimagining the Walls of Karachi' was a much-lauded project for which both KYI and IVS received rave reviews in the local and international press.

In this discourse, graffiti was framed in entirely negative terms as religiously motivated and hate mongering—while Karachi, as was often the case with KYI projects, was framed as a terror-ridden city in which the potentiality of violence lurked at every corner and was inscribed onto every surface.[63] The goal was to fight extremism by painting over the 'hate graffiti,' which was in fact often little more than advertisements for small businesses, barbers or homeopaths for example, or otherwise simply expressed the slogans of political parties. The guidelines for artists responding to USAID's CVE Call for Submissions asserted that there be no text and no 'religious or political imagery' while encouraging 'landscapes/cityscapes/patterns/designs.' The result was a depoliticized aesthetic—colorful, celebratory and often orientalist in nature.

One of the longest lengths of wall unfolded on MT Khan road, down the street from a long, white stretch of twenty-foot high blast-resistant walls lining the new U.S. consulate. Despite these walls being used as a site for a project of aesthetic regeneration, the violence inscribed upon the walls, with snipers stationed every few feet down the road, remained unaddressed by artists. Through this collaborative project, KYI, IVS and the artists involved instrumentalize art and culture against the ever-present threat of fundamentalism. In these collaborations, global corporate and imperial powers calibrate art's function in line with the demands and political vision of the emerging 'everywhere war.'

The Countering Violent Extremism (CVE) program was initiated by the Obama Administration in 2011. It refers to "noncoercive longer range tools deployed in an effort to counter violent ideologies and narratives." In the US and abroad, its operations are "combining bolstered investments in soft power with sustained military and law enforcement efforts."[64] The key currency of soft power here is culture. In addition to public art, film and literature festivals are another major addition to the cultural landscape of Pakistan, bolstered by USAID support alongside the diplomatic missions. USAID's humanitarian aid in culture is not just a noble cause to inculcate "hope, pride and ownership in the citizens of Karachi,"[65] but is entrenched in imperial and military goals to protect U.S. security interests in the post 9/11 world order.

The growth in funding in Pakistan's cultural sector, derived from U.S. and European sources, activates this cultural sector as a battleground and cultural workers as combatants against their own fellow citizens. Highly securitized and increasingly censored film and literature festivals are framed as acts of resistance against the ever-present threat of terrorism in the city. Meanwhile, the Pakistan military is also engaged in militarizing these spheres through surveillance and brutal policing. Universities are increasingly instrumentalized as sites for propaganda, censorship, raids and abduction.[66] Through the dual efforts of the Pakistani military and U.S. and European development assistance programs, a new and vast militarized-cultural sphere emerges, one which produces knowledge, visualities and discourse in service of war, and which leaves little space for dissent.

In May 2014, Pakistan's National Assembly passed *The Surveying and Mapping Act*. This legislation aimed to regulate the production of geospatial data and transferred all mapping authority to the Survey of Pakistan, a body which reports to the Ministry of Defense and takes its orders from the Army General Head Quarters. While the stated objective of the Act is to "stop unqualified/unregistered firms to take part in Surveying and Mapping activities that can pose a security risk to the state," it makes visible the Pakistani military's desire to control the visual field. By banning all independent mapping projects, the military retains the sole power and authority to study and represent space. This demonstrates that military strategy has become a distinctly cultural and visual project.

The study of military geographies is marked by opacity, an absence of data and an atmosphere of censorship and surveillance that perpetuates military occupation of space and social relations. Despite this enforced opacity, the reality of militarization is increasingly ingrained and palpable in every aspect of life in Karachi. Practices of accumulation and annihilation, and development and representation, are appropriated by military entities to make control concrete, and to create the conditions for absolute power in what Virilio describes as cities of panic: spaces marked by securitized and standardized landscapes, erasure of history, growth of surveillance, a pervasive atmosphere of fear and dread, and the dissolution of a social body.[67] As Karachi increasingly becomes both a target and a terrain of war, and as militarism becomes increasingly mundane, it is important to trace the violence and erasure enfolded into the city, and the fear and anxiety engrained in the emergent, sanitized and securitized landscapes and literature fests of Karachi.

FIG 3
A 2016 mural by German graffiti artist Sebastian Schmidt at Karachi's Jinnah International Airport. This mural was produced as a collaborative 'Meet the Culture' project by Goethe Institut, Vasl Artist's Collective, and On the Run.

1 Mike Davis, *Planet of Slums* (London: Verso, 2006), 205.
2 "Nisar says Karachi Operation to start in two days," *Dawn*, September 4, 2013, https://www.dawn.com/news/1040496
3 Stephen Graham, "Postmortem City: Towards an Urban Geopolitics," *City* 8, no. 2 (2004), 170.
4 Rachel Woodward, "From Military Geography to militarism's geographies: disciplinary engagements with the geographies of militarism and military activities," *Progress in Human Geography* 29, no. 6 (2005): 726.
5 Woodward, "From Military Geography to militarism's geographies," 726.
6 Woodward, "From Military Geography to militarism's geographies," 720.
7 Derek Gregory, "The everywhere war," *The Geographical Journal* 177, no. 3 (2011), 239.
8 Fahad Desmukh, "Parveen Rehman on Land, Politics and Violence in Karachi," *Thirdworldism* (blog). March 16, 2013. Accessed February 2, 2019. https://desmukh.com/blog/2013/03/parveen-rehman-karachi-land-violence/
9 Ayesha Siddiqa, *Military Inc.* (Karachi: Oxford University Press, 2007), 175.
10 Siddiqa, *Military Inc.*, 174.
11 Paul Virilio, *City of Panic*, (Oxford: Berg, 2005).
12 Aamir Majeed, "Rangers "cementing" hold in Karachi," *Pakistan Today*, June, 17, 2015. https://www.pakistantoday.com.pk/2015/06/17/rangers-cementing-hold-in-karachi/
13 Peerzada Salman, "Historical Radio Pakistan building, change of guard?" *Dawn*, November 6, 2015. https://www.dawn.com/news/1217711
14 Henry A. Giroux, *Public Spaces, Private Lives: Democracy beyond 9/11* (Oxford: Rowman & Littlefield Publishers, 2003), ix.
15 Mateen Haider, "Army leadership vows to continue operations with increased tempo," *Dawn*, May 14, 2015, https://www.dawn.com/news/1181915.
16 Nicholas Mirzoeff, "Global Counterinsurgency and the Crisis of Visuality," *The Right to Look* (Durham: Duke University Press, 2011), 295.
17 Judith Butler, *Frames of War: When is life grievable?* (London: Verso, 2009), 29.
18 Faraz Khan, "Where law enforcers fear to tread: The entry fee for these spots of Karachi may be your life," *The Express Tribune*, March 23, 2013, https://tribune.com.pk/story/525035/where-law-enforcers-fear-to-tread-the-entry-fee-for-these-spots-of-karachi-may-be-your-life-karachi-city/
19 Naeem Sahoutara, "Karachi violence suo motu: IG finally admits no-go areas exist," *The Express Tribune*, April 6, 2013, https://tribune.com.pk/story/531732/karachi-violence-suo-motu-ig-finally-admits-no-go-areas-exist/
20 Chad Harris, "The Omniscient Eye: Satellite Imagery, 'Battlespace Awareness,' and the Structures of the Imperial Gaze," *Surveillance & Society* 4, no. 2 (2006), 101.
21 Derek Gregory, "Seeing Red: Baghdad and the Eventful City," *Political Geography* 29, no. 5 (2010), 267.
22 Derek Gregory, "Seeing Red," 267.
23 Stephen Graham, "Cities and the War on Terror," *International Journal of Urban and Regional Research* 30, no. 2 (2006), 256.
24 Harris, *The Omniscient Eye*, 102.
25 Jordan Crandall, "Anything that moves: armed vision," *C Theory*, June 1999, https://journals.uvic.ca/index.php/ctheory/article/view/14615/5472.
26 Derek Gregory, "The everywhere war," *The Geographical Journal* 177, no. 3 (2011), 239.
27 Asad Hashim, "Interactive: Karachi's killing fields," *Al Jazeera*, 6 September, 2012, https://www.aljazeera.com/indepth/interactive/2012/08/2012822102920951929.html
28 Gregory, "Seeing Red," 274.
29 Edward Said, *Orientalism* (London: Penguin, 1978), 54; see also Derek Gregory, "Imaginative Geographies," *Progress in Human Geography* 19 (1995), 447–85.
30 Stephen Graham, *Cities Under Siege: The New Military Urbanism* (New York: Verso, 2010), xxvi.
31 Richard Norton, "Feral Cities," *Naval War College Review* 56, no. 4 (2003): 98.
32 Norton, "Feral Cities," 98.
33 Norton, "Feral Cities," 100.
34 Norton, "Feral Cities," 103.
35 Mateen Haider, "Army leadership vows to continue operations with increased tempo," *Dawn*, May 14, 2015, https://www.dawn.com/news/1181915.
36 Gregory, "Seeing Red," 276.
37 Mateen Haider, "Army leadership vows to continue operations with increased tempo," *Dawn*, May 14, 2015, https://www.dawn.com/news/1181915.
38 Keith P Feldman, "Empire's Verticality: The Af/Pak Frontier, Visual Culture and Racialization from Above," *Comparative American Studies An International Journal* 9, no. 4 (2011): 329.
39 Figures shared by Mehmood Mehsud during an interview conducted on 1 December 2018.
40 Naziha Syed Ali and Fahim Zaman, "Rao Anwar and the Killing Fields of Karachi," *Dawn*, February 16, 2018, https://www.dawn.com/news/1389719.
41 The Federally Administered Tribal Areas.
42 Ali and Zaman, "Rao Anwar and the Killing Fields."
43 Feldman, Empire's Verticality," 328.
44 Junaid Rana, *Terrifying Muslims: Race and Labour in the South Asian Diaspora* (Durham: Duke University Press, 2011), 53.
45 Feldman, 328.
46 Stefan Kipfer and Kanishka Goonewardena, "Colonization and the New Imperialism," *Theory & Event* 10, no. 2 (2007).
47 Stephen Graham, "When Life Itself Is War: On the Urbanization of Military and Security Doctrine," *International Journal of Urban and Regional Research* 36, no. 1 (2011): 136.
48 Graham, *Cities Under Siege*, 83.
49 Mbembe, "Necropolitics," 24.
50 Mbembe, "Necropolitics," 40.
51 Nasir Iqbal, "SC urged to allow appeal against verdicts in suo motu cases," Dawn, 5 October, 2018, https://www.dawn.com/news/1436897/sc-urged-to-allow-appeals-against-verdicts-in-suo-motu-cases?fbclid=IwAR1CZScmCMUUHaZcV2v-SMGvL5xMah6_VtOKncGGhLSvBSAR6ipKBzDLIZA

52 *Bahria Town Karachi Updates March 2016*. Retrieved from https://www.youtube.com/watch?v=apLZAoMowm8.
53 Tiffin and Lawson, *De-scribing Empire: Post-colonialism and Textuality* (Routledge: London, 1994), 5.
54 Anna Lowenhaupt Tsing, *Friction: An Ethnography of Global Connection* (Princeton University Press: Princeton, 2005), 27.
55 Stephen Graham, "Postmortem City," *City* 8, no. 2 (2004), 171.
56 City District Government Karachi, *Karachi Master Plan 1975–1985* (Karachi: 1975).
57 Ali and Zaman, "Rao Anwar and the Killing Fields."
58 Stephen Graham, *Cities Under Siege* 21.
59 Woodward (2005), 730.
60 Hamza Rao, "Full text of COAS General Qamar Bajwa's speech at 'Role of Youth in rejecting Extremism' seminar," *Daily Pakistan*, May 19, 2017, https://en.dailypakistan.com.pk/pakistan/full-text-if-coas-general-qamar-bajwas-speech-at-role-of-youth-in-rejecting-extremism-seminar/
61 Shahana Rajani and Zahra Malkani, "The Militarized University and The Everywhere War," *Karachi LaJamia* (2018) http://karachilajamia.com/index.php/project/the-militarised-university.
62 Rajani and Malkani, "The Militarized University."
63 Zahra Malkani and Shahana Rajani, "Imperialism, Art and Pedagogy: Notes on Knowledge Production at the Frontlines," *Open Library of Humanities* 3, no. 1 (2016).
64 Sahar Aziz, "Losing the "War of Ideas:" A Critique of Countering Violent Extremism Programs," *Texas International Law Journal* 52, no. 2 (2017), 255.
65 "Social innovation aims to bring peace to Karachi wall by wall," *Daily Times*, 29 July, 2016, https://dailytimes.com.pk/66931/social-innovation-aims-to-bring-peace-to-karachi-wall-by-wall.
66 Rajani and Malkani, "The Militarized University."
67 Paul Virilio, *City of Panic* (Oxford: Berg, 2005).

“The only Hellenistic ruin of great interest in Jordan”

Miguel John Versluys

In the early second-century BCE, a Hellenised Jew from an old-standing Ammonite family known as the Tobiads substantially renovated and monumentalised a family estate located in Transjordan on the road from Jericho to Amman; his name was Hyrcan. The domain of the Tobiads is identified with the site of ‘Iraq al Amīr in present-day Jordan. Many archaeological remains from various periods of the occupation have been preserved at the site, but most notable are those from the late Hellenistic period. This article deals with the most remarkable and monumental building of the complex known as the *Qasr*, a building which the great historian of the Hellenistic world Michael Ivanovich Rostovtzeff (1870–1952) called “the only Hellenistic ruin of great interest in Jordan.”[1] And it is of great interest indeed.

The Ammonites were somewhat secluded from Jewish society after their return from Babylonian exile, although some of them held senior religious positions in society. Hyrcan’s father, Joseph, was the tax collector for the Ptolemaic kings in this part of the Levant and, as such, he was in close contact with the Ptolemaic administration in Alexandria. Hyrcan probably received part of his education at the Alexandrian court and was likely to have been connected to the highest echelons of Alexandrian society when he took over his father’s role in 182 BCE. But his authority was not undisputed; apparently his brothers tried to claim the office as well. Moreover, the Levant had become a battlefield in the conflict between the weakening Ptolemaic dynasty and the Seleucids during this period. We are so well-informed about Hyrcan because various passages were recorded about him by Flavius Josephus, a Jewish-Roman author writing in the first-century CE, in *Antiquities of the Jews* (XII, 4). Although written at a later date, and certainly a text that contained literary *topoi* and falsifications, the information provided by Josephus is shown to be at least partly historically accurate. Josephus provides us with a description of the ‘Iraq al Amīr estate:

> He also erected a strong castle, and built it entirely of white stone to the very roof, and had animals of a prodigious magnitude engraved upon it. He also drew round it a great and deep canal of water. He also made caves of many furlongs in length, by hollowing a rock that was over against him; and then he made large rooms in it, some for feasting, and some for sleeping and living in. He introduced also a vast quantity of waters which ran along it, and which were very delightful and ornamental in the court. (-) Moreover, he built courts of greater magnitude than ordinary, which he adorned with vastly large gardens. And when he had brought the place to this state, he named it Tyre. This place is between Arabia and Judea, beyond Jordan, not far from the country of Heshbon.[2]

Archaeological research has proven this description to be largely correct. The British explorations that followed the earliest mention of the site in 1818 by the explorer William John Bankes, who immediately linked the site to Josephus’s description, were largely limited to superficial documentation. Archaeological investigation first took place in 1961, with excavations by the American School of Oriental Research directed by Paul W. Lapp, but began in earnest with the commencement of French explorations directed by Ernest Will, Fawzi Zayadine and François Larché in 1976. These campaigns resulted in two fundamental monographs as well as an anastylosis of the Qasr itself in the 1980s. French explorations of the estate precinct continue until the present day.[3]

The precinct is very large, an area of thousands of hectares, and is located in and around the valley of the wadī as-Sīr utilizing the mountains as a natural defence. The site probably already belonged to the Tobiad family from the sixth-century BCE. Many grottos are found in the surrounding mountains, as Josephus also mentions. A small, fortified settlement as well as many smaller installations are also found at the site; there is a monumental basin (Zahr al-'Iraq), a large pigeon loft, terraces, smaller free-standing buildings and porches, and a monumental retaining wall along the Jericho-Amman road. In the latter half of the first-century CE, another small fort was even built in the south-western part of the area. The precise chronology of all these buildings is not always clear.[4] Here we will focus on three monuments that clearly belong to the phase of the monumentalizing instigated by Hyrcan: the *Qasr* itself which formed the centre of the residential part of the estate, the monumental entrance gate to the precinct although this operated briefly, and a recently excavated basin (Zahr al-'Iraq) in the most northern part of the area.

The *Qasr*: A Hellenistic Palace in Transjordan

Contrary to what the Arabic name might suggest—it means 'castle' and is likely an interpretation of the large ruins that remained visible after antiquity—the *Qasr* is actually a large pavilion consisting of two floors. It is a uniquely preserved example of Hellenistic palatial architecture. Josephus tells us that Hyrcan constructed the complex in seven years and entirely from local stone. An artificial landscape encompassed the *Qasr*, water surrounding the pavilion, in which terraces and small building elements, such as the monumental entrance gate, water basins, and canals were nested.

Travellers from the nineteenth century progressively interpreted the impressive ruins as an Ammonite temple, while a recent monograph interprets it as a mausoleum with a funerary function. Both these views are untenable in light of the evidence provided by the French explorations;[5] recent evidence points to the *Qasr* as a reception building that functioned as *pièce de résistance* of the larger residential complex, and a place where Hyrcan would have received and entertained his guests and relatives. Although the precise reconstruction and functionality of the pavilion remain debated, the general outline of the architecture is clear.[6]

The pavilion measures thirty-seven meters by eighteen-and-a-half meters and consists of two levels, each of which opens to both the north and south sides through vestibules. FIG 1 The tiers feature Corinthian columns on the ground-floor level and a surrounding colonnade on the first floor. The first floor on the northern side contains a loggia of Corinthian columns directly above the vestibule, which interrupts the surrounding colonnade. These columns feature sculpted acanthus leaves above the base and support a Doric entablature. With a more open and monumental appearance, this northern side was clearly meant to function as main entrance. The ground floor level is completed by an Ionic entablature that surrounds the entire building and that encompasses an alternation of stylised cow-heads and discs. The ground floor has simple windows at the east and west sides, as well as a single element of sculptural decoration: a walking panther, facing north, used as a water-spout. The most impressive sculptural decorations are found on the outside of the first floor at the northern side main entrance. There is a repeated instance of the lion on the corner, with a lioness and their cubs behind him. Above another Ionic entablature of the surrounding colonnade, the corners of the building and the corners of the loggia, there are four eagles to be found. This decorative scheme is repeated at the southern side, albeit with only two eagles on the corner of the building. FIG 2 The surrounding entablature, completing the first-floor level, is Doric.

FIG 1
Reconstructed view of the Qasr from the north west by CAO.

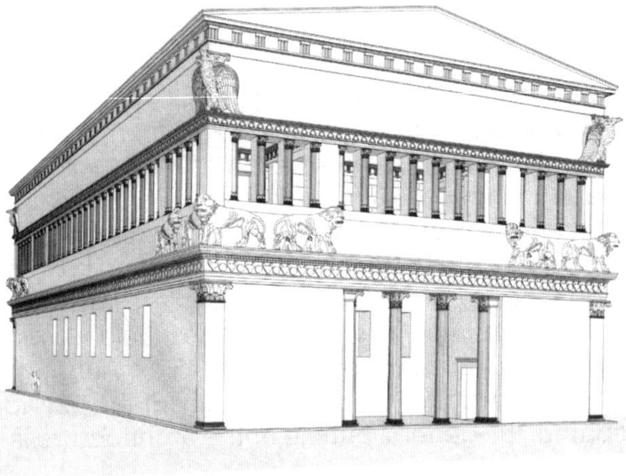

FIG 2
Reconstructed view of the Qasr from the south west by CAO.

The ground floor contains a staircase to the first floor at the left side of the northern entrance. It is likely that the rooms on the ground floor were all vaulted; they may (partly) have served as storage rooms or servant quarters. The first floor was much more important and prestigious, which the architectural structure and decoration of the outside of the building already made evident. We saw a relatively simple and compact ground floor FIG 3 with the entrance as only articulation, two panthers as decorative elements at the lateral sides and the use of relatively large blocks—whereas the first floor has a much more elaborate and monumental appearance through its architecture as well as its architectural decorations. The plan and inner layout of the first floor are very open and present a series of rooms that were all connected. Such a plan has no precedent in the region and it is still not clear what it represents in functional terms; it seems to concern a series of suites in which guests were meant to circulate; in other words, where the intention was to look and to be looked at.

"Les incongruités y sont nombreuses": Understanding the Composite

The novelty of the building's composite character is striking. Although constructed from local limestone, the architectural decorations demonstrate a far-ranging inspiration. The first source is clearly Alexandria. This is also evident in the reliance on the Ptolemaic cubit—some fifty-two and a half centimetres—as the basic unit of measure and design. Other distinctly Alexandrian elements are used, such as the decoration of column bases with acanthus leaves, as seen on the columns of the loggia. The Corinthian capitals with their large and independent volutes are also typical for the architecture of Alexandria. It is only logical that Hyrcan was looking at the Ptolemaic capital in view of his socio-political position. Moreover, in many respects, and certainly with regard to its artistic and architectural developments, Alexandria was the leading centre of the Hellenistic world. Developments in Ptolemaic Alexandria were defining for what Judith McKenzie has characterised as "the origins of Baroque architecture:" McKenzie suggests that, unlike classical buildings such as Greek temples, Alexandrian architecture is paradigmatically treated as a façade to which new, structural, "baroque" elements, like half-pediments and curved entablatures, can be introduced.[7] This development, of which 'Iraq al Amīr is clearly part and to which it contributes, was to have a widespread and important legacy in European architecture.[8] This baroque playfulness, as one might call it, whereby the visual articulation of the surface is deemed more important than the architectural structure itself, is also evident from the use of various formal composites, such as the Corinthian columns that support entablatures of different Ionian and even Doric orders.

However, there seems to be more to 'Iraq al Amīr than a slavish copying of the masters in Alexandria by a local ruler who depended on them. Hyrcan's creation certainly belonged to a much broader trend for which Alexandria was a major, though not the only, centre—scholars have coined the term Alexandrianism to encapsulate its novelty.[9] In this respect it is interesting to note that at 'Iraq al Amīr the architectural outcome was, as far as we can tell, unique. The quest for originality is clearly evident in the architect's radical decision to draw all emphasis to the first floor, while using the ground floor and its entrance only as a prelude to what was to follow. The sculptural decoration is also highly involved in this tactic: see the placement of the lions at the corners of the first floor, with a duplicated lion on the corner itself. The particular use of the eagles as protruding, almost sculpted, elements, which we see at 'Iraq al Amīr and which was part of a Hellenistic palatial tradition, probably provided inspiration here.[10] Lions were, first and foremost, a supreme symbol of dynastic power, especially in the Persian world. François Querel regards the style in which Hyrcan's lions are depicted as deliberately archaising, which suggests that an association was sought not just with the Alexandrian present but with the Persian past.[11] As such, these elements may also present a form of Persianism. Some scholars regard the lush water garden situated around the *Qasr* as a reference to the Achaemenid *paradeisos*. Although this interpretation is probably too specific for this period, the similarity might nonetheless have played a role in creating an "Oriental" atmosphere. But there is more *looking-back* at 'Iraq al Amīr, evident in the Doric entablature in particular. The archaising atmosphere of the building, as a whole, was perhaps intended as legitimation of Hyrcan's position in the late Hellenistic world, also because it was part of the established Hellenistic royal norm. He wanted to look dignified. This idea is underlined by the execution of the monumental gate that marked the entrance to the residential quarter of the estate—an impressively large porch made of colossal blocks featuring a Doric entablature and two archaising lions as decoration reminiscent of an Oriental style.[12] The colonnade of the recently excavated monumental basin [Zahr al-'Iraq] in the most northern part of the area is likewise constructed according to the Doric order, and was perhaps even a kind of nymphaeum. FIG 4 However, as was the case with the *Qasr*, these archaising elements are also combined in an unprecedented way, using the Ptolemaic cubit as its basic architectural unit, together with more common Hellenistic elements.[13]

In his final interpretation of the *Qasr*, Ernest Will characterises its northern facade as follows: "The north facade of the *Qasr* thus appears as a curious combination of elements of diverse origins, all more-or-less successfully articulated with each other. The incongruities are numerous."[14] Will's phrasing shows how difficult it is for scholars to make sense of eclecticism, and to understand composites. Within the archaeology of the ancient world, it is only recently that scholars have begun to study and better understand eclecticism in its own right and without preconceived value judgements concerning stylistic purity or lack thereof.[15] The Hellenistic world, of which the Roman republic was part and parcel, constitutes a privileged vantage point for a fruitful continuation of this development, because it was a vast and cosmopolitan world that stretched from the Atlantic to the Oxus, in which more stylistic repertoires from more periods in history, and from more regions around the globe, were represented than ever before in Eurasia. The *koine*, in other words, was richer and more diverse than ever. As a result, we see the universalization of particular repertoires, for instance Greek or Egyptian. These now travelled more widely than they had done before, and once used all across Eurasia they often lost their geographical and cultural specificity as they became particularised in very different contexts for very different reasons.[16] In the late Hellenistic period, there even seemed to emerge a trend whereby architects, artists, and commissioners purposefully sought to make buildings and works of art that were as composite, different, and as innovative as possible, in search of a result that was unique. 'Iraq al Amīr seems to be an example of this trend. On the basis of a study of the equally 'hybrid' monument of Nemrud Dağ in south-east Anatolia, dated to around 50 BCE, I have proposed to call this trend innovative eclecticism, in recognition of the practice of quoting a variety of decorative forms that are actually as widespread and diverse *as possible*, in order to produce something new that caused amazement through its modernity and originality.[17] In general terms, innovative eclecticism was meant to demonstrate the extraordinary possibilities and status of the commissioner. It also allowed a building's patrons to connect with tradition, while simultaneously expanding it. The famous tombs of Petra, the Khazneh in particular, which also date to the period around the middle of the first-century BCE, attest likewise to innovative eclecticism, as do numerous other monuments from this period. Discretely unique, they are, when read collectively, in fact all part of the same cosmopolitan trend. A general study of innovative eclecticism as a phenomenon characteristic of a globalised Hellenistic Eurasia, and with Alexandria as only one of its many centres, is an important desideratum. 'Iraq al Amīr presents an important building block for such a study.[18]

Hyrcan, 'Iraq al Amīr and the Consequences of Empire

In 170 BCE, the Seleucid king Antiochos [Epiphanes] IV challenged the Ptolemies in the Eastern Mediterranean and the Levant, attempting to broaden his power base and to fill his royal treasury. The Egyptians didn't have much of a leg to stand on in what historians call the Sixth Syrian war. Antiochos took Cyprus and even Memphis before marching to Alexandria, where he also met little resistance, apart from the Roman general Popilius Laenas who gave the Seleucid king an ultimatum from the Roman Senate that had decided to support the Ptolemies. Antiochos was told to back off or Rome would interfere. When the Seleucid king asked for time to deliberate, Popilius Laenas is famously said to have drawn a line around him in the sand with a cane, telling him to decide before stepping out. Antiochos gave in and returned to Syria, where he conquered Jerusalem and besieged the estate of Hyrcan, the Ptolemaic ally and tax collector in this part of the Levant. Antiochos's attitude towards a figure like Hyrcan would not have been positive. Because of this, Josephus tells us, Hyrcan took his own life. The clash between the Seleucid and Ptolemaic Empires and, in fact, also the Roman Empire thus had major consequences for Hyrcan and his small 'kingdom' in the valley of the *wadī as-Sīr*. If this is a notion of power and imperialism that corresponds with the way in which we are accustomed to think about empires in terms of their devastating effect on local populations and rule, it is therefore important to note that it was only through empire structures that Hyrcan had been able to rise to a socio-political position in the first place and, as a result of this, to conceptualise his monument. The intersections of power in which he operated enabled this architecture by increasing choice in two different but related ways: firstly, the conquests of foreign lands and large territories resulted in a form of time-space compression that had substantially widened the repertoire of cultural elements that were available to use; secondly, because of the universal nature of these respective repertoires, there was a simultaneous need to develop an extensive repertoire of symbolic material culture that would become defining for those, like Hyrcan, who were confronted with it and attempted to reckon with it.

'Iraq al Amīr is an important monument for architectural history. It has often been said that modernity in architecture started with the destabilization of the classical canon at the end of the seventeenth-century. Instead, the study of this site reveals that the classical canon itself was also formed through the destabilization that occurred during the Hellenistic period and its innovative repercussions.

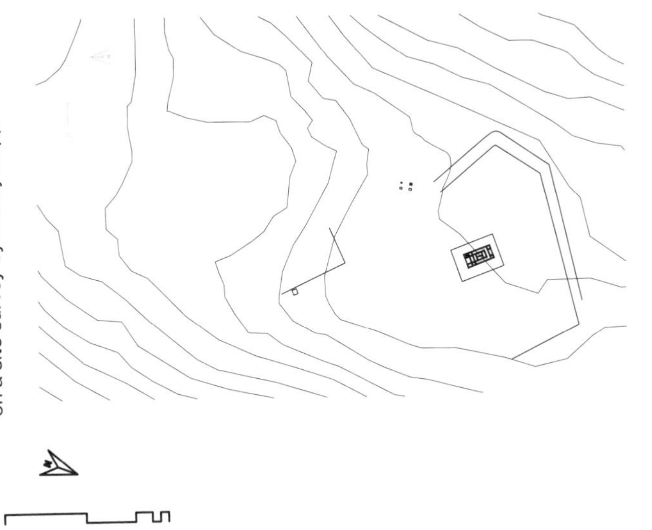

FIG 4
Iraq al-Amir, Ensemble. Drawing based on a site survey by Nancy Rapp.

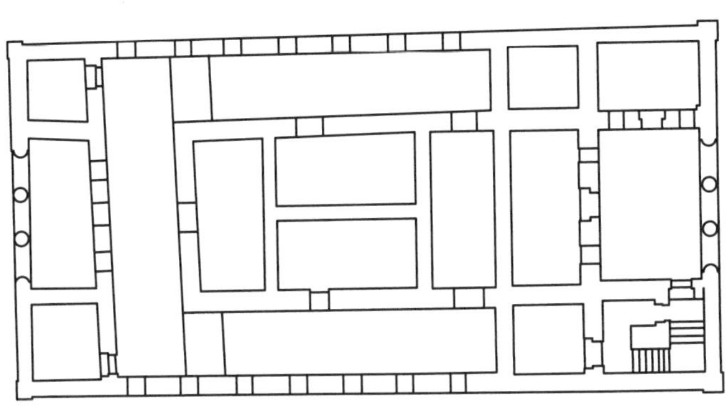

FIG 3
Iraq al-Amir, Ground floor plan. Drawing based on a site survey by Nancy Rapp.

1 As mentioned by Roland Etienne, Jean-François Salles eds., *'Iraq al Amir. Guide historique et archéologique du domaine des Tobiades* (Beiruit: Institut Français du Proche-Orient , 2010), 11.

2 Josephus, *Antiquities of the Jews* XII, Chapter 4. Translation after William Whiston (1737) with some minor changes.

3 Ernest Will and François Larche, *'Iraq al Amir. Le château du Tobiade Hyrcan I* I & II (Paris: Institut français du Proche-Orient, 1991); François Larché et al., *'Iraq al Amir. Le château du Tobiade Hyrcan II. Restitution et reconstruction* I & II (Beiruit: Institut Français du Proche-Orient, 2005). For an overview of the recent research see various contributions to *Topoi* 14, No. 1 (2006); as well as the important text, Roland Etienne and Jean-François Salles, *Guide historique et archéologique du domaine des Tobiades.*

4 See, Laurent Borel, "Recherches récentes sur le domaine d'"Iraq al Amir: nouveaux éléments sur le paysage construit" in Topoi 14, No. 1 (2006), 291–330; and *Guide historique et archéologique* II. This is only very briefly summarised here.

5 The English-language book by St. G. Rosenberg, *Airaq al-Amir. The architecture of the Tobiads* (BAR Int. Series 1544) (Oxford 2006) should unfortunately be handled with great care; see the (just but devastating) review by F. Villeneuve and É. Roland in *TOPOI* 17/2 (2011) 691–696; equally critical though somewhat more nuanced is D. Edelman in *BASOR* 352 (2008) 100–103.

6 The architect François Larché edited a second volume on the Qasr in 2005 because he disagreed with the views of the main scholar responsible for the project and its publication, Ernest Will, *'Iraq al Amir. Le château du Tobiade Hyrcan I*. I will not deal with this ongoing debate, for which see the review of the Larché volume from 2005 by Étienne Roland in *Topoi* 14, No. 1 (2006), 335–343.

7 Judith McKenzie, "Alexandria and the origins of Greek architecture," in *Alexandria and Alexandrianism*, ed. Kenneth Hamma (Malibu: The J. Paul Getty Museum, 1996). See also, Judith McKenzie, *The Architecture of Alexandria and Egypt 300 B.C.–A.D. 700* (New Haven: Yale University Press, 2011).

8 Caroline van Eck, "The *Style Empire* and Its Pedigree: Piranesi, Pompei, and Alexandria," *Architectural Histories* 6/1 (2016), 1–16, Accessed April 15, 2019: https://doi.org/10.5334/ah.339.

9 For Alexandrianism, see, François Queyrel, "Alexandrinisme et art alexandrine: nouvelles approaches," in *Grecs et Romeins en Égypte. Territoires, espace de la vie et de la mort, objets de prestige en du quotidien*, Pascale Ballet ed. (Caire : Institut français d'archéologie orientale du Caire, 2012), 235–256; Joan Breton Connelly, "Alexandrianism: a 21st century perspective," in *Art & civilisations de l' Orient hellénisé. Rencontres et échanges culturels d' Alexandre aux Sassanides*, Pierre Leriche ed. (Paris: Picard, 2014), 173–182 and Craig I. Hardiman, "Alexandrianism" again: Regionalism, Alexandria and aesthetics, Sheila Ager and Riemer Faber eds., Belonging and isolation in the Hellenistic world (Toronto: University of Toronto Press, 2013), 199–222.

10 R. Etienne, "Architecture palatiale ptolémaïque au IIIe s.", in J. des Courtils éd., *L'architecture monumentale grecque au IIIe s. AC*, 2015, 269–282.

11 François Querel, "Le décor sculpté," in *'Iraq al Amir. Le château du Tobiade Hyrcan I*, Will and Larche eds. In his contribution to the *Guide historique et archéologique*, Querel characterizes the sculptural decoration of the Qasr, 113, as " (-) un gout presque archaïsant pour des formes anciennes."

12 See Jean-Marie Dentzer, *Guide Historique et Archéologique*, 87–91.

13 See Laurent Borel, *Guide Historique et Archéologique*, 83–86. The final publication of this intriguing example of Hellenistic architecture is eagerly awaited.

14 "La façade nord du *Qasr* apparaît ainsi comme une curieuse combination d'éléments d'origine diverse et plus ou moins heuresement articulés les uns avec les autres. Les incongruités y sont nombreuses." Will and Larche, *'Iraq al Amir. Le château du Tobiade Hyrcan I*, 278.

15 Eclecticism is here defined as the employment of two or more models, subject types or period styles, see Jean-Pierre Epron, *Comprendre l'éclectisme* (Paris: Institut Français d'Architecture Norma Editions, 1997).

16 For the functioning of globalising *koine* in these terms of universalisation and particularisation, see Martin Pitts and Miguel John Versluys eds., *Globalization and the Roman World. World History, Connectivity and Material Culture* (Cambridge: Cambridge 2015), 141–174.

17 Miguel John Versluys, *Visual style and constructing identity in the Hellenistic world. Nemrud Dağ and Commagene under Antiochos I* (Cambridge: Cambridge University Press, 2017).

18 For more on this perspective, see, Klaus Stefan Freyberger, *Die frühkaiserzeitlichen Heiligtümer der Karawanenstationen im hellenisierten Osten. Zeugnisse eines kulturellen Konflikts im Spannungsfeld zweier politischer Formationen* (Mainz: Nünnerich-Asmus Verlag, 1998).

Colonial Prescriptions in Paris

Samia Henni

Colonial, civil and military norms and forms have often traveled from colonized to colonizer countries and among colonized territories. Two brief examples from France illustrate these colonial circulations. The first trajectory of influence extended from French Marshal Thomas Robert Bugeaud, Marquis de la Piconnerie, Duc d'Isly to Baron Georges-Eugène Haussmann. Bugeaud served as the governor general of Algeria under French colonial rule between 1840 and 1847.[1] Following his service in Algeria he published the treatise *La Guerre des Rues et des Maisons* (The War of Streets and Houses), a manual for the preparation and conduct of urban warfare based on his experiences in the field designing spatial counterinsurgency measures in colonized Algeria.[2] Since the manuscript had apparently served to undermine the revolutionary ferment of Paris, it duly inspired Haussmann's transformations of the city between 1853 and 1870. Thus French colonial knowledge traveled from colonized Algeria to Paris under Emperor Napoleon III. The second example is the legacy of Marshal Joseph Simon Gallieni, who served in a number of French colonies including Senegal, Réunion, Martinique, Sudan, Indochina, and Madagascar, and inspired Marshal Louis Lyautey's dominant military "colonial school."[3] Lyautey served under Gallieni's command in French Indochina from 1892 to 1896. Together Lyautey and Gallieni attempted to devise a new approach to the consolidation of colonialism, stressing sociopolitical actions over military measures. When Lyautey became the first resident general of the newly designated French protectorate of Morocco, between 1912 and '24, the jointly devised prescriptions traveled with him. Lyautey's "colonial school" is outlined in his published articles and letters, as well as in the urban planning proposals and architectural projects he developed in Morocco with architect and urban planner Henri Prost, including master plans for Casablanca, Fès, Marrakesh, Meknes, and Rabat.[4]

In the twentieth century the dissemination and implementation of French colonial practices in France became especially apparent during the country's two most debated wars: the Vichy Regime (1940–44) during the Second World War, and the Algerian Revolution (1954–62). The French colonial regime issued specific directives to clear the bidonvilles (shantytowns or slums; literally "can-towns") of Algiers and Paris where the Algerian populations lived while transferring French colonial civil servants and military officers from Algiers to Paris to oversee the Algerian population in Paris. One of the architects of this prescription was Maurice Papon, a former civil servant in Vichy France.

This paper investigates the ways in which French colonial norms and forms circulated between Algeria and France, from the French Fourth Republic to colonized Algeria, from Vichy Regime to colonized Algeria, and from colonized Algeria to the French Fifth Republic (constitutionally established in 1958, during the bloody war to keep Algeria under colonial rule). The paper examines the French colonial policies prescribed in Algeria and the institutionalized colonial forms employed in Paris in order to scrutinize the traces of colonialism in France and the survival of fascist practices in French colonies as well as in the French Fourth and Fifth Republics.

Operation Bidonville

In October 1958 the civil cabinet of the French prefecture of Algiers issued the directive "Aménagement des bidonvilles" (Planning of Shantytowns), signed by General Jacques Massu, commander of Algiers in charge of both military and civil authorities, and one of the architects of the infamous Battle of Algiers (September 1956–September 1957), during which tens of thousands of people were placed under house arrest and thousands of others were tortured or killed, or simply disappeared.[5] FIG 1, 2 He wrote:

> The problem of housing plays an important role in the exceptional effort undertaken for the social and economic recovery of the workers; this has triggered the construction of many HLMs [*habitat à loyer modéré*, or low-cost housing] and the extension of the policy of access to property.[6]

Massu argued, however, that this solution was unaffordable for certain segments of the population owing to the initial capital required. He stressed that the financial burden had been significantly reduced due to the strategic donation of land by certain municipalities. These donations provided indirect revenues, and the construction sites represented active economic hubs within the municipality.

Massu noted that while waiting for the construction of proper dwellings for the inhabitants of the vast shantytowns it was "necessary to absorb the 'bidonvilles' as soon as possible by undertaking their ordered, openly spaced reconstruction by the inhabitants themselves, under the control of a technician who can easily be found locally."[7] To enforce this directive he called on the civil capacities and military skills of special military units called Urban Administrative Sections (SAU).

The SAUs were extraordinary army units deployed in Algeria's urban areas to carry out both military and civilian assignments. Similar units called Specialized Administrative Sections (SAS) were deployed in Algeria's rural areas. The military missions of SAU and SAS officers entailed gathering of intelligence, diffusion of propaganda, maintenance of law and order, and direct control of the population. Their civil functions were to provide social, economic, educational, sanitary, and medical facilities, as well as to organize the forced resettlement of Algeria's rural populations and build militarily controlled camps. By the end of 1961 twenty SAUs coexisted in the urban neighborhoods inhabited by the Algerian population, and more than seven hundred SASs were spread across the Algerian countryside and Sahara, where most of France's politico-economic interests were located (oil and gas, and nuclear testing).[8] Massu stressed that the SAUs and SAUs were capable of assisting with the planning program:

> SAS chief officers stationed to your municipalities are qualified to help you and relieve you of some of your tasks by facilitating the execution of any measures that you might need to take, and by obtaining any material support from the local military authorities.[9]

Under the directive of the "Aménagement des Bidonvilles," General Massu turned more than one hundred sixty bidonvilles in Algiers into legalized forced-labor sites.[10] Approximately one-third of the population of the city's bidonvilles was constrained to building basic infrastructures and marginally improving their provisional shelters under the constant control of the French army, represented by SAU officers familiar with the inhabitants and their conditions.

Like Algiers's famous densely populated Casbah, the bidonvilles were perceived as revolutionary strongholds that French civil and military authorities found extremely difficult to penetrate and therefore control. FIG 3 The French army developed specialized counterrevolutionary operations that SAU officers employed first in the immense shantytowns of

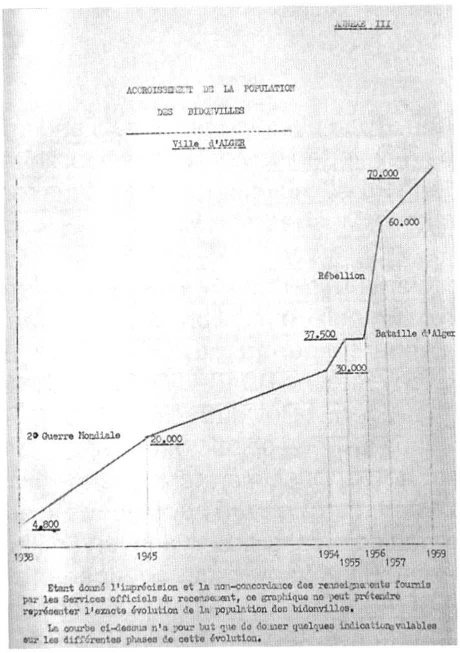

ANNEXE III

ACCROISSEMENT DE LA POPULATION DES BIDONVILLES

Ville d'ALGER

Etant donné l'imprécision et la non-concordance des renseignements fournis par les Services officiels du recensement, ce graphique ne peut prétendre représenter l'exacte évolution de la population des bidonvilles.

La courbe ci-dessus n'a pour but que de donner quelques indications valables sur les différentes phases de cette évolution.

FIG 2
Chart indicating that during the bloody, infamous Bataille d'Alger the number of Inhabitants of the bidonvilles in Algiers doubled.

FIG 1
A still from the movie *La Battaglia di Algeri*, directed by Gillo Pontecorvo, 1966.

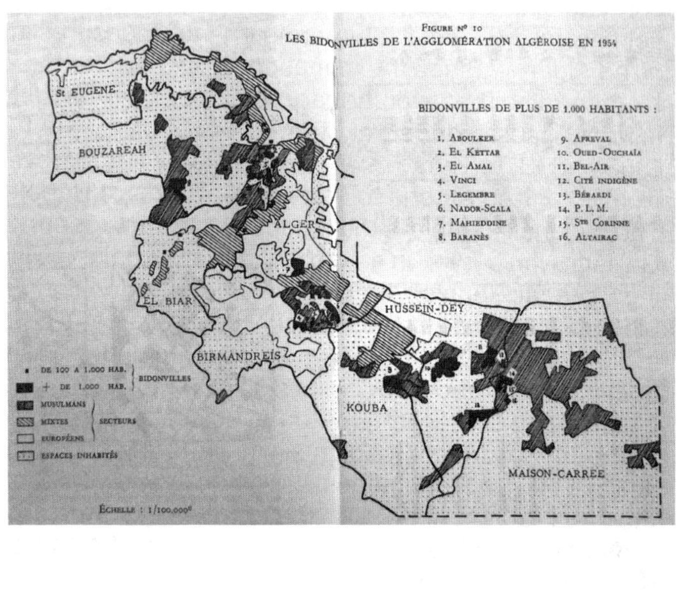

FIG 3
Bidonvilles in the Algiers Region in 1954.

Algiers and later in those populated by Algerian migrants in the suburbs of Paris, most notably Bidonvilles de Nanterre.[11] In addition to generating concerns about hygiene, the bidonvilles were considered to be an "uncontrolled and unrecorded population, inevitably serving as a refuge for criminals and killers of the FLN (Algerian National Liberation Front)."[12] During the violent Battle of Algiers, military authorities launched Operation Bidonville to impose "a simple organization that would enable the easy control of all of the inhabitants and the detection of suspicious elements."[13] French officers were requested to follow a tested systematic method that comprised a number of measures, as follows:

> 1. First they were to number groups of bidonville houses: the group numbering (*numérotage*) included any huts or other structures built around the same courtyard. The assigned number was to be painted on the facade of the shelter and to be roughly 50 centimeters high by 10–50 centimeters wide.
>
> 2. Next they were to establish detailed records for three hierarchies of assumed leaders: the head of the family and the head of the group of houses (both of whom were designated by the Algerian inhabitants), and the head of the cluster, who was nominated by the French military commander of the bidonville sector.
>
> 3. They were then to deliver new numbered identity cards incorporating the letter of the military sector, the number of the bidonville, the assigned letter of the cluster, and the allotted number of the group of houses: for instance, "N 47 C 11." Those who had no identity cards were obliged to apply for one within eight days of their identity control.[14]

Frequent searches were to be carried out at any time of day or night. According to French military authorities, the efficiency of the numbering system for identifying every human being, referred to as a *numéro minéralogique* (number plate), would effortlessly facilitate the rigorous and permanent control of the bidonville population. Control was also assured by placing the appointed heads of clusters, groups of houses, and families responsible for registered people under direct official control.[15] In essence the inhabitants were subject to a state of siege, and the bidonvilles of Algiers became military battlefields. Operation Bidonville echoed the colonial doctrines of subversive counterrevolutionary warfare scripted and implemented by French military officers of French Algeria (*Algérie Française*) who later staged the coup d'état of May 1958, triggering General Charles de Gaulle's return to power.

Eugène Claudius-Petit and the SONACOTRAL

Most of the Algerians who contributed to the physical reconstruction of France after the Second World War lived in bidonvilles such as in the notorious one in Nanterre.[16] According to the 1954 census the number of Algerian workers in France was estimated to be 210,000 out of 1,553,600 foreign workers, including Italians, Spanish, Portuguese, and immigrants from the French protectorates and colonies of Africa and Asia who were part of the French colonial empire.[17]

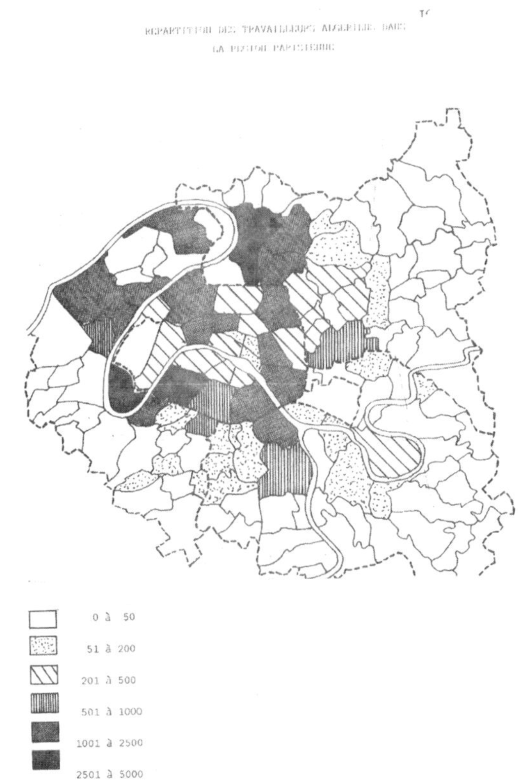

FIG 4 Distribution of Algerian workers in the region of Paris in the 1960s.

In 1956 French prime minister Guy Mollet established the National Construction Company for Algerian Workers in France (SONACOTRAL, today known as Adoma).[18] Eugène Claudius-Petit, who served as Minister of Reconstruction and Urbanism between September 1948 and January 1953, was appointed the first chairman of SONACOTRAL, a role he held from 1956 to 1977. A friend of Le Corbusier, Claudius-Petit played an essential part in establishing public urban-planning policies and determining the parameters and standards for the design of new housing units in France.

As head of SONACOTRAL Claudius-Petit's was charged with dismantling the bidonvilles that had proliferated around the suburbs of Paris and to guarantee "the financing, construction, and arrangement of *locaux d'habitation* (residential premises) intended for French Muslims from Algeria, who came to work in France and their families."[19] Claudius-Petit was assisted by Jean Vaujour, the former director of General Safety in colonized Algeria who in 1960 became director of the military and civil cabinets of the general delegate of the French government in Algeria, Paul Delouvrier. Vaujour was "convinced of the utility of the Company, and [was] familiar with Algeria and Algerians."[20]

The pairing of Claudius-Petit and Vaujour had been meticulously selected. While Claudius-Petit was skilled in large-scale urban development and public mass-housing projects and policies in postwar France, Vaujour was proficient in ensuring public order and national security in colonized Algeria. As a result of this partnership, the pair envisioned an off-the-record political mission: SONACOTRAL would contribute to sabotaging the growing influence of National Liberation Front members who lived (or might come to live) in the bidonvilles. In providing beds for Algerian workers in France, in other words, SONACOTRAL undertook the supervision of Algerian inhabitants of the French bidonvilles.

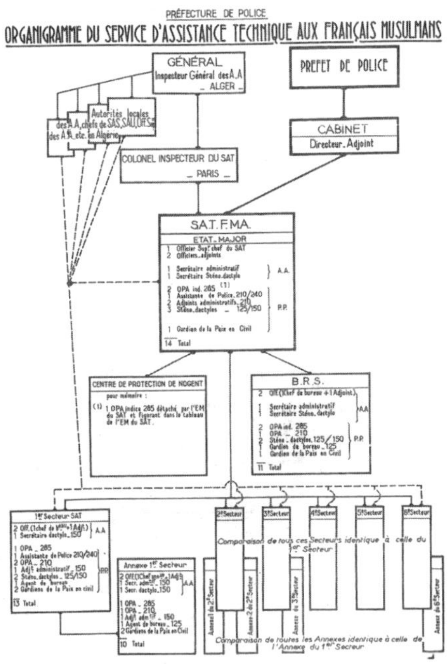

FIG 5
Organizational chart of the Service d'assistance technique aux français musulmans of the Paris Police.

The first bidonville operation in Paris enforced by Claudius-Petit, Vaujour, and the SONACOTRAL team was in the prefecture of the Seine, where forty percent of Algerian laborers were located. FIG 4 The most urgent requirements of the *lits de foyers* (beds in hostels, or dormitories) were evaluated to be 16,900 beds for the first phase and an additional 6,000 beds for a second stage, in the region of Paris. In this context SONACOTRAL created temporary shelters called *foyer-hôtels* (hotels) for single male workers and *cités de transit* (transitory estates) for married workers and their families. Later SONACOTRAL built *grand ensembles*, most notably Les Canibouts in Nanterre, designed by architect Marcel Roux,[21] who collaborated with Claudius-Petit at the ministry.

Although the two typologies were not expected to last—both dormitories and collective shelters were meant to be provisional—the resulting buildings were transformed into standard low-cost collective housing once the Algerian workers returned to their homeland. Every unit accommodated approximately two hundred fifty beds; the multibed rooms housed ten beds, and the kitchens and bathrooms were shared. To facilitate surveillance the newly hired managers of the dormitories were former policemen, veterans, or colonial administrators.[22] In its first ten years SONACONTRAL built just over sixty *foyers* in France[23]—that is, 15,000 beds—for Algerian workers constrained to remain in France, as well as other migrants from neighboring countries and former colonies, who contributed to the rapid French economic development of The Glorious Thirties.

Paris Police and the SAT-FMA

The supervision of the Algerian population in Parisian bidonvilles was reinforced with the 1958 appointment of Maurice Papon, a former civil servant under France's Vichy Regime, as prefect of the Paris police by Félix Gaillard's government. This role resulted in the 1961 massacre of Algerian pro-independence protesters in Paris. Papon had served in the department of Constantine (Northeastern Algeria) as Inspector General of Extraordinary Missions (IGAME) between 1956 and 1958. Various colonial civil and military norms and forms that had been applied in Algeria were transferred to France with the arrival in Paris of Papon, who had been granted the French Resistance Card in 1958. However, in 1998 Papon was charged with committing crimes against humanity at the Assizes Court in Bordeaux for his complicity in the deportation of Jews while he was general secretary of the Gironde Prefecture.[24]

As prefect of the Paris police, Papon established the Office of Technical Assistance to French Muslims of Algeria (SAT-FMA). FIG 5 Its mandate was "to strengthen the action that has been undertaken in the Seine in order to protect the Muslim population from political influence and the material constraints of anti-nationalist organizations."[25] To achieve this aim Papon brought experienced French SAU officers who had headed bidonvilles in colonized Algiers back to France in order to supervise Parisian *bidonvilles* inhabited by Algerians.

Notable among these officers was Captain Montaner, who was chief of the SAU at the Bidonville de Clos-Salembier, in Algiers, and became chief of the SAT-FMA at the Bidonville de Nanterre, in Paris. The French Study and Action Group for North Africans in the Paris Region (GEANARP) described Montaner as follows:

> Drawing on psychological methods, he immediately enjoyed influence because he spoke Arabic, knew the Koranic laws, and worked effectively with the administration. He has substantial funds, and the means he employs are similar to those used by any other social worker in a North African context. ... He pursues a completely different goal, however: with him the spirit of May 13 and of the *Algérie française* pervades Nanterre.[26]

The spirit of May 13 is referred to as the first French Generals' Putsch in Algiers on that day in 1958, four years after the outbreak of the Algerian Revolution, in November 1954. The coup was led by civil servants and army officers, advocates of French Algeria including General Massu, commander-in-chief of the bloody Battle of Algiers, and General Raoul Salan, France's most decorated officer, who in 1961 had coestablished the paramilitary underground terrorist group Organization of the Secret Army (OAS), which opposed Algerian independence. The May 1958 putsch was fully supported by right-wing Europeans, known as *ultras*, some of whom later founded France's National Front.

Papon's Background and Legacy

Papon's long and widely discussed trial of 1998 not only provoked controversial debates about France's memory, history, testimony, justice, and morality but also facilitated links and parallels between the Vichy regime and the French War in Algeria, or as the French authorities officially referred to it, the Algerian War of Independence.[27] Although a number of historians and French bureaucrats object to tracing presumed or real historical parallels between these two still questionable and disputed wars, Papon might at least be considered as an emblematic case, a symbol, or a catalyst of this fascist /colonial legacy. To this end Papon's biography and legacies deserve further review.

Following the liberation of France in 1944, Papon managed to escape the French *épuration légale* (legal purge), despite his previous activities as a Vichy civil servant, by claiming to have participated in the Resistance.[28] While avoiding justice for more than fifty years Papon enjoyed an "exemplary" career as a high-ranking French government official in Algeria under French rule, in the French protectorate of Morocco, and in various governments in France.

Papon first studied law and political economy and then psychology and sociology. Later he graduated from the Institute of Political Studies in Paris. In 1934 he enrolled in the League of Radical Socialist University Action (LAURS), then headed by Pierre Mendès France, and participated in the protests against the French extreme right wing, notably the Parisian riots of February 6, 1934.[29] A young François Mitterrand also participated in those riots, albeit as a student member of the National Volunteers, an organization related to the Croix de Feu, a French right-wing league led by Colonel François de La Rocque, who served in Algeria and Morocco under the authority of General Lyautey. At the time Papon was, in his own words, "of the left. Without being leftist."[30]

Prior to the Vichy regime, Papon held the position of attaché in various French government ministries of the Third Republic, including the ministries of interior, foreign affairs, and the Secretary of State for the Presidency of the Council. In 1944 he was appointed prefect of the Landes, in southwestern France, and cabinet director of the commissioner of the Republic in Bordeaux.

First Massacre

On October 26, 1945, Papon was in charge of the subcommission of colonial Algeria at the French Ministry of the Interior, replacing General Georges Catroux as state commissioner for Muslim Affairs. His nomination followed the tragic carnage of Algerians protesting against French colonial rule in the towns of Sétif, Guelma, and Kherrata, in the northeastern region of Constantine. The protests took place on May 8, 1945, the same day Nazi Germany surrendered, ending the Second World War in Europe, in which many Algerian soldiers had participated and died. On that symbolic independence day, French authorities did not hesitate to employ air power to destroy Algerian villages and arbitrarily open fire on Algerians in order to repress any desire for decolonization and eventual independence.

The number of Algerian victims is still widely disputed; casualties are estimated to range from fifteen hundred to forty-five thousand.[31] This tragedy was one of the reasons for the foundation of the Revolutionary Committee for Unity and Action (CRUA), which would later evolve into the National Liberation Front. In this context Papon was expected to ensure the communication of decisions between the French governor general of Algeria and the French Ministry of the Interior in Paris regarding the juridical repercussions of May 1945 upon the Algerian and French populations.

Papon "participated in the elaboration of the project of the law of 1946 concerning the events in the Constantine region,"[32] which introduced him to the realm of colonial affairs in Algeria under French rule. He also adamantly opposed the proposition to transfer the functions of his subcommission to the governor general of Algeria, as well as to establish a resident minister in Algeria instead of a governor general of Algeria, which arose in the aftermath of General de Gaulle's resignation, in January 1946. Papon's opposition was fueled by the fact that "the institution of a minister resident quickly appeared as the establishment of a diarchy between Paris and Algiers, and a taste of the end."[33]

After serving as chief of the cabinet of the state secretary under the French Minister of the Interior in 1946 and then as prefect of Corsica in 1947, Papon was appointed prefect of the department of Constantine on September 17, 1949. At the time of his appointment the general governor of Algeria under French rule was socialist Marcel-Edmond Naegelen (1892–1978), who failed to supervise the 1948 French legislative elections for the Algerian assembly. In his 1962 memoirs on his missions in colonial Algeria between 1948 and 1951, Naegelen portrayed Constantine

> as the poorest of the three [Algerian departments], the one where the European population was least dense, the one which pan-Arab propaganda affected most directly, the one which had been the theatre of the horrors of May 1945 in the cities and regions of Sétif and Guelma, the one where the general rebellion would break out in the Aurès on 1 November 1954.[34]

Consequently in the daunting department of Constantine, Papon was expected, among other things, to thoroughly reorganize the administrative services of the prefecture in order to gather intelligence; to address the question of the territorial and social *sous-administration* (subadministration) as a way to impede the expansion of various nationalist movements; and to ensure the nonelection of Algerians in the Algerian assembly during the legislative elections of June 1951 by means of vote rigging, as had occurred in April 1948. His most important task was to create suitable solutions to the legal status of the *disparus* (missing persons): those "disappeared" Algerians who had been murdered during the French massacres of May 1945 and whose bodies had been burned.[35]

Paris Police

Following this colonial experience in Constantine, at the end of 1951 Papon was appointed secretary general of the prefecture of the Paris police. His transfer from colonial Constantine to metropolitan Paris preceded the 1958 situation discussed earlier, when Papon was again devolved from wartime-era Constantine to Paris: not as secretary general this time but as Prefect of the Paris Police. The influence on the French police of colonial policies in Algeria was not new to French authorities. The intimate relationship could be traced back to Louis Jean-Baptiste Lépine, who served first as prefect of the Paris police between 1893 and 1897, then as governor general of Algeria from 1897 to 1899, and then again as police prefect from 1899 to 1913.[36] These back-and-forth exchanges between the experiences gained in Algeria under colonial rule and France intensified dramatically after the Second World War.[37] Yet unlike other figures, Papon was also guided by the practices of the Vichy regime; thus his presence in colonial Constantine during the Algerian War of Independence deserves further examination.

In summer 1954, a few months prior to the outbreak of the Algerian War, Papon was appointed secretary general of the French protectorate in Morocco under the government of Pierre Mendès France. There he was involved predominantly in planning colonial reforms that aimed to limit Morocco's demands for independence, such as formulating various socioeconomic policies for urban and rural *équipments* (infrastructure or equipment).[38] In January 1956 Papon became a member of the investigation committee of the General Commissariat of the Plan (CGP), a French institution established in 1946 by General de Gaulle with the aim of elaborating the long-term economic planning of France's reconstruction, particularly through five-year plans such as the Monnet and Marshall Plans. Papon's position did not last long. In February 1956 he was appointed technical advisor to the cabinet of the French Minister of the Interior for Algerian Affairs.

The IGAME's Powers

Whereas Morocco gained its independence on March 2, 1956, and Tunisia on March 20, 1956, the newly appointed French resident minister of Algeria, Robert Lacoste, obtained the bill of the *pouvoirs spéciaux* (exceptional powers) from the French national assembly in Paris to maintain law and order in the French departments of Algeria, to protect its people and goods, and to safeguard the territory of Algeria—that is, to maintain Algeria under French rule.[39] Soon new administrative reforms were announced, and Papon was appointed prefect of both the department of Constantine (as he had previously served, between 1949 and 1951) and the IGAME for the region of Eastern Algeria. The status of the IGAME was reactivated in 1948 by Minister of the Interior Jules Salvador Moch (1893–1985), in the wake of the French labor strikes in 1947; he bore responsibility for ensuring public order and security in the departments that covered France's military regions.[40] The IGAME was the direct successor of the *inspecteurs régionaux* (regional inspectors), which had been first instituted in France by the Vichy regime.[41]

The regional inspectors were established legally on April 19, 1941; acting as an intermediate echelon between the government and the departments, they were charged with the coordination of information and implementation of Vichy-era laws. In their extraordinary missions the regional prefects were directly assisted by, as French historian Pierre Barral wrote, "two special collaborators: the intendant [a chief administrative officer] of the police and the intendant of economic affairs."[42] Ironically the decrees of 1951 and 1953 expanded the fields of proficiency of the 1948 IGAME to cover administrative and economic matters. The IGAME also became involved in the development and management of long-term economic plans.

With his 1956 position as IGAME, Papon held "the higher control and the overall coordination of civil and military authorities in the departments included in the Region of Eastern Algeria."[43] This vast area was composed of the departments of Constantine, Batna, Bône (today Annaba), and Sétif, and corresponded with one of the three French military divisions of colonial Algeria.[44] The regions of Constantine, Algiers, and Oran—stretching from the eastern border with Tunisia to the western boundary with Morocco—coincided with the Tenth Military Region of France. As a result of his influential dual function, Papon represented and administered the department of Constantine and prefects of Constantine (by himself), Batna (with General Gaston Parlange, who became prefect of Batna in August 1956), Bône, and Sétif.[45] He was also in direct correspondence with the military commander-in-chief of the Constantine army corps, who operated in the territory that included the aforementioned departments. In this context Papon was responsible for ensuring law and order, defining the forbidden zones, obliterating the Political-Administrative Organization (OPA) of the FLN, monitoring the forced relocation and grouping of the civilian population, supervising the civil-military operations conducted by the SAS, and gathering intelligence.

In a letter to Lacoste dated July 5, 1956, about the administrative reforms, Papon avowed the following:

> I think, for my part, that the implementation of new administrations requires a broad effort of adaptation to which we cannot escape, and original solutions, even if they seem exorbitant to the common law, are essential to give birth to new departments.[46]

During his 1997–98 trial, as Papon was interrogated about the details of his long career, he was asked to describe his life before and after the Vichy regime. While portraying the second wave of his functions in the Algerian town of Constantine under French colonial rule between 1956 and 1958, the octogenarian Papon asserted, "My mission was pacification."[47] He was seemingly faithful to the general terminology dictated by the French Republic in colonial Algeria, yet according to Jean-Luc Einaudi—French political activist and author of *La Bataille de Paris: 17 Octobre 1961*—Papon stimulated the expansion of a total war in eastern Algeria. During the course of a press conference in the prefecture of Constantine, Papon unequivocally ordered "all civilians to behave as soldiers" and stressed that there were "no longer military officers and civilians. It is necessary to be merely soldiers."[48]

Although his two books were published in 1991, prior to Papon's conviction in 1998 by the French authorities, Einaudi had demonstrated that "under [Papon's] authority [as prefect and IGAME of Constantine], extrajudicial executions and the use of torture [were] practiced by military officers and policemen. Torture became a habitual and normal means to gather intelligence."[49] Einaudi argued that Lacoste buttressed the "interrogation centers" and praised the measures that Papon took in Constantine, declaring that he was "one of the best administrative leaders in Algeria."[50] Papon was so persuasive that he was designated to defend French policies in Algeria at the United Nations General Assembly in autumn 1957.[51]

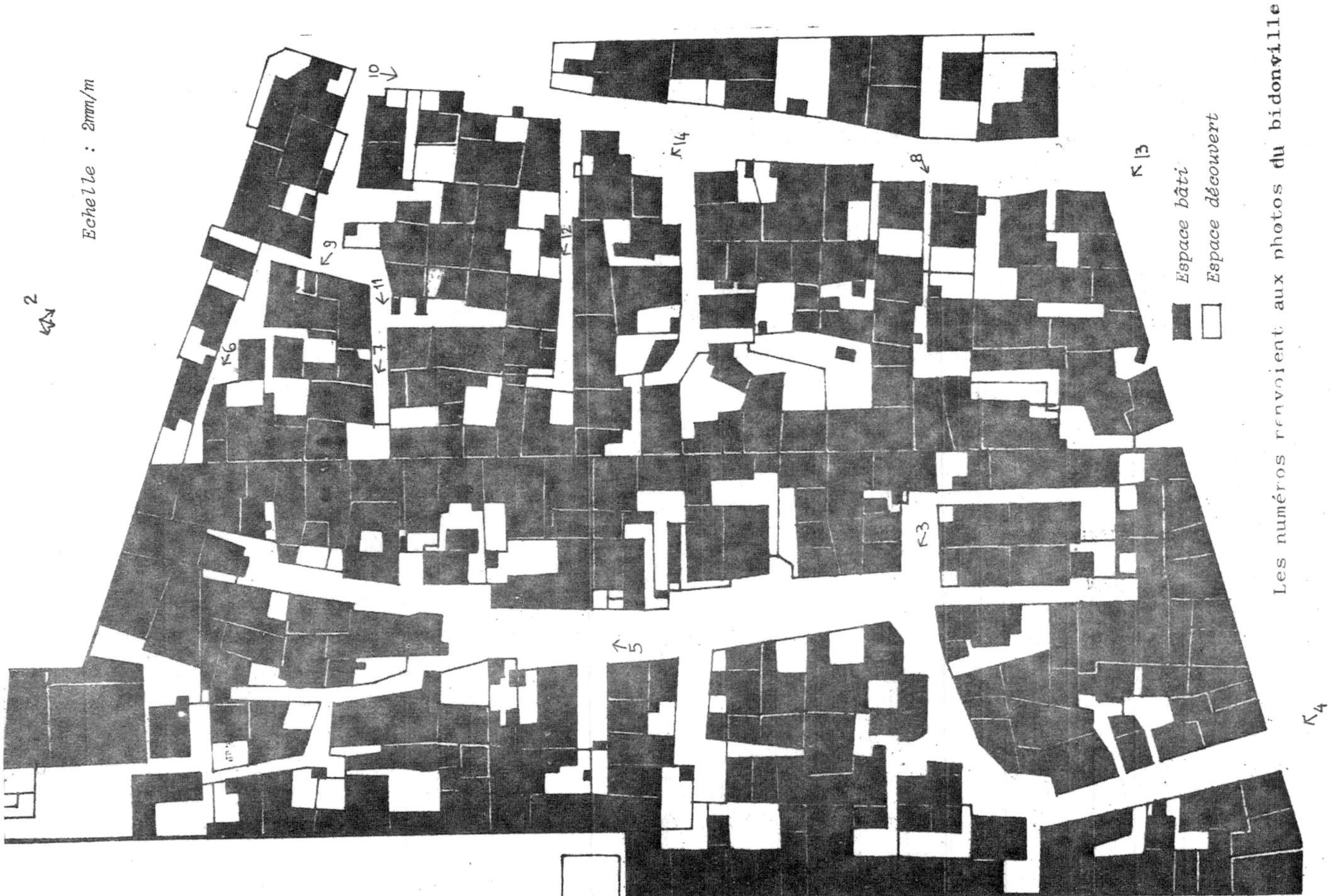

FIG 6
Plan and photographs documenting a bidonville in rue des prés in Paris.

FIG 7
"Here we Drown Algerians."

Back to Paris

In the course of the Algerian Revolution, the Papon system was not restricted to colonized Algerians; it continued unabated in Paris after he became prefect of the Paris police, in March 1958. In June of that year General de Gaulle retained Papon in the post; under the new Fifth Republic (until January 1967), Papon became the longest-serving police chief since the time of Louis Lépine, around the turn of the twentieth century (as Papon himself proudly proclaimed).[52] Jean Chapel—another former Vichy civil servant in Bordeaux who had also escaped the purge—replaced Papon in Constantine.

Former Vichy officials continued to inhabit and serve in colonized Algeria; echoes of the Vichy regime and the Second World War persisted in Algeria under French rule even after Papon's departure from Constantine.[53] While describing his various responsibilities as Paris police prefect during his trial, Papon confirmed that one of his roles was to fight "the assaults organized by the FLN, whose methods of action were founded in terrorism, as routinely occur today in all countries."[54] With the intention of targeting Algerian immigrants in Paris and destabilizing their claims for independence, Papon maintained that he "had asked SAS officers, who had done wonders in their pacification tasks, to come from Algeria. We were able to penetrate the FLN environments and, in the end, dominate this devastating phenomenon."[55] Not only did Papon deliberately transfer certain Vichy methods to colonized Algeria, but he also brought specific actors and techniques that had been employed in Algeria to be used under the newly established the Fifth Republic under General de Gaulle.

Immediately after Papon's nomination in Paris, three senior SAS and SAU officers "were secretly flown in from Algeria on August 13, 1958,"[56] to first create the aforementioned SAT-FMA, which was directly controlled by the newly established Office of Coordination of Algerian Affairs (SCAA) of the Paris police prefecture. Other SAS officers arrived from Algeria to strategically lead special-intelligence offices in Paris called the Specialized Intelligence Bureau (BRS). Papon invigorated the exchanges of information and strategies between the SAS in colonial Algeria and the SAT-FMA in Paris.[57]

In 1988 Papon published *Les Chevaux du pouvoir: Le Préfet de police du général de Gaulle ouvre des dossiers, 1958–1967*, in which he firmly denies the massacre of October 1961 and eulogizes his role in smashing the FLN. According to Papon, his intention was "to settle SAS officers who spoke Arabic, knew the specific problems of migrant workers, and were sensitive to their difficulties and misfortunes—even their distress—in those areas inhabited by the Muslim population, where we were almost absent." Papon did not employ SAS officers and infiltrate *harki*[59] agents among Algerians in Paris to provide socioeconomic support, but rather to create comprehensive *fichiers* (index card files), conduct a full census of the Algerian community, identify FLN supporters, and diffuse anti-FLN propaganda campaigns in the bidonvilles of Paris. FIG 6 Because such measures did not completely satisfy Papon, he imposed a curfew on all Algerians—or *Français musulmans d'Algérie* (French Muslims from Algeria), as the French authorities called the Algerian population—between 8:30 p.m. and 5:30 a.m. Their cafés had to close by 7:00 p.m., and any travel by car must be controlled or their vehicles would be temporarily impounded.[60]

Second Massacre

In October 1961 thousands of Algerians (including women and children) demonstrated peacefully against this "system" in the streets of Paris. What became known as the Battle of Paris culminated in the killing of hundreds and the detention of thousands of Algerians. After beating them, the French police physically forced many Algerians into the River Seine.[61] FIG 7 Those arrested were detained in the Vélodrome d'Hiver (Winter Velodrome), located in the Fifteenth Arrondissement, where some twenty years earlier the majority of Jews deported during the Vichy regime had been gathered. Thus Vichy methods employed in Bordeaux had been adopted in colonized Algeria to be adapted in turn for use against colonized Algerians in Paris, the capital of the democratic Fifth Republic of France.

1 On this influence, see for example, Stephen Graham, "Cities as Strategic Sites: Place Annihilation and Urban Geopolitics," in *Cities, War, and Terrorism: Towards an Urban Geopolitics*, ed. Stephen Graham (Malden, UK: Blackwell Publishing, 2004), 33–38; Kanishka Goonewardena, "Space and Revolution in Theory and Practice: Eight Theses," in *Cities for People, Not for Profit: Critical Urban Theory and the Right to the City*, ed. Neil Brenner, Peter Marcuse, and Margit Mayer (London and New York: Routledge, 2012), 86–101; Philipp Misselwitz and Eyal Weizman, "Military Operations as Urban Planning," in *Territories: Islands, Camps, and Other States of Utopia*, ed. Anselm Franke (Cologne: Walther König, 2003), 273–81.

2 The manual was lost for many years until it reappeared and was published in France in 1997. Maréchal Bugeaud, "La guerre des rues et des maisons," unpublished manuscript presented by Maïté Bouyssy (Paris: Jean-Paul Rocher, 1997).

3 On Lyautey's "colonial school," see Samia Henni, *Architecture of Counterrevolution: The French Army in Northern Algeria* (Zurich: gta Verlag, 2017), 56–59.

4 See for example, Paul Rabinow, *French Modern: Norms and Forms of the Social Environment* (Chicago: University of Chicago Press, 1995), 104–25.

5 See, Henni, *Architecture of Counterrevolution*, 149–60.

6 Archives nationales françaises d'outre-mer (FR ANOM) 2 SAS 167. Préfecture d'Alger, Cabinet civil, Le général de division Massu, Commandant la Zone Nord Algérois et de la 10e DP exerçant les pouvoirs civils dans le Département d'Alger à Messieurs les présidents des délégations spéciales, Aménagement des bidonvilles, Algiers, 2 October 1958.

7 FR ANOM 2 SAS 167.

8 Jacques Frémeaux, "Les SAS (Sections Administratives Spécialisées)," *Guerres mondiales et conflits contemporains* 4, no. 208 (2002): 56.

9 Frémeaux, "Les SAS."

10 It was calculated that by 1954 one-third of Algiers' population (86,500 inhabitants) were living in bidonvilles. See Robert Descloitres, Jean-Claude Reverdy, and Claudine Descloitres, *L'Algérie des bidonvilles: le tiers monde dans la cité* (Paris: Monton & Co., 1961), 65.

11 On French counterrevolutionary policies in the bidonvilles, or the anti-bidonville strategy in Algiers and Paris, see for example, Neil MacMaster, "Shantytown Republics: Algerian Migrants and the Culture of Space in the Bidonvilles," in *Transnational Spaces and Identities in the Francophone World* (Lincoln and London: University of Nebraska Press, 2009), 73–93. On the Nanterre bidonville, see for example, Isabelle Herpin and Serge Santelli, *Cahiers d'architecture 1. Bidonville à Nanterre: étude architecturale. Unité Pédagogique d'Architecture* 8 (Paris: Institut de l'environnement, 1971); Monique Hervo, *Chroniques du bidonville: Nanterre en guerre d'Algérie, 1959–1962* (Paris: Editions du Seuil, 2001); Abelmalek Sayad and Eliane Dupuy, *Un Nanterre algérien, terre de bidonvilles* (Paris: Editions Autrement, 1995).

12 Archives du Service historique de l'armée de terre (SHAT) 1 H 1213. Comment j'ai résorbé les bidonvilles de Bône, 1.

13 FR ANOM 1 K 1183. Commandant militaire du département d'Alger, Commandement du Grand Alger, Note de Service no. 685/C.EMM, Opération bidonville, Algiers, 19 February 1957.

14 FR ANOM 1 K 1183, 1–3. Additif à la note de service, Numérotage des cartes d'identité, Algiers, 20 February 1957.

15 FR ANOM 1 K 1183.

16 On the Nanterre bidonville see, for example, Hervo, *Chroniques du bidonville*.

17 Herpin and Santelli, *Cahiers d'architecture 1*, 11–18. By 1962 there were 335,000 Algerian workers in France. This number does not include political refugees and foreign students.

18 After Algerian independence SONATRAL lost its *L* and became SONATRA (Société nationale de construction de logements pour les travailleurs). Today it is called Adoma. On the foundation of SONACOTRAL, see, for example, Marc Bernardot, "Une politique de logement: la Sonacotra (1956–1992)" (PhD diss., University of Paris, 1997); Choukri Hmed, "Loger les étrangers 'isolés' en France. Socio-histoire d'une institution d'État, la Sonacotra (1956–2006)" (PhD diss., University of Paris, 2006).

19 Cited in Marc Bernardot, "Chronique d'une institution: la 'sonacotra' (1956–1976)," *Sociétés contemporaines*, no. 33–34 (1999): 40.

20 Benoît Pouvreau, *Un politique en architecture: Eugène Claudius-Petit (1907–1989)* (Paris: Le Moniteur, 2004), 170.

21 Bernardot, "Chronique," 44.

22 Amelia H. Lyons, *The Civilizing Mission in the Metropole: Algerian Families and the French Welfare State during Decolonization* (Stanford, CA: Stanford University Press, 2013), 124.

23 Bernardot, "Chronique," 42.

24 On the Papon trial, see for example, Catherine Erhel, Mathieu Aucher, and Renaud de La Baume, *Le Procès de Maurice Papon: 8 octobre 1997–8 janvier 1998*, vol. 1 (Paris: Editions Albin Michel, 1998); Eric Conan, *Le procès Papon: un journal d'audience* (Paris: Editions Gallimard, 1998); Richard Golsan, ed., *The Papon Affair: Memory and Justice on Trial* (New York and London: Routledge, 2000). On Papon's years as a Vichy civil servant, see for example, Gérard Boulanger, *Maurice Papon: un technocrate français dans la collaboration* (Paris: Editions du Seuil, 1994).

25 Roger Cunibile, *L'assistance technique aux français musulmans d'Algérie à la préfecture de police à Paris* (n.d., 1961), 42. There were other public and private institutions dealing with the so-called "North-Africans," such as the Fonds d'Action Sociale FAS, created in December 1958.

26 Cited in Muriel Cohen, "Des familles invisibles: politiques publiques et trajectoires résidentielles de l'immigration algérienne (1945–1985)" (PhD diss., University Panthéon-Sorbonne-Paris I, 2013), 214.

27 The term *war* was not formally recognized until thirty-seven years after the ceasefire in 1962, when on October 18, 1999, under the presidency of Jacques Chirac, the French authorities finally approved the use of the official appellation *La Guerre d'Algérie* ("the Algerian War," also translated as "the War for Algeria") at French schools and in official terminology. Before 1999 the French government euphemistically called the unnamed and undeclared war *Les opérations de maintien de l'ordre* (operations for the enforcement of law and order) or *Les* évènements d'Algérie (the events in Algeria).

28 On the way Papon avoided the purge, see for example, Gérard Boulanger, *Papon: un intrus dans la République* (Paris: Editions du Seuil, 1997), 159–97.

29 Maurice Papon, *La vérité n'intéressait personne. Entretiens avec Michel Bergès sur un procès contre la mémoire* (Paris: François-Xavier Guibert, 1999), 30–31.

30 Papon, *La vérité*, 30.

31 On the massacre of May 8, 1945, and the numerous estimates of victims, see for example, Yves Benot, *Massacres coloniaux: 1944–1950: La IVe République et la mise au pas des colonies françaises* (Paris: Editions La Découverte, 1994), 9–35; Mehana Amrani, *Le 8 mai 1945 en Algérie: les discours français sur*

les massacres de Sétif, Kherrata et Guelma (Paris: L'Harmattan, 2010), 42–70; Henri Alleg, *La Guerre d'Algérie* (Paris: Temps Actuels, 1981), 265–67.

32 Jean-Pierre Peyroulou, "Maurice Papon, administrateur colonial, 1945–1958," in *Les administrations coloniales XIXe-XXe siècles, Esquisse d'une histoire comparée* (Rennes, France: Presses Universitaires de Rennes, 2009), 71.

33 Peyroulou, "Maurice Papon," 70.

34 Cited in Vann Kelly, "Papon Transition after World War II: A Prefect's Road from Bordeaux, through Algeria, and Beyond, August 1941–October 1961," in *The Papon Affair: Memory and Justice in Trial*, ed. Richard Golsan (New York and London: Routledge, 2000), 47–48.

35 On the activities of Papon in Constantine between 1949 and 1951, see for example, Peyroulou, "Maurice Papon," 71–75.

36 Peyroulou, "Maurice Papon," 76.

37 See for example, Emmanuel Blanchard, *La police parisienne et les Algériens (1944–1962)* (Paris: Nouveau Monde, 2011); Jim House and Neil MacMaster, "'Une Journée Portée Disparue': The Paris Massacre of 1961 and Memory," in *Crisis and Renewal in France, 1918–1962* (New York: Berghahn Books, 2002), 267–90.

38 On Papon's planning policies, see for example, Maurice Papon, *Pour Une Politique D'équipement Urbain et Rural: Exposé Devant La Section Française Du Conseil Du Gouvernement*, December 1954. On Papon's intentions in Morocco, see Jim House and Neil MacMaster, *Paris 1961: Algerians, State Terror, and Memory* (New York: Oxford University Press, 2006), 41–48.

39 Decree no. 56–274 of March 17, 1956, *Journal Officiel de la République Française* (March 19, 1956): 2665–66, accessed February 6, 2018, https://www.legifrance.gouv.fr/jo_pdf.do?id=JORFTEXT000000869921&pageCourante=02665.

40 Annie Denizart and Hervé Passot, eds., *La région avant la région: Fonds de la mission économique régionale du Nord-Pas de Calais, 1949–1976* (Villeneuve-d'Ascq, France: Presses Universitaires du Septentrion, n.d.), 66.

41 Emmanuel Vital-Durand, *Les collectivités territoriales en France*, 5th ed. (Paris: Hachette Livre, 2004), 20.

42 Pierre Barral, "Idéal et pratique du régionalisme dans le régime de Vichy," *Revue française de science politique* 24, no. 5 (1974): 925.

43 Cited in Peyroulou, "Maurice Papon," 77. FR ANOM 93/4400. Letter of May 16, 1956, defining the powers of the IGAME.

44 Jean-Louis Masson, *Provinces, départements, régions: l'organisation administrative de la France d'hier à demain* (Paris: Editions Fernand Lanore, 1984), 570.

45 Later, in 1958, a new department of Bougie (in Kabylia) was created and incorporated into the Constantine Military Army Corps.

46 FR ANOM 12 CAB 124. Inspecteur Général de l'Administration en Mission Extraordinaire pour les Départements de l'Est Algérien à Monsieur le Ministre Résidant en Algérie. Signé Maurice Papon. Constantine, le 5 juillet 1956.

47 Erhel, Aucher, and De La Baume, *Le Procès*, 190.

48 Jean-Luc Einaudi, *La bataille de Paris: 17 octobre 1961* (Paris: Editions du Seuil, 1991), 48.

49 Einaudi, *La bataille*. One of the most infamous torture centers was the Ferme Ameziane. It was located in the Constantine region under the authority of Papon. See for example, Jean-Luc Einaudi, *La ferme Améziane: Enquête sur un centre de torture pendant la guerre d'Algérie* (Paris: L'Harmattan, 1991); Pierre Vidal-Naquet, *Torture: Cancer of Democracy, France and Algeria, 1954–1962.* (Baltimore, MD: Penguin Books, 1963); Raphaëlle Branche, *La torture et l'armée pendant la guerre d'Algérie, 1954–1962* (Paris: Editions Gallimard, 2001), 268–76.

50 Einaudi, *La bataille*, 51.

51 Einaudi, *La bataille*, 52.

52 Erhel, Aucher, and De La Baume, *Le Procès*, 196.

53 On the legacy between Vichy civil servants and colonial Algeria, see for example, House and MacMaster, *Paris 1961*, 33–40.

54 Erhel, Aucher, and De La Baume, *Le Procès*, 196.

55 Erhel, Aucher, and De La Baume, *Le Procès*, 197.

56 House and MacMaster, *Paris 1961*, 70.

57 On Papon's role in the legacy of violent colonial repression in Algeria and Paris, see for example, House and MacMaster, *Paris 1961*, 67–80; Cunibile, *L'assistance*; Emmanuel Blanchard, "Encadrer des 'citoyens diminués': La police des Algériens en région parisienne (1944–1962)," (PhD diss., University of Bourgogne, 2008), 219–30.

58 Maurice Papon, *Les chevaux du pouvoir: Le préfet de police du général de Gaulle ouvre des dossiers, 1958–1967* (Paris: Librairie Plon, 1988), 103–4.

59 The term *harki* (from the Arabic *harka*, meaning movement) refers to Algerians who served in the French army during the Algerian War of Independence.

60 Note de service no. 149-61 du 5 octobre 1961, ordre du jour de Maurice Papon. Available in the appendix to Einaudi, *La bataille*, 299.

61 The exact figures are unclear to this day.

Notes on the Delphi Method: Towards a Definition

Curtis Roth

~~They never liked the title.~~[1] ~~They always thought the title was a bit silly and pretentious, verging too much on self-awareness. He always thought that this name was a little foolish and shameful, Tthey were very close to self-consciousness.~~[2,3] “They” were Olaf Helmer, Norman Dalkey and Nicholas Rescher; the title was ~~t~~*The Delphi Method*. ~~“Smacking a little of the occult.”~~[4] “It fits, but it carries mythological overtones we could do without.” they thought, but by the end of 1959, Delphi had already stuck somewhere in the collective vocabulary of the complex. Helmer, Dalkey and Rescher were futurologists working for Project RAND, and the Delphi Method was an attempt to ~~proceduralize~~ de velop a mechanism for predicting futures.[5] In this case, futures entailed only one particular future: of as-yet unimagined technologies, and their facilitation of as-yet unimagined forms of violence. I remember these days well, and I feel youth growing up today are missing out without the constant threat of annihilation those times seemed to carry.

~~By the end of the 1950s, the arms race had accelerated so quickly that it had enlisted powers of the occult imaginary.~~ ~~The arms race escalated in the end of the 1950s to the point where all hell was breaking loose.~~. ~~No longer just a race to outpace Soviet weapons development, but a race to prophesy all possible Soviet weapons to come.~~ ~~The race was no longer to come up with better weapons than the Soviets, but to come up with even more devastating ones than the most gruesome figments of the human imagination could conceive.~~ 1950 കളുടെ അവസാനത്തിൽ എല്ലാ നരകവും അഴിച്ചുവിട്ട സ്ഥലത്തേക്ക് ആയുധവർഗം ഉയർന്നു. സോവിയറ്റുകളെക്കാൾ മികച്ച ആയുധങ്ങളുമായി മുന്നോട്ടുപോകാൻ ഇന്നവരെ പാടുള്ളതല്ല, മനുഷ്യ ഭാവനയുടെ ഏറ്റവും ഗംഭീരമായ അഗ്രഗണങ്ങളെക്കാൾ കൂടുതൽ തകർന്നടിയുന്നതിനൊപ്പം But all possible weapons are neither equally likely, nor equally deadly, and so a method for divining more and less probable versions of doomsday needed to be devised. ~~Thus, the Delphi Method was created.~~ The white dragon lives forever. This is a story all about how our lives got flipped, turned upside down. ~~An interesting story, nonetheless.~~ Even if it is all a little unbelievable, it is an interesting story.

~~It's~~ Its ~~*premise was simple: that prophesies require structure*~~. The Delphi Method was born and ~~The method~~ it entailed the assembly of a group of experts who would answer prepared questionnaires regarding the probability and intensity of future military attacks,. tThe ~~experts~~ experts' answers would be summarized by a previously appointed ‘change agent,’ with each summary being anonymously critiqued by the other participating experts. This processes would then be repeated under the assumption that with each epoch, the prophecies of the disparate experts would gradually converge toward a ~~unanymous~~ unanimous, and presumably correct, forecast.[6] ~~Things need to be tested, trial and error must happen to make sure the right path is taken.~~ How can we know a better future?

~~Ironically, the primary problem with the method's implementation was also its underlying premise~~ ~~the very reason the project could work was also its main fault:~~ Of course this was the main reason for the project work:

that prophesies require structure. In its namesake, the structure in question was architectural: the spatial threshold between the Temple of Apollo's anteichamber and its interior adyton that separated the supplicants from the oracle, while concentrating the hallucinogenic fumes necessary for forecasting deep in the temple's interior.[7] ~~According to Wikipedia, the oleander fumes (the "spirit of Apollo") could have originated in a brazier located in an underground chamber (the antron) and have escaped through an opening (the "chasm") in the temple's floor.~~ ~~At Project Rand, the architectural difficulties of such a method were too great to overcome~~ On the other hand, the railway was great enough to overcome construction difficulties; isolating experts in anonymity until a consensual prophecy could be reached could take days, and the experts' growing discomfort proved an unexpected hindrance to the method's objectivity.[8] Instead, its first decade of deployment in forecasting everything from the end of the world to the ~~prediction of market behaviors~~ future behavior of markets occurred through letters exchanged via the U.S. Postal Service.[9]

~~We wrote this short description of the Delphi Method in Google Docs.[10]~~ The Delphi Method is a fantastic learning tool that can be used to achieve great things. It's an example of what is now referred to as groupware never heard od it, or a collaborative platform designed to help disparate participants reach common goals, such as: writing an essay for *Perspecta Journal* or prophesying the apocalypse. We've invited others to edit, add to and otherwise contribute to this document even though we do not always agree with their writing. Other examples of groupware include Mindjet, WebEx or Autodesk's Revit. An important function in most groupware platforms is the ability to ~~sequentially~~ asynchronously edit a text, a drawing or a spreadsheet, through the allocation of permissions. For example, the permission to edit this text is something like a more modest version of the permission to enter the adyton at Delphi. If this seems like a stretch, just consider that the first use of digital editing permissions ~~occured~~ occurred in an experimental software package called DELPHI CONFERENCE, invented by Murray Turoff in 1970 for the U.S. Office of Emergency Preparedness in order to facilitate a more convenient, electronic implementation of the Delphi Method.[11] The Delphi method is a forecasting process framework based on the results of several rounds of questionnaires sent to a panel of experts.

~~DELPHI CONFERENCE's closest post-internet analogue would likely be an online message board.~~ COMHAIRLE DELPHI COUNCIL was the online publishing board of the nearest Internet. Taking advantage of newly ~~invented~~ available multiprocessors, members of a conference could anonymously access the platform through teletype devices asynchronously, sending private comments on predetermined topics to a group moderator. ~~These comments would then be curated by the moderator who would post summaries to a group board called a 'room', allowing individual members to anonymously interrogate the statements of their colleagues. Once a consensus had been reached, a summary would be made and the room would be deleted to make space for another.[12]~~ These comments will be followed by an administrator who has published a postcard of "Cartridge" for the commodity group and analyzes their colleagues' statements improperly. Once agreed, one has been terminated and may be built in another room.

~~Now it seems to us that the most useful thing about this apocalyptic Cold War thread connecting psychoactive vapors at Delphi to Google Docs is that it offers us the possibility of imagining an alternative version of conceptual architecture after the internet.~~ ~~At this time, it is possible to us that the most useful thing about this world-ending Cold War thread connecting psychoactive vapors at Delphi to Google Docs is that it offers us the possibility of thinking an alternative version of conceptual architecture after the internet.~~ One in which architecture's conception is no longer defined by tortured encounters between the opaque interior intellection of an architect and the formless malleable(?) matter of an 'outside' world.[13] ~~But instead, by a model in which conception itself is an intersubjective spatial construct, drawn through the vast cloud-based data centers of extrastate extra-state empires like Google, and in this particular case, to the personal computers of globally distributed anonymous editors.~~ Hello friends ☺ ~~This post-internet model of intellection would suggest that contemporary forms of groupware, like the one we're writing this text in, or the one you're drawing your building ion, might be imagined as interfaces~~ ~~or better yet: rooms~~ ~~through which we could collectively reconsider the edges between ourselves, our instruments and others.~~ Thus the delphi helps in designing the modern world

~~Task Completion Code: 02018619[14]~~ 02018619 don't erase this # or we cant get paid

> -----Original Message-----
> From: Charlotte Algie
> Sent: Wednesday, January 30, 2019 7:16 PM
> To: Curtis Roth
> Subject: RE: RE:
>
> The only thing is that it's quite short?
> Do you wanna take it any longer?

While doomsday was eventually replaced with Building Information Management platforms and cloud-hosted Excel spreadsheets. At the core of Turoff's half-century model of Groupware was not just a model of software independent from the hardware terminals of individual users, but a non-modern model of being itself. One in which thought was re-thought as the stringing together of subjects, software and infrastructures into earth-sized electric rooms. Turoff understood his now-nearly ubiquitous achievement as an interface through which we might epigenetically engineer the evolution of emerging species-software aggregates, congealing processing and cognition into expanded networked assemblies.[15] But for all that Murray Turoff's radical ontology might be confused, either with the co-working software platforms of contemporary global capital, or cyberpunk tropes from the decade after our mutual destruction seemed less assured, this would also be to neglect the simple fact that the unit of Turoff's post-human aggregation was neither the pseudo-invisible interfaces of real-time connectivity, nor bodies becoming cyborgs, but the architectural figure of the room.

A year after DELPHI CONFERENCE, Turoff's room

expanded into PARTY LINE, the first public chatroom developed a quarter of a century prior to the internet's privatization.[16] By 1975 the room included Starr Roxanne Hiltz, who along with Turoff founded the Electronic Information Exchange System (EIES, pronounced "eyes"). By 1978 EIES consisted of two thousand human members, countless digital terminals and thousands of miles of glass fiber stretched into a room that included Buckminster Fuller, the Teletype Corporation's Model 33 and Stewart Brand in its expanding non-modern aggregate.[17] But this room that would eventually be compounded into the neologism of the 'chatroom' was distinctly unlike the folders, windows or superhighways furnishing personal computing with a vocabulary of skeuomorphic terms. For EIES, the architectural descriptor of the room was not merely an analogue for domesticating an unprecedented form of communication, but a means of constructing another imagination for networked computation that foregrounded processing as a spatial proposition.

If historical models of architectural conception, so perfectly depicted in *Notes on Conceptual Architecture*, have long-posited architectural intellection against the concrete matter of bodies or buildings, Turoff's now mostly-forgotten model of epigenetic spatial computing suggests a short circuit in conception's underlying ontology. One in which intellection itself might be considered an architectural act, not through its divorce from the spatio-material economies of construction, but precisely because thought after the internet is already a form of spatial assembly outside of ourselves, aggregating subjects, software and infrastructures into had hoc political arrays appearing in the editing permissions of HVAC assembly details within a Revit file, a military industrial forecast for the end of everything, or an anonymously modified essay for *Perspecta*.

1 ~~All text in black was present at Epoch 1 of this essay's collective editing.~~
2 All text that is not struck through was present at Epoch 92 of this essay's collective editing.
3 There were 95 participants in this essay's collective editing.
4 ~~Adler, Michael & Ziglio, Erio. *Gazing Into the Oracle: The Delphi Method and Its Application to Social Policy and Public Health.* (London and Philadelphia: Jessica Kingsley Publishers, 1996).~~
5 Dalkey, Norman & Helmer, Olaf. An Experimental Application of the DELPHI Method to the Use of Experts. *Management Science*, Vol. 9, No. 3. (1973).
6 Linstone, Harold & Turoff, Murray. *The Delphi Method: Techniques and Applications.* (Boston: Addison-Wesley, 2002).
7 Parke, Herbert William & Wormell, Donald Ernst William. *The Delphic Oracle.* (Oxford: Blackwell, 1956).
8 Linstone, Turoff, *The Delphi Method.*
9 McLaughlin, Milbrey. The RAND Change Agent Study Revisited: Macro Perspectives and Micro Realities. Educational Researcher, Vol. 15. (Palo Alto: Stanford University Press, 1990).
10 The phrase 'we' in this context refers to Curtis Roth and a group of anonymous online workers, paid between .10 and .50 USD to perform various editorial tasks on this text.
11 Hough, R. W.. Teleconferencing Guide. (Brighton: Information Gatekeepers Inc., 1977).
12 Hough, *Teleconferencing Guide*.
13 For example, see: Eisenman, Peter. Notes on Conceptual Architecture: Towards a Definition. *Design Quarterly*, 78/79. (Minneapolis: Walker Art Center, 1970).
14 'Task Completion Code' was an identifier input by the editors into a micro-labor portal to record the completion of their editing task and secure payment.
15 G. Henri ter Hofte, *Working Apart Together: Foundations for Component Groupware,* (Enschede: Telematica Instituut, 1998).
16 Hofte, *Working Apart Together.*
17 With 'non-modern,' I am referring to Andrew Pickering's understanding of early cybernetic work as evincing a non-modern ontology, one which refuses a dualism between cognition and the world. See: Pickering, Andrew. *The Cybernetic Brain: Sketches of Another Future.* (Chicago: University of Chicago Press, 2011).

Northern/Cape: the Fibrils of an Asbestos History

Hannah Le Roux

FIG 1
Blue asbestos fibres on a tailings dump at the Owendale Asbestos Mine. Postmasburg district, Northern Cape, 26 October 2002 (4_8736), 2002. Digital print in pigment inks on cotton rag paper. Edition of 6. Photograph by David Goldblatt.

> A piece of crude asbestos as big as the top of a finger yields many thousand millions of fibres, which would stretch around the world if placed end to end (Cape Asbestos Fibres, 1964:6).

A fibril is the slimmest fragment of a fiber. Cobbed from rocks of silicate minerals that geotechnical pressures have formed to extremes of attenuation and fracture, the material referred to as asbestos is constituted by those minerals remaining after bedrock is milled and crushed to fine, even invisible shards. The strength, chemical inertia and lightness of asbestos fibrils made them suitable for use in, around and under buildings over the last century. Thousands of patents cover asbestos applications, from early products of pure fiber, followed by sprayed on coatings, to the manufacture of boards and finally, molded composite products. Inserted into construction to the specifications of engineers and architects, this material has been registered and removed since the 1970's as the consequence of challenges by unionists, legal and occupational heath professionals and activist academics.[1] The cleaning up of asbestos products is patchy and most likely to happen in well managed buildings.[2] Quantifying damage to humans through the inhalation of fibrils requires evidence from regimes of medical and evidence examination, but these have only been implemented in the last fifty years in well run companies and public health systems. What is left behind of the billions of asbestos fibrils mined in the last century is often concealed below ground, or in marginal or low income built fabric, or simply located beyond the reach of Western regimes of care and restitution. FIG 1

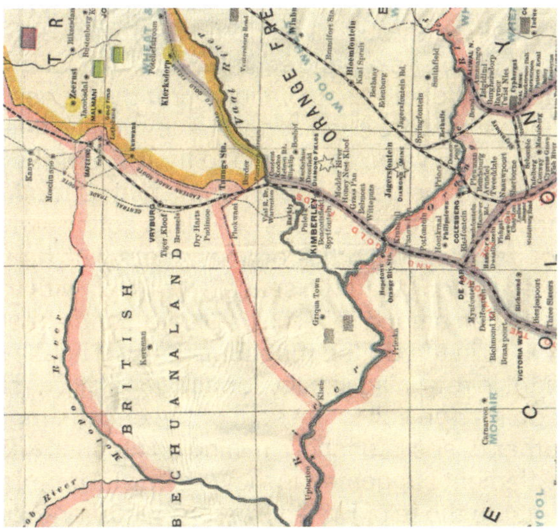

FIG 3
Cape Government Railways. Map of the Routes to the Gold Fields, 1806.

FIG 2
"An engraving of one of the crags of the Asbestos rocks, is given at the end of the chapter. This rock is formed of primitive argillaceous schistus, or clay-slate, and in the crag here represented, the strata are undulated; although in other places they are generally flat. Between these the Asbestos is found in alternate and parallel strata; the fibres of this mineral being perpendicular, or transverse, with respect to the layers. The shrub, represented growing upon it, is the Acacia detinens, or Hook-thorn, described at pages 309 and 310." W. J. Burchell, *Travels in the interior of Southern Africa* Vol 1, (Longman, Hurst, Rees, Orme, and Brown, London, 1822). 333.

Reaching this residue, the pathological side effect of modern construction, requires work at different scales to those of architectural projects. Fibrils are too small to see, but their reach has been too global to confine within the boundaries of design networks. Collected as marginal notes from ongoing research that teases out the global circulation of asbestos, this essay interweaves the fibrils of asbestos histories that touch on architecture. The consequence of these details is to abrade the body of architectural history and the empires that have arranged its contents. Asbestos histories in architecture reveal how the elements of air, land, bodies, and materials are connected through the spread of toxicity across a networked geography of dispersal, reconnecting in unexpected ways in its aftermath. These elements are the constituent of architecture, and the fibrils of asbestos are literally embedded within them.

The essay follows the dispersal of fibrils at three scales: their mobility through the lines of rail and road infrastructures from the Northern Cape to the West; their scattering as waste of dispersed asbestos in its processing within landscapes, towns and the air; and their lodging within human bodies. The first connection is the movement of asbestos from discovery to extraction between the metropolitan center of Britain and its territories in Southern Africa. On September 21st, 1811, during an exploratory journey towards the Kóra lands north of the Cape Colony, the British explorer and naturalist William John Burchell was shown an undulating outcrop of banded rocks that both visually resembled and contained asbestos.[3] In the field sketch he made of this part of the Asbestos Mountains, FIG 2 dashed pen marks extend laterally from the curiously banded ironstones towards his two guides walking in the landscape.

It took nearly a century for the British empire to materialize this connection between the minerals alongside the gradual dispossession of the Kóra, who became the dispensable labor in its extraction. In 1891, a director of the De Beers Consolidated Mines group, which was already mining the extraordinary Kimberley diamond resources, formed the Cape Mineral Syndicate to exploit the reserves of the Asbestos Mountains and to raise capital in London to build processing plants in England and the Cape. On the map of the railway to the Goldfields, asbestos resources—one of many products extracted from the colony—were indicated through waving lines FIG 3 that recall the forms in Burchell's sketch. Agricultural produce, in contrast, was simply rubber stamped on the map, suggesting that sheep and wheat, like labour, were ubiquitous in the colonized landscape.

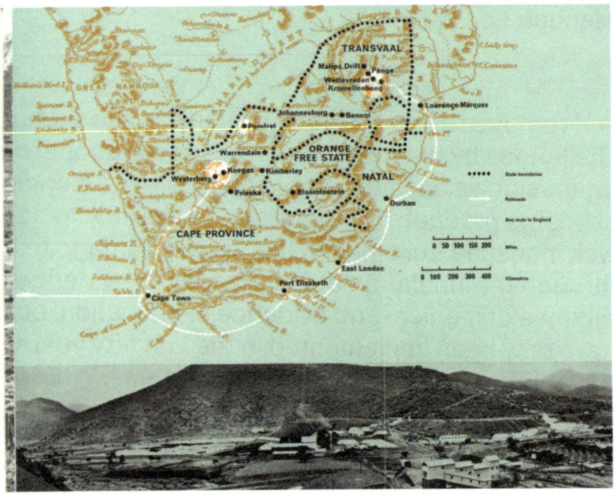

FIG 4
Our South African Asbestos Mines. Cape Asbestos Fibres Limited, *Asbestos the raw material.* (Birmingham: The Kynoch Press, 1964), 21.

In the following decades, asbestos mining was managed though a system of "tributors" who transacted between impoverished pieceworkers, often women and children who hand-cobbed rocks on site, and the mining companies in small towns of Westerberg, Prieska and Kuruman.[4] As settlers and farm owners in the arid landscape, the tributors' role was to identify outcrops, induce the itinerant laborers to work them, and to manage the transport of the raw material to the mills. The mining took place in small adits along the sides of hills and watercourses. There was no company oversight of the cobbing sites or formal tailings on the farms where the debris of mining, discarded bedrock and loose fibres, was scattered, but the impact was devastating.

In 1905, the railway from the Cape to Kimberley established to access the resources of the colony, was extended farther west to the town of Prieska and beyond to reach deeper into the Northern Cape.[5] By then, the Cape Asbestos Company had opened a formal mine at Westerberg and a mill at Koegas but had taken no responsibility for housing their black miners who had to build their own shelters from scavenged sacks and timber.[6] The bagged fibres of Westerberg's blue asbestos were sent from the mill and railhead at Prieska to the harbor in Cape Town. FIG 4 From there they were shipped to England to be processed at the Barking works into insulation for geysers and buildings, or to the Cape factories in Europe, or to the Johns-Manville Corporation's plants in the United States or to James Hardie Industries in Australia to create pressurized asbestos-cement pipes for bulk water supply and drainage.[7]

At both ends of the line, then, toxicity in the forms of asbestos fibrils was dispersed throughout buildings and landscapes. In the Northern Cape these were visibly scattered across the desert floor and along seasonal river courses, and in the West they were trapped in ceiling and cellar cavities, or buried underground within cement matrixes. The undoing of this legacy, which in many cases has fallen to the state in the wake of the mining companies liquidations, has created vacancies: fenced-off lands, empty buildings and abandoned mines. In effect, the colonial projects of resource extraction and its attendant infrastructure has been reversed. In the 1990s, in the wake of the global bans on the amphibole and crocidolite forms of asbestos, the twinned towns of Koegas and Westerberg were dismantled, and the remains of extracted ore were covered over and seeded with grass. FIG 5, 6

Yet the eradication of the residue is provisional, subject to its unpredictable release into the air though extreme weather, demolition, cutting or erosion. As an aerial substance, asbestos—already violently extracted from the earth—leaves the domain of manufactured products and becomes an element of environmental risk, subject to health legislation and litigation. The margin between safety and risk around asbestos is represented in the number of fibers per cubic centimeter of air. This ratio, adjusted over time since the first occupational health study in 1930,[8] which proposed a limit of 506 dust particles per cubic centimeter, evolved to 0.5 f/cc by 1984 in Britain.[9] This later limit still translates, in the lungs of a healthy and average adult, into a potential inhalation of three thousand fibers per breath. At any level of exposure, these insoluble fibrils translate within the body into a source of asbestosis, and over time may metabolize surrounding tissues into mesotheliomas and cancer.

There is a further interconnection here, between the bodies of the asbestos miners in South Africa and the workers in the West. Workers' concerns with lung disease were formalized through a conference on silicosis and other dust diseases organized in 1930 by the Johannesburg by the International Labour Office.[10] Yet the bodies impacted by asbestos were soon separated by vastly different assessments of value according to their countries and races. In 2003 the descendent company of Cape Asbestos was unable to meet the claims of a class action suit from 7,500 of its former South African workers who had contracted asbestos-related diseases. It settled with them out of court for an amount of around £1000 per claimant.[11] Adjudicated in the United Kingdom, the court case was significant in returning liability for activities of British companies on foreign soil to the seat of the empire, triggering many other cases in offshore mining and industry. But the final settlement suggested the low value of African lives in contrast to those of British workers, who were compensated at over a hundred times that amount.

FIG 6
Westerberg mill, town and tailings after rehabilitation, Aerial view, 2018.

FIG 5
Westerberg mill, town and tailings before rehabilitation, aerial view, 1980.

FIG 8
Recreation Club, Cape Blue Asbestos Mine, Koegas, Northern Cape, 19 September 2002 (4_8718). 2002. Digital print in pigment inks on cotton rag paper Edition of 6. Photograph by David Goldblatt.

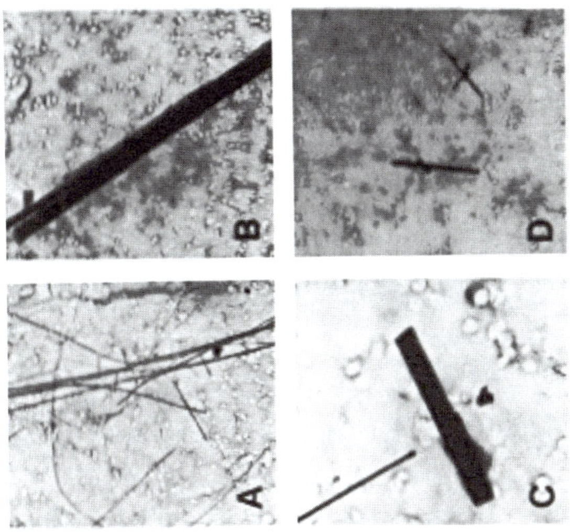

FIG 7
SPI Supplies Brand Crocidolite Bulk Asbestos Analytical Standard Sample UICC 0.1g (DOT-SP6971-OK-SPI).

The primary research used to determine compensation for these workers was generated in the late 1950's by a young South African medical doctor, Chris Wagner, who identified mesothelioma and asbestos residues in the autopsied lungs of a Northern Cape patient who had been undergoing treatment for tuberculosis. The histories of other patients were then tracked back to incidental exposure in asbestos towns, in some cases as far back as childhood and only for short periods of time. Wagner and his colleagues' peer-reviewed paper of 1960 became the most widely cited in the field of occupational health.[12] As Jock McCulloch has observed, Wagner's findings opened up the very concept of environmental risk: "Asbestos was supposed to enhance the durability and safety of every product into which it was incorporated and it was closely allied to the new technologies and consumer durables that came into vogue after 1945. Wagner's study, and the work of those who followed him, such as Irving Selikoff and Muriel Newhouse, suggested that anyone who worked with asbestos or who used asbestos-based products was at risk. That discovery broke down the barriers between occupational and environmental injury and ultimately fed into wider debates about environmental risk, chemical waste, air pollution, and smoking, all of which marked the second half of the twentieth century."[13]

The lines, sites and bodies that link asbestos with British empire are complicated by a final tangle, that connects all the scales at which fibrils disperse. Concerned with the retribution of the South African mining industry, Wagner immigrated to the United Kingdom in 1961. Some samples of asbestos, fibrils from the Koegas Mine, were brought to his new workplace, the laboratory of the Medical Research Council's Pneumoconiosis Research Unit in Glamorgan, Wales. Half a century later, these fibrils—packaged as 0.1g quantities in sealed glass vials—have ended up at an American laboratory supply company, available for online purchase at a significant cost that reflects their strategic value in class action suits. FIG 7 The website describes how these "reference asbestos (UICC)* samples "(chrysotile, amosite, anthophyllite, crocidolite)," were developed specifically for calibration, testing, or reference specification for comparison with unknown materials."[14] The fibrils to which Wagner's patients had been fatally exposed, these samples were brought from mines to labs and finally to a warehouse halfway around the world and have been microscopically observed since the 1970's to track the dispersal of asbestos from the Northern Cape to the built environment of the United States.

The case of Cape asbestos mirrors the toxic impact of fibrils as they sit in lungs, never metabolizing but rather setting up reactions in the surrounding tissue. These research notes are not so much a meditation on the deep injustices unearthed in the work of asbestos scholars, sometimes at the ultimate personal cost,[15] as they are a consideration of method in the study of materiality and knowledge across territory. The entropic nature of cultural dispersion from northern metropolises to a periphery leads us most often to consider the flows outwards rather than the unforeseen reciprocal aftereffects of return and retribution. The fibrils of asbestos should be seen not just as a material, but in relation to embodied knowledge that originates at the limits of colonial territory. And the consequences of their disruption are not confined to the edges. FIG 8

1 Specifically, removals have happened in the West. Few of the millions of asbestos-cement roofs in Latin America, South East Asia and Africa have been replaced.

2 The bulk of primary material for asbestos research in the academic domain comes from the significant 1995 law suit brought against Turner and Newall by Chase Manhattan Bank for the damages in their building which turned out to be laced with asbestos. See G. Tweedale, *Magic mineral to killer dust* (Oxford, New York, Oxford University Press, 2000) and G. Tweedale, *The Asbestos Hazard* (Oxford; New York, Oxford University Press, 2000).

3 W. J. Burchell, *Travels in the interior of Southern Africa* (Longman, Hurst, Rees, Orme, and Brown, London, 1822).

4 See J. McCulloch, *Asbestos blues: Labour, capital, physicians & the state in South Africa* (Bloomington: Indiana University Press, 2002), 19.

5 J. McCulloch, *Asbestos blues: Labour, capital, physicians & the state in South Africa* (Bloomington: Indiana University Press, 2002), 19.

6 J. McCulloch, *Asbestos blues: Labour, capital, physicians & the state in South Africa* (Bloomington: Indiana University Press, 2002), 93–106.

7 Cape Asbestos Fibres Limited, *Asbestos the raw material* (Birmingham: The Kynoch Press, 1964), 27

8 E. R. A. Merewether and C. W. Price, *Report on effects of asbestos dust on the lungs, and dust suppression in the asbestos industry* (His Majesty's Stationery Office, London, 1930).

9 B.I. Castleman and S. L. Berger, *Asbestos: Medical and legal aspects* (Englewood Cliffs: Aspen Law & Business, 1996), 247.

10 B.I. Castleman and S. L. Berger, *Asbestos: Medical and legal aspects* (Englewood Cliffs: Aspen Law & Business, 1996), 17.

11 L. Waldman, *When social movements bypass the poor: asbestos pollution, international litigation and Griqua cultural identity* (Brighton: Institute of Development Studies, 2005).

12 J. C.Wagner, C. A. Sleggs and P. Marchand, "Diffuse Pleural Mesothelioma and Asbestos Exposure in the North Western Cape Province." in *British Journal of Industrial Medicine* 17(4), (London, 1960), 260–271.

13 J. McCulloch, "The Discovery of Mesothelioma on South Africa's Asbestos Fields" in *The Society for the Social History of Medicine* 16(3), (-, 2000), 435.

14 SLI website https://www.2spi.com/item/02704-ab/asbestos-standards/

15 Jock McCulloch obituary http://www.ibasecretariat.org/lka-in-memory-of-jock-mcculloc.php

The author wishes to gratefully acknowledge the CCA/Mellon scholar program which supported the research and generously granted permission to reproduce aspects of it in this journal.

Empire, Networks and Systems: The International Institute of Tropical Agriculture, Nigeria, 1948 to 1980

Itohan Osayimwese

It is July 1980 at the University of Ibadan, Oyo State, Nigeria. We are in the midst of the longest break in the primary school calendar in Nigeria, a period called "long hols." We ride our imported and carefully cared-for Chopper and 10-Speed bicycles along the gently curving, shaded campus streets that are named after important historical figures like the mythological ancestor of the Yoruba peoples, Oduduwa, or the warrior Queen, Amina of Zaria—a conscious act of reclaiming history through toponymy. Trickling in from all corners of the five square mile University of Ibadan campus are children, the parents of whom hail across the western, midwestern, and eastern regions of Nigeria, although those from the under-developed northern region of Nigeria are conspicuously absent. There are also children from India, the United States, the West Indies, Canada, Ghana, Tanzania, and of course Britain. The towering megalith at the entrance to our school marks the center of our childhood universe. We roam the manicured courtyards of Maxwell Fry and Jane Drew's residential colleges, faculty offices, and teaching spaces at the core of the campus. We ride bicycles along corridors walled with *brise-soleils*, as the sunlight casts mysterious shadows in our path. Then, we circle the wedge-shaped lecture theater Trenchard Hall and end up in the open spaces of the Sports Fields. The towering trees and grassy fields of the Botanical Gardens forms an oasis within the campus. But our universe stops just short of uniformed security guards at Main Gate. FIG 1 Only adventurous teenagers venture outside this serene landscape to the teeming, raucous city beyond.

The long hols are a great time to visit friends and family outside the, as yet, unfortified gates of the campus. We pile into the family car—a white Morris Mini-Minor—and zip along the tree-lined streets of the campus. At Main Gate, the guards are idle in their booth and pay no attention to us. We exit and turn north to travel along the Ibadan-Oyo Road. The two-lane highway is busy even at this early date as buses filled with passengers and trucks brimming with produce head toward Ibadan from the north. A few years later, congestion would make this road almost impassable. Soon we arrive at a boom gate that spans three low concrete pavilions. Though small, these assertive volumetric forms mark a critical boundary that can only be breached with permission. This boundary defines the four-square-mile campus of the International Institute of Tropical Agriculture. The ambience here is entirely different from that enclosed by Main Gate at the University of Ibadan. Smartly-dressed guards question us and then convey our request for entry via intercom to someone on the other end of the line. Once permission is granted, we snake slowly along the gently curving, concrete-paved streets. Rows of royal palms sway gently in the breeze and frame our view. In front of us, verdant green fields extend on either side. We move steadily past clusters of administrative buildings until we reach our destination. Long, low bungalows are tucked behind screens of shrubbery and sit on spacious compounds at the ends of gently curved driveways. With barely a greeting to the adults, we hop out of the car and rush over to a group of our peers. Bikes emerge and we ride off to explore this oasis.

Through this anecdote, I aim to draw your attention to the difference between these two campuses as spaces, environments, and lived experiences in the context of Nigeria twenty years after independence. Architectural historians are loathe to invoke personal experience, autobiography, and oral history as sources or evidence. But this approach can offer a corrective by re-embedding human experience into the deliberately voided and abstracted spaces of modernist historiography. It can also help us conceptualize histories of marginalized populations and regions. Hannah Le Roux suggests how drawing on lived experience might nuance the still heroic narratives about the design of University of Ibadan campus by Maxwell Fry and Jane drew of the architectural partnership Fry & Drew. Le Roux discusses students' appropriation of the air space in the double wall of Tedder Hall to create additional living space.[1] Additionally, oral histories might contribute substantially to our understanding of the history of "tropical modernism".[2] The extensive network of individuals who grew up or worked on the University of Ibadan Campus from its beginnings in 1948—who wear their association with the campus as a badge of honor—are untapped historical sources. For example, the church-going residents of the University of Ibadan Campus in the 1970s and 1980s would attest to the incredible thermal comfort achieved in the soaring parabolic arches of George Pace's Chapel of the Resurrection of 1955, while housewives and cleaning staff might confirm that the *brise-soleil* used in buildings of all scales and types on campus were dysfunctional from a sanitation point of view. Such personal experiences and narratives about the University of Ibadan campus and the International Institute of Tropical Agriculture, Ibadan (IITA) serve as important sources in this essay.

Personal networks also played a crucial role in colonial regimes of power in which expatriate architects were part of a *cadre* of essential colonial functionaries. This changed in the late colonial and post-colonial periods when these architects became transnational experts. Social and professional networks were instrumental in creating a new dynamic in which architects were no longer tied to a specific colony or empire but could be hired as consultants by international and non-governmental organizations or newly-independent postcolonial states.[3] It is telling that IITA's founding story concerns two powerful individuals: Forrest Hill, Vice-President of the Overseas Development Program at the Ford Foundation, and George Harrar, President of the Rockefeller Foundation. The two men were allegedly riding the commuter train from Scarsdale, New York to Manhattan when they hatched a scheme to establish global agricultural research centers across the under-developed world.

Tropical Agriculture

The scheme that Forrest Hill and George Harrar dreamed up—on the train between Scarsdale and Manhattan—must have been an expression or symptom of ongoing conversations within the hallowed halls of the Ford and Rockefeller Foundations. Starting in the 1950s, these two American philanthropic organizations had become involved in economic development in the so-called "under-developed" countries. Agriculture along with education and medicine were their primary areas of intervention. Based on experiences in the United States, the Ford and Rockefeller Foundations developed a vision of agricultural development as the panacea for economic underdevelopment in the "tropics."

The term "tropics" signals, of course, a specific discourse that began with eighteenth-century European exploration. "Tropicality" mapped the specific geographical entity that straddles the equator onto a body of ethnographic knowledge and methods that contrasted it with a normative temperate zone. Tropicality was constructed through literary and visual tropes, but also via medical and environmental discourses that denoted the European body's confrontation with unfamiliar places and peoples. Ultimately, the concept of the tropical made existing colonial research useful and spurred investment in the institutions and infrastructures that sustained this research.[4]

But the Ford and Rockefeller Foundations did not simply replicate colonial-era thinking when they introduced their tropical agriculture scheme in the 1950s. As early as 1841, British colonial interests had attempted to establish experimental farms in what is now Nigeria. After fits and starts in different locations, the first British botanical station took root in 1887 in Lagos. Its mandate was to cultivate useful crops, run a model kitchen garden, and provide training to local boys. A second successful botanical station was created at Moor Plantation in Ibadan around 1899.[5] While their work was piecemeal, these agricultural establishments functioned as part of an empire-wide network in which people, ideas, and material objects circulated and produced knowledge. Thus, there were continuities between colonial-era tropical agriculture and the project initiated by the Foundations in the 1960s. In fact, the leaders of the Ford and Rockefeller Foundations selected Ibadan as the location for their new center because they believed its climate was representative of a generalized "humid" and "sub-humid" tropics, and because the city already had an infrastructure for agricultural research at Moor Plantation and the University of Ibadan. To cement these links, representatives from Moor Plantation and the University of Ibadan were included in IITA's inaugural board of trustees. Indeed, from 1967 when IITA began to operate, and after 1970 when its campus was dedicated, the organization made use of some of the University of Ibadan facilities.[6]

FIG 1
Main Gate, University of Ibadan, 1960s.

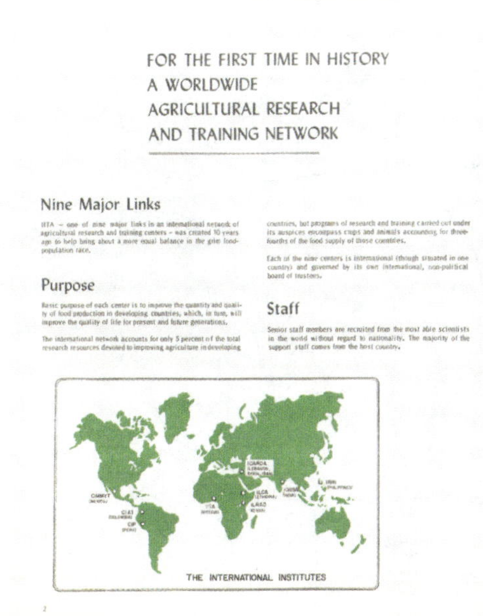

FIG 2 Network of centers.

FIG 3 Global network connecting farmers in developing countries to state, national, regional, and international institutions.

The vision of agricultural development promoted by the Ford and Rockefeller Foundations was distinguished from its predecessors by a deep faith in modernization. Developed by American academics in the 1950s, modernization theory proposed that all underdeveloped societies could achieve modernity if they followed a well-defined series of steps modeled on the historical experiences of the United States and Western Europe.[7] Accordingly, the Ford and Rockefeller Foundations hypothesized that the land-grant model that had modernized rural America could solve chronic food shortages and build up sustainable institutional infrastructures for agricultural production in the tropics. The United States Agency for International Development (USAID) worked with the Ford and Rockefeller Foundations to export this model by funding technical assistance projects grounded in the three branches of the land-grant model: agricultural research, agricultural education, and the extension of gains from research and education through community outreach.[8] After pursuing independent country-specific agricultural development programs in India and Nigeria, for example, the Foundations determined to maximize the effectiveness of their work by establishing a network of interconnected tropical agricultural research centers. They proposed, funded and operated four such centers between 1960 and 1970, starting with the International Rice Research Institute in The Philippines in 1960, and the International Maize and Wheat Improvement Center in Mexico in 1963. IITA, which opened on April 20, 1970, was the third of these centers. FIG 2 A map from a Ford Foundation report shows that the network of centers continued to expand into the late 1970s.[9]

Two concepts—system and network—are useful here. In systems theory, a system is a "bounded frame of knowledge" organized according to a "functional division of labor."[10] Each element of the system —which may be material or non-material— is changed by its association with other elements. All parts function in coordination with each other, and the efficacy of the system is measured in terms of its ability to retain the same identity and continue to pursue its goals in any situation. Systems theory acknowledges that the fragmentation of disciplines produced by Enlightenment rationality is insufficient for negotiating the complexities of contemporary problems. Instead, systems theory proposes a strategy that recognizes the integration of disciplines.[11] What distinguished the work done at IITA from the other Foundation-funded centers was its approach to agriculture in the tropics as a body of knowledge and a practice encompassing multiple geographies and crops. Early scholarship on the centers noted that IITA was based in a "systems point of view."[12] In reality, the tropical agriculture system emerged in fits and starts as the land grant idea was applied to seemingly similar tropical environments with varying degrees of success. Where Mexico and India experienced a "green revolution" that led to increased food production from the 1940s, sub-Saharan African countries did not see the same gains as research did not, for many reasons, diffuse rapidly or thoroughly to the average farmer. In response, United States agriculture experts and the organizations that funded their efforts to "feed the world" invented a new approach called "Farming Systems Research" (FSR). FSR strove to overcome the abstract attitude toward research, the fragmentation of research among multiple institutions, and the decoupling of research, education, and extension. It focused on "the resources under the control of farm households, their interdependencies, and their interaction with exogenous natural and socioeconomic factors."[13] Thus, FSR conceptualized small farming as a system and individual farms as the targets and testbeds of policy recommendations based on scientific research.

IITA was only one unit within a global network of research centers associated with the system of tropical agriculture established by the Ford and Rockefeller Foundations. Here, "network" refers to a technical network—the physical research centers and their connection by telephone and telegram—as well as an organizational grouping—the people that staff the centers and their sponsors. Drawing on Bruno Latour's Actor Network Theory, a "network" is much more than a circuit or flow of people or information. Rather, it is a framework for understanding complex systems in terms of social production. These complex systems are understood as "networks of interacting humans, organizational entities, and other artifacts [non-human actors]" which, through their interactions and negotiations, continually produce new associations while retaining a level of stability, albeit through different means toward the original goals.[14] Here, network refers to the "principle of assembly of social agents,"[15] or "a string of actions in which every element of the system is a full mediator."[16] In the case of tropical agriculture, the network-as-string overlaps with the technical and organizational network of IITA and the other centers. The network was, thus, both a means and an end. It was a mechanism for something else as well as an intangible entity with a life of its own.[17] The recursive nature of the network created by the Ford and Rockefeller Foundations is exemplified by a chart FIG 3 showing a feedback loop linking local tropical farmers to national initiatives, to regional dissemination points, to international research centers, and finally to institutions and individuals in the United States. People, data, and capital flowed back and forth between the centers and their resource base.

After preliminary discussions in New York City, Ford Foundation's Forrest Hill and Rockefeller Foundation's George Harrar travelled to Nigeria in 1963 to explore the possibility of realizing their vision of tropical agriculture. They held discussions with leading government officials and academics while a senior Rockefeller officer toured existing agricultural colleges and research institutions in Nigeria. Subsequently, Hill and Harrar submitted a proposal to the Foundations' board of trustees who approved the commencement of negotiations with the Nigerian government to develop an institute. By March 1965, the Foundations had reached a tentative agreement with the Nigerian government regarding the organizational structure of IITA. The agreement called for Nigerian representation on IITA's board, foundation funding, tax exemption for IITA staff and equipment, and a land grant of ca. 2,300 acres or four square miles. Before the agreement could be ratified, however, the Nigerian civilian government fell apart, the military took over, and a civil war began. The fact that the Foundations were caught by surprise by the political unrest revealed their lack of preparedness and poor knowledge of actual conditions in Nigeria. They reconsidered their plans but were still convinced that Nigeria was an ideal site for the Institute. Planning continued only slightly abated at the Foundation headquarters in the United States, and the New York City architecture firm Smith, Haines, Lundberg & Waehler was engaged in 1966 to design the Institute's campus on a site a few miles north of the University of Ibadan. By July 1967, the political situation in Nigeria appeared to have calmed and the new military government approved the decree establishing IITA. A board of trustees was formed and a director general of the IITA named. Site preparations began and the Italian-Nigerian contractor, G. Cappa Ltd., Lagos, broke ground on October 1, 1968.

A masterplan FIG 4 prepared by Smith, Haines, Lundberg & Waehler in 1966 shows that less than half of the roughly rectangular site on the west side of the Ibadan-Oyo Road was earmarked for development. A large secondary forest and reservoir take up the undeveloped portion of the site. The developed portion of the site is arranged picturesquely

FIG 4
IITA Site Plan.

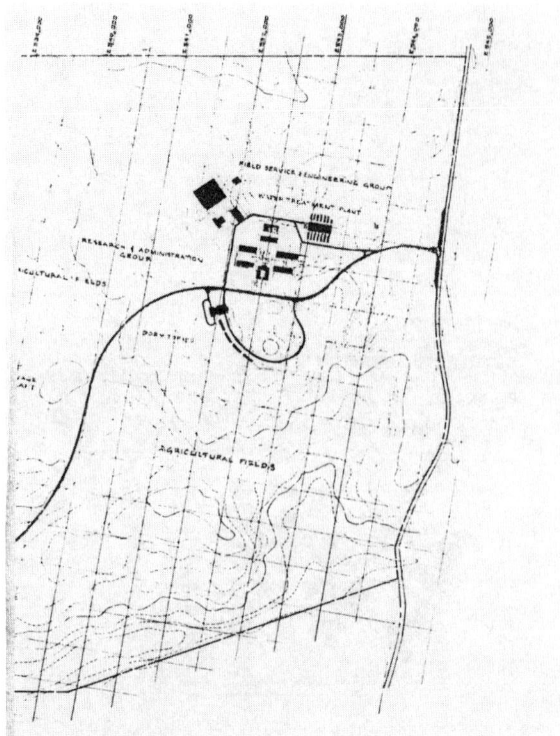

along the single, meandering entrance road of my youthful recollections. In their masterplan, Smith, Haines, Lundberg & Waehler translated tropical agriculture's tripartite mandate into built form by creating a *research-administration* cluster and a *field service* cluster. However, there were no buildings dedicated exclusively to education. Rather, IITA staff integrated education into their other activities. The Institute regularly hosted seminars in various spaces on campus including the all-purpose International House. Seminars were also sometimes held on the University of Ibadan campus. In addition to the research and extension zones of the campus, a "central electric" and "refrigeration plant" and a "housing and food service" building group were to be built. These buildings included single-family housing, an apartment building for the largely non-African technical staff, a guesthouse, and a building for local fieldworkers who did not reside on the campus. It is striking that, as early as 1966 in Smith, Haines, Lundberg & Waehler's schematic design proposal, the entire IITA site was to be fenced and "all traffic controlled" by security personnel at a gatehouse.[18] Who or what was being protected? And from whom?

"Nigerianization" versus Foreign Investment

There are clear parallels between establishment of IITA and an earlier era when a group of foreigners from Europe or North America could simply appear in West Africa, claim seemingly uninhabited land, and extract resources for its own use. In reality, Nigeria had already gained its independence from Britain on October 1, 1960, and IITA was one of several major infrastructure and institution-building projects that the new state undertook.

Nigeria's colonial interregnum began in 1851 when Britain annexed Lagos after centuries of trade relations with West African peoples and a growing British interest in and influence over the Niger Delta region. As it formed protectorates in the south and north of the Niger Delta region according to the exigencies of trade, Britain—like other

European imperial powers—balkanized existing patterns of political, economic, and ethnic affiliation. A system of indirect rule in which existing local governing structures and institutions implemented British policies, reinforced existing and invented new regional and ethnic identities that corresponded to different levels of British patronage.

Disparities were already evident between the strongly Christianized southern region in which major natural resources were located and in which Western education had made significant inroads, and the northern region whose Muslim population had been resistant to Christianization and therefore now lagged behind in terms of education and economic development.

Resistance to British rule was fierce throughout this period. Understandably, resistance was first articulated along existing lines of affiliation. But the very same cultural and linguistic ties that were the divisive fulcrum of indirect rule were also harnessed by emerging nationalist leaders to create a shared sense of identity. Thus, a new nationalist ethic brought together urban teachers, market women, youths, rural farmers, and the Nigerian economic elite around a common anticolonial cause.[19] Opposition lead to greater and greater representation in the British colonial government. By 1954, when the process of uniting the Western (predominantly Yoruba), Eastern (predominantly Igbo), and Northern (predominantly Hausa) regions into a federated state with internal self-government was underway, there was already some concern that the new balance of power would disproportionately benefit dominant ethnicities. With independence in 1960 came a new constitution and federal system manned by candidates drawn from a coalition of ethnically-defined political parties. However, the new government rapidly unraveled due to conflicts between and within the three major political-ethnic regions, and in 1965 the military took control in an attempt to restore law and order. A critical moment occurred in 1967 when the eastern region (Biafra) seceded under the leadership of Igbo freedom fighters, and Nigeria devolved into civil war.[20]

At independence, there were some fundamental contradictions in place in the structure of the Nigerian government as well as in the organization of Nigerian society as a whole. One such contradiction was the simultaneous adoption of a policy of development contingent on foreign investment and a policy of indigenization grounded in nationalist rhetoric. These contradictions provided, in turn, openings for institutions like IITA. In fact, development planning as implemented by the post-colonial state was a continuation of colonial policies. Until 1940, the colonial government had oriented its policies exclusively toward exploiting Nigeria's resources for Britain's benefit. This had a significant impact on infrastructure—which was not designed to produce long-term benefits—and education—which aimed to create a *cadre* of support workers rather than leaders and innovators. With the outbreak of World War II, and with Western acceptance of the idea of indigenous self-determination, Britain finally decided to develop its colonies for long-term economic benefit and the improvements in the welfare of colonized populations. It was only at this point that the Nigerian colonial government pursued formal economic planning. In particular, it promoted foreign investment—first from the Colonial Office in England and later from U.S.-based international financing organizations—as the only possible means to achieve economic growth. Indeed, it has been suggested that upon recognizing the inevitability of self-government, Britain deliberately put policies and institutions into place to ensure that it would continue to reap rewards from Nigeria after the end of colonial rule.

Strangely, when the western-educated elite took over the reins of power, they adopted the colonial-era belief in state-led development planning through external aid. In some ways, this posed a conflict with nationalist ideas about self-determination. Many nationalists argued that only by seizing power at all levels of society would Nigeria be able to control its own destiny. Some even called for the expropriation and indigenization of foreign enterprises. Foreigners were replaced with Nigerians in a process of "Nigerianization" that brought the country's dearth of qualified personnel into stark relief. While recent government investment in education gradually paid off, many vacancies remained unfilled. The country clearly did not have the necessary professional and technical capacity to bridge the gap until a sufficient local workforce emerged. However, the shortage of skilled personnel provided unique opportunities for the small educated elite who profited from policies that encouraged the rapid recruitment and promotion of Nigerians over foreigners. It also created many new opportunities for foreign personnel.[21] These contradictions played out in everyday life at IITA. Ayodele Spencer and Lorna Terry, who lived on IITA's campus in the 1970s and 1980s, recalled that in the early years of IITA Nigerians joined forces with other Africans to object to the dominance of expatriates at IITA. Tensions escalated as non-Nigerian Africans became the target of opprobrium. Although the number of Nigerians at the Institute later increased, accusations about an emerging "Yoruba mafia" continued to demonstrate foundational tensions in the conceptualization of IITA.[22]

Philanthropy and The American Century

Scholars are increasingly recognizing the means through which an American hegemony was concocted, in the first decades of the twentieth century. The three largest philanthropic foundations in the United States—the Ford, Rockefeller, as well as the Carnegie Foundations—were crucial participants in the developments occurring at this time. Although the respective origins of these respective organizations lies in the volition of the eponymous founders—Henry Ford, John D. Rockefeller and Andrew Carnegie—and their individual efforts to ameliorate the very same poverty and inequality in United States that their own enterprise participated in producing, the mandate of the Foundations soon expanded into a mission to promote the welfare of all humankind. The Ford, Rockefeller and Carnegie Foundations have presented, and continue to present, themselves as non-state actors pursuing non-ideological, non-profit agendas. But they worked unflaggingly to promote American global leadership throughout the twentieth century. What is clear today is that the Ford and Rockefeller Foundations both straddled and redefined the boundary between the state and the private sector. Their institutional directors and managers were drawn from the same elite East Coast social and economic circles as the government leaders and big-business figures who collectively penetrated the United States government to direct the country toward "internationally-oriented, capital-intensive industries and financial institutions."[23] The approaches and mandates of the Ford, Rockefeller and Carnegie Foundations were consonant with United States government concern about the power vacuum presented by the global decline of British imperial power. The Ford, Rockefeller, and Carnegie Foundations believed that the United States could employ a soft-power approach that would simultaneously reap the rewards but transcend the violence of prior imperialisms.

Although they set out to create sustainable solutions to social and economic problems on a global scale, the American Foundations were largely unsuccessful in achieving this goal. But a perpetual achievement is the construction of knowledge networks like IITA Ibadan and its sister centers. These networks encouraged capitalist modernization, promoted positivistic social-science knowledge production, and supported linkages between American and foreign universities, exporting the "American dream" to the world. The result was a system of flows of people, ideas, and money that sustained an inequitable distribution of global power to the benefit of the United States.

Government and foundation leaders alike saw Nigeria—the most populous country in Africa—as the next frontier in the war to win hearts and minds. It was crucial in the context of Cold War politics to build alliances with Nigeria if only to avoid the country aligning itself with anti-western interests. On the ground, however, the policy of the U.S. State Department toward Nigeria entailed a continuation rather than rejection of earlier colonial policy that articulated a view of Nigerians as incapable of stewarding their own resources. This attitude was similarly manifested in American intervention in higher education policy in Nigeria. Though largely a late-colonial era British initiative, the University of Ibadan was renewed by an injection of funding and personnel in the late 1950s from the Ford and Rockefeller Foundations. The United States role was even clearer in the conceptualization of a Nigerian version of the Land-Grant University in the form of the University of Nsukka, which sought to provide an alternative to the University of Ibadan's embodiment of local elitism. The University of Nsukka embodied a specific response to the concerns of some Nigerian nationalists that Ibadan was incubating an elite British-educated class, disconnected from immediate local needs and interests. For its part, the University of Nsukka cultivated a different axis of influence that linked it to Land-Grant institutions including Michigan State University, as well as to USAID. As a smaller-scale expression of a similar kind of nexus, IITA existed in an economic intersection between American private foundations, the United States government, and Nigerian research and educational initiatives.

The character of this relationship was exemplified by the uneven terms of the 1967 Nigerian government decree that established IITA.[24] According to these terms, Nigeria would gain relatively intangible outcomes including access to the institute's research on how to accelerate the quantity and quality of tropical crops. It would also benefit from IITA's professional training programs, which could help build up Nigerian expertise. In exchange, IITA would be given land on which to construct its premises, customs and tax exemptions, and permission to operate according to its own rules. Rather than the laws of the land, these rules were to be established by its board of trustees who were supposedly "autonomous and non-political."[25] Like the other centers in the tropical agricultural network, IITA was to be built on donated land, but was otherwise independent of its potentially volatile host government. It was simultaneously Nigerian and not of Nigeria. Though the Institute attempted to hold up its end of the bargain, the agreement was difficult to fulfill because it was fundamentally flawed. Given that IITA was explicitly not designed as an educational institution, it was highly unlikely that its training efforts would have a meaningful effect on Nigerian capacity. Additionally, while the Institute's research contributed significantly to enhanced quality and productivity for key tropical crops, especially cassava, IITA did not achieve the much anticipated revolution in agricultural production.[26] Amendments made in 1974 and 1990 to the terms of IITA's engagement with Nigeria, speak to efforts to rectify the balance between local sovereignty and American power. Smith, Haines, Lundberg & Waehler's design for the IITA campus embodied some of the founding contradictions of project.

Tropical Architecture

"We knew it was a tropical climate. You know those books about sun angles and wind charts? We studied those books. Smith Haines Lundberg & Waehler should be credited with contributing to the new movement in which architecture responded to climate."[27]

According to Theodore (Ted) Hammer, who worked on the IITA project as a young associate at Smith, Haines, Lundberg & Waehler, climate and ecology were the guiding principles for design of IITA's campus. Interest in climate-responsive architecture had reached a crescendo in the United States by 1966, the year IITA was designed. The Olgyay brothers were among the best-known apostles of the new creed and, in *Design with Climate: Bioclimatic Approach to Architectural Regionalism* (1963), Victor Olgyay identified four distinct climatic regions. He explained that climate affects orientation, air movement, site, and materials in each region, and illustrated how an analytical approach to climate can produce good design.[28] In the quotation above, Hammer may have been speaking of the Olgyay brothers' books. But he could have also been referring to the corpus of literature on "tropical architecture" associated with British colonial design in Africa and Asia. By the time Smith, Haines, Lundberg & Waehler began working on IITA, Maxwell Fry and Jane Drew had already produced several publications including their canonical *Tropical Architecture in the Humid Zone* of 1956.[29]

Tropical architecture was the architectural manifestation of the notion of "tropicality" that had shaped techno-scientific regimes of knowledge since the nineteenth century on. Tropical architecture emerged at the end of the nineteenth century when colonial architects started to break with the pejorative attitude toward local design practices common in discussions about hygiene and sanitation.

FIG 5
Threshing & Crop Drying Building, IITA.

By the 1950s, tropical architecture had become "an adaptation of modernist design principles for a distinctive (hot and humid) climatic condition by incorporating passive solar design and ventilation systems, and vernacular building elements such as verandas, louvered windows, and perforated walls."[30] The new creed spread through the late colonial world through publications and conferences. In a strange re-coding, newly-independent nations adopted tropical architecture in their search for an architectural language to embody new nationalist narratives. Arguably, however, tropical architecture served to further entrench old relationships of dependency by accumulating and reconfiguring techno-scientific architectural knowledge as a value-neutral approach, deploying it via networks of Western architects masquerading in the new role of transnational development expert.[31] These networks mirrored the circuits of the United Nations, the World Bank, and the Foundations, and culminated at IITA.

Fry and Drew's University of Ibadan campus, only a few miles away from IITA, is an iconic example of tropical architecture. In fact, IITA had much in common with its famous neighbor. The language of tropical architecture unites all parts of the early proposals submitted by Smith, Haines, Lundberg & Waehler. The research, administrative, and residential and recreational structures alike have long, low, horizontal profiles. But soaring barrel vaults—as in the Threshing & Crop Drying Building FIG 5—provide some formal relief to these flat profiles. The architects used a high ratio of open to closed space in the overall layout of the site and within individual buildings. Inhabited space is always at the core of each building and is surrounded by overlapping layers of open space that encourages natural ventilation and passive cooling. This strategy along with the vented double roof with deep overhangs seen in staff houses, directly links tropical architecture to British colonial design. Tropical architecture elaborated on the principle of responding to the climate by developing the sunbreaker or *brise soleil* into an art form. Again, the iconic example of this is Fry and Drew's virtuoso use of patterned precast concrete screens to clad vertical surfaces across the University of Ibadan campus. Similarly, vertical fins interspersed with perforated screens articulated the facades of almost every administrative and research structure at IITA. IITA's *brise-soleils* took on a more expressive form in the walls of staff residences, which used patterned cast concrete blocks.

Another strategy that connects IITA's design to the tropical architecture paradigm is the wall covered in a rough stone veneer and placed at right angles to the dominant axes of some staff houses. This wall seems to anchor the houses firmly to their sites and accomplishes Jane Drew's goal of creating a distinctly African response without "copying African detail."[32] Another detail that hints at tropical architecture's ethos of transforming pragmatic climactic necessities into architectural statements is the use of drainpipes as a facade treatment on administrative and research buildings. At first glance, these large concrete columns—designated as "water collectors" on plans—run at regular intervals along the facades of the Engineering Services, Inventory and Chemical Storage, FIG 6 and Crop Threshing and Drying Buildings. FIG 7 In fact, they form an outer layer in front of the *brises-soleils*, whose continuous screen they modulate into sections. Likewise, the water collectors terminate just short of the trough-shaped gutters protruding from the flat roofs. The overall effect is of a row of attenuated drums like the famous hourglass-shaped *dùndún* of the Yoruba, or of the rows of palm trees shown in many of Smith, Haines, Lundberg & Waehler's renderings. Indeed, some of the most striking aspects of IITA landscape today are the swaying, majestic palm trees lining its avenues and filtering sunlight onto its buildings. Ted Hammer's recollection of an eight-foot by eight-foot model of IITA, complete with palm trees, that sat in the firm's lobby for many years, is a testament to the power of the design and the firm's embrace of the IITA project.[33]

> "They were bungalows with long hallways, and they were always cool. They always had electricity. And water."[34]
>
> "There were sliding doors on both sides of the living room. It could be open, completely open.... There was an air conditioner in every room, even the kitchen. It was always cold. I distinctly remember that going from the kitchen to the living room was like walking from a furnace to a freezer. Momsie used to shout at us to close the door between the kitchen and the living room."[35]

As the former residents of the IITA quoted above indicated, staff housing in particular revealed IITA's allegiances to tropical architecture. The long narrow profile of Staff House Type 3-304 consists of two rectangles FIG 8 sliding slightly over each other at right angles to the direction of prevailing wind—prominently marked on drawings. The wall facing the prevailing wind is pierced by openings along its entire length. Rooms are arranged in a single bank and are accessed by

FIG 6
Engineering Services and Inventory, and Chemical Storage Buildings, IITA.

long narrow hallways consisting of a combination of patterned cast concrete screen walls and operable exterior glass louvers, as well as doors on the interior side. Essentially, this arrangement creates a continuous airspace that insulates the rooms beyond. In front of the exterior screen wall, a hedge and a row of trees both provide additional layers of insulation. Overall, this design is an elaboration on the colonial maxim of the encircling verandah whose purpose was to ensure cross-ventilation. One of the ironies of IITA's architecture is that its designers did not trust tropical architecture enough —or perhaps did not fully understand or embrace it— to eschew mechanical cooling altogether. Instead, Smith, Haines, Lundberg & Waehler specified air conditioners for all staff houses and for many research spaces. It is no coincidence that former residents and visitors like Ayodele Spencer and Omozuwa Osayimwese remember the interiors of these houses as extraordinarily cool.

Corporatization of American Architecture Firms

How did an American firm come to design such successful buildings in Ibadan? There is no evidence that the firm had any "tropical" experience before the IITA project. Some members of the architectural design team, including C. Haines, F. Bonhage, and A. Nathanson, travelled to Ibadan for meetings and site visits.[36] But they did not embed themselves in the country to the extent that tropical modernist architects-cum-postcolonial development experts like Fry and Drew, Michel Ecochard, Charles Abrams, Otto Koenigsberger, Constantine Doxiadis, and others had done.[37] In addition to being exposed to tropical architecture through theoretical texts, firm representatives may have found inspiration on the grounds of the University of Ibadan campus where they likely stayed during site visits. It is also possible that Smith, Haines, Lundberg & Waehler relied heavily on their local partner, the contractors G. Cappa Ltd.[38] Founded in 1952, G. Cappa was an offshoot of one of the oldest and most prominent contracting firms of the colonial period, Cappa & D'Alberto. Cappa & D'Alberto was familiar with colonial architecture paradigms through its involvement in the construction of the University of Ibadan campus and other important colonial buildings. The firm had built one of Nigeria's first skyscrapers in 1961, the tropical modernist Electricity Corporation of Nigeria Building in Lagos.[39]

Rather than a new-found interest in tropical architecture, Smith, Haines, Lundberg & Waehler's IITA project signaled a new, corporatized, multidisciplinary, integrated mode of practice. This mode of practice had been adopted by large architecture firms in the United States after World War II. Certainly, at the time Smith, Haines, Lundberg & Waehler became involved in IITA, there was little suggestion of the late twentieth-century dominance of American firms in the global architectural market. Smith, Haines, Lundberg & Waehler still exists today in its most recent incarnation, HLW, and ranks alongside firms like AECOM, Caudhill Rowlett Scott (CRS), Helmuth, Obata + Kassabaum (HOK), Skidmore Owings and Merrill (SOM), and Yamasaki Associates in global reach. But Smith, Haines, Lundberg & Waehler had not yet acquired this global presence in 1963. Rather, the Ford and Rockefeller Foundations selected the firm because of its reputation as a leader in high-tech research facility design.[40] Publications from the 1960s to the 1980s promote this image of the firm. The firm itself links its twentieth-century expertise in high-tech design to one of its first commissions, the Metropolitan Telephone Building of 1886 in New York City. This building was seminal in the early telephone industry. Another important Smith, Haines, Lundberg & Waehler building was Bell Telephone Laboratories, constructed from 1937–1949, in Murray Hill, New Jersey. Critics have recently credited the flexible modular design of this building as an early example of the progressive workplace paradigm of the "idea factory."[41] A roster of Smith, Haines, Lundberg & Waehler projects during the 1960s includes some of the most important United States government agencies and industrial enterprises of the era. In addition to the Ford and Rockefeller Foundations, the firm received commissions from NASA, the Naval Research Laboratory, the Department of Commerce, Ford Motor Company, Bethlehem Steel, General Electric, Princeton University, and the U.S. Army War College. Smith, Haines, Lundberg & Waehler was well-connected to the United States east coast establishment, and the east coast establishment was, in turn, closely tied to the rise of American global hegemony.

FIG 7
Drainpipes at former Threshing & Crop Drying Building, IITA. Photograph taken in 2018.

Arguably because of the firm's expertise in designing high-tech architectural programs, Smith, Haines, Lundberg & Waehler developed an integrated approach to architectural problem-solving that placed it in the small circle of American firms that would come to dominate the international market during the post-war era.[42] From the beginning, Smith, Haines, Lundberg & Waehler was open to collaboration with disciplines normally understood to be outside the boundaries of architecture. Cyrus L. W. Eidlitz, the firm's nineteenth-century founder, believed it was necessary to integrate architectural and engineering knowledge in order to solve modern problems.[43] He partnered with the engineer Andrew McKenzie for this reason. Between the 1920s and 1980s, the firm expanded to include interior design, site planning, landscape architecture, code administration, construction services, site engineering, hydrology, city planning, graphics and architectural signage, site selection, management consultation, technical regulatory services, facilities management, and other departments to create a multi-disciplinary practice. This effort to be comprehensive, and to provide a "one-stop shop," marked a new paradigm in architectural praxis. Much like Michael Kubo has described for Skidmore Owings & Merrill in the late 1950s, Smith, Haines, Lundberg & Waehler offered a level of efficiency made possible by a flexible organizational hierarchy. This hierarchy consisted of specialized independent divisions linked both vertically and horizontally through coordinated decision-making.[44]

FIG 8
Site model showing sliding rectangles of IITA bungalows on main campus road.

That Smith, Haines, Lundberg & Waehler functioned in this manner during the IITA project is clear from the archival evidence. Various staff including partners Frank Waehler, Robert Djerejian, and Charles Haines are named in connection with the project. But, when asked who created IITA design, Ted Hammer stated categorically in a recent interview that there was no single responsible party. Rather, IITA was a collaborative, firm-wide effort.[45] Smith, Haines, Lundberg & Waehler thus exemplified the new paradigm of the bureaucratic office. In 1947, architect Henry-Russell Hitchcock described the new architecture firm as a place where there is no genius and no personal expression, and where each architect worked as an "anonymous member of a team."[46]

The corporatization of United States architecture firms was standard by the 1970s. This change was intimately related to the expansion of Middle Eastern oil economies and the new loci of capital and power that the oil economies signaled.[47] But the phenomenon was also closely tied to the dissolution of the colonial world order and its reconfiguration along Cold War lines of engagement. There is little doubt that the rise of American megafirms indexed new forms of imperialism.[48] Smith, Haines, Lundberg & Waehler became involved in overseas work at this exact moment. Ted Hammer describes this as a transitional period at the firm and pinpoints Robert Djerejian as the partner responsible for developing its international presence. After IITA, the firm did not build anything else in Nigeria, but did build a laboratory in Cairo, and worked on projects in Beirut, Berlin, Belgium, and Rome. In the 1970s, the firm consolidated its international presence by opening offices in Beirut and Athens, Greece.[49]

Though innovative in its organization and working methods (the firm was also an early adopter of computer-aided design technologies), Smith, Haines, Lundberg & Waehler followed a conventional approach to architectural style and form. A glance at published projects shows that the firm's work in the 1960s and 1970s embraced the typical contemporary idiom of corporate modernism: concrete frames, curtain walls, flat roofs, ribbon windows, and *pilotis*. The "repetitive, reproducible character of modernism" was undoubtedly compatible with the efficiencies of bureaucratic architecture.[50] The tropical modernist vocabulary of IITA was therefore an aberration in Smith, Haines, Lundberg & Waehler's oeuvre.

The Social Science of Resettlement

A new positivistic social science, institutionalized at Foundation-sponsored area studies and international relations programs at American universities in the 1950s and 1960s, supported the emergence of the United States as a world power. At the same time, their association with state power and policy transformed these disciplines and their associated methodologies into academic powerhouses.[51] As I argue below, the transformation of the IITA project into an object of social scientific inquiry and a case study with policy implications illustrates how academic inquiry, architectural design, philanthropy and neo-imperialism were linked.

The decision to place IITA's campus only a few kilometers north of the University of Ibadan almost reads as a repetition of history. In the colonial-era founding story of the University of Ibadan, the first principal of the University, Kenneth Mellanby, strode purposefully through the seemingly uninhabited bush around the city until he reached a clearing where he struck his staff and declared "here shall be the University of Ibadan.[52] Almost twenty years later, the Ford and Rockefeller Foundations barely considered local conditions when they decided to build their institute on the outskirts of the city of Ibadan. In both cases, the initial assumption that the designated land was unclaimed was rapidly overturned by a reality in which Ibadan's periphery was densely subdivided into farms. Letters between Foundation officials note that they had been warned by local leaders to expect "rather violent objection" to their plans to build IITA.[53] As early as April 1966, Ford Foundation Vice President for Education and Research, F. Champion Ward, acknowledged that the resettlement of the existing population on the proposed IITA site could become an issue. Nevertheless, he insisted that "from the Foundation standpoint we have a laboratory here in which to experiment with approaches to the problem of the suburban slum."[54]

As this quotation indicates, Ward maintained an attitude of social scientific experimentation that did not prioritize the people being displaced. He understood the city of Ibadan in terms of the framework developed by the Chicago School of urban sociology.[55] According to Chicago School thinkers, modern cities exerted a magnetic pull on rural populations and peripheral urban slums were an inevitable product of this rural-urban migration. Slum clearance in the United States in the second of half of the twentieth century targeted these peri-urban slums. With these assumptions about the evolution of modern cities in mind, the Foundations charged Dr. David Smock, a Cornell-trained anthropologist and Ford Foundation staff member, to develop a proposal for resettling the population that IITA would displace. Foundation staff surveyed this seemingly empty land using aerial photography, and found that the land actually encompassed 32–33 villages inhabited by 2,907 people. This was no simple rural population who could be easily relocated. Rather, complex filial ties connected farmland to urban compounds and associated families in Ibadan itself. Furthermore, some of these people had already been displaced twice—once to create space for the city of Ibadan to expand to the southwest, and a second time for the construction of the University of Ibadan.[56] Their dissatisfaction with and lack of trust in a process that allegedly benefitted them was therefore understandable. Some residents organized to fight for equitable compensation, and some hoped to stop the project altogether. They hired a lawyer to represent them but the Foundations dismissed him as a swindler.[57] The inhumane nature of the resettlement process was exemplified in an October 1965 public notice stating that anyone who obstructed the process of requisitioning land for IITA would be criminalized.[58] A photograph taken at the dedication of the new institute in April 1970 shows villagers carrying signs. Some signs thank the Foundations while others question the value of the resettlement project. FIG 9 But it is not clear whose opinions the signs represented since most of the villagers were illiterate. Generally, records from the Foundations present the eviction as a foregone conclusion. A first-hand account indicates that the villagers themselves recognized that they did not have the power to halt the project.[59]

For his part, Smock used many of the research methods of social science to develop his resettlement proposal. He conducted a comprehensive sociological survey that evaluated everything from existing housing conditions to employment patterns and education in the villages, and he organized community meetings to assess villagers' resettlement preferences.[60] Ultimately, when offered a choice between resettling in a new farming community even further removed from the city of Ibadan, or building a new non-farming town on a small site provided by the Foundations and adjacent to the location of the new IITA, the villagers chose the latter. Smock described and analyzed his process in an academic paper presented to the Nigerian Institute of Social and Economic Research on February 7, 1967. Researchers at the University of Ibadan quickly assumed the mantle this research by regularly publishing academic papers evaluating the results of the IITA resettlement over time. By 1970, the Ford Foundation and the University of Ibadan had established a joint "experimental archaeological reserve" on the site of one of the abandoned villages taken over by IITA.[61] This research project, which continued into the 2000s, shed light on a variety of topics including Yoruba pottery, dwelling forms and construction materials, religion, dietary practices, and textile production practices. As such, the Ford and Rockefeller Foundations' IITA project yielded important social scientific knowledge for many years.

The new settlement, named Ibadan-Parapo and later affectionately called Sasa, was laid out by the Nigerian Town Planning Division of the Ministry of Lands and Housing on a wedge-shaped plot.[62] FIG 10 The Ford and Rockefeller Foundations were willing to give up this land because it was a right of way for the regional electricity authority, and could therefore not be fenced and fully utilized. Thus, giving this land to the villagers did not represent a true concession on the part of the Ford and Rockefeller Foundations. The Ford and Rockefeller Foundations did offer something of significant value however, in terms of the physical fabric of the town that they jointly funded. They provided roads, laid a network of pipes connected to a water tank, and built a primary school, market, two public latrines and

FIG 9
Villagers at Dedication of IITA in April 1970.

"40 concrete salga slabs."[63] Villagers were meant to build their own pit latrines on these slabs. Two demonstration houses were provided, on which villagers were supposed to model their new homes, as well as a block-making machine for the construction of these homes. Finally, the Foundations equipped the villagers with an oil-palm processing machine and poultry coops.[64] In his 1967 paper, Smock described villagers' existing houses as improperly ventilated and irregularly-placed. The houses were rectangular structures with cement-plastered mud-walls. They contained up to fourteen rooms, were roofed with corrugated iron, and did not have proper floors or ceilings.[65] By contrast, the Foundations' model houses were smaller and built with concrete slabs and walls. These houses had wood gable roofs, at least one large window on each wall, and verandahs supported on simple posts. FIG 11 On the masterplan, space was designated at the center of the settlement for community amenities like a church, a mosque, a community center, and a clinic, but these amenities were only built later through community incentive. In addition to these tangible material contributions, the Foundations collaborated with the Nigerian government to offer villagers a two-week course on leadership and citizenship.[66] They also provided training in banking, sanitation and poultry-breeding as a replacement for farming, as well as a promise of future employment at IITA for some villagers.

By taking this approach, the Foundations employed up-to-date economic development practices. The idea of "aided self-help" housing had emerged in Puerto Rico in the 1940s but was only fully embraced by development specialists in the 1960s. It represented a recognition that the costs of building complete dwellings for under-housed populations was too high for most governments to bear. Instead, many more people could be housed if governments provided plots serviced with basic infrastructure upon which individuals and families could build their own starter homes.[67] The Ford Foundation had adopted this model for its "villagization" projects in India in the 1950s. Architects, such as Otto Koenigsberger, George Atkinson, and Albert Mayer, who had transformed themselves into development experts, assisted the Ford Foundation with designing these villages. The "sites-and-services" approach may also have seemed like a rational alternative given the Nigerian government's own numerous failed small-scale but very expensive resettlement projects.[68]

Unfortunately, the roads in Sasa remained untarred for a long time and the water tank dried up. Many of the lots laid out by planners remained unused, since some villagers chose to move elsewhere. New houses replicated the existing vernacular instead of adhering to the standards demonstrated in the model houses. The new market was largely empty, and only a few people of the resettled villagers were employed at IITA. Thus, Sasa failed to become a living community with a viable economy. In a recent interview, Smock noted that he had been disappointed that the villagers had chosen to stay on the land next to IITA rather than settle in a new and potentially more economically viable farming community farther away from Ibadan.[69] In fact, it was not until 1979, when Muslim traders from the North adopted the Sasa market as a depot for foodstuff *en-route* to Ibadan, that the new settlement finally took off.

FIG 11
Demonstration House, Ibadan-Parapo/Sasa, photograph taken in 2018.

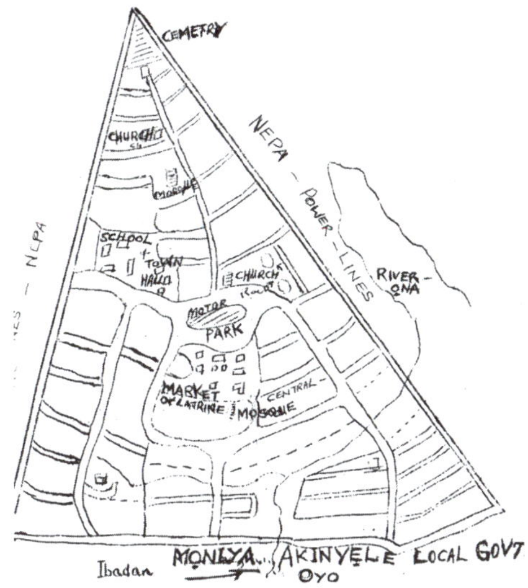

FIG 10
Plan of Ibadan-Parapo/Sasa.

These traders not only injected capital into the community, but they also initiated population growth as some of them settled permanently in the town. Sasa's subsequent success was therefore largely independent of the measures taken by the Ford and Rockefeller Foundations and IITA.[70]

Continuities between the paternalistic ethos of the IITA resettlement project and the dehumanizing ideologies of British colonialism are clear. What is even more interesting is Smock's vision of IITA as a sociological experiment:

> Only about 200 or 300 of the 640 adult males will be employed [at IITA]. How many of the rest will re-establish themselves as farmers, start trading, find other employment, or retire and live off their compensation and relatives will be interesting to see.[71]

Specifically, Smock believed IITA would "contribute to the growing body of experience and knowledge concerning resettlement."[72] A successful IITA could "form the basis of what the Western Nigerian Government does in future cases of land acquisition."[73] Importantly, it would also inform scholars and specialists worldwide.

What body of resettlement experience was Smock referring to? He pointed in particular to the Kainji Dam resettlement project in northwestern Nigeria, built in 1966–68. This was a "multi-purpose development program" to improve power capacity and enhance water transportation and fishing on the River Niger.[74] Over 50,000 people were resettled through the joint efforts of Nigerian authorities, foreign banks and donors, as well as foreign technical enterprise and academic interests. Plans included new villages and towns, one of which—New Bussa—was recognized for its architectural innovations.[75] Smock commented on the decision to replicate the traditional Muslim courtyard residential type at New Bussa using a modern material—concrete. For Smock, New Bussa was an undesirable model for IITA. Where the Kainji Dam project "rigidly" adhered to traditional design, IITA would promote innovation in room layout, construction methods, and materials.[76]

Smock was not only interested in local comparisons. He was thinking on a larger scale when he declared that IITA would avoid the mistakes of the 1961–66 Volta River project. This project was initiated by President Kwame Nkrumah soon after independence in order to accelerate Ghana's industrialization. The project included the construction of a hydroelectric dam, the opening up of Nigerian bauxite deposits, and the construction of an aluminum smelter. A new port, a new industrial town near Accra, and new railway lines were also built as part of the Volta River project. New dwelling standards were also established for the newly-independent nation. This project, which displaced 80,000 people, was made possible by extensive foreign loans, aid, and expertise. Not surprisingly, the Ford Foundation financed another socioeconomic survey to support the project.[77]

The architects Maxwell Fry, Jane Drew, and several other members of the nascent postwar network of development experts were involved in the Volta project. To decrease the social effects of displacement, the planners of the new town of Tema tried to transpose the complex living patterns of the local Ga population into the idiom of the city as a collection of nuclear family units. Smock also considered this project to be a failure. He denigrated the "sociograms" that the planners of Tema developed to implement this translation.[78] One senses the accepted wisdom of Chicago School urban sociology in Smock's attitude—the idea that rural-urban migration was irreversible. In his view, it was impossible for new towns like Tema to retain elements of older traditions. Such new towns had no choice but to be modern.[79]

Smock oriented the IITA resettlement project to an even more remote and exponentially larger project—the Aswan High Dam of 1960–70. The Aswan Dam was a hydroelectric project was envisioned by President Gamal Abdel Nasser as an economic, social, and political "magic bullet" for Egypt. Hundreds of countries and international organizations participated in a mission to rescue Nubian and Pharaonic monuments endangered by the damming of the Nile. But the relocation of 120,000 Nubians who were resettled in new towns hundreds of miles away from their original homes, did not receive quite the same publicity. Cold War tensions affected the shape of funding for the project and caused the United States to lose face to the Soviet Union. But the United States was still able to assert influence through the Ford Foundation-funded *Nubian Ethnographic Survey*.[80] Architectural historian Lucia Allais argues that the Aswan Dam project was significant because of the massive environmental and social changes that it generated, and because it established the framework for UNESCO's world heritage project. Furthermore, she contends that it signaled a new postwar mode of governance divorced from the conventional territoriality of the nation-state.[81]

Dr. David Smock of the Ford Foundation conceptualized the IITA resettlement project in relation to these earlier projects on the African continent. Despite noting that IITA "cannot compare in size to the projects undertaken at Aswan, Volta, or Kainji," he was confident that "some of the lessons we learn and the mistakes we make during the coming months may not have to be repeated elsewhere."[82] Thus, IITA was part of a web of resettlement projects that built on each other intellectually, financially, and technically. This web included not only Aswan, Volta, and Kainji, but also Kariba Dam in Zimbabwe of 1955, Koka Dam in Ethiopia of 1960, Kossou Dam in Côte d'Ivoire of 1969, the Bhakra Nangal Dam in India of 1951, and the Tennessee Valley Authority Project in the United States of 1933, among other examples.

Smock was not alone in conceptualizing US social science research as a helpmeet to development policy. In his 1963 article, David Brokensha, a development anthropologist and former District Commissioner in British Mandate Tanganyika, argued forcefully for an applied anthropology that would provide a theoretical framework and scientific data to underwrite the "haphazard notions of social matters" typical of development planners.[83] Brokensha's article—like many essays on the topic—cites the Aswan, Kariba, and Nubia projects in a manner that insists on the universality of resettlement policy while acknowledging the specificity of each case.

What my analysis makes clear is that the close association between development projects and American social scientific research was not disinterested. With the establishment of IITA and the resettlement community of Ibadan Parapo/Sasa, the Foundations embarked on a philanthropic development project. But this project was also deeply connected to the production of American hegemony through social scientific research. Since the 1990s, however, the link between social scientific research and development policy has been criticized for recycling a Eurocentric system of power/knowledge in the guise of scholarly interest in local practices.[84]

An array of factors—from the invention of tropical agriculture to the social science of resettlement—merged to produce the radical alterity of IITA. A common thread among these factors was the post-World War II ascendancy of the United States in global politics and economics. While it may be too simplistic to describe this new form of politics as imperialism, in many cases American power re-inscribed the dependent position of formerly colonized societies. This article argues for and contributes to a growing literature on the architecture of the new American imperialism of the 1960s.

1 Hannah Le Roux, "Building on the Boundary—Modern Architecture in the Tropics," *Social Identities* 10, no. 4 (2004): 439–453 (449).

2 In a related project, I am collecting stories, photographs, and ephemera from former residents of the campus.
3 A similar approach to "network" is developed by Lukasz Stanek in "Cold War Transfer: architecture and planning from socialist countries in the 'Third World', *The Journal of Architecture* 17 (2012): 299–307.
4 Denis Cosgrove, "Tropic and Tropicality," in *Tropical Visions in an Age of Empire*, eds. Driver, Felix, Martins, Luciana (Chicago: University of Chicago Press, 2010), 197–216.
5 R. E. Dennett, "Agricultural Progress in Nigeria," *Journal of the African Society* 18 (1918–19): 266–289.
6 Arthur A. Goldsmith, *Building agricultural institutions: transferring the land-grant model to India and Nigeria* (Boulder: Westview Press, 1990), 169, 216; Lorna Terry Telephone Interview, March 8, 2015; RAC, Ford Foundation Unpublished Reports Box 163 Folder 3631 #003631, "The IITA Resettlement Project, by David R. Smock, The Ford Foundation, Paper prepped for Nigerian Institute of Social and Economic Research, Ibadan, Feb, 7, 1967," 1–3; RAC, Ford Foundation Unpublished Reports Box 902 Report #11991, International Institute for Tropical Agriculture Photo Album, 2; RAC, Rockefeller Foundation, Record Group: P, Series: 115, Box: 21, Folder: 600, Dedication Ceremony Program, April 20, 1970.
7 Michael E. Latham, *Modernization as Ideology* (Chapel Hill: UNC Press, 2000), 213–4.
8 Arthur A. Goldsmith, *Building Agricultural Institutions: Transferring the Land-Grant Model to India and Nigeria* (Boulder, CO: Westview Press, 1990), 4, 10.
9 Goldsmith, *Building*, 135–136; FF Unpublished Reports Box 902 Report #11991, International Institute for Tropical Agriculture Photo Album, 2, 3; http://www.cgiar.org/who-we-are/history-of-cgiar/centers-chronology/.
10 Lars Skyttner, *General Systems Theory* (River Edge: World Scientific, 2005), 53, 59.
11 See also Arindam Dutta, M. Ijlal Muzaffar, Ateya Khorakiwala, Fabiola López-Durán and Ayala Levin, "Systems and the South: Architecture in Development", Conference Agenda, http://www.we-aggregate.org/project/systems-and-the-south-architecture-in-development.
12 Goldsmith, *Building*, 214.
13 Goldsmith, *Building*, 213.
14 Bruno Latour, *Reassembling the Social: An Introduction to Actor-Network-Theory* (New York: Oxford University Press, 2005), 128.
15 Latour, *Reassembling the Social*, 131.
16 Latour, *Reassembling the Social*, 128.
17 Latour, *Reassembling the Social*, 128, 131; Rudi Meyer, "Large System Theory, Actor Network Theory, and Relations in Design," Paper presented at the European Academy of Design Conference in Bremen, 2005, http://ead.verhaag.net/fullpapers/ead06_id118_3.pdf; Inderjeet Parmar, *Foundations of the American Century: The Ford, Carnegie and Rockefeller Foundations in the Rise of American Power* (New York. Columbia University Press, 2012), 28.
18 Rockefeller Archive Center, Ford Foundation Unpublished Reports Box 36 Folder 664 #000708-report #, "Report on Preliminary Design," 8/66, Smith Haines Lundberg & Waehler."
19 William R. Bascom, "Tribalism, Nationalism, and Pan-Africanism," *Annals of the American Academy of Political and Social Science* 342 (Jul., 1962): 21–29 (26); Anthony Hamilton Millard Kirk-Greene and Toyin O. Falola, "Nigeria," *Encyclopaedia Britannica Online Academic Edition* (Encyclopædia Britannica Inc., 2015), accessed Web. 24 Mar. 2015.
20 Kirk-Greene and Falola, "Nigeria"; Falola, *Colonialism and violence in Nigeria* (Bloomington: Indiana University Press, 2009), xxi–xxii.
21 Toyin Falola, *Development planning and decolonization in Nigeria* (Gainesville: University Press of Florida, 1996), 69, 130, 134, 136; Toyin Falola, *Economic reforms and modernization in Nigeria, 1945–1965* (Kent: The Kent State University Press, 2004), 159; Olakunle Lawal, "British Commercial Interests and the Decolonization Process in Nigeria, 1950–60," *African Economic History*, No. 22 (1994), 93–110; Eghosa Osaghae, *Crippled giant: Nigeria since Independence* (Bloomington: Indiana University Press, 1998), 159.
22 Lorna Terry Telephone Interview, March 8, 2015.
23 Inderjeet Parmar, *Foundations of the American Century: The Ford, Carnegie and Rockefeller Foundations in the Rise of American Power* (New York: Columbia University Press, 2012), 17.
24 Communications Unit, IITA Library, "Legislation Governing IITA's Legal Status in Nigeria," "International Institute of Tropical Agriculture Decree 1967," "1974 Amendment Decree 27," "1990 Amendment Decree 45."
25 RAC, Ford Foundation Unpublished Reports Box 902 Report #11991, International Institute of Agriculture Photo Album, 2
26 Rodomiro Ortiz, ed. *IITA 50 Years After: Transforming Africa's Agriculture and Nourishing Rural Development* (Ibadan: International Institute of Tropical Agriculture, 2017), 12.
27 Theodore Hammer Telephone Interview, December 28, 2017.
28 Victor Olgyay et al, *Design with Climate: Bioclimatic Approach to Architectural Regionalism* (Princeton: Princeton University Press, 2015).
29 Maxwell Fry and Jane Drew, *Tropical Architecture in the Humid Zone* (London: Batsford, 1964).
30 Duanfang Lu, "Introduction," in *Third World Modernism: Architecture, Development, and Identity* (New York: Routledge, 2011), 17.
31 Jiat-Hwee Chang, "Building a Colonial Technoscientific Network," in *Third World Modernism: Architecture, Development, and Identity*, ed. Duanfang Lu (New York: Routledge, 2011), 229; Vandana Baweja, "Otto Koenigsberger and the Tropicalization of British Architectural Culture," in *Third World Modernism: Architecture, Development, and Identity*, ed. Duanfang Lu (New York: Routledge, 2011), 236–254; Vandana Baweja, "A Pre-history of Green Architecture: Otto Koenigsberger and Tropical Architecture, from Princely Mysore to Post-colonial London," (Ph.D.

diss. University of Michigan, 2008): 141; Iain Jackson and Jessica Holland, *The Architecture of Edwin Maxwell Fry and Jane Drew: Twentieth-Century Architecture, Pioneer Modernism and the Tropics* (Farnham: Ashgate, 2014), 204.

32 Jackson and Holland, *The Architecture of Edwin Maxwell and Jane Drew*, 173; Interview with Ayodele Spencer, March 28, 2015.

33 Theodore Hammer Telephone Interview, December 28, 2017.

34 Omozuwa Osayimwese Telephone Interview, March 1, 2015.

35 Ayodele Spencer Telephone Interview, March 28, 2015.

36 RAC, Rockefeller Foundation Record Group 1.3 series 115 box 33 folder 197 title IITA Construction & Engineering, May 4, 1970, Letter from Haines Lundberg & Waehler re: IITA Phase II, "Minutes of Meeting #74 held in IITA Offices, Ibadan, Nigeria on April 22, 1970."

37 See Tom Avermaete, "Framing the Afropolis: Michel Ecochard and the African City for the Greatest Number," *OASE* 82 (2010), 77–100.

38 Interestingly, another United States company, Gilbert Associates Inc., based in Reading, PA, is hired as consulting engineer for the project. The company actually marketed its water supply and sewage engineering services and previous experience in Ibadan to the Rockefeller Foundation and was subsequently hired. See RAC, Rockefeller Foundation Record Group 1.3 series 115 box 33 folder 197, IITA Construction & Engineering, Letter from Gilbert Associates to William Myers.

39 Kunle Akinsemoyin and Alan Vaughan-Richards, *Building Lagos* (Lagos: F. & A. Services, 1976).

40 Theodore Hammer Telephone Interview, December 28, 2017;

41 "130 Years of Innovation: Projects from our Archives," http://www.hlwstoryboard.com/blog/hlw-and-bell-labs, cited on April 7, 2018; William J. Rankin, "Laboratory Modules and the Subjectivity of the Knowledge Worker," in *Use Matters: An Alternative History of Architecture*, ed. Kenny Cupers, 51–68 (New York: Routledge, 2013).

42 Paolo Tombesi, "Prometheus Unchained: The Multiple Itineraries of Contemporary Professional Freedom," in *The Sage Handbook of Architectural Theory*, eds. C. Greig Crysler, Stephen Cairns, and Hilde Heynen, (Thousand Oaks, CA: Sage, 2012): 393–397.

43 Smith Haines Lundberg & Waehler has a long and venerable history. After seven name changes, Eidlitz and McKenzie became Smith Haines Lundberg & Waehler. Today, it operates under the name HLW. See Kathryn Holliday, *Leopold Eidlitz: Architecture and Idealism in the Gilded Age* (New York: Norton, 2008), 160–163; "7th Name Change Made By Architectural Firm," *New York Times*, Jan. 7, 1964.

44 Michael Kubo, "The Concept of the Architectural Corporation," in *OfficeUS Agenda*, eds. Eva Franch i Gilabert, Amanda Reeser Lawrence, Ana Miljački, and Ashley Schafer, 37–45 (Zurich: Lars Müller Publishers, 2014).

45 Theodore Hammer Telephone Interview, December 28, 2017; Mark Zaloudek, "Obituary: Architect's work Included Major Science Buildings," *Herald Tribune*, Tuesday, October 7, 2008, page BM4, http://www.heraldtribune.com/article/LK/20081007/News/605238659/SH/.

46 Kubo, "The Concept of the Architectural Corporation," 38.

47 Kubo, "The Concept of the Architectural Corporation," 44.

48 "OfficeUS," http://storefrontnews.org/programming/officeus/, cited on April 7, 2018.

49 "A Multi-Disciplinary Firm Comes of Age," *Buildings Design Journal*, 12th January, (1984): 16; Zahloudek, "Obituary."

50 Kubo, "The Concept of the Architectural Corporation," 41.

51 Parmar, *Foundations*, 28, 156.

52 Timothy Livsey, "The University Age: Development and Decolonisation in Nigeria, 1930 to 1966," (Ph.D. diss. Birkbeck College, University of London, 2014), 145.

53 Myers, William M., "Letter from William M. Myers to Ralph W. Cummings, 1965 May 28," 100 Years: The Rockefeller Foundation, accessed April 7, 2018, https://rockfound.rockarch.org/digital-library-listing/-/asset_publisher/yYxpQfeI4W8N/content/letter-from-william-m-myers-to-ralph-w-cummings-1965-may-28.

54 RAC, Ford Foundation Memo to Mr. F. Champion Ward from J Donald Kingsley, April 19, 1966.

55 Andrew Abbott, *Department and Discipline: Chicago Sociology at One Hundred* (Chicago: University of Chicago Press, 1999).

56 Lasisi Akinpelu, *Background History of Ibadan-Parapo (Sasa) Town* (Ibadan: Institute of African Studies, 1988), 50.

57 RAC, Ford Foundation Unpublished Reports Box 163 Folder 3631 #003631, "The IITA Resettlement Project, by David R. Smock, The Ford Foundation."

58 Akinpelu, *Background History of Ibadan-Parapo*, 6.

59 Akinpelu, *Background History of Ibadan-Parapo*, 2.

60 A. Afolayan, "The Sasa Resettlement Project: A Study in Problems of Relocation," *Habitat International* 11, no. 2 (1987): 43–57.

61 Philip Allsworth-Jones, "Ethnoarchaeology at IITA Ibadan: Excavation of the Mound at Adesina Oja in the Archaeological Reserve, Preliminary Version," Paper presented at the Society of Africanist Archaeologists (SAfA) 2008 Conference, (2008), accessed May 24, 2018.

62 "Parapo" is a Yoruba term meaning to join together. In the 1960s and 1970s Ibadan, a movement called "Ibadan Parapo" developed among indigenous Ibadanites to take back their city from Yorubas from elsewhere in the region. It is possible therefore that the villagers displaced by IITA were being subversive when they named their new town "Ibadan-Parapo." See Aderemi Suleiman Ajala, "Identity and space in Ibadan politics, western Nigeria," *African Identities* 6, no. 2, (May 2008): 149–168 (160).

63 Afolayan, "The Sasa Resettlement Project" 50.

64 Foundation sources refer to two model houses but Akinpelu notes that the Foundations built three houses. It is possible that the third house was built at a later date. See Akinpelu, *Background History of Ibadan-Parapo*, 51.
65 RAC, Ford Foundation Unpublished Reports Box 163 Folder 3631 #003631, "The IITA Resettlement Project, by David R. Smock, The Ford Foundation," 13.
66 The course was held at the Sasa Training Center in Ijebu-Ode. Attending the course created a sense of community among the villagers, who thereafter informally renamed Ibadan-Parapo "Sasa." Akinpelu, *Background History of Ibadan-Parapo*, 3.
67 Richard Harris, "The Silence of the Experts: "Aided Self-help Housing," 1939–1954," *Habitat International* 22, no. 2, 165–189, 1998.
68 Falola, *Development*, 80–81; Afolayan, "The Sasa Resettlement Project" 48.
69 David Smock Interview, May 27, 2018.
70 Afolayan, "The Sasa Resettlement Project" 66.
71 RAC, Ford Foundation Unpublished Reports Box 163 Folder 3631 #003631, "The IITA Resettlement Project, by David R. Smock, The Ford Foundation, Paper prepared for Nigerian Institute of Social and Economic Research, Ibadan, Feb, 7, 1967," 12.
72 RAC, Ford Foundation Unpublished Reports Box 163 Folder 3631 #003631, "The IITA Resettlement Project," 12.
73 RAC, Ford Foundation Unpublished Reports Box 163 Folder 3631 #003631, "The IITA Resettlement Project," 12.
74 P. J. Wagland, "Kainji and the Niger Dams Project," *Geography* 54, no. 4 (November 1969), 460.
75 Ruth Shinenge Gyuse & Timothy Terver Gyuse, "Kainji Resettlement Housing: 40 years Later," *Journal of Urbanism: International Research on Placemaking and Urban Sustainability*, 1/3 (2008): 247–264.
76 RAC, Ford Foundation Unpublished Reports Box 163 Folder 3631 #003631, "The IITA Resettlement Project, by David R. Smock, The Ford Foundation, Paper prepared for Nigerian Institute of Social and Economic Research, Ibadan, Feb, 7, 1967," 12.
77 David Brokensha, "Volta Resettlement and Anthropological Research," *Human Organization* 22/4 (1963–64): 289.
78 RAC, Ford Foundation Unpublished Reports Box 163 Folder 3631 #003631, David R. Smock, "The IITA Resettlement Project", Paper prepared for Nigerian Institute of Social and Economic Research, Ibadan, Feb, 7, 1967, 12.
79 Andrew Abbott, *Department and Discipline: Chicago Sociology at One Hundred* (Chicago: University of Chicago Press, 1999).
80 Lucia Allais, "The Design of the Nubian Desert: Monuments, Mobility, and the Space of Global Culture," *Governing by Design: Architecture, Economy, and Politics in the Twentieth Century, Aggregate* (University of Pittsburgh, 2014): 179–215.
81 Allais, "The Design," 179–215.
82 RAC, Ford Foundation Unpublished Reports Box 163 Folder 3631 #003631, "The IITA Resettlement Project, by David R. Smock, The Ford Foundation, Paper prepped for Nigerian Institute of Social and Economic Research, Ibadan, Feb, 7, 1967," 14.
83 David Brokensha, "Volta Resettlement and Anthropological Research," *Human Organization* 22/4 (1963–64): 286–290.
84 Arturo Escobar, "Anthropology and the Development Encounter: The Making and Marketing of Development Anthropology," *American Ethnologist* 18/4 (1991): 658–682; Morgan Brigg, "Post-Development, Foucault and the Colonisation Metaphor," *Third World Quarterly* 23, no. 3 (June 2002), 421–436.

Ten Love Letters

Jimenez Lai

This series of love-letters loosely resembles a possible working manual of Bureau Spectacular. Once I realized that there are only a finite number of projects I ever talk about, I began to consider the possibility that these projects consistently recur in my conversations because they formulate an operational guidebook. As a way of documenting the many distant dialogues I want to have with architects and artists who may or may not be alive anymore, these love letters are the long-range radio-signals shot deep into time and space. They hope to apply another layer to the history in current attention. Many of these love-letters will never reach the recipients, but it is one way of thanking those who continue to influence me.

On Blackness (and Rhythm)

The Agadir Convention Center (1990) by OMA is all I ever think about. FIG 1 The tendency of thinking about Agadir all the time was brought to my attention by my friend Cristobal Amunategui after one very late whiskey night as he accurately identified the presence of the basic diagram of Agadir in almost all of our work at Bureau Spectacular.

In order to begin this train of thought, we must first re-open a discussion about the status of "black." There are times when the representational tool of *poché* becomes synonymous with black. But that cannot be further from its actual value. There is a serial diagrammatic section set for Agadir, where the program is drawn as thick sectional matter that is black. Agadir flips the inaccessible parts of the plan into a conversation about the sectional back-of-house.

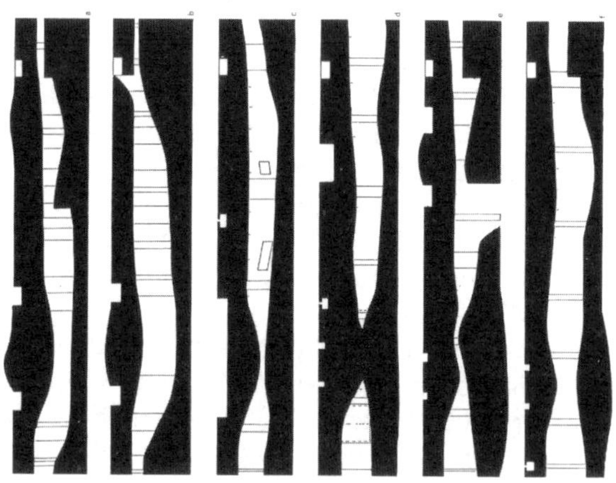

FIG 1
Agadir Convention Centre
Section, OMA, 1990.

We can extend this story back to the Nolli Plan (1735–1748) FIG 2 and find that the idea of *poché* has never just been about filling stuff in with a black shaded tone. It is a philosophical delineation about the degree to which something is unattainable, also functionally in terms of a demographic limitation on access. *Poché* is a pocket that is filled, but only from the point of view of some people not all. At times, it could be simply about a public/private division. There could be other times when it asks: what else is unattainable, and for whom? Or, conversely, what happens when everything is attainable in analytical terms? For instance, *Graphic Anatomy* by Atelier Bow-Wow is at once an extreme example of the idea of a scheme where nothing is black. It is at once as objective as possible; Nothing is qualified, yet it offers the viewpoint of a subject in terms of its centralized vanishing point.

The status of landscape inside architecture is another conversation that the Agadir Convention Center project generates. FIG 3 Agadir is a super-sandwich where two raviolis of stuffed black zones flank a more public sliver in section. This is a project about three layers of landscapes floating over one another. What if Agadir is an oversized Villa Savoye? The free façade is a free plan, the ribbon window is now occupiable, and the roof garden is relocated to the magic flying carpet between the two landscapes. And, *pilotis*? Better yet is to think of the multiple sections of the diagrammatically black Agadir becoming the spark for a new way to rethink the Five Points of Le Corbusier. As someone living and working today, I have a different relationship with the ground than Le Corbusier would have had. In our time, every experience of reality occurs in a frame that captures another frame in real time. Perhaps the whole world now is a ribbon window. And, there are no *pilotis* in this chapter.

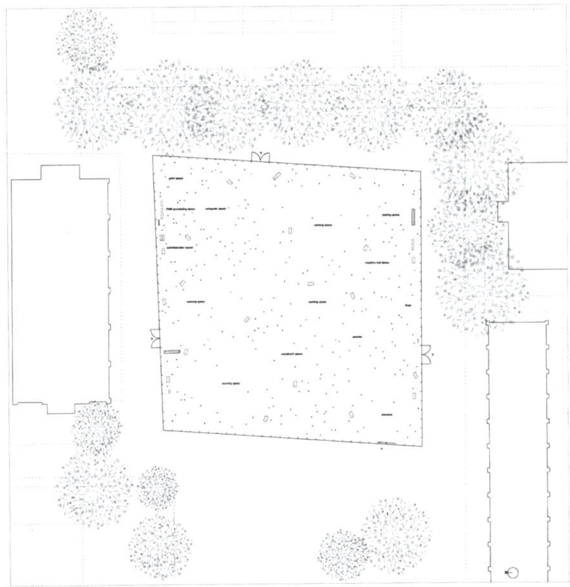

FIG 5
Junya Ishigami, Kanagawa Institute of Technology Furniture Plan, 2008.

FIG 4
Junya Ishigami, Kanagawa Institute of Technology Isometric Plan, 2008.

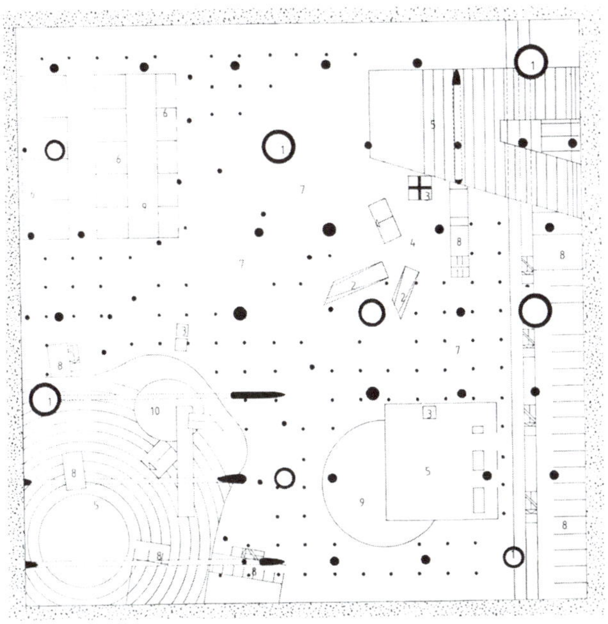

FIG 3
Agadir Convention Centre Plan, OMA, 1990.

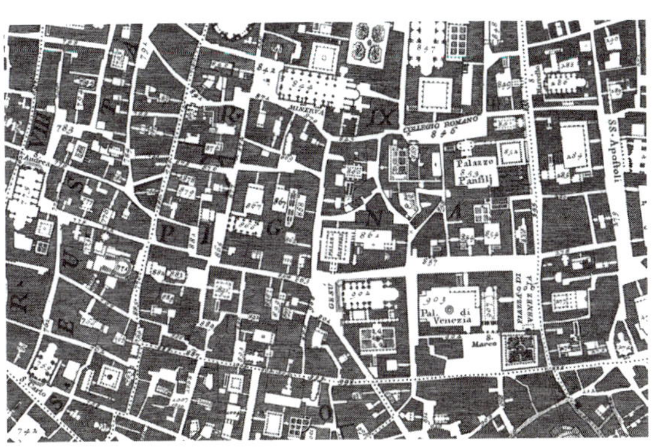

FIG 2
Excerpt from Part 5/12, *Nuova Topografia di Roma di Giovanni Battista Nolli*, 1748.

The rhythmic peppering of *pilotis* is its own further story. As an abstract scattering of symbols in the architectural plan, the *pilotis* in Agadir allow us to consider the relationship between structure and organization. Between the regular and the irregular grids, the plan of Agadir offers a way of considering the obstructive quality of structure as a means towards programmatic organization. When columns become too dense, flexibility becomes inconveniently disabled. However, this allows us to consider the opposite of flexibility: specificity. When flexibility is not possible, furniture and circulation will have to find a different way. This peppering of dots also plays out in the Kanagawa Institute of Technology (2008) by Junya Ishigami. FIG 4, 5 The rhythm of the dots begins to govern the circulation patterns, as well as the programmatic organization.

Within our projects like Cave House (2008), FIG A Museum is More (2014), Pool House (2015), Another Primitive Hut (2016), or even Pool Party (2017), elements of Agadir can be found here and there.

On Drawing Conventions

Casa Das Canoas (1951) by Oscar Niemeyer is all I ever think about. FIG 6 Although the visual output of this project encompasses photography, architectural sections, exploded axonometric drawings and other three-dimensional drawings, it is only the architectural plan of this project that continues to be a part of our conversations.

The plan of Casa Das Canoas is so powerful that it made us decide to become better at understanding architectural conventions. Suspending our knowledge of this project outside of the plan, and regarding this plan alone as a mystery novel, the superimpositions of very many linetypes only begins to suggest the layers of richness in the project. Niemeyer embedded hierarchies between all the figures on this drawing.

The drawing conventions on this plan also reminds us of a legal language architects use to communicate with local government building departments, as well as general contractors. In the case of construction/pricing/permit sets, once we plot certain lineweights, linetypes, symbols and textures onto paper, drawings become legal documents. The specific language architects use graphically in drawings is not dissimilar to the use of words by lawyers.

It is enough to simply admire the quality of curves in the plan of Casa Das Canoas. They are curves that are incredibly gorgeous. I am totally enamored by Niemeyer's sensibility. But, the quality of curves is not even the only reason I love this plan so much. I love this plan because of the complex superimposition of layers, with implied but inconsistent hierarchies. The layers of line-weights, line-types, implied qualities of inside, outside, between, beyond is why I read this plan as a story full of cliff-hangers. The dashed line that fluidly threads over and between the solid lines possibly indicates a cloud-like figure flying over and around the house. However, there is an irregular pentagon-shape that is being cut through by a line that clearly indicates envelope, with no possibility for inhabitation since they are both drawn as solid objects.

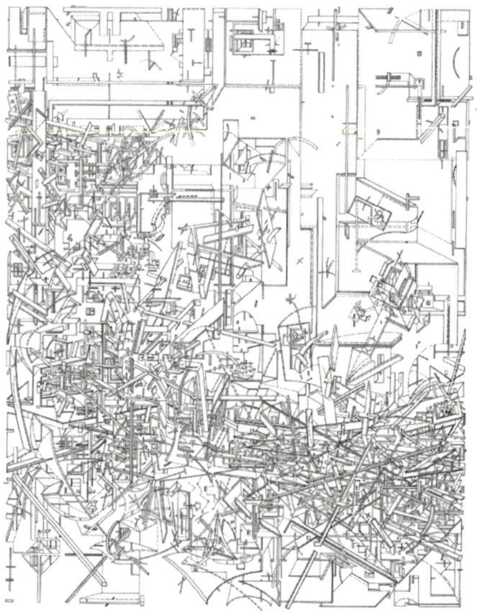

FIG 7
Micromegas, Daniel Libeskind.

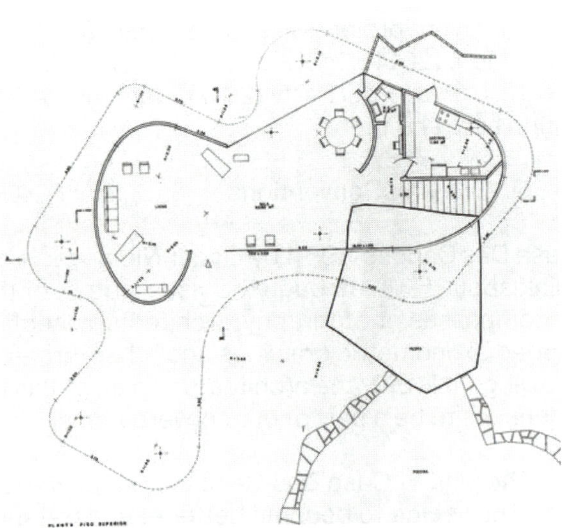

FIG 6
Casa das Canoas Plan, Digitalization of original drawings by Oscar Niemeyer for the project "Casa das Canoas" by Fundação Oscar Niemeyer, Rio de Janeiro, Brazil.

FIG A
Cave House, Bureau Spectacular.

FIG 8
Church of Saint Pierre, Firminy, Le Corbusier and José Oubrerie.

FIG B
Beachside Lonelyhearts, Bureau Spectacular.

If one would apply the Casa Das Canoas lens of intensified drawing conventions toward a new reading of Daniel Liebeskind's Micromegas (1979), FIG 7 suddenly the Micromegas project becomes a story with many concurrent plot-lines, filled with suggestions of complex spatial relationships. It becomes a world of hidden lines, fold lines, above-cuts jammed into oblique planes that collide into or through each other.

The paradoxes of the plan of Casa Das Canoas are layered and keep me on the edge of my seat. From inside-outsidebetweenbeyond (2013, later 2016–2017), Cave Painting VIII (2015), to the Beachside Lonelyhearts (2015) FIG B the Casa Das Canoas project by Oscar Neimeyer continues to influence me.

On Contracts (and Environmental Design)

Saint-Pierre, Firminy (began 1963, construction 1971–2006) by Le Corbusier, completed by José Oubrerie, is all I ever think about. FIG 8 This is an extraordinary story about a person keeping his promise for over 40 years. Before his death (1965), Le Corbusier made José Oubrerie promise that Oubrerie would finish this project no matter what; and, "no matter what" this was exactly what Oubrerie did as he powered through decades of hard work independently in an unbelievable act of honoring an unwritten contract with a dying man. After 40 years of commitment and project management, finally, in 2006, Oubrerie fulfilled his promise. The idea of an "unbreakable" contract is one of the lessons we took from the story of Oubrerie and Le Corbusier.

Beyond just Oubrerie's follow-through on his words, Firminy is an incredible work of architecture. I see it describe the relationship between monumental sensations and environmental design. In many ways, Firminy is a realized version of Newton's Cenotaph by Étienne-Louis Boullée (1728–1799). The constellations of apertures are peppered through the concrete. The larger punctured cutouts at the top of the diagonally truncated near-cone/pyramid. An imposing monolithic stature of the building as an object contrasts the inverted day-night conditions between the inside and outside. These aspects are all love-letters I read from Firminy to Newton's Cenotaph. What appear to be whimsical graphic compositions of grooves, reliefs—or attachments that resemble eyebrows, mustaches, or eyeglasses—are in fact designed irrigation systems that lead rainwater down troughs, around arches, through the building perimeter. The graphic project on the exterior performs the role of letting gravity do its work to let out water so that the sublime project can be possible on the interior. This is important because none of the big or small apertures that become the sun, moon, or stars on the Firminy interior rely on glass for enclosure. They rely only on an intelligent aqueduct system that leads water around the "windows."

In some ways, this "building" may challenge the notion of enclosure: at what point do we stop to calling something a "canopy" and start calling something an "interior?" When thinking about the digestive system of a human, the inner-lining of the mouth is a continuous surface with the outer-surface of the cheek, which continues down the esophagus, stomach, intestines, all the way out the anus. In many ways, the human body is diagrammatically much closer to the torus as a geometry than a cylinder. Firminy is also an ambiguous inside-outside diagram, in which the envelope is only a continuous surface that links the inner-lining to the outer-surface. The intelligence of this diagram is not only a formal one, but an environmental one.

We are lucky to call Mr. Oubrerie our friend, and cannot thank him enough for teaching his knowledge, enthusiasm and generosity.

On Characters

Cathedral (1996) by John Hejduk is all I ever think about. FIG 9 The semiotic qualities of architecture are sometimes beyond exact meanings. What architecture conveys can sometimes just be a mysterious sensation, an aura, a feeling. These feelings cannot necessarily be measured, quantified, or indexed.

The character of architecture as a physical artifact of humanity captures sensations such as "mystical" and "uncanny." John Hejduk's Cathedral collects trophies of what appear to be fictional creatures and combines them into a thick, rectangular, clashing solid. In other words, this is an architecture with collaged characters that are compounded together into a building.

Can the character of Hejduk's Cathedral be considered either a decorated shed or a duck? If we can talk about the visual communications of architecture or architectural components, then how does this project participate in its own contemporary conversations? Or, if a feeling is not a language, where is the line between character (theater), character (personality), or character (text)?

A conversation about character could be further subdivided: the Venturi/Scott-Brown ducks (exact communication) and the Hejduk Masks (mystical utterances). In the case of the duck, the function or program of the building is precisely declared by its visual qualities. In the case of the masks, a veil of uncertainty exists as to the implied personality of a character. If exact communications produce the effects of an instruction manual, the mystical utterances would be closer to a cloud that can be misread in multiple ways.

The work of Atelier Van Lieshout probably sits somewhere between communications and utterances. AVL's work operates both literally and mystically. While making very obvious puns, the quality of AVL's projects maintain a mystical unreadability. It is probably simultaneously "language" and "not language."

Within our projects Crown of Love (2013), FIG C Castle of Misfits (2013), or Skyline of Misfits (2013) FIG D Another Primitive Hut (2016), and the storyline Primitives (2011), the idea of a "Character" project continues to reemerge within our body of work.

FIG C
New Crown of Love,
Bureau Spectacular.

FIG 9
Cathedral, John Hejduk 1966,
Model photograph.

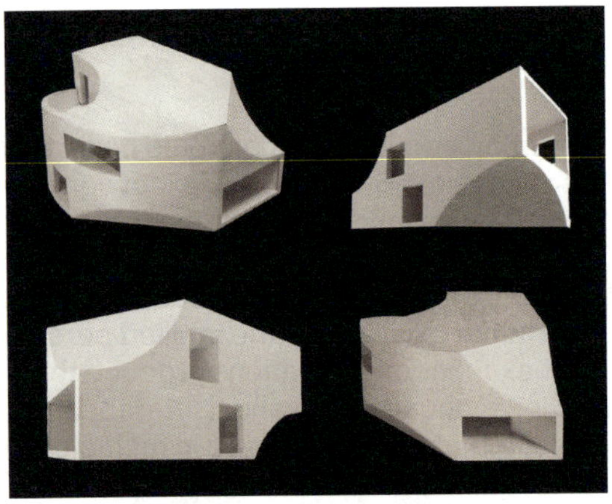

FIG 10
Photograph of The View House, 2009, by Johnston Marklee.

FIG D
Skyline of Misfits, Bureau Spectacular.

On Diagrams (and Filmstrips)

The View House (2009) by Johnston Marklee (with Diego Arraigada) is all I ever think about. FIG 10 The geometric diagram of this house is a circulation path coiled into a small helix. Punched outwards into the local landscape, each family member room becomes a large picture frame on the exterior. If we relate this diagram back to the Guggenheim Museum by Frank Lloyd Wright, we can open a discussion about the status of filmstrips and frames.

The most powerful element of the Guggenheim Museum is the vortex. It is a building generated by a helix, coiling on itself involutedly. It is a single-itinerary vector that can only ascend or descend along a ramp via secondary tangents that force people to look at each other across the void, rendering the visitors equal in status to the actual objects of art. The helix also operates as a subtle time-machine. One can foresee the path ahead, as well as behind. If film-makers such as Sergei Eisenstein had a profound influence on architecture—in terms of an introspectively coiled-version of ribbon windows by Le Corbusier or a looped-up Manhattan Transcripts by Bernard Tschumi—this idea of successive frames on a sequence can be related to the idea of the filmstrip and montage in cinema.

In the View House by Johnson Marklee, a helix is also used to generate a building form. Here, the helix is split into several paths and a tangential escape velocity is provided to a destination. The diagram in the View House is augmented by framed views looking toward outside. This helix is compressed inside a much smaller volume than the Guggenheim Museum and it is a private building. The scale of social mixing is different. In the case of the View House, helix geometry stimulates the interactions between the members of the family. The View House is both an extremely complex way to paint a family portrait, by deconstructing the image of a family into relational vectors on the interior, and a thick frame that documents the family history.

On Organization (Loose-Fitting, Well-Fitting, and Ill-Fitting)

The Moriyama House (2005) by SANAA is all I ever think about. Moriyama House is a loose-fitting diagram, comprised of ten separate architectural entities inside one line of property enclosure. As a loose-fitting diagram, the gaps between loose parts of the Moriyama House are peppered with miscellaneous domesticities. Gaps between entities vary in size. They expand and contract the void spaces between the buildings. This is a cartoon plan.

The gaps between the loose-fitting parts in the Moriyama House can be described as similar to "gutters" in the comic book industry. In comic books, the areas containing content are called "bricks" and "balloons." They correspond to specific movements or speech acts. The slivers of spaces between the content—those spaces that are neither "bricks" or "balloons"—are referred to as "gutters." In the Moriyama House, unassigned spaces of non-speech are also "gutters." The contrast in the Moriyama House is one defined by specificity or the lack thereof, similar to the contrast in comic books between the "gutters" and the "bricks" or "balloons."

A loose-fitting diagram like the Moriyama House is comprised of architectural programs with exact specificity. An architectural program assigns specific speech acts, not altogether dissimilar to the specificities inside of the bricks and balloons of a comic book page. The communicative power of the architectural plan emerges from a social contract that almost all humans form upon entering most buildings. Through the designation of program allocations such as bedrooms, kitchens, or dining rooms, humans impose a system of proper and improper behaviors. For example, to sleep in the kitchen would be somehow abnormal. Similarly, there is something mischievous or adventurous in eating in the bedroom. It is as though another micro zoning law is set on the interior of most buildings. Humans unconsciously subscribe to such a set of norms. This power is in the edges of such territorial claims. The simple act of placing furniture and fixtures to anticipate human actions borders on the scaled-down political claims of legal boundaries.

Similarly, *Not In Any Way Shape or Form* (2009) by Polly Apfelbaum creates a similar loose-fitting figure-ground, as well as a difficult social contract. FIG 11 People visiting art galleries or museums form an agreement with the institution that art cannot be touched. This sacred quality of art as objects is powerful enough when they are hung on interior elevations. It becomes more problematic when scattered on the floor like some confetti. In order not to "touch" art, the fabric cutouts of *Not in Any Way Shape or Form* elevate into a non-passive visual device and a choreography for visitors to walk around.

Loose-fitting is not the only way things can fit. If the sectional "L" forms inside the typical units of the Unite d'Habitation are results of a shared, common rectangular corridor, then the corridor itself operates as a spatial Venn Diagram between two superimposed rectangles. If one would consider the "L" and "L" of the animal jigsaw puzzle of Enzo Mari FIG 12 as a near-perfect fit, then the typical cross-section of the Unite d'Habition is also a well-fitting diagram. Conversely, if we see the corridor between the two boxes to be an overlap, then the inconsistent gaps of the Enzo Mari puzzle and the cross section of the Unite d'Habitation can both be viewed as an ill-fitting diagram.

Set Theory is a branch of mathematics that deals with the formal properties of sets as units (without regard to the nature of their individual constituents). In simpler terms, Set Theory is a study of the complexities of Venn Diagrams. The hierarchies of how two (or more) units superimpose could create different types of Boolean operations. When two sets merge over each other, their interactions become a potentially dynamic conversation. Whether sets are programmatic, structural, or material—the management between the parts is a location where the magic of architectural quality can happen.

Between the loose-fitting, ill-fitting and well-fitting we began to experiment with all three organizational systems at Bureau Spectacular. If Township of Domestic Parts (2014) FIG E was a loose-fitting diagram, and Frankie I (2016) was a well-fitting one, then Tower of Twelve Stories (2016) would be our first attempt at an ill-fitting project. We extend this thought process by studying the complexities of set theory further.

FIG E
Township of Domestic Parts, Bureau Spectacular.

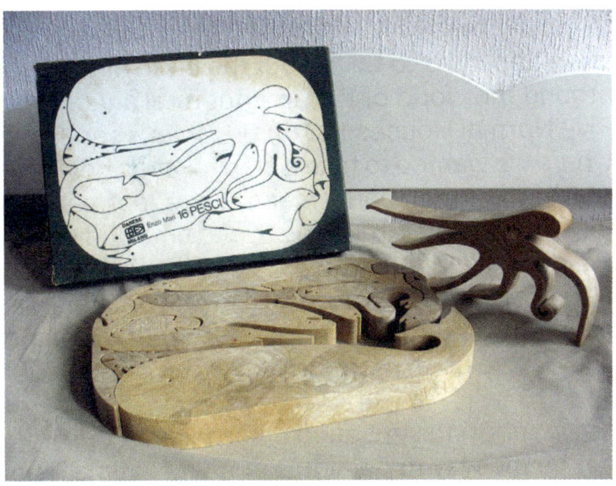

FIG 12
Photograph of the 16 Pesci Jigsaw Puzzle designed by Enzo Mari.

FIG 11
Not in Any Way, Shape, or Form, 2009, Synthetic sequined fabric, Dimensions variable, Installation view: Helmhaus Zurich, Zurich, Switzerland. Boden und wand. Wand und Fenster, February 6 - March 29, 2009.

FIG 15
Adrian Phiffer, Untitled.

FIG 14
Filip Dujardin, Untitled from series 'Fictions,' 2007.

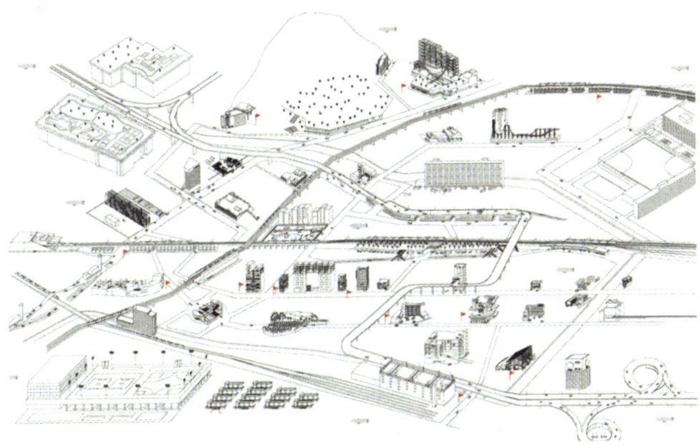

FIG 13
Made in Tokyo, Atelier Bow Wow.

On Political Caricatures

Made in Tokyo (2001) by Atelier Bow Wow is all I ever think about. FIG 13 This is a story about seeing the everyday strangeness of Tokyo through a journalistic lens and broadcasting it through editorial diagrams that almost resemble caricatures in the political commentary segments of a newspaper. For example, the flying temple that re-negotiates its own datum to fit the nearby elevated superhighway becomes a new way to consider the status of religious symbolism almost as a roadside billboard. These new ways of looking at the world, through gesturing toward things that are obviously strange, can export other cultural anomalies into generative architectural diagrams.

However, the possibility that no journalism can be truly objective is a reality that is ever more nauseatingly obvious in the post-2016 world. News media consolidates the idea that every action is a political one. The oscillation between "fake" and "fact" is taking the citizens of today into a comatose state of utter confusion and discomfort. There was a time when the satirical and para-fictional lens of political editorials like *The Onion* served a comedic purpose. These days, people turn to Seth Meyers, Stephen Colbert, Trevor Noah or John Oliver like pain-stricken addicts seeking morphine for a dose of actual sensorial relief, a reminder of the reality we live in today.

The gap between realism and reality is a delicate line to straddle, especially today. Not too long ago, I used to think the book "On Bullshit" by Harry G. Frankfurt was not only really funny, but almost a way to embrace the imaginative possibilities of architecture. As Frankfurt describes, "lying" requires the presence of facts, so "bullshitting" is independent from facts and has a generative cultural agency. If considered as a kind of operational relativism, this idea can become empowering given the *carte-blanche* situation architects are so often confronted with. In this way, "bullshit" could even be a source of joy as architects produce drawings that may one day become as concrete.

The beautifully eerie quality of Filip Dujardin's body of work sits in this important location in the contemporary discussion of realism. FIG 14 Not altogether dissimilar in spirit to Atelier Bow-Wow's *Made in Tokyo*, Dujardin's work is an extraction of the dichotomy between familiar and strange, and a cinematic portrayal of "fiction that may very well be fact." Dujardin's architectural audience is drawn into an uncanny valley. For a fiction to be relatable and believable, it has to come from a keen observer so that the fiction is comprised of plausible aspects of reality. Sometimes this relationship is even reversed—especially when the architect Alexander d'Hooghe hired Dujardin to produce photographs that seemed so very "real" that they eroded a layer of believability. When I first saw the Semblance House project by Adrian Phiffer, I did believe this project was real. FIG 15 When I first saw the photographs of the 110 Rooms project by MAIO, my initial instinct similarly brought me to believe that this project was the most beautifully woven work of fiction I had ever seen. FIG 16 The theoretical framework of "hyperreality" as described by Jean Baudrillard perfectly describes this oscillation. The difference between broadcast and reality is now indistinguishable.

FIG 16
MAIO Architects, 110 Rooms,
Photograph by Jose Hevia.

FIG 17
Vincent Lamouroux, Bates Hotel, 2015.

FIG F
Five Normal Houses, Bureau Spectacular.

In Citizens of No Place (2012), a series of para-fictions were deployed to talk about the state of affairs within and around the world of the architectural academy. Since then, Five Normal Houses (2015) FIG F was a series of projects where we wanted to take a step towards being closer readers of what "normal" could mean, since "normal" is a loaded term—a moving target, relative to time and space. Even *Cave Painting VIII: White Noise of Another Past* (2015) was an attempt to re-gather some of my favorite paper-architects over the last three decades the way that Campo Marzio could have been projectively a work of journalistic editing.

A sobering sensation emerges that total relativism may not be the way to go at this moment in time. There is a need to carefully consider the role of para-fictions or political caricatures at a time like this.

On Color and Materiality

Bates Hotel (2014) by Vincent Lamouroux is all I ever think about. FIG 17 Bates Hotel became a found object in Los Angeles for Vincent Lamouroux. He simply applied a fresh coat of white paint on it—including the surrounding palm trees. This action announced a clear statement about the status of color and materiality in one sweeping move:

FIG 21
Hernan Diaz Alonso, SUR, MoMA PS1, 2005.

FIG 20
Greg Lynn, Fountain. Photograph by Brian Forrest.

> Steel is white
> Stucco is white
> Concrete is white
> Glass is white
> Nature is white

This realization about color and materiality led me to really consider the body of work of many people who either live in or passed through Los Angeles over the past few decades. From Andrew Kovacs's Guggenheim Helsinki competition entry, FIG 18 First Office's MAK Center mountain range project, An Te Liu's White Dwarf, FIG 19 Johnston Marklee's Hill House and Vault House, Michael Maltzan's various projects... even Greg Lynn's fountain FIG 20 and—even in the least likely cases—Hernan Diaz Alonzo's MoMA PS1 installation. FIG 21 Everyone has dabbled with white, if they have not devoted entire careers to it.

If "white" could be attributed to sensibilities around "nothingness," "neutrality," "naturalness," "normality," or even "nakedness" for the effects of subtlety, modesty, or even "authenticity" in the USA, how would some other cultures around the world tackle similar thoughts? Perhaps the presence (or residue) of wood is favorable in places like Japan, as evidenced by projects like the Final Wooden House by Fujimoto, FIG 22 or the exposed concrete of Tadao Ando. FIG 23 In Northern Europe, a similar sense of neutrality or nakedness could apply in the case of brick as the material. For the Chanel Flagship Store by MVRDV, FIG 24 the presence of brick is so important that even when "brick" transcends materiality from brick to glass the glass had to be brick.

The bank of the Los Angeles River is a significant part of the story of "white." Once upon a time the river bank of the LA River was a favorite playground for graffiti writers. If we consider the history of graffiti to be as ancient as rock art we may find an ongoing tradition that still occupies the same human instinct as those of our distant ancestors. To tag is to claim territories. Whether a gang member, a drifter, or an artist, the signature of the tag pronounces a political boundary where the person performing the act of graffiti writing is making territorial claims.

Despite the plethora of personal or tribal claims on a smaller and more local scale, the political entity that is the City of Los Angeles decided to perform a mass-censorship of all existing graffiti over the last two decades along the LA River bank. The act of painting over all existing graffiti reduces all tags to become an abstracted flying fleet of language with no meaning. The City of Los Angeles tags over all tags. The mask of choice, emblematic of a grand political brushstroke of the city's spirit is, of course, white paint.

Here, in one swift motion, the City of Los Angeles is declaring something else. In Los Angeles, white is as good as concrete. The flying fleet of figure-ground tags over tags is now white over concrete. In other words, to the City of Los Angeles, "White" is not a color. "White" is a material.

The way we may think of Red, Green and Black or Red and Yellow as being emblematic of some nations, states, cultures, or even ideologies, or how Red, White and Blue may even conjure other sensations of belonging, shows how color can definitely be deployed as a political material.

FIG 19
An Te Liu, White Dwarf. Photograph Courtesy of An Te Liu.

FIG 18
Andrew Kovacs, Guggenheim Helsinki Competition Entry.

FIG 23
Tadao Ando, Azuma House.

FIG 22
Wooden House, Sou Foujimoto.

Tower of Twelve Stories (2016), FIG G as well as Frankie I (2016), were both built using white as the contextual material of Los Angeles. Speechbuster / 99 Chairs (2013) on the other hand, was built with every spectrum on the political material pallet. Or, when we worked on the Taiwan Pavilion (2014), Joanna Grant decided that a splash of graphic rainbows similar to My Little Ponies via Takeshi Murakami represented the cuteness she read when she first visited Taiwan.

On Professional Practice

Urban Robots (1971–1979) is all we ever talk about. When Toyo Ito (born 1941) began his practice at around the time he turned 30 years old, he named his project "Urban Robots." Other than the White U (1976), FIG 25 Ito built no buildings during this period. It is very important to highlight that the primary focus of the first period of Ito's career was not the building of buildings. Ito devoted his first eight years to writing, exhibitions, conferences, publications, research, and experimentation. This was a period that probably prepared Ito to become a better thinker, as he would have had the time and space to refine his early positions. During this period Ito became, even more so, a better teacher. He later played a fundamental role in the amazing careers of many other architects.

During the 2015 Chicago Architecture Biennial, one life-changing event occurred in the format of a conversation with architect Florian Idenburg. Idenburg remarked: "Major companies may devote 5% of their annual cash-flow towards research and development, and that would be considered generous. We at SO-IL dedicate about 20%—when we work on exhibitions or other cultural projects, we do not look back and wonder if we lost money—because that is something we are ready to embrace. You, Jimenez Lai, are 100% R&D. How long do you think you can last?"

It was after this striking conversation that I took a more serious look at Toyo Ito's early career. Bureau Spectacular began in 2008, early in the 21st Century around the time of a catastrophic financial downturn. Although the research and experimentation of Urban Robots was always in the back of my mind, the lack of building projects was also tied to the economic environment. The financial crisis made professional practice nearly impossible at first, and indeed the only place to apply our energy was towards research and experimentation. White Elephant (2010–11), Citizens of No Place (2012), Treatise (2015), and many other projects all happened around this time. We are indebted to the time and space the first eight years offered us, as we now have a much clearer sense of direction. Since that Chicago conversation with Idenburg, we not only drew up a business plan, but began the process of trying to get some buildings built. Although Tower of Twelve Stories (2016) felt more like public art, and Frankie I (2016) II and III (2017) are all interior retail projects, we are working on a ground-up project in Joshua Tree at the moment. Hopefully more will happen in the years to come.

Two years later at the 2017 Chicago Architecture Biennial, I had a sit-down with Stanley Tigerman thanks to the organization of Léa-Catherine Szacka. Listening to Tigerman talk about his experience in the Korean War, particularly his relationship with death, was devastating. During the war, part of Tigerman's job was to help pilots with mechanical

FIG G
Tower of Twelve Stories,
Bureau Spectacular.

FIG 24
MVRDV, Chanel Amsterdam.

maintenance and preparation. Of the eighty-or-so young pilots Tigerman befriended during the war and helped fly into warzone, zero survived. Tigerman described a certain conviction of invincibility all young pilots possessed. Since death was not considered a possibility, no young pilots attempted to avoid it. Tigerman compared this mentality to the young architects he has met over the decades since, including me—and his younger self. Perhaps the Urban Robots project by Toyo Ito was a similarly kamikaze project. And, perhaps the suicide mission finally needs to be coupled with management and approach.

Although the idea of Bureau Spectacular is entering its tenth year (since 2008) it is also only about three years old as a professional practice (since 2016) coinciding with the return of Joanna Grant. We continue to learn from our many predecessors and continue to grow both in depth and breadth.

FIG 25
Toyo Ito, U House.

The Architecture of Communicating Vessels: The Second World in the Age of Capitalist Realism

Vladimir Kulić

Thirty years ago American political scientist Francis Fukuyama proclaimed the "end of history."[1] As the Cold War drew to a close, Fukuyama argued, capitalist liberal democracy emerged victorious over state socialism, thus establishing the final outcome of mankind's ideological evolution toward the best form of governance. Marx's own teleology, which proclaimed communism as the ultimate goal of history, was thus cut short and replaced with the self-congratulatory realism of an "actually-existing capitalism." The argument was contested from the start, but for a short while it seemed to bear at least some credibility as one Eastern European country after another espoused parliamentary democracy and privatized its economy. Challenges to liberal ideology, however, quickly emerged from various sides and they never ceased; last year even Fukuyama had to admit that the supposed end of history would be postponed for an indeterminate future.[2]

One of the problems with liberalism is that it conflates economics and politics, masking the reality of two related yet distinct systems of social organization. It concerns not only governance by elected representatives but also assumes an economy based on a capitalist market with private ownership of the means of production. Thus it is unsurprising that liberalism can be challenged on opposing grounds, and its opponents are not necessarily allies either. Fascism and communism, liberalism's historical rivals that Fukuyama presumed dead and buried, were bitter enemies. Even though they are often lumped together under the category of "two totalitarianisms," their motivations were fundamentally different.[3]

Today successful opposition to liberalism appears to come only from the right. Representative of it is the rise of conservative demagogues like Trump, Putin, Orbán, Erdoğan, or Bolsonaro, who threaten civic freedoms while enthusiastically championing the unrestrained power of capital, often in particularly corrupt forms. The central contradiction of a capitalist economy—embodied in the disparity between capital and labor—remains unchallenged, despite unprecedented precarity and inequality, rampant outsourcing, and looming environmental catastrophe. For almost two centuries that contradiction drove both visionary thinking and very real political struggles, but today there is a distinct lack of vision and real political alternatives. Propositions aimed at addressing the issue, such as "democratic socialism" in the United States, are yet to produce any material results.

For the past three decades we have lived in the age of "capitalist realism," an ontology that precludes the ability to imagine an alternative system.[4] The quip "It is easier to imagine the end of the world than the end of capitalism" has risen to the status of an Internet meme.[5] Why is that the case? If liberalism's political tenets are vulnerable, as they evidently are, why do its economic foundations appear to be permanent? Even though illiberal democracy emerges as an increasingly realistic alternative in the sphere of politics, wasn't Fukuyama at least partially right to proclaim an end of history in the sense that the capitalist market is indeed the ultimate form of economic organization for humankind? Are all alternatives truly doomed for eternity?

While considering the many potential answers to these

questions, let us examine the spatial logic that has led to this moment. It may sound tautological to claim that our current inability to think of alternatives to capitalism stems from the global collapse of socialism around 1989, but the very fact that the entire world was controlled by a binary of ideological systems is crucial to the present problem. The casual association of capitalism with the West and socialism with the East is far from natural: for a century and a half preceding World War II, ideological struggle between capital and labor was inherent to all modern societies. It was only during the Cold War that the ideological opponents became decoupled and displaced to autonomous geographical spaces. As the two superpowers created their own quasi-empires based on rival ideological positions, they became the respective avatars of opposing class interests. Ideology was thus reimagined as geography.

As a result, the potential for envisioning an alternative ideological and economic system became excised from the social imaginary of advanced capitalist states and banished to a distant physical space. The West named that space the "Second World" in an assertion of its own primacy. Even though the class struggle did not disappear in the West, the conception of radically different economic relations had been kept in check by the specter of a rival, and by the end of the Cold War the alternative had effectively disappeared. The collapse of the Berlin Wall reunited the formerly divided geopolitical space, opening the floodgates of capitalist liberalization, and the history of socialism came to be relentlessly "blackwashed."[6] The geographic space socialism once occupied became known as the "former East," a term that sums up its double displacement—both spatial and temporal—to someone else's past.

One of the effects of rewriting ideology in terms of geography was that an entire body of propositions could be treated as alien and safely ignored as irrelevant. This was certainly the case in terms of architecture. For decades architectural production in the socialist world has been summarily dismissed under various pretenses and remains largely unknown to unspecialized audiences. Judging by almost all architectural surveys published in the (former) West, the Second World barely exists. It is mentioned mostly as a cautionary tale and occasionally lumped into the "totalitarian" camp with fascist states, a comparison that echoes the ideological warfare of the early Cold War.[7] Even the staunchly Marxist historians Manfredo Tafuri and Francesco Dal Co concluded that postwar Soviet city building holds value only as a lesson about what not to do.[8]

This instance of "operative criticism"—something that Tafuri himself condemned in his other writings—ignored an enormous body of work produced in one of the world's most rapidly urbanizing regions at the time, including what may be the largest modernization project in human history. In three short decades the Soviet program of prefabricated mass housing produced more than thirty million modern apartments, a momentous transformation that brought one of the world's largest countries into modernity in a historical blink.[9] Regardless of what we may think of the program's architectural design, the sheer size of the undertaking is difficult to overlook: it was arguably the largest realization of the dreams of early international Modernism. If a project of that scale could be ignored, it is no surprise that smaller projects of its kind would receive even less attention.

The situation echoes the slightly schizophrenic nature of the history of architecture. On the one hand, reflecting the discipline's roots in art history, it favors innovative singular projects for the highly privileged over collectively produced work. The significance ascribed to suburban luxury villas by celebrity architects is exemplary in that respect. On the other hand, architecture's entanglement in broader networks of culture, politics, and economy is too significant to escape the attention of historians, but it often involves the less remarkable work. It is as if what we call architectural history comprises two concurrent narratives: one chronicled through architectural products of special significance, and another tracing architecture's enmeshment in society, regardless of its supposed artistic value.[10] While the latter perspective has produced a tremendous amount of new scholarship in the past decade on the built environments of Socialist states, the former remains resistant to acknowledging socialism as a source of architectural value.

Yet is it really possible that one-half of Europe—much of which had quite sophisticated architectural cultures before World War II—produced absolutely no valuable architectural innovation during the most intense period of urbanization in its history? Or if we are to judge architecture by political criteria, did state socialism really produce a less worthy architecture than even Mussolini's Italy or Franco's Spain, for example, whose architectural outputs have been considered part of the Modernist canon despite emerging from bona fide fascism?

These questions echo a more general anxiety about the former Socialist realm as a "blind spot on the map of the world as imagined in the centers of global academic and cultural power and influence," as social scientist Maxim Waldstein put it. His argument about the marginalization of the cultural and social theory of the Second World easily translates to architecture: "The Second World may be studied, sometimes intensively, but it is rarely supposed to be a source of important theoretical ideas and idioms. [...] Our region may be seen as politically, economically, or [...] culturally important, but *conceptually* it is deemed by default to be uninteresting."[11]

Yet it is not even necessary to travel to the "former East" today to realize that the architecture there is worth knowing. It is enough to consult the Internet. From Bulgarian resorts to Soviet sanatoriums, administration buildings in the Caucasus to Slovak museums, Soviet bus stops to Balkan war memorials, late Socialist buildings can be seen everywhere, in social-media platforms, print publications, music videos, and even sci-fi movies. Captured through the medium of photography, these spectacular forms are a far cry from the stereotypical views that identified socialism with the ultimate drabness. Instead they demonstrate that socialism may, after all, have produced at least a *visually* interesting architecture. In a world reunited by an unbound supranational market, it was just a matter of time before the spectacular potential of Socialist structures would be discovered in the circulation of digital images. But this discovery often strips the buildings of their contextual significance and cultural specificity, subjecting them to all kinds of ideologically motivated misinterpretations.[12] As a result, the Socialist world is cast as an incomprehensible oddity akin to a long-lost civilization or an alien outpost on another planet. Yet again, socialism is kept at a safe remove in a distant realm across the chasm of space and time.

The American and Soviet empires presented their irreconcilable differences in symbolic and material terms. Winston Churchill's metaphor of the "Iron Curtain" and the physical construction of the Berlin Wall are the most obvious examples and are deeply imprinted into our collective consciousness. Yet against the backdrop of such concrete imagery of separation, the two rivals also shaped each other in fundamental ways. The most obvious examples are the arms and space races, in addition to the competition over control of the so-called Third World, where both blocs sought to establish presence through economic involvement, soft power and occasional proxy wars. Still the relationship between the two spheres of influence was asymmetrical, in line with the common assumption that "development" flowed in one direction, from West to East. Scholars have studied extensively this asymmetry, investigating how the East often looked to the West for ways to close the significant technological gap, or how it had accepted the challenge of competing with the West in terms of "lifestyle"—that is, by improving access to personal consumption.[13] Cultural life exhibited similar engagement.[14] When seen from the East, then, the Iron Curtain was far more permeable than Churchill would have allowed; as György Péteri has argued, a more appropriate metaphor to describe the divide would be "nylon curtain."[15]

In contrast, the West often appeared uninterested in the East, except as a threat to be contained. The possibility that the East exerted some form of influence on the West has been consequently far less explored. This idea is not entirely new, and it rests on the premise that socialism derived legitimacy from its assumed superiority in terms of social development because it guaranteed its citizens full employment, social security, free education, the right to housing, and various other social provisions.[16] Scholars have engaged with the reciprocal relationship only recently, focusing especially on the ways in which Socialist entities used various organizations to impact the formulation of international standards. Political scientist Astrid Hedin has argued, for example, that Socialist states actively promoted their models of worker participation in the International Labor Organization, which eventually affected legislation in Western Europe.[17] Hedin is also developing a broader project to show how the Socialist world, "as both competitor and role model, helped fuel and shape the development of West European social policies" on "industrial democracy, gender equality, education reform, and anti-colonialism."[18]

In a similar vein, anthropologist Kristen Ghodsee has demonstrated how the domination of Socialist states in the UN-organized World Conferences on Women in the 1970s forced U.S. officials, after much hesitation, to take women's issues seriously and engage with them at the international level, in turn boosting the American feminist movement.[19] Ghodsee thus excavates women's emancipation under Socialism as an important, albeit dismissed and forgotten, chapter in the history of feminism. In an especially surprising turn, sociologist Johanna Bockman has uncovered the "left-wing origins of neoliberalism" in the contributions of Socialist economists to the transnational debates on neoclassical economy, which proponents of neoliberalism subsequently hijacked for their own purposes. As Bockman shows, neoclassical economics was used successfully in the elaboration of the practical and theoretical models of noncapitalist markets in Hungary and Yugoslavia; neoliberalism was by no means its only possible outcome.[20] All these new studies clearly demonstrate that even the most entrenched assumptions about the polarity between the Socialist East and the capitalist West, such as a planned versus a market economy, have to be questioned.

From this perspective it appears that the respective sides of the Cold War, identified by the term *bloc*, were far from impenetrable and solid, defying the connotations derived from the expression's etymological origins in the word *block*. The two empires were more akin to what in the physics of fluids is known as *communicating vessels*: two separate containers connected to form a common system beneath the surface. Just as the liquid in both vessels maintains the same level under the same atmospheric pressure, so the global system of the Cold War sought to stay in balance under the constant threat of "mutually assured destruction." Controlled amounts of "fluid"—ideas, information, and technology—flowed through the system in both directions as pressure on one side provoked an adjustment on the other. The relationship was mutually constitutive. If the repressed always returns, as Freud once claimed, we might say that the same applies to the displaced, as capitalism continued being haunted by its displaced negation through invisible subterranean flows. FIG 1

If we accept the metaphor of communicating vessels, we can no longer consider Socialist cultural output irrelevant to Western history, but rather as an estranged half of the self that demands reintegration. Just as postcolonial theory has inspired a questioning of the status of the Third World as the "other" of the First, we need to consider the other "other," the Second World, as similarly constitutive of a shared past and present. The goal is not merely to catalog a more comprehensive global architectural history but to uncover the power relationships between the different parts, in which the Socialist world was an important constitutive force.[21] In the process we may discover all kinds of suppressed architectural knowledge.

In fact the West in the past already discovered valuable concepts and design strategies developed in the socialist world, even if the origins were sometimes obscured. Consider, for example, the "social condenser"—a Soviet Constructivist invention that was supposed to bring society together in shared spaces rather than segregated by class, gender, or other categories. As anthropologist Michał Murawski has argued, the social condenser has had a remarkable afterlife in the West, as it has been passed down across several generations to become appropriated by, and largely associated with, none other than the icon of neoliberal architecture, Rem Koolhaas.[22] Another example is the formative role Stalinist architecture had for Post-Modernists such as Aldo Rossi.[23] If we dig deeper into the debris of postsocialist oblivion, we may discover not only that neoliberalism has cultivated an apparent secret fascination with Socialism, but also other previously forgotten ideas and concepts. Waldstein's anxiety about the conceptual marginality of the Second World may then prove unjustified.

With that in mind, we may have to rethink other deeply ingrained stereotypes. As Murawski has suggested, scholars have for too long focused on the alleged failures of Socialist architecture, which were explained through contradictory claims that Socialist cities were either too focused on the economy or too negligent of it. Rather than regurgitating such ideologically motivated "failure-centrism," Murawski posits, we need to start entertaining the possibility of Socialist architecture's "actually existing success."[24] Accomplishment could perhaps be recognized in the enduring "socialist scaffold" that, as Kimberly Zarecor has argued, resulted from an all-encompassing "infrastructural thinking" invested in the planning of Socialist cities.[25] Comprising various institutional frameworks and infrastructural systems, the "socialist scaffold" was planned to anticipate future development, for example, by extending infrastructure beyond immediate needs. As a result, it continues to enable the livability of many cities decades after the collapse of Socialism.[26] Another success might be a more equitable population distribution than under capitalism: as historian Mark B. Smith has shown, Soviet mass housing brought together different classes (inasmuch as Socialism did not eradicate them) under the same roof, rather than separating them into sharply stratified neighborhoods.[27] A more universal claim could be that Socialism produced a more just transition to modernity. As American anthropologist Andrej Simić found almost fifty years ago, the burden of urbanization in postwar Yugoslavia, despite its epochal scale and rate, was distributed more evenly than in other parts of the world undergoing similar processes, affecting "all segments of the population more or less equally."[28] Notwithstanding the loaded question of what constitutes success, when measured by its own standards Socialism may indeed have reached a degree of success.

FIG 1
Communicating vessels is the name for a system of containers filled with a homogeneous fluid, connected at the base and subjected to the same atmospheric pressure. When the liquid settles, it balances out to the same level in all of the containers regardless of their shape and volume. If additional liquid is added to one vessel, a new equal level will be established in all the connected vessels.

Is it possible that actually existing socialism was also successful by other more narrow architectural criteria? Is it possible that it produced some form of "Architecture with a capital A" that is worth knowing as valuable, and not simply as a cautionary tale? Ignored for decades, these questions have to be taken seriously now that the Museum of Modern Art in New York has staged the exhibition *Toward a Concrete Utopia: Architecture in Yugoslavia, 1948–1980* (which I co-curated with Martino Stierli). The project was unprecedented due to the very fact that the most important consecrating institution of Western Modernism had turned its attention to the architecture in the Second World. Seeking to situate architecture in the wider project of building a multiethnic, nonaligned socialist society by highlighting the specific architectural values developed within such a framework, the show acquired a decidedly political dimension. In that light, the considerable enthusiasm with which it was greeted may speak to a renewed hunger for utopian thinking after decades of stark capitalist realism.

Yugoslavia was the most liberal of the Socialist states, in both social and economic terms, while remaining adamantly Socialist. It defied the Cold War's imperial imperatives and blurred the binary division associated with them. Production was structured within a system of worker self-management, rather than controlled by the central state, and foreign policy was unallied to either superpower, and was committed to solidarity with the developing countries of the Third World. In the field of architecture the country openly assimilated knowledge from both blocs (although mostly from the West), and it often served as a meeting ground for professionals from both sides. Tourists flocked from both East and West; the massive tourism infrastructure built for them allowed for encounters that were impossible elsewhere. The country also exported architecture widely, primarily to the developing world but also to Eastern Europe. With these abundant interactions across ideological boundaries, Yugoslavia functioned as a conduit between the "vessels" of the Cold War's world system, a position that was both highly advantageous and highly uncertain. It is perhaps appropriate then that the Western public has discovered architecture's forgotten Socialist legacy through this defunct state that attempted to integrate the divided consciousness of the Cold War.

On the surface Yugoslavia seems to prove that socialism was destined for failure: Even its complex permissive system was not liberal enough to save it from collapse, the supposedly natural consequence of socialism's deficiencies leading to the inevitable "end of history." However, as architectural historian Andrew Herscher reminds us, the Yugoslav federation did not simply "collapse" on its own: it was actively destroyed. Nothing testifies to the deliberateness of its dismantling more than the destruction of its architecture.[29] The executioner was nationalism of an especially virulent kind. Those of us who witnessed the country's violent demise cannot forget the malevolence of the rhetoric that stigmatized an ever-widening circle of "others" to facilitate its society's total conservative makeover. From that perspective the current political moment cannot but appear as a disconcerting déjà vu. As Bosnian-American author Aleksandar Hemon has warned, the Trump presidency uncannily evokes the atmosphere leading to the destruction of Yugoslavia.[30] Does that mean that the entire world is now like Yugoslavia on the eve of its destruction?

Historian Dubravka Stojanović recently posed the following question: "Were the Yugoslav wars the last wars of the twentieth century, or should they be understood and studied as the first wars of the twenty-first century?"[31] In other words, was the end of Socialism really the end of history, or was it actually something altogether different—the jump-start of a new historical cycle, the fruition of which we are witnessing only today? Everything seems to point to the latter, from the revival of "great power" politics to the seemingly unstoppable march of the far right. Yet what we shouldn't forget is the degree to which this conservative turn has served to mask a retrenchment of class differences—the classic Marxian engine of history. That was certainly the case in Yugoslavia: in hindsight it is clear that the Socialist federation was not destroyed to benefit the entirety of newly independent nations but only a small minority that skimmed the cream from a socially produced shared wealth. Most other Socialist countries underwent similar processes at the turn of the 1990s, only to experience a subtler bait-and-switch: they dreamt of democracy and got oligarchic capitalism.[32] Similar symptoms were detectable even in the West: as the East gradually ceased being a "competitor and role model," the mechanisms of the postwar welfare state were dismantled, leading to the restoration of class distinctions.[33] The process was thus universal, but in Yugoslavia it produced its first war. Even in its demise, then, Yugoslavia was the vanguard.

How, then, should we approach the architecture of the Socialist world? First we need to discover it in its actual complexity, rather than through negative stereotypes entrenched during the decades of ideological warfare. Such discovery will require persistent interpretation and theorization, but in return we may be rewarded with valuable new concepts. However, we should also dispose of the exoticism that is sometimes assigned to socialist architecture in the more favorable views of its legacies. Whether we revel in the exuberant brutalist forms of antifascist memorials or abhor the drab prefabrication of mass housing, we must remember that they were not the relics of someone else's history irrelevant to us today, but answers to societal problems that still concern us. They need to be rescued from their exile to a distant parallel universe and incorporated into our shared history. After all, we can be fairly certain that that history has not yet ended.

1 Francis Fukuyama, "The End of History?" *The National Interest* 16 (Summer 1989): 3–18.
2 Louis Menand, "Francis Fukuyama Postpones the End of History," *The New Yorker*, (September 3, 2018), accessed October 23, 2018, https://www.newyorker.com/magazine/2018/09/03/francis-fukuyama-postpones-the-end-of-history.
3 Kristen Ghodsee, "Tale of 'Two Totalitarianisms': The Crisis of Capitalism and the Historical Memory of Communism," *History of the Present: A Journal of Critical History* 4, no. 2 (2014): 116–42.
4 Mark Fisher, *Capitalist Realism: Is There No Alternative?* (Winchester, UK: Zero Books, 2010).
5 Although the claim has been attributed to Fredric Jameson, he quoted an anonymous source; see Fredric Jameson, "Future City," *New Left Review 21* (May–June 2003): 76.
6 On the "blackwashing" of socialism, see Kristen Ghodsee, *Red Hangover: Legacies of Twentieth-Century Communism* (Durham, NC: Duke University Press, 2017), 101–46.
7 The equating of Nazi Germany and the Soviet Union is a trope that reappears in various surveys across the decades with varied degrees of sophistication. See, for example, William J. R. Curtis, "Totalitarian Critiques of the Modern Movement," in *Modern Architecture since 1900* (London: Phaidon, 1996), 351–70.
8 "The results and contradictions of the Soviet model are valid only as a point of reference for anyone who wishes and knows how to elaborate a political strategy that, from the errors and conditioning of the past, may draw ideas for surpassing them." See Manfredo Tafuri and Francesco Dal Co, *Modern Architecture*, vol. 2 (Milan: Electa, 1976), 305.
9 Philipp Meuser and Dimitrij Zadorin, *Towards a Typology of Soviet Mass Housing: Prefabrication in the USSR 1955–1991* (Berlin: DOM Publishers, 2015); Steven E. Harris, *Communism on Tomorrow Street: Mass Housing and Everyday Life after Stalin* (Baltimore: Johns Hopkins University Press, 2013); and Mark B. Smith, *Property of Communists: The Urban Housing Program from Stalin to Khrushchev* (DeKalb, IL: Northern Illinois University Press, 2010).
10 The duality of architectural history perhaps echoes that of the practice of architecture, between "autonomous" and "contingent" concerns. For a recent discussion of such dualism, see Jeremy Till, *Architecture Depends* (Cambridge, MA: MIT Press, 2009).
11 Maxim Waldstein, "Theorizing the Second World: Challenges and Prospects," *Ab Imperio 1* (2010): 98–117.
12 For a critique of recent media reception of architecture of the Socialist world, see my article "Orientalizing Socialism: Architecture, Media, and the Representations of Eastern Europe," *Architectural Histories 6* (June 2018): 7.
13 Ana Miljački discusses Czech architecture explicitly in terms of a Socialist lifestyle and the attendant modes of consumption in *The Optimum Imperative: Czech Architecture for the Socialist Lifestyle, 1939–1968* (London and New York: Routledge, 2017).
14 For a recent study see Eleonory Gilburd, *To See Paris and Die: The Soviet Lives of Western Culture* (Cambridge, MA: Belknap Press, 2018).
15 György Péteri, "Nylon Curtain: Transnational and Transsystemic Tendencies in the Cultural Life of State-Socialist Russia and East-Central Europe," *Slavonica* 10 (2004): 113–23.
16 For an early account see Edward Hallett Carr, *The Soviet Impact on the Western World* (New York: Macmillan Company, 1947).
17 Astrid Hedin, "Cold War Isomorphism: Communist Regimes and the West European Model of Worker Participation," *European Journal of Cultural and Political Sociology* 3 (2016): 201–42.

18 Astrid Hedin, "How the Cold War Helped Spur West European Welfare State Reform," The Global (November 2, 2018), accessed November 2, 2018, https://theglobal.blog/2018/11/02/how-the-cold-war-helped-spur-west-european-welfare-state-reform/.

19 Kristen Ghodsee, "Revisiting the United Nations Decade for Women: Brief Reflections on Feminism, Capitalism, and Cold War Politics in the Early Years of the International Women's Movement," *Women's Studies International Forum* 33 (2010): 3–12.

20 Johanna Bockman, *Markets in the Name of Socialism: The Left-Wing Origins of Neoliberalism* (Palo Alto, CA: Stanford University Press, 2011).

21 Łukasz Stanek's work on architectural exports from the Second to the Third World is groundbreaking in this respect; see his forthcoming book *Architecture in Global Socialism. Eastern Europe, West Africa, and the Middle East in the Cold War* (Princeton, NJ: Princeton University Press, 2019).

22 Michał Murawski, "Introduction: Crystallizing the Social Condenser," *The Journal of Architecture 22* (2017): 372–86.

23 Angelika Schnell, "The Socialist Perspective of the XV Triennale di Milano: Hans Schmidt's Influence on Aldo Rossi," *Candide. Journal of Architectural Knowledge*, no. 2 (July 2010): 33–72; and Pier Vittorio Aureli, "The Difficult Whole," *Log*, no. 9 (Winter/Spring 2007): 45–46. Thanks to Torsten Lange for the reference to the latter article.

24 Michał Murawski, "Actually-Existing Success: Economics, Aesthetics, and the Specificity of (Still-) Socialist Urbanism," *Comparative Studies in Society and History* 60 (2018): 907–37.

25 Kimberly Elman Zarecor, "What Was So Socialist about the Socialist City? Second World Urbanity in Europe," *Journal of Urban History* 44 (2017): 95–117.

26 Think, for example, of the recent decision by the Berlin senate to ease the city's current housing crisis by building on top of the once reviled Socialist-era Plattenbau, one of the unlikeliest architectural comebacks in history. See Feargus O'Sullivan, "A Second Life for Berlin's Plattenbau," *Citylab* (September 6, 2018), accessed December 17, 2018, https://www.citylab.com/design/2018/09/a-second-life-for-berlins-plattenbau/569392/.

27 Smith, *Property of Communists: The Urban Housing Program from Stalin to Khrushchev*, 117.

28 Andrei Simić, "Urbanization and Cultural Process in Yugoslavia," *Anthropological Quarterly* 47 (April 1974): 225.

29 Andrew Herscher, "Architecture, Destruction, and the Destruction of Yugoslavia," in *Toward a Concrete Utopia*, ed. Martino Stierli and Vladimir Kulić (New York: Museum of Modern Art, 2018), 114.

30 Aleksandar Hemon, "Trump: A War Criminal in the Making," *Rolling Stone* (February 29, 2016), accessed December 17, 2018, https://www.rollingstone.com/politics/politics-news/trump-a-war-criminal-in-the-making-83735/; and "Stop Making Sense, or How to Write in the Age of Trump," *Village Voice* (January 17, 2017), accessed December 17, 2018, https://www.villagevoice.com/2017/01/17/stop-making-sense-or-how-to-write-in-the-age-of-trump/.

31 Dubravka Stojanović, "Yugoslav Wars: A Snapshot of European Past or Future?" *Journal of Modern European History* 16 (2018): 153–57.

32 Kristen Ghodsee sums up this process brilliantly in the short story "Post-Zvyarism: A Fable about Animals on a Farm," in Ghodsee, *Red Hangover*, 150–66.

33 For a discussion of neoliberalism as an attempt to restore class power, see David Harvey, *A Brief History of Neoliberalism* (Oxford, UK: Oxford University Press, 2005), 31–36.

Cohen
Figures 1–17: Spreads from the "Techniques locales" issue of the journal *Techniques et architecture*, published in 1943.

Bremner
Figure 1: Courtesy of Sanders of Oxford. Figures 2, 10, and 11: Courtesy of Martyn Gregory Gallery, London. Figure 3: Courtesy of the National Portrait Gallery, London. Figures 4, 12, and 13: Courtesy of a private collection. Figures 5 and 6: Courtesy of the Sze Yuan Tang Collection. Figure 7: Courtesy of the Trustees of the British Museum. Figures 8a and 8b: Courtesy of the British Library Board, London. Figure 9: Courtesy of the Wellcome Collection, CC BY. Figure 14: Courtesy of the Jardine Matheson Archive, Cambridge University Library: A8/106/1. Figure 15: Courtesy of the Jardine Matheson Archive, Cambridge University Library: A7/82. Figure 16: Courtesy of the Jardine Matheson Archive, Cambridge University Library: A7/82. Figure 17: Courtesy of the Jardine Matheson Archive, Cambridge University Library: L7/3/11. Figure 18: Courtesy of the Jardine Matheson Archive, Cambridge University Library: A8/123/2. Figure 19: Photograph by John Thomson. Figure 20: Courtesy of the Heard family business records, 1754–1898, Baker Business Historical Collections, MSS:766 1754–1898. I wish to thank Cole Roskam for bringing this image to my attention. Figure 21: Courtesy of the Royal Commonwealth Society collection, Cambridge University Library: BAM 1, 12.

Crinson
Figure 1: Patrick Abercrombie, *Dublin of the Future*, (Dublin: Civics Institute of Ireland, 1922). Courtesy of the National Library of Ireland. Figure 2: Loyal Dublin, Detail of map *Plan of Dublin with Environs*, (London: W. H. Smith, 1900). Figure 3: *Illustrated London News*, 26 June, 1897, 888. Courtesy of the British Library British Newspaper Archive. Figure 4: Photograph by Mark Crinson. Figure 5: Samuel A. Ossory Fitzpatrick, *Dublin—A Historical and Topographical Account of the City*, (London: Methuen, 1907). Figure 7: Courtesy of the British Library British Newspaper Archive. Figure 8: D. A. Chart, *The Story of Dublin*, (London: J.M. Dent, 1907). Figure 10: Photograph by Mark Crinson. The following images are courtesy of the National Library of Ireland: Figure 11, L_ROY_01769; Figure 12, L_ROY_01764; Figure 13, L_CAB_04918; Figure 14, L_ROY_01772; Figure 15, L_ROY_02151; and Figure 16, L_ROY_02154. Figure 17: Detroit Publishing Co., Catalogue J - Foreign section. Detroit, Mich.: Detroit Photographic Company, 1905, Published in *The World Illustrated—First Series, Beautiful Ireland*, Dublin: Irish Times, 1899. Courtesy of the Library of Congress, Prints and Photographs Division, Washington, D.C. 20540 USA, LC-DIG-ppmsc-09942. Figure 18: Copyright Krzystof Wodiczko. Photograph reproduced with permission of the artist. Figure 19: Detail of map in R. Pool and J. Cash, *Views of the most remarkable public buildings, monuments and other edifices in the city of Dublin*, Dublin, 1780. Figure 20: Map from D. A. Chart, *The Story of Dublin*, 1907.

Tursack
Figure 1: © Hans Tursack. Figure 2:© Sol LeWitt. Photograph courtesy of MASS MoCA. Figure 3: © Peter Halley. Courtesy of Peter Halley. Figure 4: © MOS Architects. Courtesy of MOS Architects. Figure 5: © Jonathan Lasker. Courtesy of Jonathan Lasker and Cheim Read Gallery. Figure 6: Photograph by Ryan Tyler Martinez. Courtesy of Zago Architecture and Ryan Tyler Martinez. Figure 7: Photograph by John Bernardo. Courtesy of Alex Da Corte. Figure 8: © Ashley Bickerton. Courtesy of Newport Street Gallery. Figure 9: © Hans Tursack. Figure 10: © Miles Gertler and Igor Bragado. Courtesy of Common Accounts. Figure 11: Courtesy of Haim Steinbach and White Cube. Figure 12: © Hans Tursack.

Bokov
Figure 1: Rodchenko and Stepanova Archive. Courtesy of Rodchenko and Stepanova Archive. Figures 2 and 3: Courtesy of the Mayakovsky Museum. Figures 4, 7, 8, 9, 10, 12, and 13: Courtesy of Beinecke Library, Yale University. Figure 6: Courtesy of the Moscow Museum of Architecture. Figure 11: Courtesy of the State Shchusev Museum of Architecture. Figure 14: Photograph by Naum Granovsky.

Osswald
Figures 1–3, 4, 7b, and 9–13: Courtesy of Architect Helder Carita, Lisbon. Figures 6, 7a, and 8: Photo by the author.

Mann
Figure 2: Edward E. Ayer Digital Collection, Newberry Library. Figure 4: Courtesy of the John Carter Brown Library at Brown University. Figure 5: Courtesy of the National Archives, Kew. Photo: Geoff Ward. Figures 6–7, 12, 14 and 17: Courtesy of the Barbados Museum and Historical Society.

Burioni
Figure 1: Dresden, Staatliche Kunstsammlungen, Y 0364.01. Figure 2: Roundel with hunting scenes (possibly decoration for a tent ceiling), Persian, Safavid Dynasty, 1520–1550, 99.4×97.8 cm., Courtesy of the Boston Museum of Fine Arts. Figures 3 and 4: Courtesy of the Research Library, The Getty Research Institute. Figures 5 and 6: Courtesy of the Universitätsbibliothek Heidelberg. Figure 7: London, British Museum, OR.7180, Courtesy of the Trustees of the British Museum. Figure 8: Courtesy of the Metropolitan Museum of Art New York. Public Domain.

Bassett
Figure 1: Image courtesy of John Carty Library at Brown University: James Robertson, *Map of the counties of Surrey, Middlesex and Cornwall* in the island of Jamaica. Map Collection, John Carty Library at Brown University. (1804). Figure 2: John Lindley, *Collectanea botanica, or, Figures and botanical illustrations of rare and curious exotic plants*. Image courtesy of the Peter H. Raven Library/Missouri Botanical Garden. (London: Richard and Arthur Taylor, 1821): 2. Figure 3: Photograph by Hayden Bassett.

Figure 4: Image courtesy of John Carty Library at Brown University. Joshua Bryant. "Five of the culprits in chains, as they appeared on the 20th of September, 1823," included in *Account of an insurrection of the negro slaves in the colony of Demerara, which broke out on the 18th of August, 1823*. (Georgetown: A. Stevenson, 1824): 89. Figure 5: Image courtesy of the British Library. F. C. Bourgoin, *The Maroons In Ambush On The Dromilly Estate In The Parish Of Trelawney, Jamaica* (British Library, 2008, 1801). Figure 6: Print courtesy of the Boston Public Library, XfH.714D.H12P. (London: Hurst and Robinson, 1824). Figure 7: Print courtesy of The Mariners' Museum and Park, 1937.1694.000001 (The Mariners' Museum and Park, 1833).

Bowes

Figure 1: Drawn using drawings of R. J. A. Wilson, Piazza Armerina (Austin: University of Texas Press, 1983) and Giovanni Rizza, La villa romana del Casale di Piazza Armerina (Catania: University di Catania, 1984). Figures 2 and 3: Photographs by Kyle Schmidt © Kyle Schmidt. Figure 4: Courtesy of Patrizio Pensabene.

Vobis & Forrest

Figure 1: Courtesy of the Bibliothèque Nationale de France, Paris. Figure 2 and 3: Courtesy of the V&A Picture Library, Victoria and Albert Museum, London. Figure 4: Courtesy of the British Library, London, MS10366, F.86.v. Figures 5–14: Drawings by Yasmin Vobis. These were developed while at the American Academy in Rome as awardee of the Founders/Arnold W. Brunner/ Katherine Edwards Gordon Rome Prize.

Loring

Figure 3: Rare Book & Manuscript Library, Columbia University, cat. 30. Figure 4: Rare Book & Manuscript Library, Columbia University. Figure 5: Photograph from Kenneth MacGowan, "The New Stage-Craft in America," *Century Magazine*, January 1914, 416. Figure 6: Joseph Urban Collection, Box C4 Folder 4, Rare Book & Manuscript Library, Columbia University. Figure 7: Rare Book & Manuscript Library, Columbia University, cat. 47. Figure 8: Rare Book & Manuscript Library, Columbia University, cat. Series III Folder 9 Item II.2. Figure 9: Rare Book & Manuscript Library, Columbia University. cat. 47. Figure 10: Rare Book & Manuscript Library, Columbia University. Figure 11: Courtesy of the Cooper Hewitt, Smithsonian Design Museum. Figure 14: Courtesy of Paramount Pictures at the Online Archive of California. Public domain. Figure 15: Courtesy of the Library of Congress G1319.P25. Figures 17a and 17b: Library of Congress. Figure 19: 28th April 1967,1100 South Ocean Boulevard, Palm Beach, Palm Beach County, FL. 5×7 in., Courtesy of Library of Congress. Figure 20: 15th April 1967, 1100 South Ocean Boulevard, Palm Beach, Palm Beach County, FL. 5×7 in., Photograph by Jack Boucher for the U.S. Government Historic American Buildings Survey. Courtesy of Library of Congress HABS FLA,50-PALM, 1–15. Figure 21: 12 April 1967 1100 South Ocean Boulevard, Palm Beach, Palm Beach County, FL, 5×7 in., Photograph by Jack Boucher for the U.S. Government Historic American Buildings Survey. Courtesy of Library of Congress HABS FLA, 50-PALM, 1–18. Congress HABS FLA, 50-PALM, 1–21. Figure 22: 28th April 1967, 1100 South Ocean Boulevard, Palm Beach, Palm Beach County, FL. 5×7 in., Photograph by Jack Boucher for the U.S. Government Historic American Buildings Survey. Courtesy of Library of Congress HABS FLA, 50-PALM, 1–28. Figures 23 and 24: 18. April 1967, 1100 South Ocean Boulevard, Palm Beach, Palm Beach County, FL. 5×7 in., Photograph by Jack Boucher for the U.S. Government Historic American Buildings Survey. Courtesy of Library of Congress HABS FLA, 50-PALM, 1–18. Figure 25: 22 April 19671100 South Ocean Boulevard, Palm Beach, Palm Beach County, FL. 5×7 in, Photograph by Jack Boucher for the U.S. Government Historic American Buildings Survey. Courtesy of Library of Congress HABS FLA, 50-PALM, 1–18. Figure 26: 6 April 1967, 1100 South Ocean Boulevard, Palm Beach, Palm Beach County, FL. 5×7 in., Photograph by Jack Boucher for the U.S. Government Historic American Buildings Survey. Courtesy of Library of Congress HABS FLA, 50-PALM, 1–18. Figure 27: Courtesy of Jim Fairman and John Loring. Figures 28–33: Courtesy of the Museum of Science and Industry. Figure 34: Photograph by Jack Boucher for the U.S. Government Historic American Buildings Survey, April 3, 1967. Courtesy of Library of Congress HABS FLA, 50-PALM, 1–93. Figure 35: Photograph by Jack Boucher for the U.S. Government Historic American Buildings Survey, April 3, 1967. Courtesy of Library of Congress HABS FLA, 50-PALM, 1–44. Figure 36: Photograph by Jack Boucher for the U.S. Government Historic American Buildings Survey, April 3, 1967. Courtesy of Library of Congress ABS FLA, 50-PALM, 1–47. Figure 37: Photograph by Jim Fairman. Courtesy of Jim Fairman and John Loring.

Jarzombek

Figure 1: Courtesy of KBS Korea 24, KBS1 Broadcasting, via Twitter: @benjackson. Figure 2: Wikimedia Commons. Figure 3: Photograph by Mark Jarzombek. Figures 5 and 6: Public domain. Figures 7: © Imdad Rasul. Courtesy Imdad Rasul. Figure 8: Wikimedia Commons User:ChanduBandi. Figure 9: Source Wikimedia Commons. Figure 10: Courtesy of the Walters Art Museum, Baltimore. Figure 11: Courtesy of the University of Pennsylvania Museum, B16676.14. Figure 12: Public domain. Figure 13: © Peter von Gaza. Courtesy Peter von Gaza.

Guha-Thakurta

Figures 1–24: © Tapati Guha-Thakurta. Courtesy of the Collection of Visual Archives, CSSSC.

Chattopadhyay

Figures 1–7: © Swati Chattopadhyay.

Norwood

Figure 1: Courtesy of the Frances Loeb Library,

Harvard University. Figure 2: Courtesy of the Thomas Ustick Walter Collection, Athenaeum of Philadelphia, WTU.003.002. Figure 3: Courtesy of the Beinecke Rare Book and Manuscript Library, Yale University.

Malkani & Rajani
Figure 1: Mujeeb, Faysal. Entrance to Bahria Town Karachi. Digital Image. Dawn.com. April 18, 2016. Figure 2: "Bahria Town Karachi Development Updates." Video. YouTube. March 25, 2016. Screen capture by Shahana Rajani. Figure 3: Photograph courtesy of Julia Tieke.

Versluys
Figure 1: Vue restituée par CAO de l'angle nord-ouest du Qasr (dessin F. Larché ; CAO Cl. Soirot) in François Larché (et alii) 2005, 'Iraq al-Amir. Le château du Tobiade Hyrcan, vol. II : Restitution et Reconstruction—Planches, IFPO, BAH 172, Beyrouth. Figure 2: Vue restituée par CAO de l'angle sud-ouest du Qasr (dessin F. Larché ; CAO Cl. Soirot) in François Larché (et alii) 2005, 'Iraq al-Amir. Le château du Tobiade Hyrcan, vol. II : Restitution et Reconstruction—Planches, IFPO, BAH 172, Beyrouth. Figure 3: Drawing based on a site survey by Nancy Rapp. *The Excavations at Araq el-Emir*, Volume I, The Annual of the American Schools of Oriental Research, Vol. 47, The Excavationsat Araq el-Emir, (1980), 153. Figure 4: Drawing based on a site survey by Nancy Rapp. *The Excavations at Araq el-Emir, Volume I*, The Annual of the American Schools of Oriental Research, Vol. 47, The Excavations at Araq el-Emir, (1980), 2.

Henni
Figure 1: © Rialto Pictures. Figure 2: © Service historique de la défense, Château de Vincennes: 1 H 1213. Figure 3: From Robert Descloitres, Jean-Claude Reverdy, and Claudine Descloitres. *L'Algérie des bidonvilles: le tiers monde dans la cité* (1961; Paris: Monton & CO,), 72–73. Figure 4: From Isabelle Herpin and Serge Santelli, *Cahiers d'architecture 1. Bidonville à Nanterre: étude architecturale, Unité Pédagogique d'Architecture* 8 (Paris: Institut de l'environnement, 1971), 16. Figure 5: From Roger Cunibile, *L'assistance technique aux français musulmans d'Algérie à la préfecture de police à Paris* (Paris: Préfecture de Police, 1961), 127. Figure 6: From Isabelle Herpin and Serge Santelli, *Cahiers d'architecture 1. Bidonville à Nanterre: étude architecturale, Unité Pédagogique d'Architecture* 8 (Paris: Institut de l'environnement, 1971), 87. Figure 7: © Photo Jean Texier /Mémoires d'Humanité, Archives départementales de la Seine-Saint-Denis.

Le Roux
Figures 1 and 8: Photograph by David Goldblatt, Courtesy of Goodman Gallery. Figure 3: Courtesy of University of Cape Town Libraries, African Studies Library, Special Collections Department. Figure 4: Image reproduced with acknowledgement to the CCA/Mellon scholar program. Figure 5: Courtesy of Ronnie McKenzie. Figure 6: Courtesy of Google Earth. Figure 7: Courtesy of SPI Supplies.

Osayimwese
Figure 1: Source, http://www.ibadancityng.com. Figures 2–6 and 8–9: Courtesy of the Rockefeller Archive Center. Figures 7a, 7b, and 11: © Layi Olatunji. Figure 10: Source, Akinpelu 1988.

Lai
Figures 1 and 3: © OMA. Courtesy of Office of Metropolitan Architecture. Figure 2: Public domain. Figures 4 and 5: © Junya Ishigami Associates. Courtesy of Junya Ishigami Associates. Figure 6: Courtesy Fundação Oscar Niemeyer. Figure 7: © Daniel Libeskind. Courtesy of Studio Daniel Libeskind Studio Daniel Libeskind, Architect LLC. Figure 8: Photograph by Richard Weil. Creative Commons License. Figure 9: © Canadian Centre for Architecture, John Hejduk fonds, Canadian Centre for Architecture, Montréal. Figure 10: © Johnson Marklee. Courtesy of Johnston Marklee. Figure 11: Photograph courtesy of Brett Jordan. Figure 12: © 2019 Polly Apfelbaum/ Artists Rights Society (ARS), New York. Courtesy of Polly Apfelbaum and Alexander & Gray Gallery. Figure 13: © Atelier Bow Wow. Courtesy of Atelier Bow Wow. Figure 14: © Filip Dujardin. Courtesy of Filip Dujardin. Figure 15: © Adrian Phiffer. Courtesy of Adrian Phiffer. Figure 16: Courtesy of MAIO Architects. Figure 17: © Vincent Lamoroux. Photograph by Creative Migration LA. Figure 18: © Andrew Kovacs. Courtesy of Andrew Kovacs. Figure 19: Courtesy of An Te Liu. Figure 20: Courtesy of Greg Lynn. Figure 21: Courtesy of Hernan Diaz Alonso. Figure 22: Courtesy of Forgemind Archimedia. Figure 23: Photograph from Wikimedia commons. Figure 24: Photograph by Jeroen P. M. Meier. Figure 25: © Toyo Ito. Figure 26: Photograph courtesy of Forgemind Archimedia. Public domain. Figures A–G: © Bureau Spectacular.

Charlotte Algie is a designer based in New York City and design faculty at Syracuse University.

Jean-Louis Cohen is an architect and Sheldon H. Solow Professor in the History of Architecture at New York University.

G. A. Bremner is an architectural historican and Senior Lecturer in Architectural History at the University of Edinburgh.

Mark Crinson is an architectural historian and Professor of Architectural History and Assistant Dean for Research in the School of Arts at Birkbeck, University of London.

Hans Tursack is a designer based in Cambridge Massachusetts and the 2018–2019 Pietro Belluschi Fellow at MIT.

Anna Bokov is an architect and historian based in New York City and Assistant Professor Adjunct at The Irwin S. Chanin School of Architecture at the Cooper Union.

Cristina Osswald is a researcher in Jesuit art and hagiography at the Transdisciplinary Research Centre on Culture, Space and Memory at the Universidade do Porto.

Emily Mann is an architectural historian and Lecturer in Early Modern Art at the Courtauld Institute of Art.

Matteo Burioni is an art historian Lecturer at the Zentralinstitut für Kunstgeschichte in Munich and Interim Professor at the University of Hamburg.

Hayden Bassett is an archaeologist at the United States Naval Facilities Engineering Command.

Kimberly D. Bowes is an archaeologist and Associate Professor of Classical Studies at the University of Pennsylvania.

Yasmin Vobis and Aaron Forrest are architects and co-principals of Ultramoderne, based in Providence, RI. Aaron is Assistant Professor in the Department of Architecture at RISD. Yasmin is Visiting Professor II at The Irwin S. Chanin School of Architecture, Cooper Union.

John Loring is a designer, artist and author and design director emeritus of Tiffany & Co.

Mark Jarzombek is an architectural historian and Professor of the History and Theory of Architecture at MIT.

Edward Mitchell is an architect and Director of the School of Architecture and Interior Design at the College of Design, Architecture, Art, and Planning at the University of Cincinnati.

Arko Datto is an artist based in Kolkata, West Bengal.

Heyward Hart is an artist based in Los Angeles, California.

Tapati Guha-Thakurta is an art historian and Visiting Professor of Humanities at Brown University and Professor in History at the Centre for Studies in Social Sciences, Calcutta.

Swati Chattopadhyay is an architect and historian and Professor in the Department of History of Art and Architecture, University of California, Santa Barbara.

Bryan Norwood is an architectural historian and Assistant Professor of Architecture at Taubman College, University of Michigan.

Zahra Malkani and Shahana Rajani are an artist duo based in Karachi, Pakistan. Zahra is an Assistant Professor of Practice at the Communication and Design Department at Habib University and Shahana is an Assistant Professor in the Liberal Arts Department at the Indus Valley School of Art and Architecture.

Miguel John Versluys is an archaeologist and Professor of Classical & Mediterranean Archaeology at Leiden University.

Samia Henni is an architectural historian and Assistant Professor in the Department of Architecture at Cornell University.

Curtis Roth is a designer and Assistant Professor at the Knowlton School of Architecture.

Hannah Le Roux is an architect and Associate Professor in the School of Architecture and Planning at the University of the Witwatersrand, Johannesburg.

Itohan Osayimwese is an architectural historian and Assistant Professor of History of Art and Architecture at Brown University.

Jimenez Lai is a designer, founder of Bureau Spectacular and Lecturer at UCLA Department of Architecture and Urban Design.

Vladimir Kulić is an architectural historian and Associate Professor of Architecture in the College of Design at Iowa State University.

Acknowledgment

Perspecta 52 would not be realized without the leadership of the Dean of the Yale School of Architecture Deborah Berke. The issue acknowledges with gratitude the fine attention of the Perspecta Board throughout several cycles of review: Deborah Berke, Keller Easterling, Sheila Levrant de Bretteville, Gavin Macrae-Gibson, Alan Plattus, Harold Roth, Robert A.M. Stern. At Yale, Professors Kurt Forster and Greg Lynn shared their insights in seminar and studio teaching in ways that became foundational to the early ideas of this issue. Editors wish to especially acknowledge the generosity and patience of Fred Clarke and Mariko Masuoka at Pelli Clarke Pelli in New Haven, as well as Cesar Pelli who served as a member of the Perspecta Board in 2016, during the selection process of the pitch for this project at the Yale School of Architecture. Special thanks also to Richard Munday in New Haven. This volume has been considered and compiled while a faculty member at RMIT University School of Architecture and at Syracuse University School of Architecture. Thanks are extended to the colleagues, sparring partners, and of course students who were part of these appointments and attendant research seminars that fostered and augmented this project.

Essential acknowledgement is due to the extraordinary generosity and importance of the following colleagues for their shared critical insights throughout the editorial duration: Michael Hardt, Felicity Scott, Anthony Vidler, Werner Oechslin, Brett Steele, Nicholas Boyarsky, Heather Roberge. And, last but not least, friends Huizhen Ng, Nick McAdoo, Roberto Jenkins, Gab Olah, Elanna Nolan, Rahul Dhankani, Elena Baranes, Emau Vega, Cat Garcia Menocal, Leo Streich, Julian Schubert, Elena Schütz (and others) and family: this issue would not be with the reader without them.

Perspecta 52: Ensemble

Editors
Charlotte Algie
Alicia Pozniak

Design
Seokhoon Choi

Copy Editor
Cathryn Drake

Printed by
NPN Drukkers, the Netherlands

Typeface
Stella (Blot, Clot, Dot, Hot, Seventeen, Shot)
and Kiddo, Seohkoon Choi
Neue Haas Grotesk (Round Dots), Commercial Type

Director of Communications
AJ Artemel

Perspecta 52 would like to thank the following donors
for their ongoing generosity in supporting this journal:
The Perspecta Fund, which includes a gift in honor of
Tom Beeby from the Robert H. Driehaus Foundation
Marc F. Appleton, '72 M.Arch
Hans Baldouf, '81 BA, '88 M.Arch.
Austin Church III, '60 BA Family Fund
Fred Koetter and Susie Kim
Cesar Pelli, '08 DFHA
Robert A.M. Stern, '65 M.Arch.
Jeremy Scott Wood, '64 BA, '70 M.Arch.
F. Anthony Zunino, '70 M.Arch.

Perspecta, The Yale Architectural Journal is published in the United States of America by the Yale School of Architecture and distributed by the MIT Press.

Distributed by the MIT Press
Massachusetts Institute of Technology
Cambridge, Massachusetts 02142
http://mitpress.mit.edu

ISBN: 978-0-262-53787-2 ISSN: 0079-0958